Pollution, Untouchability and Harijans

Pollution, Untouchability and Harijans

A South Indian Ethnography

Yasumasa Sekine

RAWAT PUBLICATIONS

Jaipur • New Delhi • Bangalore • Hyderabad • Guwahati

ISBN 978-81-316-0385-7

Published by
Prem Rawat for **Rawat Publications**
Satyam Apts, Sector 3, Jawahar Nagar, Jaipur 302 004 (India)
Phone: 0141 265 1748/7006 Fax: 0141 265 1748
E-mail: info@rawatbooks.com
Website: www.rawatbooks.com

New Delhi Office
4858/24, Ansari Road, Daryaganj, New Delhi 110 002
Phone: 011 2326 3290

Also at *Bangalore, Hyderabad* and *Guwahati*

Typeset by Rawat Computers, Jaipur
Printed at Chaman Enterprises, New Delhi

Contents

Part Two
POLLUTION THEORY

Part Three
HARIJAN STRATEGIES

Note on Transliteration

The transcription used for Tamil words in this book is in principle the strict transliteration adopted by the Tamil Lexicon [University of Madras, 1982: lxviii] with the exception that proper names for places, temples, kingdoms and persons follow the Anglicized version without diacritical marks, indicating approximate pronunciation or customary usage. Caste names written with diacritical marks are found only in Tables 4.5 and 4.6. As shown below, Roman letters are used for the Tamil characters [Tokunaga, 1981: 1].

[Vowels]

short		long	
a	அ	ā	ஆ
i	இ	ī	ஈ (ஈ)
u	உ	ū	ஊ
e	எ	ē	ஏ
o	ஒ	ō	ஓ

ai ஐ au ஔ

[Consonants]

	Guttural	Palatal	Retroflex	Alveolar	Dental	Labial
Stop	k க்	c ச்	ṭ ட்		t த்	p ப்
Nasal	ṅ ங்	ñ ஞ்	ṇ ண்	ṉ ன்	n ந்	m ம்
Lateral			ḷ ள்	l ல்		
Vibrant : flap				r ர்		
trill				ṟ ற்		
			ḻ ழ்			
Semi-vowel		y ய்				v வ்
Fricative	[h] ஹ்	[j] ஜ்	[ṣ] ஷ்	[s] ஸ்		

[kṣ] க்ஷ்

In general, I transcribe the Tamil orthography given to me on the spot in Kinnimangalam. Otherwise I follow the spelling found in the Tamil lexicon. The Tamil language has differences between colloquial and literary language, and there are again various dialects of the colloquial language. In this book literary expressions are basically adopted, except for a few cases of ritual words circulating in the village.

Preface

This book is a monographic study of the ideological practices observed in a Tamil village, especially the practices of the Harijans (formerly known as Untouchables). It is intended to make theoretical contributions to two important themes of South Asian anthropology: (1) Hindu pollution concepts and (2) the culture of the Harijans. A new understanding of the concept of pollution in the Tamil cultural context is presented as the fundamental basis on which the ideological practices of the Harijans are analysed. For this purpose, the research attitude is characterized by a "decentripetal" (i.e., "interpretative" "other-worldly" and "bottom-up") viewpoint. Thus the immediate aim of this book is to establish a theoretical perspective in which "untouchability" in caste societies is properly understood. At the same time, however, I regard this book as the foundation of a larger task, which is to construct what I call a "common-ground" anthropology. In this Preface I will explain that latter aim in order to provide a better grasp of what is meant by the term "common-ground" anthropology, and also to clarify the location of the present work within the anthropological arena.

In its obvious appearance this book is an ethnography of a South Indian village focusing especially on concepts of pollution and the everyday life of Harijans. It should be noted that the present work has been generated from my motif of reflexive anthropology, which always requires making clear the position of an ethnographer. During the writing of this ethnography, I kept the following inner voice in my mind: "Why do I, a Japanese anthropologist, have a concern with an Indian society and especially with its repressed people like Harijans?" Listening to this inner voice is deeply connected with my following intention. The argument discussed in this ethnography is not simply confined to a cognitive understanding particular to a South Indian village, but is expected to provide some insights in terms of an ontological comprehension of human society in general, which seems to be the ultimate purpose of social anthropology.

Writing culture, i.e., an ethnography written while holding such an inner voice naturally must reflect the relationship between objectified people and an ethnographer. Among the many challenging arguments and attempts connected with the writing of ethnography, my attempt in this book has some features in common with so-called experimental ethnography in terms of its basic motif. The motif is to overcome the conundrum of representation of the other culture, and particularly to avoid the Orientalistic manner of representation in Said's sense. My attempt, however, focuses mainly upon the theoretical perspective for contributing to the motif, and thus differs somewhat from the attempts of experimental ethnographies in a narrow sense which are much concerned with how empowerment of informants reflects upon the way in which ethnography is written. Compared to such a polyphonic appearance of ethnography, the style of writing adopted in this book is, therefore, still an old-fashioned one. For it seems to me that the investigation of an effective theoretical perspective (horizon), in which understanding of others (other cultures) is made possible, is most crucial and fundamental in seeking a disorganization of the writing hegemony monopolized by an ethnographer. The reason is as follows.

Dialogue in a true sense is not simply a so-called conversation (exchange of words), but the creative process of participating in the sphere of understanding where the other's life and the self's life are synchronized. The sphere must have the common basis of "singularity" [Karatani, 1994 (1989)], which means a uniquely alienated situation lacking any shared code between others and self (see note 1 of Conclusion). It is paradoxical that the communicative open sphere in a true sense is built on "singularity", which means an ultimate discommunicative situation lacking any shared code. I would call this creative sphere, where one faces the intrusion of unknown otherworldly-ness (other-ness), the horizon of "common ground". In sum, the central task of anthropology is to more consciously investigate and clarify the features of the "common-ground" horizon through the dialogue with "other culture". It should soon be noted that "other culture" is a hypothetical concept used at the beginning of investigation, which corresponds to Sartre's "*autrui-objet*" that is ultimately negated in order to access the "*autrui-sujet*", again in Sartre's sense [Sartre, 1943].

I repeat that a superficial dialogue (i.e., exchange of words), even though it looks to be polyphonic and provide empowerment to the other, is not dialogue in the true sense. The distinction between true dialogue and disguised dialogue depends on whether or not the ethnographer holds a reflexive attitude, which requires awareness of the limitations of one's perception. Hence dialogue in the true sense is made possible by a monologue on a deep level which maintains the reflexive attitude and finally leads to the liminal experience of facing others. At the ultimate point, then, the difference between dialogue and monologue vanishes. This suggests conversely that if the ethnographer lacks the reflexive attitude, the ethnography even if it adopts the form of dialogue would be a superficial and closed monologue. It is an unavoidable fact that the ethnography written by a particular anthropologist is basically a monologue, but that fact need not lead simply to a negative connotation. It means the beginning of an ontological dialogue in the true sense.

The above recognition was not derived through deductive top-down philosophical thinking, but was realized through my long-term intellectual experience of doing fieldwork and writing ethnography, in which particular and concrete problems were found and analysed. In my case, the objectified problem was "discrimination against Harijans in an Indian social context", as presented in this book. My efforts to understand this concrete problem naturally led me to acquire the recognition described above, in which a "common ground" is found as a key concept.

The anthropological perspective based on the "common ground" is not only proposed in order to cope with the problematic representation of others that produces discrimination, but also expected to contribute to overcoming the predicament of cultural relativism. Because our fundamental aim is to understand others in a less discriminative manner. In order to accomplish this it is inevitable to find the third way based on singularity, that is, the "common-ground" horizon, which escapes from the simplistic dichotomy of generalization (positivist universalism) vs. particularization (relativism). It should be here again remembered that the original intention of cultural relativism was not to spread "a kind of cognitive apartheid" [Sperber, 1985] but to understand others with an attitude of respect which promotes to access towards the other's emic viewpoint. This original intention is doubtlessly invaluable so that our undertaking aims at a theoretical renovation to make the intention materialize in a positive manner.

In the context of this book, a so-called "social evil" found in a caste society, that Harijans are discriminated as a category of impure people, provides an important field of discussion in terms of the salvage of the original intention of cultural relativism. This topic directly illuminates the problem of anthropology and ethics. One of the main criticisms of cultural relativism, presented by (Euro-centric) universalists, is that it can not condemn the "inhuman" activities carried out by people in other cultures. There is a circulated idea shared among the modern Western universalists that discrimination against "Untouchables" must be a social evil still practiced in the caste society of South Asia. What must immediately be pointed out is that such criticism strongly reflects modern Western values, and premises that those critics can never be in a dirty position; in other words, it lacks the reflexive attitude. My criticism of such the universalistic criticism of cultural relativism in a sense resembles Renato Rosaldo's arguments on headhunting among the Ilongots. "I could no longer speak about headhunting as one of the clean addressing the dirty. My loss of innocence enabled me and the Ilongots to face each other on more nearly equal ground, as members of flawed societies. We both lost positions of purity from which to condemn the other, without at the same time having to condone what we found morally reprehensible in ourselves and in the other" [Rosaldo, 1989: 64]. As headhunting seems to be a fearful custom for Rosaldo (and me, of course), discrimination of Harijans also seems to be a terrible social evil. Nonetheless, we cannot simply condemn the discrimination as a problem found specifically and exclusively in caste societies. This is the standpoint I take wittingly. Not only do I know that there is still a similar problem of discrimination against "Buraku-min" equated with "Untouchables" in Japanese society, and in other societies as well, but I also recognize that there is a discriminating mind in me and most probably in all humans. Others have discriminated against me and I may have discriminated against others, even though I have tried not to do so. The self-recognition that I am already in a dirty position, to use Rosaldo's term, is placed at the starting point for understanding what is actually taking place in discrimination of Harijans. The reflexive attitude is absolutely opposed to that of naively believing in the modern Western values that (Euro-centric) universalists adopt. Therefore, we have the unavoidable task of inventing a theoretical perspective based on the self-recognition associated with a reflexive attitude.

In order to respond to the claims of naive universalists, it is necessary to change the static and self-contained image of culture that universalists premise, because the combination of such a premise and cultural relativism in a superficial sense logically leads to an impossibility of understanding the other culture. The concept of "other culture" does not refer to a substantial and self-contained entity at all, but is seen as an initial indicator of the comprehension process of finding another structuralist sense of universal horizon where the original intention of cultural relativism is maintained. In other words, we should pay attention not to the functionalist similarity of manifest cultural substances between different cultures, but to the structuralist similarity of relationship (structure) found in the liminal, peripheral or tabooed phenomena of each socio-cultural systems. My understanding of culture is close to Rosaldo's view, in which culture is conceived as "a busy intersection", that is, a bundle of liminality in my term, where heterogeneous social processes are crisscrossing [Rosaldo, 1989: 20–21].

This thought leads to the structuralist and *dynamic* concept of "common ground" based on "singularity". It is too early to pass a death sentence on cultural relativism on the grounds of a superficial universalist criticism. There is no contradiction between an investigation by another deeper level of universalist view based on "singularity" and the original intention of relativism. It is no more allowed to objectively describe the other culture in general from the substantialist standpoint. An ethnography inevitably reflects the synchronicity between other life in a different society and the ethnographer's life. It has to be written on the horizon of the "common ground". In this book, I have attempted to elucidate the "common-ground" horizon by focusing upon concepts of pollution and Harijan lives as liminal or peripheral phenomena.

Overview

With the prologue of the theoretical reviews in Part One, the main body of this work consists of Part Two, a discussion of pollution theories that lays the groundwork for Part Three, and Part Three, which reconsiders our representation of the culture of the Harijans (Untouchables).

The "pure-impure" ideology, or the key ideology of Louis Dumont's theory that has acquired the position of a strong paradigm for understanding Hindu society, supports centripetal thinking, or the dominant ideology. In the discussion in Part Two, drawing upon my own fieldwork in an Indian village, I criticize this Dumontian understanding because of its "top-down" or one-sided nature. In the "pure-impure" ideology, polluted phenomena (*tīṭṭu*) are only seen as objects of repression and rejection, as "impure". I argue that in reality, the very marginal nature of pollution (*tīṭṭu*) makes it a creative space (a space with hidden potential for decentralization) where it is possible to radically change one's own sense of order through encounters with others. It is possible to observe this on the ground, and in order to clearly depict this creative nature of pollution, which maintains the basis of the lives of the villagers, it was necessary to distinguish it as "pollution" from "impurity", which is an unequivocally negative concept.

Pollution (*tīṭṭu*) is a concept used to indicate a chaotic situation that destroys the conventional order. It is an alarm that indicates the social necessity for a renewal of order. Society can deal with the chaos in two ways: it can reject it as "impurity" or it can accept it and share it as "pollution". As a response to the pollution of death, relatives, villagers, and friends gather and place themselves amidst the pollution in the house of the dead. In this way, the receptive attitude towards pollution is still very evident today where pollution marks the critical phases of a human life (birth, puberty, death, etc.). The funeral, as a ritual sharing of pollution, is a creative device that converts the pollution of death into vitality for the future of the people left behind. For example, the ritual enactment of the conversion of the pollution of death into prosperity, such as the fruits of the harvest or the birth of the next generation, shows that such a clear delineation of pollution is deeply connected to the villagers' need for survival. Observation of actual life in the village provides a glimpse into the fact that the Harijans (Untouchables), who are considered to be polluted, are not necessarily regarded as unequivocally negative, or objects of repressed "impurity". Of course in the eyes of the dominant castes, there has been a history of the "impurity"-based view of the Harijans overpowering the "pollution"-oriented view (historians have shown a shift from Untouchables being dreaded to Untouchables being despised).

If we fail to describe the reality of this creative aspect of pollution, that I term "pollution", we cannot accurately depict actual Indian society. In this light, a theory of pollution such as Dumont's, which emphasizes only a "pure-impure" framework, is similar to the "Orientalist" representation of modern Western society, which stereotyped the Orient including Indian society as a stepping-stone to the acquisition of self-identity of the Occident and can be criticized as representing the dominant caste-centred point of view. Nonetheless, no systematic study has yet been made that criticizes the basic biases and errors in Dumontian theory of pollution (though there have been various but partial criticisms of Dumont's theory and plenty of reports that present fragmentary information corresponding to the aspect of "pollution" in my terms). This is the principal contribution of the present work to the anthropology of Indian society. This discussion overcoming the limitations of Dumontian theory also provides important suggestions concerning the general theory of pollution in anthro pology.

In Part Three I attempt to examine the actual reality of the culture of the Harijans (Untouchables), based on the views expressed above. Up to now there have been two opposing theories of Harijan culture, the consensus theory, which assumes that the Harijans (Untouchables) have been copying the culture of the dominant castes, and the disjunction theory, which maintains that the Harijans have possessed their unique cultural traditions. However, such a reductionist oversimplification distorts and obscures the actual lifestyle of the Harijans (Untouchables). The results of a multifaceted study of ritual and everyday behaviour across socio-economic position, caste level, lineage level, and individual level within the context of a comparison to the upper castes make it clear that the Harijans are led by a desire for self-aggrandizement (desire for improvements in the quantity and quality of life) and live strategically within the same core reality of "pollution" ideology as the upper castes. In doing so, although they may sometimes manipulate and make use of the "pure-impure" ideology, they do not necessarily accept the ideology that labels them as "impure".

The upper castes and the Harijans in the village are no different in their basic values of living within the reality of "pollution" ideology and seeking their respective self-aggrandizement. Yet because the Harijans are in the completely disadvantaged position of lacking capital and facing social discrimination, there are many restrictions on their behaviour, which result in a tendency to make it fragmented and inconsistent. As a consequence, it is important to avoid oversimplifying the relationship between their behaviour as it appears on the surface and the values they actually believe. Consensus theorists readily consider the existence of rank relationships among the Harijans as copying and acceptance of the "pure-impure" ideology. Disjunction theorists idealize the Harijans' behaviours of rejecting or turning over the "pure-impure" ideology as proof of the their unique value system. Both arguments are far from the reality. Therefore, both consensus and disjunction theorists should free themselves of the error of reductionism (an exclusionary view) with respect to the culture of the Harijans. It is noted that theorists should regard the diversity of the Harijans' behaviour in the context of the adversity brought on by their position on the fringe of society (*misères de condition* in Bourdieu's terms) as the whole of the Harijans' strategic or tactical attempts to live a better life, even as they remain concerned about what Bourdieu calls the *misères de position* (e.g., jealousy of competing neighbours), which anyone, including the upper castes, experiences.

If the Harijans' lifestyle and community appear to be alien, this is not due to cultural differences that can be reduced to some core essence. Rather, they appear alien as a result of the Harijans' weak social position, which is on the margins of the social order (they have been made to play the role of boundary-setters). The present work criticizes substantialist and centripetal cultural theories that are tied to an exclusivist position (i.e., view from the centre of the social system) and points out the necessity of understanding the community of the Harijans through the relationalist and decentripetal approach that takes a more receptive position (i.e., view from the margins of the social order and from within the on-boundaries). This is the second contribution of the present work to the study of the culture of the Untouchables in India.

This type of reevaluation of concrete ways of understanding the community of the Harijans shows us how to approach the communities of repressed peoples (*subaltern*) in general. The reevaluation described above does not view repressed communities as alien cultures that cannot be understood, but rather makes possible a shared understanding that any people put on the boundary of society will behave the same way. Just as sharing the pollution of death was a source of socially creative energy, sharing the position of those on the boundaries of society can orient us towards the creative locus where social boundaries are dissolved, i.e., social discrimination is vanished.

If we express this point of view in Karatani's terms, it suggests a position that aims to convert an order built on exclusivity residing within the "generality vs. particularity" domain to an order established on the basis of sharing and acceptance resting on a "universality vs. singularity" domain. In this sense, the present work offers a basic theory to begin studies on discrimination.

A major goal of the present work is to free Indian society from its stereotyped image as "an alien and incomprehensible society that still maintains a discriminatory caste system". On that account, I contemplated the standpoint which we need to adopt to understand Indian society, being free from bias. I term this attempt a "common-ground" anthropology.

Acknowledgements

The book is produced on the basis of my Ph.D. thesis that was submitted to and accepted by the University of London in 1993. The concerns discussed in the book have been gradually developed since my first encounter with Tamil society, which took place during fieldwork in 1980 and 1982 in the Jaffna Peninsula, Northern Sri Lanka. During my stay in Jaffna one of my most impressive experiences was that when a Vellalar (the dominant caste of Jaffna society) man told me about pollution, he did not make any distinction between pollution associated with life crises and pollution associated with caste, by using the same term *tuṭakku* (the most popular expression of ritual pollution in Jaffna society). This incident evoked my simple questions of how and why he could deal with these two different kinds of pollution together. I myself attempted to answer these questions in my 1984 article on birth and death ceremonies among the Jaffna Tamils [Sekine, 1984]. The discussion on pollution among the Jaffna Tamils is indirectly reflected in Part Two of this book in which ritual pollution (*tīṭṭu*) among the South Indian Tamils is dealt with. At that time, however, my attention to the lowest castes or "the Untouchables" was not very strong. This is partly because Jaffna society does not draw as clear a line between the Caste Hindus and "the Untouchables" as South Indian Tamil society does. Therefore, my conscious concerns with the "Harijans" practices were rather developed by fieldwork in the Madurai region, Tamil Nadu, which has been conducted intermittently from 1985 to 1989. Part Three of this thesis is penetrated mainly by these concerns.

The series of fieldwork trips undertaken was made possible by a grant from the Niwano Peace Foundation (1986) and by grants from the Japanese Ministry of Education, Science and Culture (1980,1982 and 1987–1989). The research work at SOAS, University of London was supported by a grant of the Japan Foundation (1989).

My deepest gratitude for this project is owed to the people of Kinnimangalam who received me with kindness and hospitality and helped me with my research in various ways. Though it is impossible to list them all, I cannot avoid special mention of the late Mr S. Balasubramanian who gave me all-out cooperation, with his gifted intelligence and affectionate manners. He was almost a joint researcher during my fieldwork. So this book is dedicated to the soul of my brilliant "brother" who reached *mukti* (salvation) too early (See plate 1).

I revisited Kinnimangalam in 1996 even for a short period and had a very good time with the villagers. They welcomed me with their unchanging hospitality. This

1996 field experience in the village reflects especially upon plates included in the book, which show the change of the village.

I express my special thanks to Professor R. Venkataratnam, Head of the Department of Sociology of the Madurai Kamaraj University, whose generous support made it possible for me to carry out the fieldwork without any mishap. I also thank Dr V. Sobhana Bai, a student of Prof. Venkataratnam, who helped me much during my stay in Madurai. I express my gratitude to the following members of the Department of Anthropology of Madras University: Professor N. Subba Reddy, Dr U.C. Mohanty, Dr. V. Karuppaiyan, Dr M.A. Kalam, Dr V. Sudarsen, and Dr A. Chellaperumal for their kind cooperation with my research work in Tamil Nadu. Professor. S. Subbiah of the Department of Geography, Madras University is acknowledged for his kind cooperation in my data-collection and especially for his friendship. Furthermore, he prepared an opportunity in which the present book is fortunately published from Rawat Publications. I show my most appreciation for his unchanging long-term cooperation and support.

I owe a very great debt to Professor Lionel Caplan (SOAS, University of London) who supported me from the beginning to the completion of the Ph.D. thesis as my supervisor. I especially thank him for having given me various precise comments and useful advice during the work and for finally suggested me to publish the thesis in a book form and kindly introduced me to the editor of Oxford University Press (London). I also would like to record my appreciation to Professor Adrian Mayer (SOAS) and Dr Andrew Turton (SOAS) who encouraged me to continue to study at SOAS when I completed the Masters course and from whom I benefited much through personal communications. I must acknowledge the teaching I received from 1983 to 1985 from other members of SOAS, University of London, including Dr A. Cantlie, Professor D. Parkin, Professor B.D. Moeran, the late Dr R. Burghart, Dr P. Spencer, and Dr R.L. Tapper. Dr J. Parry (LSE, University of London) kindly read my 1984 article mentioned above and gave me useful comments.

It is particularly emphasized that the present work owes much to Professor Keiji Iwata (Tokyo Institute of Technology and National Museum of Ethnology) who was my first teacher of anthropology and whose anthropological thoughts (cf. [Iwata, 1995]) profoundly reflect upon my present work. He is not just an anthropologist but an outstanding thinker. The present book is also dedicated to my *Guru*, Professor Iwata.

I especially mention Professor Shigeru Iijima (Tokyo University of Foreign Studies) who helped me when I began my post-graduate course at SOAS. Professor Shigeharu Tanabe (National Museum of Ethnology) encouraged me to embark on this project. I also thank Professor Yasuke Ikari (Kyoto University), a luminary in the studies of Vedas who provided many stimulating insights.

The present book have some overlapping sections and extended and expanded pages of my earlier publication from the National Museum of Ethnology. Osaka, and in this context, the support and permission received from the National Museum of Ethnology is fondly remembered, appreciated and duly acknowledged.

My special thanks are due to my former classmate at SOAS, Miss Susan Steele, whose friendship helped me a lot during my stay in London. I most regret that she went far away but I never forget her pure, tender and warm heart.

I note that I may have used the former titles of the aforementioned people.

Finally, and most importantly, I must mention my wife, Mitsue, who has given me her long and patient support, without which the completion of this book would have been impossible. I should also note that my eldest son Yasuhito had to live in London against his will while I was reading my postgraduate course at SOAS. My most longstanding debt of gratitude is to my parents and my parents-in-law, whose moral support made possible the accomplishment of this project.

Yasumasa Sekine

Illustrations

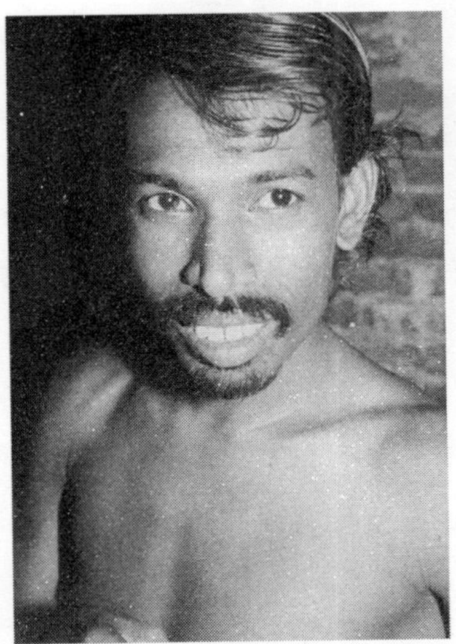

Plate 1 The late Mr S. Balasuburanmanian Pillai as a joint researcher.

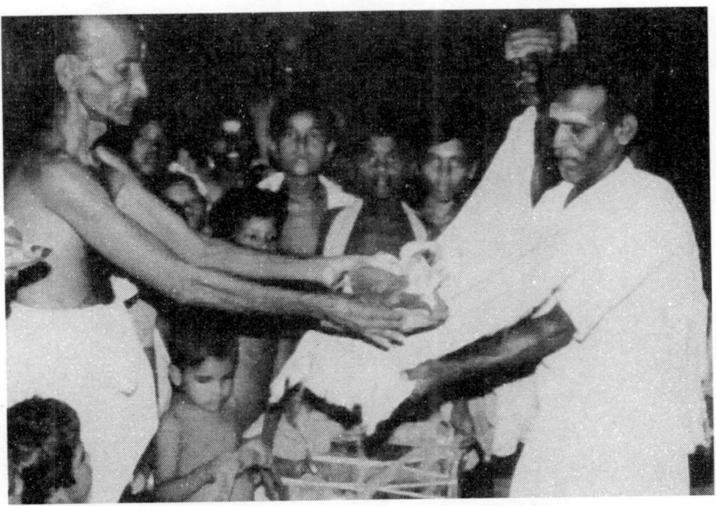

Plate 2 *Tōṭṭi* and *maṭaiyaṉ* (village servants), who are selected from the village Harijans (the Paraiyars), participate in the worship of Vinayakar Caturtti and receive *piracātam* (consecrated leftover) last in the order of precedence (*mutaṉmai*), in which they live between enjoyment of god's grace and acceptance of degraded status. What are they thinking at the moment?

Plate 3 The main traditional occupation assigned to the Paraiyars is drum beating. They spread the message around the village by beating a drum called *ṭamāram* with leather drumsticks. What do they see at the moment?

Plate 4,5,6,7 The marching band of the Paraiyars on the occasion of the Kecavan lineage festival (The two instruments above are *uṟumimēḷams*, below left is a *nātasvaram* and below right a *ṭamāram*.)

Plate 8 Cow dung cake-making.

Plate 9 *Ammi* and *kuḻavi* (front), and *āṭṭukkal* (back).

Plate 10 A mortar (*ural*) and a mallet (*ulakkai*).

Plate 11 Commensality.

Plate 12 When my fieldwork started in 1985, the villagers planted a sapling of neem tree . (*vēppamaram*) on the bank of the Eastern Tank in commemoration of my visit.

Plate 13 I revisited the village in 1996 and stood under the 11 year old neem tree.

Map of India and the Location of the Village Studied

Chapter 1

Introduction

In Search of a "Common-Ground" Anthropology

Transformation and Sustainment of Caste Culture

The notion that the caste culture observed broadly in South Asian societies has formed changeless and stagnant societies has rapidly been relativized in recent years. Caste culture is also an emanation of history. It has undergone many transformations and will continue to change in the future [Breckenridge and van der Veer, 1993: 8]. In recent years, in the critical tide against Orientalism, there has been a trend to re-examine in a radical manner the concept of the "caste", which originated in the West (detailed descriptions regarding this are given in [Sekine, 1994b]). At any rate, a considerable length of time has elapsed since the caste concept, which is strongly characterized as "invented tradition" [Cohn, 1983], was introduced in South Asian societies. In the meantime, that which was first invented by the imagination of Orientalism was materialized (or objectified), gradually permeating the reality. Anthropologists of the latter half of the twentieth century encounter societies embracing a solid idea of caste developed through the aforementioned processes. Accordingly, to our eyes, castes appear as essential qualities that provide an important social framework in actual life. Caste society, a historical emanation as mentioned above, has indeed been transformed along with rapid modernization and urbanization. However, in actuality, it is unimaginable that castes will disappear in the near future. According to Kolenda's analysis, for example, the societal unit that will continue to exist in the future as a strong fort protecting the nature of castes in the Hindu society is "kin community", while the caste system has been somewhat dissolved by modernization in the sense that castes correspond to occupational divisions [Kolenda, 1978]. Béteille maintains that, even in the trend of modernization, loyalty to the family acts as a conservative drive which paradoxically preserves caste, especially in urban areas [Béteille, 1991a and 1992]. Many scholars have pointed out that as modern occupational and social structures had penetrated and grown in the society, a transition to a relaxed caste system occurred as exemplified by lowered barriers between adjacent castes and broader intermarriage ranges. However, the Harijans (nearly identical to the former untouchables) are still differentiated clearly from Caste Hindus.[1] Government measures intended to close the gap in small ways cannot do away with the fundamental cleavage. Notwithstanding that the educational and occupational reservation policies implemented by the government for the Harijans are gradually producing an effect, the label "impure people" remains persistent. Why does not that dividing line fade away? Discrimination against the Harijans continues to exist as an insolvable problem after all.

Doubts about the Conscientious Criticism of the Caste System

A possible, and actually occurring, general response to the aforementioned state of affairs is that the caste system, a relic of feudalism, which allows the discrimination against the Harijans, is the parent of vices and therefore should be banned. Accordingly, that response proposes an alternative, which is what is known as the modern democratic system and advises its introduction. It should be noted, however, that such a response neglects the history of the re-inventing and strengthening of the caste system in the process of modern colonial rule. At the same time, it is naive affirmation of modernization believing that modern systems are more advanced than pre-modern systems. As a result, that response takes a form of social reformism that appeals to the conscience of those who are rationalistic. The question, then, is whether it is possible to truly solve the state of affairs. The answer appears to me to be in the negative.[2] I cannot accept straightforwardly conscientious actions lamenting the reality of discriminated people in India as miserable from the standpoint of modern reason and emphasizing the urgency of social reforms. Such actions indeed tend to pass judgement upon people looking down from the viewpoint of respectable and perfect individuals. I feel that such tendencies fail to grasp ontological issues essential to human beings.

It is certainly possible to recall and describe the misery of the unjustly discriminated Harijans, even from my limited experience in India. However, my experience in India had other effects on me. A great change occurred in me through the actual experience of meeting and having conversations with real people of village Harijans A and B. The image that I had of hopelessly miserable Harijans, created due to my ignorance before leaving Japan, vanished spontaneously. They were indeed crying, laughing, getting angry, telling lies and so forth, they were hardily alive. I realized that the Harijans there were people as imperfect as myself, and then I felt a sense of relief. What constituted their misery was not solely what Bourdieu terms *misères de condition* (misery of condition) [Bourdieu, 1993], caused by being confined in a social position of discrimination. I saw with my own eyes that they were also suffering from *misères de position* (misery of position) [ibid.], as they were anxious not to lose to their immediate neighbour Harijan C. I felt they were really closer to myself. Considering that personal experience of mine, I cannot help but feel odd when I read instructive books or hear lectures that report the actual conditions of discrimination against the Harijans focusing on misery of condition, and reduce, as a natural consequence, the responsibility for their misery to the villain of India's indigenous caste system, and accuse the system. Such books and lectures somehow appear as if they compulsively assert that everybody must have a good heart, in which case I no longer know where I fit in. Rather, I feel strongly that there should be some other approaches to overcoming discrimination from the standpoint of an unenlightened person who has both virtues and vices. My struggle for liberation is not to head off with a good heart for the salvation of others. Rather it is an inevitable struggle because I sense that there is a person within myself who compulsively suppresses myself. Liberation in this context is not simply setting someone free, but becoming aware of the fundamental passivity of human beings. I have fully internalized the three devices of modern democracy, that is, freedom, equality, and progress, and therefore need to make a conscious effort to become aware of that passivity. This must be equivalent to a statement made by Poirié while discussing thoughts of Lévinas: "Humaniser la Justice, avoir conscience que la Justice n'est jamais *assez* juste …" [Poirié, 1987: 39]. This point must not be forgotten. At least I do not place trust in an understanding of caste society if it lacks this point of view.

"Common Ground" between Self and Others

Embracing the above-mentioned thoughts, I very easily understand the following remarks made by Seiji Takeda in the book *Sabetsu to iu kotoba* (literally, "The Term 'Discrimination'"):

> Concerning discrimination, my basic point of view is as follows: Avoid first setting a goal to change society and then thinking of discrimination as a means to that goal. Conversely, if one can identify the nature of discrimination and persuade others to agree on that identified nature, only then does it become possible to link ordinary life with the goal to change society; in other words, to link the mind directed towards oneself with the mind directed towards society. Therefore, of a variety of views on discrimination (anti-discrimination), one must carefully reject those that reduce discrimination to an issue of social reform and those that resolve discrimination into humanism (high-sounding rhetoric). [Shibatani and Ikeda, 1992: 172]

These words articulate the problem that I should tackle, which is to elucidate the nature of discrimination and reach agreement on the clarified nature. Moreover, it should become possible to establish a link between oneself and society, or self and others, by making efforts towards that goal. The present work is a milestone on the course of my efforts to do so. In the context of this ethnographic work, I attempt to examine the true nature of discrimination on a common ground (link) between myself and others who are the discriminated people, the Harijans in India. I look for a horizon where my thoughts on them merge with my contemplation about my own way of life. The location of that common ground is a phenomenological field that develops as an intersubjectively constructed reality. This is exemplified by the writing process of the present work. I write this work in the hopes of obtaining an equalized viewpoint by parenthesising natural attitudes and getting down to a recognition that as incomplete people they and I exist to discriminate against others in search of order, while being aware that those who discriminate against some people are not clearly distinguishable from the discriminated. We should watch for the pitfall of natural attitudes concealing a salvation theory, characterized as hierarchical binary opposition, that there exist you who must be saved and I who must save you. The chances are great that contemporary Japanese see the discriminated people in India as being confined to the bottom of a double hierarchy (an image of the misery of oppressed people in a "southern" country) and have an ideally amplified and excited compassion towards them. We should always remember that, although they appear to be different, oppression and compassion are derived from the same root, that is, a desire for power.

Transcultural Quality of the System of the Untouchables

The intention of doubting the conscientious criticism of the caste system and searching for a common ground between self and others is to cast off the way of seeing caste society with an emphasis on the differences, regarding it as an exceptional society, and then to change direction towards the discovery of commonality. The understanding that people living in a caste society and oneself are in the same world on a common ground opens the way to a broader perspective that allows one to examine the reality of the caste system, including discrimination against the Harijans, as one's own problem. At least my experience in India, although limited, does not allow me to consider India a unique country characterized by discrimination. Historically, scholars have argued over whether to treat the caste system as indigenous to India, connected to the *dharma* and *karma* concepts, or see it as a universal type of society, that of the stratified society. That difference in viewpoint determines whether one regards castes as an "ethnographic category" or a "sociological category" [Leach, 1971: 1]. Seen from the former viewpoint, Dumontian structural theory [Dumont, 1980 (1966)] adopting the former viewpoint illuminates the contrast between the traditional, totalitarian hierarchy in India (an ideology giving priority to general social order over individuals) and the modern western, individualistic equality (an ideology that considers hierarchy inequality). This structural theory is representative of the India-is-unique argument in that it is consistently a dualistic theory paying attention to differences between India and modern Western countries. On the contrary, the latter viewpoint, for example, Berreman-style cross-cultural analysis (e.g., [Berreman, 1966, 1973]), is valuable in that it attempts to make note of commonality; in other words, it is open to comparisons between the Indian caste society and other stratified societies. Dumont and Berreman stand at opposite poles but on an equal footing because they develop their thoughts within the same structural outline of relativism versus universalism. However, Berreman is vindicable because of the attention brought to commonality. My standpoint is close to Berreman's, as I agree that the Indian society should not be viewed simply as unique. Yet, there is a clear difference in how and where we find a common ground. My standpoint in search of commonality is outside the confrontational framework of relativity versus universality. I look for the "common ground" not in the commonality of centring structures but in decentring, boundary events (a detailed analysis will be given in the final section of Conclusion). Recently scholars have been steadily tracing how stratified societies were established in the historical contexts of individual societies in many parts of the world including South Asia, and what influences colonial rule had on that process. This marks a step forward from intellectual conflicts arguing over particularity or generality from the viewpoint of contemporary studies disregarding historicity (pertaining to South Asia, refer to [Carroll, 1978], [Cohn, 1983], etc.). As a result, it is becoming possible to make comparisons taking into consideration internal contexts of social configuration, going beyond simple comparisons of external forms.[3] It is certainly necessary to avoid careless comparisons of different societies. However, the accumulation of historical studies as mentioned above is beginning to reveal that discrimination equivalent to the existence of Untouchables under the Indian caste system is a historical phenomenon frequently found in other hierarchically stratified societies. Moreover, in a broad sense, one can discover traits common to each of such phenomena, although they respectively have their indigenous historical contexts. There is also a loose contemporaneousness, in that each group of dreaded people underwent solidification and became an object of discrimination from the middle of the medieval era into the modern era. It is also noteworthy that homomorphy is found concerning occupations and social roles of the lowest groups who are the objects of discrimination.[4]

Re-examination Based on Theories of Pollution

Concerning the above-mentioned contemporaneousness and homomorphy, it should be noted that there is an evident fact that discrimination against the repressed people is always spoken of as fear of touching the polluted. It is a common fact of vital importance that discrimination/differentiation is based on a somesthetic notion, pollution. Therefore, examination in depth of the meaning of the common boundary phenomenon called pollution will serve as a means of coming down to what I call "common ground".

To understand the aforementioned fact completely, it is necessary to review properly these fundamental questions: what kind of people are polluted (impure)? In other words, what in the first place is pollution (impurity)? Why do pollution concepts play a role in discrimination so often and act so effectively? Efforts to answer these fundamental questions are indispensable for seeing discrimination in depth and throwing off the popular understanding (misunderstanding) that leads to the reduction of discrimination to a humanitarian problem. The necessity of such questions arises from a blind side of the history of discrimination studies that is, the unfortunate neglect of efforts to focus on pollution concepts independently, without placing them within the frame of the hierarchy of caste society. In my view, the content of studies relating to pollution concepts is poor in contrast with the obvious quantity of their accumulation in South Asian anthropology. Most studies tend to discuss "pollution" within the framework of caste system theories. It seems that there have been few scholars who intentionally adopted a method of reviewing caste system theories from an independent standpoint of pollution theory. In practice, the caste system theory-oriented study stance is likely to devise an explanation identifying "impurity" of the Harijans with the pollution associated with death when researchers uncritically accept remarks made by dominant castes, such as "the Harijans are impure because they deal with dead people and dead cattle" (for example, refer to [Dumont, 1986 (1957): 463]). My approach, which is a re-examination based on a pollution theory, will first of all closely examine pollution itself. On the basis of findings gained through that approach, I would offer insights into the power-oriented nature of the discourses that construct the social space called caste society. A clear answer will be given in a relativized manner to the question asking in what context identification of the "impurity" of Harijans with that of death occurs.

Bottom-up Anthropology: Bridge-Building between Pollution Theory and Harijan Culture Studies

As regards the above-mentioned problems, the present work deals with pollution and the Harijans which are regarded as boundary-type phenomena from the viewpoint of an order-centred paradigm. By doing so, this book aims at clarifying a new point of view for boundary phenomena, namely, a dimension where boundary areas, as they are, are recognized as the core centres of culture. Thus, the main arguments of this book consist of two parts, i.e., pollution theory and Harijan culture studies, which are bridged such that the former serves as grounding for the latter. In advance of these main arguments, a theoretical perspective is provided in Part One with a review of preceding studies and identification of problems in them.

My primary and ultimate aim is to investigate the practices of the Harijans in a Tamil village, locating them within the entirety of social relations of the village so as to illuminate their real ideologies and the features of their behaviour. The theoretical and direct contribution of such investigation is a more inclusive understanding of the Harijans' socio-cultural situation, going beyond both cultural disjunction and cultural consensus theories in a productive manner. In addition, as a wider effect, my contribution lies in the reconstruction of the caste society theory from a decentring "bottom-up" viewpoint. This project requires fundamental work in which the pollution concept as a key idea to the understanding of caste society is re-examined, as stated previously. In fact, fundamental re-examination is required because a correct understanding of cultural situations in which the Harijans are placed is actually interlocked with a proper understanding of caste society. Actual work will focus on a method of breaking the strong spell of the Dumontian theory of Hindu/caste societies on which Orientalism casts its shadow [Sekine, 1994b: 41–47], namely, Dumont's general understanding based on a hierarchical binarism in which every social phenomenon is encapsulated by an ideology of "purity" and "impurity" [Dumont, 1980 (1966)]. Again, re-examination is an unavoidable task not only for better understanding of the socio-cultural situations of the Harijans, but also for renovating the understanding of the entirety of Hindu/caste society [Parry, 1974: 115].

In order to adopt a new point of view, it is necessary to reform the research methodology. Generally speaking, in the first place, we need at least to depart from the approach of substantialists (essentialism) and take a relational and interpretative approach [Geerts, 1973] in a thoroughgoing manner. It is methodologically necessary to look at individual behaviours of people as symbols, refrain from assuming inherent meanings of symbols, and successively grasp how symbols are interpreted in the relational context where symbols are located. Processes producing "thick description" consisting of interpretation of interpretations imply reciprocal and cyclical movements between ethnographic details and general explanatory conceptions. It seems equivalent to the *understanding* reaching causal *explanation* which Weber attempted; namely the grasp of *Sinnzusammenhang* (dialectics or mutual reversal of denotation and connotation) (refer, for example, to [Koto, 1975] and [Shindo, 1990: 52–53]). Through these processes, deep, ideal-type cultural features become apparent that the very people are not aware of in their everyday life, although they actually display them [Giddens, 1977: Chapter 3].

In comparison with the posture of the above-mentioned research methodology, Dumontian totalitarian theory which can be summarized as a "this-worldly," "top-down," and "static" approach, will be discussed in detail in Chapter 2. Dumont's presentation of an objective structure, which reflects his functionalist substantialism dressed in relationalism, results in overlapping with the household Brahmin's standpoint looking down at social boundaries as peripheries from the height of the centre of order (off-boundary centripetal viewpoint) as exemplified by their way of thinking. Therefore, in order to overcome the one-sided substantialist and dominator viewpoints, the present book adopts the reverse approach to the Dumontian methodological standpoint, namely, the "other worldly",[5] "bottom-up," and "dynamic (generative)" approach (explained later), as an attempt to make the interpretative standpoint apparent and come close to the viewpoint of gazing at order from within the "gap" at the boundary of the inside and outside of order (on-boundary decentripetal viewpoint).

This methodological reversal postulates a contrast between explanation and understanding that has roots in two traditions in the history of thought, i.e., positivism (the philosophy of enlightenment) and hermeneutics (historicism). However, as pointed out previously, it is not only a shift in placement of importance from the former to the latter, but also an attempt to link the two traditions (see [von Wright, 1971] [Naka, 1990]). The "dynamic" approach introduced here, on the one hand, is based on Weber's and Geertz' interpretative standpoint [Shindo, 1990: 57] and, on the other hand, takes into consideration Bourdieu's concept of generative structuralism, namely, structuralization process (cultural reproduction) by *pratique* (everyday practices) founded on *habitus* (incarnated history-society or objective structure developed into subjective structure).[6] Specifically, the "strategy" concept that has roots in *habitus* is useful for describing and analysing Harijan behaviour (for example, [Bourdieu, 1977]). Bourdieu avoids concepts of substantialists, such as individuals and groups, and uses the agent (actor) concept instead. This book incorporates that idea of Burdieu's, but does not necessarily adopt that expression. Furthermore, in the sense of supplementing Bourdieu's theory that places importance on reproductive aspect, the three categories proposed by T. Imada may be of some help to analyse Harijan behaviour. They are "rule-governed customary behaviour" demanding analysis at deep levels, "rule-applied rational behaviour" at conscious levels, superficial levels heading to a target, and "rule-examining self-reflexive behaviour" involving new differences (fluctuation) [Imada, 1989: 20]. These efforts to avoid substantialism are made for fear of unconsciously mixing the observer's analytical viewpoint and the doers' (especially, dominators') viewpoint in the target society. Without the aforementioned conversion of the methodological standpoint, it is impossible to look from within at what are boundary phenomena when viewed from the this-worldly (secular) centre of order, including rites of passage and pollution (impurity), faith and sacrificial acts, and the Harijans' everyday practices.

Thus, the main arguments of this book consist of two parts. Part Two (Chapters Five to Eight) aims at establishing my basic viewpoint for understanding Tamil society, one of the components of South Asian society, by focusing upon the concept of pollution. In doing so, I critically and systematically re-examine the Dumontian theory (pure/impure ideology-centred theory) that is still a strong paradigm for understanding Hindu/caste society. An interpretative field of vision is established through these analyses, which makes a distinction between "pollution" and "impurity". Within this vision, Part Three (Chapters Nine to Twelve) analyses everyday practices of the Harijans and clarifies characteristics of the ideological world in which they actually live.

Notes

1. In 1991, about 15 per cent of total population of India are occupied by Scheduled Castes (SCs). This means 140 million people are categorized under SCs. So far as Tamil Nadu is concerned, the population of SCs is about 18 per cent of the state population. The terms of SCs and STs have been used in administration since the Government of India Act in1935 and until today for referring to the people called the "Untouchables" or the "repressed classes", both of which had used under the British rule. After independence the term Harijans, invented by Mahatma Gandhi, which literally means "The Children of God", started to be used socially for expressing ex-Untouchables. There is, however, a criticism that such a replacement of name does not make any difference and it is jokingly said that others may become "the children of Saturn". Hating such a given name, awakened ex-Untouchables consciously began to use the word Dalit for themselves as an inclusive term from the 1970s. Furthermore, we can find a recent tendency (less than ten years old) that they tend to extend the meaning of Dalit to a more inclusive social category including not only SCs and STs but also BCs and the minorities like Muslims. Therefore, I should explain why I still use the word Harijans in this book. In my experiences in the village, the Paraiyars call themselves Harijans, SCs, or Adi Dravidas, avoiding the term Paraiyars when they introduce themselves to me. Generally speaking, Dalit is not used by the village Paraiyars, at least it was not in 1980s. I, of course have to avoid using the term Untouchables. Then, after taking into consideration the above observation in the village, I here compromised and decided to adopt the more inclusive term Harijans out of three terms in order to clarify that this book deals with Untouchability. Because, although I think that SCs and Adi Dravidas seem to be a little better than Harijans from the viewpoint of discrimination, the administration word SCs is too mechanical and the word Adi Dravidas is too localized in the context of this book.
2. For example, in the case of the discrimination of African Americans in USA, the policy of integration known as a "melting-pot theory" on the basis of modernist humanism could not work out the problem and, as the result, a secessionist ideology has become more dominant at present, as shown by the PC (Political Correctness) movement, the excess form of which causes a reverse-discrimination [Sawada, 1994]. In this connection, it is regarded as a parallel phenomenon with the case of the USA that the rise of Hindu nationalism and the repulsion against affirmative actions like the reservation for ex-Untouchables in contemporary India have taken place after the ideal of Nehruvian democracy was betrayed by reality.
3. Shozo Omori proposes the theoretical perspective of "extension of meaning of thinking through experiences" in order to explain the process of "poesis of other ego". The proposal seems to be useful for the present context. That is to say, when concerning societies are compared after knowing the details of historical change of social formation of each society, it is made possible to acquire the more reliable comparison based on the more dense "extension of meaning of thinking through experiences".
4. It is not difficult to find similar examples all over the world. For instance, the lowly executioner in Europe, the Cagos in the Basque dominated area, the Questas of Mallorca Island, the Pakucho of the Korean Peninsula, the repressed people called *buraku-min* in Japan and so forth have been, or were, discriminated under the name of impure or pollution. It was around the 10th century AD that the discriminative village social system associated with Untouchability was established in India [Kotani, 1989: 206], though it is reported that there were already Untouchables in the latter period of the Veda era. In Europe, the lowly were

socially recognized in the 8th century AD when the Christian world view began to swallow the world of folk traditions and were clearly distinguished until the 13th or 14th century AD. It seems that, after the rise of Basque Nationalism around in the 10th century AD, the discrimination against the Cagos, which clearly appears in a document of the 13th century AD was started. In Japan, a group of peripheral people called *hinin* who played ambiguous social roles was formed around the 10th century AD, when the idea of avoidance of pollution was spread and emphasized among the aristocrats. Those people were fixed as a discriminated class towards the 14th or 15th century AD. This is the dominant understanding of the origin of the repressed *buraku-min*, though there is a different opinion, in which the *buraku-min* derived from those who believed in a particular Buddhist sect called *Ikko-shu* and were ill-treated as the repressed under the political intention of the ruler.

5. Dumont himself defines the value of pure and impure as religious, which contrasts with politico-economic. However, Dumont's understanding of religion, which seems to me a secular one adhering to a worldly viewpoint, betrays religion that in its nature must have holiness, i.e., a horizon beyond secular understanding. This limitation of Dumont's understanding is self-evidently verified by the fact that it cannot explain sacrifice properly (see Chapter 2). Since religion inevitably has to cope with liminal phenomena occurring at the boundary an absolute other worldliness, it is obvious that this-worldly thinking is not enough for considering the religious sphere. It is, therefore, necessary for overcoming the limitation to shift the standpoint from the center to the periphery, that is to say, from a this-worldly viewpoint to an other-worldly one. The latter viewpoint, which has the more potential, is called here an on-boundary decentripetal viewpoint.
6. Although Bourdieu is conscious that he is also under the influence of Weber, he criticizes Weber's substantialist tendency and emphasizes the difference between his approach and interactionalism in the USA, which is derived from Weber's tendency [Bourdieu, 1990: 179]. Thus, Bourdieu is keen on following the structuralist stance but one can criticize Bourdieu in that the shadow of a substantialist stance still remains in his approach. This chain of criticism of substantialism ironically shows how difficult it is to get out of it.

Part One

Theoretical Perspective and Setting

Chapter 2

Reconsideration of Theories of Pollution

Beyond the Orientalistic View

An investigation of the concept of pollution is essential to an understanding of the caste society prevailing in South Asia. Yet this does not imply that pollution theory must inevitably be reduced to caste society theory. Pollution theory should be maintained as an independent realm of discussion. It is of great significance as a basic theory that allows researchers to recapture caste society theory in a broader and deeper perspective. This claim is justifiable by the fact that although it is impossible to discuss caste society without pollution concepts, it is possible to assume the existence of pollution concepts that are not necessarily associated with the caste system, and such concepts do exist. The present work is firstly focusing on pollution concepts, instead of a caste society itself, because I believe caste society theory should not be closed off as arguments dealing with one particular society, but rather should be opened in the direction of a general theory of human society, based on scrutiny of the "singularity" of a society [Karatani, 1994 (1989)] (see note 1 in Conclusion). My aim is to use the concept of pollution as a means of communication between people who live in a caste society and myself who is, in their view, a member of "other culture".

The Limitations of Society-Oriented Studies

Functionalist Approach

Today, it can doubtlessly be claimed that we cannot avoid a discussion on concept of pollution in terms of the understanding of caste society. Bouglé was one of the earliest writers who asserted that the decisive principle of the caste hierarchy is purity-impurity [Bouglé, 1971 (1908): 29–40]. Among modern social anthropologists who began to work in South Asia, Srinivas made clear the folk knowledge of ritual purity (*maḍi*) and ritual impurity (*polé*) in his ethnography on the Coorgs of South India [Srinivas, 1978 (1952): 102–123]. He reports that the normal ritual status, called *mailigé,* is opposed to both *maḍi* and polé, as the sacred states. On the basis of these folk concepts, on the one hand, he notes that "the concept of ritual purity and impurity systematize and maintain the structural distance between different castes" [ibid.: 103]. On the other hand, he emphasizes that "these concepts also occur in certain non-structural contexts" like "praying or sacrificing to an ancestor or deity" [ibid.: 104]. It is notable that Srinivas distinguishes ritual state in non-structural (religious) context from that in structural (social hierarchical) context and makes clear the subjective viewpoint of the Untouchables in which they consider themselves as being "as subject to the various ritual states as any one else" [ibid.: 110]. Srinivas' distinction between the structural and non-structural contexts contrasts with Dumont's connection between them in his ethnography [1986 (1957)],[1] as is clarified later.

Stevenson [1954] is the earliest work in which a systematic argument on pollution in Hindu culture is attempted. He firstly differentiates secular status from ritual status. The latter is then divided into group ritual status and personal ritual status. Further, he classifies several binary concepts of pollution, like permanent/temporary, voluntary/involuntary, and external/internal.[2] He tries to clarify status evaluation, namely, the relationship between pollution and ritual status, by formulating "the Hindu Pollution Concept".[3]

Harper [1964] formulates tripartite concepts, as does Srinivas, but the point Harper makes is in a sense represented by his concept of "respect-pollution" (a sort of expression of respect in which impurity of the higher status being is absorbed by the lower status being with the purest condition), which is exemplified by a wife towards her husband, a Brahman priest towards a deity etc. [Harper, 1964: 181–183]. The concept "respect pollution" reflects, or is deeply connected with, his notion that these tripartite concepts penetrate into every domain, such as the individual state, the social structure and the pantheon. This clearly explains his deep concern with hierarchical status. In this sense, Harper and Dumont share the same concern. The principle of purity and impurity extended to the divine world by Harper and Dumont elucidates as well the vertical distinction between the pure (vegetarian) god and the impure (meat-eating) god from the Pramalai Kallars' religious practices [Dumont, 1986 (1957)].

As is suggested by the contrast between Srinivas and Dumont, Srinivas' natural attitude towards purity and impurity seems to be more empirical than Harper's or Dumont's. Harper's and Dumont's views are biased by their attaching too much importance to the hierarchical aspect of the principle of pure-impure. Their views could be criticized for two reasons. Firstly, I recall Fuller's statement in his paper on the relationship between caste system and Hinduism, "the gods themselves cannot be polluted" [Fuller, 1979: 459], which contradicts Harper's extension of the pure-impure principle to the divine world. I heard almost the same statement in the village I studied; "If a temple was polluted, a god could not reside there and would leave out. But it never happens that a god himself is polluted". Secondly, my investigation of village deities (Chapter 6) and lineage deities (Chapter 11) does not support the idea of a divine hierarchy. In the village there is no "impure god", which is a contradictory expression. The problem basically lies in their one-sided attitude that makes them pay attention to hierarchy but ignore the fact that viewpoints differ according to caste status. Therefore, the dominant Brahmanical view, which posits ritual caste hierarchy, unwittingly dominates their research viewpoint. This tendency furthermore results in their contradictory claims in the following sense. It is a contradiction that they extend such a "secular" notion of caste hierarchy, implying social discontinuity, to the "sacred" divine world, whose nature is transcendental and continuous (*vide infra*, see [Bataille, 1976]). Their work can thus be regarded as society-oriented, even though they deal with religious or ritual matters. Let us examine Dumont's work further.

Dumont's Work and Its Critiques

In his outstanding and polemical work "Homo Hierarchicus" [1966], Dumont clearly asserts that caste society can be principally understood by the hierarchical "ideology" (*vide infra*) of purity and impurity, though it seems that he already had presented such a basic motif in his early ethnographic work on Pramalai Kallars [Dumont, 1986 (1957)]. As already mentioned, the pure-impure dichotomy for an understanding of Hindu society is not new,[4] but the decisive difference between Dumont and the functionalists mentioned in the previous section lies in the fact that Dumont adopted the relationalist standpoint[5] from which the complementarity between purity and impurity was taken out as "structure" and presented the Brahmanical pure-impure principle as an encompassing "ideology" of Hindu hierarchical society. His work can be regarded as pioneering, in that it connects the studies of caste society with the general field of discussions on ideology, even though he did not intend to use "ideology" in the post-structuralist's sense [Dumont, 1980: xxvi] (*vide infra*). Rather he wittingly attempted as a structuralist,[6] or a French intellectualist, to elucidate the central value which penetrates caste society, as the "structure", i.e., a system of binary opposition. He presents his cultural consensus model, in contrast to the model of the so-called disjunction theorists, like Redfield, Srinivas and the early Marriott [Marriott 1955], who posit a disjunction between the little tradition and the great tradition within a single civilization [Keyes and Daniel, 1983: 8].[7] This central value encompassing the whole society is called "ideology" by Dumont.

Though Dumont's intention at that time (1960s) is understandable, there is no doubt that his theory has several limitations, as many critics[8] point out. Dumont himself organizes the criticisms of "Homo Hierarchicus", by comparing them to the four branches of a tree: "condemnation for betrayal of empirical data; condemnation for an approach focussing on ideas and representations (and for French intellectualism); condemnation for the inclusion of ancient texts in the study of contemporary society; and finally and most important, condemnation for the distinction proposed in H. H., and in fact central to it, between status and power..." [Dumont, 1980: xvii–xviii]. The former three condemnations are related to the methodological problem of H. H., which is pointed out from the viewpoint of the empiricists, on the basis of which the last condemnation of his primary claim is proposed. That is to say, Dumont's distinction between status and power and his theoretical device of encompassing-encompassed become the main target of his critics' attacks. It is questioned whether this distinction is empirically valid or not (for instance, [Leach, 1971], [Tambiah, 1972], and [Marriott, 1976]). Burghart also states, "Dumont has deprived politico-economic power of its former religious status" [Burghart, 1978: 520]. That is, Dumont has been criticized for his theory of status/power distinction being derived from modern Western dualism. Marriott's monism (see [Marriott, 1976 (1973)], and [Marriott and Inden, 1977]) challenges Dumont's dualism but it does not seem to be successful.[9] Moreover, Dumont's emphasis of ritual hierarchy of "status" as the encompassing ideology over "non-ideological power" (in Dumont's terms) has caused heated responses of disagreement. Roughly speaking, we can distinguish three lines of argument, namely, (1) the emphasis of kingly ideology ("power"), (2) the emphasis of transcendental value based on a ritual sacrifice, and (3) the emphasis of egalitarian value.

The first argument is that kingly ideology (politico-economic power) as another hierarchical value is not always encompassed by Brahmanical ideology (e.g., [Quigley, 1993][10] [Dirks, 1987], [Hoek, 1979]). Several critics use this line of argument. For example, Marglin and Raheja attach importance to kingly ideology through their re-evaluation of concepts of auspiciousness/inauspiciousness ([Marglin, 1985] and [Raheja, 1988]). In the present context, important works are Malamould [1981] and Burghart [1978] because both theories take into account an interpretative (dynamic) and therefore multi-dimensional viewpoint. Malamould introduces the concept of "revolving hierarchy" for going beyond Dumont's theory [Malamould, 1981: 41]. Using this concept, he explains that both Brahman and king can claim superiority over each other [ibid.: 49]. Burghart beautifully illustrates the inter-relationships among three different axes of hierarchy which are embodied by the Brahman, the ascetic and the king respectively [Burghart, 1978]. Of value is the fact that he pays attention to the internal viewpoint of each domain.

Burghart's argument already covers the second line of argument in which the values of asceticism become fundamental. This standpoint is typically represented by Heesterman [1981, 1985]. Though Dumont also focuses on renunciation [Dumont, 1980: Appendix B (1959)], it is suggested by Heesterman that Dumont's view overlaps with that of a Brahman householder. Heesterman properly clarifies, with its inner viewpoint, the transcendental sphere of the institution of renunciation which is embodied by "internalized sacrifice" [Heesterman, 1981: 252, 269], and asserts that "the preeminence of Brahmin is not based on his priesthood, but on his being the exponent of the values of renunciation" [Heesterman, 1985 (1964): 44] (See also [van der Veer, 1988: 193]). This difference between Dumont and Heesterman makes it clear that Dumont's theory consistently has a this worldly or society-oriented tendency and, at the same time, that sacrifice must be focused upon in order to acquire an other worldly (transcendental) viewpoint.[11] In this connection, Das' work [1976, 1977, 1983] which concerns sacrificial acts is important, and I will discuss it later.

The third line of argument consists of two streams. One, e.g., Das and Uberoi, [1971] or Parry [1979], underlines the significance of egalitarian values in contrast to Dumont's emphasis on hierachy.[12] Another stream is more radical and fundamental. This stream refutes Dumont's assertion that the whole of society is encapsulated by a hierarchical top-down ideology and claims rather that an independent bottom-up view can be found. This stream was founded by Marxian exploitation theorists like Mencher, and stratification theorists like Berreman. It has been developed by broader concerns which mainly consist of studies of popular culture ([Caplan, 1980, 1981, 1985], [Singer, 1966], [Holmstrom, 1971, 1976], [Obeyesekere, 1977, 1981], [Fuller, 1976] etc.), and studies of the Harijans (see the details in chapter 3). In this respect, Parry [1974] is seen as a pioneer in emphasizing the significance of studies of various religious movements, such as conversion, sectarianism and *bhakti*, which are deeply connected with the standpoint of the socially repressed people (See also [Deliège, 1992: 168–169]). In the context of this book, McGilvray [1974] seems to be important and suggestive, for he proposes matri-clan ideology as the dominant social value from his fieldwork in Eastern Sri Lanka. Namely, he provides an actual example of "sharedness of 'ordinary values' " in Caplan's term (see [Caplan, 1980:

235]), which are different from theological values. In other words, McGilvray suggests that there is an indigenous cultural tendency based on a logic of kinship which is shared among all the villagers, regardless of caste, and which cannot be fully reduced to the Brahmanical culture or a logic of caste. In short, we can learn of cultural depth from his work. The example shown in his work should not be made light of, though Dumont regarded such an example as a dismantled caste system found in a peripheral society of South Asia.

These criticisms of Dumont suggest the following three related points, which we should take up more seriously: (1) The first and second lines of argument imply that an ideology should not be seen as objectively and unambiguously defined but should be understood as "interpretation" from each subject's viewpoint like the king's, Brahman's or ascetic's. This "interpretative" point of view is the fundamental basis on which the following two points are based; (2) The second line especially suggests that it is crucial for refuting Dumontian this worldly (society-oriented) understanding to investigate the inner view of other worldly liminal situations which are for example represented by a world renouncer because this means the move from a this worldly viewpoint to the "other worldly" one; (3) The second stream of the third line of argument strongly suggests that proper understanding of popular culture and the investigation of socially repressed people's inner view is required in order to revise the Dumontian one-sided top-down view. This attitude can be called the bottom-up approach.

In sum, it is necessary to adopt the "interpretative", "other worldly" and "bottom-up" viewpoints in order to overcome Dumontian limitations.

The "interpretative" viewpoint is further discussed as the post-structuralists' sense of ideological approach and the "other worldly" point of view is considered by reviewing liminality theories in the following sections. Then, the "bottom-up" viewpoint is more seriously dealt with in Chapter 3 (The Problem in Studies of "Untouchables").

The Ideological Approach

The necessity of the "interpretative" viewpoint requires leaving Dumont's non-interpretative usage of ideology for the neo-Marxist sense of ideology. For this, it is necessary to clarify the difference between the two.

Let us start from a famous passage of *The German Ideology*; "The ideas of the ruling class are in every epoch the ruling ideas, i.e., the class which is the ruling *material* force of society, is at the same time its ruling *intellectual* force." [Marx and Engels, 1970: 64]. This passage at least is suggests "a theory of incorporation", even though there is disagreement as to whether it is actually claimed, and the neo-Marxists, like Althusser and Habermas, more clearly tend to emphasize the ideological incorporation of the working class [Abercrombie et al., 1980: 7–9].[13] In this sense, we can find a kind of similarity between such modern Marxists and Dumont in terms of the emphasis of superstructure and of incorporation. Nonetheless, there is a decisive difference between their research concerns and approaches. Dumont aims at clarifying the static "structured structure" in Bourdieu's term [Bourdieu, 1979a], whereas the neo-Marxists are concerned with the dynamic mechanism of how "The dominant ideology does incorporate the subordinate classes" [Abercrombie et al., 1980: 29], rather than merely with social morphology. Dumont's sense of ideology is naturally very different from the modern Marxist sense of ideology. This difference is well described by Turton as follows: "The concept of the ideological is used to refer not to fixed or systematic meanings, but to the moment of formation of consciousness in practical activity: in work, social and cultural reproduction, and in struggle" [Turton, 1984: 19]. This view coincides with Therborn's statements that "We see ideologies not as possessions or texts but as ongoing social process" [Therborn, 1980: 77] and, moreover, that "Ideologies differ, compete, and clash not only in what they say about the world we inhabit, but also in telling us who we are, in the kind of subject they interpellate" [ibid.: 78]. Though Dumontian ideology is thought of as a fixed text type, I adopt Therborn's or Turton's view of ideology in the present book. It is noted that the latter sense of ideological viewpoint is doubtless found in Bourdieu's notion of "practice" [Bourdieu, 1977] (see [Good, 1987: 80]). This thus suggests that my adoption of this viewpoint must invite a conception of "strategy" or "strategic process" for my argument (cf. [Bourdieu, 1979 (1977)], [Cohen, 1974: 80–82]).[14]

This methodological standpoint is necessary not only for reviewing pollution theories here but also for the studies of the "Untouchables", as is discussed later.

Reconsideration of Liminality Theories

The Shift from the This Worldly to the Other Worldly

It was suggested that the field of discussion must be shifted from the this worldly social domain to the other worldly religious domain. This does not simply mean the change of the object of discussion, but the important point is the change of point of view from the this worldly to the other worldly. In other words, what is necessary is the shift from the *off-boundary* viewpoint to the *on-boundary* viewpoint (*vide infra*).

The shift can be described as that from the value of *dharma* to the value of *mokṣa* in the South Asian context. The necessity of the shift is supported by Glucklich, who is conscious of the gap between *dharma* ("transferable") and *mokṣa* ("non-transferable"), as follows; "*Mokṣa* was a later addition to the *trivarga* of *dharma*, *artha*, and *kāma* of Vedic thought and according to many writers, it never did fit the *pravṛtti* ('transactional') tradition" [Glucklich, 1984: 28]. In his article [ibid.], he clearly points out that the Hindu ideas of pollution are not exhausted by the understanding derived from the transactional domain, or the domain of "transferable *karma*", but require more extended understanding based on the dimension of *mokṣa* as "non-transferable *karma*". He rightly suggests that "the full implications of Das' observations have yet to be developed" [ibid.: 27]. This statement is a good introduction to our reconsideration of liminality theories of pollution, which enable us to overcome the limitations of the society-oriented (this worldly) studies.

Liminality Theories

The point is whether the so-called liminality theories actually embody the inner viewpoint of the other worldly domain (*mokṣa*) or not. It is, therefore, necessary to carefully examine each theory in terms of this point. In the course of the examination, what the inner view of the liminal domain is, and how sacrifice is understood, are also made clear.

Liminality theories have been developed on the basis of van Gennep's inspiring classic [1960 (1909)]. They include, for instance, the time theory (or the sacred/profane theory) [1961] and the taboo theory [1972 (1964)] of Leach, and the "communitas" theory [1969] of Turner. In connection with the present topic of pollution, Douglas [1966] is important. She proposed the notion of anomaly or liminality[15] as a key concept for understanding pollution (impurity). Das [1976], who deals with Hindu culture, explains that she is a descendant of van Gennep, and in her work she takes a critical attitude to Dumont. Das herself notes that her work owes much to Durkheim's concept of "sacred", and to van Gennep's concept of "marginality" or "liminality". Firstly Leach's taboo theory is critically re-examined and the significance of Bataille's theory of religion is emphasized. Then, Douglas' and Das' studies and other related works are reviewed.

Leach's Taboo Theory and Its Critiques

The essence of Leach's taboo theory is summarized by Figures 3 and 4 in his work [Leach, 1972 (1964): 48].[16] According to Leach, "We are taught that the world consists of 'things' distinguished by names; therefore we have to train our perception to recognize a discontinuous environment. ... Language gives us the names to distinguish the things; taboo inhibits the recognition of those parts of the continuum which separate the things (Figure 3)" [1972 (1964): 47]. This explanation of Figure 3 which attaches an importance to named "things" and regards taboo as an instrument for clarifying them is naturally criticized as follows; "the complex interaction between the development of logical-operational structures and linguistic structures does not justify the exclusive function that Leach attributes to verbal categories *per se* in perception" [Platenkamp, 1979: 174] (See also [Halverson, 1976: 507–508]).

The problem of Leach's language-centred understanding of the world basically derives from his static (non-interpretative), top-down and this-worldly view, as self-evidently shown by his adoption of objective explanatory diagrams like Figures 3 and 4. His standpoint is, therefore, the very opposite of that of recognizing the

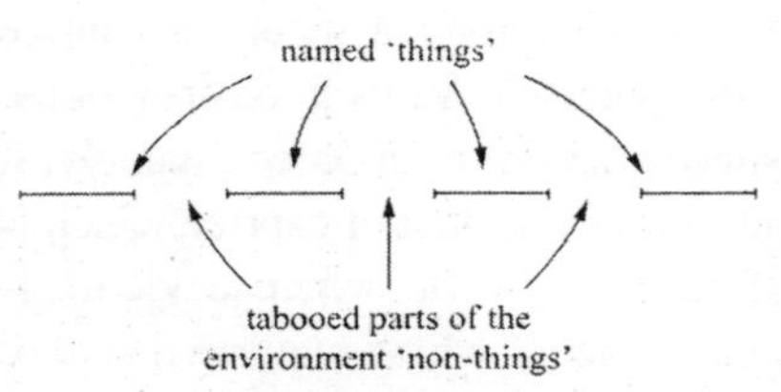

The Relationship of tabooed objects to the world of names
[Leach 1972(1964): 48, Figure 3]

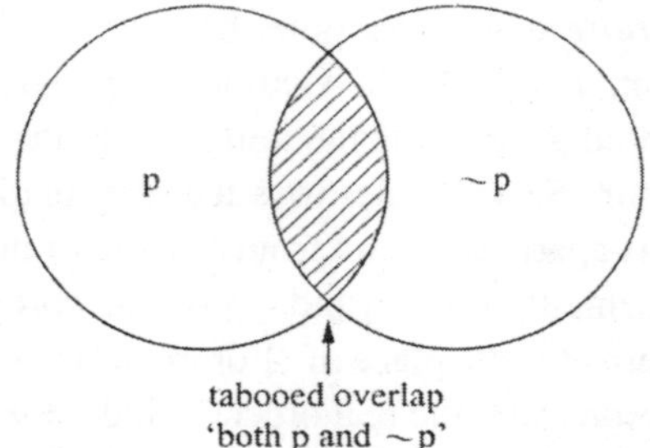

The relationship between ambiguity and taboo
[Leach 1972(1964): 48, Figure 3]

generative potentiality of poetic language, that is, a rather taboo-centred standpoint associated with the on-boundary viewpoint in which language becomes instrumental for watching a deep sea of taboo. As Platenkamp also points out, though Leach insists on the connection between anomaly on the structural categorical level and taboo on the empirical level, he fails to explain systematically how such a connection is actually possible (see also [Halverson, 1976: 513]). In this sense, Leach's theory is indifferent to dynamic processes such as who interprets it and how such an interpretation is possible. As a result, his generalized theory, which is produced by the dogmatic (reductionist) approach lacking a contextual and interpretative viewpoint, is unwittingly fused with the ruling top-down ideology.[17] This top-down and non-interpretative viewpoint never pays attention to the inner or on-boundary view of the liminal tabooed area and therefore confines his theory to the this worldly domain.The limitation of Leach's theory is more clearly found in his understanding of the other world and of rituals or sacrifice (see [Leach, 1976: 81–82]). According to his understanding, the other world is also seen as one of discontinuous categories like named "things", which has the opposite character of a category of this world. There is no doubt that the other world in Leach's sense reflects his this worldly thinking [Leach, 1976: 81–82]. This results in the two parallel categorical domains in the same level, that is, this world as a human domain and the other world as a gods' domain, as shown in Figure 4. As long as we are not conscious about where our viewpoint is positioned and our view is confined to the this worldly view, like Leach, we cannot properly access the other worldly domain. If we entered into the boundary confronting the other worldly domain, we would be led to the religious experience in a true sense of leaving the discontinuous world for the world of "continuity". This exactly coincides with what Bataille points out in his book, *Theory of Religion* [Bataille, 1976 (1948)], as is explained next.

Bataille's Theory of Religion

According to Leach, sacrifice is "purposefully" dealt with as a topic of "communication between Man and Deity" or "changing the social status of individuals" [Leach, 1976: Ch.18]. However, religion in its nature must be free from usefulness, as Bataille deliberately argues [Bataille, 1976]. Bataille notes, "Le principe du sacifice est la destruction, … . C'est la chose—seulement la chose—que le sacrifice veut *détruire* dans la victime. Le sacrifice détruit les liens de subordination réels d'un objet, il arrache la victime au monde de l'utilité et la rend à celui du caprice inintelligible. (It is the thing – only the thing – that sacrifice wants to destroy in the victim. Sacrifice destroys the real relation of subordination of an object, namely, it pulls apart the victim from a world of utility and returns it to that of caprice which is not intelligible.)" [ibid.: 307]. According to Bataille, a world where a victim is returned is the place of "l'ordre intime (the intimate order)", which requires denial of "l'ordre réel (the real order)" [ibid.: 308], where it is realized that "qu'il n'y a pas de différence entre elle (la mort) et la vie (there is no difference between death and life)" [ibid.: 308]. More precisely, he explains about the difference between "l'ordre intime" and "l'ordre réel": "L'ordre réel rejette moins la négation de la réalité qu'est la mort que l'affirmation de la vie intime, immanente, dont la violence sans mesure est pour la stabilité des choses un danger, et qui n'est pleinement révélé que dans la mort. (The real order rejects the affirmation of the intimate and immanent life, in which unmeasured violence is dangerous for the stability of things and which is perfectly revealed by death, rather than the negation of the reality represented by death.)" [ibid.: 309].

These statements of Bataille make clear that Leach's notion of sacrifice remains within the domain of usefulness ("l'ordre réel") and is, therefore, confined within a this-worldly view. In other words, Leach's this-worldly theory of liminality produces or reinforces the hierarchical discontinuity between the central and the marginal because of its outer point of view towards the liminal domain or the off-boundary viewpoint. To the contrary, if one moved into the liminal area and acquired its inner viewpoint or the on-boundary viewpoint, one would experience a continuous world where liminality is shared by everybody, namely, liminality disappears, as Bataille proposes.

Thus, we have learnt that liminality can be interpreted from two different viewpoints, namely, the this worldly ("the real order") and the other worldly ("the intimate order") or the outer view and the inner view of the liminal domain. The this worldly view results in the repression of liminality for maintaining a order whereas the other worldly view leads to the acceptance of liminality for creating a new order.

Douglas' Theory

In Douglas' theory, anomaly is connected with pollution, by which taboo in Leach's theory is replaced. The essence of Douglas' theory is to some extent represented by her statements; "dirt ... was a by-product of the creation of order" [Douglas, 1966: 160] and "dirt is essentially disorder. ... it exists in the eye of the beholder," [ibid.: 2]. Thus, her theory of pollution is usually circulated by the following generalized dictum: "uncleanness is matter out of place" [ibid.: 40]. Although there is no doubt that a linkage between pollution and anomaly (as disorder or danger) is her major contribution, it creates problems as well.

The principal problem is said to lie in the simplistic and rather psychological connection between pollution and anomaly. In other words, she proposes a sort of generalized theory in which different kinds of taboo situations are not distinguished [Ardener, 1967: 139], [de Heusch, 1971: 10–12]. As many writers have already noted,[18] Douglas' theory fails to explain clearly how anomaly can be linked with pollution, because it lacks an "extensive body of ethnography" [Bulmer, 1967], or a "social historical context" [Uberoi, 1967].[19] In this sense, at least in terms of her 1966 theory, it perpetuates the shortcoming of uprooted "generalization", which is shared with Leach, though she revised her original theory in her later essay [1975 (1972)], in which Leach is clearly criticized by her [ibid.: 287–288].

It seems to me that it is unjust and partial to evaluate Douglas' work only from the above-mentioned viewpoint. For Douglas' intensive study focusing on pollution goes beyond Leach and succeeds in showing a complexity and an abundance of pollution concepts. The merit is derived basically from her materials supporting her argument, which are collected from a broad range of religions, from primitive religions to world religions.

Her investigation of primitive religion naturally leads to her broad interests in pollution, ranging from its social control to its ritual treatment, or from the negative (suppressive) response to the affirmative response [Douglas, 1966: 39–40]. This broad interest in pollution, including her concern with the ambiguous or creative power of pollution (see [ibid.: Chapter 10]) prevents her theory from being a Leach type of rigorous society-oriented study. Douglas' understanding of pollution, which is crystallized especially in Chapter 10 of her book, is insightful and stimulating, going beyond the above-mentioned shortcoming. It is unjust that her dictum of "matter out of place" is over emphasized. Rather than this, we should pay attention to her statement that "The moral of all this is that the facts of existence are a chaotic jumble." [ibid.: 163]. This fundamental recognition is crucial. Her remarkable contribution to the theory of pollution lies in her proper understanding of William James, and on this basis, her adoption of a two-dimensional framework of dirt-affirming and dirt-rejecting philosophies [ibid.: 164]. This distinction between two types of philosophies can correspond with Bataille's concepts of "the intimate order" and "the real order".[20] Moreover, Das' theory, to be explained subsequently, is supported by Douglas' clear statement that "when someone embraces freely the symbols of death, or death itself, then it is consistent with everything that we have seen so far, that a great release of power for good should be expected to follow." [ibid.: 178] Thus, the other worldly viewpoint, or the inner viewpoint of the liminal domain, is acquired by Douglas, and her theory is judged as a firm foundation for my later argument.

Das' Theory: Liminality of Death

Das' work [1976] which deals with liminality in the broad sociological perspective has the feature of her argument being constructed consistently on the basis of a particular ethnographic context of Hindu society [Das, 1976: 249]. On the conceptual bases of Durkheim's original sense of "sacred" and van Gennep's "marginality" [Das, 1976: 246–248], Das rejects Dumont's emphasis of the pure-impure dichotomy, and replaces it with the religious (transcendental) concept of the "sacred", namely, a cosmic order as a source of axiomatically legitimizing social institutions [ibid.: 247]. Das defines pollution as the liminal (marginal) situations in which "an individual experiences his social world as separated from the cosmic" [ibid.: 248] and which have a threatening nature. Religion provides the means by which liminalities are positively overcome. Das states the important dictum that "the paradigm of liminality *par excellence* is death" [ibid.: 252]. The essential meaning of "ritual" for her is to "convert death (birth) from an accidental, contingent event capable of questioning the entire social order to a part of a design of a cosmic order" [ibid.: 256]. A sacrifice or a death ritual (cremation) is, therefore, the most typical "ritual" in this sense (see also [Kaushik, 1976]).

It is made clear that Das' argument can also be regarded as one of the attempts taking into consideration the dimension of "the intimate order", especially in the Hindu social context. However, I feel that Douglas' expression, "a great release of power through embracing death", is more suitable than Das' expression of "the restoration of cosmos through a sacrificial rite". Das' contribution, mentioned above, is basically due to her special attention to the sacrificial aspect of death,[21] which cannot be reduced to the this worldly principal of pure-impure. This is the point which

Gluklich wants to make when he recommends Das' argument, as previously mentioned. In sum, Das' discussion makes clear that Hindu ideology holds the transcendental value of the "sacred" which is reproduced according to the logic of sacrifice, or the logic of death and the regeneration of life. This naturally explains Das' standpoint from which she criticises Dumont's identification of life process pollution with caste pollution.

Metaphor of Dying

In order to expand the point that Douglas and Das made clear, it is useful to take up Meigs' work on pollution, which challenges Douglas' theory on the basis of her monographic data from the Hua people of the New Guinea Highlands [Meigs, 1978]. Here I focus only on the merits of her work and ignore its shortcomings.[22]

Meigs also questions a point, which is repeatedly pointed out as a critique of Douglas' theory by many writers: "how can Douglas account for the fact that most anomalous, disordered phenomena are not polluting? Consider, for example, in that same context of the dining room table not shoes but a toy ship, or stationery, or a roll of paper towels, or a new dress. Each of these is as out of place as the shoes. Yet we do not feel them to be dirty or polluting. "Messy" is the appropriate term" [Meigs, 1978: 310]. Meigs asks what makes the difference between pollution and a mess. In response, she defines pollution as: "(1) substances which are perceived as decaying, carriers of such substances and symbols of them; (2) in those contexts in which the substances, their carriers, or symbols are threatening to gain access to the body; (3) where that access is not desired" [ibid.: 313]. In this definition, "the perception of decaying" is seen as the first key notion. This notion is based on the Hua view that "Anything that is polluting is a form of *nu* (vital essence)" [ibid.: 307]. "*Nu* is viewed as the source of life, vitality, sexuality, youth. Its loss or contamination may result in loss of health, ageing, or death" [ibid.: 306]. Meigs illustrates that *aune,* which is defined as the animating substance of matter, is *nu* in its positive, health-enhancing aspect; whereas *siro na* is *nu* in its negative, health-reducing aspect [ibid.: 308]. She reports that menstrual blood and parturitional fluids are the most dangerous and polluting but are, at the same time, regarded as "the means *par excellence* of *aune* transfer" [ibid.: 309].

Thus, Meigs shows that the perception of decay or of losing *nu*, is recognized as pollution, and pollution is, therefore, evoked by the liminal situation of dying. Moreover, as is suggested by *aune* typically being embodied by menstrual blood, pollution, namely, the perception of death, is the moment of the regeneration of life. Through these arguments an important point is raised. That is, pollution is not death itself but perception of dying. Meigs regards as the sources of pollution, "substances which are perceived as decaying, carriers of such substances and symbols of them". This suggests, in sum, that the "metaphor of dying" evokes pollution. Though Meigs does not use this expression, she insists that the "perception of being drawn into death" is the point that distinguishes pollution from messiness.

Thus, we find the following equation: *liminality (matter out of place) plus "metaphor of dying" (the intrusion of other-worldliness) equals pollution.* Meigs fails to formulate this point well, although she touches on it in her description.

Although the claim that the definition of liminality itself includes the metaphor of dying is not impossible, adding metaphor of dying is intended to more unambiguously define pollution, keeping away the danger of the uprooted generalization. In other words, the added definition makes it clear that pollution always premises a subjective viewpoint from which it is narrated in some particular context. If liminality was understood as between different categories within this-worldly order from the privileged analytical (transcendental) viewpoint, it would not always generate pollution. In this sense, it is indispensable for the definition of pollution to have a subjective view of insider of the order, because pollution appears in the insider's perception of destruction of the order, i.e., the metaphor of dying. This interpretative fact is clarified by the above-mentioned equation.

Pollution and Context

The above-mentioned equation vividly suggests that pollution must be defined in each individual context because the "metaphor of dying" is not an absolute or objective feeling but a subjective perception which reflects different internal and external conditions.

In order to clarify this point, let us take up the topic of "foreignness" described by Khare [1962–63]. According to his work, which deals with an Indian society, people often see manners or things having a "foreign" origin as being ritually polluting in the phase of social change. Khare gives several examples. The Western manner of sitting on chairs and placing food on a table is thought of as polluting by old people. Tomatoes and carrots were treated as non-vegetarian (ritually pollution) foods due to their "foreign" origin. Here we have to notice the fact that the pollution of the first example was strongly recognized by the old generation and by people of the higher castes who were conservative and against European contact, and was not recognized by other people. Similarly, concerning the second example, tomatoes and carrots are usual vegetables for today's Indians who never say that these things are polluting. Even in those days it was not a matter of concern for non-vegetarians. Therefore, we can learn from these examples that it is indispensable to take into account the contextual settings in the definition of the concept of pollution. That is, when, where, and how pollution is felt and who feels pollution should not be missed. This logically leads to the possibility that everything could become a polluting thing depending upon the context in which it is placed.

Towards Theories of Pollution: The Distinction between "Pollution" and "Impurity"

The discussion so far can be summed up as follows:

1. The complete definition of pollution requires not only the generalized cognition of liminality (anomaly), which is expressed as "matter out of place" or "disorder", but also the "perception of being drawn into death" or the "metaphor of dying". In short, pollution is thought of as the "metaphorical perception of liminality of death". In this sense, pollution is not an innate attribute of a carrier, but an "interpretation" of a particular subject in a particular socio-cultural context.

2. Once pollution is defined, as described above, pollution can be seen to invite two different attitudes towards it, namely, the negative and the positive, which correspond with Douglas' distinction between the dirt-rejecting philosophy and the dirt-affirming one. The former attitude comes from the off-boundary viewpoint confined in the secular realm (the viewpoint of the outsider of the liminal domain). This negative attitude towards pollution is penetrated by the principle of pure-impure and makes a hierarchical discontinuity between a pure non-carrier of liminality and an impure carrier of liminality.
   In other words, the attitude confines one to "the real order" in Bataille's sense, in which pollution is segregated and suppressed. To the contrary, we can imagine another positive attitude towards pollution which reflects the on-boundary viewpoint of the sacred realm (the viewpoint of the insider of the liminal domain). This shift of viewpoint from the outsider to the insider is described as participation in the liminality of death, which is comparable to the sacrificial act. There, "the intimate order" in Bataille's sense, or a world of continuity, is accessed through the principle of sacrifice (death and the regeneration of life), i.e., the cosmic dialogue with the other-worldliness.

We can extract two different attitudes to coping with pollution. One is an attitude of "elimination", in which pollution is regarded as a dangerous alien substance destroying the order of the system so that it must be eliminated out of the system or suppressed in the peripheral part of the system. This attitude is naturally connected with the social hierarchy defined by the principle of pure-impure. The theories of Dumont and Leach reveal this aspect of pollution. Another is an attitude of "acceptance", in which pollution is seen as cosmic pollution, so that it is once accepted and then converted into a creative power. In this sense, the sacrificial act is inevitable, as Douglas and Das make clear.

These differences in the attitudes towards pollution imply that there are two different dimensions hidden under the conventional concept of pollution. In order to differentiate these two dimensions of pollution, *I propose that the dimension of pollution directed by the attitude of "elimination" is called "impurity", while the dimension of pollution directed by the attitude of "acceptance" is named "pollution"*. "Impurity" always appears as the opposite of "purity", so that Dumont's ideology can be placed in this dimension; whereas "pollution" is seen as an independent notion, on the basis of which Das criticizes Dumont. Thus, my understanding of pollution provides the map on which both theories of pollution can be properly placed.

Notes

1. Dumont notes, "The passage from occasional individual impurity to permanent group impurity is exemplified here, as Hocart has stated, by the washerman …, or the barber …" [Dumont, 1986 (1957): 463].
2. Orenstein [1968] deals with "a grammar of defilement in Hindu Sacred Law", in which he classifies pollution types into "relational pollution" based on kinship relations and "act

pollution" caused by contact with biological phenomena. He further classifies "act pollution" into "internal pollution" and "external pollution", but these are not the same as Stevenson's concepts.

3. "The Hindu Pollution Concept" is a particular corpus of beliefs concerning purity and pollution, by which ritual status, both group and personal, is defined. The following, for example, are included in "the Hindu Pollution Concept": to commit the taking of life, to deal with a corpse, to treat human excretions, to slaughter a cow and eat its meat or deal with its skin, to take an alcoholic drink, remarriage of a widow and so on. These polluting actions cause a decline in ritual status.
4. It is said that Dumont's theory has two strong foundations, Bouglé and Hocart. Dumont developed the theory of Bouglé especially in terms of the concept of pure-impure [Kolenda, 1978: 38], though the connection between the pure-impure ideology and the dualism of the *varṇa* system (Brahman/Kshatriya) is Dumont's contribution [Kolenda, 1976]. Dumont doubtless learnt a lot from Hocart's work [Hocart, 1970: xvi]. For example, Dumont cites Hocart's idea in support of his argument of the passage from occasional individual impurity to permanent group impurity [Dumont, 1986: 463].
5. Nonetheless, Dumont's relationalist standpoint is not enough to escape the substantialist one. For example, if the relationship between Brahman and Harijan is once understood by the dichotomy of pure-impure, its understanding soon starts to be fixed. Therefore, it is always required to prevent substantializing pure Brahman and impure Harijan regardless of context, but Dumont fails to do so.
6. In this connection, Burghart's evaluation of Dumont is this. He notes that "Dumont's approach has often been characterized as 'structuralist'. … Dumont appears to be more a Weberian sociologist than a Lévi-Straussian structuralist" [Burghart, 1985: 6]. He suggests a contact between Lévi-Strauss' universalist structuralist approach and Dumont's culturally specific structuralist approach.
7. More broadly speaking, Dumont intends to refute the empiricism of Anglo-American anthropologists [David, 1977: 239]. This is clearly stated in his Preface to the 1980 edition [Dumont, 1980: xviii–xx].
8. There have already been two review symposiums on Dumont's contributions, namely, [Madan et al. 1971] in "Contributions to Indian Sociology" and [Richards and Nicholas et al. 1976] in "The Journal of Asian Studies".
9. Marriott's theory is called the transactional, ethnosociological, monist, or substance-codes theory, which was originally inspired by Schneider's concepts of natural identity and code for conduct [Schneider, 1968]. According to Marriott's notion, the theory tries to explain the "superior value" ruling the caste system by transactions of "substance" in order to overcome Dumont's dualistic thought. Marriott notes, "Transactors and transactions are oriented ultimately neither towards "purity" nor towards "power" as usually understood in social science, but towards a unitary Indian concept of superior value – power understood as vital energy, substance-code of subtle, homogeneous quality, and high, consistent transactional status or rank." [Marriott, 1976: 137]. Transactional theory also invites much criticism. The criticism of Barnett, Fruzzetti and Oster [1976] is convincing and they point out the partiality of the monist theory and conclude, "The exchanges and sharings of substances defining genera and creating rank … add little to our understanding of what Indian society is all about." [ibid.: 632–634]. (see also [Marglin, 1977: 268]) Another problem is that Marriott's theory is textual and "reductionistic" [McGilvray, 1982: 88], and seems to be derived from the Samkhya guna theory [Glucklich, 1984: 38]. While some field

research (e.g. [Davis, 1976: 9–21]) supports Marriott, other (e.g. [McGilvray, 1982: 91]) does not. Moreover, Good's critique of ethnosociology is fundamental and important. He points out the insensitivity of ethnosociologists to the distinction between "data" and "theory" [Good, 1978: 511]), which makes it impossible to introduce an interpretative viewpoint. The defect remains unchanged in the recent integrating work of Marriott and his students (Special Issue: "Towards an Ethnosociology of India" [Marriott et al. 1989]).

10. Quigley undermines the superiority of Brahman by pointing out the fatal contradiction that Brahman priests have to receive *dāna* from secular people in the post-colonial perspective (see [Sekine, 1994b]).
11. Burghart [1983] more consciously analyses renunciation from the ascetic's point of view and clarifies the partiality of the Brahman householder's construction of asceticism.
12. While Das and Uberoi pay attention to an egalitarian mutuality or reciprocity which is observed in the removal of pollution among the lower castes, Parry extracts an egalitarian ideology of "brotherhood" though his extended ethnography, which not only is found within the intra-caste relationship but also spills over into inter-caste relationships. Raheja's concept of "mutuality" also falls into this stream [Raheja, 1988]. Parry criticizes Dumont by comparing Dumont's theory to Polanyi's substantivist view, which is thought of as the reverse projection of modern Western thought [Parry, 1974: 105–107].
13. The standpoint of Abercrombie et al. is not the same as that of the Althusserians. Thompson comments, "The authors of *The Dominant Ideology Thesis* may have been right to criticize Althusserian Marxist theorists of ideology, and the Parsonian functionalist theorists of common culture, for over-stressing the incorporation of people into a community of shared values as a prerequisite for the reproduction of the relations of production or the maintenance of social order in late capitalism." [Thompson, 1986: 48]
14. This claim can be supported by Dirks' statement, "History – viewed more as process than as chronology – is fundamental to this concern with practice" [Dirks, 1987: 12]. In this sense, going beyond Dumont is symbolic because this shift can be linked with the more general argument on the change of paradigm from the science of "reversibility" (timeless) to the science of "irreversibility" (time) [Prigogine and Stengers, 1984]. Foucault's view, in which a concept of discourse as a historical phenomenon is adopted and the notion of a pre-existing system is refuted [Fowler, 1987 (1973): 64–65], can be placed in the same theoretical stream.
15. Douglas explains that anomaly is not synonymous with ambiguity but that there is little advantage in distinguishing between these two terms [Douglas, 1966: 37]. Furthermore, ambiguity, marginality and liminality are interchangeable, as is suggested by the fact that she cites van Gennep in her important arguments.
16. It is noticed that there is a logical contradiction which is found in Leach's identification of Figure 3 with Figure 4. I am puzzled how Figure 3 can be replaced by Figure 4, because "tabooed parts" in Figure 3 are obviously outside of named things but "tabooed part" in Figure 4 overlaps a particular verbal category P (see [Halverson, 1976: 510], [Platenkamp, 1979: 177]).
17. The following aphorism of Eagleton is valid for this problem. "Such 'pure' literary theory is an academic myth: some of the theories we have examined in this book are nowhere more clearly ideological than in their attempt to ignore history and politics altogether." [Eagleton, 1983: 195]

18. For instance, [Hershman, 1974: 293], [Bulmer, 1967: 21], [Meigs, 1978: 310], [Bradford, 1983: 320–321], [Uberoi, 1967: 90] and [Platenkamp, 1979].
19. Douglas herself later accepts such criticism and recognizes that anomaly is not always regarded as pollution or taboo [Douglas, 1975: 287–288].
20. Douglas notes, "Thus we have to reckon with two tendencies in Lele religion: one ready to tear away even the veils imposed by the necessities of thought and to look at reality direct; the other a denial of necessity, a denial of the place of pain and even of death in reality." [Douglas, 1966: 171] The former dimension, which is realized by the mysteries of the pangolin [ibid.: 160–170], is related to "the intimate order"; while the latter is related to "the real order".
21. Das' later work entitled "Language of Sacrifice" [1983] examines Vedic sacrifice in the light of the same concern.
22. It seems to me that Meigs' work is problematic as an independent study. For Meigs interestingly challenges Douglas' theory but finally fails to overcome its shortcomings because Meigs does not leave her this-worldly and non-interpretative (functionalist) viewpoint. This limitation is clearly found in her humble statement that: "at best pollution could only be a particular kind of marginality or ambivalence, a subclass of the larger class of ambivalent things" [Meigs, 1978: 317, n. 9].

Chapter 3

The Problem in Studies of "Untouchables"

Is a Harijan Community Special?

Introduction: A Contrivance of "Impure" Harijans

Harijans have been discriminated as "impure" people by Caste Hindus. The Harijans have been necessary people for a village life not only as labourers engaging in degraded services and manual work but also as a symbolic marker indicating the boundary between a village social space and its outside. Every institution requires such a boundary marker by which the shape of the institution is made clear and its identity is guaranteed. This mechanism can be in principle extended to the relationship between life and death. One's life could be vividly recognized when one confronts a crisis of dying. There is, therefore, a structural correspondence between the polluting experience of dying for a living person and socially defined polluting Harijans for the ruling people of the village sphere. Such boundary markers indicating the end of the inner order must be seen as the pollution or the impure that is a sort of social alarm.

The Indian village holding the above-mentioned contrivance clearly appeared in the modern era in a broad sense. According to Kotani, the change from an ambiguous discrimination to an unambiguous discrimination against a particular peripheral group of people, later called Harijans, had taken place towards the modern era [Kotani, 1989: 112–119]. The change of perception in terms of the peripheral people can be described in my terms as the transition from pollution to "impurity" in social interpretation about them. Here, it is useful to recall Foucault's concept of "normalization" for explaining modern discipline. If the concept was applied for understanding the social position of Harijans, they would be regarded as " 'abnormal' members of a normalizing hierarchy" [Pinny, 1988: 147], who instrumentally play a crucial role for maintaining the village caste system. To know this ruling contrivance in the modern era, which reflects the centripetal viewpoint of the ruling people, is an important outset for studies of Harijans.[1]

It is now clear that the "impurity" attached to Harijans is not innate but a product of a modern social order ruled by the dominant caste. However, it is also the fact that such a dominant ideology has a permeating power among the villagers including Harijans themselves. Not only that, but the scholars studying caste societies have been more or less dazzled by the dominant viewpoint and have deviated from the proper understanding.[2] As already mentioned, the typical example is their inadequate understanding of phenomena of pollution or impurity.

At any rate, our quest is to disclose the real lives of Harijans living under the pressure of the top-down viewpoint and in the trap of the modern contrivance as mentioned above.

Mencher's Aphorism: The Significance of the Bottom-up Viewpoint

First of all, the following aphorism of Mencher in terms of the Harijans' viewpoint should be noted, because it strongly advocates the necessity of seeing a caste society from the bottom-up viewpoint. Mencher points out not only that the idea of *ḍharma*, which is embodied by the *jajmānī* system, has been used as an instrument of repression, but also that many people at the bottom of the social hierarchy have been aware of this [Mencher, 1974: 470].[3] Furthermore, she makes the important remark that "Untouchables may accept these notions (*dharma* and *karma*) to some extent, but it is important to distinguish between the overt acceptance of such values and the holding of other values usually unexpressed to outsiders" [ibid.: 476].[4] This suggestion must be kept in mind when the socially repressed people are investigated. This furthermore reminds us of another more basic problem, which is related to what the unexpressed other value is. Prior to the problem of expression, the values in which the socially repressed believe are actually not always clear to them, because the indigenous or popular culture which is deeply internalized in their minds and bodies does not have a clear-cut shape like the superimposed dominant ideology, as Caplan, for example, points out [Caplan, 1980: 235]. Thus, a study of the Harijans requires a more careful approach than that of Caste Hindus because we have to take into account both the Harijans' complex representations (expressions) and the less explicit ideology (values) they hold. It is, therefore, presupposed that there are complex relationships between the given social status and conditions, the given ideological configuration, and their contradictory behaviour.

Moffatt's Consensus Model

Our primary question are in what kind of ideology the Harijans actually believe and what kind of relationship is found between such a less explicit ideology and the dominant ideology.

At the outset, Moffatt's classification regarding the studies of "Untouchables" since 1950 is useful, though it is problematic, as I will show.[5] He sets up three categories, i.e., (1) outcaste images (lack of culture),[6] (2) models of diversity (other culture),[7] and (3) models of unity (replicated culture), and he then classifies his own work into the third category [Moffatt, 1979: Chapter 1].[8] It is clear that Moffatt's categorization is basically made according to whether "Untouchables" share or replicate the dominant ideology. This criterion distinguishes (1) and (2) from (3). In this sense, the difference between (1) and (2), both of which are thought of as disjunctive theories, is subtle. According to Moffatt, the outcaste images imply that Untouchables have some awareness of their own oppression, while models of diversity contain no such implication [ibid.: 21]. Moffatt claims that the main shortcoming found in theories professing the disjunctive models (e.g., Gough, Mencher, Berreman, and Miller) lies in their attitude in which the world of the Untouchables is described as if it was a self-contained whole, "emphasizing distinctiveness and failing to weigh continuities with the larger culture" [ibid.: 23]. The criticism itself that he raised is worth attention, but since his research is confined to the Harijan community I wonder whether he has enough qualification to say so. Anyhow, he asserts that the models of unity, in which his own theory is placed, are based on the structural model of Dumont and the "ethnosociological" models of Marriott, Inden and Nicholas, and that both models, "contain principles of diversity, but in each model diversity is either 'encompassed by', or generated from, a more basic unity" [ibid.: 24]. Moffatt, who emphasizes a cultural consensus [ibid.: 98], concludes as follows: "Those persons who are, in egalitarian terms, among the most oppressed members of Indian society are also among the truest believers in the system that so oppresses them" [ibid.: 304]. This statement indicates that Moffatt is not only a strong supporter of Dumontian theory, but also a representative of the consensus theorists in the field of Harijan studies.

Moffatt's work is rather welcomed by Indianists, because his work contributes to undermining – as he himself intends – the empathetic attitude often found among the disjunction theorists, which reflects the researcher's personal distaste for caste hierarchy [ibid.: 22–23]. Mayer, for example, objectively evaluates Moffatt's book as follows; "the value of this … book is to suggest an answer to the question of why it is that it is often the lowest castes which are the most conservative, and the most exclusive among themselves" [Mayer, 1980: 398]. Deliège, who also studied the Paraiyars, says of Moffatt's work that it doubtlessly provides a good illustration of the Harijans' internalization of caste hierarchical values [Deliège, 1988: 109–110; 1992: 156–160].

Criticism of Moffatt's Work: The Necessity of an "Interpretative" Viewpoint

I certainly understand the importance of Moffatt's paradoxical conclusion, but there are a lot of doubts in the process of discussions through which his conclusion is reached from the empirical data. The following methodological problems are found in Moffatt's works. One is that Moffatt fails to properly take into account the historical changes in the caste system when he discusses the position of the Harijans, though he himself provides such data (see [Moffatt, 1979: Chapter 3]). This problem appears because of his underestimation of the important role of high-handed repression (politics) for maintaining the caste system, and his improper understanding of the economic dependence of the Harijans which limits their activities, as Deliège also points out [Deliège, 1988: 110–111].[9] This shortcoming is not unique to Moffatt, but is related to the typical conundrum of anthropology of "ethnographical presence" which tends to neglect historical change. Anyhow, Moffatt fails to properly take account of the power relationships based not only on ritual values but also politico-economic values (see also [Parry, 1970], [Mines, 1984]).

Another more fundamental criticism is the matter concerning the epistemological order. As has already been pointed out (in Note 4), Moffatt fails to distinguish the Harijans' experiences (what they actually do) from their representations (what they express to an outsider) [Deliège, 1988: 112] [Deliège, 1992: 162]. It is claimed that this failure leads Moffatt to overestimate the Paraiyars' profession of Brahman-like orthodoxy [Deliège, 1988: 112]. Deliège concludes that, even though the Paraiyars accept the imposed hierarchy, this does not mean that the hierarchical ideology penetrates the Paraiyars' beliefs[10] but that there is an egalitarian value within their community [ibid.: 287] (see also [Deliège, 1992: 168; 1987: 235–236]). Related to this, Deliège reports that the hierarchical divisions within the Harijans that Moffatt found in Endavur [Moffatt, 1979: 216] are not found among the Paraiyars he studied [Deliège, 1988: 114; 1992: 160–161].[11]

The distinction between what the Harijans experience and what they represent, which Deliège points out, can be translated into a slightly different distinction between what they actually believe and how they behave. The recognition of this distinction naturally suggests that we cannot take how they behave at its face value, but that we have to take into account how it is interpreted. It is necessary to adopt an "interpretative" approach for the investigation of the complex social processes of the Harijans and for resolving the superficial opposition between disjunction and consensus theories. In other words, the Harijans' behaviour does not hold fixed and objective meanings, but their subjective interpretation of their own practices must be taken into account.

From this point of view, Moffatt's approach is rather naive and problematic, for he short-circuits the observable morphological level, like replicated social and ritual structures, with the level of consciousness, like consensus, without any mediatory explanations [Moffatt, 1979: 291–292].[12] The connection is made by his speculation based on "pure-impure" ideology [Deliège, 1992: 167] rather than by the Harijans' own interpretations which seem to be motivated by their self-esteem. Such one-sided speculation by Moffatt is often problematic (e.g. [Moffatt, 1979: 115]). This shortcoming arises from his static investigation. That is, he does not deal with dynamic incidents reflecting the Harijans' interpretations in his ethnography. In short, the replicated morphology found among the Harijans does not always mean that beliefs are replicated too. The more dynamic relationships between replicated morphology and their actual beliefs need to be carefully investigated from the "interpretative" viewpoint.[13]

In this respect, McGilvray's study of Sri Lankan Tamils provides an interesting example: "the first major permanent temple to be constructed in the village was for Pillaiyar and not for Mariyamman, despite the fact that the cult of Mariyamman remains the most important focus of religious observance among the Paraiyars" [McGilvray, 1983: 111]. This shows that the temple which is fine and big in appearance is not always in proportion to the significance of the actual religious beliefs. Another clear example is found in Maloney's work in Tamil Nadu [Maloney, 1975], in which he systematically examines the villagers' interpretations of philosophical concepts like *dharma, karma*, *saṁsāra* etc. and the world view. For example, regarding their feelings about *dharma*; "Brahmans and many other villagers who value piety define it in terms of morals, behavior, and thoughts. ... The non-Brahman landowners, merchants, and many farmers define *dharma* essentially as charity, for they are better at charity than at piety. ... But the third class level in Tamil Nadu, the Harijans, and other lower castes too, can vaunt neither piety nor charity and reject the idea that a donor can acquire merit at the expense of the recipient. For them, real *dharma* is giving at the temple. ... at least its purpose is to engender prosperity rather than to accentuate class or status distinctions." [Maloney, 1975: 175].[14] He concludes that most of the lower castes (the Harijans) maintain their subcultural identity through their own interpretation [ibid.: 189].

It is notable that all of them who provide the above examples and attach importance to interpretative approach are commonly critical to Moffatt.

Thus, it is now clear that the introduction of an interpretative viewpoint is inevitable for investigating the rather complicated social practices of Harijans. The interpretative approach, then, requires a consideration of the following two points: (1) What kind of *ideology* basically defines the Harijans' interpretations, even though it is difficult to be aware of? (2) What kind of *motivation* penetrates their interpretations?

Ideology and Interpretation: Beyond Disjunction and Consensus

Let us think about the ideology of the first point. The problem of opposition between a disjunction theory and a consensus theory in Harijan studies can be paraphrased to the question whether a particular unique ideology exclusively corresponds to a social section of Harijan. In fact, this problem in Harijan studies is a reflection of the opposition between the double-layers theory of early Marriott (dualism consisting of "great tradition" and "little tradition") and the Dumontian structural theory (monism consisting of a binary opposition) in Hindu social studies.

Solving the problem and going beyond the opposition is made possible by the dialectical dialogue between both theories, that is, by taking up merits and removing defects from both theories. A good point of a disjunction theory is having discovered two different cultural tendencies, while a defect is its functionalist and substantialist understanding. A merit of a consensus theory is, even though inadequately, having extracted a hierarchical and complementary relationship between two components, i.e., the centre and the peripheral in the name of ideology, while a defect is taking up only an explicit dominant ideology, in other words, only the centripetal viewpoint. Though Dumont uses ideology as the encompassing dominant value in a static manner, ideology in nature means a consistent subjective interpretation from the particular viewpoint and suggests the possibility of plural viewpoints. It also should be remained that the usage of ideology, as mentioned before, is the neo-Marxist one in which a key concept is a generative discourse depending on context.

The dialectical consideration based on merits of both theories thus leads to a better sketch of the dynamic (interdependent) configuration of two ideologies having different vectors, that is, the centripetal ideology having the off-boundary viewpoint and the decentripetal ideology having the on-boundary viewpoint. As discussed in the previous Chapter, this dynamism is exactly found in the connection and distinction between the "pure-impure" ideology and the "pollution" ideology.

Let me explain a little more about the dynamic relationship between both ideologies. A centripetal ideology like "pure-impure" ideology is a ruling one that constructs and justifies a social hierarchical order from the off-boundary viewpoint. The yardstick of "normalization" consisting of a binary opposition of "the highly A vs the lowly non-A" such as "pure-impure" opposition is adopted by the centripetal ideology. Non-A is a necessary counterpart of A, because the existence of non-A as a boundary marker guarantees the identity formation of A. On the contrary, the decentripetal ideology like "pollution" ideology is basically a passive and paradoxical ideology which is produced by the superimposition of the ruling ideology but at the same time has a moment of escaping from it. Since this ideology is born from the boundary between the inside and outside of the social space defined by the ruling ideology, it must have a potentiality of undermining or disorganizing the superimposed distinction between A and non-A, due to its unique feature of confronting the outside. It can be ironically called a *passively independent* ideology.

For example, although the action of animal sacrifice is judged as "impure" (non-A) by the centripetal ideology, the same action could be attached a different independent value B like "pollution" indicating a power generated from the boundary, that is the interpretation of the decentripetal ideology. In actual social life the ruling ideology is overwhelmingly strong and explicit so that interpretation B related to confusion (e.g., "pollution") is obliged to be suppressed and concealed by interpretation as non-A (e.g., "impurity"). This is an ideological struggle being deployed in an unsymmetrical power relationship. Furthermore, in order to understand the dynamic and temporal connection between the centripetal and the decentripetal ideologies, Kristiva's theoretical distinction between "*Symbolique*" and "*Semiotique*" [Kristiva, 1974] seems to be useful. According to Kristiva, *Symbolique* is the value holding an intention towards the ordered state and *Semiotique* is the value accepting the dynamism of maternal chaos which is dismantling but at the same time holds latent capability. It is, then, obvious that the relationship between "pure-impure" ideology and "pollution" ideology corresponds to that between *Symbolique* and *Semiotique*. This suggests that the two ideologies are two poles of views in terms of one same world that is changeable by the shift of viewpoint from the off-boundary to the on-boundary and vice versa.

The implication of the above argument for the problem of disjunction and consensus is this: there are inevitably two connected and different ideologies, i.e., the centripetal and the decentripetal, but this does not mean the objectivity of two substantial cultural entities but the possibility of two subjective interpretations (viewpoints). Furthermore, within each ideology its interpretation of the world is consistent. In sum, I agree to an inter-related ideological disjunction and at the same time accept ideological consensus within each ideology. Let us take one example. It is often said that there are "Theological Hinduism" and "Popular Hinduism" in Hindu societies. What does it mean? This statement is very much misleading and problematic, because such a distinction is made possible only by the interpretation from the ruling viewpoint, but it appears an objective classification. As a result, it is easily understood as the coexistence of two kinds of Hinduism. After the above discussion, I have to say that such naive disjunctive understanding is wrong. The statement should be grasped as two ideologies on the same reality that are inter-dependent or inter-reflexive.

The Dimension of Ideology and the Dimension of Social Section

Now we can come back to the question whether Harijans live in their own cultural world or whether a particular unique ideology exclusively corresponds to a social section of Harijan. Miller, one of the disjunction theorists who to some extent holds an viewpoint, provides an interesting bottom-up perspective. In his argument on the culture of the Mahar caste, one group of Harijans, Miller illustrates a series of themes of a "Great Tradition" for the Mahar caste, which is the antithesis of the Brahmanical

Great Tradition, as follows; "equality ..., individual ability ..., emotionalism ..., escape *from* the system ...," [Miller, 1966: 28]. Miller's bottom-up illustration of the Mahar culture seems to have an important byproduct beyond his intention. That is to say, not only this example but also other examples like Deliège's[15] suggest that most of the cultural traits which the disjunction theorists raise as the elements of the Harijan proper culture are not confined only to the Harijans but are shared among a broader section of the villagers. It is rather natural to think that those cultural traits belong to "non-Brahmanical popular culture" which is disposed in the periphery of the Brahmanical culture-centred domain.

Although eating beef or dead cattle meat, different clothes, a custom of bride-price etc. are thought of as the cultural traits showing the peculiarity of Harijan culture, most of them are not the difference of cultural quality but are caused by social suppression and economic disability and moreover forcibly reproduced by the pressure of the ruling people. It is, therefore, important to recognize that there is no a priori correspondence between a social section of Harijans and "a Harijan proper culture" imagined by disjunction theorists and that the cultural (?) gap between Caste Hindus and Harijans is not an ideological (qualitative) difference but a quantitative difference or a difference of fragmented cultural traits historically reproduced by institutionalized compulsion. As is subsequently clarified in this book, the ideological rupture is not found between Caste Hindus and Harijans but is found "between the Brahmanical theology and the popular ideology" [Caplan, 1980: 234]. The above consideration gives us a significant lesson that there is a discrepancy between the dimension of social section and the dimension of ideology. Listening to the lesson makes us free from the presupposition that Harijans must have their proper culture (ideology). The peculiar cultural traits found among the Harijans should not be regarded as their independent proper culture but is seen as a distortion produced through a long history of discrimination. This is the fundamental recognition on the basis of that the studies of Harijans would be properly developed.

Motivation and Strategy of Self-Aggrandizement

Let us shift to the second point of *motivation*. What is the driving force of the Harijans' interpretations? As many writers point out, there is a contradiction in appearance or "half-way" situation in the Harijans' cultural practices. Parry notes, by citing Fuchs [Fuchs, 1965 (1908)], "they (SC and ST) frequently contain a strong element of ambivalence. On the one hand the inequality of man is explicitly denied, while on the other hand, cult members are urged to adopt a style of life and a set of customs calculated to enhance their standing in the eyes of orthodox society" [Parry, 1974: 117]. In order to understand such complex social processes of the Harijans' behaviour, a closer examination is indispensable.

In this respect, Freeman's attempt [1979], in which the life history of an Untouchable called Muli is reconstructed, is remarkable. In this work, Freeman throws light upon a very ordinary (non-elite) Untouchable's experiences, behaviour and thoughts, and tries to describe his inner viewpoint, though he does not sufficiently analyse the rich source materials in his book.[16] From his book, we learn of the Harijan's strong desire for "self-aggrandizement"[17] which ultimately penetrates

Muli's diversified activities ranging from opportunistic to defiant. Most impressive is Muli's split attitude, on the one hand, aspiring to the power of the higher castes and being keen on acquiring friendship with them, but, on the other, ridiculing the shamefulness of the higher caste people and cynically enjoying the servile attitudes shown in front of him. Though it is true that his attitudes appear contradictory, these acts in fact suggest his consistent desire for escaping from his socially oppressed position. In this sense, it is especially interesting and notable fact that Muli, who has no hope of an institutional reform of the discriminative system, is much concerned with the dimension of *dyadic relationships* in which he can have something left to his discretion. This dimension is defined as "the pair imaginary sphere" in Yoshimoto's terms,[18] and includes family, marriage relationships, sexual affairs, and friendships. Here one can be freer from the social and formal sphere such as the oppression of caste hierarchy, which is defined as "the communal imaginary sphere" by Yoshimoto.

In the present context, Vincentnathan's work [1987] is outstanding, because the complex behaviour of the Harijans are systematically analysed in it. Her theoretical framework for explanation of contradiction among complex social processes (of the Harijans) is based on a Parsons' system theory, which can simultaneously take into account the plural systems such as personality, society and culture that are not fully interchangeable, rather than on Dumontian "structure" (not structuralist) theory [Vincentnathan, 1987: 81, 110–118]. The attempt of understanding Harijans' conducts in the framework of the relationship among the above-mentioned three systems naturally leads us to take a strategic viewpoint. Her key assumption is "that people have a basic need for self-esteem or a positive identity, and for positive communal esteem, from which their self-esteem is in part derived" [ibid.: 81–82]. She seems to see a basic need for self-esteem not only as motivation (or an incentive for action), but as a key need integrating several other basic needs, like security, social ties, cognitive needs [ibid.: Chapter 2].[19] She thus claims that the Harijans' self-esteem management within the given socio-cultural conditions is a consistent theme which penetrates their diversified and contradictory actions, in other words, that this consistent theme self-esteem produces, and at the same time integrates, their various strategic behaviours.

On the basis of Marriott's four strategies corresponding with four *varṇas* [ibid.: 63] (see [Marriott, 1976: 122]),[20] she lists the Harijans' social strategies as follows: in the spheres of intercaste relations, passing, avoidance and withdrawal, positive transactions, defiance, political movements and protests, escape, non-caste-based status [Vincentnathan, 1987: Chapter 4]; and in the spheres of intracaste relations, an *optimal* strategy (disassociation, exemplary behaviour), an *optimal* and *maximal* strategy (political power), a *minimal* strategy, a *pessimal* strategy (cognitive reversal, deviant behaviour) [ibid.: Chapter 5]. This list of strategies, all of which are motivated by self-esteem, provides a useful map for understanding the various behaviours of different types of Harijans ranging from passive, illiterate and rural Harijans to positive, educated, urban Harijans. In this sense, Freeman's book can also be to a considerable extent analysed by using Vincentnathan's theory.[21]

Here, I would like to follow especially her basic notion of self-esteem management. This notion is applicable for my present inquiry into what kind of motivation penetrates the Harijans' interpretations. However, I prefer to adopt a slightly modified concept of self-esteem, namely, the more inclusive concept of "self-aggrandizement", for the following two reasons. The first reason is that, though Vincentnathan uses the concept of self-esteem in two ways, i.e., as one of basic needs and as a central need integrating other needs, I take up here the latter broader sense of self-esteem. The second reason is that I would like to adopt Bourdieu's sense of volition working as a fundamental motivation of strategy (see Note 17).

Thus, the coexisting attitudes of both accepting the system and blaming the system can be explained without contradiction as part of the Harijans' strategies for seeking self-aggrandizement. This viewpoint doubtlessly leads us to a horizon where the unproductive dispute between disjunction and consensus theories is overcome and synthesized. This dynamic understanding of their activities, which allows for the coexistence of different theories, furthermore makes it possible to properly take into consideration the influence of the socio-cultural changes due to westernization and modernization[22] upon the Harijans' strategies, such as disconnection from the village system, mass or individual conversion, caste associations, conscious manipulation of pollution as a social weapon and so on (see [Miller, 1966], [Kolenda, 1960], [Barnett, 1975], [Cohn, 1955], [Searle-Chatterjee, 1979, 1981] etc.).[23]

The Dominant Ideology to be Replicated and Harijan Strategies

The above discussion on their ideology and motivation in terms of the interpretative approach can be in a sense synthesized by carefully rethinking "the Harijans' replication of the upper castes' culture", which was proposed by Moffatt. In this connection, Vincentnathan provides an interesting example in which the recent shift of the deity of the Anbur (her studying village) communal festival from Kaliyamman to Murugan is understood not as the conflict "between power, which is inherently contaminating, and purity", but as that "between supernatural power and a desire to increase communal esteem through purity" [Vincentnathan, 1987: 347]. This example vividly shows that the Harijans' replication is not due to their being "the truest believers" or "Sanskritization", but is seen as an act aiming at self-aggrandizement.[24]

The replicatory acts of the Harijans cannot be explained adequately by the non-interpretative usage of the concept of Sanskritization which disregards whether they are true believers or not, but should be described as conscious and strategic borrowing from socially evaluated cultural models which is expected to enhance their self-aggrandizement.

Lastly, I should make clearer what the dominant ideology to be replicated is. When we consider the Harijans' replication in the village sphere, it is necessary to take into account two levels of social space, namely, the space within a particular village, and the broader social space beyond villages.

As to the village space, we can imagine two different cases according to the dominant caste of the village system, that is, the Brahman-dominated village and the non-Brahman-dominated village. In the former case the upper caste culture is of course the Brahmanical one; whereas in the latter case the upper culture is more or less different from the Brahmanical one, even though it has been Sanskritized in various ways. In the larger outside social space where modernization (urbanization) prevails, "class" ideology based on a market economy and the Brahmanical ideology which is reintroduced as the middle class ethics coexist and occupy the dominant position in a complex manner [Kolenda, 1960: 286]. The village Harijans today thus logically have two-layered models of dominant values to emulate, namely, the local dominant caste's values and the more widely accepted dominant value which is a cultural complex of modernity and Brahmanical culture, i.e., "the contemporary popular Brahmanical culture" in my term.

If Moffatt's work is placed in this framework, it is evident that he is a bit careless because, as a Dumont-follower, he wittingly or unwittingly confuses the upper caste culture with the Brahmanical ideology ("pure-impure" ideology) in his argument. Since the village I study here is a non-Brahman-dominated village, I naturally have to be conscious of such a distinction.

Needless to say, village Harijans also live in the contemporary world where people's social spaces are rapidly expanding and multi-layered. Therefore, it is more and more indispensable for the studies of Harijan strategies to properly ascertain the extension of social space and its ideological configuration.

Notes

1. The way of elimination with an expression of pollution or impurity, if it was once internalized, could be very effective for reproducing and sustaining a hierarchical order of the social due to its connection with a embodied sense. The implication becomes obvious when the sensory expression of pollution is confused with ethical expression of bad, because, though the latter axis of good and bad allows consideration based on reason, there is little room for reasonable thinking in the former axis of pure and impure. Therefore, the way using the former expression more directly resorts to the people and, as a result, works for concealing the crude from of the dominant ideology.
2. Although this is a problem of relationship between the level of data and that of analysis, it is, in fact, not a simple and small problem. Why does the dominant ideology of the society studied so often reflect upon the theory of social analysts? One of my basic answers is that it is because there is a structural similarity between the system of normalization (in Foucault's sense) realized by the dominant ideology in the observed society and the Orientalist structure of Modern Western knowledge in which the analyst is deeply involved.
3. Mencher seems to imagine the people at the lower end of the social hierarchy as conscious subjects like an awakened proletariat, who reject the dominant ideology [Mencher, 1974: 469]. She is classified as an "outcaste images" theorist by Moffatt [Moffatt, 1979: 10], and is regarded as a theorist professing "countercultural models" by Vincentnathan [Vincentnathan, 1987: 74].
4. Deliège also makes the same point, namely, the distinction between an actual experience and its representation, in his criticism of Moffatt [Deliège, 1988: 112]. There, he raised the example that the Paraiyars do not usually accept that they are beef-eaters, even though they actually eat it. This example reveals that the Harijans have a strong desire for self-respect [ibid.: 112]. The point is further developed by Vincentnathan, who investigates the Harijans' behaviour under the concept of self-esteem [Vincentnathan, 1987].
5. The following studies of "Untouchables" soon come to mind: [Cohn, 1954, 1955, 1958], [Miller, 1966, 1967], [Mencher, 1974], [Maloney, 1975], [McGilvray, 1983], [Kolenda,

1960, 1964], [Sachchidananda, 1977], [Moffatt, 1975, 1979], [Freeman, 1979, 1986], [Vincentnathan, 1987], [Deliège, 1987, 1988, 1992, 1993], [Khare, 1984], [Houska, 1981], [Searle-Chatterjee, 1979, 1981], [Mosse, 1994b] etc., though the list is not complete.

6. Moffatt claims that Gough [1956], Mencher [1974], and Berreman [1971] can be classified into this category.
7. For this category, Cohn [1955], Kolenda [1964], Gough [1960, 1973], Miller [1966], etc. are mentioned by him.
8. Vincentnathan also takes up a similar categorization to Moffatt's. Her tripartite models are the consensus model, subcultural model and countercultural model [Vincentnathan, 1987: 70–75]. It seems to me that these models correspond respectively with models of unity, models of diversity and lack of culture in Moffatt's sense.
9. This shortcoming of Moffatt seems to be derived from Dumont who, as Dirks argues, separated caste from the politico-economic sphere [Dirks, 1987: 7–10]. Dirks notes that this problematic view is commonly found in comparative sociology which tends to remove politics from societies [ibid.: 8].
10. Deliège clearly states elsewhere that: "there is no necessary link between these two concepts: replication does not imply consensus." [Deliège, 1992: 160].
11. Deliège's conclusion should not be, however, simply thought of as an argument for disjunction. On the one hand, when he notes that the contrast between the Brahmans' customs and those of the Harijans [Deliège, 1988: 115] can be seen as the two poles of one continuum which is bridged by Sanskritization [ibid.: 116], this aspect of his theory seems to come closer to Moffatt. On the other hand, since Deliège emphasizes the complexity and contradiction of the Harijans' behaviour and values [Deliège, 1992: 171], his approach looks like a conciliation between the disjunction and consensus theories. The argument of Deliège is rather similar to Cohn's on the Camars [Cohn, 1955]. In this sense, it seems that the categorization of the disjunction model itself is idealized in the disputes. In this connection, it is due to Mosse's article [1994b] that the latest work still supports Moffatt's view after learning of Deliège's critical works of Moffatt. It seems to me that the arguments between Mosse and Deliège do not meet each other and it is problematic that Mosse's way of argument remains unchanged without learning properly from the previous studies of "Untouchables" (see [Deliège, 1994]).
12. A link between replication and consensus is claimed by Moffatt on the basis of the Harijans' replication observed in the following three major areas: an inter-caste relationship among the Harijans, an intra-caste relationship within the Paraiyars and the Harijans' religion (see also [Deliège, 1992: 157]).
13. Here, one is reminded of Miller's claim, based on Bailey's [Bailey, 1959: 91] criticism of Dumont; "shared components are *not* the indicators of participation in a *single* system ... or tradition. It is the perceived relationship between components, the organization of the meaning of these relationships and components which gives body to a 'tradition' " [Miller, 1966: 41]. Not only is this claim suggestive, but Miller clearly points out the significance of an "interpretative" approach [Miller, 1966: 28].
14. Furthermore, in terms of *karma*, he sums up: "Brahmans define *karma* in moral and behavioral terms. Most farming and middle castes define it simply as sin. The majority of Harijans define it as misfortune, and in so doing they absolve themselves of responsibility for hard times, sickness, or ritual pollution." [Maloney, 1975: 176]. Maloney's conclusion on the Harijans' definition of *karma* almost corresponds with the theory of fate (*karma*) among a group of North Indian sweepers (UP) which is described by Kolenda [1964]. Kolenda also

claims that the sweepers do not believe in practice in the higher castes' philosophical understanding of the transmigration-*karma* idea [Kolenda, 1964: 74].

15. The comparative list of cultural traits between Brahman and Harijan [Deliège, 1988: 115] is useful.
16. Freeman's later article [1986], which is produced on the basis of his ample monograph, makes his theoretical position clear.
17. Although I have already used the term "self-aggrandizement", my usage of the term is based on Bourdieu's idea of a basic motivation of strategy, that is, "the volition for seeking the perpetuation of one's social existence". For example, "A family is a conatus in Spinoza's sense, that is, a corporate body that holds the volition for enduring its social existence without losing all of its power and priviledge and the family adopts a marriage strategy, an inheritance strategy, a economic strategy and especially an education strategy as its reproduction strategy"[Bourdieu, 1990: 84].
18. T.Yoshimoto proposes the hypothesis that the super-structure in the Marxist sense, or "the total imaginary domain" in his terms, consists of three imaginary spheres, namely, "the personal imaginary sphere", like art and literature; "the pair imaginary sphere", like family and sexual relations; and "the communal imaginary sphere"; like state and law [Yoshimoto, 1982 (1968)]. According to him, the former two spheres are incompatible with the third sphere. In this sense, Muli's aspiration for having a pair relationship going beyond caste boundaries, namely, his friendship with a Caste Hindu, can be regarded as a challenge by him to caste feelings, even though made unwittingly.
19. Though she repeatedly reminds us that the need for self-esteem should not be regarded as a single determinant of the personality system [Vincentnathan, 1987: 84, 86], there is no doubt that she deals with self-esteem as the focal concept throughout the thesis.
20. Vincentnathan's explanation of *varṇa* strategies is as follows: "(1) The *optimal* or Brahman strategy, in which less gross substance codes are received and more given; (2) the *maximal* or Kshatriya strategy, in which there is a vigorous giving *and* receiving of substance codes among closely ranked castes, often for political reasons to maintain a wide network of alliances; (3) the *minimal* or Vaishya strategy, in which there is less giving, because those above refuse, and less taking (from those above or at same level, as well from below) to maintain a pose of being higher; and (4) the *pessimal* or Shudra strategy, in which there is less giving because those above refuse, and more receiving, because it will not lower their position further, and often because they cannot financially afford to refuse." [Vincentnathan, 1987: 62]
21. Muli's behaviour, described by Freeman, can be analysed like this. "Positive transactions", like friendship, and "defiance" seem to be predominant in the sphere of intercaste relations, and "pessimal strategy" is mainly adopted in the sphere within his community.
22. For example, from religion to ideology [Kolenda, 1960: 287]; the change of caste culture [Barnett, 1975: 151]; or the increase in the importance of non-caste-based status, like education, economic class, and military position [Vincentnathan, 1987: 248–263].
23. The change of socio-economic positions of the Harijans make possible more diversified strategies and these changes naturally cause new dilemmas in that the differential between the socio-economically better off Harijans (the Harijan elites [Sachchidananda, 1977]) and those less well off (the backward Harijans) has been increased, and as a result both sections suffer from severe problems. It is said that the Harijan elites tend to have great psychological disturbance, caused by falling short of their raised expectations [ibid.: 253]; while

the backward people are put into a more unstable economic condition than before [ibid.: 88] (see also [Gough, 1989]).

24. Although the tendency that Harijans themselves are averse to inter-caste marriage is sometimes taken up as an example to explain their conservatism in terms of caste boundary or their replication of the dominant ideology [Mayer, 1980: 398], this is absolutely misleading. This does not imply their conservatism but is the product of their practical sense. It is the Harijan side that always submits to severe social sanctions in the case of inter-caste marriage so that such harsh experiences they have had repeatedly naturally discourage them from conducting inter-caste marriage from the viewpoint of self-defence. Generally speaking, their negative experiences for a long time tell them the non-reality of seeking social integration and they incline to choose the way of forming a separate social domain for protecting their security.

Chapter 4

Setting

Village, Caste and Kinship

On Fieldwork

The field materials for this book were collected through a series of fieldwork excursions in Tamil societies, conducted intermittently from 1980 to 1989. The total period of fieldwork among Tamil societies was roughly eighteen months, consisting of two stages. In the first stage, I did fieldwork in the Jaffna Peninsula, Northern Sri Lanka, between July and September 1980 and between July and August 1982.[1] At the end of the first stage I had a one month trip to Tamil Nadu, Kerala and Karnataka for an extensive survey of house forms, in September 1982. Nonetheless, the present book is produced mainly on the basis of the second stage of field research carried out in the Madurai area, Southern Tamil Nadu, over twelve months between July and September 1985, between July and October 1986, between August and October 1987 and between February and March 1989. The first stage of fieldwork among the Jaffna Tamils could be seen as a preliminary one for my Tamil study, in which my various concerns with caste society were developed. In contrast, the second stage of fieldwork was more purposefully undertaken, because I had started to follow my post-graduate course in 1983. The periods during which my fieldwork was carried out were concentrated on the same season-from the end of the dry season to the beginning of the rainy season, with the exception of the last visit in 1989, which to some extent compensated for this seasonal partiality. In this respect, my fieldwork is not the most anthropologically desirable one, but I had no option other than to carry out my fieldwork in that period due to my college duties. However, I think that this does not cause decisive damage to the arguments in the book because the main issues discussed here are rather free from seasonal change, though I did my best to collect more reliable information in terms of the incidents I could not directly observe.[2]

The outbreak of the Colombo riots in the summer of 1983 made it impossible to continue fieldwork in Jaffna, and I decided to shift my field to Tamil Nadu. Apart from this negative reason, I had the more positive purpose of making a comparison between a society of island Tamils and one of continental Tamils. In the course of my village selection in Tamil Nadu, I had gradually become conscious about my present attempt to reconsider the ethnographic basis on which Dumont established his powerful theory of purity and impurity. As a result, I decided to choose my field in the Madurai area, where Dumont's field of Tengalapatti is located, as I thought that Dumont's monograph, focusing on the intra-caste relations of the dominant caste

Pramalai Kallar (*sic*) [Dumont, 1986 (1957)], should be reconsidered by a study of inter-caste relations in the same type of village. I was encouraged by Dumont's statement, "I have not exhausted the empirical complexity of my South Indian ethnographic work" [Dumont, 1980: xix]. After visiting several villages around Madurai city, Kinnimangalam, which is located on the southern side of Tengalapatti, was finally chosen.[3]

The first villager I talked to in Kinnimangalam was an ex-president of the Kinnimangalam panchayat, P. Cinnacami (a Kallar) who happened to be chatting on the village *mantai*[4] when I visited the village for the first time in 1985. At that time there was no president of the village panchayat because the local government had postponed having an election for nearly ten years due to political reasons. Therefore, he was in a sense acting village president and he gave me permission to conduct research work in the village, after hearing a brief explanation of myself and of my research purpose. He then took me to the village priest's house where I was served a coconut juice, and I chatted with the village priest, N. Mutturamalingampillai (a Pantaram), and with the ex-president's elder brother's son, K. Cataccaram (a person of Cattayi lineage of the Kallars). The following day, as soon as I reached the village, I was taken to the front of one of the biggest houses along the village's main street. There I was welcomed by a young, but dignified, man named S. Balasubramanian (a Pillai), the son of the late *nāṭṭāṇmai* (village *muṉcīf*), who ultimately gave all-out cooperation with my research work.[5] When I met him, I was convinced that my village selection was right and that I was almost formally accepted by the village. Other villagers also gradually recognized me as a Japanese researcher doing a village survey for a Ph.D. thesis. I was accepted basically as a guest of the *nāṭṭāṇmai* family and this almost meant that I became a guest of the village (more precisely, the Kinnimangalam hamlet). This process of establishing rapport was very natural from the viewpoint of the village power structure, so that most villagers naturally accepted this situation.[6]

In order to carry out my fieldwork in this village, I had no option but to accept this initial situation in which I established my rapport with the villagers, even though it had both merit and disadvantages. That is to say, this was the position I had to accept when I considered how to make contact with the village Harijans.

I always kept in mind that the aim of my fieldwork was to collect data equally from all the castes of the village, and I consciously thought that this fieldwork aim distinguished me from Dumont and Moffatt, who concentrated upon a particular caste community.[7] Nevertheless, I had to recognize the practical fact that I was deeply involved, generally speaking, with the dominant castes but, more specifically speaking, with Balasubramanian's family. Thus, I was put in the dilemma that I could not neutrally carry out fieldwork both among the dominant castes and among the dominated. More simply, the problem was how the village Harijans would respond to me while I was identified as a friend or a guest of the dominant castes.

The Harijans seemed to have an antagonistic feeling towards the dominant castes, especially towards the Kallars, though there were some factional relationships in which the dominant caste members and the Harijans to some extent cooperated. In this sense, when I talked with the Harijans, I had to be aware of at least two types of fabrications in their replies, invented in order to protect their own positions or to save their faces, i.e., one invented against the dominant castes and another against the opposing Harijans belonging to other factions. It was possible to see through these fabrications by interviewing from many angles and repeatedly the same person, and at the same time combining the opinions collected from Harijans of other factions or from the Caste Hindus and, moreover, by observing a person's actual attitudes.[8] In this connection, the recent progress of urbanization proved an advantage for disclosing such fabrications, because it encouraged the Harijans' economic independence from the dominant castes, which to some extent released the Harijans from their oppressed position in the conventional village system (see [Moffatt, 1979: 84]). No doubt nowadays the Harijans are more or less protected from the rude attacks of the Kallars by the Untouchability (Offence) Act, as a result of which today's Harijans do not have extreme hesitation in speaking about their village matters.

I think that my strong friendship with a Pillai family, not a Kallar family, helped to place me a little outside the direct oppressive power relationships between the Kallars and the Harijans. The Pillais are not regarded as a caste to be feared by the village Harijans. They are rather seen as "good" people by them, due to the fact that not only are there only three Pillai households in the village, but also that, as can be historically verified, their behavior is far more modest than that of the Kallars. This means that my friendship with the Pillais was more acceptable to the Harijans than my friendship with the Kallars.

It seems to me that my fieldwork conducted intermittently, as mentioned above, to some extent prevented me from being entirely identified with a particular caste. On the one hand it cannot be denied that I was identified with the status of the Pillais, but on the other hand I tended to preserve my outsider's position as a Japanese visitor until the end of fieldwork. This interruption of identification left open the possibility that the Harijans would confide in me rather more freely because of my perceived outsider's position.

When I interviewed the Harijans, I basically followed a process in which I started from rather neutral questions, with no direct reflection of village power relations, such as kinship relations, processes of rituals and festivals. Only after judging that I had established a good personal relationship with that Harijan, did I touch on more sensitive points, like inter-caste problems and inter-lineage conflicts. When interviewing, I always visited each Harijan's own house and often entered inside the house in order to avoid the presence of unnecessary people, especially of dominant caste persons. When I could not segregate a Harijan from other people, I avoided more sensitive questions, and rather tried to observe how the Harijan responded both to other people and me.

I recognize that my fieldwork holds various limitations, as indicated above. However, at the same time, I believe that my "data" collected among the Harijans has enough reliability for reconstructing their social and cultural situation, for I always took efforts to pay attention to the contextual connotations of our conversations in the given interviewing situation. "Data" in my sense is not simply crude information about what people say or how they behave, but rather is interpretative information, found by placing people's statements and behaviour in the context of data collection including my presence (cf. [Peacock, 1986]). In this connection, it is important to make clear the difference between Moffatt's attitude and mine in terms to data collection. Moffatt fastidiously attempted to exclude any "suspicion in the minds of the local Harijans that I (Moffatt) might be reporting what they told to the high castes" [Moffatt, 1979: xxvi]. Though I of course admire Moffatt's sincere attitude in terms of his fieldwork, I rather suspect that this attitude corresponds to his static understanding of data, which lacks an interpretative viewpoint, as already pointed out in the previous chapter. I do not deny his efforts in seeking the neutrality of a fieldworker especially in the study of the Harijans, but it seems to me that if he naively believed he could collect data free from any suspicion, his thinking would be a product of the ideal. I think that it is more significant how a fieldworker interprets the collected data distorted by the informants in the given context. It seems to me that this attitude of data-collection is more "anthropological" than that excluding the informants' bias from the beginning.[9]

Before starting the ethnographic description, it is necessary and helpful for readers to know the change of value of the rupee during the 25 years from 1985, when I began my fieldwork, till today. If the consumer price index for rural labourers in 1986–87 is 100, that of December 2009 will be 537 in all India, and as to the exchange rate, while 1 Rupee equalled about 20 Yen in 1985, 1 Rupee was about 2 Yen in December 2009. Readers should keep in mind that the present time of this ethnography is the latter half of the 1980s.

Geographical and Historical Sketch

Geographical Sketch

The Tamil village Kinnimangalam (*Kiṇṇimaṅkalam*), where I conducted fieldwork, is located about 15 kilometers west of Madurai city, the capital of the Madurai district of Tamil Nadu state.[10] The villagers of Kinnimangalam can easily travel to and from this historic city by bus. Besides the bus service between Kinnimangalam and Madurai which operates three times daily, Kinnimangalam villagers can also use the more frequent buses from their nearest town, Chekkanurani, which is situated at the junction of the Madurai-Teni and the Tirumangalam-Dindigal roads. Another town that Kinnimangalam villagers sometimes need to visit is Tirumangalam,[11] which is 10 kilometers south of Kinnimangalam, because there is a Taluk office there. A bus service to Tirumangalam operates hourly from Chekkanurani. Chekkanurani is located within walking distance of Kinnimangalam, being located only one mile away from it. Chekkanurani thus functions as part of the everyday life space of Kinnimangalam villagers. Data pertaining to the shops and services of Chekkanurani, the total number of which are 258, is shown in Tables 4.1 and 4.2. Most of these shops deal in goods and services which directly support villagers' everyday activities. In this respect, the town, which originated from a Saturday weekly market, is still in germ and very dependent on the surrounding villages.

Needless to say, a town attracts villagers not only to meet their practical needs, but also to offer them opportunities for recreation, such as the cinema.[12] In addition, villagers can enjoy being relatively free from the caste hierarchy in a town. Even though Chekkanurani is a very small town in which face-to-face relationships are still maintained, the feeling of caste discrimination is much reduced there compared to the situation in the village. The town, therefore, to some extent plays the role of being a refuge for the Harijans (Untouchables) of the surrounding villages.

Kinnimangalam is situated on flat land extending from the southern side of a range of mountains called the Nagamalai[13] (literally, snake hill).

Agricultural villages in South India are classified into "wet land area" or "dry land area", but even wet land areas have only around 1100 mm annual rainfall, so that it is difficult to maintain waterfield rice cultivation without an irrigation tank. According to the classification, Kinnimangalam is seen as a village just close to a wet land area. In fact, the villagers make their living mainly by agriculture of tank and well irrigated land, which occupies about 51 per cent of the cultivated land, and non-irrigated land.[14] Villagers claim that recent agricultural production has been unstable because of irregular and inadequate rainfall, though their claim is not fully supported by the official statistics of rainfall (cf. [Government of Madras, 1933: 46], [Government of Tamil Nadu, 1986: 58–61]).

Table 4.1

Classification of the Shops and Services in Chekkanurani

Category	*Shops or Services (No. of shops)*
Agriculture/Stock raising (17)	chemical fertilizer (5), cotton brokerages (3), tyre repairs (3), chemical fodder (2), motor pump repairs (2), Milk Cooperative Society (1), farm tractor repairs (1)
Daily life (65)	bicycles (13), barbers (12), firewood (7), florists (7), hardware (6), cleaning (3), bullcart repairs (3), bicycle parts (2), iron scrap (1), charcoal (1), astrology (1), frame making (1), iron smith (1), oil (1), pantal (a hut for rituals) making (1), key repairs (1), clay pots (1), stone statues (1), Saturday market (chickens and goats) (1)
Food Stuffs, (56)	greengrocers (19), groceries (12), butchers (mutton) (5), fruiterers (5), grinding (5), rice dealers (3), steamed bread (3), snacks and sweets (2), dry fish (1), beans (1)
Factory (6)	soft drinks (2), aluminium products (1), calcium (1), cement boards (1), soap (1)
Others/Urban elements (115)	tea stands (35), tobacconists (20), textiles (14), tailors (10), restaurants (7), stationers (5), radio sales and repairs (4), clinics (3), drug stores (2), electrical goods (2), fancy goods (2), studios (2), police station (1), post office (1), cinema theatre (1), bank (1), tape recorder repairs (1), furniture (1), printing (1), cram school (1)
Total (258)	

Table 4.2

Shopkeepers' Castes

Caste	*Number of shops*	*Caste*	*Number of shops*
Kallar	122	Pillai	2
Natar	57	Ravеji	2
Acari	17	Nayakkar	1
Ampattar	14	Valluvar	1
Cettiyar	11	Christian	1
Pantaram	5	unknown	20
Vannar	3		
Aiyar	2	Total	258

Historical Sketch

The outline of the macro history of the Madurai area is as follows. The Pandya Kingdom ruled the Madurai area from just before or after the beginning of the Christian era. The prosperity of the Kingdom is recalled, for example, by Tamil Sangam Literature. From the 4th century AD to the 6th century AD, the Pandya Kingdom was under pressure from the adjacent Chola Kingdom and the Kalabrah Kingdom. Although the Pandya Kingdom revitalized, it was ultimately conquered by the powerful Chola Kingdom at the end of the 9th century. The Pandya Kingdom was again restored in the 13th century and ruled over the weakened Chola Kingdom. At the beginning of the 14th century, these local kingdoms were defeated by the invasion of Muslim powers from the north. At that time, the Madurai area was severely hit especially by the first invasion of the Afghan power. In the middle of the 14th century, the rule of the Vijayanagar Empire reached this area and the Muslim power was chased out from the south. During one century from the fall of the Chola Kingdom to the rise of the Vijayanagar Empire, enormous social changes and confusions were caused by those Muslim invasions [Karashima, 1980: 104]. According to Shigematu [1976: 57–58], the ruling system of the Vijayanagar Empire was changed both before and after the middle of the 16th century from "centralized feudalism" to "decentralized feudalism". From the latter half of the 16th century the local lord, the Nayaka, became the major independent power and finally established a regional dynasty in the Madurai area. The middle of the 17th century, particularly, was the golden period of the Nayaka dynasty, when Tirumalai Nayaka (1623–1659), called "a king of kings", was very active. The Nayaka rule, however, became unstable before

Plate 14 Chekkanurani town.

the power of the Mughal Empire reached this area in the middle of the 18th century, partly due to the foreign pressures of the Mysore Kingdom and the Maratha Kingdom and partly because of the internal contentions between Madurai and Tanjavur. According to Rajayyan [1974: 33], the political picture of the southern part of Tamil Nadu in the middle of the 18th century, when European contact began in this area, can be divided into three areas, that is, the one ruled by the Nayaka (Tiruchirapalli, Madurai, Tirunelveli), the one ruled by the Tevars (Marawars, Kallarnadu) and the one ruled by the poligars (little kings, *pāḷaiyakkārars* [Dirks, 1987: 19, 52–54]). According to this political picture, it seems that the village I am studying, Kinnimangalam, was located between Madurai (the area ruled by the Nayaka) and Kallarnadu (the area ruled by the Tevars).[15]

It seems to me that the connection between the above-mentioned macro history of the Madurai area and the micro history of the village being studied can be confirmed from approximately the 14th Century AD, even though the evidence is not all that clear. The period called *paṭaiveṭṭukālam* (literally, the age of the warring states) by the villagers, which can be traced through their oral history, almost corresponds with the period during which the Muslim powers who had conquered this area were chased out by the power of the Vijayanagar Empire. The villagers' claim that *paṭaiveṭṭukālam* was about 500 years ago also becomes circumstantial evidence to support my judgement.

The history of Kinnimangalam, which I reconstruct from what the villagers told me, is as follows. At the time known as *paṭaiveṭṭukālam,* two Zamindars, namely the Muslim Zamindar and the Zamindar of the Kauntar caste, controlled the village, and the people suffered much under their despotic rule. At that time, the village consisted of three separate hamlets, Amganampatti (which was located 500 meters north-east of the present Kinnimangalam), Konampatti (which was located 400 meters south-east of the present Kinnimangalam) and Mangalapatti (which was developed just on the southern side of the present Kinninmangalam). Mangalapatti was the head hamlet of the three, where the Zamindars lived. It is said that under the control of the Zamindars there were several castes, such as *Ācāri, Ampaṭṭar, Vaṇṇār, Vaḷaiyar, Kucavar, Nāṭār, Paṟaiyar and Piḷḷai.* The Pillai person, who is an ancestor of three Pillai families of the present village, worked as *nāṭṭāṇmai* (a village headman and a village police) under the rule of the Zamindars (see [Fuller, 1989: 38]). It is noted that there was no Kallar living there at that time. During the period of *paṭaiveṭṭukālam,* the migrations of various castes took place because of the social instability of the Madurai region. It seems to be at about this time that the early settlers of the Kallar caste, such as the *Kēcavaṉ* lineage and the *Kāmaṇaṉ* lineage, reached Mangalapatti.[16] As was commonly found in this area [Dumont, 1986: 20], the Kallars took over the dominant positions by chasing out the former rulers. This was the case in Kinnimangalam, where the two Zamindars were killed by the Kallars.[17] Thus, the basic caste structure as the foundation of that of today's village was almost in place when, after this incident, the village began to be constructed on its present site. That is to say, Amganampatti and Konampatti were united with Mangalapatti, and the name of the village was changed from Manggalapatti to Kinnimangalam.

On the one hand there is no doubt that Kinnimangalam as a village dominated by the Kallars was under the influence of the regional politics of the Kallarnadu.[18] On the other hand, the village, the whole of whose land was an *iṉām* (a grant of land) of the Minaksi Amman Temple, in other words, a *tēvastāṉam* or a *kōvil māṉiyam* (land donated to a temple),[19] was economically connected with the Nayaka kings who granted these *iṉām*. According to the Panchayat president, Javaharlal, in the pre-British days *kaṇakkappiḷḷai* (a village accountant) collected *tēvatāyam* (Skt. *dēvadāya*, grants to temples) in the form of grain (in kind) and handed it to a collector sent by the Minaksi Amman Temple. Even after British rule, *iṉām* grants to the Temple were allowed, but they were redefined as land revenue to be collected in cash [Fuller, 1984: 94], because the British government was eager to establish the Ryotwari administration in South India.[20] As far as Kinnimangalam is concerned, the major *iṉām*s were abolished and shifted to Ryotwari by the Madras Estates (Abolition and Conversion to Ryotwari) Act (26 of 1948), as the Detail Notes (*Vivarakkuṛippu*) of Kinnimangalam revenue village clarify (see also [Gough, 1981: 43]).

Although "Zamindari estates and private *iṉām* estates were abolished shortly after the independence of India" [ibid.: 43] (see [Mencher, 1978: 81–83]), the offices of *karṇam* (village accountant) and *nāṭṭāṇmai* (village *muṉcīf*), which were originally appointed for the Ryotwari administration by the British government, remained until 1980 when they were finally abolished. The post of V.A.O. (village administrative officer) was introduced in 1982 after a two-year gap. There is no doubt that these historical changes in the revenue system have contributed to the weakening of the village communal unity by the enforcement of direct cash taxation on individual landlords and the introduction of externally appointed revenue officers.[21]

On Village Community

The concept of "village" is one of the problematic topics in the study of Hindu societies.[22] Though I have used words such as village and hamlet without any precise definition, I must now explain how I use these terms here. At the same time, it will be made clear why the hamlet of Kinnimangalam is seen as a proper field to be studied in the light of the present research aims.

There are two main streams of arguments in terms of the understanding of Hindu villages. On the one hand the actual existence of village as a social unit is claimed by one stream of people and on the other hand another stream of people criticizes such a claim as an anthropological myth. As notable examples of the former, Srinivas' idea of mental condensation of a village that is mediated by "the dominant caste" [Srinivas, 1987: 60–115] and Bailey's concept of a village reality in a politico-economic sense [Bailey, 1959] are raised. This stream seems to have deep roots both textual and practical. The textual ones are the works of Karl Marx and H.S. Maine, which advocated a village integrity [Good, 1978: 155], and the practical one is the movement of Panchayat Raja (village autonomy) in the independent era. The representatives of the latter stream are Dumont and Pocock. They claimed that it is caste and kinship that are important in a Hindu village and the regional ties of a village occupy only a secondary position [Dumont, 1986 (1957), 1980 (1966)], [Dumont and Pocock, 1960].[23] When those opposed opinions are reconsidered, it is useful to recall Mayer's statement: "the external relations mostly exist within the village, whereas the internal order of the caste group is based to a large extent on kinship relations within the population of a number of adjacent villages" [Mayer, 1960: 5–6]. Even after taking into account that Mayer's village of study is a North Indian type following village exogamy, we can learn from the statement that it is necessary to carefully investigate how caste and kinship relationships are connected with a village framework. In this respect, Good [1978] and Raheja [1988] are invaluable because their works attempt to analyse not only prestations among castes but also those within kinship at the same time. As a result, for example, Good proposes a concept of "micro-region",[24] which is similar to Mayer's concept "region". The above review of several arguments seems to suggest that a meaningful regional unit is not objectively defined but is set up according to the analyst's purpose (cf. [Mayer, 1960: 4]).

In the case of Kinnimangalam (hereafter K, but not always), there are three levels of village congregation, that is, a political level of panchayat village, an administrative level of revenue village, and a spatially congregated "natural" village that I call a hamlet. As shown in Table 4.3, K panchayat consists of seven hamlets and K revenue village is formed by six hamlets. The table shows that K hamlet has the most balanced caste structure and obviously occupies the central core position in K panchayat village, coming closer to Good's sense of micro-region. In fact, as discussed later, the principal social relationships (inter-caste and intra-caste relationships) of K hamlet residents are by and large observed within the hamlet and, if necessary, they extend their hamlet-based relationships towards the broader social space. Why I emphasize the point is not to claim that K hamlet is a social entity separated from the broader social space, but rather to make clear that K hamlet provides a sufficient field to think about the topic of the present book, i.e., reconsideration of pollution concepts and analysis of Harijan practices.

The landlords of the hamlet consist mainly of the Pillais, the Kallars, the Natars and the Pantarams. If these candidates of the dominant castes were checked by Srinivas' original criteria such as numerical preponderance over the other castes, preponderance of economic and political power, and a not too low status in the local caste hierarchy [Srinivas, 1955: 18],[25] it could be concluded that the Kallars pass almost all these conditions, since their ritual status is neither high nor too low; the Pillais sufficiently fulfil the criteria, except for the numerical condition; the Natars are limited only to economic dominance; and the case of the Pantaram priest managing large temple lands is too unique to be considered. It would appear, therefore, that the Kallars and the Pillais are the dominant castes of the hamlet. Nonetheless, as Mayer suggests [Mayer, 1958: 425] and Good points out [Good, 1978: 177], I also think that the concept of "dominant caste" is too vague to describe the actual village situation, and that attention should also be paid to the unit of "dominant family", even though my case is not as complicated as that of Good. At any rate, the relations between these dominant castes and the dominated Harijans (the Paraiyars) form the principal vertical axis of the social structure of the hamlet, on which the so-called *jajmānī* relationships are based (*vide infra*). Let us briefly consider the relationships between villagers' actual activities and the hamlet.

Table 4.3

Caste Structure of Hamlets of the Kinnimangalam Panchayat

	Hamlet name (Word No.)	*Pallai*	*Pantarm*	*Kallar*	*Kavuntar*	*Konar*	*Acari*	*Natar*	*Vannar*	*Ampattar*	*Kucavar*	*Kucavar*	*Valaiyar*	*Paraiyar*	*Cakkiliyar*
Revenue Village 203 kinnimangalam	*Kinnimangala m (No. 1 No. 2)	3	1	202	—	—	10	10	7	—	—	1	—	174	—
	*Pottuluppatti (No. 3)	—	—	—	—	—	—	—	—	—	—	—	—	35	—
	*Puvaracampatt i (No. 3)	—	—	90	—	—	—	—	—	6	7	—	—	—	—
	*Alampatti (No. 3)	—	—	—	—	—	—	—	—	—	—	—	—	44	—
	*Minakucipatti (No. 4)	—	—	—	—	10	—	—	3	—	—	—	90	—	—
	*Putumangalam (No. 5)	—	—	43	—	—	—	—	1	1	—	—	—	—	—
	Mavelipatti (No. 5 No. 6)	—	—	119	9	3	—	3	1	—	—	—	—	—	40
	Total	3	1	454	9	13	10	10	14	8	7	1	90	253	40
	Grand Total 913														

Note: Revenue Village 203 Kinnimangalam consists of six hamlets marked by *.

It has become more and more difficult today to look upon the hamlet as a confined unit of economic relations, though it is true that the hamlet is still the focal place where the villagers' main economic activity, agricultural production, takes place on the basis of a reduced degree of *jajmānī* relationships. The rapid fall of big landlords during the past two generations doubtlessly damaged the "traditional" socio-economic framework. Related to this, the recent general tendency of agricultural labourers being hired as day-labourers (*kūliyaḷ)* has eroded the convention of agricultural labourers being supplied within the hamlet on the basis of permanent or annual contract.[26] Moreover, many villagers have to go outside the village to earn their living (see Chapter 9). Though there is no doubt that these tendencies have been enhanced and accelerated by recent rapid urbanization, it is also true that the introduction of the Ryotwari system by the British government in the 19th century, as a starter, fundamentally more basically prepared an economic environment which caused the discrepancy between individual activities and local unity.

As to the political aspect, it is undeniable that the institution of the "village (elected) panchayat (*kirāmap pañcāyattu*)", superimposed administratively after Independence, has weakened the power of the "traditional panchayat", called *ūrātci maṉṟam* (a village assembly) or periya mantai (a big gathering), based on the hamlet (cf. [Mayer, 1960: 113–131]).[27] Corresponding to this change, troubles within the hamlet tend to be taken to public institutions, such as the police and law courts. However, the "traditional panchayat" still functions for managing village festivals, appointing *tōṭṭi* and *maṭaiyaṉ* (village menial workers chosen from the Harijans), arbitrating between *paṅkāḷis* (lineages) or between *vāricus* (sublineages) and settling minor village problems in its own way.[28] In the Kinnimangalam hamlet, there are two

Plate 15 *Kāriyakkāraṉs* of the Kallars.

Plate 16 Playing cards on *periya mantai*.

Plate 17 *Ciṉṉa mantai* located in Cluster II.

separate "traditional panchayat", i.e., the main one mentioned above, *periya mantai*, which consists of *kāriyakkāraṉs* or *periyamaṉitaṉ* (influential persons or big men)[29] of the Caste Hindus, mainly those of the Kallars; and *ciṉṉa mantai* (literally, a small gathering) which consists of *kāriyakkāraṉs* of the Harijans (see Table 4.4). Until a little while ago, the Harijans sometimes took their problems to *periya mantai* when they failed to solve them in *ciṉṉa mantai*.

Table 4.4

Distribution of Influential Persons

Caste (No. of household)		*Lineage (No. of households)*	*Kāriyakkāraṉ*
Caste Hindus	Pillai (3)		—
	Kallar (202)	Kecavan (23)	2
		Kamanan (21)	2
		Cattayi (28)	4
		Panniyan (65)	5
		Kattappinnai (18)	2
		Cuntravalliyamman I (17)	2
		Cuntravalliyamman II (4)	1
		Cataci (4)	1
	Pantaram (1)		1
	Acari (10)		1
	Natar (10)		—
	Vannar (7)		1
	Kuravar (1)		—
Harijans	Paraiyar (174)	Kartananti (29)	3
		Cinnananti (15)	3
		Mataiyan (41)	1
		Cahalan (19)	1
		Tankalan (44)	3
		Cappataiyan (3)	1
		?	1
Total			35

The survival of these *mantais* indicates that at some levels the unity of the hamlet has been preserved. Moreover, hamlet unity has to some extent been demonstrated by the recent election of the president of the village panchayat. Though the election was contested between one candidate supported by the K hamlet and another supported by the adjacent M hamlet (a big hamlet next to K hamlet, which belongs to a different revenue village), it is interesting that the people of K hamlet united in their support of one candidate and thus wittingly or unwittingly showed their "hamlet loyalty".

Hamlet unity can more clearly be seen in the annual festivals of village deities because these festivals are held basically by the hamlet community. Even if at a politico-economic level villagers' activities threaten hamlet unity, their feeling of loyalty to or love of their home hamlet still forms the basis of their support for their village festivals. In this sense, the word *ūr* (village) well reflects one's subjective attachment to one's native place. That is, *ūr* basically involves the connotation of "my village" (see [Daniel, 1984: Chapter 2]). In this sense, *ūr* contrasts with the word *kirāmam*, which means village in an objective sense, and which is suitable for expressing an administrative sense of village, like a panchayat village or a revenue village (see [Sekine, 1993b]).

Nonetheless, it would be hasty to conclude from the above discussion that hamlet unity is disintegrating except for subjective feelings of attachment, because it still remains to consider the aspect of kinship relations. The lineage network extends beyond the hamlet boundary, but at the same time it is also noted that in Kinnimangalam the lineage tends to be strongly connected with the locality of the hamlet. For example, the lineage festivals of the principal lineages are sponsored basically by lineage members living in the hamlet, while other lineages represented by only a few households virtually give up their festivals. In this sense, lineage identity is not always incompatible with local identity in this case. In other words, there is a tendency that locality rather confines the lineage network. This tendency is clearly demonstrated by the geographically confined nature of the sphere of intermarriage (see Table 4.10). Most of the villagers, except the Pillais who are numerically fewer and ritually higher, take a bride within the hamlet or from neighbouring villages. The kinship network that is drawn towards locality to some extent prevents the hamlet from losing its social unity completely.

After these empirical observations, since it is not my present task to define the boundary of the "micro-region", I feel that it is much more important for me to recognize the actual situation of the hamlet as it presently is. Fortunately, K hamlet provides sufficient data on various social relations so that my purposes can be accomplished mainly by concentrating on the K hamlet, while at the same time taking data from the broader sphere into account if necessary. Hereafter, K hamlet and the village are used interchangeably and if I refer to a panchayat village or to a revenue village it will be clarified each time.

An outline map of K hamlet is shown in Figures 4.1. and 4.2. K hamlet is located between two large tanks, east and west, and it consists of four residential clusters (not in Dumont's sense), one for the Caste Hindus and three others for the Harijans (the Paraiyars).[30]

1. Cluster I: This is the central cluster called "*ūr*" where the Caste Hindus live. Whereas the dominant castes like the Kallars and the Pillais occupy the central part of it, other service castes such as the Acaris, the Vannars and the Kuravars have their houses in the peripheral area of the cluster.

2. Cluster II: This is the oldest residential area of the Paraiyars, which is adjacent to cluster I, and therefore called "*Paṟaiya-vīṭu* (Paraiyars' residence)" by other castes. This is a so-called *cēri*[31] However, the Paraiyars living there tend to think of it as part of *ūr*. This interpretative difference should be noted. Nearly half of the houses of this cluster were rebuilt or newly constructed using house loans from the Uslampatti Cooperative Society.

Figure 4.1

Map of the Kinnimangalam Hamlet and Location of Village Deities (Scale: 1 cm = 50 m)

Residential Areas of Caste Hindus
(Cluster I)
a. Piḷḷai
b. Paṇṭāram
c. Kaḷḷar
d. Nāṭār
e. Ācāri
f. Vaṇṇār
g. Kuṟavar
Residential Areas of Harijans
(Cluster II, III, IV)
h. Paṟaiyar
★ T1-T11: village deities
Notes
1. figures on the mat correspond to sruvey numbers on the land register
2. The sign indicates a well
3. The sign indicates a cemetery
West Tank
East Tank
Primary School

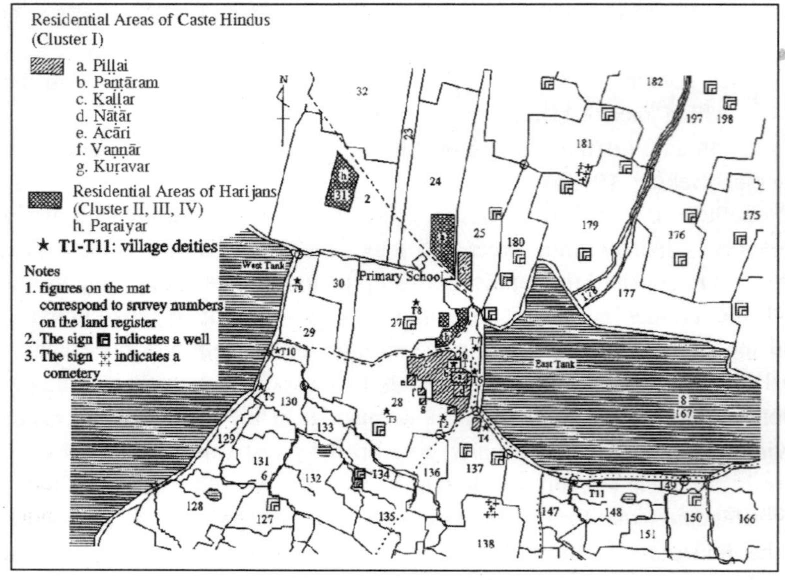

Figure 4.2

Classification of House Patterns According to Building Materials

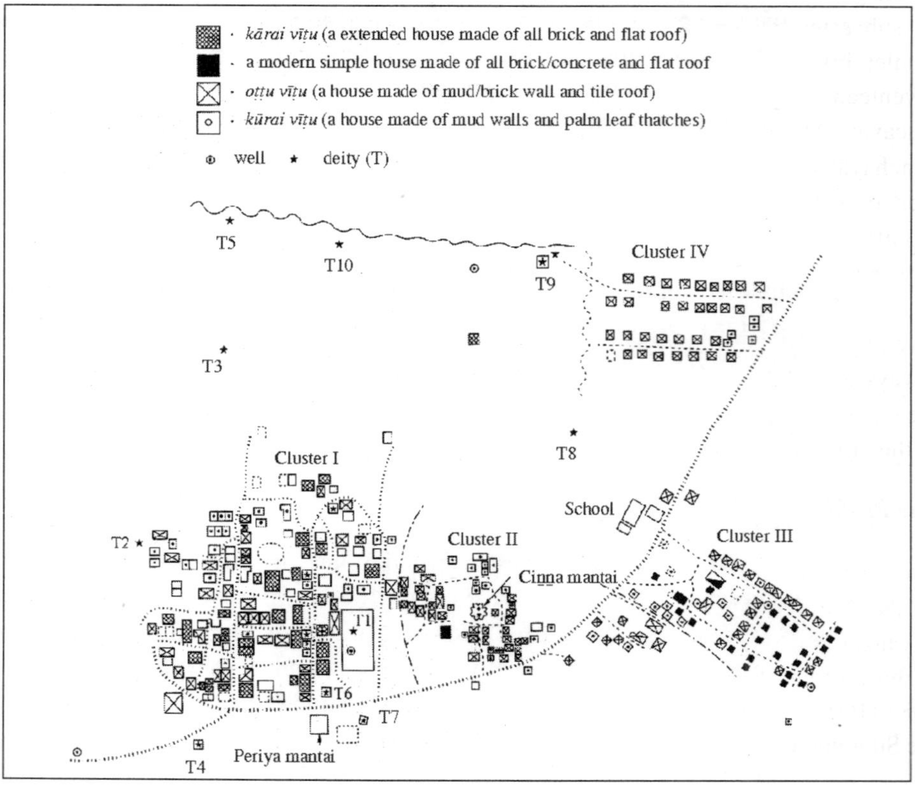

kārai vīṭu (a extended house made of all brick and flat roof)
a modern simple house made of all brick/concrete and flat roof
oṭṭu vīṭu (a house made of mud/brick wall and tile roof)
kūrai vīṭu (a house made of mud walls and palm leaf thatches)
well
deity (T)
T5
T10
T9
Cluster IV
T3
T8
Cluster I
School
T2
Cluster II
Cluster III
Cinna mantai
T1
T6
T7
T4
Periya mantai

3. Cluster III: This is a newly developed residential area for the Paraiyars. Except for a few, almost half of the houses were provided without charge under the Congress state government in 1960, and another half were again provided free of charge by THADCO (Tamil Nadu Harijan Development Corporation) during 1974–5 under the DMK state government. Other castes call this cluster "*Paṟaiya-kalaṉi* (Paraiyars' colony)", but the Paraiyars themselves seem to prefer the name of "*Āti Tirāviṭar kuṭiyiruppu* (Adi-Dravida residential area)". It should be noted that about ten Kallar houses were recently constructed between cluster II and cluster III.

4. Cluster IV: This is the newest colony for the Harijans, located to the northern side of, and a little away from *ūr*. Under the AIADMK state government, most of the houses here were built using house loans from the Uslampatti Cooperative Society in 1981, and another five houses got house loans from the Tirumangalam Panchayat Union in 1982. Because it is the newest development, it is often called "*putukkalaṉi* (new-colony)". Sometimes it is called "*Vatakku Āti Tirāviṭar kuṭiyiruppu* (North Adi-Dravida residential area)" by the Paraiyars.[32]

Caste Composition

Though the K hamlet consists of only eight "castes" (more precisely speaking, "sub-castes"),[33] fourteen kinds of castes are found in the panchayat village (see Table 4.3). Furthermore, if I asked a knowledgeable person what kind of castes are found in the wider area, such as Tirumangalam taluk to which Kinnimangalam belongs, I would get a list of caste names, as shown in Table 4.5, which includes the names of 41 subcastes. Nonetheless, the so-called *jajmānī* relationships[34] found in the K hamlet involve 17 castes (*vide infra*), listed in Table 4.6. Eight out of these seventeen castes live in the Kinnimangalam hamlet, and another three castes, Kucavar, Ampattar and Cakkiliyar, are present in the adjacent hamlets of the K panchayat village. Therefore, villagers get the services of the remaining six castes from outside the panchayat village, mainly from Chekkanurani town. Thus, today's modified *jajmānī* relationships of the K hamlet are almost confined within the area between the hamlet and Chekkanurani.

Table 4.5 shows caste names in the descending order of caste ranking which is given by the Pillais, the ritually highest caste in the village, though the order is not always accepted by other castes (see Table 10.2 in Chapter 10). For the sake of convenience, I will briefly describe 15 castes involved in the present arguments, according to the order given by the Pillais.

The Profiles of Castes

The Aiyars (the Smartha Brahmans)

In the Tirumangalam area, two kinds of Brahmans, Aiyar as the Saivites and Aiyankar as the Vaishnavites, are usually recognized by non-Brahman people. Aiyar in this area can be classified as the Smartha, who recognize Trimurti [Thurston et al. 1987 (1909): Vol. 1, 269], or who worship both Siva and Vishnu but regard Siva as the Supreme being [Gough, 1981: 28]. As in Thanjavur [Gough, 1981: 28–29], in this

Table 4.5
Castes (sub-castes) in the Tirumangalam Area

Caste	*Traditional occupation*	*Ritual status*
Aiyar (Smartha Brahman)*	Priest	
Aiyaṅkār (Vaishnava Brahman)	Priest	
Celarāṣṭirar	Weaver	
Kārkāttār (Piḷḷai)	Farmer	*High*
Vīrakōṭi (Piḷḷai)	Farmer	
Ceṭṭiyār	Merchant	
*Kāraikkattār (Piḷḷai)****	Farmer	
Tuḷuvavēḷāḷar	Farmer	
Illattuppiaḷḷi (Piḷḷai)	Farmer	
Koṭikkāppiḷḷai (Piḷḷai)	Farmer	
*Kollācāri (Acāri)**	Blacksmith	*Higher-Middle*
*Taṭṭācāri (Acāri)**	Goldsmith	
*Taccuācāri (Acāri)**	Carpenter	
*Kallācāri (Acāri)**	Mason	
*Piramalaikkaḷḷar****	Farmer, Watchman	
Maṟavar	Farmer	
Akampaṭiyār	Farmer	
Cērvai	Farmer	
Nāyakkar	Farmer, King, Musician	
Reṭṭiyār	Farmer	Lower-Middle
Kavuṇṭar	Farmer	
Mukamatiyar	?	
Kōṉār	Herdsman	
(Kiṟittuvar)	Christian	
*Paṇṭāram****	Non-Brahman Priest, Florist	
Kaṉṉār (Īyampūcumācāri)	Brazier	
*Cattiriya Nāṭār****	Merchant	
Maram ēri Nāṭār	Toddy-tapper	
Tōṭṭakkāra Nāṭār	Farm labourer	
*Vaḷḷuvar**	Priest for Harijans	*Low*
*Kucavar (Vēḷāḷar)**	Potter	
*Vaṇṇār****	Washerman	
*Kuṟavar****	Basket maker	
Vaḷaiyar (Muppar)	Catcher of small animals	
Ampaṭṭar	Barber	
Oṭṭār	Stone-cutter	
Pallar	Farm labourer	
*Paṟaiyar****	Farm labourer, Tomtom-beater	*Harijan*
*Cakkiliyar**	Leatherworker	
*Potaravaṇṇār**	Washermna/Barber for Harijans	
Narikkuṟavar	Gypsy	

*** being present in the Kinnimangalam hamlet

* trading from adjacent villages or towns

Table 4.6

Caste Composition Around Kinnimangalam Hamlet

Caste	*No. of household*	*Traditional occupation*	*Traditional position*
<inside the Kinnimangalam hamlet>			
[Caste Hindus]			
Piḷḷai	3	Landlord	village *muṉcīf* accountant
Kaḷḷar	202	Landlord Watchman Herdsman	
Paṇṭāram	1	Temple priest Florist Landlord of temple land	*pūcāri*
Taccuācāri	10	Carpenter Landlord	
Nāṭār	10	Merchant Toddy-tapper Landlord	
Vaṇṇār	7	Washerman	
Kuṟavar	1	Basket maker	sweeper
[Harijans]			
Paṟaiyar	174	Tomtom-beater Farm labourer	*talaiyāri, tōṭṭi, maṭaiyaṉ* (menial workers)
Total	408		
<outside the Kinnimangalam hamlet>			
[Caste Hindus]			
Aiyar (Brahman)		Domestic priest	
Kollācāri		Blacksmith	
Taṭṭācāri		Goldsmith	
Kallācāri		Mason	
*Kucavar**		Potter	
*Ampaṭṭar**		Barber	
Vaḷḷuvar		Priest for Harijans Astrologer	
[Harijans]			
*Cakkiliyar**		Leather worker	
Potaravaṇṇār		Washerman and Barber for Harijans	

*Inside the Kinnimangalam Panchayat village

Note: The *Vaḷḷuvar* is often regarded as one of the Harijans by Caste Hindus.

area, the Telugu Brahmans are employed as domestic priests basically by the Sanskritized non-Brahmans, such as the Pillais and the Acaris.[35] Thus, the non-Brahmanical tendency of the village is demonstrated by the fact that only about 3 per cent (13/408) of the villagers to some extent have a stable connection with the Aiyars.

Plate 18 The Eastern Tank and Tirupparankunram.

Plate 19 The Western Tank.

Plate 20 The main street of Cluster I.

Plate 21 Cluster II.

Plate 22 Cluster III.

Plate 23 Cluster IV.

Plate 24 The Pillais: Chatting with a Vannar, an Acari and a Kallar at the hall of SB's house.

Plate 25 The Kallars: a woman having tattoos on her arms and earlobes with a hole.

Plate 26 Bull-racing (*jallikkaṭṭu*) in which the Kaḷḷar men show their braveness.

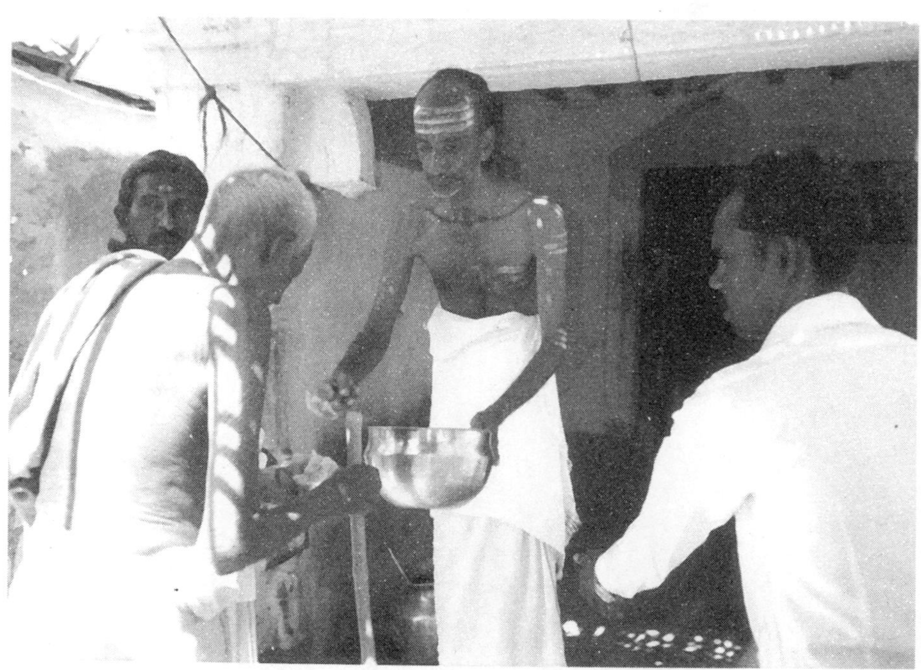

Plate 27 The Pantaram village priest gives *piracātam* to devotees At Ekanatarcuvami Temple.

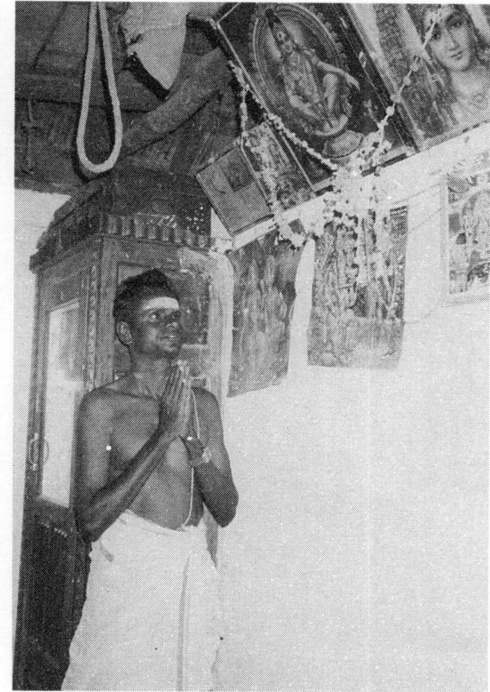

Plate 28 The Taccuacaris (carpenters) wearing a sacred thread.

Plate 29 *Kamalai* is maintained by the Taccuacaris.

Plate 30 The Kollacaris (blacksmiths).

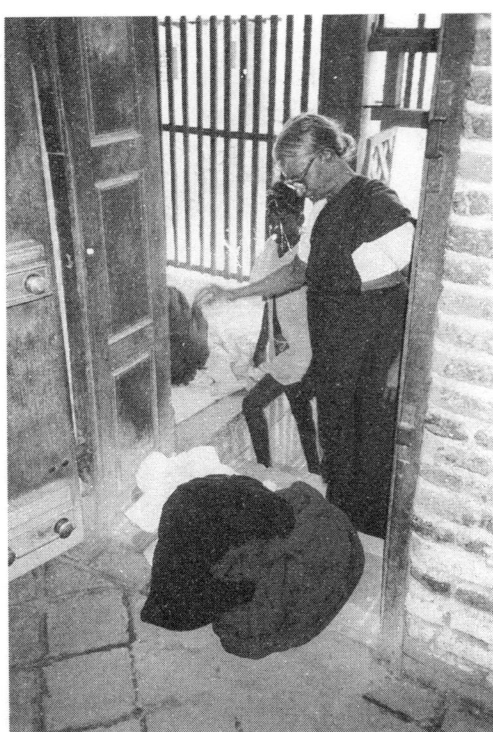

Plate 31 A Vannar boy collects clothes to be washed from his family's clients' houses.

Plate 32 A Vannar wife collects evening meals from her family's clients' houses.

Plate 33 The Vannars: beating and washing.

Plate 34 An evening scene at the Vannars' quarters in Cluster I.

Plate 35 The Ampattars: a barber's shop in Chekkanurani.

Plate 36 The Kucavars.

Plate 37 The Paraiyars as messengers.

The Pillais (the Vellalars)

The Pillais or the Vellalars are one of the typical agricultural castes, which spread across the whole of Tamil Nadu. Their own explanations and the description of Thurston et al. make it clear that the Pillais of the hamlet can be identified as the *Kāraikkattār* subcaste, one subdivision of the Pandya Vellalars [Thurston et al., 1987: Vol. 7, 373–375]. In the village sphere, the village Pillais as *nāṭṭāṇmai* (village *muṉcīf*) and as *karṇam* (village accountant) have enjoyed the highest social position both ritually and politico-economically. Even after the abolition of the system of *nāṭṭāṇmai* and *karṇam*, they successfully proceeded to higher status professions, such as station master, government official, school teacher etc. It is also a clear difference between the Pillais and other village castes that they have conducted distant marriages and therefore hold a Tamil Nadu-wide social network ranging from South Arcot to Tirunelveli. This means, however, that their lineage unity is very loose and is almost dismembered into individual families.

The Piramalai Kallars

The Kallars are said to be a subdivision of the *Mukkulattōr* (the people of three clans), which consists of the Kallars, the Maravars and the Akampatiyars [Natarajan, 1978: 29]. Among the Kallars, there are two separate endogamous groups, *Kīḻ Nāṭṭu Kaḷḷar* (the Eastern Country Kallars) and *Mēl Nāṭṭu Kaḷḷars* (the Western Country Kallars), which are roughly separated by the Nagamalai hills. Whereas the former group is sometimes called Ica *Nāṭṭu Kaḷḷar* (the North-Eastern Country Kallars), the latter, who inhabit the western side of the Nagamalai, are usually addressed as *Piramalai Kaḷḷar.*[36] It is said that the name *Kaḷḷar* is derived from the Tamil word "*kaḷḷaṉ*" which means thief [Natarajan, 1978: 34–35]. The Kallars do not mind this interpretation and rather tend to be proud of their reputed boldness. As is suggested by this, they are relatively less sophisticated and less Sanskritized and are, therefore, not regarded as a ritually high caste, though there is no doubt that they have dominant power politico-economically. They are classified into the Other Backward Classes (OBC)[37] by the government. Unlike the Pillais, the Kallars attach importance to their lineage unity, which will be further clarified in Chapter 11.

The Acaris (the Taccuacaris)

Acari or Kammalar which originates from Kannalar [Thurston et al. 1987: Vol. 3, 106] denotes any of the five kinds of artisan castes, that is Kollacari (blacksmith), Taccuacari (carpenter), Kallacari (mason), Tattacari (goldsmith) or Kannar/Iyampucumacari (brazier). The Acaris living in Kinnimangalam are the Taccuacari so that villagers must get the services of the other four sections of the artisan trade from outside the village, especially from Chekkanurani. Their mythology claims that the Acaris are descendants of *Vicuva-karumā* (Skt. *Viśvakarmā,* the greatest architect of the cosmos since Rig-veda).[38] As is suggested by this and indicated by their wearing *pūṇūl* (a sacred string), the village Acaris are far more Sanskritized than the dominant caste Kallars. The Brahmanical tendency of the Acari culture is originally derived from their profession as house-constructors, which requires them to study treatises of architecture (for example, *maṇaiyaṭi*

Table 4.7
Numbers of Clients of the Acaris

Acari persons / Clients		A2		A7				No service
		B1	*B2*	*B3*	*B4*	*B5*	*B6*	
[The Kinnimangalam hamlet]								
(Caste)	(Lineage)							
Kallar	Kecavan	4	6	1	7	5	1	0
	Kamanan	2	3	0	8	6	1	0
	Cattayi	11	6	1	2	3	0	5
	Panniyan	16	10	8	13	7	3	5
	Kattapinnai	0	1	5	5	3	2	1
	Cuntara-I	5	7	0	1	0	4	0
	Cuntara-II	0	0	0	2	0	2	0
	Conai	0	4	0	2	0	3	0
	Kanni	0	2	0	1	0	0	0
	Cetti	0	0	0	1	2	1	0
	Tarakan	0	0	0	2	0	0	0
	Cataci	0	2	0	0	0	0	2
	Veriyan	0	0	0	0	0	0	1
	(Subtotal of Kallar)	(38)	(41)	(15)	(44)	(26)	(17)	(14)
Pillai		0	0	0	3	0	0	0
Pantaram		1	0	0	0	0	0	0
Natar		0	0	1	3	0	1	4
Acari		—	—	—	—	—	—	—
Vannar		0	0	0	0	0	0	7
Kuravar		0	0	0	0	0	0	1
Total-I		39	41	16	50	26	18	26
		80		110				
[Other adjacent hamlets]								
(Hamlet)								
Putumangalam		20	0	0	0	5	10	
Minakucipatti		0	0	15	0	0	0	
Mavelipatti		5	0	0	0	0	0	
Cikkanpatti		5	0	0	0	0	0	
Total-II		30	0	15	0	5	10	
Total (I + II)		69	41	31	50	31	28	
		110		140				

cāstiram) systematized in the Sanskritic tradition. As shown in Table 4.7, the six active carpenters out of the ten households each have client families, who are allotted by almost equally dividing their father's clients among the sons residing in the village.[39] It is known that their clients consist mainly of the Caste Hindus of the Kinnimangalam hamlet. Apart from these *jajmānī* relationships, the Paraiyars (the Harijans) who hold land can obtain the services of the Acaris if they pay in cash for each piece of work. This means that the Acaris do carpenter work for the Paraiyars as *vēlai*,[40] not as *to<u>l</u>il* which is rewarded on the threshing floor, on annual occasions or in the domestic ceremonies of the life course.[41] In this connection, it should be note that the rewards in the *jajmānī* relationships are not enough for them to support themselves and their families so that the village Acaris are engaged in working as carpenters outside the village to earn cash. They also manage farms for themselves.

The Pantarams

It is said that Pantaram was originally the name of an occupation, and was later recognized as one of the caste names. They tend to affiliate to Siva temples and there engage in making garlands for decorating Sivalinga, and in blowing brazen trumpets when offerings are made or processions are organized [Thurston et al. 1987: Vol.6, 45]. Though the Pantarams have occupied the position of assisting in Siva temples, at the village level they very often work as priests (*pūcāris*) of the village temple. This is the case in Kinnimangalam. The head of the pantaram household engages in the *pūcāri* of the biggest village temple *Ēkanātarcuvami Ālayam* (or *kōvil*). He is given the right of cultivation of the *kōvil maniyam* (land donated to a temple)[42] for his management of the temple. The social status of this Pantaram family in the village is ambiguous. Whereas the villagers show respect to the *pūcāri* because he plays the role of their village priest and is a man of knowledge, the villagers' conventional underestimation of the Pantaram caste in general works to degrade his status.

The Natars

The Natars are very famous as a typical caste who have succeeded in socially raising themselves through the exhaustive effort of the whole caste. The process of their social rise, which took place at the beginning of the 19th century under British colonial rule, is well described by Hardgrave [Hardgrave, 1969]. The Natars, who originally resided in the Tirunelveli area, migrated into Madurai or Ramnad and there accumulated their economic stocks especially through the trade of Palmyra sugar, and they ultimately succeeded in establishing their socio-political position in the social circumstances resulting from British rule. As a result, they were split into two different groups, the traditional Natars mainly engaging in toddy-tapping in the Tirunelveli area,[43] and the Natars of the Madurai or Ramnad areas who are active in the commercial field. It is judged that the Natars of Kinnimangalam belong to the latter group. In this respect, the village Natars are not fully involved in the village social structure, because they tend to depend upon the outside economy, even if they hold some land in the village. Although nowadays the Natars are administratively classified into the OBC, as are the Kallars, other castes do not always accept the social status which the Natars themselves claim, because they stick to the view that the Natars were originally a very low caste, almost equal to the Untouchables.

The Vannars

There are seven Vannar households in the village, whose houses are located at the south-west corner of *ūr* (cluster I). Donkeys with their forelegs tied are an indication of Vannars' residence. Though they classify themselves into the second-graded subcaste Pantiya Vannars among the five subcastes, they prefer the name *Ēkāli* rather than Vannar because they feel that the former is more dignified.[44] The Vannars are obviously one of the main service castes, indispensable for the *jajmānī* relationships so that, as shown in Table 4.8, they have a strong relation with the dominant castes, like the Kallars and the Pillais and their activities are basically confined to the hamlet. Since out of seven households, one (V4) left the village and another (V1) retired due to advanced age, only five Vannars actually engage in the services of washermen.[45] They do not give their services to the Ampattars (barbers), the Kuravars (basket makers) or the Harijans because they think that these castes are regarded as lower than the Vannars. The essential function of the Vannars is to carry out ritual roles

Table 4.8

Numbers of Clients of the Vannars

Client		*V1*	*V2*	*V3*	*V4*	*V5*	*V6*	*V7*	*No service*
	Vannar persons								
Kallar	Kecavan	0	4	2	0	4	7	5	0
	Kamanan	0	6	6	0	1	6	0	0
	Cattayi	0	14	6	0	4	0	1	3
	Panniyan	0	18	19	0	14	9	1	0
	Kattapinnai	0	2	6	0	9	0	1	0
	Cuntara-I	0	5	5	0	7	0	0	1
	Cuntara-II	0	0	2	0	1	0	1	0
	Conai	0	1	0	0	1	9	0	0
	Kanni	0	1	2	0	0	0	0	0
	Cettikularn	0	0	0	0	4	0	0	0
	Tarakan	0	1	1	0	0	0	0	0
	Cataci	0	2	1	0	0	1	0	0
	Veriyan	0	1	0	0	0	0	0	0
	(Subtotal of Kallar)	(0)	(55)	(50)	(0)	(45)	(32)	(9)	(4)
Pillai		0	1	2	0	0	0	0	0
Pantaram		0	0	0	0	0	1	0	0
Acari		0	4	0	0	0	6	0	0
Natar		0	1	3	0	2	0	0	4
Vannar		0	0	0	0	0	0	0	7
Kuravar		0	0	0	0	0	0	0	1
Total		0	61	55	0	47	39	9	16

rather than the usual laundry work. Moreover, there is general recognition that the Vannars are holders of magical power.[46] Even if the village Vannars were replaced by the town laundry service for secular washing under the ongoing process of urbanization, they would still play an important role in the ritual sphere in the village. The split between *vēlai* (secular sense of work which is paid in cash each time) and *tol̲il* (traditional work as a calling which is rewarded by the year) will become more distinct in the course of time. Even today, the village Vannars as the *kamin* type of service caste engaging in their *tol̲il* are deeply involved in conventional *jajmānī* relationships, showing their extensive dependence upon the dominant castes. For example, it is clearly only the Vannars who collect cooked food from their patron-clients (the households of the dominant castes) every morning and evening, which is part of their reward. This custom is also described by Good as an indication of *kuṭimakan̲ ("son of the village")* [Good, 1982: 28].

The Ampattars

The villagers of Kinnimangalam obtain services from eight Ampattars living in the adjacent hamlets, or from 12 barber salons in Chekkanurani. Whereas most of the villagers go to Chekkanurani for haircuts, they tend to invite the Ampattars of the adjacent hamlets for ritual purposes. In particular, their role in the funeral ceremony is highly important. On the occasion of a birth, the Ampattar wife helps in the delivery as a midwife. In this manner, the Ampattars, like the Vannars, carry out the indispensable role of removing pollution. Today the division between *vēlai* and *tol̲il* is also found in the case of the Ampattars. Although there is a report which states that the original occupation of the Ampattars was as medicine men, today barber work tends to come to the fore and supercede the aspects of medicine men or magicians (see [Thurston et al. 1987: Vol. 1, 32, 39–40]. As is shown by the fact that hair-cutting causes *Ampaṭṭan tittu* (barber's pollution), their social status is very low. Generally speaking, the villagers regard the Ampattars as a lower caste than the Vannars, because they believe that the Ampattars are more likely to directly touch a polluting body, especially the lower half of the body.[47] In the aspect of *tol̲il*, there is no doubt that the Ampattars are again deeply involved in *jajmānī* relationships. To the extent that they are involved in their traditional rights and duties, they have to be placed in a lower position of the social hierarchical ladder.

The Kuravars

Only one household of the Kuravars lives in Kinnimangalam. The head of the family is hired as the village sweeper by the Kinnimangalam village panchayat (salary-Rs 150/month), though the traditional occupation of his caste is basket making. Besides sweeping work as his main duty and his side work of basket making, this Kuravar servant sometimes takes part in ear-piercing ceremonies or supplies a special string made of the stems of palm leaves for tying the joint of an agricultural tool, due to his traditional skills in dealing with grasses and leaves. It is said that the Kuravars are probably one of the early tribes of Southern India. It is well known that they do not mind eating meat or drinking alcohol. They are also famous for eating cat meat. When I asked the village Kuravar directly of his preferred order of various kinds of meats, he answered very frankly as follows: (1) goat, (2) sheep, (3) cat, (4) pig, (5) hen or cock, (6) fish, (7) cow or bull.[48] It is very impressive that he did not shown any feelings of shame about eating cat meat, and that he put beef at the last of his preferred order. His straightforward attitude towards eating cat's meat can be explained by the fact that his position in the village is not a hereditary one, but is a contract-based one, so that he is somewhat free from the constraints of the village social structure. Nonetheless, it seems to me that his attitude to beef-eating demonstrates his competitive feeling towards the Paraiyars (Harijans).

The Kucavars

There are no Kucavars in Kinnimangalam, but there are seven households in Puvaracampatti. The traditional profession of this caste is pottery. Today it is more important for the Kucavars to provide pots and plates for religious or ceremonial purposes at no charge to the villagers with whom they are involved, because nowadays villagers can buy vessels for secular use in towns. It is also notable that the Kucavars make the deity statues for the annual festival and they often hold the office of the priest of the village goddess, such as Muttalamman (see Chapter 6). They are, thus, very conscious of their social status and are keen on claiming higher status than that which they actually enjoy.

The Paraiyars

The Paraiyars numerically occupy the dominant position, after the Kallars in this village. Most of them, however, as a dominated caste, engage in agricultural labour. Though the Paraiyars as *aṭimaikārars* (bonded labourers) were originally more deeply involved with the landlords of the dominant castes,[49] today they are usually employed as *kūliyāḷs* and partly as *paṇṇaikārar* in the sense defined in Note 26. The agricultural labour, which they engage in as *aṭimaikārars*, is a quasi-*toḻil* for the Paraiyars of Kinnimangalam. The Paraiyars have, as Moffatt notes, five distinct roles as their original *toḻils*: (1) *parai* drummers, (2) cattle scavengers, (3) cremation ground attendants, (4) *varayan* announcers and (5) village watchmen [Moffatt, 1979: 111]. These roles are valid for the Paraiyars of Kinnimangalam and are indispensable for village life. Whereas the Paraiyars are regarded as people holding the unusual powers of being able to chase out evil and of managing pollution, the dominant castes see them as a heavily polluted caste, basically due to their traditional calling dealing with death pollution and the custom of beef-eating. However, as far as today's village Paraiyars are concerned, they tend, in practice, to look upon these works not as their *toḻils* but rather as their *vēlai* by which they can earn their basic living (see Note 41 about the basic definitions of *vēlai* and of *toḻil* This viewpoint of the Paraiyars seems to reflect the mental detachment of the Paraiyars from the dominant ideology which has confined them to a repressed position under the name of *toḻils*.[50] In Kinnimangalam, the above-mentioned *toḻils* are jointly carried out under the responsibility of menial village servants called *tōṭṭi* (grave-digger, cattle scavenger, cremation ground attendant and messenger) and *maṭaiyaṉ* (caretaker or the sluice of the village tank), which are the offices allotted to the Paraiyars and held in turn every year by members of the different lineages.[51] Besides this, *talaiyāri*, traditionally an assistant of the village *mun̲cīf*, who is chosen from the Paraiyars, is today appointed as a menial government servant to assist the V.A.O.

Generally speaking, there is no doubt that the Harijans today are quite conscious of their status, which is a result of social discrimination. It is said that their social awakening has progressed remarkably since 1946, when Congress came to power [Moffatt, 1979: 80]. The Harijans have acquired a much better position than that which they held previously, due to administrative efforts under the protection policy for the Harijans, even though this change is still not sufficient, especially in the villages.[52] It is of particular practical importance that the *Tiṇṭāmai Oḷippu Kāvalnilaiyam* (the special police for the abolition of Untouchability) and the *Tiṇṭāmai Oḷippu Aluvalakam* (the section for abolition of Untouchability) of the District Office were set up under the Untouchability (Offences) Act, promulgated in 1955. The fear of being arrested under the Act has much suppressed the crude persecution of the Harijans. In this respect, it is very interesting that the Paraiyars, who have suffered from discrimination based upon Brahmanical "pure-impure" ideology, have myths explaining their caste origin in which brotherhood between the Brahmans and the Paraiyars is claimed (see Appendix). Even though the myth narrating their caste origin as having fallen from the status of the Brahmans is broadly shared by the Paraiyars, it should not be overlooked that they feel that verbalizing this myth will not help them to change their low status. The village Paraiyars thus rather try to follow their own paths and to minimize their contact with the dominant castes, as long as they are not intolerably disturbed by them.

The Potaravannars

The Potaravannars are traditionally washermen and barbers serving exclusively the Paraiyars. Until about 50 years ago they were thought of as the Unseeables, people lower than the Untouchables. One Potaravannar moved from Kinnimangalam to Chekkanurani six years ago, but he still comes to the village if necessary. Compared with the service castes for the Caste Hindus, Moffatt points out three roles of the Potaravannars for the Harijans, the roles performed by the Vannar (washerman), the Ampattar (barber) and the Vettaikarar (*pūcāri*), [Moffatt, 1979: 132], which support his theory that the Paraiyars replicate the position of the dominant caste. The role of Vettaikarar (*pūcāri*)is not directly recognized in Kinnimangalam [ibid.: 136], but it is played by the lineage *pūcāris* of the core lineages of the Paraiyars. A Paraiyar elder, MK explains the relationship between the Paraiyars and the Potaravannars as follows: "They (the Potaravannars) are lower than us because they cannot live without depending upon us. This is exactly the same as the situation where we are seen as a lower caste than the Kallars because of our economic dependence on them." It is important here that the Paraiyars do not explain the low status of the Potaravannars by means of ritual pollution. It seems to me that this rational attitude found among the village Paraiyars, in which caste hierarchy is interpreted as the differential of economic power, cautions against Moffatt's hasty conclusion.

The Valluvars

The Valluvars play the priest's role for the Harijans, which is comparable to the Brahman priesthood for the Caste Hindus. Therefore, the Caste Hindus often regard the Valluvars as the highest-ranking Untouchables, although this view is not always accepted by either the Valluvars themselves or by the village Paraiyars.[53] In so far as Kinnimangalam is concerned, the relationship between the Paraiyars and the Valluvar priest is rather limited, compared with the case of Endavur [Moffatt, 1979: 102–9].[54] In this sense, compared with Moffatt's case, the Paraiyars in K hamlet show far more self-sufficiency, being dependent on kinship rather than on caste relationships (see Chapter 10). The Valluvars are also famous for being *cōtiṭārs* (astrologers). As *cōtiṭārs*, the Valluvars have contact not only with the Harijans but also with the Caste Hindus. The traditional connection of the Valluvars with the dominant castes is found at harvest time, when a Valluvar visits the threshing fields of the dominant castes and sings paeans to the gods in celebration in order to acquire auspiciousness. For this magical act, the landowner rewards him with a small amount of crops.

The Cakkiliyars

There is no Cakkiliyar in the Kinnimangalam hamlet, but there are 40 households in neighbouring Mavelipatti. They are regarded as one of the Harijans because their traditional profession of leatherwork (not tanning) is defined as polluting work. In the past their *jajmānī* relationships involved them making or mending *kamalaittōl* (a leather bag for drawing water from a well), but this work has become unnecessary as a result of the recent introduction of an engine pump. Another traditional job, the covering of the drumhead of a *tampattam* (a kind of small drum), is still dependent on their skill. Whereas the former job of supplying a leather bag was rewarded with a yearly payment in kind, the latter is paid for in cash each time.

In the standard opinion both of the Caste Hindus and of the Paraiyars, status ranking becomes lower in the following descending order: the Pallars, the Paraiyars, the Cakkiliyars and the Potaravannars. It is noted that this is different from Moffatt's case [Moffatt, 1979: 140–143].

The Narikkuravars

The Narikkuravars are a Gypsy-like wandering group, who are said to be one of the subcastes of the Kuravars. For example, the Tamil Lexicon defines the Narikkuravars as a people of the Kuravar subcaste who hunt jackals for food. This claim makes the sedentary Kuravars lose face because the wandering Narikkuravar are regarded as a more unclean caste than the Harijans, so that other Kuravars are afraid of being degraded by the negative image of the Narikkuravars. Not only their appearance of uncleanliness, but also their alleged habit of not caring about eating other people's leftovers, are raised by the sedentary villagers as the reasons why the Narikkuravars are looked upon as the most polluting people. I can guess that their own view is different from that of the villagers, but I do not, regrettably, have such data.[55]

Inter-caste Relationships

The jajmānī relationship

It should be noted that there is no inclusive Tamil expression corresponding to the "*jajmānī* system", which has been used by South Asianists, as if it were a universal concept, since Wiser [1958 (1936)]. It is reasonable that Good asks, "Is this notion applicable to parts of India which lack the actual word '*jajmānī*'?" [Good, 1982: 24], in order to challenge the notion of the "*jajmānī* system". Good ultimately dismisses the notion of "*jajmānī* system" as a universal concept and claims that the "*jajmānī* relationship (not a system)" in a limited sense can be used as an aspect of the broader prestations found in village life [Good, 1978: 250–251].[56] In so far as Kinnimangalam is concerned, *kuṭiurimai* (literally, tenants' right) seems to refer to some aspect of the *jajmānī* relationship, especially from the standpoint of the service castes called *kuṭimakkaḷ* (literally, subjects). Whereas the service castes of the Caste Hindus, such as the Acaris and the Vannars, are called *kuṭiyāṉavarkaḷ*, the service people of the Paraiyars were designated *aṭimaikālar* or *aṭimaippaṟaiyar*, these terms recently being replaced by the term *paṇṇaikālar*. There is, however, no word equivalent to *jajmānī* which holds not only the connotation of landlord but also that of *yajamāna* (sacrificer or institutor of a sacrifice), though the words *nilaccuvāṉtār* or *nilattukkārar*, which simply mean a landlord, could refer to a patron (see also [Good, 1978: 245] and [Good, 1982: 32]). *Kaḷḷarkaḷ* or *Tēvālkaḷ* is useful in practice for indicating a patron because the Kallars form the majority of the dominant castes in Kinnimangalam. This expression comes a little close to *jajmān*. In everyday conversation, the expression of "*enka* (our) …" is used more naturally when the landowing patron and the people of the service castes directly refer to each other. Such an expression, which evokes a feeling of involvement in the minds of both the speaker and the listener, conveys the hereditary inter-dependence between the dominant castes and the service castes, that is to say, the *jajmānī* relationship.[57] I anew note that agricultural production depends upon the Paraiyar labourers (see Plates 38–42).

Plate 38 Well-irrigation by *kamalai*.

Plate 39 Plowing at rice nursery.

Plate 40 Hoeing.

Plate 41 *Puṭaittal* (winnowing by women).

Plate 42 Threshing using bulls.

Plate 43 *Poli* (a heap of paddy).

Plate 44 *Kaṭakapeṭṭi* (having one *marakkāl* capacity).

It is recognized that the ritual aspect of *toḻil* of the service castes still persists in village life, even since urbanization [Commander, 1983: 310]. This reveals that the *jajmānī* relationship has not only an economic function but also a ritual function in its nature.[58] It seems to me that the *jajmānī* relationships found in Kinnimangalam, in which the Kallars dominate the village community as patrons and the Pantaram priest and other service castes carry out their ritual roles, is regarded as a much modified example of a Hocartian understanding of the *jajmānī* relationship, namely, the view of the king-centred religious relationship. Dumont's model, which claims that the *jajmānī* system is a Brahman priest-centred institution, would not be valid for the Kinnimangalam case. Firstly, the relationship between the Kallars and the Pantaram priest does not embody that of *jajmānī* and *purohita*.[59] Secondly, the primary values of the Kallars is not "pure-impure" ideology but "pollution" ideology, as will be gradually clarified. In this sense, Raheja's argument, which basically follows the Hocartian view, seems to be important [Raheja, 1988], even though her approach is different from mine.[60]

On the Threshing Floor: Prestations at the Paddy Harvesting

I provide here a standard example of the prestations associated with paddy cultivation, which are made by a Kallar landlord holding a relatively large cultivated land. First, at the time of making a rice nursery (*nāṟṟankāl* in the month of *Purattāci* (September–October), one *mukkai* (three handfuls) of paddy is given to the service castes such as the Acaris, the Vannars, the Ampattars, the Kuravars, the Kucavars, the *tōṭṭi* and *maṭaiyaṉ* and the Cakkiliyars. At the harvesting (*aṟuvaṭai*) in the month of *Tai* (January–February), the prestations on the threshing floor, as shown in Table 4.9, are given as the main part of the yearly rewards of the *jajmānī* relationships. The details of the prestations on the threshing floor are these.

Labourers, both men and women, carry paddy bundles from the fields to the threshing floor. The people start threshing after worshipping the goddess of the earth, *Pūmadēvi*. The threshing process consists of two steps, and the distribution is also divided into two stages. The first step of threshing is to hit the bundles on a stone by hand, which is called *katir aṭittal*. Then winnowing is firstly done by the men, using a winnow made of steel (*muṟam*). This work is called *muṟam potutal*. Only the paddy dropped leeward is again winnowed by the women, using a winnow made of a palm leafstalk (*cuḷaku*). This second winnowing is called *puṭaittal*. After this work, a small conical shape of cow-dung, which symbolizes the God Ganesh, is put on the top of a *poli* (a heap of paddy). The paddy dropped the most leeward, which is not good, is kept separately in a vessel called *nārpeṭṭi*. This vessel of paddy is shared among *aṭimaikārar* and *paṇṇaikārar* of the Paraiyars, after the master ritually takes a small portion. The *mukkai* is taken by the service castes from the *poli*. The rest of the heap, after giving *mukkai*, and the paddy left in the winnows is taken by *aṭimaikārar* and *paṇṇaikārar*. The second step of threshing is necessary because the ears of rice still have undropped paddy. The paddy straws are again spread on the threshing floor and cattle or buffaloes walk on them. This is called *cūṭu aṭittal*. Again, through the same process of winnowing, *poli* and *nārpaṭṭi* are separately prepared. Then the prestations are made by following the same procedure as in the first step. A small difference, however, is the participation of the Valluvar. After *cūṭu aṭittal*, a Valluvar comes to the threshing floor and sings celebratory songs there. For this service, he takes *mukkai* from the *poli*. Prestation (1) *varucakūli* are usually given sometime later after finishing this harvesting work.

Table 4.9

Prestations on the Threshing Floor
(in the Case of 1 Acre of Paddy Field with Well-irrigation Using Kamalai)

Prestations / *Service castes or servants* *works in the village	(1) *varuca-kūli*	(2) *first mukkai*	(3) *second mukkai*	(4) *katir-kaṭṭu*	(5) *cutantiram*	(6) *other*
	[1 *marakkāl*=8 *paṭi*=6.5 litre, 1 *kaṭṭu*=12 *ari*, 1 *ari*=2 *paṭi*, 1 *pati*=0.8 litre]					
Acari * making & mending farming tools & bullcarts * making kamalai (#) * gifts of life course ceremonies * mending houses * construction of a new house (SS)	7 *mara-kkāl*	2 *paṭi*	2 *paṭi*	1 *kaṭṭu 3 marakkāl*	2–3 *paṭi per one kamalai*	
Vannar * services in life-course ceremonies * services in village festivals	6 *mara-kkāl* Rs 25	2 *paṭi*	2 *paṭi*	2–3 *ari* (4–6 *paṭi*)		
Ampattar * services in life course ceremonies * services in village festivals * circumcision (#)*cutting hair ($)*cutting pubic hair (#)	6 *mara-kkāl* Rs 20	2 *paṭi*	2 *paṭi*	1-2 *ari* (2–4 *paṭi*)		
Kuravar * mending farming tools * ear-piercing*basket making ($) * sweeping ($$)		2 *paṭi*	2 *paṭi*	1–2 *ari* (2–4 *paṭi*)		
Cakkiliyar * making & mending a leather bag for *kamalai* * covering a drumhead ($$)	3 *mara-kkāl per kamalai*	2 *paṭi*	2 *paṭi*	1–2 *ari* (2–4 *paṭi*)		

Cont'd ...

Cont'd ...

Kucavar * providing pots & plates in village festivals and in life course * making pots ($$)	2 *paṭi*	2 *paṭi*	1–2 *ari* (2–4 *paṭi*	peddy straw
Valluvar * singing celebratory songs * astrologer ($$)		2 *paṭi*		
totti & mataiyan * announcement with drumming * grave-digging * cattle scavenging * menial services at funerals & marriages * village watching * caretaking tank-sluices (*mataiyan* only) * menial services on village occasions	2 *paṭi*	2 *paṭi*	5 *ari* 1 *marakkāl* 2 *paṭi*	
aṭimaikārar & paṇṇaikārar * supervising farm labourers * menial domestic work * farming works	*nār-peṭṭi* the rest of the heap the rest in the winnow (8 marakkāl)	*nār-peṭṭi* the rest of the heap the rest in the winnow (8 marakkāl)		
kūliyāl * harvesting works			1 kattu	24 *mara-kkāl* divided among *kūliyāḷ*
kūliyāl * trasplaning (women only)		2 *paṭi*		1–2 *paṭi* (the rest of the winnow)

Notes: 1. *Kamalai* is a traditional facility for raising water.

2. # : work no longer carried out or disappearing,

3. $: work requiring part cash payment

4. $$: work requiring full cash payment

5. 1 *marakkāl* : the full among of a cylindrical box called *kaṭakapeṭṭi* (see Plate 44)

These rather complex prestations are found only during the paddy-harvesting time, i.e., in *Māci* month (February-March). In the case of the harvesting of millet or of that of nuts and beans, the landowner gives *mukkai* only, or a combination of *mukkai* and *katirkaṭṭu* (one bundle of sheaves). As to vegetables, there is no fixed regulation, and the people of the service castes can take at any time a certain amount for their food from the master's field. It is also added that the service castes can enjoy some reward (clothes and meals) on the occasions of the domestic rituals of their masters and of annual festivals, though they also give *moy* (a gift) to their masters. These prestations are basically made in kind, but today are sometimes paid in cash. This is partly because of the recent inadequate agricultural production and partly due to the increased production of cash crops.[61]

Table 4.9 shows that there are several kinds of prestations for the service and labour provided for paddy cultivation, as follows: (1) *varucakūli* (a yearly-stipend), (2) *mukkai* (three handfuls), (3) *katirkkaṭṭu* (sheaves of paddy or of millet) and (4) *cutantiram* (a perquisite). Good reports, from a Tamil village of Tirunelveli, that there are three types to prestations on the threshing floor, that is, *sampaLam* ("salary"), *sāshtiram* (literally, "branch of specialized knowledge") and *sandōsham* ("mutual satisfaction") [Good, 1978: 180–185, 1982: 24–27]. It seems to me that *varucakuli* corresponds to *sampaLam*, that *mukkai* can be equated with *sāshtiram*, and that *katirkkattu* can be regarded as *sandōsham*. Scince *cutantiram* is a very specific reward given only to the Acaris for their preparation of the equipment of *kamalai* (a traditional well irrigation system), I look upon it as part of *sāshtiram* for the Acaris. A comparison of the examples of Good [Good, 1978: 180–181] and mine, makes it clear that the Acaris (carpenters), the Vannars (barbers), the Ampattars (washermen), the Valluvars (priests for the Harijans), the *maṭaiyan̲* (channel controllers) and the *aṭimaikārar/paṇṇaikārar* (house servants) are commonly raised as the important receivers of presentations in both cases. However, the Cakkiliyars, the Kucavars and the Kuravars also join in the sharing on the threshing floor in Kinnimangalam. In my case, it is obvious that the service castes expressed by "*eṅka-*" receive all *varucakūli mukkai* and *katirkkaṭṭu*. The connection with other necessary service castes is displayed by giving *mukkai* and *katirkkaṭṭu*, which are the reward for their *toḻil*.

Today, since not only the agricultural labour force itself is basically secured by a daily payment in cash rather than by prestations in kind, but also the craft works done by the *eṅka* artisans tend to be replaced by outsiders' services or by machine-made items, it seems to me that the *jajmānī* relationships are diminishing and becoming very limited.

Kinship System

There is no doubt that the kinship system which defines intra-caste relationships reflects inter-caste relationships, namely, village dynamism and vice versa. In this sense, it is necessary to understand an outline of the kinship system of the village castes.

Parallel Relatives

Generally speaking, the village castes consist of one, or plural, patrilineal lineages as a clear kinship unit, which is called *vakaiyaṟā* (literally, division or kind)[62] or *paṅkāḷi* (shareholders of property).[63] *paṅkāḷi* in a general sense means a group of blood relations (*ratta uṟavu*) or parallel relatives traced through the father's line (*appāvaḷi*), which can be replaced by the expression of the *aṇṇaṉ-tampi* (eB-yB) relationship.[64] *Uṭaṉpaṅkāḷi* which denotes a group of people sharing a blood relationship and a common lineage god, *kulateyvam*, should be distinguished from *muṟaikkupaṅkāḷi* ("conventional[65] a group of people who believe they are brothers, although this relationship cannot actually be traced by them (see Figure 4.3). *Uṭaṉpaṅkāḷi* works as a basic cooperative unit, whereas *muṟaikkupaṅkāḷi* simply provides a framework of èxogamy. In this sense, *Uṭaṉpaṅkāḷi* can be equated to *vakaiyaṟā* which usually consists of several sublineages called *vāricus*. These categorical systems are directly applied both by most of the Caste Hindus and the Paraiyars with the exception of the Pillais. In the case of the Pillais, the larger social framework of *kōttiram* (Skt. *gōtra*), which can be seen as a patri-clan, works as an exogamous unit. This difference reflect the contrast that the Pillais are conscious of and attach importance to the title of *kōttiram;* whereas the Kallars, for example, recognize the title of *vakaiyaṟā* as the significant one. It is said that the *kōttiram* of the Pillais have a common clan god but it is difficult for them to carry out their clan festival in practice because of their dispersed residence, which is indicated by the survey of marriage distances shown in Table 4.10. In contrast, other Caste Hindus and the Paraiyars in the village mostly marry partners within the village or from the neighbouring villages. It is notable that about 30 per cent of the marriages recorded in the village can be categorized as village-endogamous.

Figure 4.3

Muṟaikkupaṅkāḷi of the Kallars as Exogamous Units

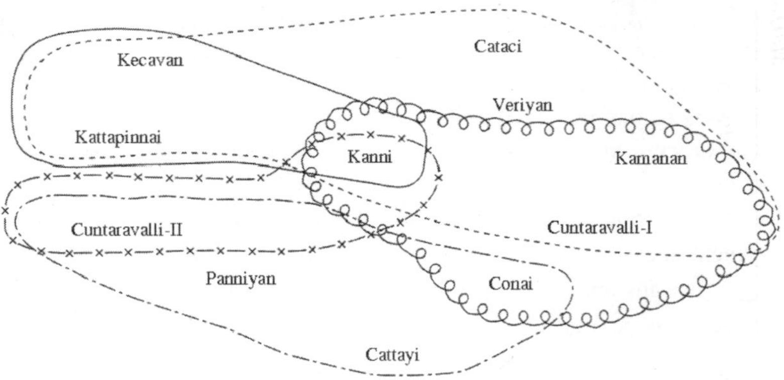

As shown in Table 4.11, the village Kallars consist of more than 13 *vakaiyaṟās* and the Paraiyars have more than 8 *vakaiyaṟās.*[66] Furthermore, Figure 4.3 displays my reconstruction of the villagers' knowledge of the *muṟaikkupaṅkāḷi* relationship among the Kallars. It is common knowledge among villagers that *Iraṇṭu-Tēvār* = *Nāṟ-Paṅkāḷi* (literally, Two Heads of the Kallars and Four Paraiyar lineages) form the fundamental axis of the village structure. On the one hand, *Iraṇṭu-Tēvār* (Two Tevars) are the representatives of the Kallars as the dominant caste and they are chosen from the Kecavan and the Kamanan lineages as the earliest settlers. On the other hand, *Nāṟ-Paṅkāḷi* (Four Pankalis) refer to the Kartananti, the Cinnananti, the

Table 4.10

Marriage Distance (km)

Castes / *Distance*	*Inside village*	*Below 5*	*5–10*	*10–15*	*15–20*	*20–30*	*30–40*	*40–60*	*Above 60*	*Other districts*	*Total*
Pillai	0	0	0	0	0	0	0	0	0	3	3
Kallar	66	84	13	9	2	2	0	1	0	0	177
Pantaram	0	0	0	0	0	0	0	0	1	0	1
Acari	1	0	1	3	0	0	0	0	0	0	5
Natar	3	1	2	1	1	0	1	0	0	0	9
Vannar	0	4	3	0	0	0	0	0	0	0	7
Kuravar	0	0	0	0	0	0	1	0	0	0	1
Paraiyar	25	34	30	10	6	1	4	7	1	0	118
Total	95	123	49	23	9	3	6	8	2	3	321
%	29.6	38.3	15.3	7.2	2.8	0.9	1.8	2.5	0.61	0.9	100.0
Accumulated %	29.6	67.9	83.2	90.4	93.2	94.1	96.0	98.4	99.1	100.0	

Table 4.11
Lineages and Lineage Deities

Caste	*Lineage*	*Lineage deities*	*Place of temple*	*Festive month*
Pillai (3)	Kiravan (*kūṭṭam*)	Puvayammal (F)		
	Kanicamar (*kōttiram*)	Ankalaisvari (F)	Cittalai	*Māci* (Feb.-Mar.)
Kallar (202)	*Kecavan (23)	Kottamantai-karuppu (M) Cilailcari (F)	Karumattur	*Māci*
	*Kamanan (21)	Ankalaisvari (F) Virapattiran (M)	Kinni —	*Māci*
	Cattayi (28)	Cattayi (F)	Kinni	*Māci*
	Panniyan (65)	Virumanti (M) Pecciyamman (F)	—	*Māci*
	Kattappinnai (18)	Sivan (M) Pinniyammal (F)	Cikkanpatti	*Māci*
	Cuntaravalli-yamman I (17)	Cuntaravalli-yamman (F)	Cittalai	*Māci*
	Cuntaravalli-yamman Il (4)	Cuntaravalli-yamman (F)	Cittalai	*Māci*
	Conaikamatci (9)	Conaicarmi (M) Kamatciyamman (F)	Tirali	*Māci*
	Kanni (3)	Kamatciyamman (F)	—	*Māci*
	Cettikulam (4)	Periyakarrupu (M) Pecciyamman (F)	Karumattur	*Māci*
	Tarakan (2)	Sivan (M)	Cinnavakaikulam	*Māci*
	Cataci (4)	—	—	—
	Veriyan (1)	—	—	—
	? (3)			
Pantaram (1)	—	Ankalaisvari (F)	Kampam (Curuli)	Aippaci (Oct.-Nov.) or Tai (Jan.- Feb.), Cittirai (Apr.-, May)
Acari (10)	Palikkanciyacari	Irulappacami (M) Ayamman (F)	Kamatcipulam	*Māci*
Natar (10)	—	Muttaiyacami (M) Cilaikari (F)	Kinni.	*Māci*
Vannar (7)	—	Irulappacami (M) Ankalaisvari (F)	—	—
Kuravar (1)	—	—	—	—
Paraiyar (174)	*Kartananti (29)	Periyanatcci & Ariyanatcci (F)	Kinni.	*Paṅkuṉi* (Mar.-Apr.)
	Cinnananti (15)	ditto	ditto	ditto
	*Mataiyan & Vettaiyan (41)	Meyyanamurtti (M) Marattiyamman (F)	Kinni.	*Vaikāci* (May-June) (*Āṭi*) (July-August)
	*Urkalan (19)	Urkavalcami (M) Cilaikari (F)	Kinni.	*Vaikāci* (*Āṭi*)
	Tankalan (44)	Muttaiyacamii (M)	Kinni.	*Vaikāci*
	Manakuli (6)			
	Necavan (1)			
	Cappataiyan (3)			
	? (16)			

Note: Lineages having * form *Iraṇtu-Tēvār* = *Nār-Paṅkāḷi*

Mataiyan (including the Vettaiyan) and the Urkalan. This fundamental axis forms the core of the village caste structure. Nonetheless, it is obvious today that other Kallar lineages such as the Cattayi and the Panniyan, have increased their lineage members and the Tankalan of the Paraiyar community has also developed as a big lineage. Since these lineages are late comers, they tend to stand a little outside the sphere of traditional rights and duties. This is true especially in the case of the Tankalan, for, as is clarified in Chapter 11, the lineage often shows an outsider-like character as compared to the *Nāṟ-Paṅkāḷi* who occupy a central position in the Paraiyar community. There is, in practice, a social gulf between the *Nāṟ-Paṅkāḷi* and the Tankalan lineage and their members have never married each other.[67]

Cross Relatives

Besides *paṅkāḷimuṟai* or *aṇṇaṉ-tampi muṟai* mentioned above, there are the another two distinguishable kinship relations, that is, *māmā-maccinaṉ muṟai* and *cakalaṉ*.[68] *Māmā-maccinaṉ muṟai* are regarded as cross-relatives kinship having affinal relations, which include relations through the mother (*tāyvaḻiccontam*), relations through the wife (*maṉaivivaḻiccontam*), relations through the father's sister and relations through the sister.

Table 4.12 shows the kinship "terms of reference" of the Kallars (male ego-centred). Good precisely studied the relations between "relationship terms"[69] and uncle (MyB) – niece (eZDy) marriage broadly found among Dravidian societies and extracted a clear perspective of this problem [Good, 1980: 492–3, 1991: 54–74]. There, Good criticizes Dumont's classic work on the Dravidian kinship system, in which a kin/affine framework was adopted, and claims that the distinction between "parallel-relatives" and "cross-relatives" is more appropriate for understanding the Dravidian kinship.[70] That is, *aṇṇaṉ-tampi muṟai* are thought of as parallel-relatives and *māmā-maccinaṉ muṟai* as cross-relatives. The terms of reference shown in Table 4.12 can, therefore, be classified into parallel or cross. As to male members of cross-relatives, for example, the members older than ego consist of *māmaṉ* (+1) and *maccāṉ* (+0) and those younger than ego are referred by *maccinaṉ* (–0) and *marumakaṉ* (–1). As this example tells, generation and relative age work for defining terms of reference. The list of terms of reference of the Kallars (Table 4.12) resemble the Maravar type which is said to suppress uncle-niece marriage by Good [Good, 1991: 56]. In so far as K hamlet is concerned, Good's distinction between the Maravar type and other types harmonious with uncle-niece marriage is not supported. Because, (1) the Kallar's terms of reference shown in Table 4.12 are basically shared by all castes in K hamlet except several caste-specific expressions (cf. [Dumont, 1986: 303], [Good, 1980: 416], [Trautmann, 1981: 34-5] etc.), and (2) as shown in Table 4.13, there is the fact that every caste has a custom of uncle-niece (*māmaṉ-marumakaḷ*) marriage (although no cases for Pillai, Pantaram and Kuravar appear in the Table because of fewer households, it is confirmed by interview that those castes also have the custom outside the village). The correspondence between relationship terms and the custom of uncle-niece marriage, that Good claims [Good, 1991: 69], should be treated with caution.[71] Good, who emphasizes the necessity of distinction between terminological identification and genealogical identification,

Table 4.12

Kinship Terminology of the Kallars (by a Male Speaker)

Kinship term	*Genealogical referents*	*Level*
cīyāṉ	FF, MF, FFB, MFB, FMB, MMB	+2
appattā	FM, FFZ, FMZ	+2
ammattā	MM, MFZ, MMZ	+2
appā, appaṉ	F	+1
periyappaṉ	Feb, MeZH (periyayyā)	+1
cittappaṉ	FyB, MyZH (nallayyā)	+1
attā	M	+1
periyattā	MeZ, FeBW	+1
ciṉṉattā	MyZ, FyBW (nallattā)	+1
māmaṉ	MB (tāymāmaṉ), FZH	+1
māmaṉār	WF	+1
periyamāmaṉār	WFeB	+1
ciṉṉamāmaṉār	WFyB	+1
attai	FZ, MBW	+1
māmiyār	WM	+1
periyamāmiyār	WFeBW	+1
ciṉṉamāmiyār	WFyBW	+1
aṇṇē, aṇṇaṉ	Be, FBSe, MZSe	+0
akkā	Ze, FBDe, MZDe	+0
tampi	By, FBSy, MZSy	–0
taṅkacci	Zy, FBDy, MZDy	–0
maccāṉ	MBSe, FZSe, WeB, eZH	+0
matiṉi	MBDe, FZDe, WeZ, eBW	+0
macciṉaṉ	MBSy, FZSy, WyB, yZH	–0
koḻuntiyāḷ	MBDy, FZDy, WyZ, yBW	–0
makan	S, BS, WZS	–1
aṇṇaṉmakaṉ	eBS	–1
tampimakaṉ	yBS	–1
matiṉimakaṉ	WeZS	–1
koḻuntiyāmakaṉ	WyZS	–1
makal	D, BD, WZD	–1
aṇṇaṉmakaḷ	eBD	–1
tampimakal	yBD	–1
matiṉimakal	WeZD	–1
koḻuntiyāmakaḷ	WyZD	–1
marumakaṉ	ZS, WBS, DH	–1
marumakaḷ	ZD, WBD, SW	–1
pēraṉ	SS, DS, BSS, BDS, ZSS, ZDS,	–2
pētti	SD, DD, BSD, BDD, ZSD, ZDD	–2

Notes: 1. The above-mentioned kinship terms are the written form of expression.

2. Though the Paraiyars' kinship terminology is primarily similar to that of the Kallars, there are a very few differences such as *aiyaṉ* as F and *ammai* as M.

3. The Pillais' terminology is also almost same as that of the Kallars. Some differences are as follows; *tāttā* instead of *cīyāṉ*, *pāṭṭi* instead of *appattā* or *ammattā*, only *appā* as, F, only *ammā* as M.

points out that the principle of relative age works more dominantly and the principle of generation (genealogy) is regressive in the case of the kinship terminology holding uncle-niece marriage [ibid.: 70]. This claim seems to be supported by "terms of address" (*viḷippeyar*) in the case of K hamlet, which directly reflect their practices of uncle-niece marriage. Let us take two examples. First, as Dumont also reports, at the level of terms of reference, *maccaṉ* e.g., MBSe) is differentiated from *macciṉaṉ* (e.g., MBSy) according to both principles of generation and relative age, but at the level of terms of address, the principle of generation regresses and for example MBSe is called *māmaṉ* and MBSy is called *māppiḷḷai* or by name. Secondly, FZ is *attai* (or *māmiyār*) at the level of reference, but becomes *akkā* at the level of address. Since *akkā* denotes eZ in reference, the principle of generation regresses in this example. These examples of terms of address are compatible with Good's argument of relationship terms around eZDy marriage.[72] At any rate, it is here important to confirm that *māmā-macciṉaṉ muṟai* is the whole stock of ego's cross-relatives which might supply a marriage partner to ego.

Another category of kinship relation should be touched on. *Cakalaṉ* relations refer to those among a wife's sister's husbands, and are thought of as types of parallel relatives (a pseudo-*paṅkāḷi*) through being cross-relatives of ego's cross-relatives.[73]

There is no doubt that the three kinds of kinship relations mentioned above correspond well with the three categories of relatives proposed by David, that is, "sharers" (*sakotarar*), "uniters" (*sampantakkarar*) and "non-uniters" (*sakalar*) [David, 1973: 525]. By citing these tripartite categories of David, Good criticises Dumont's analysis based on the "consanguine/affine" distinction [Dumont, 1961: 81] which ignores the category of "non-uniters", i.e., *cakalaṉ* relations [Good, 1980: 482–483].

Close Relatives and Distant Relatives

Kinship relations are not exhausted by the above-mentioned lineage-centred categories of kinship. The extension of ego-centred recognition of relatives is also taken into account. It consists of a three-layered concentric structure from inside to outside; family (*kuṭumpam*), close relatives (*neruṅkiya contam*) and distant relatives (*tūrattu contam*). As shown in Figure 4.4, the husband-centred case differs from the wife-centred one. The difference reflects the patri-lineal society where wife joins to husband's lineage. Wife is, therefore, required to have not only self-centred recognition but also her husband-centred recognition. It is, however, notable that this concentric structure has bilateral extension. That is, the *kuṭumpam* or in *neruṅkiya contam* depends on person, and this opinion may affect the border between *neruṅkiya contam* and *tūrattu contam.* Kinship system of K hamlet is fully understood by taking into account the principle of ego-centred *contam* as well as the principle of patrilineal lineage or clan (cf. [Good, 1980], [Barnard and Good, 1984: 44–47]). The disorganization of a joint family tends to reduce the sphere of *kuṭumpam,* but in their recognition it still includes lineal ascendants of both husband and wife, direct brothers and sisters of both husband and wife and their children (husband's side only). Whether husband's father's brothers and husband's sisters' children are included in *kuṭumpam* or in *neruṅkiya contam* depends on person, and this opinion may affect the border between *neruṅkiya contam* and tūrattu contam.

The consideration of the above kindred-like *contam* has an important connotation in that *neruṅkiya contam* becomes a basic core group which sustains *kuṭumpam* rituals and in those functions one generation above cross-relatives among *neruṅkiya* contam, that is *tāymāmaṉ* (MB) and *attai* (FZ) in descriptive sense play crucial roles. The importance of the ego-centric distinction between *neruṅkiya contam* and *tūrattu contam* has some evidences. One is that, as is shown in Table 4.13, there is no MBDy spouse in the classificatory sense, and another is that ego's descriptive MB is sharply distinguished from *māmān* as a classificatory term by having the special term of reference *tāymāmaṉ*.

The people outside the concentric structure of *contam,* i.e., the unknown people beyond *tūrattu contam* are called *aṉṉiyam* (unrelated person).

Preferential Marriage

After having discussed several concepts for an understanding of the kinship system, a discussion on marriage practice follows. The traditional right and duty of marriage preference called *karai,* which is regarded as the "jural" level of social reality in the sense of Good [Good, 1978: 499–500] and Barnard and Good [Barnard and Good, 1984: 9–14], is basically found regardless of caste difference, though there are some caste-specific characteristics. It is claimed that "prescribed" spouses [Barnard and Good, 1984: 100–104] in their tradition are, genealogically speaking, FZDy, MBDy and eZDy, which are expressed terminologically as *koḻuntiyāḷ* for the former two and as *marumakaḷ* for the third (commonly a female junior cross-relative), from the male viewpoint. This is the case not only among the Pillais but also among the Kallars and the Paraiyars. Though Dumont reports that "the Kallar vigorously condemn sister's daughter marriage and their genealogies show almost no such marriages" [Dumont, 1986: 204], as already explained, this statement is wrong in so far as my data from K hamlet is concerned. Since the possibility that MBD and ZD can overlap is logically verified by Good, as shown in Figure 2 of Good [1980: 486] or in Figure 5.3 of Good [1991: 67], it is known that "the preference for the matrilateral cross cousin" [Dumont, 1986: 203] as an *urimai* preference [Dumont, 1957b: 14] found among the Kallars is not incompatible with sister's daughter marriage. Thus, Dumont can be refuted not only from this logical viewpoint, but also by the fact that eZDy marriages are found in practice among the Kallars, as shown in Table 4.13.[74]

In this connection, it is traditionally the general tendency for the villagers to have *pūrvīkaccontam* (literally, "hereditary relatives"), who have successively exchanged the "prescribed" spouses mentioned above with each other. Table 4.14 shows the list of *pūrvīkaccontam* claimed by each lineage and of lineages from which spouses are most taken. The custom of "hereditary relatives" is, logically speaking, realized through "restricted" exchange, that is, a bilateral exchange of FZDy and MBDy[75] or that of eZDy and MBDy; and also through "generalized" exchange, i.e., a patrilateral exchange of FZDy. This logic is in practice supported by the "statistical-behavioural" level of data shown in Table 4.13.

There is no doubt that *tāymāmaṉ* (MB) is a focal person in the selection of a marriage partner, because the MB can claim three possible "prescribed" marriages for his sisters' sons and daughters. That is to say, MB himself can marry eZDy (an eZDy

Figure 4.4

Family, 'Close Relatives' and 'Distant Relatives'

(1) Husband-centred case (Ego-1)

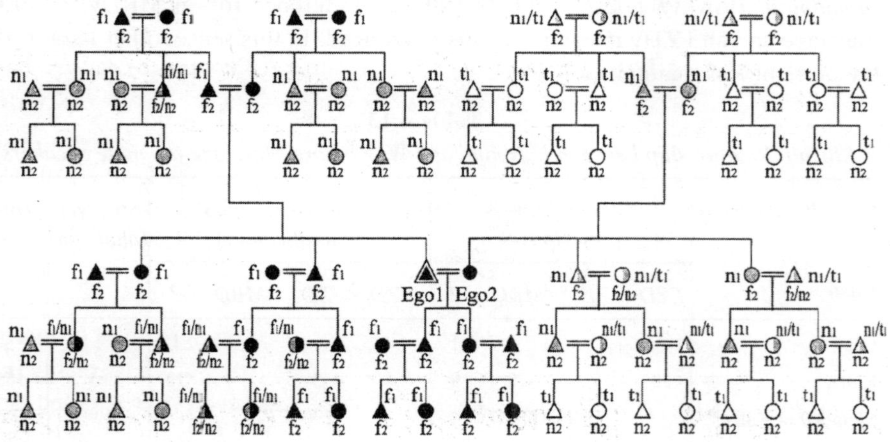

(2) Wife-centred case (Ego-2)

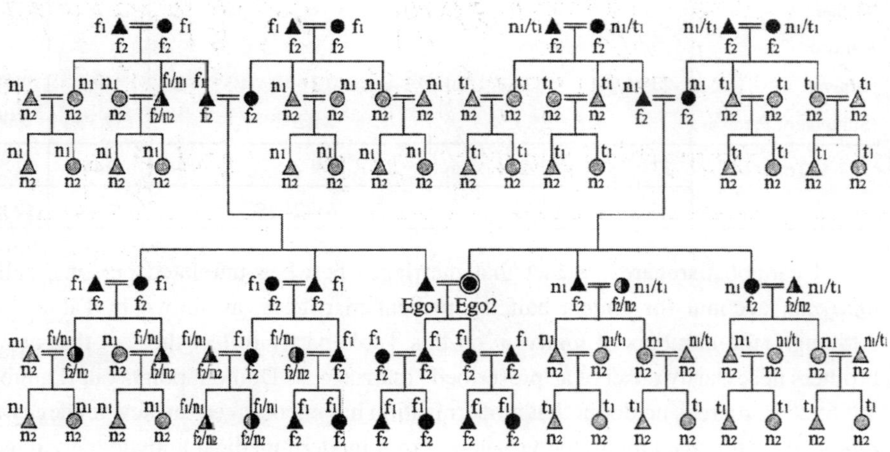

Notes: 1. f and ▲/ ● refer to family.
2. n and △/ ◉ refer to 'close relatives'
3. t and △/ ○ refer to 'distant relatives'
4. Number 1 indicates husband's viewpoint
5. Number 2 indicates wife's viewpoint.

marriage), MBS can marry MB's ZDy (an FZDy marriage) and MBD can marry MB's ZSe (an MBDy marriage). *Tāymāmaṉ,* therefore, holds three possible rights and duties in his hands. Due to their *urimai* preference for an MBDy marriage, the *tāymāman* of the Kallars, especially, insists on his regulated right that his ZS should marry his D. Therefore, if his ZS fails to marry his D, MB can require his ZS to pay a special fine called *karaip peṇṇukku tīrval* (literally, a fine for the karai girl).[76] I also know a Kallar man who got divorced due to the interference of his wife's *tāymāman.* However, despite their regulated preference for an MBDy, an eZDy marriage and an FZDy marriage are also practiced. In this sense, other karai rights are more or less maintained.

Table 4.13

Kinship Relationship between Husband and Wife before Marriage (by male speakers)

Relationship / *Caste*	*Close relatives (descriptive)*				*Distance relatives (classificatory)*				*Stranger (aṉṉiyam)*	*Total*
	FZD	*ZD*	*MBD*	*?*	*FZD*	*ZD*	*MBD*	*?*		
Pillai				1				1	1	3
Kallar	10	7	15	9	4	3		22	85	155
(Subtotal of Kallar)	41(26.4%)				29(18.7%)				(54.9%)	(100%)
Pantaram			1							1
Acari			1			2		1	3	7
Natar				1		1		2	4	8
Vannar			1	1		1		2	2	7
Kuravar										
Paraiyar	23	1	9	14	4	2		18	46	117
(Subtotal of Paraiyar)	47(40.2%)				24(20.5%)				(39.3%)	(100%)
Total	33	8	27	26	8	9		46	141	298
	94 (31.5%)				63 (21.1%)				(47.4%)	(100%)

I cannot disregard the fact that marriages between unrelated persons, called *aṉṉiyam,* account for almost half the present marriages, as shown in Table 4.13. Although the numbers of *aṉṉiyam* on this Table partly reflect the fact that not all brothers necessarily observe a "prescribed" marriage, as Dumont points out [Dumont, 1986: 207], there is no doubt that modernization has encouraged the new tendency for *aṉṉiyam* preference among the villagers. From modern medical knowledge villagers are aware of the harmful effects that may result from marriages with close relatives.[77]

Lastly, the prohibition of inter-caste marriage, which is very well observed in the village is touched on. As to actual examples of inter-caste marriages, I know of only one couple (a Paraiyar husband and an Acari wife) living in the Paraiyar quarter of the village, and have heard of another two couples (a Kallar husband and a Valaiyar wife, and a Kallar husband and a Brahman wife) residing outside the village. Though the former couple is legally married, the latter couples, legally speaking, are not regarded as formally married [Dumont, 1986: 198–199]. Thus, inter-caste marriage is still exceptional for the villagers. One day a Kallar youth said to me, "We make love with other caste women but don't get married to them."

Table 4.14
Pūrvīkaccontam of Main Lineages

Caste	*Lineage*	*Lineage as pūrvīkaccontam claimed*	*Linage from which spouses are most taken (1) mainly (2) secondly*
Pillai	Kiravan		—
Kallar	Kecavan	Conaikamatci	(1) Conaikamatci
			(2) Panniyan
	Kamanan	Panniyan	(1) panniyan
			(2) Kattapinnai
	Cattayi	Kanni	(1) Kanni
			(2) Kattapinnai
	Panniyan	Kamanan	(1) Kanni
			(2) Kattaminnai
	Kattapinnai	Panniyan	(1) Viramanti
			(2) Kamanan
	Cuntaravalli-I	—	(1) Cuntara-II
			(2) Panniyan
	Cuntaravalli-II	—	(1) Cataci
	Conaikamatci	Kecavan	(1) Kecavan
	Kanni	Panniyan	(1) Panniyan
Pantaram		—	—
Acari		Pettanacami	(randam)
Natar		—	Kamatci
Vannar		Karuppacami	Karuppacami
Kuravar		—	—
Paraiyar	Kartananti	Vettaiyan,	(1) Kumpakaran
		Urkalan	(2) Vettaiyan
	Cinnananti	Mataiyan,	(1) Cappataiyan
		Urkalan	(2) Mataiyan
	Mataiyan and Vettaiyan	Kartananti,	(1) Cinnananti
		Cinnananti	(2) Kartananti
	Urkalan	Kartananti,	(1) Pucari
		Cinnananti	(2) Kartananti
	Tankalan	Manakuli	(1) Manakuli
		Pattain	(2) Catayanti

Plate 45 *Paricam pōṭutal* at the Kallar engagement after finalizing the amount of *varataṭciṇai*.

Plate 46 The procession of *Āṭi cīr* (a gift from the bride's side in the first *Āṭi* month after marriage).

Notes

1. On the basis of fieldwork among the Jaffna Tamils, I wrote several articles related to the topic of this book [Sekine, 1984, 1985].
2. For example, I left my camera in the hands of S. Balasubramanian, who was my best friend and research partner, and asked him to take photographs of a village festival which is held in *Paṅkuṉi* (March–April).
3. I should note that my field selection was to some extent influenced by the statement of Good that "such villages (those without a Brahman community), though much the more numerous in the region to be studied, had so far received a disproportionately small amount of attention in the ethnography of Tamil Nadu" [Good, 1978: 5].
4. *Mantai* is an open-air raised floor for a village meeting or court. It is also used as a place for resting and play by male adults.
5. S. Balasubramanian was at that time (1985) in his early thirties but he had already earned enormous popularity and the respect of villagers not only for being a son of a village *muṉcīf*, but also due to his being an intellectual in the true sense, and a paragon of honesty and uprightness. In this sense, his acceptance of me produced an atmosphere in which other people trusted me. His cooperation was far more than I expected. I was very much impressed by his scholarly sense and ability so that he naturally became almost a co-researcher. One day he told me delightfully, "I really like this sort of research work". Hearing it, I was happy and grateful that I had met him. I now remember the happiest of times with him, regretting his too early, accidental death.
6. A culture of hospitality still remains in the village. The villagers warm-heartedly accepted me, not because they understood what I was doing in their village, but mainly because of the fact that I was a visitor from a distant place, and because of the incidental fate that had caused me to select their village from many others for my work. In this connection, I am reminded of two statements of villagers. One day soon after starting fieldwork, an old woman asked me, showing her sympathy, "You're lonely, aren't you? How do you manage your board? If you have trouble about meals, you could come to my house, for my son's wife is a good cook", and she then told the people accompanying me, "You all must look after him well". Another occasion was when I was invited to lunch, my host told me, "You have to eat plenty, because it will be the shame of our village, if you lose weight".
7. Moffatt describes the caste structure of Endavur in Chapter 3 of his book [1979] only as the background of his main argument on the Harijan community.
8. An interesting example is taken from the experience of interviewing two sons of an influential Harijan together. When the younger brother said, replying to my question whether he ate dead cattle meat, "I don't eat dead cattle meat even though other people do it. I only eat meat bought from a shop", the elder brother cut in on us and said to me, "He's lying. He also eats dead cattle meat". The younger brother laughed and accepted what the elder brother said. It seems to me that these examples show us not only how we can see through the fabrications in their replies but also that the interactive process itself found in the example gives us much information about their thoughts. I think that the latter point is most important for an anthropological study.
9. My methodological claim here comes closer to what Dirks argues as his understanding of ethnohistory. Namely, fieldwork is regarded as a process of "textualization" in J. Clifford's terms [Dirks, 1987: 15].
10. There are several opinions as to the etymology of the word Madurai. One is that the word Madurai is derived from a Sanskrit word "Madura", which means sweetness. Another is

that it is a metathesised form of "Marudapuri", the original meaning of which is a fort-city surrounded by local trees called maruda. As is well known, Madurai flourished for a period as the ancient capital of the Pandya (*Pāṇṭyaṉ*) Kingdom from just before or after the beginning of the Christian era, and later as the centre of the Nayaka (*Nāyakkam*) dynasty until the beginning of British rule. Today (the latter half of the 1980s) Madurai, whose population is about eight hundred and twenty thousand, has two faces, one old, the other new, that is, both a traditional, religious facet and a modern, industrial one. The former is symbolized by the famous temple *Mīnākṣī Ammāṉ Kōvil,* and the latter by the newly developing factories, such as the T.V.S. motor company, the Kothandaram spinning mill, and the Madurai Coats and Sri Minaksi textile industries.

11. Tirumangalam, the population of which is about thirty thousand, is a more urbanized area, indicated by the availability of luxury items, such as tape recorders, television sets, autobikes, scooters, jewelry, fashionable garments, photocopiers, and high grade soft drinks. Facilities such as pharmacies and a taxi service are also available.
12. Watching movies is the most popular amusement among the villagers. There are more than thirty cinema theatres in Madurai city. The late chief minister, M.G. Ramachandran, was a famous cinema actor and his outstanding popularity as a politician among the Tamil masses was basically derived from the image of the good man he played in his films. There is no doubt that the cinemas are a strong influence on the Tamil masses. This aspect is investigated in depth by Dickey [1988], Hardgrave [1973] and Sivathamby [1981].
13. According to the Gazetteer of the Madurai District [Government of Madras, 1960], local legend tells that Nagamalai is the remains of a giant snake which was produced by the magic of the Jains and finally defeated by the God Siva.
14. According to "Season and Crop Report of Tamil Nadu for the Year 1983–84" (Tamil Nadu Bureau of Statistics), the average ratio of irrigated land to actual cultivated lands is 40.4 per cent.
15. As to the relationship between the rule of the Nayaka and that of the poligars, Good notes that until the latter half of the 18th century there were 48 auxiliary chiefdoms (ruled by the poligars) in the southern part of Tamil Nadu under the rule of the Nayaka or the Maravar chiefs, and that such poligars were often transformed into zamindars (*jamīṉtārs)* under British rule [Good, 1978: 70–78] [Ludden, 1985: 49].
16. The tendency of the expanding migration of the Kallars continued until the British government suppressed it [Dumont, 1986: 15].
17. It is said that the Kecavan people (the pioneer lineage of the Kallars), with the cooperation of the Kartananti=Cinnananti (the core lineages of the Paraiyars), jointly killed the Kauntar Zamindar, while the Kamanan people (another core lineage of the Kallars) and the Urkalan (one of the Paraiyar lineages) slew the Muslim Zamindar.
18. According to a village elder, Tangaraj, the socio-political system of the Kallarnadu is said to consist of 8 *nāṭus* (provinces) and 24 *upakirāmams* (secondary villages). A *nāṭu* again consists of 18 *paṭṭis* (hamlets) (also see [Dumont, 1986: 159–169]). The head office of the Kallarnadu was called *Nāṭṭupuratāni,* and it was given to Karamanikariyanitevar of the Pinnattevar lineage by Tirumalai Nayaka, at his own request, as a reward, since he discovered a thief wanted by the King (see also [Dumont, 1986: 155]). This indicates both aspects of the Kallarnadu, independence and subordination, in the decentralized character of Nayaka rule. The political centre of the Kallarnadu, the *rājatāni,* where the *Nāṭṭupuratāni* lives, is Urappanur and the religious centre is said to be Karumatur, where the *mūṉucāmi* (three great gods of Hinduism, namely, Siva, Visnu and Brahma) are said to

reside. In Karumatur today, there are various important temples, the number of which is more than three, such as the Kaluvanadan, the Angala Isvaran, the Nallakurumbaiyar, the Virumandi, the Chittraputran and the Kotta Mandai Karuppu.

19. It is reported that at the end of the Nayaka dynasty, nearly 200 villages, most of which were located in the north-west direction of Madurai city, were defined as the *kōvil mān̲iyam* of Minaksi Amman Temple [Fuller, 1984: 92]. See also [Kumar, 1965: 12].
20. The revenue system of Ryotwari was introduced, especially in southern India, in the 1830s, by the English East India Company, after a 30 year debate starting from the grant of the Permanent Zamindari Settlement in Bengal (1793) [Ludden, 1985: 170]. In theory, it is a system of taxation in which the government imposes a tax on each landowning cultivator as a ryot. Nonetheless, as Kumar clarifies [Kumar, 1965: 14–17], the British government faced complicated problems, caused not only by the Zamindari system and the Inamdari system, but also by the Mirasdari system, which was, originally at least, a communal system of landholding and was later often modified. It took more than half a century to shift to the Ryotwari system in practice.
21. It seems to me that the replacement of the *nāṭṭāṇmai* and *karṇam*, who are members of the village (*ūr* in Tamil), by the V.A.O., who is a purely administrative officer, foreign to the village, was the final step that completely wiped out the little remaining communality on the revenue level in the village. See also [Mukherjee, 1962: 249–250] and [Good, 1978: 79–81].
22. Dumont used the concepts of "residential cluster" and of "territorial unit" (a social unit consisting of plural "residential clusters") instead of village in his ethnography of the Pramalai Kallar community [Dumont, 1986 (1957)]. Since the settlement pattern shows a congregated type in this area, it is easy for us to grasp Dumont's sense of "residential cluster", which is almost the same as what I call a hamlet (see the editor's footnote in [Dumont, 1986: 33]). There is no doubt that Dumont's attempt aims at pointing out the danger for students of Hindu societies in unwittingly believing in the actual existence of the "village".
23. It is a matter of course that how we understand a village is deeply related to how we understand *jajmānī* relationships. While Fuller [1977, 1989] takes Dumont's side, Raheja [1988] tends to protect the significance of a village social sphere.
24. Good basically accepts Dumont's standpoint and evaluates Beck's definition of dominance, in order to explain his notion of "micro-region", consisting of several hamlets, as a necessary analytical framework [Good, 1978: 152–264]. Good clearly notes, concerning how he delineated the micro-region, "if I wished to 'make sense' of the social structure of TV—my original primary intention—it was essential that I should take VV and KP into consideration too" [Good, 1978: 263].
25. Later he adds the fourth criterion of "Western", which indicates the number of people in a caste who have a Western and thus non-traditional education [Srinivas, 1987 (1959): 97].
26. The present villagers distinguish three types of employment when the Paraiyar work under the dominant caste landlords (*nilaccuvān̲tār)* is explained that they work (1) as an *a aṭimaikārar* (a hereditary bonded labourer attached to a particular family or lineage of the dominant castes), (2) as a *paṇṇaikārar* (a labourer employed on a one-year contract) or (3) as a *kūliyāḷ* (a day labourer). The former two are regarded as traditional types and have been rapidly disappearing in recent times. The third type, *kūliyāḷ,* is commonest today. Cf. [Kumar, 1965: 41] and [Moffatt, 1979:67].
27. The introduction of an institution of panchayat was attempted in the 1920s under British rule but it failed [Retzlaff, 1962: 45, 48]. A new "village panchayat" system was introduced

to Tamil villages in 1958 (the Madras Panchayat Act) [Gough, 1989: 15] according to the recommendation of the Balwantrai Mehta committee (1957), which stood for the ideal of "democratic decentralization". The present panchayat is in its third term, and its current members were elected in 1986, after a ten year interval.

28. The "traditional panchayat" (*periya mantai*), as a judicial system (*pañcāyattuk kūṭṭam*) has dealt with problems concerning (1) *karai* (a traditional right and duty of marriage preference), (2) *vivākarattu* (divorce), (3) *kaṟpaḷippu* (rape), (4) *kaḷavu* (stealing), (5) *canṭai* (fighting), (6) *vivacāya payir iḻappu* (agricultural crop damage), (7) *caṭaṅku* (puberty ceremonies), (8) *iḻavu* (death ceremonies) and so on. They have various methods of judgement, called *cattiyam,* to be used when they find difficulty in identifying who is in the wrong.
29. A *kāriyakkāraṉ* is not formally selected, but is informally admitted by the lineage members and the villagers due to his abilities, especially due to his skills of oratory at meetings.
30. A detailed description and discussion of house forms in each cluster is found in my article [Sekine, 1993a]
31. The word *cēri* is an insulting expression today, so that villagers usually avoid using it.
32. It is noted that, in this Paraiyar cluster, there is an Acari household where an Acari widow and her children live. This reminds me of Moffatt's argument on caste structure, where he shows that the second subset of the third set of castes, like the Chettiyars, the Pantarams, and the Acaris will come into the Harijans' colony to perform their *toḻils* [Moffatt, 1979: 96].
33. I basically follow Kolenda's definition of caste and subcaste [Kolenda, 1978: Ch.1].
34. I also hesitate to use the concept "*jajmānī* system" naively so that I adopt, for convenience's sake, the term "*jajmānī* relationships" as an analytical concept, according to the suggestions of Fuller [1989: 41] and of Good [1982].
35. According to Gough [Gough, 1981: 24–5], a subcaste of the Brahman Kurukkal which is engaged as priests of Siva temples is given a lower status than other non-priestly subcastes of the Smartha Brahmans because of their priesthood (see [Fuller, 1984: 50–51]). The status of domestic priests serving non-Brahmans, like the Telugu Brahmans, is lower than that of the *cāstiri* serving his same caste, the Brahmans.
36. The difference between *kīḻ Nāṭṭu Kaḷḷar* and *Piramalai Kaḷḷar* is marked by their different titles. Whereas the former has the title *Ampalam,* the latter holds the title *Tēvār.* There are several opinions as to the origin of the name *Piramalai* [Natarajan, 1978: 32].
37. Under its protection policy, the government has set up several social categories such as that of the Backward Classes (BC), which consists of Other Backward Classes (OBC), Scheduled Castes (SC) and Scheduled Tribes (ST).
38. Their caste association *Vicuvakarumā Toḻilāḷarkaḷ Caṅkam* holds the temple of Kamatciyamman.
39. A2 and A7 have 6 brothers, but the other brothers have left the village. As a result, A2 and A7 divided their father's clients roughly in half. The fact that the number of each Acari's clients is not exactly the same suggests that there are other factors which cause this difference. The main factors are the skill by which they acquire their reputation and declining health which reduces their number of clients.
40. This is different from Moffatt's explanation in which the Acaris come to the colony to perform their *toḻils* [Moffatt, 1979: 96].
41. The definitions of *vēlai* and *toḻil* in Kinnimangalam are as follows: *toḻil* is one's hereditary job associated with special skills or knowledge, and *vēlai* generally refers to all jobs except

toḻil, and rather connotes simple labour which does not always require special knowledge. According to Good, "*Vēlai* refers to job in the normal western sense, namely one's actual, current paid employment. *Toḻil* refers to one's hereditary, caste-specific speciality, which one may or may not follow in practice." [Good, 1982: 26]. He points out that "Work in the sense of *vēlai* seems therefore to be external to oneself", but this is not the case with *toḻil* [ibid.: 26]. The use of these terms in Kinnimangalam seems to be slightly different from that in Good's case in terms of the dichotomy of the skilled and the unskilled found between *toḻil* and *vēlai.* Moffatt's definition emphasizes the aspect of "right" which *toḻil* holds and connects *toḻil* with caste ranking [Moffatt, 1979: 91].

42. The *kōvil Māṉiyam* consist of 14 acres of *puṉcey* (non-irrigated land) and 2 acres of *naṉcey* (irrigated land). The *pūcāri* has the biggest lands in the village today, because the holdings of other big landowners have been dissolved.
43. The Natars as toddy-tappers were rather known as the *Cāṉār*, whose status was just above that of the Untouchables.
44. According to the village Vannars, they also have other honorific names, such as *Irkuli Veḷḷāḷa* and *Rajakaṉ.*
45. The youngest Vannar, V7, has only 9 clients because he is engaged mainly in agricultural labour, whereas the other four Vannars make a living by being washermen.
46. This recognition has been reinforced by men who are exorcists, medicine men and sorcerers, and women who are midwives being relatively commonly found in the Vannar caste. The late grandfather of the present active village Vannars was such a powerful person, and he had a good command of various *mantras.*
47. Attending funerals, shaving the pubic hair of the Kallars and conducting circumcisions degrade the status of the barber.
48. The preferred meat order given by the usual non-vegetarian villager is: 1. goat or sheep, 2. hen or cock, 3. fish. Compared with the Kuravar's list, we can easily see the singularity of the Kuravars
49. There is a hereditary connection between the Cattayi lineage (the Kallars) and the Cinnananti lineage (the Paraiyars), and one between the Kamanan lineage (the Kallars) and the Urkaran lineage (the Paraiyars).
50. For example, as Moffatt notes, the dominant ideology claims that to carry out *toḻil* seriously is an action of *dharma.* [Moffatt, 1979: 92, fn. 12]
51. Though the Paraiyar community of Kinnimangalam consists of five major lineages, it is their traditional custom that *tōṭṭi* must be selected from one of the following three lineages: the Kartananti, the Cinnananti and the Urkalan. The *maṭaiyaṉ* is chosen from the Mataiyan lineage. The office of *tōṭṭi* is rotated among these three lineages every year, in order that each lineage can equally enjoy the privileges of *tōṭṭi.*
52. The Paraiyars of Kinnimangalam are still not allowed to draw water from the well of the Caste Hindus, to enter the temples of *ūr* (the residential cluster of the Caste Hindus), or to enter the houses of the higher castes. Cross-caste marriage between the Paraiyars and the Caste Hindus is still strongly prohibited.
53. The village Paraiyars simply regard the Valluvars as Harijans and do not have a clear idea that the Valluvars, as priests, are higher than them. This is different from what Moffatt reports [Moffatt, 1979: 102]. However, the Valluvars strongly reject being categorized with the Harijans, because they are proud of their "clean" life in which they follow a Brahman type of lifestyle.

54. The occasions on which the Valluvar priest is invited by the Paraiyars are (1) the sixteenth day ceremony of a funeral, called *karumāti* (the ceremony for sending the soul of the dead to Heaven), (2) the thirtieth day ceremony of a funeral in the case of the death of the *pūcāri* (a lineage priest) or of the *cāmiāṭi* (a shaman possessed by a particular god or goddess) and (3) the simple ceremony of purification for cooking vessels at the beginning of the marriage ceremony. The first occasion is not always observed by most Paraiyars, an exception being made in the case of an influential person. The second occasion in only for *pūcāri* and *cāmiāṭi*
55. I have heard that they have a strict regulation that they will allow a woman to go out in the daytime but that she must come back home before sunset. If she fails to observe this rule, she will be punished by caste banishment. This suggests that they have their own independent moral code.
56. Raheja who studies prestations in a North Indian village seems to share a similar view as Good that the *jajmānī* relationships should be placed in the broader sense of prestations [Raheja, 1988: 13]. However, Raheja criticizes Fuller by saying that he should not too quickly "dismiss the possibility that the ensemble of *jajmānī* relationships constitutes a culturally meaningful entity" [Raheja, 1988: 25] (cf. [Fuller, 1977] and [Fuller, 1989]).
57. This reminds me of Raheja's report that *phaslana* (harvest prestation) is given to the service castes holding "one's own" relationship with the *jajmāns* [Raheja, 1988: 204–205].
58. As is well known, there is a debate between a group which regards the ritual relationship as fundamental and another group which understands the *jajmānī* system as an economic institution. The former group includes two streams, the Hocartian [Hocart, 1950] and the Dumontian [Dumont, 1966]. The Hocartians claim that Brahman (Skt. *purohita*) and *kamīn* are similar in terms of "priestly" duties, whereas the Dumontians exclusively attach importance to the relationship between *purohita* and *jajmān* [Raheja, 1988: 25–26]. The latter group again holds two different standpoints [Prinde, 1977: 288]. One standpoint, which can be called the exploitative theory, emphasizes the coercive force of the dominant caste and the irrationality of payments (e.g. [Beidelman, 1959], [Berreman, 1962] and [Mencher, 1974]). The other group evaluates the "economizing" aspect and recognizes the bargaining power of the *kamīn's* side (e.g. [Wiser, 1958 (1936)] and Leach [1960]). See also [Kolenda, 1963].
59. Though it is true that the Pantaram priest plays an important role in village affairs, like annual festivals and village festivals, he is never invited to the domestic rituals of the villagers. Not only that, but also neither the Pillais nor the Kallars recognize the Pantaram priest as ritually higher than them. In this sense, the dominant castes tend to see the Pantaram priest as a *kamīn*, i.e., as one of the service castes, like the Acaris, the Vannars and so on. Exceptionally in the village, the Pillais, who are much Sanskritized, invite a Brahman priest for their domestic occasions. Even if I took into account this Pillai situation, it would still be difficult to naively agree with the Dumontian understanding, partly because the Pillai primary value can again be the "pollution" ideology even though they are Sanskritized and partly because, since Brahman priests in this area economically much depend on the dominant castes, like the Pillais, the statement that status encompasses power sounds vain.
60. She elucidates the horizontal dimension of the village structure with her theories of "centrality" and of "mutuality" on the basis of concepts of auspiciousness and inauspiciousness. I basically admire her stimulating theory which has the challenging aim of criticizing the conventional understanding of a village structure which has been strongly limited by the concept of the Brahman-centred "pure-impure" hierarchy. Her viewpoint, which embodies the concepts of auspiciousness/inauspiciousness, is to some extent shared by my argument represented by the decentripetal concept of "pollution", which attaches

importance to "productivity", though Raheja's understanding seems to still retain the bias of a top-down view and the problem of a non-interpretative approach due to her underestimation of the politico-economic power of the dominant caste.

61. The main agricultural crops produced in Kinnimangalam are as follows: 1. *nel* (paddy), 2. *kēḻvaraku* (ragi), 3. *kampu* (millet), 4. *parutti* (cotton), 5. *karumpu* (sugar cane), 6. *kattari* (eggplant), 7. *takkāḷi* (tomato) and 8. *veṅkāyam* (onion). All the crops except paddy are cash-crops. The introduction of these cash-crops has enhanced payment in cash.
62. The villagers sometimes use *kūṭṭam* (union, group, class or kind) instead of *vakaiyaṟā.*
63. In Kinnimangalam, there are no castes without unilineal groups, such as the Konars and the Paraiyars of TV in Good's field area [Good, 1980: 483].
64. *Paṅkāḷi* in a narrow sense refers especially to the unity of the male members of the same generation.
65. According to Dumont, *muṟeikki Paṅkāḷi* is the brother relationship between the male descendants of two sisters [Dumont, 1986: 203]. This is different from the definition that I heard in Kinnimangalam.
66. The numerically minor castes such as the Pantarams, the Natars, the Vannars and the Kuravars do not know the name of their *vakaiyaṟā,* though they are conscious of their lineage gods.
67. The people of the Kartananti and Cinnananti tend to explain that they have not married Tankalan people because of the *muṟaikkupaṅkāḷi* relation between them. This is a way to avoid plainly exposing the social gulf between them.
68. Other than this, there are several expressions of kinship relationship such as *ōrppaṭiyāḷ* (a relation between brother's wives), *campanti* (a relation between husband's parents and wife's parents), and *cakkalatti* (a relation between two wives of one husband).
69. Since Needam's proposal [Needam, 1971] the relationship terms theory has developed from the standpoint of which terminology indicates cultural categories of people beyond expressions of genealogical relationship, so that it is necessary to make precise investigations in each culture before proceeding to comparison. People taking this standpoint avoid using "kinship term" and adopt "relationship term". Good seems to be regarded as a relationship term theorist. Although I accept the point they raise, I still use the expression "kinship term" and the distinction between terms of reference and terms of address, because of their usefulness. Good's claim of the importance of relative age beyond generation is to some extent resolved by the distinction between the basic usage of term and the applied usage of term, which overlap the distinction between terms of reference and terms of address.
70. Good evaluates Dumont's works as "the most satisfactory account" [Good, 1980: 476] among the various analyses of Dravidian kinship terminology, and then criticises it. The interrelated points on which Good's criticism are based are these. (1) Terminological identity is not always equated with genealogical identity; (2) Besides the structural analysis, in the light of "kin/affine" distinction, more attention should be paid to ego-centred modes of classification; (3) There is a strong tendency for cross-relative kinship terms to reflect relative age rather than genealogical position such as generation [Good, 1980]. Directly on the bases of the second and third points, Good clearly notes that "Not only does *maman* (term 9) apply to the MBe (who belongs, in terms of Figure 1, to the +1 level), but to the elder male cross-cousin (of level +0), and even to the opposite-sex sibling's son (of level-1), should the latter be older than Ego." [ibid.: 493] Though Dumont also reports the distinction between maccan elder than ego and maccunan younger than ego

within ego's generation the point of relative age is not developed systematically, as Good has developed it.

71. The Maravar, Nadar and Kallar have been said not to have a custom of uncle-niece marriage, but the data from K hamlet deny such a view. Natarajan's work on the social organization of the Kallars also clearly refer to the fact that they have eZD marriages [Natarajan, 1978: 216]. Therefore, Good's explanation for the lack of the custom among those castes becomes meaningless [Good, 1991: 70].
72. The reason why FZ is possibly called *akkā* is that there is a fundamental tendency of looking upon the marriage imaginarily as if it was a MB-eZDy union, so that, even though ego marries FZD, FZ is seen as eZDy's mother, that is, *akkā* (eZ). In the light of this tendency, MBW is also "addressed" as *akkā*. It is explained that since ego's sister is a potential wife of MB (tāymāmaṉ), according to marriage with eZDy as the "prescribed" [Good, 1991: 100–104] spouse, MBW can be regarded as *akkā*-like. In this sense, if I follow Bourdieu's concepts of "official kin and practical kin" [Bourdieu, 1977: 33–38], an eZDy marriage can be regarded as a sort of "official marriage".
73. *Māmā-maccinaṉ* relationship is regarded as a joking relationship (*kēliccontam*), in which it is rather strange to have serious talk. It is not unusual for sexual topics to appear in conversations among the same generation, especially in the case of the Kallars. To the contrary, the relations where joking should be avoided are said to be *paṅkāḷi* and *cakalaṉ*.
74. The Kallars in K hamlet provide the somewhat contradictory statement that eZDy marriage is ideal but MBDy marriage should be given the first priority in practice. I presume that Dumont focused upon the later regulation among the Kallars. As shown in 4.13, the reality of the Kallars to some extent deviates from the regulation. It seems to me that their strict regulation of the MBDy marriage preference can be regarded as a traditional device by which they try to prevent their kinship relations from becoming part of a narrowly closed system.
75. The bilateral exchange of FZDy and MBDy is an exchange of sisters, which is called *koṇṭāṉ māṟṟuc campantam* (literally, husband-subsequent-alliance). Aiyavu, a middle-aged Kallar man, told me that this sort of marriage tends to be avoided because a fight between one couple easily spreads to other brothers' or sisters' couples and then it is very difficult to settle the problem.
76. The amount of the fine is said to be Rs 8,000–10,000 for ordinary Kallars. Nonetheless, the fine is, in practice, decided according to the payer's economic ability, though the minimum Rs 500 must be paid in each case.
77. For example, Tangaraj stopped the convention of taking wives from their "hereditary relatives", the Conaikamatci lineage, because he judged that the sterility of their lineage was due to the long "restricted" exchanges between the Kecavan and the Conaikamatci. As a result, he successfully had four children from his marriage with an *aṉṉiyam*.

Part Two

Pollution Theory

The fundamental basis of the book's assertion is constructed in Part Two. The deliberate consideration of pollution conceptions elucidates a new horizon of pollution theory which cannot be reduced to Dumontian type of pure-impure theory. Setting up the fundamental viewpoint of an interpretative distinction between "impurity" and "pollution", it is made clear that "pollution" ideology, which tends to be concealed by "pure-impure" ideology, is a basic ideology shared among the Tamil villagers.

Chapter 5

"Pollution" and "Impurity"

Configuration of Folk Conceptions

Tīṭṭu (Pollution) and its Essential Connotations

Denotation of Pollution and Folk Terms

As far as Kinnimangalam is concerned, the folk terms which are expressions related to pollution include *tīṭṭu, aciṅkam, acuttam, cuttam illai, tuppuravu illai, tuymai inmai, nalla illai,* and *ācūcai.* Among these terms, *aciṅkam, acuttam,* and *ācūcai* are derived from the Sanskrit words *asahya, aśuddha*, and *āśauca* respectively. *Cuttam illai* is a combined expression of a Tamilized Sanskrit word *cuttam,* and a pure Tamil suffix of negation *illai.* It is literally proper that both *acuttam* (Skt. *aśuddha*) and *acucai* (Skt. *āsaūca*) are translated as "impurity" as they are antonyms of "purity (Skt. *śuddha* or *śauca*)". It is important that the pair words, *acuttam* and *cuttam,* are actually used for expressing a relative ritual ranking, as is more precisely discussed later. The most popular words, regardless of caste difference, are *tīṭṭu, aciṅkam* and *acuttam.*[1] Although *aciṅkam* is often used as a synonym of *acuttam, aciṅkam* has its own implications, referring to things and happenings which are ugly, unpleasant, or unusual. Therefore, *tīṭṭu* and *acuttam* are the two most important words directly referring to pollution or impurity, which are mainly investigated here. It should be remembered that even if the same words were adopted in the village, the meanings of these words in their practical usage would differ depending on the speakers' situational context.

There are three categories of folk terms which are deeply connected with the concept of pollution mentioned above. The first is a group of words denoting sin, crime or fault such as *pāvam* (Skt. *Pāpa*), *kuṟṟam,*[2] *tappu* and *tavaṟu.* The situations referred to by these words are described not only as *aciṅkam* but also possibly as *tīṭṭu.* The second is *tukkam* (Skt. *duḥka*) which means sorrow and mourning, and which is strongly related to death pollution. The third is an astrologically inauspicious situation, called *tōṣam* (Skt. *dōṣa*), in which people behave as if they were in *tīṭṭu.*

Ordinary Interpretations of tīṭṭu

What causes tīṭṭu?

Firstly I take up *tīṭṭu*, which is deemed an indigenous Tamil word. There is a fundamental consensus among villagers of all castes as to what causes *tīṭṭu,* with one exception—the Paraiyar's disagreement over the view that Caste Hindus look upon the Paraiyars as a people of *tīṭṭu*.[3] This exception is discussed later in Chapter 7. There is strong agreement among the villagers that four "incidents" occurring in the life course, namely childbirth (parturition), puberty, menstruation and death inevitably cause *tīṭṭu*. Only for the Kallars, was the circumcision of a boy, a custom no longer followed by the present generation, a source of *tīṭṭu*, as is puberty for a girl.[4] Besides these, it is also said that sexual intercourse causes *tīṭṭu*. These "incidents" generating *tīṭṭu* are always associated with some physical pollutants, like "persons" or "things". Physical pollutants of childbirth are blood from the delivery, a woman in childbirth (a mother) and a newborn baby; those of puberty and menstruation are menstrual blood and a menarcheal woman; those of circumcision are blood resulting from the treatment and a circumcized boy; that of death is a dead person (body); those of sexual intercourse are semen and female sexual fluids. Furthermore, it should be noted that there is a group of objects which to some extent provokes a feeling of *tīṭṭu*, though they are at the same time described as things *acuttam* and *aciṉkam* (this is not the case in reverse). Among these objects, nail clippings, fallen hairs and spat saliva are to some extent distinguished from the rest, such as decayed food, a nosebleed, bloodshed, a dead animal, a body with parts amputated or malformed, smallpox or a lizard falling onto the body. The former three are generally regarded as *tīṭṭu*; whereas the evaluation of whether the latter miscellaneous objects are *tīṭṭu* or not differs from person to person, and moreover, depends on the situation.[5] The polemical act of beef-eating should not be disregarded. Though it is claimed at least by the Caste Hindus that beef-eating is undoubtedly an act of *tīṭṭu*, today's Paraiyars never accept this opinion and openly deny this view of the Caste Hindus.[6] The upper caste people think that eating dead cattle meat is more abominable than just beef-eating (because the cattle most probably died due to some disease). Since the argument on beef-eating and eating dead cattle meat is directly related to the problem that the Paraiyars are regarded as *tīṭṭu* people, it will be taken up in later discussions.

Ordinary Metonymical Explanation and their Limitations

There are two characteristics to be noted in terms of the villagers' explanations of *tīṭṭu*. Firstly, the feelings of *tīṭṭu* are very negatively explained as being dangerous, unpleasant, disgusting and allergic. Secondly, they tend to recognize *tīṭṭu* as feelings brought about by certain pollutants (things and acts) which are themselves visible and tangible.

The clear example in which the cause of *tīṭṭu* is reduced to a visible pollutant is found in the cases of *tīṭṭu* of puberty and of menstruation. It is usually claimed that the source of *tīṭṭu* is a menarcheal woman due to her menstrual bleeding. This view leads to their custom that she is kept in a separate hut or room, in theory, for about 5 or 7 days during the period.[7] This usual explanation in which *tīṭṭu* is due to some physical pollutant, however, cannot cope well with the following facts: (1) that puberty pollution lasts 30 days (see Table 5.1 in which more details are given) which exceeds the actual bleeding period; (2) that puberty has the longer pollution period even though both share the same cause of menstrual bleeding; and (3) that, though both share the same cause of menstrual bleeding, there is a difference in terms of their influence. In the case of puberty, it is basically claimed that *tīṭṭu* automatically spreads to a girl's whole family,[8] whereas *tīṭṭu* associated with usual menstruation is confined only to the menarcheal woman, according to standard opinion.[9]

Table 5.1

General Opinions as to Periods of Pollution Associated with Life Course Incidents (days)

Inciden / *Caste*	*Chilbirth*	*Puberty*	*Usual menstruation*	*Death*	*Circumcision*
Pillai	30 (13/14 for *puṇṇiyatāṉam*)	15 (11/13/15 for *caṭaṅku*)	7	30 (16 for *karumāti*, 1 year-mourning)	—
Kallar	30	30 (7/9/11/15/16 for *caṭaṅku*)	7	30/31 (7/9/11 for *karumāti*, 1 year-mourning only for *pūcāri* & *cāmiāṭi*)	15/16
Pantaram	30 (odd number day before 16 for *puṇṇiyatāṉam*)	30 (7/9/11/13/15 for *caṭaṅku*)	7 (4 days-segregation)	16 (7/10/11/16 for *karumāti*)	—
Acari	30	30 (16 for *caṭaṅku*)	7	16/30 (16 for *karumāti* 1 year-mourning)	
Natar	30	30 (before 15 for *caṭaṅku*)	7	16/30 (3 for *karumāti*)	—
Vannar	30	16	7	30 (16 for *karumāti*)	—
Paraiyar	30	30 (11/13/15 for *caṭaṅku*)	7	30 (16 for *karumāti*)	—

The limitations shown by this example, therefore, suggest that the cause of *tīṭṭu* must lie in the symbolic meaning of these incidents, rather than in the physical phenomena in a crude sense.[10]

Birth pollution (*tīṭṭu*) in a roundabout way addressed by the expression "*avaḷukku koḷantai peṟantirukku* (she had a child)". The villagers' ordinary view is as follows: A woman in childbirth is regarded as a direct source of *tīṭṭu* due to bleeding associated with the delivery. Thus, she and her newborn baby must be traditionally segregated in a detached hut or in a separate room for 30 days.[11] This ordinary view leads to the opinion that her baby is not basically *tīṭṭu* but is polluted by the mother's bleeding, so that if the baby was given a bath, the *tīṭṭu* of the baby would go away. It is also obvious that the metonymical explanation reducing *tīṭṭu* to a physical pollutant of blood can again be shown to have limitations. Firstly, there is another opinion that the newborn baby itself is also polluting so that, even after giving it a bath, the baby maintains *tīṭṭu* until the 30th day. Secondly, as in the case of puberty, other family members also become *tīṭṭu* due to childbirth, even though the degree of their *tīṭṭu* is not as strong as that of the baby's mother.[12]

In the case of death, there is the same tendency to try to find the source of *tīṭṭu* in a visible or tangible thing. It is, therefore, claimed that a decaying dead body causes *tīṭṭu,* so that *tīṭṭu* would increase if the dead body was left without any treatment. The bad smell from the dead body is also seen to evoke the feeling of *tīṭṭu*. In this view, *tīṭṭu* of death must be much decreased after the burial or cremation of a dead body. At the same time, it is thought that death brings about 30 days *tīṭṭu* which is fully removed with the ceremony of *mokṣa viḷakku* (a light offering for salvation) on the 30th day.[13] Further, the chief mourner becomes the main pollutant after a dead body is no longer present. When I pointed out the contradictions found in their explanations to several respondents from the Kallars, the Pillais and the Pantarams, a Pantaram young man who is a graduate of a Hindu college proposed the following rather rational solution. According to him, though physical *tīṭṭu* disappears after the burial or the cremation, mental *tīṭṭu* remains until the 30th day after the death. Although other people are not fully convinced by this logical explanation, it at least refers to the symbolic aspect of *tīṭṭu*. In other words, this indicates that they doubtless recognize the nature of *tīṭṭu* which cannot be fully reduced to a physical cause. Moreover, the fact that death *tīṭṭu* is shared strongly by the family of the dead person and, even if to a lesser extent, by the patrilineal members,[14] again requires the cause of *tīṭṭu* to be found in the incident of death itself rather than in physical phenomena, such as the dead body, the polluted house and the chief mourner.

Deep Connotations of tīṭṭu: Beyond an Ordinary Level of Consciousness

In order to overcome the limitation and the contradiction of the villagers' ordinary interpretations of *tīṭṭu*, described in the previous section, it is necessary to throw light upon the incident itself. This means that the deeper connotation of *tīṭṭu,* hidden under the villagers' ordinary consciousness, needs to be investigated.

Tīṭṭu Associated with Death

For this, let us start from the incident of death. Death is an incident by which, on the social level, society loses a member and, on the personal level, a family experiences mental sorrow and upset. The existing order in both senses is broken down and a situation of confusion arises. It is natural that the dead person's family and patrilineal relations (*uṭaṉpaṅkāḷi)* directly experience most intensely the disorder due to the loss of their member. A funeral ceremony, therefore, is regarded as a ritual attempt through which the chaos can be brought under control and a new order introduced. Thus, it is reasonable to regard *tīṭṭu* as the villagers' expression referring to the state of disorder or of confusion, which is brought about by death. Though this interpretation of *tīṭṭu* is mine, elucidated from my observations of funerals in the village, this is at the same time a social meaning of funerals which has been generally accepted since Radcliffe-Brown's understanding of death among the Andaman Islanders [Radcliffe-Brown, 1922]. This idea does not, in fact, contradict the villagers' practices that *tīṭṭu* is shared by the family concerned and by the patrilineal relations, and that *tīṭṭu* is step by step decreased by having a funeral ceremony consisting of the management of the dead body (burial or cremation), *karumāti* (a ceremony for sending the dead person's soul off to heaven) and *mokṣa viḷakku.* (See Chapter 10 in which details of a funeral ceremony are described. See also [Sekine, 1984].)

This understanding of death *tīṭṭu* reminds us of Douglas' theory that anomaly as a danger to symbolic or social order is connected with pollution [Douglas, 1966].

Though the above argument basically supports her theory, I must point out two inadequate aspects of it. As I have already pointed out in Chapter 2, these are her disregard (1) of the otherworldly character of pollution, and (2) of its contextual character of subjective interpretation.[15] These criticisms are clarified in the following discussion.

The first point of otherworldliness is related to Douglas' revised argument that "not all symbolic anomalies must be coded as polluting" (see [Buckley and Gottlieb, 1988: 27]). In this statement she clearly confesses that pollution cannot be defined only by the condition of anomaly. In order to define pollution more correctly, the single condition of anomaly is not enough and another condition needs to be added. I propose that the other condition is otherworldliness. It is obvious for the villagers that death is a departure on a journey from this world to the other world, as their funeral rites themselves verify. In other words, death is looked upon as an anomalous situation between this world and the other world, which is recognized as an intrusion of other worldly power into this world. This recognition is described as the command of *Yamatarmarājaṉ* or as the God Siva's invitation by the villagers.[16] This indicates that "death *tīṭṭu*" is not simply the result of an anomaly or from matter out-of-place spoiling categorization, but that it is necessary to add the condition of otherworldliness to the condition of anomaly (liminality). The addition of the condition of otherworldliness aims at emphasizing the point that an incident of death is not simply an anomaly between different known categories within this world (see also [Douglas, 1975 (1972)], but that between a known category of this world and an unknown category of the other world. It must be recognized that the anomaly of death provides people with the experience of actually confronting the intrusion of the otherworldly power, namely, the experience of "the menace of death".

This fundamental recognition about the *tīṭṭu* of death naturally leads us to the second point, dealing with the contextual character of pollution, because "the menace of death" is a subjective recognition. Therefore, it is necessary to ask who feels "the menace of death". On the occasion of death, the subject must be a person living in this world, namely, an insider of the known category of this world. This suggests the following two interrelated points. Firstly, it shows that it is necessary to pay attention to who claims *tīṭṭu* and to notice that there are many-sided viewpoints even within one specific culture.[17] Secondly, it logically suggests that, though "the menace of death" takes place in its direct sense in the case of death as an incident between this world and the other world, the liminal incidents between the known category and the unknown category are also associated with "the menace of death" in a metaphorical sense. For an insider of the known category, the intrusion of the unknown category means the intrusion of a threatening power destroying the order of the familiar known category. What should be emphasized is that anomaly is defined as "the menace of death", or pollution, from the viewpoint of the subject standing within the known category. An anomaly of death which becomes the archetype of the subjective feeling of "the menace of death" is thus seen as the paradigm of pollution in general. Therefore, Das' statement that "the paradigm of liminality *par excellence* is death" [Das, 1976: 256] would be more meaningful if it was connected with the subjective viewpoint or a contextual character.

Plate 47 Prayer for conception at the precinct of Muniandi Temple near Madurai city.

Plate 48 *Cumaitāṅki* as a memory of death of an expectant mother.

Thus, I insist that *tīṭṭu* (pollution) is the expression of a subjective feeling of "the menace of death". I think that this is the necessary definition to be adopted for bridging anomaly and pollution.

After this consideration, the villagers' ordinary explanation of *tīṭṭu,* that is, the propensity of villagers to reduce the source of *tīṭṭu* to a visible or tangible pollutant, can be comprehended as follows. Those physical pollutants such as a dead body, a chief mourner with a shaven head and a dead person's house can be regarded as the symbolic indications referring to "death *tīṭṭu*" at a deeper level of connotation which evokes the feelings of "the menace of death". It is difficult to directly obtain this understanding from the villagers themselves, since they are not usually conscious of such a relation between indicators and the indicated.[18] It seems to me, however, that, for the villagers, the word *tukkam* rather holds a closer meaning to the deeper level of connotation of "death *tīṭṭu*" in my sense.

Plate 49 A girl attending the coming of age ceremony (the Natars).

Other tīṭṭus and "The Menace of Death"

It is the present task to consider how the paradigmatic statement that *tīṭṭu* is caused by an incident which subjectively evokes a feeling of "the menace of death" can be applied to other incidents and things coded as *tīṭṭu*.

Plate 50 *Tāli* tying in marriage ceremony (the Pillais).

What about *tīṭṭu* associated with childbirth? An incident of childbirth has two facets, one related to the newborn baby which tends to be socially repressed, and the other to the mother in childbirth. A newborn baby is regarded as a transitory being, coming from the other world to this world. This other worldly character of childbirth coincides with people's opinion that childbirth itself is seen as a divine act (*viti*). A newborn baby can be compared to a dead person, even though their directions of movement are opposite, because both are in the unstable liminal position between this world and the other world.[19] The fact that both birth and death are associated with the same time-span of pollution, 30 days, strongly supports this similarity (see [Kolenda, 1978: 19]).[20] For a baby, delivery must be the difficult experience of crossing a boundary, where the baby may have to overcome the confusion of adapting to this world, a sphere which is the unknown for the newborn baby [O'Flaherty, 1988: 98, 100]. From the social point of view, childbirth can be described as the social experience of accepting a new member of the family and of the *vakaiyaṟā* (patrilineal lineage), so that it requires a renewal of the order of the family or of the lineage. As to the mother, she also experiences drastic changes, both socially and physically. If she is having her first baby, the change in her social position is very big because she acquires the additional strong position of mother besides being a wife. Delivery with severe bleeding is physically very dangerous for a mother. According to the belief of villagers, it makes her body very "hot" and it takes 30 days for the recovery of the confusion of her body system by "cooling down".

Tīṭṭu associated with childbirth can be thus possibly interpreted by the paradigm of *tīṭṭu* associated with death. Childbirth must be a harsh liminal experience, for both the baby and the mother, in which the feeling of "the menace of death" is provoked by their encounter with the unknown situation.

The incident of puberty provides an anomalous experience to both a girl and her family. She experiences for the first time the unknown phenomenon of menstrual bleeding, and she may be upset and uneasy for some time.[21] This experience can be interpreted as her confrontation with the intrusion of the unknown post-pubescent sphere, in other words, the death of her childhood. Through a ceremonial process of coming of age, the girl mentally overcomes the gap between pre-pubescence and post-pubescence and becomes conscious of her fertility. At the same time, it puts a family having a marriageable post-pubescent girl into a new social situation. There is a clear propensity that the villagers see puberty as being auspicious, as they tend to avoid directly using the word *tīṭṭu* for puberty, or as it is said, a family having "puberty *tīṭṭu*" is thought of as a *nallavīṭu* (good-house). It is possible to say that "puberty *tīṭṭu*" indicates the drastic change from childhood to adulthood which embodies death and the regeneration of life in a metaphorical sense. In this sense, the experience of puberty basically means the process of life-renewal at the cost of the death (sacrifice) of the former order. Thus, it is not impossible to understand puberty *tīṭṭu* as the expression of "the menace of death (destruction of order)".

Monthly menstruation as a part of everyday life is associated with less ceremonial than is puberty, but is seems to repeat the motif found in the case of puberty in a minimal way. For supporting this claim, it is useful to know how menstruation is understood by the villagers. For example, a Kallar man explains that a woman becomes *tīṭṭu* because "bad" blood gradually increases in her body, and that the monthly bleeding of this "bad" blood, that is, menstruation, makes her body "clean (*cuttam*)". He insists that she would have a "good" child if she conceived just after menstruation, because her body is then "clean". There is no doubt that the speaker regards menstrual blood itself as the source of the woman's *tīṭṭu* recognized the cleansing power of menstrual bleeding,[22] and regards women as being most fertile just after the menstrual flow.[23] This explanation should be understood by connecting it with the following opinion I heard from several Kallar men that what is *tīṭṭu* is the menarcheal woman herself, not the menstrual blood, which is just *acuttam* (unclean). The latter opinion indicates that *tīṭṭu* associated with monthly menstruation refers to the dynamic state of the menarcheal woman as a whole, not just to "unclean" or "bad" menstrual blood. "Menstrual *tīṭṭu*" indicates the whole dynamism in which "bad and unclean" blood is replaced by "good and clean" blood once a month. It, therefore, seems to me that these Kallars' opinions reflect their basically positive view of menstruation.It is notable here that these positive remarks are made by Kallar males. This suggests that the extent to which women's views are repressed by men's views is not so large among the Kallars, though it is also true there is to some extent a bias reflecting the male's viewpoint. The negative view of menstruation, expressed by them, is that women's menstrual bleeding provokes allergic feelings in men. There is no doubt that there is a consensus among all castes as to the primary value of placing importance on women's reproductive powers. However, while there is not much difference between the Paraiyar and the Kallar men as to the understanding of menstruation and the women's position, it is noted that the Pillai men, the most Sanskritized people in the village, tend to more strongly show their negative view on menstruation and degrade women's position (see [Allen, 1982: 18]). Apart from these male-centred viewpoints, a positive evaluation of menstruation is more naturally found in women's view.[24] This claim is supported by the following remark I heard from a Pillai female informant (middle-aged and married). According to her, a family properly having *tīṭṭu* is called "*nallavīṭu* (good-house)", from which people like to take a bride. This shows that not only is the menstrual flow not a fearful incident for a mature woman, but she may also be conscious of the social recognition that having menstrual *tīṭṭu* is evidence of her fertility, and therefore an honour for her.[25] Today, with modernization, some women have a more pragmatic understanding of menstrual *tīṭṭu*. They explain that the segregation of a menstruating woman in the name of *tīṭṭu* gives her publicly recognized resting periods for coping with her unusual body condition, called "menstrual vacations" by Harper [1964: 160].

There is a fundamental consensus, regardless of gender, that menstruation is an inevitable painful experience, which is regarded as a temporal disorder, for acquiring the renewed fertility of a woman's body. Menstruation can be culturally thought of as a sort of sacrificial process for re-creation, in other words, as a dynamic process of positively coping with "the menace of death".[26] This essential connotation of menstruation has been referred to as menstrual *tīṭṭu* by the villagers.

After the discussion of *tīṭṭu* associated with these four occasions, it is interesting to note that the intensity of the feeling of "the menace of death" seems to correspond with the length of the *tīṭṭu* period which the villagers claim, as shown in Table 5.1.[27] This table indicates that there is a decisive difference between the incidents associated with rites of passage, such as death, childbirth and puberty,[28] which commonly require one month of *tīṭṭu* and the more usual incident of menstruation, having only 7 days *tīṭṭu*. The more discontinuous an incident, the longer the time it takes to cope with it. It seems that setting the *tīṭṭu* period is a type of traditional wisdom in which this situation of vulnerability, marked by *tīṭṭu*, is overcome or protected against with the cooperation of the family and of the relatives (both kin and affine) concerned, which is described as the sharing of *tīṭṭu* [Buckley and Gottlieb, 1988: 38].

Lastly, I have to consider that there are things such as fallen hair, nail clippings, spat saliva and ejaculated semen which not only are seen as *acuttam* but also to some extent provoke feelings of *tīṭṭu* in the minds of most villagers. As mentioned above, the essential nature of *tīṭṭu* does not lie in the physical object itself, but in a subjective incident which evokes the feeling of "the menace of death". From this point of view, these things must thus hold some incidental factor which brings about the feeling of "the menace of death", even slightly. That is to say, it is necessary to find a factor which distinguishes these things from other bodily wastes or bodily excretions, which are simply thought of as *acuttam* (unclean) or as *aciṅkam* (ugly). This investigation also reveals the inadequacy of Douglas' theory of "matter out of place", because even her revised theory cannot explain adequately the villagers' differentiation between *acuttam* and *tīṭṭu*. For example, Douglas' theory cannot clearly distinguish ejaculated semen from discharged faeces, a distinction which is recognized by the villagers. Their opinions that semen is equal to blood as the seat of life,[29] and that sexual intercourse makes a man weak are important.[30] This is the point which distinguishes semen as being *tīṭṭu* from other bodily wastes as being just *acuttam*. On the basis of this view, it is believed that semen has a vital force, and that the loss of vital energy due to the loss of semen is an incident which evokes not only the feeling of *acuttam* but also that of *tīṭṭu*. Ejaculated semen is thus again metaphorically associated with the feeling of "the menace of death". In this respect, it seems to me that Meigs' insight into pollution concepts of the New Guinea Highlanders supports my present argument and extends it. According to her, "Anything that is polluting is a form of *nu* (vital essence)" [Meigs, 1978: 307] and "Its loss or contamination may result in loss of health, ageing, or death" [ibid.: 306]. In this sense, the other three things associated with *tīṭṭu*, fallen hair, nail clippings and spat saliva, were initially alive as bodily elements and after their removal from the body can also be seen to provoke the perception of a loss of vital force, even though slightly.[31] The argument on semen is thus basically valid for them. As circumstantial evidence, I can cite the fact that, for his magic, the *mantiravāti* (a sorcerer) particularly is said to use menstrual blood and these four *tīṭṭu* things, rather than other things such as faeces, urine, and so on, which most people regard as being just *acuttam*. This is because these things coded as *tīṭṭu* provoke a sense of the loss of vital force, namely the feelings of "the menace of death", and at the same time are useful for contagious magic due to their strong identification with the person from whom they are removed. It is kept in mind here that these *tīṭṭu* things as incidents do not simply indicate the loss of vital energy but they are believed to have a potential power which is generated in practice by other worldly manipulation.

Thus, it is necessary to more consciously add the conditions of other worldliness and of context (subjectivity) to Douglas' theory of anomaly in order to define an incident of *tīṭṭu* fully. It is concluded that the evocation of the feeling of "the menace of death", which is theoretically *the subjectively defined integration of anomaly and other worldliness*, is the essential or deep connotation of *tīṭṭu*.

Two Kinds of Attitude towards *Tīṭṭu* (Pollution) and *Puṉitam* (Sacredness)

The Distinction between "Impurity" and "Pollution"

It has been argued that *tīṭṭu* is regarded as the indispensable disorder for regenerating a new order. This essential connotation of *tīṭṭu* is referred to by the expression of "the menace of death". In this sense, *tīṭṭu* indicates a situation that is ambiguous, risky and at the same time potentially powerful, and the situation of *tīṭṭu* therefore requires proper management, guided by various taboos and rituals in order not to invite a bad result.

Plate 51 *Kōtāṅki.*

Firstly, there is a belief that *tīṭṭu* negatively invites misfortune (see also [Ferro-Luzzi, 1974: 113], [Yalman, 1963: 29]. For example, it is said that "you would be attacked by *pēy* (an evil spirit) if you went out without taking a bath after sexual intercourse", and that "you had better avoid going out on the day you have had a hair-cut, otherwise you will have an accident". In these cases, an attack of *pēy*, or having an accident, can be thought of as the negative symbol of the other worldly unknown force. God's anger is another form of misfortune believed to be invited by *tīṭṭu*. The actions of polluting a god are thought of leading to the god's punishment. It is, therefore, necessary to eliminate *tīṭṭu* before facing a god.[32] A menarcheal woman or a person who has just had sexual intercourse, for instance, should not enter the praying room.[33] As far as the negative aspect of *tīṭṭu* is concerned, then, the elimination of *tīṭṭu* is of first importance.

This understanding of *tīṭṭu* can be seen operating in reverse in the thought process shared by the villagers in which an inexplicable misfortune tends to be attributed to *tīṭṭu*. *Tīṭṭu* even in a negative way, contributes to connecting a this-worldly incident with the other-worldly sphere. In other words, *tīṭṭu* provides an opportunity for the villagers to become conscious about their cosmology. This suggests that one could draw unusual cosmic power from the

Plate 52 A scarecrow for protection against evil eye.

cosmological sphere if one succeeded in manipulating *tīṭṭu* after careful preparation. This can be called the positive aspect of *tīṭṭu*, which I focus upon next.

In this respect, the *mantiravāti* (a sorcerer) can be taken as a good example. The *mantiravāti* is said to have his own individual god, and he gains the supernatural power to manage *tīṭṭu* by praying to this god.[34] According to the villagers, he can use this power for both good and bad purposes, depending on his client's will. For example, in black magic, something attached to the target person such as a fallen hair, nail clipping, or a cloth stained with menstrual blood, which are *tīṭṭu*, is said to be indispensable. In the case of white magic in which, for example, the betterment of the husband-wife relationship or the realization of love is aimed at, the *mantiravāti* again is said to use a cloth stained with menstrual blood (see also [Buckley and Gottlieb, 1988: 34–35]). It is most striking that the skull and the brain of a dead foetus or of a baby who has died within 30 days of its birth are said to be the most powerful objects for charming because they are the most *tīṭṭu* due to their double pollution, of death and of birth. This shows that the strength of magical power is proportional to the degree of *tīṭṭu* of the object used for charming. The stronger the *tīṭṭu* the more powerful, it is believed, is the other worldly power generated under the operation of the *mantiravāti*.[35]

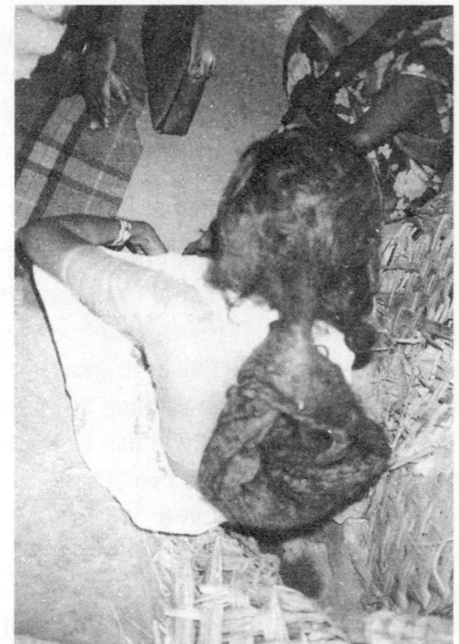

Plate 53 *Śakti* (power) residing in matted hair.

There are other instances showing the positive aspect of *tīṭṭu*. One is a ritual dining on the first day after a marriage ceremony, through which the unification of husband and wife is realized. The essential point of the co-dining is that the wife takes her meal from a banana leaf which has already been used by her husband. The used leaf is regarded as being *eccil* (anything defiled by contact with the mouth, i.e., saliva), a sort of *tīṭṭu*. It is noted that unification is thus realized through *tīṭṭu*. Another example is the traditional wisdom in the village that one should take a wife from a *nallavīṭu* (good-house), which means a wholesome family regularly having *tīṭṭu* associated with life crises, like birth, puberty, menstruation, and death. This indicates that the occurrence of *tīṭṭu* guarantees future fertility of the new family.

The examples mentioned of the positive aspect of *tīṭṭu* suggest that an acceptance of *tīṭṭu* under careful management produces unusual creative power, which is indispensable for the continuance of the villagers' lives. This is the fundamental reason that the concepts of *tīṭṭu* associated with life crises have been observed among the villagers, as part of their traditional wisdom. The acceptance of *tīṭṭu* is regarded as the metaphorical experience of death and the regeneration of life, or of a sacrificial death.[36] This positive attitude towards *tīṭṭu,* which tends to be hidden under the ordinary level of consciousness, undoubtledly reveals the essential connotation of

Plate 54 Sivalinga of Ekanatarcuvami Temple placed on the *camāti (Skt.samāthi)* of an eminent renouncer.

Plate 55 Village cemetery under the big tree.

tīṭṭu. This suggests that people's everyday lives consist not only of the shallow (ordinary) level of consciousness of regarding *tīṭṭu* as a negative disorder to be eliminated, but also of the deep dimension of wisdom of positively accepting *tīṭṭu* and changing it to an energy for living.

For analytical purposes, I would like to call the ambiguous but positive aspect of *tīṭṭu* associated with an attitude of acceptance as "pollution"; whereas the unambiguous and negative aspect of *tīṭṭu* corresponding with the attitude of elimination is referred to by the term "impurity".[37] What is important is that the distinction is a subjective and interpretative one, which is defined by differing attitudes (views) towards *tīṭṭu*.

Two Kinds of Attitudes towards Sacredness (Puṉitam)

The positive management of *tīṭṭu* is believed to generate unusual cosmic power transcending the secular sphere. This means that "pollution" in my sense potentially holds sacred power and is, therefore, intimately associated with the sphere of sacredness, *puṉitam*. From this point of view, it will be made clear that there are two paths to sacredness.

The village cemetery can be taken as a typical example for the present argument, for most of the villagers, regardless of caste, claim that the cemetery is sacred. It is because, according to them, God resides in the cemetery,[38] so that it must be *puṉitam*. They say that the cemetery is far from a fearful place because the presence of God prevents *pēy* (an evil spirit) from coming there. This claim is very impressive to me because it is absolutely the opposite of the Jaffna Tamils' opinion that the cemetery is a den of *pēy* and a very dangerous place [Sekine, 1984: 29].[39] The question arises why most of the villagers can regard the cemetery, which must be polluted by corpses, as *puṉitam*. There would be a contradiction in their outlook if we seriously adopted their view, previously mentioned, that *tīṭṭu* spoils *puṉitam*. For answering this question, the following argument may be proposed. They recognized some difference between the *puṉitam* of the cemetery and the *puṉitam* of the temple. For example, it is said that a sacred tree, the bo-tree, is suitable for the temple but is unsuitable for the cemetery, because corpses are buried in the cemetery, even though it is *puṉitam*. In this connection, Good's observation about the cremation ground comes closer to my point. "It is not a shrine as such and worship is never performed there but it does hold a divine presence in the form of Siva in his poisoned aspect (Good, 1980)." [Good, 1985: 123] Though it is difficult to expect further systematic answers to this question from the villagers, it is possible to give a logical answer on the basis of the distinction between "impurity" and "pollution" in my sense. For there is a clear contrast that *puṉtam* of the temple rejects (excludes) *tīṭṭu* whereas *puṉitam* of the cemetery accepts (includes) *tīṭṭu*. This contrast indicates that there are different attitudes towards *tīṭṭu* associated with the temple and the cemetery. While *tīṭṭu* associated with the temple is seen as "impurity", that associated with the cemetery is seen as "pollution". It is thus necessary to distinguish two kinds of attitudes towards sacredness (*puṉitam*), which correspond with the kinds of attitudes towards *tīṭṭu* crystallized by the concepts "impurity" and "pollution". The temple type of *puṉitam* always requires "purity" by eliminating "impurity"; the cemetery type of *puṉitam* is associated with "pollution" as the potentially creative. I thus propose the distinction between "purity-sacredness", exemplified by the temple,[40] and "pollution-sacredness", exemplified by the cemetery. "Purity-sacredness" reflects the protective attitude of avoiding "impurity", through which sacredness is sought out;

whereas "pollution-sacredness" expresses the sacrificial attitude which concerns the creation of sacredness due to "pollution" as the ambiguous power.[41]

This distinction cannot simply be regarded as a binary opposition on the same plane, but refers to two different ideological spheres. Furthermore, it is made clear that "pollution-sacredness" is more fundamental than "purity-sacredness", because sacredness has to be originally acquired through sacrifice.[42] For example, it is obvious that the *puṉitam* of the cemetery, or "pollution-sacredness" in my sense, corresponds with Parry's understanding of Benares as "sacred to Siva, the Great Ascetic, the Lord of the Cremation Ground and the Conqueror of Death; and the cornerstone of its religious identity is its association with death and its transcendence." [Parry 1982: 75] In this connection, though its details will be described in Chapter 6, it is suggestive that the Ekanatarcuvami (Siva) temple which is the biggest and most Sanskritized temple in Kinnimangalam, was built on the tomb *(camāti)* of the ascetic, Arulanantacuvamikal, and is a good example for elucidating the dynamic relationship between "purity-sacredness" and "pollution-sacredness". As the origin myth of the temple shows, this Siva temple, professing "purity-sacredness" in the ordinary level of consciousness (e.g. no entry of Harijans), crystallizes the dynamic relationship in that "purity-sacredness" (embodied by the God Siva) can be derived from the basis of "pollution-sacredness" (embodied by the *camāti* of the ascetic). In this sense, just as O'Flaherty points out that the asceticism (*tapas*) and eroticism *(kāma)* of Siva should be understood as "the problem of cycles" [O'Flaherty, 1973: 313], it would be very reasonable to regard the relationship between "pollution-sacredness" and "purity-sacredness" as the cyclical change of "creation (religious generation)" and "maintenance (social preservation)", rather than as a simple opposition. In other words, the transformation from "pollution-sacredness" to "purity-sacredness" can be seen as a shift from the religious cosmic sphere to a this-worldly social sphere, where the hierarchical measure of "purity-impurity" works. It is obvious that Brahman priests mediate this risky process. In nature, a way of "purity-sacredness" is a contradictory practice between the reduction of pollution to "impurity" and the necessity of sacrifice requiring "pollution". The demand for solving this contradiction resulted in the development of complex rituals holding various sacrificial metaphors. This is a refraction called sophistication.

This argument, in which the fundamental significance of "pollution-sacredness" and its relationship to "purity-sacredness" is revealed, suggests a dynamic relationship between "pollution" and "impurity", rather than a simply opposed distinction, as is further discussed below. This means that an unambiguous and negative notion, "impurity", is reared by a broader foundation in the ambiguous and potentially positive notion of "pollution", but betrays it.

The Configuration of Folk Terms and Analytical Concepts

Cuttam and Acuttam

As already noted, when the villagers express the hierarchical difference of ritual status among castes, they often use the words *cuttam* and *acuttam* which are derived from the Sanskrit word *śuddha* and *aśuddha*. The words *cuttam* and *acuttam* can be unambiguously defined and therefore can be translated exactly into the paired concept "pure and impure" in Dumont's sense, which provides the ideological expression reflecting the this worldly (social) power relationship.[43]

Acuttam and tīṭṭu

It was shown that *tīṭṭu* manifests two aspects according to the subject's attitude towards it, namely "impurity" and "pollution". Whereas *tīṭṭu* appears as "pollution" in its essential connotation, *tīṭṭu* in a shallow sense can be equated to "impurity". Since *acuttam* can be translated as "impurity", the meaning of *tīṭṭu* in the shallow sense and *acuttam* overlap in the analytical concept of "impurity". In the overlapping area, named "impurity", there is no difference, other than intensity, between *tīṭṭu* and *acuttam*. That is, an intense *acuttam* can be regarded as *tīṭṭu* within the domain of "impurity". This explains the ordinary view among villagers who often use *tīṭṭu* and *acuttam* interchangeably.[44]

The Caste Hindus' usages of *acuttam* and of *tīṭṭu* in reference to the Paraiyars provides a good example for revealing the categorical relationship between these folk terms and the analytical concepts "impurity" and "pollution". The dominant castes, like Kallars and the Pillais, claims that the Paraiyars are not only *acuttam* but also *tīṭṭu*. In contrast, they never describe the lower service castes as *tīṭṭu* people, but just as *acuttam* in a relative sense.[45] This shows that the Paraiyars only socially carry *tīṭṭu* in a fixed sense. The clear differentiation between Paraiyars and lower castes in the eyes of the dominant castes reveals the special position of the Paraiyars. The Paraiyars are assigned a role of a boundary marker, i.e., the position of insider's outsider of the village social space, the decentripetal character of which evokes the feeling of "menace of death" in a metaphorical sense in the minds of those who take a centripetal viewpoint. In fact, I heard that some dominant people describe the Paraiyars as the uncultured people who cause confusion and evoke allergic feelings. At any rate, in so far as Harijans are defined as *tīṭṭu* they essentially have an ambiguous power of "pollution". However, today the "pollution" aspect of the Paraiyars appears to be repressed and their "impurity" aspect can be seen to be dominant in the eyes of the dominant castes. Thus the Paraiyars are today unambiguously regarded as the most intensely "impure" people and placed at the bottom of the social ladder, and their creative "pollution" aspect is found only in limited situations, as in the case or the Paraiyar priest of one of the village temples, the Mataikaruppacuvami Temple (see Chapter 6).

The above-mentioned subjective view of the dominant castes is shared by other lower Caste Hindus, like the Vannars and the Kuravars. It is, however, also true that the village Paraiyars today never accept this top-down view, where they are regarded as *tīṭṭu* mainly in the negative sense. The Paraiyars never think in their real intention that non-vegetarian dishes or beef-eating make the eater *acuttam* or *tīṭṭu*. Most of them claim affirmatively that beef-eating is their own traditional custom.[46] Today's Paraiyars are not so naive as to merely accept the dominant view. Though the Paraiyars' practices are to be seriously investigated in Part Three, I very briefly mention this point here. The Paraiyars tend to deny the ritually defined social-hierarchy, but they have to recognize the actually existing hierarchy in which they are placed. As a result, they prefer to explain the social hierarchy by the differential of economic power, rather than in ritual terms. However, this does not mean that the Paraiyars are indifferent to ritual language. My overall impression of the Paraiyars' verbal discourse is that they basically do not like to use words such as *cuttam*, *acuttam* (*cuttam illai*), and *tīṭṭu* for referring to the ritual status differential of the social sphere. Rather, they tend to limit using these words to the religious context, like a village festival and a lineage festival. That is, on those occasions it is important for them whether a person or a thing is suitable for facing god or not. *Cuttam* in this usage means a suitable condition for worshipping god, in other words, a state holding enough positive power for attending a sacrifice and receiving god's grace properly; whereas *tīṭṭu*, *cuttam illai* or *acuttam* refer to the conditions unsuitable for this. The Paraiyars say that ritual fasting and eating only vegetarian dishes, for example, make a person *cuttam* so that the *pūcāri* (a lineage priest) should observe such regulations for some time before a festival. It is specially noted that their positive attitude to vegetarians is not associated with the view that non-vegetarians are degraded compared to vegetarians. They never think that non-vegetarian dishes cause *acuttam*, but they recognize that fasting or eating vegetarian dishes makes body conditions suitable for meeting gods, in other words, makes them shift from "the normal ritual status" to "the sacred ritual status" [Srinivas, 1978(1952)].

There is a tendency for the context in which these ritual words are used to be not the man-man hierarchical relationship but rather the man-god relationship, professing egalitarianism in front of the god. The latter usage of ritual words by the Paraiyars is not limited to them, but is shared by the Caste Hindus as well. In other words, the Paraiyars basically share with the Caste Hindus the same verbal world in the religious sphere but they attempt to limit their involvement in the social hierarchical sphere.

Cuttam and *Puṉitam*

The relationship between *cuttam* and *puṉitam* seems to be parallel with that between acuttam and *tīṭṭu,* discussed above. I try to make clear here the relationships between the folk terms, *cuttam* and *puṉitam*, by using my analytical concepts "purity-sacredness" and "pollution-sacredness".

Generally speaking, the village Caste Hindus see the Aiyar (Brahman householders) as the most cuttam caste and place them in the highest ritual position in the social sphere.[47] Nonetheless, the villagers also claim, in general, that a world renouncer is more *cuttam* than a Brahman householder, because the former has no sexual pleasure. This shows that a renouncer who takes a vow of celibacy can be placed in the overlapping area of *cuttam* and *puṉitam*, since he can be categorized among the houseless renouncers who seek transcendence (*puṉitam*) with celibate lives [Burghart, 1983: 642], namely, with the attitude of "purity-sacredness", at least at the beginning. For clarifying the villagers' view that a celibate renouncer is ritually higher than a Brahman householder, the Pantaram village priest's description of the world renouncer is useful. According to him, there are four successive stages within the inclusive category of a world renouncer (*caṉṉiyāci*) as follows:

1. The first stage: "*Caṉṉiyāci*" is a trainee renouncer who stays in a temple or in a monastery and thinks only about God, under the guidance of a Guru. He goes about asking for alms and observes a vegetarian way of life.
2. The second stage: "*Cittar*" is a self-supporting renouncer who has acquired a certain level of *cakti* (sacred power) and who is pleased to use his *cakti* for

saving people. In this stage, although he usually eats fruit and drinks milk, he does not reject any food offered to him as alms, even if it is *tīṭṭu*. It is said that his use of *cakti* for secular people carries two disadvantages, namely, a disturbance of his meditation and a decrease of his power.

3. The third stage: "*Muṉivar*" is an advanced ascetic who leaves the secular world and lives in a remote forest. There he is lost in meditation and it is said that he possesses enough *cakti* to control himself and to do anything he wants, but he never uses this power for the people. He does not take cooked food, but eats only wild grasses and fruits.
4. The fourth stage: "*Ñāṉi*" is an ascetic who has attained the final and the highest stage, in which he holds perfect knowledge and power controlling the senses. He breathes, but takes no food so that he is almost equal to the immortal. He fervently continues to meditate in the forest, being segregated from the secular world. His meditation is so deep and his *cakti* is so strong that no one can come near and disturb him. He never uses his power for secular people.

The above description is suggestive for the present argument. The fourth stage ("*Ñāṉi*") can be regarded as true renunciation or as reaching the *puṉitam* state, completely separated from the secular social sphere. In contrast, since "*Caṉṉiyāci*", as a beginner in world renunciation, would be still vulnerable to secular influence, this stage is described as *cuttam* rather than as *puṉitam*. The second "*Cittar*" stage and the third *muṉivar* stage are placed between these two. Nonetheless, there is a big leap between "*Cittar*" and "*Muṉivar*" in terms of separation from a secular world. This four stage framework suggests that the renouncer begins to seek out *puṉitam* through the principle of "purity", i.e., the principle of elimination, which is realized by refraining from sexual intercourse and by restriction of meals, and ultimately reaches the transcendental state of *puṉitam* where he is fully engaged in self-sacrifice.[48] The transcendental state is a locus of creation where a renouncer ceaselessly sacrifices himself and, therefore, is never influenced by secular pollutants or the logic of "pure-impure". This can be called the path of "pollution-sacredness", but, if a renouncer once reaches the state of *puṉitam*, there would be no difference between "purity-sacredness" and "pollution-sacredness". This implies that a logic of "pollution-sacredness", which is embodied by ceaseless meditation, i.e., ceaseless self-sacrifice in the liminal position between life and death, is most essential for reaching *puṉitam* in a true sense.

In other words, the religious essence of generation of sacredness is more straight-forwardly expressed by the way of seeking "pollution-sacredness" through "pollution" in which the highbrow way of "purity" by cutting off external pollutants is not taken, but the ultimate pollution situation of the death threat is accepted and internalized for *jumping into* to sacredness. In this respect, the adoption of rituals using sexual methods or dead bodies in Tantrism is regarded as the direct way of "pollution-sacredness". The ultimate state of *puṉitam* is a realization of a world of continuity where every dividing logic is powerless. In this sense, "pollution-sacredness" comes closer to *puṉitam* than "purity-sacredness", because the latter is still caught by the dividing logic of "pure-impure". Thus, world renouncers start from "purity", proceed to "purity-sacredness" and finally transform it to "pollution-sacredness", that is, a true sense of *puṉitam*. This process has a reverse implication. When non-divided *puṉitam* flows into the secular sphere that is full of divisions, *puṉitam* is unavoidably interpreted by the secular logic of "pure-impure". Here, the important point to be focused upon lies in the difference between the householders' secular point of view and the renouncers' sacred point of view.

The above consideration well explains the villagers' evaluation that world renouncers are "more *cuttam*" than household Brahmans. The real connotation of the statement is that the *puṉitam* embodied by renouncers is more important than the *cuttam* of Brahmans, or more clearly that *puṉitam* is a source of *cuttam*. Thus, the way of understanding of the villagers in terms of *puṉitam* and *cuttam* as folk terms is as follows. (1) In the this-worldly hierarchical sphere, or from the householders' secular viewpoint, renouncers are thought of as relatively more *cuttam* than Brahmans. (2) In the other-worldly religious sphere, or from the renouncers' sacred viewpoint, renouncers are absolutely defined as generators of *puṉitam*. (3) In this sense, the concept of "purity-sacredness" plays a crucial role of mediation between both spheres secular and sacred, when *puṉitam* as "pollution-sacredness" flows into the secular sphere from the top end of the hierarchical society, that is, through the Brahmans' mediation.

Conclusion

What I have discussed here is summarized in Figure 5.1, which shows the configuration of folk terms and my analytical concepts. In sum, the this worldly (social) hierarchical values of *cuttam* and *acuttam* ("purity" and "impurity") are contrastingly sandwiched between two other worldly and cosmic concepts, *puṉitam* and *tīṭṭu*. Both spheres, indicated by *puṉitam* and *tīṭṭu* can be commonly seen to include the cyclical shift between the two different facets (attitudes), namely, the this worldly (conservative) facet and the other worldly (creative) one. The point is that the creative aspect can be the essential dimension of *tīṭṭu* or of *puṉitam*, where "pollution" and "pollution-sacredness" come closer by means of the act of sacrifice, and the conservative aspect is strongly adopted by the dominant people in order to maintain their social control. This aspect forms the "purity-impurity" ideology. In so far as *puṉitam* is the source of *cuttam*, the secular social world cannot be basically maintained without sacrificial creation in the sacred world, or, in my terms, the acceptance of "the menace of death" and its transcendance. Once creative power (*cakti*) is acquired, the power can be used for maintaining the social hierarchy of the secular world. This is the hierarchical usage of *cuttam* and *acuttam* under the conservative attitude, which produces the hierarchical caste differences. Thus, it is possible to say that conservative household Brahmans are sustained by creative world renouncers. Besides this hierarchical (vertical) understanding of *cuttam* and *acuttam* in the social context, it should not be disregarded that in the religious and horizontal context *cuttam* and *acuttam* have a rather casteless and egalitarian value in front of a god. This dimension can be connected with the notions of auspiciousness/inauspiciousness (see [Raheja, 1988: Chapter 2]). *Cuttam* in this usage means a positive preparation which is necessary in order to attend sacrifice and receive a god's grace properly.

Figure 5.1
Configuration of Folk Terms and the Analytical Concepts in Terms of Pollution, Purity and Sacredness

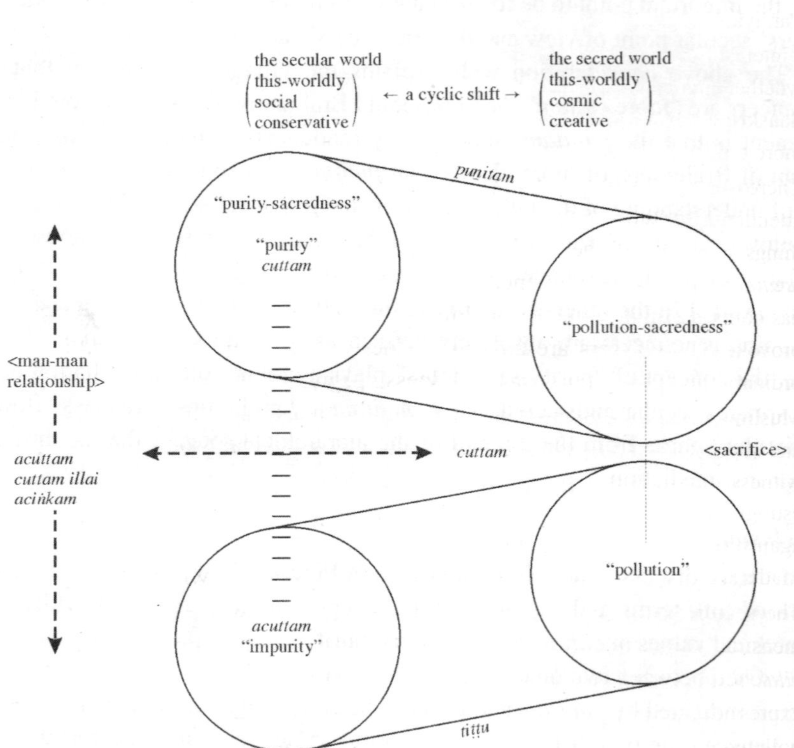

Though the ideological configuration shown in this Figure is valid regardless of caste, it is a different matter how each caste manipulates or interprets it in practice. In particular, the Paraiyars' interpretation should be separately investigated. This is the topic of Part Three.

Notes

1. The uses of *tuppuravu illai* and *tuymai inmai* tend to be limited to the context of physical uncleanness, so that they are less frequently heard. *Ācūcai* is used only by the educated elders.
2. Villagers sometimes use both the words *pāvam* and *kuṟṟam* interchangeably, but they are also conscious of the distinction between the two. It is said that *pāvam,* which originates from a Sanskrit word, refers to other-worldly sin that is punished in the next life and is, therefore, connected with *karma* theory; whereas the Tamil word *kuṟṟam* is this-worldly sin, that is punished within this life. This difference between *pāvam* and *kuṟṟam* provides one of the examples of the contrast between the Brahmanical cultural tendency and the basic Tamil cultural tendency.

3. The low castes of Caste Hindus are not referred to as *tīṭṭu* but only as *acuttam* in a relative sense, by the dominant castes. It is noted that the Paraiyars alone are defined *tīṭṭu.* In everyday conversation, the *tīṭṭu* of the Paraiyars is euphemistically referred to by expressions such as "*arcaṉattai toṭṭuttiyā* (Have you touched a Harijan?)", and "*toṭak kūṭātavar* (untouchable people)", because it is obvious for both the speaker and the hearer that the Paraiyars are *tīṭṭu.*
4. I interestingly witnessed a heated argument between two middle-aged Kallar men about whether circumcision causes *tīṭṭu*, or not. It is impressive that the one who followed a more Sanskritized behaviour strongly denied the *tīṭṭu* of circumcision, while the other, who was a more typical Kallar, agreed to its *tīṭṭu* more readily.
5. There is a general tendency that religious people, regardless of caste difference, pay more attention to *tīṭṭu,* so that they tend to apply the word *tīṭṭu* to a broader range of acts and things, compared to less pious people. That is, less pious people see these things just as *acuttam*, but pious people think of them as *tīṭṭu*. The contextual situation in which a person has contact with these things is also important for making the decision of whether they provoke the *tīṭṭu* feeling or not. For example, food cooked on the previous day is not *tīṭṭu* in ordinary time, but becomes *tīṭṭu* during periods of fasting.
6. Muslims are also regarded as being *tīṭṭu* by Caste Hindus because Muslims are beef-eaters and often deal with beef as butchers. The village Paraiyars, however, often told me that they witnessed Caste Hindus sometimes secretly eating beef in towns. The same attitude is interestingly found among the Kallars, when the Kallars defend their non-vegetarian habit against vegetarian values. Some Kallars told me that there are Brahmans who eat mutton in Madurai city.
7. The segregation of a menarcheal woman reflects upon the euphemistic expression of menstrual *tīṭṭu*, namely "*vīṭṭukku tūramāyirukku* (to be remote from a house)" or "*vīṭṭukku vilakku* (to be shut out from a house)". As to the Kallars, they sometimes use a direct expression including the word *tīṭṭu* for menstrual *tīṭṭu*, namely, "*tīṭṭāyirukku* (being polluted)". Generally speaking, more positive expressions are used for *tīṭṭu* caused by puberty, such as "*vayacukku vantuṭṭāl* ([she] has attained her majority)", and "*caṭaṅku āyittal* ([she] is ready for marriage)", because puberty is seen as an auspicious incident. The auspiciousness of puberty is a clear indication of the positive aspect of *tīṭṭu*, which is developed in the later argument.
8. Though it is said that a girl at puberty carries *tīṭṭu* for one month, it seems that the degree of *tīṭṭu* decreases after the celebration of the coming of age ceremony held on the 7th, 9th, 11th, 13th, 15th or 16th day after the onset of her first period. *Tīṭṭu* carried by other family members almost vanishes after the ceremony. Some Paraiyars claim that only after the 30th day they can give meals to them, while other Paraiyars say that only the girl at puberty is polluted. These oral claims of the Paraiyars, which differ widely, indicate the complexity of their situation. This point is developed in Part Three.
9. It is said in the present village that menstrual *tīṭṭu* does not spread to other family members without touching. This claim seems to be a result of modernization, and it does not necessarily exclude the possibility that there was a traditional custom that a husband shared his wife's pollution, which is interpreted by the notion of shared substance between husband and wife, according to Buckley and Gottlieb [Buckley and Gottlieb, 1988: 33].
10. Ferro-Luzzi also makes the same point by saying that "the independence of pollution from the physical fact is clearly shown by the preferred numbers of segregation days"

[Ferro-Luzzi, 1974: 122]. She repeatedly claims that the length of segregation "can only be culturally explained" [ibid.: 134].

11. The Paraiyars also claim 30 days *tīṭṭu* for childbirth and explain that mother and child must be segregated for a week.
12. I presume that the recognition of *tīṭṭu* of family members in those days was stronger than is presently the case. As a reference, I cite the Jaffna Tamils' case in which pollution associated with childbirth spreads to blood relations as a whole, as does death pollution [Sekine, 1983: 133; 1984: 27].
13. Among the Sanskritized castes like the Pillais and the Pantarams, one year *tukkam* (mourning) is observed even after the period of pollution has ended.
14. As is shown by the villagers' expressions for death pollution, such as "*kēta vīṭu*" or "*tukkavīṭu*" which means "a house under mourning", the most intense *tīṭṭu* is carried by the family members living together with the dead person in the same house. It is important that the family members living separately also have considerable *tīṭṭu*. Moreover, other patrilineal relatives automatically become *tīṭṭu*, even though it is not as strong and it recently tends to be limited to close relatives.
15. Although her theory here basically refers to the theory shown in "Purity and Danger" [1966] and in "Pollution" [1968], her revised position, found in "Self-evidence" [1975(1972)], is also taken into account. In the latter work she accepts some defects of her initial generalized theory. She emphasizes there the importance of a culturally specific context for deciding what are anomalous beings [Douglas, 1975 (1972): 282]), and recognizes that anomaly is not always coded as polluting [Douglas, 1975 (1972): 287–288]. It seems to me that these revisions are useful but my criticism of her theory is still necessary.
16. They tend to regard death as a divine act, *viti*, because it is basically an inexplicable incident. For example, when Mr Balasubramanian had a traffic accident and died, his elder brother wrote to me that he had been invited to heaven by the God Siva because he had accumulated enough *karma* for reaching *mukti*.
17. From this point of view, Douglas' revision of her initial theory is still not sufficient, because her failure lies in her objective analysis of anomaly defined in one way and in her disregard of the subjective and dynamic point of view. A good example is Buckley and Gottlieb's criticism of Douglas. They point out the methodological prejudice of her male-dominated analytic standpoint [Buckley and Gottlieb, 1988: 30].
18. However, it seems to me that the deeper level of connotation of *tīṭṭu* is intuitively understood by the villagers, who state that *tīṭṭu* is pollution which cannot be removed by bathing.
19. For example, a verse of the *Tirukkural*, "*Uṟaṅkuvatu pōlum cākkāuṭu uṟaṅki viḻippato pōlum piṟappu* (Death is falling asleep, birth is awakening from that sleep)" expresses this idea. One of the clear pieces of evidence for the correspondence between birth and death is a villager's comment on the posture of a dead person lying in a burial pit. According to him, the posture can be compared to a baby suckling.
20. Most *Smṛtis* also prescribe the same length of pollution of 10 days for both birth and death [Ferro-Luzzi, 1974: 115].
21. In order to mitigate her worry, there is a custom that she is accompanied by her grandmother or another old woman and is given useful knowledge and advice by this older woman.
22. This cleansing aspect of menstrual bleeding is also pointed out by Hiltebeitel [1981: 203] and by Hershman [1974: 286].

23. This can be connected with the indigenous opinion that conception in the most purified womb, just after a woman's periods, is preferred (cf. [Hiltebeitel, 1981: 204–5]).
24. As Buckley and Gottlieb [1988] claims, it is necessary to carefully take into account women's opinions on menstruation because in Hindu societies women's views are usually repressed under the formal social norms which strongly reflect men's domination.
25. This positive attitude to menstruation can be logically connected with the ideology of "embryo murder" in which a child is formed from menstrual blood so that a woman's menstruation should be rendered fruitful [Krygier, 1982: 77].
26. As is discussed in the next section, this sacrificial nature of menstruation is used for various types of magic. The deep connection, in general, between sacrifice and menstrual blood is pointed out in Buckley and Gottlieb [1988: 36].
27. There is no doubt that the intensity of "the menace of death" chiefly determines the length of the pollution period, though there are some influences of other factors, as Ferro-Luzzi shows [Ferro-Luzzi, 1974: 142–3].
28. Pollution associated with marriage is exceptionally reported among the Kaikatti section of the Kanakkan (a Tamil accountant caste), according to Thurston and Rangachari. "After the marriage ceremony, the girl is kept inside the house, and not allowed to move about freely, for at least two or three days. She is considered to be under some kind of pollution. It is said that, in former times, she was confined in the house for forty days, and, as occupation, had to separate dhal (peas) and rice, which has been mixed together." [Thurston and Rangachari, 1987 (1909): 152] This case seems to be remarkable, because, as is suggested by the fact that the focus of pollution is the bride, who experiences a more radical change in social status than does the bridegroom, marriage logically satisfies the condition of pollution. In this connection, Parry notes that "in folk dream-analysis a naked woman or a bride is a presentiment of impending death" [Parry, 1982: 81]. I therefore understand that people generally repress marriage pollution by attaching more importance to the auspiciousness of marriage.
29. According to Davis, men's semen can be equated with women's uterine blood among the Bengali Hindus [Davis, 1976: 19].
30. Daniel provides a detailed account of Tamil understandings of sexual intercourse in Chapter 4 of his book [Daniel, 1984].
31. It seems to me that villagers' special attention to hair and nails as vital elements of the body reminds us of the description of embryology in *Mārkaṇḍeya Purāṇa*, because it specifically mentions nails and hair growing out of subsidiary limbs [O'Flaherty, 1988: 97].
32. It is said that it is necessary to observe one *maṇaṭalam* (40 days or 41 days) of continence in order to meet god in a true sense. An example is found in the pilgrimage to the Ayyappa temple at Sabarimalai [Daniel, 1984: Part 2]. As to the number 40, Ferro-Luzzi discusses its significance [Ferro-Luzzi, 1974: 148–152].
33. In this connection, the story that a Kallar told me, half jokingly, is impressive. According to him, a god himself is not polluted by the invasion of *tīṭṭu*, but a god cannot stay in a polluted place. Thus a thief may throw a cloth with menstrual blood into a temple compound and steal the treasures of the temple, because the god will not be present once the site is polluted. This reminds me of Fuller's statement that "the gods themselves cannot be polluted" [Fuller, 1979: 459].
34. According to Buckley and Gottlieb, the logic is as follows; "potent, negatively valued substances such as menstrual blood may be manipulated for positive ends by those who are

themselves spiritually potent enough to reverse the valence and make it positive" [Buckley and Gottlieb, 1988: 37].

35. It is noted that the social position of the *mantiravāti* itself is marginal in a village-centred society. This is partly verified by the fact that Muslims, who are socially peripheral in Hindu society, often become sorcerers in this area. There is another type of magician (or shaman) called *kōṭāṅki* or *cāmiāṭi* who is recruited from ordinary villagers and who tends to be engaged in white magic, such as exorcisms and healing. There are several contrasting points between *mantiravāti* and *kōṭāṅki*, respectively as follows: an outsider of the village: an insider of the village:: worship of an individual god: worship of lineage gods:: indispensable *tīṭṭu:* indispensable *cuttam*:: more fearful and powerful: less fearful and powerful.
36. A sacrifice in this context reminds me, for example, of the necrophagous ascetic, "a group of ascetics who are intimately associated with death, corpses and the cremation ground", discussed by Parry [Parry, 1982: 74–110]. More generally, the necessity of a sacrificial death for the regeneration of life is pointed out by many scholars. For example, Shulman notes, "To attain more life … the life of the victim must be extinguished" [Shulman, 1980: 90].
37. In their book on the study of menstruation, Buckley and Gottlieb clearly point out the limitations of conventional pollution theory and attach importance to the creative power of pollution [Buckley and Gottlieb, 1988: 33–38].
38. There is no doubt that this notion is derived from *ruttiratāṇṭavam* (Skt. *Rudra-Tāṇḍava*, Siva's dancing in the cemetery).
39. I should note that there are a few people who see the cemetery as *keṭṭa iṭam* (literally, a bad place). This naive view is an important clue to understanding the ambiguous *tīṭṭu* of the cemetery which is strongly suppressed by the absolute notion of *puṉitam* embodied by the presence of Siva.
40. Though I have so far dealt with the temple in a simplified way in order to emphasize its contrast with the cemetery, it will be revealed in Chapter 6 that the village temples themselves can be associated with two kinds of attitudes towards sacredness.
41. This distinction of sacredness reminds me of the various examples and arguments in terms of woman and of the renouncer. Allen, for example, provides a typical example as follows; "the orthodox renouncer *avoids* women as dangerous distractions; … ; while the Tantric *uses* them as a necessary means of attaining spiritual liberation" [Allen, 1982: 18]. This shows the contrast between Vedic Brahmanical *sannyasin* [Burghart, 1983] and the necrophagous ascetic [Parry, 1982]. Obeyesekere's distinctions in the Sri Lankan context are also noted. He presents a series of dichotomies such as (1) the Hindu view of celibacy and the Buddhist view of celibacy, (2) matted hair and the shaven head, and (3) personal symbols and psychogenetic symbols [Obeyesekere, 1981]. Stirrat's discussion on the sacred, in which the Durkheimian sacred and the Eliadean sacred are distinguished, is also suggestive in the present argument [Stirrat, 1984].
42. As noted by O'Flaherty [1073], Parry [1982], Heesterman [1981], Das [1976, 1983], Shulman [1980] and Sahi [1980], the logic of sacrifice (death and the regeneration of life) in Bataille's sense, whether it is explicit (animal sacrifice) or implicit (*pūjā*) [Biardeau, 1976: 138–153], exteriorized or interiorized [Heesterman, 1981: 252], has consistently penetrated not only Tamil thought (see Shulman [1980]) but also Hindu thought in general, in terms of transcendance [Parry, 1982: 100].
43. It is said that *śudh*, which is the original verb form of *śuddha* means an action of beautifying or purifying by bathing and adorning. This suggests that *cuttam* and *acuttam* seem to be

more or less manipulated under this-worldly control, compared with *tīṭṭu*, which is deeply connected with uncontrolled other-worldly power.

44. It seems to me that Moffatt simply accepts this villager's ordinary view of pollution and never investigates it deeply [Moffatt, 1979: 87].
45. The reason which is raised by the Caste Hindus especially for explaining the difference between the lower Caste Hindus and the Paraiyars is the eating of beef and the meat of dead cattle. Nonetheless, this seems to be a tautological reasoning for justifying the already fixed distinction. For, in reply to my question, a Kallar said, "No, they (the Paraiyars) could not leave their *tīṭṭu* position even if they stopped their custom of eating beef, just as higher education could not change it. Because it is tradition (*pāramparai*), in which there is no room for argument". In this connection, I am reminded of Pfaffenberger's statement that it is necessary for the Vellalars to "depict the Untouchables as *lower* than the impure, ..." [Pfaffenberger, 1980: 207].
46. Several Paraiyar informants told me that if their economic conditions became better they would stop eating beef. However, this does not mean that beef-eating is regarded as being polluting by them, but their intention of stopping beef-eating lies in their strategic calculation for reducing its associated social stigma.
47. The Paraiyars' attitude towards the Aiyars seems to be ambivalent. Some Paraiyars deny the special value of the Aiyars but other Paraiyars give value to the Aiyars' religious background, like vegetarian lifestyle and their knowledge of *mantras*.
48. For example, Heesterman notes that "the renouncer does not reject vedic sacrifice, he 'internalizes' it" [Heesterman, 1981: 252].

Chapter 6

Blood Sacrifice and "Pollution" Ideology

The Cults of Village Deities

The purpose of this chapter dealing with village deities (Skt. *grāmadevatā*) and their cults is to support and deepen my argument on the understanding of pollution, purity, and sacredness, which was discussed in the previous chapter. In particular, the dynamic relationship between "pollution-sacredness" and "purity-sacredness", which is based on the distinction between "pollution" and "impurity", is clarified by focusing upon blood sacrifice, which is frequently found in the festivals of the village deities. It will be argued that from the viewpoint of "pollution" ideology, the dynamic (cyclic) relationship can be understood as "creation" and "conservation" of sacred power. This will naturally provide a different interpretation of village deities from the Dumontian understanding, which adheres strongly to the "purity-impurity" dichotomy. Not only that, but also the question how my interpretation is related to Dumontian interpretation is answered in a productive manner.

Pali (Skt. *bali*) means "offering given to gods, manes, etc., in sacrifice", which is the first meaning of the Tamil Lexicon. *Pali*, therefore, is not necessarily limited to animal sacrifice. Nonetheless, in the village *pali koṭuttal* (literally, giving sacrifice) is often used as the expression for the ritual act of holding a blood sacrifice.[1] In Kinnimangalam, there are two kinds of village deities, namely, those deities which accept animal sacrifice and those which reject it. Though the former deities are deemed as degraded "impure" gods from the Brahmanical point of view (for example, [Dumont, 1986: Part 3]), they seem to be more familiar to, and are regarded as being more reliable by, most of the villagers than are the latter Sanskritic gods (see [Whitehead, 1921: 16], and [Srinivas, 1978(1952): 214]).[2] I want to take up here the fact that villagers tend to believe that the gods'grace is acquired by means of the so-called "polluting" acts of bloodshed and death.[3]

An Outline of Villagers' Religious Life

The following five categories of deities (gods and goddesses) in which the villagers believe can be distinguished:

1. *ūr potutteyvam* or *kirāma teyvam* (a village deity: a common god or goddess worshipped by the villagers).
2. *cāti teyvam* (a caste deity: a god or goddess worshipped by a particular caste).
3. *kulateyvam* (a lineage deity: a god or goddess worshipped by a particular lineage).

4. *vīṭṭu teyvam* (a family deity: a god or goddess worshipped by a particular household).
5. *iṣṭa teyvam* (a personal deity: a god or goddess worshipped by a particular individual).

Of the five categories, caste deities are not possessed by every caste, and in the case of Kinnimangalam only the carpenter caste (*Taccuācāri)* has a caste deity. *Kāmātciyammaṉ*, who has attractive and passionate eyes, is worshipped by this caste as their guardian deity, and their caste association possesses the goddess's temple.[4] The other four categories of deities mentioned above are possessed by all village castes, including the Paraiyars. Even though they worship these plural deities, this does not mean that they are polytheists, because they themselves claim that there is only one God. In this view each deity can be seen as a kind of medium for the acquisition of the grace provided by transcendental sacred power, which is unique. For the villagers of Kinnimangalam, Siva is usually the God which represents such transcendental power, because they are basically followers of Saivism.[5] Therefore, the villagers can rather be described as being pantheistic monotheists [Tokunaga, 1985: 41].

Personal Deities

The selection of a personal deity is to some extent influenced by the lineage one belongs to, but most villagers tend to prefer one of the great Gods of Saivism. The overwhelmingly popular God among the villagers is the God Murugan. The God *Ēkanātārcuvāmi* (Siva) is also often chosen as a personal God, mainly because he is the main deity of the biggest village temple. Although a few villagers prefer the God Visnu or the *Mūṉṟucāmi* (Three Gods), and some women like the Goddess Minaksi Amman, there is little doubt that the Hindu Gods belonging to the so-called great tradition, especially the male deities of Saivism, tend to be adopted most commonly as the villagers' personal deities. The most obvious expression of their devotion (*pakti*, Skt. *bhakti*) to such great gods is to conduct a pilgrimage.[6] The motivations of pilgrimage vary from the pure enjoyment of meeting God to seeking a solution for diseases or problems. Dreams or suggestions of a *kōtāṅki* (a shaman) sometimes encourage the villagers to attempt a pilgrimage. Making a vow and its return is often an important reason for a pilgrimage. However, a long pilgrimage requires a lot of expense and time so that many villagers cannot afford to do so due to financial reasons.[7]

Lineage Deities

Chapter 11 is devoted to the description and discussion of lineage deities, so that I here only briefly touch on their characteristics. It is obvious that a lineage deity holds a collective character reflecting a lineage group, which contrasts with the individuality of a personal deity. Though every lineage claims that there are 21 gods and goddesses as its lineage deities,[8] as a whole, goddesses are relatively more significant in the case of lineage deities than they are in the case of personal deities which are dominated by male deities (see Table 4.11).[9] This is because, without exception, a goddess is either the chief-main or the sub-main deity of lineage deities. It can be also pointed out that a family deity tends to be a goddess who is the main or sub-main lineage deity. These facts suggest that there is a profound relationship between a goddess and a collectivity based on blood relations.

Another important point derives from the fact that a lineage festival inevitably has a blood sacrifice. The 21 lineage deities by and large consist of local deities, though the main deities tend to be identified with the great Hindu God or Goddess. In this sense, the main deities are regarded as *cuttamuka teyvam* (literally, a pure-face-deity), who reject blood sacrifice, while most of the rest (guardian deities) are *tuṭiyāṉa teyvam* (literally, a fearful deity),[10] who require blood sacrifice. Hereafter, I call *cuttamuka teyvam* "a deity rejecting blood sacrifice" and *tuṭiyāṉa teyvam* "a deity accepting blood sacrifice".[11] To conclude, although blood sacrifice is said to be offered only to the guardian deities, as far as the number 21 symbolizes a complete whole, the blood sacrifice is interpreted as an action for revitalizing lineage deities as a whole, including main deities.

Village Deities

Here "village" refers to Kinnimangalam hamlet, *ūr* in a broad sense. The village deities I deal with here are basically worshipped by the people of K hamlet. These village deities guard the hamlet people exclusively. In other words, they reflect the collectivity based on a particular region. In this sense, the local expression of *ūr potutteyvam* (*ūr* common-deity) is more relevant than *kirāma teyvam*. The actual disposition of the 11 village deities obviously shows the Caste Hindus' centricism, for these deities' temples are located around the Caste Hindus' residential area (cluster I), *ūr* in a narrow sense, as shown in Figure 4.1. This spatial centricism corresponds to the fact that the Caste Hindus financially support the village deities' festivals. This does not mean that the Paraiyars are perfectly excluded from the festivals. The Paraiyars rather tend to interpret *ūr* in a broader sense, within which they are included, and they believe they are protected by these village deities, even though they do not contribute financially[12] and live outside the *ūr* boundary marked by these village deities (cf. [Daniel, 1984: 72–79]). Table 6.1 displays 11 village deities' names and some related details. Though the details will be discussed later, casting a glance at the list, it is obviously rich in local colour due to the predominance of local gods and goddesses.[13]

This brief general view reveals that village religious life chiefly consists of the cults of the personal deity, of lineage deities, and of village deities. It is suggested that there is an interesting contrast between the individual cult, like the worship of a personal deity, and the collective cult, such as the worship of lineage deities or village deities. The former cult depends upon the great Hindu God (*kaṭavuḷ* type), especially on male deities, whereas the latter cults tend to require local deities (*teyvam* type), in which goddesses are inevitably included. This point will be developed later.[14]

Village Deities and Their Festivals

The characters of eleven village deities are described here. The focus of the description is how each deity responds to blood sacrifice. The numbers of the 11 deities, T1-T11, correspond with the numbers in Figure 4.1 and the numbers in Table 6.1. Except for T1, enshrined in a big temple, and T4, T5, and T9, enshrined in small temples, the rest have no temple buildings and their statues are placed in the open air. It should be noted that the size of the temple building does not correspond simply with the popularity of the deity enshrined in it (see [McGilvray, 1983: 111] and [Dumont, 1986: 349]).

Table 6.1
ST List of Village Deities

	Name	*Sex*	*C/T*	*Festive month*	*Animal sacrifice*	*Priest's caste*
T 1.	Ekanatarcuvami	M	C	Maci	No	Pantaram (i)
T 2.	Vinayakar	M	C	Avani	No	ditto
T 3.	Perumal	M	C	Avani	No	ditto
T 4.	Urkkavalcuvami	M	C	Maci	Yes	Kavuntar (o)
T 5.	Aiyanar	M	C	Purattaci	Yes	Kucavar (o)
T 6.	Muttalamman	F	T	Pankuni	yes	Kucavar (o)
T 7.	Kaliyamman	F	T	Vaikaci	yes	Kallar (o)
T 8.	Vatakkuvacelliyamman	F	T	Purattaci	yes	Pantaram (o)
T 9.	Pattattaraciyamman	F	C (T)	ditto	No (Yes)	Kavuntar (o)
T 10.	Mataikaruppacami	M	T	ditto	Yes	Paraiyar (i)
T 11.	Nakammal	F	T	(Maci)	No	Kavuntar (o)

Notes: 1. C means "a deity rejecting blood sacrifice", whereas T means "a deity accepting blood sacrifice".
2. (i) means an insider and (o) means an outsider.

Ēkanātarcuvāmi (T1)

The Ekanatarcuvami temple originated in the tomb *(camāti)* of the outstanding world renouncer ("*cittar*") called *Arulānantacuvāmikaḷ* who played an active part in this area during the ruling time of Tirumalai Nayaka (the latter part of 17th century). The temple was built by putting a Siva linga on the place where the renouncer is said to have reached salvation (*camātinilai*) and is, therefore, identified with the Siva temple. It is said that Arulanantacuvamikal announced beforehand to the people, "You will see my figure in five different places at the same time when I reach salvation",[15] and what he said actually happened. This episode explains why the deity is called Ekanatarcuvami, which means an "omnipresent god". The present village name of Kinnimangalam is also derived from the achievements of the renouncer.[16] These origin episodes associated with the renouncer who once lived, are to some extent useful to the villagers for regarding Ekanatarcuvami as a familiar god, even though he is identified with Siva as a *kaṭavuḷ.*

The Ekanatarcuvami temple, facing east, is located almost at the centre of the *ūr* in a spatial sense, and exactly in the centre of the *ūr* in a cosmic sense. It has a big walled compound in which the main God Siva is enshrined in the centre and the Gods Vinayakar and Murugan are also enshrined at the back corners. This large and fine temple is formally the representative of village temples, though this does not simply mean that it enjoys the most ardent worship of the villagers. The present temple buildings and compound were constructed by architects sent by the Nayaka king. The origin of the temple indicates that the temple is not purely indigenous but reflects power superimposed from outside.[17] This is an important point, which contrasts with the character of the village deities mentioned below, which were from the beginning connected with a particular region.

This temple has been managed for generations by the Pantaram priest *(pūcāri)* who has settled in the village. The priest has been given the right of cultivation of the land associated with the temple called *kōvil māṉiyam* (18.12 acres) because of his priesthood. This means that he must bear all the expenses of temple management and his family's living costs by means of agricultural production from the land. Since he serves the great Hindu God Siva, he observes a Brahman priest-like lifestyle. He also has to take care of another two village deities, Vinayagar and Perumal, who reside on the southern borders of the village, because they are also great Hindu Gods. It is the Ekanatarcuvami temple that is responsible for the celebrations of the Tamil annual festivals, shown in the rightmost column of Table 6.2, as the representative of the village temples. Besides this, the festival peculiar to this temple, Guru *pūcai* (the anniversary of Arulanandacuvamikal), is celebrated on the day of *pūram*(the eleventh *nakṣattiram*) of *Vaikāci* month (May–June) and the withdrawn offering (*piracātam*) is given to "*caṉṉiyācis*" who gather from Tiruparankunram.[18] The most important festival for Ekanatarcuvami is *Makācivarattiri*, which is celebrated on the night of the new moon in *Māci* month (February-March). On the same day, most of the Caste Hindus' lineages also conduct their lineage festivals, even though not every year, so that the whole village is enveloped in a festive mood. In these important annual festivals, a special elaborate *pūjā*, including five kinds of *apiṣēkam* (Skt. *abhiṣēka*),[19] is often offered to the Siva linga. After this, the priest gives *mutaṉmai* (the order of honour)[20] by distributing *piracātam* to the participants. It is further noted that, on the five occasions marked by *p.* in Table 6.2, *pacanai* (an act of chanting hymns) is offered to God by a voluntary group consisting of 17 male members recruited from the Caste Hindus (1 Pillai, 1 Pantaram, 12 Kallars, 2 Acaris, and 1 Natar). In everyday life, God is served every morning and evening, and on every Tuesday and Friday the priest does a *pūjā* associated with a *poṅkal*.[21] There is little doubt that Ekanatarcuvami professes a Brahmanical tendency. As a result of this, the Paraiyar people are even today prohibited from entering the temple compound.[22]

Plate 56 The front view of Ekanatarcuvami temple (T1) in 1996.

Plate 57 *Poṅkal* as an important offering.

Plate 58 Chanting of devotees in front of Vinayakar shrine in Ekanatarcuvami temple.

Plate 59 Puja at Vinayakar temple by the village priest.

Plate 60 Perumal temple (T3) in 1987.

Plate 61 Urkkavalcuvami temple (T4).

Plate 62 Aiyanar temple (T5).

Table 6.2

Festivals of Village Deities and Annual Festivals

Tamil month	*Festival of village deity*	*Annual festivals conducted in the Ēkanātarcuvāmi temple*
Cittirai (April-May)		*Varatap pirappu*[*1]
Vaikāci (May-June)	Kālīyammaṉ (Tuesday)	*Guru pūcai (pūram)*
Āṉi (June-July)		
	the beginning of dakshinayanam	
Āṭi (July-August)		
Āvaṇi (August-September)	Perumāl Vināyakar	*Kokulaṣṭami (p.)*[*2] *Vināyakar caturtti (p.)*[*3]
Puraṭṭāci (September-October)	Vaṭakkuvācelliyammaṉ (Tuesday) Pattattaraciyammaṉ (Tuesday) Aiyaṉār (Thursday) Maṭaikaruppacuvāmi (Friday)	*Puraṭṭāci varapacaṉai (p.)*[*4]
Aippaci (October-November)		*Āyuta pūcai (p.)*[*5] *Tīpāvalip paṇṭikai*[*6]
Kārttikai (November-December)		*Cokkappan koḷuttutal*[*7]
Mārkaḻi (December-January)	Perumāl (*Vaikuṇṭa ēkātaci (p.)*)	*Tirupaḷi eḷuci*[*8] *Tiruvātirai*[*9]
	the beginning of uttarayanam	
Tai (January-February)		*Tai poṅkal*[*10] *Māṭṭu poṅkal*[*11]
Māci (February-March)	Ūrkkāvalcuvāmi Nākammāḷ	*Makācivarattiri*[*12]
Paṅkuṉi (March-April)	Muttālammaṉ (Tuesday)	

Notes: 1. p. means that *pacaṉai* (chanting hymns) is carried out.
2. This column shows only the important festivals for the Ekanatarcuvami temple, according to the priest.

*1: *Varutap pirappu*: the Tamil new year day
*2: *Kokulaṣṭami*: the celebration of the birth of Krsna
*3: *Vināyakar caturtti*: the celebration of the birth of Ganesa
*4: *Puraṭṭāci*: varapacaṉai or *Puraṭṭāci* caṉivaram: chanting hymns every Saturday of Purattaci month
*5: *Āyuta pūcai*: a service for books, agricultural tools, carpenters' tools etc.
*6: *Tīpāvalip pàṇṭikai*: offering lamps in commemoration of the victory of Krsna against Narakasura
*7: *Cokkppan koḷuttutal*: the fire festival for worshipping Siva, which is associated with the story of the competition between Visnu and Brahma.
*8: *Tirupaḷḷi eḷuci*: the early morning worship on the day corresponding with the daybreak of God's one day, which means the end of the dark half of a year.
*9: *Tiruvātirai*: worshipping Siva who dances on the day of *tiruvātirai nakṣattiram* of Markali month
*10: *Tai poṅkal*: the harvest festival in which *poṅkal* is offered to the god of the sun and the god of the wind and the lineage gods are worshipped as well
*11: *Māttu ponkal*: giving a share of *poṅkal* to the bullocks
*12: *Makācivarattiri*: the festival in honour of Siva as the God of destruction

The characteristics of the Ekanatarcuvami temple can be pointed out as follows. Firstly, the temple is clearly connected with "purity-impurity" ideology and, therefore, tends to come closer to Sanskritic Hinduism in Srinivas' sense. Secondly, Ekanatarcuvami is continuously "sacralized" [Hubert and Mauss 1964 (1899): 95] by the regular *pūjā* conducted by the village *pācari* (priest) as an insider. These characteristics promise a continuous and stable provision of God's grace for the villagers.

Vināyakar (T2)

The God Vinayakar, facing east, is enshrined at the southern boundary of the village. It is said that there is a Vinayakar shrine in the compound of Ekanatarcuvami Temple but it does not allow women's worship, so that this Vinayakar was built. Vinayakar is said to be the God of wisdom and fortune, and promises success for new undertakings if he is worshipped beforehand [Good, 1985: 122].[23] Why is the Vinayakar temple located at the southern border? One knowledgeable person says that the Gods enshrined at the southern borders, such as Vinayakar and Perumal, protect the village from the influence of the world of the dead, where *Yamatarmarājaṉ* (Skt. *Yama*) is said to reside. This indication could be connected with Good's statement that Vinayakar is also a gatekeeper [ibid.: 122]. Vinayakar is classified as a Sanskritic god but he was enshrined originally by simply putting a statue on the ground, and, more recently, on a little raised base (about 50 cm in height). Thus anybody can come close to this statue. During my period of observation, not many people participated in the *pūjā* in the festival of *Vināyakar caturtti*, which is conducted by the Pantaram priest of the Ekanatarcuvami temple.[24] Nonetheless, the necessary persons, like the panchayat president, the Two Tevars and the Four Pankalis, and *tōṭṭi* and *maṭaiyaṉ*, at least attend the *pūjā* and, afterwards, they receive *mutaṉmai*. It was observed that the Paraiyars (the Four Pankalis, and *tōṭṭi* and *maṭaiyaṉ*) stood at a distance, without joining the queue before the god. Though the Vinayakar temple in the compound of the Ekanatarcuvami temple is completely isolated from the Paraiyars, this outdoor temple does not spatially reject the Paraiyars' approach.

Perumāl (Visnu) (T3)

Perumal is also located at the southern boundary of the village, and faces towards the east. Apart from his significance as a boundary god in this village, the villagers' worship of Perumal is not very enthusiastic because they are basically believers in Siva. This god's statue has been moved to the Ekanatarcuvami temple temporarily because a roofed building is under construction.[25] Once he was managed by a Brahman, who left for Madras more than 50 years ago, but he is today served by the Ekanatarcuvami priest. As is the case with Vinayakar, there is no regular *pūjā* and only two occasions, namely, *Kokulaṣṭami* (Krisna's birthday) and *Vaikuṇṭa ēkātaci* (the day when the gateway to heaven is broadly open to believers), provide an opportunity to worship Perumal.

The above-mentioned three gods, as Sanskritic gods, reject blood sacrifices. In addition, temple celebrations which are prepared and conducted solely by the Ekanatarcuvami priest involve the participation of important village officials and do not necessarily require the attendance of all the villagers. This clearly differs from the celebration of the following more localized deities, whose communal festivals are held with the all-out cooperation of the villagers. It should be noted that the lack of regular *pūjā* and the emphasis on the village boundaries are two points which distinguish both Vinayakar and Perumal from Ekanatarcuvami. Next, I deal with the local male deities who are classified into the category of *cuttamuka teyvam*, unassociated with blood sacrifice.

Ūrkkāvalucuvāmi (T4)

Ūrkkāval literally means "village-guardian". As indicated by this name, the villagers regard this god as their main village protector. Urkkavalcuvami, facing east, is enshrined in the roofed temple[26] on the bank of the eastern tank, in order to protect the tank, which is the lifeline of the villagers, and ultimately to guard the village territory as a whole. The god Ayyanar, with whom I deal next, is symmetrically located on the bank of the western tank, for the protection of both the tank and the village. Urkkavalcuvami is described as follows: (1) he has two consorts, (2) he does not accept blood sacrifice, (3) he can be identified with Siva, and (4) he patrols the village boundary at midnight. These characteristics obviously overlap with those of Aiyanar. In fact, several villagers agree with this identification of Urkkavalcuvami and Aiyanar.[27] Thus, there is little doubt that Urkkavalcuvami of Kinnimangalam is part of the so-called Aiyanar cult, popular in Tamil Nadu. It should be noted that the discussion on Aiyanar in the next section is, therefore, applicable to Urkkavalcuvami as well.

The annual festival for Urkkavalcuvami is held in *Māci* month (February-March). The highlight of this festival is the offering of 5 clay horses to the gods as the village watchmen. Urkkavalcuvami is offered three horses by the villagers, by V.A.O. (traditionally, *karṇam* and *nāṭṭāṇmai*), and by Two Tevars respectively. Apart from this, Aiyanar and Mataikaruppacami are also offered one villagers' horse each.[28] The festival process is as follows. The villagers go to the village boundary to meet the Kavuntar priest, who carries *cāmipeṭṭi* (the sacred chest) symbolizing the god, from Puliyankulam, and they form a procession to the temple. It is emphasized that women, except those after menopause, should not approach the procession. Urkkavalcuvami, as the main deity, receives only a vegetarian offering, whereas his 21 guardian deities, such as Cinnacami and Pecciyamman,[29] enjoy blood sacrifice. Therefore, when a young male goat (*cattikkuṭṭi*) is killed, not only is the sacrifice made behind the temple, but also the main deity Urkkavalcuvami is curtained, so as not to be polluted by the animal sacrifice. The priest offers a goat's head in whose mouth the right leg is held, and conducts *kappālapūcai* (literally, a skull-*pūjā*). The priest brings the head back to his village the following day. He is seen off by the villagers at the village border. Thus, the festival emphasizes the following points: (1) the collectivity of the village, (2) the village boundaries, (3) the role of the outsider priest, (4) the purity of Urkkavalcuvami, and (5) the significance of the goat's sacrifice.

Aiyaṉār (T5)

The cult of a Tamil local deity Aiyanar is very popular, especially among the people of central and southern Tamil Nadu. Aiyanar, who is enshrined on the bank of the western tank,[30] is in the southwest direction from the village. Three deities, whose statues are carved on one stone, are placed facing the east in the open air. The central main deity Aiyanar, who has a sitting posture called *cukācaṉam* (Skt. *sukha+āsana*), a Yogic posture characterized by ease and comfort, one of nine Yogic postures[31], is associated with the virgin goddess *Kaṉṉimā* (a worshipper of Aiyanar) on his right side, and the guardian deity *Muṉṉōṭum Karuppu* (literally, the Karuppu who recites a mantra at the lead) on his left side. Though Kannima here is the sole goddess, it seems to me that the goddess can be understood in two ways, namely, (1) as the southwest directional deity *Kaṉṉi* who represents the dynamic ambiguity of death and the regeneration of life in the Tamil area [Reiniche, 1981: 47–55] and (2) as the seven virgins, *Kaṉṉimār* [Oppert, 1978 (1893): 511]. Oppert's description of the Aiyanar temple structure suggests that *Muṉṉōṭum Karuppu* could be identified with *Mannadiyar*, two gigantic guardians standing at the gates of the temple [Oppert, 1978 (1893): 511]. The Karuppu is sometimes simply called *Kāvalkāratteyvam*.

In the village, it is said that Aiyanar rides on a white horse with a green coloured saddle during his inspections (hunting), and he is preceded by a dog.[32] It is said that if a woman alone meets Aiyanar's party during its midnight patrol, she will definitely die (see [Oppert, 1978 (1893): 505]). The fundamental communal role of Aiyanar is to protect the tank water for agriculture (see [Dumont, 1970: 22]), and to guard the village as the night watchman. It is also believed in the village that he is effective in curing diseases and in facilitating conception.[33] In connection with the latter personal benefits, one who makes a vow and whose desire is fulfilled, often offers a clay horse figure as a return.

As is well known, Aiyanar is one of the polemical local deities in the Tamil area. Though there is not a big difference in the description of the observed features of Aiyanar, it is not easy to agree how we should define the character of Aiyanar.The earlier notable works are Oppert [1978 (1893)] and Whitehead [1921 (1907)], which contrast with one another. Oppert regards Aiyanar as a portion of the Guada-Dravidian belief [Oppert 1978 (1893): 509], whereas Whitehead looks upon him as a Brahmanized deity [Whitehead, 1921 (1907): 18]. Both inquire whether Aiyanar should be seen as Aryan or non-Aryan. A dichotomous framework, consisting of an Aryan cultural layer and a non-Aryan one, was refuted by Dumont, who strongly professes his theoretical viewpoint that royal power is encompassed by Brahmanical status based on "purity-impurity" ideology. Dumont defines Aiyanar as the Lord or the Master by saying that Aiyanar combines the real (and original) values of the temporal chief with the rather official values of the Brahmanical quality [Dumont, 1986: 448]. This conclusion is reached after a discussion of the relationship between Aiyanar and Karuppucami on the one hand, and that between Aiyanar and the goddesses (his two wives) on the other hand [Dumont, 1986: 440–448] [Dumont, 1970: 31–32]. Dumont claims that both Aiyanar's relationships with Karuppu and with the goddesses (wives) hold two kinds of hierarchies, namely, the Brahmanical and the royal. In these discussions, the identification between Aiyanar and Siva is made clear by him raising their common characteristics, like their connection with a bull, and having two wives (*pūrṇa* and *puṣkara*), as many people point out. The villagers generally recognize this. Dumont's conclusion appears to hold for the case of K hamlet as well. In fact, Aiyanar is said to have two wives, and the above-mentioned stone statue shows Aiyanar associated with Karuppu and Kannima as iconographical evidence, though Kannima is said not to be his wife. As Dumont points out, Aiyanar's annual festival is held in *Puraṭṭāci* (September–October) on

Thursday soon after the festivals of the goddesses Vatakkuvacelliamman and Pattattaraciamman (see Table 4.2 and [Dumont, 1986: 424–448] [Dumont, 1970: 24, 31]) and shows a deep association between them (see [Good, 1985: 131]). The relationship between Aiyanar and Karuppu is made clear in the scene of the goat sacrifice of the annual festival.[34] Aiyanar and Kannima are curtained so as not to see the blood sacrifice which is offered to the 21 guardian deities, including Munnotum Kruppu. There is little doubt that this fact emphasizes the contrast between Aiyanar as the Brahmanical chief deity, and Karuppu (and others) as one of the non-Brahmanical surbodinate deities. Nonetheless, even though I have this data supporting Dumont's observations, I am still not sure whether I would reach the same conclusion on Aiyanar's character as Dumont does. In his analysis, he uses a hierarchical ideology based on the dichotomy of Brahman and Kshatriya, namely, "Brahmanic qualities" ("purity-impurity") and "royal qualities" (master-servant) in his terms [Dumont, 1986: 448].

My main criticism of Dumont is that he persists too strongly with the monistic explanation from the dominant viewpoint. As a result, he fails to properly throw light on the indigeneous cultural elements. Therefore, in his theory, these local elements tend to be interpreted as inferior aspects, such as the "impure" against the "pure", or the royal against the Brahmanic from the viewpoint of the encompassing Brahmanical ideology. It seems, therefore, that in his understanding of Aiyanar the puzzling character of Aiyanar which cannot be reduced to Brahmanical qualities is deemed to have royal qualities.

In order to overcome this limitation, it is important to notice a fundamental pattern commonly penetrating the local cults, including both the cult of the lineage deities and that of the village deities. In this context, Oppert's description of Aiyanar, in which he is defined as "the Lord of ghosts", can be re-evaluated. Oppert seems to observe the festival sequence as a whole, which includes blood sacrifice, and the ambiguous character of Aiyanar is therefore properly emphasized [Oppert, 1987 (1893): 505–506, 512].[35] The fundamental point lies in the fact that the cult of Aiyanar as a whole inevitably requires blood sacrifice, even though Aiyanar himself is said to be segregated from seeing it. The whole process of the cult of Aiyanar can be understood as an integration in which the villagers' two requirements which appear contradictory from the Brahmanical viewpoint are fulfilled at the same time. These requirements are (1) the necessity of blood sacrifice and (2) the necessity of "pure" main deities (the Brahmanization of the main deities). The former necessity is fulfilled by the blood sacrifice dedicated to the 21 subordinate deities, represented by Munnotum Karupu, while the latter requirement of the conservation of sacred power is met by Aiyanar and Kannima being the main *cuttamuka teyvam*s (the deities rejecting blood sacrifice). The logic of my argument for explaining the Aiyanar cult thus is this. Firstly, I recognize the villagers' fundamental religiosity, which requires blood sacrifices for their cults of folk deities, even though this sacrifice is dedicated to subordinate deities. From this point of view, I ask why the villagers want to segregate the main deity Aiyanar from blood sacrifice. The answer is in their need for stabilizing sacred power and preserving the god's grace. Thus, the Aiyanar cult itself has a dynamic sacrificial process, namely, the dynamism of the generation of sacred power and its conservation. In other words, the festival can be seen as an act bridging "pollution-sacredness" and "purity-sacredness". This interpretation, which is different from the Brahmanical one, is more appropriate for understanding the villagers' thought, in which the above-mentioned two requirements are not contradictory.

This non-Brahamanical understanding is also to some extent supported by the character of Kannima. For, Kannima is not Aiyanar's wife but an independent goddess, though she is seen as *cuttamuka teyvam*. That is, the relationship between Aiyanar and Kannim is not a marriage relationship, which is an indication of the degree of Sanskritization. This halfway situation of Kannima, between her independence, and her residing at the side of Aiyanar, reflects the real character of the Aiyanar cult which is not fully Brahamanized, but basically preserves local ideas attaching importance to productivity. Thus, in my concept, Aiyanar embodies the dynamism of productivity by manipulating both "pollution-sacredness" and "purity-sacredness", though the former is more fundamental.

I believe that the difference between Dumont and me has been clarified. What I understand by the concept of "pollution-sacredness" seems to be explained as the royal (Kshatriya) quality by Dumont.[36] However, it is problematic that both are equated, for I understand the cult of Aiyanar as a whole by including blood sacrifice, whereas Dumont takes up Aiyanar separately and deals with him as the "pure" god, even when he argues the royal aspect of Aiyanar. The point is that the cult of Aiyanar does not refer to the sole worship of Aiyanar himself, but is formed by a group of deities consisting of not only Aiyanar, but also other subordinate deities. This group of deities as a whole, like the lineage deities, represents the dynamism of the Aiyanar cult, which reflects upon the festival processes. As I have already mentioned, the present argument on Aiyanar, which is deemed as a category of god [Dumont, 1986: 441], is valid for Urkkavalcuvami as well.

Plate 63 Muttalamman temple (T6).

Plate 64 Kaliyamman temple (T7) in 1987.

Plate 65 Vatakkuvacelliyamman temple (T8).

Plate 66 Pattattaraciyamman temple in 1996.

Plate 67 Mataikaruppacami temple (T10).

Plate 68 Nakammal temple (T11).

Next, I shift to the local goddesses.

Muttālammaṉ (T6)

The goddess Muttalamman is enshrined in the centre of the village square, near the *mantai*, and faces east. Though her temple itself is small and lacks a compound, Muttalamman is doubtlessly the most important village goddess, indicated by the fact that the grandest festival is held for her. There is no goddess's image in the temple, where only the palanquin used in the festival is found (*vide infra*). Muttalamman literally means "a pearl goddess" and she is, therefore, possibly identified with the goddess of smallpox, Mariyamman [Dumont, 1970: 24]. However, both the icon carved on the facade of the temple and the goddess's statue, which is made only during the festival, show characteristics of the goddess Durga. Nonetheless, it seems that the proper names of goddesses are not very important for the villagers. A member of the Kallars, for example, says that the goddesses, like Muttalamman, Kaliyamman, Pecciyamman, and Durgayamman, are basically the same, but are revealed in different forms, each goddess sharing the duty of destroying a particular demon (see [Moffatt, 1979: 249]). But, as Kinsley warns [Kinsley, 1988: 197], the identification of a local goddess with a great Hindu goddess (*Mahādevī)* in terms of their icons or their names does not always mean that the village goddess carries the characteristics of the great Hindu goddess.

As is well known, Mariyamman is characterized by her dualistic nature, which is symbolized by "the split body theme", that is, her figure consisting of the head of a Brahman woman and the body of an Untouchable (Chakkiliyan) woman (for example, [Beck, 1981: 127] [Moffatt, 1979: 249]). How she became such a combined figure is explained in the legend of her origin. I also collected the legend of the origin of Muttalamman, which is very similar to that of Mariyamman (for example, in South

Indian villages, [Moffatt, 1979: 248–249]) [Beck, 1981: 126–127], though an Untouchable woman does not appear in the Muttalamman legend.[37] In this respect, the duality of Muttalamman is not claimed by the shape of her figure, but the contrasting change from the chaste wife to the angry independent woman is at least recognized by the story as a whole. Actually, the villagers regard Muttalamman as a goddess having two natures, a calm and kind aspect, and a dangerous and harmful aspect. The former nature is found in the strong tendency in which Muttalamman is drawn towards (identified with) the goddess Minaksi of Madurai, who is to a considerable extent encapsulated by "Brahmanical Hinduism" [Kinsley, 1988: 202–203].[38] This tendency is indicated by the placing of Muttalamman in the main position among village goddesses. It is confirmed by the following facts: (1) Her temple place was shifted from the boundary to the center (all other goddesses reside in the peripheral area), (2) Her temple faces east (all other goddesses face north), (3) The annual festival of her temple is held in *Pankuni* (March–April) (The festivals of other goddesses are held mainly in *Purattaci* (September–October), and (4) Her temple festival is on the biggest scale, not only among the goddesses' festivals but also among the village festivals. This attempt at emphasizing the benevolent aspect of Muttalamman, who is described as *cantama teyvam* (a calm deity) by the villagers, shows the people's desire to seek the goddess' grace in a stabilized way, not to follow Sanskritized religion.

Nonetheless, the villagers share the recognition that another ambiguous and dangerous aspect of Muttalamman, symbolized by her anger, is part of her basic nature. In fact, the dangerous and powerful aspect is regarded as a reflection of her independent and topocosmic character. This aspect is clearly revealed through the observation of her annual festival in which blood sacrifice is included. The following points should be noted: (1) A *low caste* potter living in the adjacent village, who makes the statue of Muttalamman, is the goddess' priest. It is noted that the priest is an *outsider*. (2) The goddess' statue which appears only during the festival (for two days) is put and directed towards the *north* in a *pantal* (a hut built temporarily for a ritual) in front of her temple. (3) There is a ceremony called *kaṇtiṟattal* (a ceremony of putting the eyes into the goddess' statue) conducted at the village *boundary* (in the northeast direction) where Muttalamman was originally enshrined.[39] (4) The *goat sacrifice* is conducted by the hand of Two Tevars (the Kecavan and the Kamanan representatives)[40] on the morning of the second day of the festival. (5) At the end of the festival, the goddess's statue is *broken* at the *northern boundary* of the village,[41] because otherwise, it is believed, she would destroy or burn the whole world by means of her excessive power. Though the dangerous aspect is clarified by analysing her festival process, I also note that the festival is an indispensable device for the villagers to generate (release) and acquire (enjoy) the goddess's powerful grace. This shows that it is thought that Muttalamman cannot regenerate her power without returning to her fundamental nature as a local goddess, which is commonly shared by other village goddesses. Here, the focal point is the relationship between the generation of sacred power and the goat's (blood) sacrifice.

As is well known, the animal sacrifice in the cult of the goddess can be understood by the theme of "the demon devotee" [Shulman, 1980: Chapter 5]. It is thought that the blood sacrifice of the male victim makes him transform into a devotee of the goddess, or realize union with the goddess. By this process, the creative sacrifice, which adopts the shape of the divine marriage in south India, is embodied. Moreover, Shulman claims that Tamil myths introduce the demon devotee instead of the death of the god himself in order to avoid the god's contact with the polluting act of death (see [Shulman, 1980: 317]). Beck also discusses the marriage of Mariyamman with the demon in the villages of Tamil Nadu [Beck, 1981]. Her discussion, which is obviously based on Turner's communitas theory, leads her to the conclusion that the metamorphosis of the male victim finally appeases the anger of the goddess [Beck, 1981: 113–115]. Nonetheless, there is a decisive difference between both the interpretations of the blood sacrifice of the male victim, namely, the creative sacrifice by Shulman and the appeasement of the goddess' anger by Beck. I support Shulman rather than Beck, for Beck's interpretation does not work well in terms of my example of Muttalamman. If Beck was right, the goddess would not no longer be dangerous after the goat's sacrifice on the second morning. However, this is not the case with Muttalamman, who is still ambiguously powerful even after the sacrifice, so that her statue must be broken or removed from the village in the final moment of the festival. In this respect, and as far as my observations are concerned, it is more natural to understand the situation as follows. The people recognize that Muttalamman's ambiguous power is continuously active throughout the festival, namely, as long as the goddess is present in the village (or in the world). Therefore, it is important to clearly mark out her appearance (*kaṇtiṟattal*) and disappearance (the ritual destruction of her statue) on earth, which take place at the northern boundary. Her perceived birth and death is also expressed by the movement of her statue in and out of the village border. In this sense, it is more logical that blood sacrifice itself forms the climax of the festival. This is deemed as "the creative sacrifice" [Shulman, 1980: Chapter 3], rather than as the ritual for the appeasement of the goddess. In other words, I argue that the condensed act of the creation of sacred power is basically embodied by the goddess's presence throughout the festival (see [Shulman, 1980: Chapter 4]).

This argument is supported by the remarkable fact that the degree of women's participation in the festival is much higher than in the case of the male deities' festivals, like Urkkavalcuvami or Aiyanar. Firstly, women take the initiative in dedicating the offerings to the goddess, such as *māviḷakku* and *poṅkal*[42] on the first day, and *muḷaippāri*[43] on the second afternoon. Secondly, women in general are not banned from approaching the goddess' procession, though, as was already noted, Urkkavalcuvami rejects women except those who are post-menopausal. As is directly symbolized by the dedication of *muḷaippāri*[44] there is little doubt that the productivity of the woman is deeply connected with the creativity of the goddess. This means that there is a clear correspondence between the women's productivity, realized through menstrual "pollution" (as discussed in Chapter 5), and the "creative sacrifice" embodied by the goddess who cannot avoid slaying, which is a "polluting" act (see [Shulman, 1980: 317]). In this sense, the festival of Muttalamman should not be reduced to an understanding within Turner's framework [Turner, 1969], but, as a whole, should be regarded as the generation of sacred power or as the realization of "pollution-sacredness".

Thus, Muttalamman can be defined as the goddess who embodies "pollution-sacredness" in her fundamental nature but, at the same time, she is on the way to being a Minaksi type of goddess, who is said to be not simply Sanskritic but still to preserve her topocosmic nature. In other words, she is required to reply to the villagers' greedy desire for her, through not only the creation of sacred power but also the conservation of it. In sum, from the Brahmanical viewpoint, Muttalamman is deemed and expressed as a slightly Sanskritized Hindu deity. Nonetheless, from the villagers' viewpoint, she is a most powerful deity, i.e., a source of *cakti* (as an aspect of creation) and at the same time a calm deity who definitely give her grace to them (as an aspect of conversation). Compared to Urkkavalcuvami or Aiyanar, the former aspect is more fundamental and stressed in Muttalamman.

Kālīyammaṉ (T7)

Kaliyamman is placed at the north-east corner of the *ūr* (the Caste Hindus' residential cluster) and faces north. The goddess is symbolized by the trident (*tiri-cūlam*, Skt. *Tri-śūla*)[45] laid on the raised stone base. This open-air temple is said to be the newest village temple, built by the contribution of the Kecavan lineage. In this sense, it is not surprising that, since the temple was purposefully built, there is more textual knowledge about the temple, compared to the cases of the other older village temples. Actually, the most knowledgeable man of the Kecavan lineage says that the goddess Kaliyamman was enshrined there as *Mahiṣāuramardinī* (the goddess slaying the buffaloe demon), which is another name for *Mahādevī* Durga (see *Devīmahātmya*, a part of *Mārkaṇḍeya-purāṇa*). Therefore, even though Kaliyamman, as one of village goddesses, holds the localized character of granting the villagers' requests, such as curing smallpox or cholera, and removing misfortune, there was a conscious will, at least among the temple builders, that the goddess bears the image of *Mahādevī*. As a result, she has several different points which to some extent distinguish her from the other goddesses protecting the village at the northern boundary, namely, Vatakkuvacelliyamman (T8) and Pattattaraciyamman (T9). One is the difference of the festive month. Kaliyamman is celebrated in the hottest and most difficult month Vaikaci (May–June), independently. Another difference is found in the scale of the festival. The festival of Kaliyamman is considerably grand, second only to that of the Muttalamman festival. Moreover, the tendency towards *Mahādevī* is suggested by the fact that *karakam*, which is deemed *ammaṉ eḻuntaruḷutal* (the symbol of the goddess)[46] during the festival, is made by the Ekanatarcuvami (Siva) temple priest.[47] These subtle differences seem to indicate that the villagers seek to increase the certainty of the protection of the goddess having the name of *Mahādevī*.

In the festival of Kaliyamman, blood sacrifice is conducted on the first day. The highlights of the first day are the goat sacrifice in front of the *karakam*, and then the dedication of 200 *uruṇṭai* (a rice ball mixed with pieces of cooked meat of the sacrificial goat) to the goddess. The main ceremony of the second day is the dedication *muḷaippāris* by women, after the individual offerings of *poṅkal* and sometimes an animal (chicken etc.) sacrifice. Finally the *karakam* and the *muḷaippāris* are thrown into the eastern tank water, because it is believed it is necessary to cool down the excessively powerful goddess's *shakti* to a suitable level for everyday activities. It is noted that the first day animal sacrifice in this two-day festival again does not support Beck's interpretation.

Vaṭakkuvācelliyammaṉ (T8)

The goddess Vatakkuvacelliyamman, the spelling of whose name was given by a knowledgeable villager, is the same as *Vaṭakku-vācaṟcelvi* [Tamil Lexicon], *Vaḍakku vāsal selli amaṉ* [Dumont, 1986: 426], or Vaḍakku-vāsal Celviyamman [Good, 1985: 119],[48] which can be translated as "the north-gate goddess". In fact, a pair of goddess statues, who are said to be sisters, are laid in the fields of the northern side of the *ūr,* and moreover face north. These are accompanied by *Kaṉṉimārkaḷ* (seven virgin goddesses) nearby. This goddess typically embodies the deep connection between the goddess and the north (see [Shulman, 1980: 48, 138] and [Good, 1985: 123, 127]). It is said in the village that Vaṭakkuvācelliyammaṉ, not only holds the character of *Mahiṣāuramardinī* but also works real miracles for the diseases peculiar to women (see [Good, 1985: 120]). In this sense, the participation of women in her festival is again notable.[49]

Vatakkuvacelliyamman has her annual festival on a Tuesday of *Puraṭṭāci* (September–October).[50] The festival starts with the *pūjā* conducted by the Pantaram priest living in the neighbouring village (Kokkulam),[51] in which only the village representatives participate and dedicate offerings. Then the Paraiyars' music of the procession returning from the goddess's temple to the *ūr* tempts the people to gather in the central square. There, a big procession attended by the other villagers is again formed and proceeds to the goddess's temple. It becomes dark. In the darkness, the dedication of *taḻukai* and *māviḷakku*[52] and blood sacrifice are carried out in front of the goddess.

Pattattaraciyammaṉ (T9)

Pattattaraciyamman has a small roofed building, in which her statue, facing north, is enshrined. Her temple is located in the north-west direction of the *ūr*. Pattattaraciyamman literally means "the goddess as the queen" and she is identified with Kamacciyamman, having attractive eyes, so that she is regarded as a very powerful goddess in the village. It is believed that she not only cures smallpox and leprosy, but also that she has the special power of curing eye-diseases. Mental diseases and leg pains are sometimes included in the list of illnesses which this goddess can cure.

Furthermore, there is also a view that she can be one of the agricultural deities, that is, a topocosmic deity. In this connection, it is notable that, in front of the goddess, there is a statue of the guardian deity Karuppacami, which faces east, on the foot of the western tank bank.[53] It is said that Karuppacami resides there in order to protect the goddess, as is stated in the origin story of Karuppacami, which is obviously derived from the story of Dakṣa's *yāga*.[54] The attendance of the 20–30 dancing Paraiyars, whose sides are hooked by pins and are pulled by ropes, at the final stages of the goddess's annual festival is very suggestive when the relationship between Pattattaraciyamman and Karuppacami is considered. For, when the origin story of the goddess, based on the story of Dakṣa's *yāga*, is connected with these Paraiyar practices of penance, called *kavaṟukuttutal*, and their carrying out a blood (cock) sacrifice dedicated to Karuppacami, one is again reminded of the theme of "the demon devotee" (see the section on Muttalamman). In this respect, the most meaningful fact is that the cock brought by the Paraiyars is beheaded by the Kavuntar priest of Pattattaraciyamman, though the goddess herself does not accept blood sacrifice. Taken seriously, through the mediation of Karuppacami and the Paraiyars, namely, through her sanction of the Paraiyars' blood sacrifice to her guardian deity Karuppacami, the theme of "the demon devotee" would still be preserved in Pattattaraciyamman's festival. In this sense, it seems to me that Pattattaraciyamman herself replicates the Sanskritic tendency of avoiding the direct contact of a god (or a goddess) with the polluting act of death [Shulman, 1980: 317], by transferring her blood-thirsty nature to Karuppacami. Nevertheless, this transference does not seem to be completed because the goddess accepts a non-vegetarian offering in *Makācivarattiri*. In this connection, it is interesting that there is confusion among the villagers as to whether she accepts blood sacrifice or not. This confusion seems to be further complicated both by the goddess's blood thirsty image being deeply rooted in their minds, and by the cock sacrifice conducted at her festival.Since the Kavuntar priest comes from Mavilippatti, an adjacent hamlet, the people of Mavilippatti also attend this goddess' festival. This case of having participants from outside the Kinnimangalam hamlet is unique.

The next temple with which I deal with is unique, in that a Paraiyar priest manages it.

Maṭaikaruppacāmi (T10)

Since *maṭai* means sluice, Mataikaruppacami literally designates the guardian deity of the sluice of the bank. In this case, the god is located on the western bank. Mataikaruppacami is regarded as an agricultural deity because he guarantees the production of irrigated land (*naṉcey*) by guarding the tank bank and controlling the tank water. The most striking fact is that this god is served by a Paraiyar priest, who is always selected from the Mataiyan lineage, one of the *Nāṟpaṅkāḷi* (Four Pankalis). How a Mataiyan person acquired the priesthood of Mataikaruppacami is explained in the origin legend of this god.[55] This recalls a similar god, *Pēykkāmen* Karuppacāmi, found in Dumont's report [Dumont, 1986: 355]. Nonetheless, if the fact that the Paraiyars are most probably the previous occupants, as Dumont also suggests, is taken into account, it can be imagined that the legend describes the process by which Mataikaruppacami, who was originally the local deity of the Paraiyar community,[56] was seized by the Caste Hindus, as late comers, and was transformed into one of the village deities (cf. [Dumont, 1986: 355]).

The annual festival is held on the Friday of *Puraṭṭāci* following the festival of Aiyanar. The date of the festival, which is decided at the meeting of *Nāṟpaṅkāḷi* finally fixed with the permission of the Caste Hindus. The expense of the festival is covered by the Caste Hindus and both the Kecavan and the Kamanan are responsible for collecting money and preparing the necessary things, including a sacrificial goat. The balance of the money is given to *Nāṟpaṅkāḷi*. The festival starts in the evening at *ciṉṉa mantai*. The Mataiyan priest (*pūcāri)* asks the god-dancers (*cāmiāṭi*s) of the Kartananti-Cinnananti lineage, who are in a trance, whether people can proceed towards the Mataikaruppacami temple on the western bank. After getting their permission, Two Tevars give the garlands to the *pūcāri* and the *cāmiāṭi*s and then the procession, in which both Caste Hindus and Paraiyars are mixed, leaves *ciṉṉa mantai*. In front of the stone pillar symbolizing Mataikaruppacami, *poṅkal*, which is made by using water taken from the western tank with the hands of the priest, is offered, and the goat's sacrifice is conducted by the hands of Two Tevars. The Paraiyar *pūcāri* then distributes sacred ash and *piracātam* (offerings blessed by the deity) to the gathering people, including *nāṭṭāṇmai*, *karṇam*, and Two Tevars, according to the order of *mutaṉmai*. Though the Caste Hindus return to their homes, the Paraiyars remain there, because they must cook the goat meat and eat it there. It is said that the cooked meat should not be taken to their homes because it is sacrificial meat for *tuṭiyāṉa teyvam*.

I have briefly described the details of this festival process because phenomena which cannot be explained by the logic of "purity-impurity" are recognizable in it. It is obvious that if the Caste Hindus regarded the Paraiyars simply as "impure" people, they would not accept the priesthood of the Paraiyars. There is no doubt that the Caste Hindus give priority to the status of the priesthood rather than to the status of the Paraiyars during this festival. More positively, the festival itself seems to be evidence for the Caste Hindus' appreciation of the Paraiyars' (especially, the Mataiyan lineage's) special power of drawing the grace of Mataikaruppacami, which is based on the deep connection between the Paraiyars and the god. It is a very important fact that Mataikaruppacami is a unique village male deity, in terms of directly accepting blood sacrifice, compared to other village male deities who reject blood sacrifice. This shows that this uniqueness, namely, the main male deity as *tuṭiyāṉa teyvam*, must be controlled by the Paraiyar's power. In this situation, the Paraiyar is looked upon as the indispensable agent for drawing the positive power of guarding the village from *tuṭiyāṉa teyvam* through the polluting act of animal sacrifice. This verifies that the Caste Hindus do not simply confine the Paraiyars to the "impure" category, but that they recognize and use the ambiguous and, therefore, positive aspect of the Paraiyars, namely, their "pollution" aspect through which "pollution-sacredness" is acquired. However, at the same time, it should be remembered that this positive character of the Paraiyars is realized only in very temporally and spatially limited situations such as the festival night and at the temple site.

Though I have finished explaining the importanı village deities, another minor goddess, who is not so significant structurally, remains. I deal with her last.

Nākammāl (T11)

Nakammal literally means "a snake-mother", and this goddess is said to protect people working in the fields from snake-bites. The goddess's statue, placed on the inside of the eastern tank bank, is located at about 300 meters distance from the *ūr* in the southeast direction. This goddess reminds us of the snake goddess *Manasā* of the Bengal area, reported by Dimock [1962], but Nakammal here, at least today, does not have much importance as a village deity.[57] Though there is no annual festival for this goddess, a small *pūjā* is held in *Puraṭṭāci* and in *Māci* by the Kavuntar *pūcāri* living in Mavilippatti.

Structure and Interpretation

Structure

In the previous section, the characteristics of the village deities have been considered, but the aim of this final section is to integrate these descriptions and discussions, and to elucidate the total structure in which these deities are placed. As a result, it is possible to find two levels of binary oppositions from the above descriptions, as is shown in Figure 6.1. Firstly, there is the main opposition between the central group and the peripheral group. Secondly, amongst the sub-categories of the peripheral group, another opposition between the northern group and the southern group is found. Needless to say, these binary oppositions are not simply opposed but are rather regarded as part of the complementary relationship by which the total structure is formed. It should be remembered that these oppositions are basically presented as relationships in the semantic domain, rather than in the objectified spatial sense, although in K hamlet there is some correspondence with physical spatial relationships.

Figure 6.1

Locations of Village Deities and Their Semantic Structure

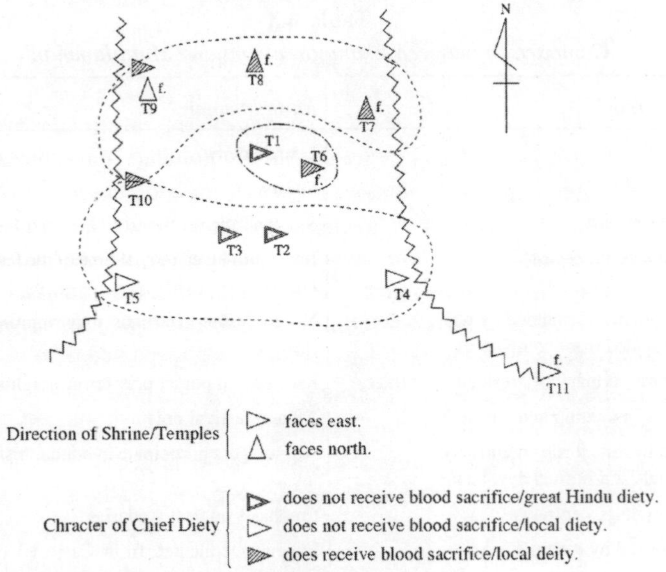

N

T1 T2 T3 T4 T5 T6 T7 T8 T9 T10 T11

Direction of Shrine/Temples: ▷ faces east. △ faces north.

Chracter of Chief Diety: ▶ does not receive blood sacrifice/great Hindu diety. ▷ does not receive blood sacrifice/local diety. ▶ does receive blood sacrifice/local deity.

The Central Group and the Peripheral Group

Ekanatarcuvami and Muttalamman form the central group among the village deities. Ekanatarcuvami represents the male deities who reject blood sacrifice, while Muttalamman occupies the chief position of the female deities who accept blood sacrifice. This centrality reflects upon the fact that both their contrastive shrines are located in the village centre.

What is the relationship between Ekanatarcuvami and Muttalamman? To discover this, it is useful to sum up the characteristics of both (see Table 6.3). As is shown by the origin of the temple, the Ekanatarcuvami (Siva) temple, which originated from the tomb of the *cittar,* was not established purely on an indigenous religious basis, but rather has a Brahmanical tendency, which was to some extent imposed by the policy of the Nayaka Dynasty. In this sense, Ekanatarcuvami tends to profess "Brahmanical Hinduism" which is associated with the "purity-impurity" ideology and, therefore, avoids blood sacrifice, even though the temple priest is a non-Brahmin (a Pantaram). It is, furthermore, characterized by the following points: (1) The priest is a vegetarian and lives inside the village; (2) The regular *pūjā* and the annual events according to the Tamil calendar are constantly held, but such functions do not always involve the villagers as a body, but rather there is a tendency to limit the participation to village representatives and ardent devotees; (3) The production from the farm land donated to the temple covers the expense for these occasions. On the other hand, Muttalamman, who can be basically regarded as a deity of "Popular Hinduism",[58] encourages the villagers' cordial religious sentiment and acquires the most remarkable popularity among them. She has the following characteristics: (1) She is celebrated only on the unique occasion of her annual festival, during which the goddess's statue, made by the potter priest, appears before the people; (2) The priest is a non-vegetarian of a low caste, and lives outside the village; (3) the annual festival is participated in by basically all the villagers; (4) The festival processes emphasize the village boundaries; (5) Since blood sacrifice is inevitable for the goddess's celebration, the goddess can be seen to embody "pollution-sacredness" in my sense.

Table 6.3

Comparison between Ekanatarcuvami and Muttalamman

Ēkanātarcuvāmi	*Muttālamman̠*
Male deity	Female deity
kaṭavuḷ	*teyvam*
Big temple faces east	Small shrine faces east
Permanent image faces east	Image produced only at time of the festival and faces north
Temple compound surrounded by walls (Harijans excluded from compound)	No enclosure (Harijans may approach vicinity of shrine)
Pantāram priest permanently resident in village	Kucavar temporary priest from neighbouring village
Daily services (including annual rites)	Annual festival only
Participation in annual rites mainly by village officials and limited devotees	All villagers participate in annual festival
Emphasis on village centrality	Emphasis on *ūr* boundaries
Expenses covered by earnings from cultivation of temple land	Expenses collected from Caste Hindus at time of festival
Not receiving sacrifice	Receiving blood sacrifice

How can we understand that the villagers need both the "Brahmanical Hindu" god, Ekanatarcuvami, and the "popular Hindu" goddess, Muttalamman? The answer lies in the division of labour found between Ekanatarcuvami and Muttalamman. Muttalamman can be deemed as an indispensable device for the generation of sacred power (*cakti*) through blood sacrifice, whereas the "pure" god Ekanatarcuvami can be seen to play a role in stabilizing such rather ambiguous power in order to guarantee the villagers' well being. It is noted that Muttalamman herself tends to be transformed into a more stable and meeker character, like the goddess Minaksi. This Sanskritic tendency makes Muttalamman move from the northern border to the centre. Nonetheless, Muttalamman is never deemed to be the wife of Siva, and is therefore still very independent.[59] In this sense, the goddess basically retains her "popular" character unchanged ever after having some Brahmanical cultural elements. This suggests that the adoption of Brahmanical elements does not mean Sanskritization but stabilization of a god's or goddess's grace.

The Northern Boundary Group and the Southern Boundary Group

The northern boundary of the *ūr* is protected by a group of goddesses accepting blood sacrifice, while the southern boundary is guarded by a group of gods rejecting blood sacrifice.[60] Table 6.4 shows not only this fundamental contrast, but also some variations included in each group. The southern group consists of two kinds of gods, that is, the "Brahmanical" deities, like Vinayakar and Perumal, and the local gods identified with Siva, like Urkavalcuvami and Aiyanar, whose guardian deities require blood sacrifice. As for the northern group, though Pattattaraciyamman tends to avoid blood sacrifice, even though imperfectly, there is no doubt that the motif of "the demon devotee" is repeatedly carried out by these goddesses. It is also noted that Mataikaruppucami cannot be easily categorized into either group. He must be placed in the marginal area between both sides, because he requires blood sacrifices even though he is a main male deity. It is also ambiguous that Mataikaruppucami has a Harijan priest, who is an insider of the village but at the same time an outsider from the viewpoint of the Caste Hindus (the *ūr* people). Nonetheless, if importance was attached to the dedication of the clay horse to Mataikaruppucami, as is done to Aiyanar, it would not be unnatural that he was regarded as one of the southern group of male deities. Table 6.5 is the integration of the above-mentioned two axes, that is, of Table 6.3 and 6.4. It can be seen in Table 6.5 that the opposition and the complementarity found between the main deities of the central group is extended repeatedly in the total structure of the village deities. Thus, the villagers' religiosity holding the above structure of village deities appears to be a combination of two different cultural tendencies, i.e., the Brahamanical and the popular. However, this sort of substantialist (Great Tradition – Little Tradition theorist) view should be abandoned and, instead of that, an interpretative and ideological approach should be taken here. The phenomena of the structure of village deities wait for ideological interpretations, by which villagers' religiosity is properly understood.

Table 6.4

Contrast between the Northern Boundary and the Southern Boundary Groups

<table>
<tr><th colspan="3">The southern boundary group</th><th colspan="2">The northern boundary group</th></tr>
<tr><td>Vinayakar (T2)
Perumal (T3)</td><td>Urkkaval (T4)
Aiyanar (T5)</td><td>Mataikaruppu
(T10)</td><td>Pattattaraciyamman (T9)</td><td>Kaliyamman (T7)
Vatakkuvacelliyamman (T8)</td></tr>
<tr><td colspan="2">male deities</td><td></td><td colspan="2">female deities</td></tr>
<tr><td colspan="2">temple facing east</td><td></td><td colspan="2">temple facing north</td></tr>
<tr><td>insider-priest
(Pantaram)</td><td>outsider-priest</td><td>insider/outsider-
priest (Paraiyar)</td><td colspan="2">outsider-priest</td></tr>
<tr><td colspan="2">main deity avoids blood
sacrifice</td><td colspan="3">(T9 avoids) main deity enjoys blood sacrifice</td></tr>
<tr><td>festival has no
blood sacrifice</td><td colspan="4">festival has blood sacrifice</td></tr>
</table>

Table 6.5

Structure of the Village Deities (pre-interpretation)

Centre	*Southern boundary*	*Centre*	*Northern boundary*
Ekanatarcuvami		Muttalamman	
	Vinayakar (S)		Pattattaraciyamman (NW)
	Perumal (S)		(Karuppacami)
	Aiyanar (SW)		Kaliyamman (NE)
	Urkkaval (SE)		Vatakkuvacelliyamman (N)
	Mataikaruppu (W)		
	(Nakammal)		
dominance of male deity		dominance of female deity	
main deity rejects blood sacrifice propensity to "purity-sacredness"		main deity accepts blood sacrifice "propensity to "pollution-sacredness"	
interpretation from "pure-impure" ideology ⇨			⇦ interpretation from "pollution" ideology

Interpretation

The actual meaning of the above-mentioned structure does not lie in the static juxtaposition of two different cultural tendencies, but rather in the struggle between different ideological viewpoints, or between different interpretations. To conclude, the cult of the village deities should be regarded as the arena where the debate (the struggles) between interpretation from "pure-impure" ideology and that from "pollution" ideology is conducted.

I will explain the developmental process of the arguments through which I have reached the above conclusion. First of all, the predominant understanding of the functionalist approach, found in Srinivas and the early Marriott, in which the village cult in southern India is seen to embody the juxtaposed structure of the Sanskritic culture and the Dravidian culture, was refuted by Dumont and Pocock, who profess a monistic theory. It seems to me that their criticism of the functionalist dualism is reasonable because it is difficult to imagine that two different religious attitudes towards the village deities coexist in the same villager's mind simultaneously. In this sense, the juxtaposition theory is a superficial description of village cults from an outsider's viewpoint. Dumont and Pocock claim that the village cult should be understood from the viewpoint of monism, based on the binary opposition between "purity" and "impurity" (e.g., [Dumont and Pocock, 1959a: 45]). Though I agree that the structuralist approach contributes to theoretical progress, this theory also has limitations. In my view, there can be no doubt that the Dumontian monistic theory is useful for describing a religious belief found in a villager's mind, but this does not mean that village cults are exclusively dominated by the Brahmanical "pure-impure" ideology [Dumont, 1980 (1966)]. There is no doubt that the decentripetal ideology in the form of "popular Hinduism" or in the appearance of "indigenous culture" exists in village religious space. In this connection, there is another point made by Marriott and Srinivas which tends to be forgotten under the strong influence of Dumontian theory but which should be reconsidered [Keyes and Daniel, 1983: 8]. That is, while it is true that Srinivas's concept, "Sanskritization", or Marriott's concepts, "universalization" and "parochialization", are inadequate because they lack an ideological viewpoint, these concepts do pay attention to the transaction (the dynamic relationship) between "Sanskritic Hindusim" and "Local Hinduism", a point which deserves reevaluation. Thus, my standpoint is formed by adopting the merits of both the functionalist approach and the structuralist one.[61]

It is necessary for further argument to clarify the limitations of Dumont. As has sufficiently been argued, the fact that blood sacrifice is indispensable for the cult of the village deities cannot be underestimated by being confined to the framework of "purity-impurity". If not only my own data, but also Shulman's work [1980] and other important works on the religious notions and behaviour of the Tamils[62] were referred to, there would be no doubt that Dumont's view leans to the Brahmanical side of ideology. Thus, it can be confirmed that the logic of "purity-impurity" is not the unique ideology of village religion but, far from it, the villagers rather attach fundamental importance to "pollution" ideology. What is significant here is to consciously adopt the concept of ideology in the post-structuralist sense (e.g., [Therborn, 1980: 77–78]), in order to make use of the merits of Dumont's monistic understanding. It is necessary to always invoke the relative view that a given outlook is the interpretation from a particular subjective position. In other words, using the term ideology aims at keeping a distance from the naive view that a meaning (a value) is *a priori* attached to an object. From this point of view, though Dumont is rather unaware of it, it is obvious that his theory unwittingly overlaps with the Brahmanical top-down ideology. In this sense, it is reasonable to understand that his theory provides an integrating interpretation from the "purity-impurity" ideological viewpoint. This suggests that there can be another uniting interpretation based on "pollution" ideology.

The "pollution" ideological view is typically expressed by the festival of the goddess which embodies the dynamism of death and the regeneration of life. Through the mediation of blood sacrifice, namely, the destructive death "pollution", sacred power (*cakti*) is acquired. As has been discussed, I called this creative process, which realizes the motif of "a demon devotee", "the paradigm of the goddess".[63] In this connection, I have argued that the local gods also practise "the paradigm of the goddess", even though in an indirect way. It cannot be denied that the sublimation of "pollution" into "pollution-sacredness" takes place in such a creative process.

How can the village gods who profess the "purity-impurity" ideology and, therefore reject blood sacrifice, be understood from this "pollution" ideological point of view? To conclude, Sanskritic or Sanskritized gods can be seen as religious devices for stabilizing sacred power, which is excessively and dramatically generated by bloodthirsty goddesses, in order to support the villagers' everyday activities. This understanding is obviously different from the Dumontian interpretation of the binary and hierarchical opposition between the "pure" god and the "impure" goddess, but it provides the complementary dynamic process of the "creative" goddess and the "maintaining" god. This is the integrating interpretation from the "pollution" ideological viewpoint (see also [Marglin, 1985: 78–79]). The "creative" goddess can be regarded as a powerful device for inviting the villagers who are at the level of *l'ordre réel* in everyday life, towards the deeper dimension of *l'ordre intime*, in which "continuity of existence" is revealed. The "maintaining" god can be seen as playing the role of preserving the sense of sacredness which originates from the deep experience in people's minds.[64]

As is clarified by this discussion, the structure shown in Table 6.5 can be compared to an icon, which awaits interpretation. More concretely speaking, the dualistic structure of Table 6.5 is compared to the icon of the great god of Hinduism having two wives. For example, Siva and *Umā* (*Pārvatī*) and *Kālī;* Visnu has *Lakṣmī* (*Śrīdevī*) and *Bhūmidevī;* and Murugan has *Tēvayāṉai* and *Vaḷḷi*. If I tried to read these icons, it would be soon noted that there are inevitably two different interpretations which correspond with the above-mentioned two different ideological standpoints. According to "purity-impurity" ideology, the former wife represents the "pure" and good aspect, whereas the latter is unambiguously deemed to be the degraded "impure" wife. Nonetheless, if we adopt the "pollution" ideological viewpoint, the latter wife, who accepts "pollution", contributes to the creation of sacred power, and the former wife bears the role of stabilizing and maintaining this power. What is emphasized is the need to distinguish a binary opposition of a dimension of observed materials (e.g., whether there is blood sacrifice or not) from that of a dimension of interpretation (e.g., whether a blood sacrifice is deemed to be a degrading act or a creative act) (see also [Sekine, 1999]).

In sum, although a unified understanding is necessary for appreciating the villagers' religious beliefs, the interpretation is not fixed in one way. As I have shown above, two ideological interpretations are possible in terms of the same matter. Why two? Because it is inevitable that one is a centripetal ideology and the other is a decentripetal ideology and that both are interdependently defined. In the religious or ritual context, the former is "pure-impure" ideology and the latter is "pollution" ideology. The villagers attempt to form their integrating interpretation of their religious lives within the struggle between these two ideologies. In K hamlet, most villagers share the common attitude in which their religious lives are fundamentally defined by the "pollution" ideological view. It is also to be remembered that there are some villagers such as Pillai families and the Pantaram priest family who more strongly adopt "pure-impure" ideology. This, therefore, suggests that it is necessary to investigate more precisely how the different groups construct their own interpretations (ideological formations) according to their given social conditions. This point will be investigated and developed in Part Three.

Notes

1. In his paper, after recognizing that *pūjā* also has an idiom of sacrifice, Fuller emphasizes the contrasting relationship between *naivēdya* (a part of *pūjā*) and *pali* (*bali*) in the village context [Fuller, 1988: 24]. He also notes that "the ordinary people who practice it usually refer to it by a literally descriptive phrase, such as 'cutting the goat' " [ibid.: 23]. This is a little different from the case in Kinnimangalam.
2. Srinivas's classification of "All-India Hinduism", "Peninsular Hinduism", "Regional Hinduism", and "Local Hinduism" based on the concept of "spread" is convenient for

distinguishing cultural levels neutrally, and I use it in order to make clear the contrast between "All-India Hinduism" and "Local Hinduism". However, the classification itself is somewhat misleading, because it invites the idea that "All-India Hinduism" is most universal and "Local Hinduism" is most parochialized. Nonetheless, I use his classification in the following sense. My argument is based on the concept of "sharedness", rather than the concept of "spread". For, from this standpoint, "Local Hinduism", even though it looks diversifying, is rooted most deeply and widely, even beyond culture and, in this sense, the degree of "sharedness" diminishes towards "All-India Hinduism". With this modification, a god accepting blood sacrifice can be classified into "Local Hinduism"; whereas a god rejecting blood sacrifice can be classified into "All-India Hinduism" or "Sanskritic Hinduism".

3. In her discussion on who kills a sacrificial animal, Beck points out that "the beheading of any living being is a demonic or polluting act" [Beck, 1981: 115].
4. The cult of *Kāmātciyammaṉ* is not limited to *Taccuācāri* (carpenters), but is shared by five kinds of artisan castes, which are called *Ācāri* or *Kammāḷar* generically.
5. In this connection, the distinction between *teyvam* and *kaṭavuḷ* which was recounted to me by several villagers, seems to be interesting. According to them, they cannot make contact with *kaṭavuḷ* the unseeable great God, without the mediation of *teyvam*s, the seeable and more familiar gods. They also say that the villagers are more concerned with sacred power itself than with each deity having a proper name. This sacred power corresponds to "the divine" in Dumont's sense [Dumont, 1986: 458], "shakti" in Wadley's sense [Wadley, 1975], and "sacred power" in Harman's sense [Harman, 1989: 98]. According to Yamasita, this hierarchical split between *teyvam* and *kaṭlavuḷ* took place towards the middle ages [Yamasita, 1989].
6. First of all, the famous pilgrimage centres, such as the *Mīnāksi* Amman temple in Madurai city, the *Alagār* temple in the eastern side of Madurai city, and the Murugan temple in Tirupparankuṉṟam (one of *āṟupaṭai vīṭu)* are easily accessible to the villagers. In addition, they also sometimes visit Palani, one of the six holy places of Murugan (*āṟupaṭai vīṭu*), the Ayyappaṉ, temple in Cabarimalai, Kērala, and so on. The pilgrimage to the great Hindu gods itself is deemed an act of self-sacrifice [Shulman, 1980: 17–29].
7. According to Harman, 80 per cent of South Indian Hindu believers are devotees of village deities and devotion to Hindu Great Gods outside villages is relatively limited [Harman, 1989: 98].
8. The lineage members do not always know all the names of their 21 lineage deities. There is a consensus about the names of the main deities and several guardian deities, but the names of the rest of the lineage deities often vary from person to person.
9. According to Table 4.11, the composition of the main deities of the Kallar lineages are 5 goddesses, 3 gods, and 3 pairs (god and goddess), and, in the case of the Paraiyars, the main deities consist of a pair of goddesses (elder and younger sisters), 1 god, and 2 pairs (god and goddess). This undoubtedly shows that goddesses are indispensable for their lineage cults.
10. *Tuṭiyāṉa teyvam* is described as a deity which easily possesses a person and, if necessary, punishes a person within this life, not in the next life, like a king.
11. As is well known, Dumont adopts the dichotomy between "pure (*cuttam*) god" and "impure (*acuttam*) god" or between "vegetarian god" and "meat-eating god" [Dumont, 1986]. However, as Fuller [1988: 21] argues, Dumont's analytical translation, which results from his naive application of the "purity-impurity" ideology to the gods' world, seems to be far from the truth from the villagers' viewpoint.

12. *Tōṭṭi* and *maṭaiyaṉ*, and *Nārpaṅkāḷi* of the Paraiyars have to do various types of menial work for the festival. This means that the festival provides the Paraiyars with the opportunity of receiving some reward from their patrons.
13. The deep relationship between the goddess and the particular bounded area of village (*ūr*) has been repeatedly pointed out (e.g., [Whitehead, 1921: 17], [Kinsley, 1988: 198–200].
14. This contrast recalls Whitehead's distinction between the Dravidian deities dominated by goddesses, and the Aryan deities dominated by gods, and Srinivas's distinction of four levels from "All-India (Sanskritic) Hinduism" to "Local Hinduism".
15. It is said that the renouncer sat in the meditation form on the day of the twenty second of *tiruvōṇam nakṣattiram* of *Cittirai* month and appeared in the following five places simultaneously: Kinnimangalam, Solavantan, Madurai, Periyakulam, and Cinnamanur.
16. The following legend shows why the old village name, Mankalapatti, was changed to Kinnimangalam. One day, Arulanantacuvamikal, who lived in the forest of Nagamalai, asked a young shepherd to milk a barren cow, handing him a bottomless bowl (*kiṇṇi*). Though the man wondered how it was possible, he did so and strangely he was able to get a full bowl of milk. The news of this miracle spread at once among the people of this area and they started to ardently worship the renouncer. He became more and more popular as he did good things for the people. Since various village people asked him to come and settle in their villages, after consideration he proposed to them that he would live in the village where his bowl (*kiṇṇi*) fell, and he threw it in the air. The bowl fell in the place where the Ekanatarcuvami temple is located, and the renouncer came to this village, as he had promised. After this incident, the villagers began to call their village Kinnimangalam after *kiṇṇi*. The story continues further, but I mention only the relevant part of it.
17. This provides evidence that the Nayaka dynasty carried out a policy of encouraging Hinduism by constructing Hindu temples in the areas under its rule. This policy was adopted mainly with the aim of displacing the Muslim power.
18. According to the priest, the *Cittar* Arulanantacuvamikal is sitting in the form of meditation at the right side of the linga.
19. (1) *cantaṉa* (sandalwood) *apiṣēkam*, (2) *paṉṉir* (rose-water) *apiṣēkam*, (3) *iḷanīr* (young coconut juice) *apiṣēkam*, (4) *pañcamirta* (a mixture of banana, honey, sugar, ghee, and grape) *apiṣēkam*, (5) *pāl* (milk) *apiṣēkam*
20. According to the priest, the order of *mutaṉmai* is as follows; (1) *karṇam*, (2) *nāṭṭāṇmai*, (3) the Kamanan lineage, (4) the Kecavan lineage, (5) the Acari, (6) *tōṭṭi*, *maṭaiyan* and the representatives of *Nārpaṅkāḷi* (selected from the Paraiyars), (7) other villagers.
21. It is interesting that a *pūjā* associated with *poṅkal* is not conducted on Monday, which is normally said to be suitable for worshipping Siva, but on Tuesday and Friday which are said to be good days for the worship of the goddess. According to Dumont, "Generally ... the Goddess priest is a Pandaram" [Dumont, 1986: 355]. I presume that this convention influences the choice of the days for more elaborate worship. See also [Good, 1985: 139].
22. One Paraiyar tells me that the Pantaram priest himself never says that the Harijans should not enter the temple compound, but they do not do so because they are afraid of the Kallars' physical force.
23. In the village, a Kallar man explained that Vinayakar is the god holding *porumai* (meekness or patience). Details of Vinayakar are found in Sekine [1995]
24. There is no regular *pūjā* to Vinayakar enshrined at the southern border. *Vināyakar caturtti* is the unique occasion on which the god receives *pūjā*. On the festival day, a sweet called

kolukkaṭṭai, *poṅkal*, and boiled Bengal gram is prepared, and an unglazed statue of Vinayakar is brought by the people. After having a *pūjā*, statues of Vinayakar are thrown into the Eastern tank water.

25. The construction was started in 1982 but was still not completed in 1989.
26. It is said that the statue was made more than 200 years ago and that the temple building was built about 50 years ago. This temple is a branch of the main temple of Puliyankulam, a neighboring village, which is located in Panjamalai (a part of Nagamalai), so that the priest of the main temple holds concurrently the priesthood of the Kinnimangalam temple. The main temple priest is a Kavuntar, who came originally from Karnataka. In this connection, the movable statue of the main temple visits the temple of Kinnimangalam during the Purattaci festival of the main temple.
27. According to a Kallar person, the god *Ūrkkāvalcuvāmi* is deemed to be *Puracṭṭāi Aiyan*, which means a Brahmanic god guarding the village. See also [Dumont, 1986: 447] and [Oppert, 1978 (1893): 505].
28. It is said that Urkkavalcuvami, Aiyanar, and Mataikaruppacami patrol the village from 12 midnight to 2 a.m. One guardian deity, whose name I failed to identify, patrols the village in the evening, and Kaliamman is said to inspect the village at daybreak. It is said that these guardian deities are located at the village borders, in order to protect it.
29. 21 subordinate gods are not fully identified by the villagers, as is the case with the lineage deities. Therefore, it seems to be that the number 21 again symbolizes one set of wholeness.
30. It is said that since Aiyanar was born on the riverside, the people made the temple near the water. Dumont also reports that Aiyanar, associated with a goddess, is enshrined on the tank bank [Dumont, 1986: 354] [Dumont, 1970: 25]. The connection between Aiyanar and tank/river is touched on by Oppert as follows: "Under his special charge are the boundaries, forests, tanks and rivers" [Oppert, 1978 (1893): 506]. As to the connection between Aiyanar and the west, see [Oppert, 1978 (1893): 510].
31. As is described by Oppert [Oppert, 1978 (1893): 511–512] and as Dumont notes [Dumont, 1986: 448], Aiyanar iconographically holds both the characters of an ascetic (*tavaci*) and a hero (*vīran*).
32. Oppert notes, "Mounted on a wild elephant or on a horse, he rides sword in hand over hills and dales to clear the country from all obnoxious spirits. It is generally believed that at midnight, preceded by heralds, and followed by his retinue, Aiyanar leaves his residence to go a hunting" [Oppert, 1978 (1893)]. See also [Whitehead, 1921 (1907): 33].
33. Oppert lists the various functions of Aiyanar from the contents of prayers as follows; "to grant wealth, to bestow sons, to destroy enemies, to avert drought, to secure the favour of women, to destroy the evil effects or omens caused by lizards, and similar boons" [Oppert, 1978 (1893): 506].
34. The priest of the Aiyanar temple is a Kucavar (a potter) living in the neighbouring village, as is usual [Dumont, 1986: 442–443] [Brubaker, 1979]. The sacrificial goat is beheaded not by the Kucavar priest but by the Kecavan with a knife handed over by a Kamanan.
35. In contrast to Oppert, Whitehead overestimates the aspect that blood sacrifice is not offered to Aiyanar.
36. The villagers' use of the adjective "kingly" is different from the royal in Dumont's sense. For example, when they explain *tuṭiyāṉa teyvam* (a deity accepting blood sacrifice), they use it. In this context, *tuṭiyāṉa teyvam* is compared to a "kingly" deity because it punishes the people in this life, as a king does.

37. According to Gail, the legend originates from the incident of Rama in the "Mahabharata", in which his mother Renuka is beheaded by Rama, and began to be narrated with the name of Parasurama in the Puranas after the first half of the 6th century AD [Gail, 1977: 221–228]. The Muttalamman legend I collected from a Kallar elder is as follows, though I presume that it is only one of several variants found in the village. "Once upon a time, an ascetic lived in the forest and strove for meditation. His wife who lived with him cared for him. One morning, as usual, the wife went to the river and was making a mud pot for a *pūjā,* after which she took a bath. At that time, she noticed the flying figure of Ghandharva reflected on the river. Since he was so beautiful, she looked up at him in the sky and was attracted to him. After this, she could not make the pot, so she returned home without one. She told her husband honestly what had happened at the river. The husband got angry on hearing it, and decided to punish his wife. First, the husband commanded his first son to behead her, but the first son refused. Then he asked the second son Parasurama to do this. Since Parasurama did so instantly, the ascetic was much satisfied and promised the second son he would grant any request of his. Parasurama asked his father to revive his mother. The ascetic fulfilled his request by connecting her body with her head, which was kept on *muccanti* (according to a villager's explanation, the raised base near the junction). The revived wife, however, could not tolerate her husband's cruel conduct. She got so angry that she left him. This angry wife, as a matter of fact, is the goddess Muttalamman. Therefore, that is why people have to break the goddess' statue at the end of the festival, in order to avoid her fearful anger." It is very obvious that this Parasurama legend is incomplete due to various omissions, but it seems to narrowly preserve the basic story. That is, the story is that a wife who fails to control her desire (Renuka) is beheaded by her son Parasurama under the command of her husband but, after she is revived again by virtue of Prasurama's request, she shows her strong anger against her husband. It therefore embodies the general motif that a woman who is very badly treated by a man transforms into a fearful goddess with unbearable anger [Kinsley, 1988: 201].

38. It is, however, difficult to simply say that Minaksi is a Sanskritic goddess because, as has been already argued in various places, such as [Fuller, 1984: 17–20], [Shulman, 1976: 138–146], [Shulman, 1980: 138–139] and [Harman, 1989: Chapter 4], Minaksi is said to still hold the indigenous aspect of an independent and topocosmic deity as her basic character. This sort of argument cannot be productive without adopting an interpretative approach.

39. On the first morning of the festival, Two Tevars and other Caste Hindus go to the potter priest's house in order to receive the goddess' statue. They bring the palanquin for the procession, the goddess's clothes and decorations, and the necessary things for a *pūjā*. After the *pūjā* in the priest's house, the goddess's procession leaves the house for Kinnimangalam. When the procession reaches the entrance of the *ūr* (near the elementary school), the goddess is taken down and *kaṇtiṟattal* is held there. During this ceremony, many Paraiyar people gather there and worship the goddess.

40. This is different from Beck's argument that the sacrificer often introduces an outsider to behead the sacrificial animal, and that this results in an easier identification of the sacrificer and the sacrificial animal [Beck, 1981: 115].

41. After finishing the dedication rites of *muḷaippāri* (see Note. 43), important people like *nāṭṭaṇmai, karṇam*, Two Tevars, and the potter priest bring the goddess's statue and *taḷukai* (vegetarian offerings) to a place under a milk tree, called *pālai maram*, standing at the

northern village border, and there the goddesss statue is broken by the hands of the potter priest after a small *pūjā*. At the same time, *muḷaippāri*, which is sometimes claimed as the goddesss symbol, is thrown into the eastern tank.

42. *Māviḷakku* (literally, a rice flour lamp) is a special oil lamp having a small cotton wick on its base, made from a mixture of rice flour, water, sugar, cardamom, ginger, etc. *Poṅkal* is boiled ritual rice. *Māviḷakku* and *poṅkal* are put in front of the goddess and then the priest conducts a *pūjā*. According to Beck, *Māviḷakku* and *poṅkal* must be dedicated before the animal sacrifice [Beck, 1981: 113]. She also suggests that there is a symbolic equation between the sacrifice, the head of the sacrifice, and the *Māviḷakku* light [Beck, 1981: 114].
43. *Muḷaippāri* is a little grown sprout of nine kinds of grains planted in a small bowl, which is nursed in a dark room by the hands of a small girl before the onset of menstruation or of a woman after menopause. She has to take a bath before watering it. In this sense, *muḷaippāri* is not made by all the households of the Caste Hindus but is planted by several lineage-based families chosen from the suitable families at the rate of one per 10 or 15 households. Of course, voluntary participation is allowed due to personal reasons. They begin to make *muḷaippāri* eight days before the festival starting day. The dedication of *muḷaippāri* is associated with the women's dancing, called a *kummi*, around the *muḷaippāris* in a circle (*kummi pāṭal*), and is followed by personal animal sacrifice or by penance such as *cēṭṭaṉṭi vēṣam* (dancing done by a person with mud applied to his body and having magosa leaves) and *akkiṉicaṭṭi* (a penance of carrying a fire bowl in which firewood is burning) in return for the personal vow.
44. It is said that the workmanship of *muḷaippāri* tells the fortune especially in terms of the fertility or productivity of the house (or the household) which the woman taking care of it belongs to, because it indicates the goddess's will. There is little doubt that these sayings suggest a symbolic equation between *muḷaippāri*, the woman, her household (which could be extended to her lineage), and the goddess in terms of prosperity based on productivity.
45. According to *Devīmahātmya* compiled in the 5th or 6th century AD, *Mahiṣāuramardinī* (the great goddess slaying the buffalo-demon) was given various weapons by the gods witnessing her birth. At the time, Siva gave her a trident drawn out from his own trident. Therefore, a trident is one of her weapons, showing her connection with Siva.
46. *Karakam* is a pot filled with sacred water, on which margosa leaves and a coconut are put [Beck, 1981: 116, footnote 44]. I heard of another explanation, that *karakam* is a favourite thing of Kaliyamman.
47. The local deity in whose festival the Ekanatarcuvami temple priest, even partially, participates is only Kaliyamman among the village deities, with the exception of the Sanskritic Gods, like Siva, Vinayakar and Perumal.
48. It seems that Vaḍakku-vāsal Celviyamman in Good's report rather occupies a similar position to that of Muttlamman as the central village deity. This shows that it is necessary to take into account the position of the deity concerned, within the whole structure of the village deities, in order to identify the character of the deity.
49. The women attend the function by dedicating *poṅkal, muḷaippāri, and pīṭṭu* (a conical shape of confectionery made from black gram flour) to the goddess. Since, in the village, the shape of *pīṭṭu* is looked upon as a breast, these offerings doubtlessly symbolize fertility or productivity.
50. The actual festival date and each household's share in the festival cost is decided at the Caste Hindus' meeting (*periya mantai*). The villagers are informed of the date by *tōṭṭi*, and

their share is collected by the members of the Kecavan and of the Kamanan. Though the 1987 festival cost nearly Rs 300, it is said that Rs 2 each was collected from the Caste Hindus' households.

51. The priest is given a small portion of the temple land but the festival is held at the Caste Hindus' expense.
52. It is noted that there was no dedication of *muḷaippāri* in this festival.
53. This spatial relationship reminds us of the division of labour according to which the goddess protects the north direction exclusively, whereas Karuppacami watches other directions in the village [Dumont, 1986: 427].
54. The story I heard from a Kallar elder is as follows. "Pattattaraciyamman was born as the daughter of Tatcan (a carpenter), so that she was named Tatcayini. After having grown up, she married Siva. Her father, Tatcan, was so envious of Siva's great power that he plotted to steal this power from Siva. For this, he conducted a special *pūjā* called *yākam* (Skt. *Yāga*). Siva noticed it and became angry. He commanded Virapattiram and Vairava to kill Tatcan. They failed to do so however. Then Tatcayini herself went to her father and destroyed the *yākam*. Soon after, she entered into deep meditation. At that time Karuppacami, as an incarnation of Visnu, appeared and protected her. Since then, she has been guarded by Karuppacami." This story obviously originates from that called "the destruction of Daksa's *yāga*" in the Puranas so that Tatcan and Tatcayni are easily identified with Dakṣa and Satī [O'Flaherty, 1973: 128–129].
55. The story I learned from a Mataiyan elder is this. "One day, an ancestor of the Mataiyan lineage happened to find a water leak from the western tank bank. The tank was full of water due to the rainy season and the tank bank might have broken at any moment. He made a desperate effort to stop the leak, but he failed. He was upset. Suddenly, Karuppacuvami appeared and said to him, "Don't worry. I will protect the bank while you inform the villagers of the water leak. So you hurry and go." Hearing this, he hurried back to the village and explained what was happening. Nonetheless, the villagers surprisingly killed him on the spot, because they judged that if they went back to the bank with him, Karuppacuvami would disappear, and the bank would break. Since then, Karuppacuvami has resided there and has guarded the bank. By virtue of this incident, the right to monopolise the priesthood of Karuppacuvami was given to the Mataiyan lineage as compensation for its member becoming a victim."
56. Another Mataikaruppacuvami is enshrined on *ciṉṉa mantai* which is located in the square of the oldest residential cluster of the Paraiyar. This Mataikaruppacuvami is clearly recognized as their community god.
57. As is recorded in the village history, there were hamlets called Konampatti near the Nakammal temple, so it is guessed that the goddess enjoyed a more active worship in the past.
58. "Popular Hinduism" cannot be defined as a substantial entity but refers to the decentripetal ideology which springs up at the edge of the social space dominated by the ideology of "Brahmanical Hinduism".
59. The contrast between the independent goddess who engages in the fight against the demons, and the goddess tamed by her consort (the god) is clearly discussed, for example, in [Tapper, 1979: 15–16] and [Kinsley, 1988: 202–203].
60. As I noted before, a knowledgeable Kallar explains this contrast as follows. On the one hand the southern side deities defend against the intrusion of death coming from the southern

world ruled by *Yama.* On the other hand, the goddesses protect the village against the evil power symbolized by *Mahiṣāsura* on the northern boundary and invite the grace of the god of wealth, *kupēraṉ* (Skt. *Kubera*). This knowledge is not always shared by the ordinary villagers, but it cannot be denied that the present village deities were placed according to the guidance of knowledgeable leading persons.

61. The development from functionalism through structuralism to the post-structuralist theory of ideology is concisely summarized by Fardon in his Introduction to "Power and Knowledge" (1985).
62. For example, [Beck, 1981], [Good, 1985], [Moffatt, 1979], [Reiniche, 1979, 1981], [Hoek, 1979], [Brubaker, 1978] and [Whitehead, 1921] support my present argument.
63. In this connection, Hiltebeitel's work [1981] which deals with the dynamism of "polluting" menstrual blood by focusing on the Draupadi of Mahabharata strongly supports my argument. His extended argument on the Draupadi cult in general [Hiltebeitel, 1988, 1991] is also suggestive and important.
64. It seems to me that the arguments found in [Beck, 1981: 118] and [Kinsley, 1988: 211] come close to the present understanding of a goddess.

Chapter 7

Pollution Concepts Manipulated I

Practices of the Dominant Castes and the Harijans

I have attempted so far to reveal the significance of the cosmic ideology represented by such concepts as "pollution" and "pollution-sacredness", which cannot be dealt with properly from the Dumontian standpoint based on "purity-impurity" ideology. Not only have I refuted the Dumontian view by introducing the dimension of "pollution" but also the dynamic relationship between "pollution" ideology and "purity-impurity" ideology has been made clear.[1]

I have concentrated on an investigation of the ideological configuration *per se*, especially through a consideration of pollution concepts. On the basis of that, I proceed to the next investigation. As Burghart suggests,[2] it is necessary to inquire into the villagers' practices from a subjective viewpoint, in other words, how these ideologies are actually manipulated by different social sections. Taken into consideration are the differences between the view of the dominant castes and that of the Harijans or the difference between the male-centred dominant view and the female-centred view. Such investigation brings the ideological configuration to life, because ideologies actually work and are reproduced in socio-economic power relationships. The following two chapters deal with the manipulation of pollution concepts: the practices reflecting the caste hierarchical difference in this chapter; and in the next chapter gendered space focused upon woman's body is described as an arena of ideological struggles over pollution concepts. These two chapters present a logical foundation for Part Three, in which the Harijans' practices are discussed in greater depth.

Practices of the Dominant Castes on Pollution

I will mention several examples which cannot be logically explained only by "purity-impurity" ideology. Other explanatory logics or ideologies must be found to explain these examples.

Example 1: It is usually said that contact with the Harijans pollutes the Kallars. Nonetheless, it is not uncommon for a Kallar man to keep a mistress of the Paraiyar caste (the Harijans). How is this possible? A Kallar man who openly told me that he had a Paraiyar mistress explained that this love affair was different from other usual matters. Hearing his answer, other Kallar men added with much laughter that such pleasure was free from pollution. I asked the first Kallar, "You said you could visit your Harijan mistress but, if she came to your house, would you be polluted by her?"

Responding to this, he shouted, "If she did so, I would behead her". How is it possible to understand this contradictory behaviour?[3]

Example 2: The dominant castes basically do not allow the Harijans to use the wells of the Caste Hindus, though there are several opinions concerning the result of the Harijan's contact with the well. While one Kallar man says that the Harijan's contact pollutes the well but not the well water itself,[4] another Kallar man claims that the water is also polluted by the Harijan's use and that it must be purified by pouring milk. A Pillai man says that he will fight the Harijan who draws water from the Caste Hindus' well. On the one hand, as mentioned above, there is a prohibition against the Harijan's use of the well. On the other hand, it is also said that there is no problem if a Harijan uses the well of the Caste Hindus while on his master's business.[5] I know of a Paraiyar boy who was hired as a servant for carrying a water pot from the Caste Hindus' well to the Kallar master's house, though the boy himself did not draw water from the well. In this case, needless to say, he touched not only the pot, but sometimes also the water itself. How can we understand this contradiction?

Example 3: The Paraiyars (the Harijans) work as agricultural labourers in the fields of the dominant castes. Why do the dominant castes not mind eating the products that the Harijans touch in the course of this production? Many Kallars support the idea that cooking changes things from the neutral state to the polluted or unpolluted state depending on who cooks them. In this sense, raw materials are open to cooking, namely, a change of pollution level. Due to this logic, the Brahman can take raw rice and vegetables from ritually lower people. However, I still wonder how it is possible to claim such logic without arbitrariness.

It is obvious that the contradictions or arbitrariness shown in these examples cannot be consistently explained by "purity-impurity" ideology, but rather strongly reflects the convenience of the dominant castes. It is, moreover, noted that there is a characteristic common to the above-mentioned examples in which the dominant castes can be free from the logic of "purity-impurity". That is, the dominant castes do not feel polluted by contact with the usually polluting Harijans in those cases where the dominant castes have the positive motivation of fulfilling their own needs or interests. In other words, such subjectively positive motivation works for suspending "purity-impurity" ideology temporarily.[6] However, it is obvious that such a temporal suspension is made possible by the social superiority of dominant castes. To know this sort of arbitrary materialization of "pure-impure" ideology based on power relations again makes us recognize the necessity of stressing a concept of ideology.

With this preliminary suggestion, the problem of inter-caste marriage, in which the hierarchical status difference is dependent on "purity-impurity" ideology, can be dealt with. As was mentioned earlier, inter-caste marriage in a formal sense is practised only very exceptionally in the village. There is no doubt that every caste strictly observes the prohibition of inter-caste marriage even today, though there are a number of inter-caste relationships which are not legally regarded as formal marriages. There is little doubt that the strict prohibition of inter-caste marriage found in the village seems to be basically derived from the so-called South Indian (Dravidian) type of marriage system, in which "various forms of exchange marriages including the patterns of cross-cousin marriage" [Milner, 1988: 149] are predominant as a response to the inferiority of wife-givers, as Milner suggests.[7] By asking theoretical questions in terms of inter-caste marriage, I do not purport to investigate the attitudes towards hypergamy or hypogamy as an institution prevailing in North India, but to explore the views on deviations from the South Indian culture tendency of isogamy, by which status homogeneity is preserved. An understanding of their notions of inter-caste marriage, which would break such status homogeneity based on the "purity-impurity" ideology, must suggest the principles of their practices.

These are the replies of several Kallar informants. Firstly, in the setting of inter-caste marriage with a caste lower than the Kallars, it is claimed that a hypergamous union (e.g., a Kallar husband – a Valaiyar wife) is associated with lighter excommunication than a hypogamous union (e.g., a Valaiyar husband – a Kallar wife). This response is not relevant for the case of inter-caste marriage with castes higher than the Kallars. For example, the hypergamous union between a Brahman husband and a Kallar wife is said to be unforgiven by and intolerable to the Kallar community. If such a marriage was forced, the Kallar woman would be expelled from the Kallar community. By contract, the hypogamy between a Kallar husband and a Brahman wife (evena Pillai wife) is rather proudly accepted by the Kallar community, far from being rejected. The explanation given by one Kallar and supported by other Kallars is this. A woman is regarded as the property of her family, of her lineage and of her caste, so that it is desirable that a woman is kept within her own community. In this sense, giving a woman to another caste means a loss of her caste property, which is thought of as dishonour for the caste. Taking a purer woman from a higher caste (a hypogamous union with the higher caste) is regarded as honourable, due to the acquisition of valuable property. This is the logic with which both a hypergamous union with a higher caste and a hypogamous union with a lower caste are disapproved of. The Pillais also have the same sort of response as the Kallars, though they do not show their feelings of pleasure openly even in case of getting a higher caste woman. Though the above-mentioned view on inter-caste marriage is completely different from the so-called North Indian type of outlook, in which hypergamy is accepted but hypogamy is rejected,[8] what should be paid more attention to is the dominant caste's interpretation of regarding a woman herself as their property.

How can I interpret the dominant castes' views mentioned above? In this connection, Kolenda's work [1984] is suggestive, in which she makes clear the contrasting images of women between the North Indian Rajput and the South Indian Nattati Nadar.[9] The contrast can be expressed symbolically as "woman as tribute" in the North, and "woman as flower" in the South. This clearly indicates that the North Indian woman is seen as a means for bridging the hierarchical relations, whereas a woman in the South tends to be given an independent value as a property possessor. This claim is, for example, made clear by a discussion of property-transfer in marriage, such as the brideprice, groomprice, and *cītaṉam* [Kolenda, 1984: 108]. In the North, the choice between a groomprice marriage and a brideprice marriage directly depends upon the hierarchical power relations between wife-taker and wife-giver; whereas in the South, the bride's side's economic contributions are free from the hierarchical differential found between the couple because *cītaṉam* is not property transferred from bride's side to groom's side, but is moved from a bride's parents to a bride.[10] Two fundamental features of the South Indian type of marriage can be seen from the above argument: (1) that its marriage pattern has an egalitarian tendency and is rather free from caste hierarchy [Dumont, 1983: 167], and (2) that a bride (woman) herself is the focal person as a property holder, namely, "as flower".

As this first feature indicates, the dominant castes in Kinnimangalam, who observe caste endogamy almost perfectly, in practice, look upon marriage as an opportunity for creating or reproducing the unity of affinal relations, rather than for seeking an increase in their status. Moreover, the above-mentioned second feature is also found in the village. The marriage payment of the Kallars and of the Pillais basically consists of *paricam* (bridewealth), *varatatṭciṇai* (groomprice), *cītaṉam* or *stiritāṉam* (property given by the bride's parents to the bride), and other occasional *cīrs* (gifts by the bride's side to the couple, especially in the first *Āṭi* month and in the first *Tai* month).[11] It is said that *cītaṉam* is usually given to a wife after she has had her first child, because having a child is regarded as evidence of the couple's stable relationship.

The above-mentioned two features help us to understand the Kallars' responses to inter-caste marriage. Since they see a woman herself as valuable property, their welcome of a higher status woman and conversely their rejection of the loss of their own women can be consistently understood by their concern with the increase or the protection of productive power in which ritual status is not literally accepted but is translated into a form of power. Whether the Kallars clearly distinguish between "status" and "power", in Dumont's sense, seems to be very doubtful because, for them, "status" is rather encapsulated by "power". In other words, a *cuttam* woman is not a means for climbing the status ladder, but is seen as being powerful property for them. Thus, this interpretation typically found among the Kallars is continuous with "pollution" ideology, for both seek to increase power by attaching importance to women's potentiality.

If the Pillais' response to inter-caste marriage is examined, it will be clear that they share the same tendency as the Kallars. However, the Pillais, who are the most Sanskritized in the village, tend to adopt the "purity-impurity" ideology more strongly than the Kallars.[12] The relative difference between the Kallars and the Pillais in their responses reflects their respective social positions. "Role theory" can be applied to the situation. Whereas the Kallars are deemed to be politico-economically powerful but are never expected to follow a ritually higher attitude, the Pillais are thought of as the more sophisticated people because of their high ritual status.[13] In order to reproduce or reinforce the Pillais' high social status, it is important for them to meet these social expectations. They behave so wittingly or unwittingly. This explains the relative difference between the Kallars' practices and the Pillais' practices, despite both sharing the popular cultural tendency stressing productivity.

Practices of the dominant castes cannot be consistently understood by simply applying a single objective standard, like the "purity-impurity" ideology. To understand their pollution concepts or practices requires properly taking into account their subjective interpretations, which reflect their social positions. Furthermore, their subjective interpretations are basically motivated by their need for seeking productivity, namely, self-aggrandizement. A subjective account sometimes leads to the situation where "purity-impurity" ideology fades behind (is suspended by) their primary value of productivity, "pollution" ideology. The dominant castes wittingly or unwittingly manipulate the "purity-impurity" ideology under their primary value of "pollution" ideology and this arbitrary manipulation aims at self-development.

Practices of the Paraiyars on Pollution

Apart from the dominant castes, the socially dominated caste, the Paraiyars, will be focused upon here as a prelude to Part Three, where the practices of the Paraiyars are dealt with in more depth.

It is clear that the village Paraiyars today wittingly negate the caste hierarchy based on the "purity-impurity" ideology (c.f. [Pfaffenberger, 1980], [Gough, 1959]), in which they have been placed in a repressed social position. In particular, the younger generation more explicitly and more radically express their feelings of hatred against this hierarchy, more so than do their elders.[14] The elders tend to agree on caste *distinction* itself, though they no longer believe in the caste *hierarchy* in a ritual sense. The Paraiyars today, young and old, think that there is no reason for them to be said to be polluting (*tīṭṭu*) and they reject the ritual hierarchy. However, since the social hierarchy doubtlessly persists even though they oppose it, they tend to recognize the hierarchy by describing it in economic terms.[15] Therefore, as shown in the examples mentioned in the previous section, the one-sided attitude of the dominant castes, especially that of the Kallars, in which the "purity-impurity" ideology is arbitrarily applied or suspended is unacceptable and intolerable for the Paraiyars.

In order to confirm their view on hierarchy, it is helpful to know the Paraiyars' outlook on inter-caste marriage. Their response is quite similar to that of the Kallars. For them, the acceptance of a woman from another caste is more tolerable than the loss of a woman from their own caste, though they also basically avoid inter-caste marriage. Their view is made clear by the fact that hypogamy with a Kallar woman is welcomed but hypergamy with a Kallar man is not acceptable.[16] According to this, the Paraiyars share the ideology of "woman as flower" as well. It is also pointed out that today's custom of marriage payments again closely resembles that of the Kallars. There are two features of their marriage payments, compared with the Kallar's. That is, (1) the usual amount of *paricam*, *varataṭṭcinḷai* and *cītaṉam* is relatively small due to their economic position and (2) the equal balance between the payments of the bride's side and the groom's side is more basically emphasized (though the bride's side pays a little more).[17] Thus, this indicates that their negation of the "purity-impurity" hierarchy not only results from their resistance to the caste hierarchy, but is also a result of their cultural tendency of attaching importance to productive power, not to the value of purity, which is basically shared with the Kallars.

Although there is no doubt that this outlook of the Paraiyars is in the mainstream today, there are two factors to be considered which make their attitudes complicated, namely, they not only simply reject the socially dominant view but, in addition, they may also sometimes accept or replicate it. The first factor is their desire for a rise of social grade, or at least for saving face socially. This desire for self-esteem in Vincentnathan's terms prevents the Paraiyars from being free from the dominant values, by which the dominant castes preserve their social status. For example, their own opinions on the habit of beef-eating or of eating dead cattle verifies this. On the one hand, denying the Caste Hindus' view that the habit causes *tīṭṭu*, most of the Paraiyars I interviewed positively claim that the habit has been part of their tradition and that meat-eating, including beef-eating, is good for the body and provides it with necessary physical energy. On the other hand, several Paraiyars, comment that though they personally do not mind eating beef, they would like to stop the habit if it were possible, in order to reduce the social dishonour caused by it, but poverty has prevented them from doing so. This comment well indicates that in their attitude, account is taken of the prevailing negative evaluation of the habit. This, therefore, suggests that they adopt the dominant castes' view not because they believe it, but because they can benefit by avoiding the act which is perceived as degrading them.

This problem cannot be exhausted by a consideration of their strategic replication under such cool calculation. Their religious loyalty also influences or supports their attitude towards the "replication" of the dominant view. This is the second factor. In this connection, their ambiguous evaluation of vegetarianism, which naturally includes the argument on beef-eating, provides a good example. Some insist on the nonsense of the distinction between vegetarian and non-vegetarian, whereas others accept the idea that the vegetarian is purer (more *cuttam*) than the non-vegetarian. This complex attitude seems to have at least two causes, namely, (1) their strategic calculation, as has been explained above in terms of beef-eating, and (2) their religious beliefs. Though there is no doubt that they never think non-vegetarian dishes makes them *acuttam*, on religious occasions they accept the idea that vegetarian dishes are useful for preparing a *cuttam* (pure) body, which is suitable for worshipping gods, as is verified in their observance of *viratan̲* (fasting) before a festival. This attitude also helps to understand their view that a world renouncer is more *cuttam* than a Brahman. Thus, as has already been explained in Chapter 5, their acceptance of the concepts of "purity" and "impurity" in the religious context (not in the social hierarchical context) seems to make their arguments on vegetarianism/non-vegetarianism complicated.[18]

In sum, since the Paraiyars today basically reject the caste hierarchical system based on the "purity-impurity" ideology, they tend to understand the actually existing social hierarchy as an economic hierarchy. It can be noted, moreover, that this rational understanding is not only derived from their defiance, but is also based on the shared "pollution" ideology, which attaches importance to increases in productivity. Nonetheless, this basic ideological tendency associated with a rational thinking is made complicated by their practical attitudes, such as (1) their strategic attitude for saving face or seeking a rise in social grade and (2) their religious attitude in depending upon the grace of the Hindu deities. Since the former attitude sometimes includes their observation of the dominant value of "purity-impurity", even for mere form's sake, they can be seen as followers of the dominant values (or look to be "a true believer" in Moffatt's expression), or they can at least not be seen as opposers criticizing it, even though they do not believe in it. The latter attitude leads to their acceptance of the "purity-impurity" concepts in the context of the man-god relationship, which ironically provides a moment for mystifying the "purity-impurity" ideology defining the man-man hierarchical relationship, or which at least weakens their power to criticize this hierarchical sense of the "purity-impurity" ideology.

Thus, the rationale for the practices of the Paraiyars can again be thought as being a subjectively strategic attitude for seeking self-aggrandizement or an increase of productivity. In this sense, it is argued that Moffatt, who simply emphasizesthe Harijans' replication of the dominant ideology, lacks this interpretative and strategic viewpoint. It seems to me that if the interpretative and strategic viewpoint is adopted, the achievements of these Harijan studies, which I reviewed in Chapter 3, would be more positively revived.

This summary provides only a preliminary perspective on the Paraiyars' practices, which has been elucidated from a limited discussion of their attitudes towards pollution concepts. What I have discussed in this section is more extensively investigated in the following chapters of Part Three.

Notes

1. As is well known, Dumont and Pocock [1959] discussed the related topic in their review article of Srinivas' work on the Coorgs [Srinivas, 1978 (1952)]. I should touch on their work here, even briefly, though it is not easy to argue the relationship between their theory and mine, because their argument is formed on a different basis. That is, the difficulty comes from their lack of adequate analysis of pollution (impurity). As I have sufficiently argued, they fail to find the depth of pollution, i.e., the distinction between "impurity" and "pollution" in my sense. My theory is constructed on the basis of this distinction, and, moreover, the concept of "pollution" is a very dynamic one which refers to the generation of positive and productive power. For example, one wonders how the binary concepts "bad-sacred" and "good-sacred", that derive from Srinivas and that Dumont and Pocock focus upon, are related to my distinction between "pollution-sacredness" and "purity-sacredness". Not only that, but also another axis of auspiciousness and inauspiciousness comes in their argument. According to Srinivas, "bad-sacred" includes impurity and inauspiciousness, while "good-sacred" includes purity and auspiciousness [ibid.: 102]. Basically I refute their static (non-interpretative and non-generative) view. I understand that auspiciousness (Skt.: *maṅgala*, Tamil: *maṅkalam*) means a positive change, like a marriage [ibid.: 93], and inauspiciousness (Skt.: *amaṅgala*, Tamil: *amaṅkalam*) implies a negative change, like a funeral. Both commonly indicate a change, that is, a happening which is regarded as a source of creation. This point of view leads to the following understanding that a funeral rite plays a role of transforming a negative change to a positive change. That is, a funeral cannot be seen simply as a "bad-sacred" ritual but is deemed as a dynamic process of transforming "bad-sacred" to "good-sacred". My interpretative concepts "pollution" and "pollution-sacredness" which are associated with an affirmative attitude towards pollution describe this dynamic and positive transformation itself. Therefore, "bad-sacred" is quite different from "pollution-sacredness" in my sense. However, I think that "good-sacred" comes much closer to my concept "purity-sacredness", though, precisely speaking, one should still remember that there is a decisive difference between them, for "purity-sacredness" must be understood in the interpretative dimension. This is the reason that I do not adopt their static binary concepts "bad-sacred" and "good-sacred" and use my own concepts. As I argued at the end of Chapter 5, I agree with Dumont and Pocock's understanding of purity in the cosmic order (purity as the *means* of contact with the sacred) [Dumont and Pocock, 1959b: 31] and, if this

understanding of purity is connected with my concept "pollution", there will be no contradiction that "mourners offering food to the departed must do so after a bath" [ibid.: 27].

2. Burghart claims here that the institution of renunciation should be interpreted from the ascetic's viewpoint in order to overcome the partiality of an understanding from the Brahman's standpoint [Burghart, 1983]. I am influenced by his emphasis on the significance of the subjective interpretation of each social category.
3. A Paraiyar youth consciously points out contradictions found in the Kallars' behaviour. Another example is that, according to him, there are several Kallars who, after drinking spirits, come to Paraiyar houses and eat beef curry there.
4. A Kallar man says, "We can drink water drawn from the Harijan's well if we do not use their vessels."
5. It is claimed that the Kallar people often hire Harijan labourers for digging their well, but they insist that the well water is never polluted by these Harijans.
6. I can provide another example to show that a positive motivation of a higher caste person suspends "purity-impurity" ideology. A Paraiyar, MK, who acquired the skill of massage during his army career, is in high demand for his services from the higher caste people, such as the Kallars and the Acaris. I actually observed him touching a higher caste person's body while giving a massage. The latter, who wanted to improve his well-being, did not mind this touching.
7. Milner [1988] provides a good perspective on the South Asian marriage system in general. He shows the two polar responses to the inferiority of wife-givers as a pan-Indian phenomenon, that is, institutionalized hypergamy in the North and exchange marriage in the South, by taking into account the ideology of *kanyadan*. As cited by Milner, Parry [1979] elucidates a typical North Indian type in which intra-caste relations and inter-caste relations work together, whereas Trautmann [1981] contributes to clarifying the characteristic of the South Indian type. Milner's argument is clear and interesting, but I rather doubt his premise that the ideology of *kanyadan* penetrates throughout India when I follow Kolenda's insight which distinguishes "woman as flower" in the South from "woman as tribute" in the North [Kolenda, 1984].
8. Milner explains logically that hypogamy is eliminated by "the patriarchal components of *kanyadan*, and Hindu society in general" [Milner, 1988: 150].
9. As Miller points out in her extensive exploration of marriage payments in India, not only differences between the upper and the lower social class, but also north/south differences should be taken into account [Miller, 1980: 103]. Miller's Tables 2 and 3 [Miller, 1980: 106–111] indicate that it is necessary to carefully deal with variety due to regional and class differences.
10. In South India, the custom of *cītaṉam* or *stiritāṉam*, which is given to a bride by her parents, is important.
11. In the bride's side's house, an engagement ceremony is held. Both parties, who are represented by *tāymāmaṉs*, discuss the marriage payment. Firstly, the amount of *varataṭciṇai* (literally, offering to bridegroom) is stated by the bride's *tāymāmaṉ*, in front of both parties. Then, *paricam* as bridewealth, is given to the bride's *tāymāmaṉ* (*paricam pōṭutal* in the case of the Kallars, *niccaya tāmpūlam* in the case of the Pillais), and half of the *paricam* is returned to the groom's side a little later. *varataṭciṇai* is equated with dowry in the sense of groomprice, which is clearly different from *cītaṉam* as bride's property. According to Kolenda, *cītaṉam* recently tends to have been replaced by groomprice (*varataṭciṇai*) [Kolenda, 1984: 108]. *The point is that cītaṉam* is a bride's own property. The distinction

between *cītaṉam* and groomprice is doubtlessly crucial, as Kolenda righly points out, but Tambiah and Dumont fail to recognize this [Tambiah, 1973] [Dumont, 1957b] [Miller, 1980: 103].

12. For example, the Pillais have a type of marriage called *kaṉṉika tānam* (literally, virgin gift) in which the bride's side bears all expenses for the marriage. It seems that, though *kaṉṉika tānam* takes place within the same caste, it embodies the ideology of *kanyadan* which attaches importance to the ritual hierarchy. Compared with this, the Kallars tend to regard such a marriage as shameful for the bridegroom's side because it publicly shows the powerlessness of the groom's family. Therefore both the Kallars and the Pillais basically share the same ideological basis of pronouncing power but the Pillais are relatively more Sanskritized than the Kallars.
13. Most villagers comment that the Pillais are good people because they are said to behave gently. This reputation of the Pillais rather contrasts with that of the Kallars. The Pillais are encouraged not to behave roughly, like the Kallars do, by other villagers' conventional view of them. Therefore, for instance, the crude ill-treatment of the Paraiyars, as shown in Example 1, will not much harm the Kallers' reputation but will definitely degrade the Pillais' dignity, if they did so.
14. For example, Muttaiya, a young Paraiyar told me, "The unnecessary caste system is dying actually and I think what we need is only two castes (*jātis*), namely, man and woman". Tottikkaruppan, one of the influential elders of the Paraiyar community, explained to me about the caste difference as follows: "*Jāti* is like a different kind of tree. A mango tree and a banana tree are of course different, so that they cannot be mixed with each other. Like this, people belonging to different castes cannot marry each other."
15. When I asked an old Paraiyar man, over 60 years old, about the hierarchical relationship between the Paraiyars and the Potaravannars, he explained, "We do not think they (the Potaravannars) are more impure (*acuttam*) than us, but they are socially lower than us because they depend upon us economically. This is exactly the same as our situation of depending on the Kallars for making a living."
16. The hypogamous union with a higher status woman is very positively accepted by them. There is an actual marriage between a Paraiyar husband and an Acari wife in the village and the couple is happily accepted by the Paraiyar community.
17. Miller's Table 3 [Miller, 1980: 111] shows only bridewealth of the lower class (unpropertied people) by citing from [Moffatt, 1979] and [Gough, 1956]. However, Thurston's report on the Tangalan Paraiyars [Thurston et al. 1987 Vol. 5: 100] and my data are different from Millar's. The point is that the Paraiyar have not only bridewealth (*paricam*) but also the custom of dowry (*cītaṉam* even if this custom is little followed due to poverty. It is said that the amount of dowry should exceed the value of bridewealth.
18. Their main concern in being *cuttam* lies in their religious aim of enjoying god's grace, not in the rise of their ritual status. In other words, they do not believe in the ritual hierarchy but believe in Hindu gods. In this respect, it is also suggestive that none are followers of the DK movement (the Dravidian nationalistic movement, which stands for the negation of belief in Aryan gods as the root of all evil).

Chapter 8

Pollution Concepts Manipulated II

Women as an Arena of Ideological Struggles

The statement that Hindu women combine within their being the two opposing poles of a positive (or bright) aspect and a negative (or dark) aspect would seem to have become almost a *cliché* when discussing Hindu society. The present chapter attempts to shed fresh light on this seemingly clear-cut yet static and essentialist proposition and to both criticize it by throwing the one-sidedness of its definition into relief and to present a more valid theoretical framework for understanding Hindu women. This clarifies the mechanism of gendered space of Hindu societies, in which woman's body plays an indispensable role, being focused upon as an arena of ideological struggles over pollution concepts. I will begin by describing pollution and purification in everyday life and then focus in particular on the coming-of-age ceremony for girls performed in the village. Then, following an examination of the Tamil view of women, I hope to extend the scope of the discussion to embrace the wider context of Hindu women in general. My objective is not only to criticize the current situation, in which an interpretation based on "pure-impure" ideology has come to be understood in substantialist terms and has won social acceptance, but also to demonstrate that consideration of an interpretation from the perspective of "pollution" ideology is indispensable for accurately describing the realities of Tamil women, and those of Hindu women in general.

Pollution and Purification

Pollution and Purification in Daily Life

For a time every morning the area around the pump house by the well in the fields on the south side of the village becomes alive with villagers bathing. This is a typical scene in a Tamil village in a corner of south India. Water gushes forth from the pump of the well used for irrigation, providing a bathing site popular with the villagers. When they rise in the morning, the villagers first go to the edge of the reservoir to answer the call of nature and then bathe themselves. These morning ablutions are not merely for the sake of personal cleanliness, but also represent an act of purification to remove the pollution caused by sleep. After having bathed, the villagers return to their homes, offer up prayers, and apply holy ashes to their forehead and arms. A refreshing start is thus made to the day.

The villagers usually bathe in one of two ways. In rivers or ponds they will repeatedly immerse themselves completely in the water, or else, when using water drawn from a well, they will pour bucket after bucket of water over themselves. I have seen a young villager pouring close to fifty buckets of water over himself in this manner. After seeing this, and also doing it myself, I realized that the aim of bathing is not simply to remove the soil from one's body, and I discovered just how enjoyable and also how necessary for the preservation of health it is to remove the heat from one's body in this way in a tropical region such as south India. In particular, bathing after having rubbed oneself down with sesame oil has a great cooling effect and is most invigorating.

The woman who always prepares my meals when I stay in the village, a member of the Vellalar caste, invariably bathes in a corner of the kitchen after returning from town and then changes her sari. She says that she does this because going out, especially into town, makes her dirty *(acuttam)*.

Nowadays it is not only members of the higher castes that are assiduous in purifying themselves, and I heard the following observations from an elderly man belonging to the Paraiyars.

> When I was young (until shortly after independence), I would be totally exhausted after a day's work, and because it was bothersome bathing at night and also sometimes cold, I would often go to sleep as I was. We Harijans were thus really dirty, and I thought that it was only natural that the gods would be angry if we entered the temples. But as a result of the reforms under the Indian National Congress Party the awareness of the Harijans, including myself, rapidly changed, and now we all bathe frequently and keep the area around our houses clean too.

By thus calling to mind just one or two scenes from everyday village life, it becomes evident that apparently casual acts of purification are not meant simply to remove physical dirt, but are also vested with a ritual significance, namely, that of removing pollution felt mentally (really speaking, feeling of pollution on body and in mind may be inseparable). In addition, the remarks made by the Paraiyar hint at the popularization of the act of purification brought about by the winds of modernization after the independence. In other words, it could be pointed out that modernization, which brings about popularization of the upper class culture, has spread the enthusiasm for purification amongst greater numbers of people and is actually promoting Sanskritization.

The Mechanisms of Pollution and Purification

At this stage it will probably be helpful to touch briefly on the mechanisms of pollution and purification in Brahman culture, which continues to exert influence not because of any historical continuity but as a reference point for the villagers' actions in the context of today's new Sanskritization. Let us first consider what the *Manusmṛti* (Laws of *Manu*), of which Brahmans have always been mindful, has to say about pollution and purification.

According to N. Watase, because of the identification of pollution and sin and because these are regarded as substantive entities, "purification is nothing other than the removal of the entities of pollution and sin" [Watase, 1990: 153]. Here we have a succinct expression of the value world of Brahmans, in which purification and the expiation of sin are regarded as one. Watase also points out on the basis of terms relating to purification that purification signified "the 'removal,' 'cleansing,' 'destruction' or 'burning' of, or 'emancipation' from, pollution and sin, which adhere to one's person as physical entities". [ibid.: 167–168], while typical means of purification included "fire, earth, water, cow dung, sacred grass *(kuśa),* sesame, clarified butter, gifts, wind, sun, sacred phrases, words spoken by a Brahman, austerities, religious ceremonies, time, knowledge, true words, meditation, breath control, punishment by a king, renunciation of worldly pursuits, etc." [ibid.: 168].

This being so, what then are the actual mechanisms governing pollution and purification in Tamil villages today? The villagers also seem to believe that sin and misdeeds give rise to pollution, but the karma theory or the theory of transmigration, involving the atonement of sins through rebirth, are by no means obvious to them. As far as I have been able to ascertain through my own enquiries, there seems to be a strong tendency to believe that retribution for one's pollution and sin will occur during the lifetime in which they were committed.

Be that as it may, the generation of pollution requires an appropriate response, namely, purification. If we now consider firstly some of the terms corresponding to "purification," it is found that dynamic expressions conforming to different situations, rather than vocabulary items removed from context, function as actually living words. Therefore, a grasp of verbal expressions and accompanying actions in accordance with their context can conversely provide clues for an understanding of the actual content of purification. For example, giving a newborn baby its first bath is referred to as *tīṭṭu kaḻuvutal* ("washing away pollution"), while the term *muḻukutal* ("washing down the whole body") is used when referring to the ablutions of a woman who has just given birth, and there is also the expression *mañcaḷnīrāṭṭuviḻā* ("ritual for bathing with turmeric water"), used as the name of the coming-of-age ceremony for girls that takes place with the onset of menstruation. In general, expressions and actions indicative of washing away with water are those that are the most common. One other commonly performed action is that of using milk to remove pollution. For instance, after a cremation the site is "cooled" by "pouring milk" *(pāl ūṟṟutal)* over it, thereby restoring the earth's fertility. Methods of purification by smearing cow dung and drinking or sprinkling cow's urine also fall into the same category. These are all methods of purification that rely on the five products *(pañcakaviyam)* of the sacred cow *(kōmātā).* A cow is so pure that even its dung and urine are capable of purifying human beings. Other methods of purification include shaving one's hair, eating food that is regarded as "cold," and using objects that are *paccai* ("raw, fresh, cold") as ritual implements.

The most involved method of purification is the purificatory rite to which a Brahman is invited. For example, in the case of the Vellalar caste, the highest caste in the village, a purificatory rite called *puṇṇiyatāṉam* (lit. "sacred gift for accumulating merit") is performed on the thirteenth or fourteenth day after birth in order to remove the pollution of birth, and on this occasion not only sacred gifts but also the power of the *mantras* chanted by the Brahman play an important role. But it should be pointed out that ritual acts associated with a high degree of abstract thinking such as this particular rite are generally confined to certain ritually high-ranking castes, and in the non-Brahman village where I stayed they were quite irrelevant to the majority of villagers.

When viewed in this light, it becomes apparent that pollution is perceived as a "hot" state *(cūṭu),* and therefore various means must be devised to "cool" *(kuḷir)* it [e.g., Beck 1969]. Pollution, a "hot" state, is a state of disorder in which things are in flux and mix with one another [Daniel, 1984: 188]. The act of cooling serves to reinstate the mixing and confusion in a new order and to stabilize them. This principle underlies all methods of purification, ranging from the exoteric method of pouring water over oneself, which can be performed by anyone, to the esoteric method of chanting mantras, which has been monopolized by Brahmans. One other point that should not be overlooked when considering purification is the fact that the very lapse of time expunges pollution. A certain period of time is necessary for the subsiding of confusion, just as something that is hot will cool down only slowly, and the length of time will depend upon the caste and the event in question [for details see Ferro-Luzzi 1974]. Thus, on a phenomenal level, purification may be understood first of all as the act of bringing order (or equilibrium) to pollution, representing a "hot" state of disorder, by various means, including the lapse of time.

"Purification for Elimination" and "Purification for Creation"

Next let us consider whether or not this understanding of purification to be observed in the villages is identical to the aforementioned Brahmanical conception of purification as the removal of the substantive entities of pollution and sin. This will be discussed in concrete terms in the following section on the pollution and purification associated with menarche, but here I wish to anticipate my conclusions in general terms.

In the case of the Brahmanical view, pollution is regarded as something that is substantive and primarily negative (or evil), and therefore, because of a need to remove it, adherents of this view tend towards "purification for elimination". It is, however, extremely doubtful whether this Brahmanical perspective can fully explain the realities of purification carried out in the villages. These doubts become even stronger when observing rites of passage, which are closely related to the generation of pollution. It must, in other words, be realized that although on one level pollution is indeed treated as a "thing", essentially it originates in events or "incidents" such as birth and death, as argued in Chapter 5. One is thus led to examine the content of the purification that follows from pollution representing an "incident" irreducible to a "thing". To wit, understanding pollution as an "incident" signifies a switch to a generative perspective liberated from any substantialist view, and because pollution is understood from this perspective as the locus of the manifestation of productive forces, it involves the dynamism of death and the regeneration of life, that is, a process that might be called "purification for creation".

I have been advocating the differentiation of two ways of interpreting the content of what is expressed as pollution and the validity of making this distinction. Defining the essence of pollution as "the experience of the destruction of order, which causes a sense of fear of death (or being drawn into a world of continuity)," I have shown that there are two ways of interpreting or responding to this experience. That is, I designate as "pollution" that which ensues from an affirmative and receptive attitude born of abiding within the marginal state of pollution, and this I distinguish from the negative manifestation of pollution, which I call "impurity", that results from standing outside the marginal state of pollution and looking down on it from the centre of the established order. It could also be said that the former regards pollution as an "incident" and has a generative and dynamic perspective that looks outwards from within pollution, while the latter represents a standpoint that treats pollution as a "thing" and considers it in fixed terms from without.

These two ways of interpreting pollution lead of themselves to two forms of purification, namely, "purification for creation" and "purification for elimination". In the case of "purification for elimination," which is predicated on the existence of an external authoritarian viewpoint, pollution is merely pushed away to the fringes of established power or under the carpet, as it were, and this results in no more than a state of constant fear and apprehension. In this respect, L. Dumont's theory of purity and impurity [Dumont, 1980 (1966)], which conceals this type of authoritarian viewpoint, is able to deal only with "purification for elimination", and it affords no scope for discussing "purification for creation". There is a need to aim at greater precision in such debate by disentangling the confusion in discussions based on essentialist substantialism taking the form of relationism, as in Dumontian theory, and setting the situation to rights from the standpoint of a more thoroughgoing hermeneutics by remaining constantly aware of the positions of those who speak of pollution.[1] "Purification for creation" extracts "pollution" or the positive interpretation of pollution—that is, its latent power and fertility—in such a way that it may be utilized on a social level, while "purification for elimination" adopts the path of coercive purification by suppressing the aspect of "impurity" inherent in the ambiguous chaos of pollution and preserving its aspect of "purity".

On the basis of the above observations, the points at issue may now be summarized in the following manner. For a correct understanding of the content of acts of purification accommodating the rich ambiguity of pollution, a simple centralized understanding that merely removes the "impure" and, if necessary, arbitrarily transforms it into the "pure" is inadequate, and consideration of the interpretative vector of what I call "pollution", with its orientation towards decentralization, is indispensable. It is this point that I wish to make clear here. This is because I fear that, with an above-mentioned centralized understanding that retains the stratified dichotomy between "purity" and "impurity", one may misconstrue the villagers' true motives.

I now wish to consider this question in more concrete terms by taking up as an example the coming-of-age ceremony for girls that accompanies the onset of menstruation. This celebration of menarche in the form of the coming-of-age ceremony is highly distinctive of south India, for in north India not only is little importance attached to menarche, but it tends to be concealed [Wadley, 1980: 163]. Moreover, insofar that the rites surrounding menarche are directly related to views of women, kinship and marital relations, they are also worth taking up in that they represent an important node in the cultural structure of south India [e.g., Beck, 1974; Reiniche, 1981].

Pollution and Fertility among Tamil Women

The Tamil Coming-of-Age Ceremony for Girls

The purpose of the coming-of-age ceremony for girls is to make socially explicit on the occasion of a natural occurrence in the form of menarche the change from a girl, hitherto referred to as a child *(ciṉṉapiḷḷai),* to an unmarried woman or virgin *(kaṉṉi).* This coming-of-age ceremony is generally called *caṭaṅku,* but as is suggested by its alternative name *mañcaḷnīrāṭṭuviḻā* noted earlier, the ritual as a whole may be viewed as a process of purification for overcoming the pollution associated with menarche. It could also be described as a process for culturally interpreting and incorporating within society the inescapable natural changes entailed in menarche. The way in which it is incorporated into society constitutes the actual content of its purification. First I wish to sketch the main elements in the process leading from menarche to the coming-of-age ceremony with reference to the Vellalar caste, which evidences the most highly evolved ritual process in the non-Brahman village where I conducted my fieldwork.

1. The Tamil term for "menarche" is *kaṉṉippūppu,* but it is worth noting that *pūppu* not only means "menstruation", but also has the connotation of "flowering" [Kolenda, 1984: 114]. First of all the relatives are informed, with priority being given firstly to the mother's brothers *(tāymāmaṉ)* and their wives *(attai)* and secondly to the father's sisters *(attai).* That is, these closely related cross-kin play an indispensable role in the ceremony. This is closely linked to the practice of cross-cousin marriage [Reynolds, 1980]. Other village women are also invited. This is called "village message". *(ūr colli).* It is customary for those who have been invited to the ceremony to bring bananas, flowers and milk. The ritual begins with an odd number of five or seven women, starting with the wives of the mother's brothers and followed by the father's sisters, sprinkling holy water containing turmeric *(mañcal)* and flowers over the girl, who sits facing a direction that is auspicious for her on that day. This is looked upon as "ordinary" bathing. Next, the girl changes into a new sari given to her by her mother's brothers and sits facing east in an open area such as a courtyard. Then, after a tray bearing bananas, flowers, milk, rouge *(kuṅkuman),* and sandalwood powder *(cantaṉam)* brought by the mother's brothers has been placed in front of the girl, an odd number of women, again starting with the wives of the mother's brothers, apply rouge to the girl's forehead and sandalwood powder to her cheeks and hands. This is called *nalaṅku,* which also refers to a rite during the marriage ceremony in which the bride and groom apply rouge and sandalwood powder to one another, and one may thus read into this action a metaphor of marriage. Next, the waving of lamps, or *āratti,* is performed in order to exorcise the girl of, and also protect her from, the malevolent influence of the evil eye *(tiruṣṭi kaḻikkiratu).* This also starts from the mother's brothers' wives. Slaked lime, turmeric, and betel leaves and areca nuts *(veṟṟilai-pākku)* are placed on a tray, and the girl is exorcised of evil by means of the tray bearing a camphor lamp (but no money). Because the objects on the tray are believed to have absorbed the evil, they are discarded on the road outside the house. In this fashion the vulnerable girl is placed in a liminal state in which she is protected from the evil eye and other malevolent influences, and, as was hinted at by the metaphor of marriage, preparations are made to direct her towards auspiciousness and prosperity. (This represents the prelude to sacred symbolic conception.) The girl could indeed be identified with the initiate *(dīkṣita)* in the initiatory rite of return to the womb (*dīkṣā*) [Eliade, 1965: 104–108]. Following the performance of *ārratti*, the girl is given bananas and milk, and the remaining milk is

boiled and consumed by the other participants. It is considered meet to give the girl gruel *(kūḻ)* made from the powder of black grams, this being regarded as "cold" food.

2. The girl is kept in seclusion in a room inside her home until the coming-of- age ceremony *(caṭaṅku),* which is performed on the sixteenth day. Usually a room in the southwest *(kaṉṉimūlai)* part of the house is used for this period of segregation. During her segregation, the girl's mother delivers her meals in such a way that the mother does not touch her daughter's eating utensils. "Hot" dishes are avoided, and the girl bathes daily with water brought to her room. During this time she wears worn-out saris, and the washerman's wife comes regularly to collect her soiled garments. When explaining the reasons for her segregation, the Vellalars themselves state that she is segregated because she is in a state of menarcheal pollution *(kaṉṉittīṭṭu),* but at the same time they also say that it is an "auspicious event" *(maṅkaḷamāṉa kāriyam).* These statements merit attention in that they explain the seemingly negative phenomenon of segregation from a perspective that would comprehend the pollution associated with menarche in a positive light. It is true that this explanation gives clear expression to the villagers' perception of menarche as being both an auspicious *(maṅkaḷa)* and a polluted *(tīṭṭu)* event, but if anthropologists then simply classify menarche as a point of intersection of the two axes of auspiciousness and pollution, they have done no more than superficially rehash the villagers' words without having grasped the essence of the matter.[2] As will be discussed below, the question of how to interpret the southwest quarter where the girl is segregated and the villagers' above explanation must be considered in greater depth.

3. On the sixteenth day, when the period of menstrual pollution is over, the house is cleaned and purified (with the floor and walls being recoated with cow dung or lime), and then the coming-of-age ceremony is performed. Letters of invitation to the ceremony already sent out, although personal visits are made to the mother's brothers and the letters of invitation are delivered directly together with bananas, betel leaves, areca nuts, and one-rupee coins. On the day of the ceremony, the mother's brothers bring with them numerous gifts, including silk saris, rice, eggs, crystallized sugar, sweetmeats, fruit, betel leaves, areca nuts, and makeup implements. The Brahman priest sits facing north, while the girl sits facing east. In front of them are placed three water vessels *(karakam)* full of turmeric water and a small water pot symbolizing the gods, ritual utensils, the saris and other gifts. After the priest has chanted mantras to sacralize them, the girl is taken to the bathing site and purified by her mother's brothers' wives with holy water from the water vessels. (It has also been reported that the priest besprinkles the girl with holy water [Good, 1978: 284, 290]. This represents a type of consecration *(apiṣēkam),* and it should be interpreted not just as an act of purification, but also as a form of sacralization.

4. The girl changes into a silk sari and returns dressed up like a bride to where everyone else is waiting. Then wicks are stood in sweets called *piṭṭu* and in sweetmeats such as the pudding-like *kaḷi* and thin bread *(aṭai)* made from the powder of raw rice *(paccai arici),* and the act of *āratti* is performed by waving trays bearing these sweetmeats with their wicks lit to and fro in front of the girl. The tray of *piṭṭu* is first brought down in front of the girl, from her head down to her knees, and then it is similarly brought down parallel to her back. This is performed by the mother's

brothers' wives and the father's sisters. The same actions are then performed using the tray of *kaḷi.* In this manner the girl is gradually purified, and the tray of *aṭai* is rotated three times near her head expressly in order to ward off the evil eye, after which the *aṭai* is discarded in the four quarters. The Brahman priest first sacralizes the girl with fire that has been offered to Gaṇeśa and then gives the holy ashes to the girl and other participants. The women, starting with the mother's brothers' wives, apply a mixture of sandalwood powder, rouge and flowers to the girl's forehead, this being the second time that the ritual act of *nalaṅku* is performed. When this has been completed, the mother's brothers rub holy ashes on the girl's forehead, and the girl then pledges respect and obedience to her parents, her mother's brothers, and others.

5. Lastly gifts of money and other valuables which are called *moy* are presented to the girl, and then a banquet *(viḻuntucāppāṭu)* is held. On either the following day or three days after the coming-of-age ceremony, *piṭṭu* and *aṭai* are prepared and distributed among the relatives, who are again notified that the girl has indeed come of age.

Interpreting the Coming-of-Age Ceremony: "Pollution" and "Purification for Creation"

As is indicated by the numbers used in the foregoing section, the above ritual process surrounding menarche has, roughly speaking, five phases: (1) "ordinary" bathing prior to segregation, *nalaṅku,* and *āratti*; (2) segregation due to the pollution associated with menarche; (3) ritual bathing after segregation; (4) *āratti* and *nalaṅku* of the finely dressed maiden; and (5) presentation of gifts and banquet. If we compare this with, for example, my own observations of a menarcheal ritual among the Jaffna Tamils of Sri Lanka [Sekine 1983: 101–103] and Good's report from *Tirunēlveri* in southern Tamilnadu [Good, 1978, 1991], the basic structure of the ritual is identical in all cases. However, one point deserving special mention is to be found in the instance described by Good, for it clearly incorporates a mock marriage in phase (4) in which the role of groom is often played by a matrilateral cross-cousin (viz. a daughter of one of the mother's brothers) [for details see Good, 1991: Chapter 7]. In the ritual that I have described above, it is also quite possible to regard the ritual act of *nalaṅku,* which is performed twice (in phases (1) and (4)), as a metaphor of marriage. At any rate, through the consecration ritual of phase (3) and this phase (4) the pollution associated with menarche is transformed into a sacred fertility and firmly incorporated into the culture that the girl belongs to. In other words, after having absorbed her wild, untamed power, culture moulds her into a fertile woman. As is noted by Good, these ritual actions are not simply expressions of culture, but have a "performative" content whereby a woman conforming to a particular cultural pattern is created through the performance of these actions. The girl is not merely imitating her cultural rules; instead, Tamil culture is being generated through the performance of a ritual in the form of the girl's coming-of-age ceremony.

But here we are concerned with the question of what exactly the cultural patterns generated and moulded in this fashion actually are. In this respect, when compared with Good, who has produced analytical interpretative diagrams of the ritual sequence in which he unthinkingly uses the objective concepts of purity and impurity [see Good, 1991: 195, 209], the observations of S. Wadley, who espouses a cultural approach and attaches special importance to women's own powers of self-control (regarding the celebration of menarche in Tamil society as a ritual the objective of which is to control the ambiguous energy that manifests as the "heat" of a woman's body and to convert it both internally and externally into a power of abundant beneficence [Wadley, 1980]), would seem to come closer to the ideas of the Tamils themselves, notwithstanding certain shortcomings.[3]

Bearing these facts in mind when interpreting the above coming-of-age ceremony, I would now like to focus on the girl's segregation in the southwest room. Those segregated in this room are not restricted to girls experiencing menarche, for pregnant women about to give birth and the bodies of the dead are also transferred here. This room may be described as a marginal place within the residential sphere that borders on the otherworld. The deity presiding over the southwest is the goddess Kaṉṉi, a virgin goddess who died unmarried.[4] As is suggested by the fact that the southwest is associated not only with this virgin goddess, but also with the god of chastity, Gaṇeśa, the southwest may therefore be looked upon as a direction replete with powerful sexual potentiality [Daniel, 1984: 126]. Thus the southwest, also said to be linked to the earth, becomes a uterine direction which, similar to the return to "the forest (or the wildness)", incorporates within it as a single process the ambiguity of death and birth or destruction and creation [see Reiniche, 1975]. The creative power of the southwest, comparable to the forest, can be confirmed in the importance attached to the southwest and northeast in architectural rites and in their interchangeability [Sekine, 1993b]. It is found, namely, that the southwest can be substituted for the northeast (Īsāna), which is associated with both fertility and good fortune [see also Moore, 1989].

What we must clearly realize through these observations on the southwest is the fact that the dynamism of destruction and creation (representing a single process rather than a dichotomy) embodied in the uterine direction of Kaṉṉi is indicative of the essence of "pollution", which abides on the borderline between untamed nature and tamed culture, and that it is here that the generation of the extraordinary power of *śakti* becomes possible. We should note that the essence of this "pollution" corresponds to the ambiguity found at the boundary point between in and out of a culture (i.e., at the edge of a cultural system), and under no circumstances is it the ambiguity being reduced to an negative sense of anomaly (= the "impure") located within the cultural system that consists of the "pure-impure" ideology. The usage of the word pollution when it is said that the segregation of the girl is due to the pollution associated with menarche must not be confused with "impurity". It is not appropriate to reduce this pollution only to the "impurity" that has been interpreted within the authoritarian cultural order of "pure-impure ideology" as having primarily negative connotations. When this point is clearly understood, then the real intent of the villagers in identifying menarche with both pollution and auspiciousness becomes clearer. In a word, this embodies the villagers' wish to allow this untamed power, once its existence has been basically recognized, to circulate within society in a productive and stable manner. Śakti, which has its origins in the chaos corresponding to the marginal point where culture encounters nature, is the fountainhead of the villagers' lives, and they embrace it in such a way so as not to damage them and then transform it into a productive and reproductive power in their daily life. The girl's segregation (being a metaphor of death and the regeneration of life) corresponds to the generation of this power in a uterus, while the aim of the *āratti* and *nalaṅku* (a metaphor of marriage) following her ablutions is to ensure the stabilization of this generated power. Stated in more figurative terms, it constitutes a single process of "purification for creation" in which first the power of the red "hot" blood is accepted in positive terms and then a white "cold" enclosure is installed in order to stabilize it as an auspicious force [cf. Beck, 1969: 553]. This differs from the methods of "purification for elimination", in which red, having been ascribed a negative value, is then decolorized and eliminated so as to leave only white, marked by tranquillity. The character of "purification for creation", interpreted with a view to accepting this power in its entirety, points to the existence of a cultural pattern (or ideological dimension) differing from "pure-impure" ideology, namely, the dimension which I have termed "pollution" ideology. This is fundamentally the same as the villagers' affirmative view of menstruation (—"the menstrual flow cleanses a woman's body") and their assertion of the need to make blood sacrifices to the village gods (—"blood sacrifices purify both the temple and the worshippers"). It could also be argued that this ideological dimension is linked to the south Indian view of women, which discovers within the being of women themselves a fertility value, expressed by P. Kolenda, who compares views of women in north and south India, as "woman as 'flower' " [Kolenda, 1984].

However, it is not necessarily correct to maintain that the ideological dimension represented by the concepts of "pollution" and "purification for creation" is peculiar to south Indian culture, nor is it my intention to make any such assertion. Rather, it should be considered that Tamil society, being doubtlessly situated within Hindu society, is a place where ideological expression of "pollution" on menarche is more visible, compared to the case in north India. Women is regarded as *śakti* (the source of power) in north India too, and expression like "woman as 'tribute' [Kolenda, 1984] are very often used. Irrespective of overt or covert approaches to the pollution of menarche, there is no fundamental difference between the north India and the south India in the view that women's reproduction power is invaluable sources for maintaining their society. In so far as this "social fact" exists, it is not a baseless assertion that the "pollution" ideology penetrates into the Indian society as an underlying ideology, even in the social space dominated by the "pure-impure" ideology. The assertion is enough supported by the ethnographic descriptions on pollution conceptions associated with birth and death not only in south India but also in north India, as shown in the next section. Here an important question arises. What is the difference between pollution associated with menarche and pollution associated with birth and death? The answer is clear. The former is associated with women only. This suggests that north Indian societies, in which ritual responses to menarche are covert and oppressed, tend to more elaborately manipulate womanhood in producing the societal order. This point is further discussed in the next section.

At any rate, using as a theoretical framework of the existence of the two ideologies belonging to two different dimensions that I have educed mainly on the basis of observations in Tamil society—namely, "purity-impurity" ideology, which looks down on the marginal state of pollution from without, and "pollution" ideology, which seeks to abide within this marginal state—I now wish to set about correcting the biases inherent in ideas concerning "the ambiguous character of Hindu women", which have won wide but ill-considered currency. This I shall do by reviewing the relevant literature. Consequently, in the following section the scope of the discussion will be extended from Tamil society to Hindu society in general.

Rethinking "the Ambiguous Character of Hindu Women"

It seems to be one of several remarkable phenomena in Hindu culture that women possess a split character combining the negative with the positive. In this context, menstrual blood, which clearly distinguishes a woman from a man, becomes a focus of the symbolism of women. That is to say, menstruation itself is considered to have a dichotomous character, with elements of the destructive and the creative. More correctly speaking, menstruation, which is connected with a woman's reproductive power, represents the mediating character of women that converts the polluting to the prosperous. For example J. Krygier notes that "[i]n India there is the remarkable notion of embryo murder" [Krygier, 1982: 77]. This notion includes the view that menstrual blood is associated with conception and a child is formed from menstrual blood, so that a woman's menstruation must be rendered fruitful [ibid.: 77]. This type of Hindu ideology (or cultural interpretation) evidently shows the preeminence of "a metaphor of birth" [e.g., Nicholas, 1981: 378; Hershman, 1977: 287]. In any case, it is my task here to clarify how I understand these phenomena.

The Limitations of an Understanding Based on "Pure-Impure" Ideology

The ambiguous character of Hindu women is commonly expressed stereotypically in various social contexts. Expressed simply, Hindu women possess aspects of both "purity" and "danger," or "compassion" and "sexuality (passion)" [Tapper, 1979: 1]. M. Allen clearly exemplifies the dual character of Hindu women by means of pairs of terms such as pure/impure, sinister/benign, creative/destructive, ally/opponent, and goddess/witch [Allen, 1982: 1]. More precisely, according to P. Hershman, "[v]irginity and motherhood are both highly esteemed states in Punjabi society but wifehood and sexuality are those aspects which devalue a woman and make her the inferior of a man" [Hershman, 1977: 275].

These descriptions of Hindu women are not incorrect, but their cultural analysis, the standpoint of which is static and top-down, still remains vague and confused. The vagueness of the analysis is due to the lack of a clear understanding that pollution has two different interpretations or dimensions, namely, "impurity" and "pollution", depending upon whether one's standpoint is centralized (top-down) or decentralized (bottom-up). In this connection Allen's conclusion is suggestive, although it juxtaposes several views of women and does not show the dynamic relationship obtaining among them. According to Allen, "the orthodox renouncer *avoids* them *(viz.* women) as dangerous distractions; the seeker after high social status *controls* them in order to maintain his status through their purity;... the low status worker *values* them as providers of material satisfaction...; while the Tantric *uses* them as a necessary means of attaining spiritual liberation" [Allen, 1982: 18]. This statement of Allen's naturally invites the application of my distinction between "impurity" and "pollution" to the present context. We notice that Allen's four categories can be broadly classified into two major ideological tendencies, with the former two being separated from the latter two. The distinctive feature that divides these two groups is the difference of attitude towards female sexuality. The former group tends to negate or segregate it, while the latter enjoys or accepts it. This contrast clearly corresponds to the distinction between "impurity" and "pollution", which is typified in the contrast between the orthodox renouncer and the Tantric. The high status seeker is eager to keep the "purity" of women under his control because an uncontrolled woman is seen as "impure", and so he joins the group of the renouncers. Since the low status worker, because of his distance from the dominant ideology, does not exhibit an explicit attitude of rejection towards women, he tends to accept her as she is, and this is the reason that he and the Tantric form one group.

Thus it becomes clear that Hindu women must be understood in terms of an analytical map consisting of the two dimensions, or ideological tendencies, of "impurity (pure-impure)" ideology and "pollution" ideology. In this respect, I am convinced that the accounts by Allen, Hershman and perhaps Tapper, cited above, are the results of confusion in that they fail to distinguish between these two ideologies because of the strong influence of what I call "impurity" ideology here, that is, Dumontian "pure-impure" ideology. Although in "pure-impure" ideology women have to be segregated as the "impure", it is impossible for secular people, who must live together with women, to chase them away altogether. Therefore, they are required to resolve this contradiction. Then, as a last resort, within this ideology they invent the dual character of woman, such that she is "pure" and at the same time "impure". For example, according to H. Orenstein, the code-writers as typical symbolic producers of the dominant ideology touch on the "pure" as well as the "impure" aspects of women [Orenstein, 1968: 122]. It is, then, natural to pose the question of what makes it possible for such contrary ideas to coexist. This conundrum can never be solved within the confines of "pure-impure" ideology alone, and it is to be concluded that in actual fact use is made of the logic of sacrifice as a device for achieving the coexistence of the "pure" and "impure". In this sense, we notice that "pure-impure" ideology is in fact supported by "pollution" ideology, the central logic of which is sacrifice *(viz.* death and the regeneration of life), but the Brahman code-writers hide this fact in order to protect the preeminence of "pure-impure" ideology. Moreover, most South Asianists superficially describe what they have read or observed with regard to Hindu women without, however, analysing it in depth, and they just repeat the above Brahman-biased and male-biased view, which is circumscribed by "pure-impure" ideology.

Generally speaking, the limitations of this attitude naturally reflect upon one's understanding of menstruation, which is the key phenomenon in ideological discourse about Hindu women. For instance, in his discussion of Draupadi's hair, A. Hiltebeitel notes that "conventional notions of menstrual blood as defiling are somewhat one-sided. To the women, at least, menstrual blood is also purifying". Furthermore, "[t]here are numerous statements in the Dharmaśāstra Saṃhitās to the effect that women are cleansed by the menstrual flow" [Hiltebeitel, 1981: 203]. Outside textual sources, Hershman reports that "Punjabi women do not look upon menstruation as a curse but rather see it as a necessary bodily process in order to purge themselves of pollution and make clean their wombs" [Hershman, 1974: 286].[5]

These accounts provide very interesting material because they not only indicate the "pure" aspect of women but also touch on the dynamic process in which the menstrual flow changes women from "impure" to "pure'. Nonetheless, these materials still await a deeper analysis going beyond the confines of "pure-impure" ideology. In other words, menstruation has to be dealt with as a dynamic "incident" rather than as a "thing". For that, one has no choice but to consider women from the viewpoint of "pollution" ideology, which is based on the logic of sacrifice.

From the Viewpoint of "Pollution" Ideology

In order to investigate the "pollution" dimension of women, it is useful to focus on the position of wifehood, which is degraded as "impure" from the viewpoint of "pure-impure" ideology.

Firstly, let us take up the topic of *satī* in connection with widowhood. Especially among the higher castes, whose culture is more Brahmanical, a widow tends to be regarded as very "impure" and as inauspicious, and she is, therefore, excluded from normal social life. For example, "a common term of abuse in Kannada is *randi,* a word which means both widow and whore" [Bradford, 1983: 316]. This implies that a widow is "impure" not only because of the effect of death pollution but also because of her sexuality, which has lost its controller (her husband), as E.L. Stutchbury also points out [Stutchbury, 1982: 62]. Therefore, it is usual for the "impure" widow to be socially segregated as a mourner throughout the rest of her life. However, there is one other drastic way of responding to her husband's death. This is the custom of *satī. Satī* is a form of self-sacrifice in which a widow throws herself into the cremation fire of her husband. According to Stutchbury, through *satī,* "the widow, extremely polluted by her husband's death, is transformed into the purest of wives by sacrifice" [ibid.: 62]. This is followed by her explanation that, by this sacrificial death, the threat that the widow presents to the patrilineage is completely removed and the honour of the purest wife makes her lineage prosperous.

A wife, especially among the socially higher castes, is also required to sacrifice herself for her husband in everyday life, though in not so drastic a fashion as *satī.* The sacrifice is to serve her husband faithfully. For example, it is a sacrificial action when a wife eats dinner by using the plate which her husband has used and after having served him his meal. This action is conceived of as absorbing and removing pollution from her husband, so that if the wife accumulated pollution in her body through this action and ultimately died, this could be equated with *satī as* the result of her everyday efforts of self-sacrifice.

In the same context, it is said that the devotion of a wife to her husband has the value of renunciation in this world [Ojha, 1981: 255]. In short, a husband is a god to his wife [Harper, 1964: 181]. Thus we are convinced that a wife's devotion to her husband in this world is regarded as a *religious* act participating in the sphere of the sacred. In this connection, it is C.J. Fuller who tries to give a systematic explanation of this phenomenon. According to him, the relationship between wife and husband is similar to that between man and God [Fuller, 1979: 471]. As evidence in support of this statement, he points to the resemblance of the patterns of giving meals: although in the usual *social* sphere the status of a giver is necessarily higher (or purer) than that of a taker, the situation is reversed in both the wife-husband relationship and the man-God relationship. Namely, in both situations the lower-status party gives a meal (or offering) to the higher party, i.e., husband or God. This indicates that these relationships belong to the *religious* sphere, where the logic of the *social* sphere does not operate, as is indicated by Fuller when he states that "the gods themselves cannot be polluted" [ibid.: 459].

These examples suggest that the self-sacrificial actions associated with wifehood belong to the *religious* (or sacred) sphere, not to the *social* (or profane) sphere. It is to be noted that there is a clear contrast between these two spheres. The underlying logic of the *social* (or profane) sphere is the "pure-impure" ideology in which women are regarded as "impure" while at the same time the "purity" of women is also stressed. In this sphere, importance is attached to "self-preservation", i.e., stability of social hierarchical position. By way of contrast, the *religious* (or sacred) sphere requires "self-abandonment" leading to metamorphosis, namely, self-sacrifice, which represents the underlying logic of "pollution" ideology. In the *religious* sphere, women are seen as a source of energy and their "sacredness" is stressed. Therefore, although it is said in the *social* sphere that the self-sacrificial actions of a wife change her into the "pure" (or "purest"), the "pure" in this context should be regarded as the "sacredness" from the viewpoint of "pollution" ideology. This argument obviously implies that a "pure" wife is a misleading expression which both wittingly and unwittingly ignores the distinction between the two ideological spheres. It is logically impossible to change women from the "impure" into the "pure" within the *profane* sphere (or secular world), and, therefore, it is necessary for the proper understanding of women to go beyond the *profane* sphere. It must be taken into account that such a change inevitably requires a sacrificial action like *satī* that is equated with world renunciation, that is to say, an incident in the *religions* sphere or a "pollution"-ideological action. Thus, our task is to see through the above-mentioned code-writers' attempt to hide this fact and to correctly demonstrate the actual ideological configuration in terms of Hindu women.

Women as an Arena of Ideological Struggles

It is clear from the above arguments that images of Hindu women are made up of two different ideological dimensions, namely, "pure-impure" ideology and "pollution" ideology. Therefore, we can say that the ambiguous character of women has to be investigated on the basis of the fact that they embody these two ideologies, each with its own logic. In other words, women on the one hand submissively conform to the hierarchy governed by the logic of "pure-impure" and contribute to the preservation of the this-worldly *social* (or profane) system, while on the other hand they violate or transcend the hierarchical social order and produce the other-worldly sacred power through the logic of sacrifice which makes the social order renew.

If we now reconsider the ambiguous character of Hindu women after having taken cognizance of the differences between these two ideological dimensions, it becomes evident just how indifferent to the distinction between these ideological dimensions the popular stereotypical image of Hindu women is. That being so, by way of conclusion I wish to delineate the characteristics of the images of women corresponding to each of these two ideological dimensions. The important point that I wish to confirm is that ideological differences do not simply reflect different types of value orientation, but attest to fundamental differences in terms of the standpoint in which their respective interpretative perspectives are produced.

In other words, the essence of "pure-impure" ideology lies in a secular attitude that objectifies from without that which it regards as marginal conflonting other-worldlyness or having a window for cosmos. It thus represents a top-down interpretation from the standpoint of the centre of the dominant order, and in the present instance, from its position at the centre of a male-centred and Brahman-centred order, it defines women as peripheral and marginal entities and looks upon them as "impure". Yet at the same time, because women are a *sine qua non* for society, it moulds women who are pure by imposing various kinds of self-sacrifice in the form of social restrictions and then extolling their observance, and the power of women is in actual fact incorporated into the dominant order. This is put into practice by means of the act of "purification for elimination". In this manner, on the basis of the reciprocality of the centre and the periphery, which manifests as subservient devotion and domineering protection and is predicated on an uneven distribution of power, women are forced to embody a veritably split and ambiguous character combining the contradictory aspects of the "impure" and the "pure".

By way of contrast, the essence of "pollution" ideology lies in an attitude grounded in a perspective from within that which the socially dominant view defines as marginal, and it therefore represents a world that places value on the dynamics of living on the borderline linking chaos and cosmos, which are not embraced by nomos. Here there is maintained an attitude that seeks to accept in a positive light the existence of the pollution brought about by a woman's physiology (equivalent to chaos) as an independent latent power corresponding to what I call "pollution", and the efflorescence of its productivity and fertility (equivalent to cosmos) is enjoyed as something sacred. Because this sacredness is reached via the path of "pollution", I shall designate it "pollution-sacredness". This process whereby pollution is regarded as "pollution" and "pollution-sacredness" is attained corresponds to what I have referred to as "purification for creation".

The fact to which we must now turn our attention after having recognized the above ideological differences is that, as has already been pointed out, "pure- impure" ideology, with its viewpoint centred on the dominant order, comprehends the phenomenon of a woman's flowering fertility by translating it into the acme of "purity" (which might be described as "purity-sacredness"), thereby attempting to keep it within the confines of the nomos of the centralized ideology. In this fashion, the interpretations made by two different ideologies of one and the same phenomenon *(viz.* fertility) occurring in the person of Hindu women run into direct conflict. This is why I would suggest that women are an arena of ideological struggles.

It might assist the reader's understanding of my arguments if I were to borrow K. Karatani's concepts of "particularity" and "singularity" in order to characterize this ideological struggle that takes place between "pure-impure" ideology and "pollution" ideology as a struggle between the dimension of "particularity" and that of "singularity". The distinction between "particularity" and "singularity", which Karatani illustrates by means of the expressions "me" and "this me (and none other)", is explained as follows: "Whereas particularity represents individuality as seen from generality, singularity represents individuality that can no longer belong to generality" [Karatani, 1994 (1989): 11]. Karatani thus equates differences that can be compared by means of a common yardstick with the individuality of "particularity" and differences for which there is no common yardstick, and which thus reject comparison, with the individuality of "singularity". Restated in my own terms, the gist of his argument would seem to lie in the fact that he makes explicit the rupture existing between the discovery of the relative other and the discovery of the absolute other. The discovery of the relative other takes place in this world through the comparison of known objects premised on the existence of a common yardstick, whereas the absolute other represents that which is no more comprehensible by this worldly yardstick, and its discovery takes place through the experience in which we encounter the otherworld (the world of death) at the ends of this world. When we consider that the absolute marginal experience of death which embraces the logic of sacrifice represents the essence of pollution, as I have explained above, it becomes clear that Karatani's purpose in separating "singularity" from "particularity" in general evidences close parallels with my arguments for separating "pollution" from "impurity" in general. Just as the essence lying at the root of individuality is "singularity", so is "pollution" the essence lying at the root of pollution. What I mean here by "essence" could be "structure" in Levi-Strauss' sense, and is the nature of the world that becomes visible when one consistently adopts a perspective from within the marginal sphere, and this is the key point underlying both "singularity" and "pollution".

When considered from such a viewpoint, it becomes evident that the image of women that is produced by relatively particularizing women with the dominant values of Hindu society *(viz.* male-centred or Brahman-centred values) as a common yardstick—that is, the view of women as being "impure" but also "pure" when certain conditions are fulfilled—represents a discourse or narrative emanating from the world of "particularity" predicated on the existence of a this-worldly common yardstick in the form of "pure-impure" ideology [Foucault's *normalization* (Foucault 1975)]. By developing a suppressive narrative typical of a centralized ideology which, as was pointed out earlier, would regard menstrual blood and sexual intercourse, representing the starting point of reproductivity, as "impure" while interpreting the resulting fruit of fertility as exalted "purity" (or "purity-sacredness"), the existence of "pollution" as representing the dimension of "singularity" (and corresponding to the process of "pollution-sacredness") ends up being concealed. If the situation is understood in this manner, it will be realized that the popular conception of the ambiguous or two-sided character of Hindu women has unwittingly rehashed this thesis of the dominant ideology. What I am trying to clarify here is the fundamental difference in positions of viewpoint to be observed between the dimension of "particularity" and that of "singularity", a difference which this worldly and dominant ideology conceals and obscures, for the clarification of this difference becomes a focal point when reconsidering the popular understanding of the two-sidedness of Hindu women.

A typical illustration of this difference in positions of viewpoint is the contrast between obedient and compassionate goddesses who represent the consorts of male gods and ambivalent, bellicose and independent goddesses as already described in Chapter 6. According to my theory, these are regarded as classic manifestations of "purification for elimination" based on "pure-impure" ideology and "purification for creation" based on "pollution" ideology respectively. Therefore, one must take care not to interpret this contrast from the perspective of the dominant value of "pure-impure" ideology, thereby drawing both back into a relative stratified system of values with the former goddesses being regarded as "pure" and the latter as "impure". As will have become clear in the above discussion, it is important to squarely recognize the fact that Hindu women are themselves an arena in which two fundamentally different ideologies clash with one another, and it should not be considered admissible to reduce this conflict to a stratified bipolar contrast characteristic of the dominant ideology's view in the form of an image of women as being both "pure" and "impure", which represents an interpretation based on "pure-impure" ideology. I wish to again point out that the "pure-impure" ideological interpretation of Hindu women is based on this-worldly ambiguity produced within the *social* sphere, while the "pollution" ideological interpretation of Hindu women is derived from other-worldly ambiguity encountered at the end of the *social* sphere. By "pollution" ideology, I hope to reclaim the dangerous but powerful creative horizons, which have hitherto been obfuscated, of the dimension of "pollution" or "singularity". As was noted earlier when citing Hiltebeitel and Hershman, without a clear and systematic understanding along these lines, one is able to analyse but inadequately the intriguing data on the purifying powers of menstrual blood. The arguments developed by Hiltebeitel and Hershman seem to be positioned merely in a vague state of limbo in the arena represented by women, or in between the above two interpretative dimensions, and as such they fail to formulate any systematic theory.

Lastly, I wish to return to the point made by Allen and bring this chapter to a tentative close with a comment of my own. The "pure-impure" ideology is more strongly imposed among castes of higher social standing, and therefore the higher the social standing of those concerned, the greater the degree to which the two-sidedness of women as denned by the dominant ideology is forced to embrace within itself the intense conflict between the above two ideologies in a suppressed form (that is, in the form of the conflict between "pure" and "impure" aspects) [e.g. Ortner, 1978]. The higher status women, therefore, can be a more vigorous arena. By way of contrast, the bifurcation into two ideologies is usually quite negligible among lower-status people, and so the ambiguous character of lower-status women is not so distinct. This means that the ambiguous image of Hindu women is not always the property of lower-status women, whose image is more unified and is more simply characterized by the productive aspect. In this manner, the difference between the images of women dependent upon their hierarchical positions can be systematically elucidated in the light of my scheme positing two different ideologies, with a distinction being made between "impurity" and "pollution." Conversely, through the above discussion of women, the explanatory power of my insistence on distinguishing between "impurity" and "pollution" seems to some extent to have been substantiated.

Notes

1. In this regard M. Douglas's differentiation of "dirt-affirmative philosophies" and "dirt-rejecting philosophies" is important [Douglas, 1966: 164].
2. In this respect the discussions presented by Das [1977: 143] and Good [1991: 200], although of considerable interest, are inadequate.
3. Namely, the fact that because she has not freed herself sufficiently from a viewpoint centred on the established order, she is still encumbered by "pure-impure" ideology.
4. On the differences between *Kaṉṉi* and *Nirrti*, the latter a goddess of calamities associated with the southwest in north Indian Hinduism, see [Reiniche, 1981].
5. This report from Punjabi society is exactly the same as what I heard in the course of my investigations in a Tamil village.

Part Three

Harijan Strategies

Part Three is devoted to an elucidation of the actual features of the ideological practices of the village Paraiyars through a comparison of their practices with those of the dominant Caste Hindus, in other words, through an understanding of the whole social context of the village. At the outset, Chapter 9 reveals the socio-economic position of the Paraiyars in the village context as the fundamental basis to their practices. The following three Chapters elucidate real features of the Paraiyars' practices in terms of ritual or religious facets, such as funerals (Chapter 10) and lineage festivals (Chapter 11), and in terms of politico-economic aspects which more vividly reflect recent social changes (Chapter 12).

Chapter 9

The Socio-Economic Position of the Paraiyars (The Harijans)

In Chapter 7, I pointed out the Paraiyars' general interpretation of their socially repressed position. The Paraiyars people tend to think that the disadvantages of their social position are caused by their economic dependence on the dominant castes, and they dislike reducing them to ritual reasons. It is, therefore, an indispensable task to understand their present economic condition, which provides the basis for this interpretative statement. Furthermore, in order to fully explore the social power of the present Paraiyars, not only their economic situation, but also their educational background and their political circumstances need to be taken into account.[1] The former two, namely the economic position and the educational level of the Paraiyars in the village setting, are dealt with in this chapter. Their political behaviour and conditions will be discussed in the arguments on the Milk Cooperative Society (Chapter 12). Since I aim to elucidate the Paraiyars' socio-economic position within the village social framework, it is necessary to describe the other castes' socio-economic conditions as well.

The Economic Position of the Paraiyars and Government Aid

Agricultural Lands

Classification of Cultivated Lands

Agricultural lands are primarily classified into two categories, namely, *puṉcey* (irrigated land) and *naṉcey* (non-irrigated land). Both can be, moreover, divided into two sub-categories according to whether water supply from a well is available or not. If well-irrigation is available, the land is called *tōṭṭam*, and if not, it is simply called *kāṭu* Therefore, there are logically four categories of agricultural land,[2] but, in the villagers'everyday conservation, they usually adopt only three categories: (1) *puṉcey* or *puṉcey kāṭu,* (2) *puṉcey tōṭṭam*, and (3) *naṉcey*. The reason that in practice they reduce these categories to three is understandable, because whether the land is *tōṭṭam* or not makes the decisive difference in the case of *puṉcey* but not in the case of *naṉcey*. Hereafter, I adopt these three divisions, according to the villagers' use.

On the Survey of Land Possession

A survey of land possession in the village is very problematic. Firstly, the administrative register[3] is not up to date. Dumont has already pointed out such a time lag [Dumont, 1986: 137]. The name of the owner in the register, therefore, does not always refer to the actual possessor of the land. Secondly, there is the serious problem of the register not distinguishing between *puṉcey kāṭu* and *puṉcey tōṭṭam*. This detail is vital for an understanding of the actual economic situation. Thirdly, the usefulness of the register is further decreased by the customary and popular institution of loans, called *otti* or *pōkkiyam*. *Otti* is property, such as land or houses, as a mortgage to the lender for the loan of money, the usual purpose being to raise money for marriage, medical expenses, repayment of a debt, gifts etc.[4] (cf. Table 9.1) *Otti* is associated with the shift of the right of use to the taker of the mortgated land.[5] These informal transactions in the right of cultivation never appear on the register, despite the fact that they take place frequently and are significant for villagers.

Table 9.1

Transaction Price of Agricultural Lands (Round Figures, 1987)

	Sale (transfer of ownership)	*Otti (transfer of cultivation right)*
puṉcey kātu	Rs 10,000 acre	Rs 7,000 acre
puṉcey tōṭṭam	Rs 20,000 acre	Rs 15,000 acre
naṉcey	Rs 30,000 acre	Rs 20,000 acre

Thus, the problem lies not only in the time lag or in the categorization of the register, but also in this informal movement in the use right through the *otti* institution (see [Document, 1986: 137]). This, therefore, suggests that it is necessary to understand the movement of the usufruct in order to understand the villagers' actual economic situation. I eventually decided, as did Dumont [Dumont, 1986: 137], to collect information on both the cultivated lands that are actually possessed, and on the *otti* lands taken or given, though I use the official register as a reference.[6] Table 9.2 shows the 1987 conditions of the cultivated land holdings of each caste, using the data I myself collected. This Table distinguishes the cultivated land actually owned, and the cultivated land taken by *otti*.[7]

Changes in the Distribution of Land Possession

Table 9.2 indicates that even the dominant caste, the Kallars, do not possess enough agricultural land to support themselves, even if the 20 per cent gap (see Note 7) is revised. It is said in the village that the combination of 5 acres of *puṉcey tōṭṭam* and 2 acres of *naṉcey* would be enough for maintaining one average household of five family members, providing the rainfall was average. This is the minimum standard for maintaining a family by agriculture alone. The *tōṭṭam* is usually used as a garden for vegetables and cash crops, while the *naṉcey* is used as a rice-field. As is shown in Table 9.3, today only five Kallar households are able to reach the above-mentioned standard for maintaining a family by agriculture alone.[8] Even if the standard was lowered a little, only another two Kallar households (No. 148 and No. 160) would

Table 9.2

Caste-wise Cultivated Landholdings (1987)

(acre)

Caste	*puṉcey kātu (PK)*		*puṉcey tōṭṭam (PT)*		*naṉcey (NA)*		*Total*	
	gr.	*av.*	*gr.*	*av.*	*gr.*	*av.*	*gr.*	*av.*
Pillai (3)	0.70	0.23	0.00	0.00	0.22	0.07	0.92	0.31
							*13,600	*4,533
Kallar (202)	138.43	0.69	142.90	0.71	53.85	0.27	335.18	1.66
	48.94	0.24	24.12	0.12	11.65	0.06	84.71	0.42
							*6,795,180	*33,640
Pantaram (1)	11.00	11.00	5.00	5.00	2.12	2.12	18.12	18.12
							*273,600	*273,600
Acari (10)	8.25	0.83	0.63	0.06	1.85	0.19	10.73	1.07
	3.00	0.30			0.25	0.03	3.25	0.33
							*176,600	*17,660
Natar (10)	4.00	0.40	7.00	0.70	1.50	0.15	12.50	1.25
	4.90	0.49			0.45	0.05	5.35	0.54
							*268,300	*26,830
Vannar (7)	0.00	0.00	0.00	0.00	0.00	0.00	0.00	0.00
Kuravar (1)	0.00	0.00	0.00	0.00	0.00	0.00	0.00	0.00
Paraiyar (174)	15.34	0.09	0.00	0.00	0.94	0.01	16.28	0.09
	11.80	0.07	3.18	0.02	2.12	0.01	17.10	0.10
							*354,300	*2,036
Total (408)	177.72	0.44	155.53	0.38	60.48	0.15	393.73	0.97
	68.64	0.17	27.30	0.07	14.47	0.04	110.41	0.27
Estimation from the Detail Notes	556.63				92.79		649.42	

Notes: 1. The upper row refers to the cultivated land actually owned and the lower row refers to the cultivated land taken by *otti*.
2. Figures with an asterisk(*) — refer to land value which is caluculated by the following expression (O means *otti*): Total value (Rs) = PK × 10,000 + PKO × 7,000 + PT × 20,000 + PTO × 15,000 + NA × 30,000 + NAO × 20,000.
3. gr. = gross, av. = average.

come near to this level. As to the other castes, only the Pantaram priest's household (No. 166) and one Natar household (No. 31) exceed this standard. Thus, it is revealed that only the top nine landholders out of 408 households can maintain a family by agriculture alone. It is also remarkable that there are no longer any big landlords in the village, except for No. 15, who has in total 50.8 acres.[9]

This notable fragmentation of landowning (cf. [Gough, 1989:132]) is made clearer when the current situation is compared with that in the previous generation (30 or 40 years ago). Table 9.4 shows a list of large landlords at that time. If you compare Table 9.4 with Table 9.3, it will be noted that, firstly, Table 9.3 has no descendents of the families listed in Table 9.4; and, secondly, that there were in the previous generation several big landlords who monopolized the village economy, the two largest of whom were Pillai families. Therefore, there is no doubt that the fragmentation of agriculture holdings rapidly took place in the process through which the previous generation's property was handed over to the present generation. In this process of charge, the agricultural lands were dispersed from the two Pillai families and a few influential Kallar families who had long dominated the village. The positions they occupied were replaced by the newly socially rising lower-middle class Kallars and Nadars who succeeded in acquiring their lands. A typical example showing such change is found in the case of the *nāṭṭāṉmai* family (the line of AK pillai). The grandson, who is the present head of the family explains the process as follows. His father, the son of AK pillai, to a considerable extent used his property for family concerns, especially for the higher education of his three sons. In addition, large sums of money were consumed for generously welcoming various visitors, in his position as the village headman. He also emphasizes that his fathers taste and behaviour was very regal. Thus, it can be easily understood that his father had to sell off his lands to cover these expenses, because the rapid extension of monetization associated with modernization required cash rather than kind. Furthermore, such dismemberment of the big landlords had been basically accelerated by the rapid changes towards modernized agriculture, because the big landlords in K village failed to cope with the wave of switching to modern agricultural methods. Although villagers tend to explain things by visible and immediate causes, they usually relate the dispersion of land to low agricultural production due to the irregular rainfall and the series of changes in land legislation dealing with land ceiling and the protection of tenancy rights (see [Gough, 1989: Chapter 3]). These changes which affected the Pillai landlords in this village, are very similar to what the *mirasdārs* of the Tanjore village described by [Béteille, 1965: 201–202] experienced.[10]

Table 9.3

Landholders Reaching the Standard for Specializing in Agriculture (The standard is 5 acres of puṉcey tōṭṭam and 2 acres of naṉcey)

(acre)

Caste	*House No. (Lineage)*	*puṉcey tōṭṭam*		*naṉcey*		*puṉcey kāṭu*	
		own	*Otti*	*own*	*Otti*	*own*	*otti*
Kallar	7 (Catayi)	5.15	2.00	2.00	0.00	6.40	0.00
Kallar	15 (Kattapinnai)	15.00	1.00	15.00	1.80	15.00	3.00
Kallar	123/124 (Kecavan)	3.75	0.00	2.00	1.72	4.60	1.00
Kallar	129/130 (Kecavan)	4.25	0.00	5.00	0.00	9.25	3.75
Kallar	9 (Catayi)	3.81	3.63	0.29	0.87	1.38	4.14
Kallar	148 (Panniyan)	6.00	0.00	0.00	0.00	0.00	–5.50
Kallar	160 (Panniyan)	6.20	0.00	0.00	0.00	0.00	1.50
Pantaram	166	5.00	0.00	2.12	0.00	11.00	0.00
Natar	31	7.00	0.00	0.00	0.00	0.00	0.00

Table 9.4
Large Landlords of the Previous Generation

(acre)

Name (in abbreviated form)	*Caste*	*Approximate Landholding*	
		puṉcey	*naṉcey*
AK pillai	Pillai	25	40
CK pillai	Pillai	25	40
KN tevar	Kallar	10	15
PN tevar	Kallar	35	20
MP tevar	Kallar	20	to
VT natar	Natar	20	5

Nonetheless, it should be noted that the loss of agricultural lands of the traditionally influential families does not simply mean a decline in their socio-economic power in the village context. This is because their descendants have succeeded in acquiring stable urban employment, for example as station masters and government clerks. In other words, holding agricultural land is no longer the only source of maintaining one's economic position today. It is obvious that they cannot afford to show their "generosity" as their ancestors did, as the patrons of the village *jajmānī* relationships, because their salaries are fixed. The families shown in Table 9.3 who have achieved a rapid economic rise in the present generation (see [Gough, 1989: 45]), do not play the role of traditional patrons, but rather have contract-based (capitalistic in Gough's sense [Gough, 1989: 233]) relationships with day-labourers.[11] Their behaviour is rather individualistic and is influenced by the new value of "economy" or "cutting down expenses". This is completely opposite to the traditional value of "generosity" which the patron should show. However, there is no doubt that "generosity" is still important for understanding social hegemony. In this respect, as Béteille clarifies in his work [Béteille 1965], the domains of politics and administration have become significant arenas where the village leaders newly embody the attitude of "generosity". This point will be developed in Chapter 12.

Plate 69 The descendants of the Kallar big landlord and their house.

The Income and Expenditure of the Caste Hindus

I now deal with some details of the economic lives of the villagers. Firstly, in order to understand the economic position of the landed farmer, I examine the agricultural production of household No. 7 (see Table 9.5) which enjoys relatively better economic conditions. Secondly, I examine the cost of living of six households chosen from different castes (Table 9.6), and take up the characteristics of the expenditure of each household, which reflect the social situation of each caste.[12]

Table 9.5

Annual Income and Expenditure of No. 7's Agricultural Production (1986-87)

Kind of land	*Product*	*Area (acre)*	*Expenditure (Rs)*	*Income (Rs)*	*Net profit (Rs)*
puṉcey kātu	*peanut	4	5,000	9,000	4,000
	*red bean (side crop)		25	300	275
puṉcey tōṭṭam	*onion	2	4,000	6,000	2,000
	*rice	1	2,000	4,000	2,000
	*eggplant	1	1,500	2,500	1,000
	*tomato	1	1,500	3,000	1,500
	*millet (*kēppai*)	0.5	200	500	300
	*lady's finger	0.5	100	1,000	900
	*cotton	1	1,000	3,000	2,000
	*peanut	1	1,000	3,000	2,000
	*drumstick	0.25	50	200	150
naṉcey	(not cultivated due to tank water shortage)				
Total			16,375	32,500	16,125

Household No. 7 is an extended family consisting of two old parents, their son, and his wife, and their five grandchildren (two boys and three girls). Table 9.5 shows, in round figures, the annual income and expenditure of Household No. 7's agricultural production in 1986–1987.[13] According to this Table, the annual net profit is roughly Rs 16,000, and it provides Rs 148 per person per month. What does this mean? It can be noted that Household No. 7's income is never high, if the amount is compared with the expenditures of other households shown in Table 9.6, which range from Rs 107 to Rs 250 per person per month. This comparison only provides a rough guide. The recent rapid increase in cash expenses can be made clearer if the present situation (1987) is compared with that at the end of the 1940s, as reported by Dumont [Dumont, 1986: 126–127].[14]

Before shifting to the economic condition of the Paraiyars, I sum up the points shown:

1. Whether the household concerned specializes in agriculture or not makes a difference in terms of the cash expense of food. According to Table 9.6, even in the case of partial self-supply, Rs 700 per person per year is necessary for having simple meals (rice or millet with one side dish). If more than Rs 1,000

Table 9.6

Cash Expenses in 1986

(yearly, Rs)

Caste / *Item*	*Pillai* *A:1*	*Kallar* *A:4, C:2*	*Acari* *A:2, C:2*	*Pantaram* *A:4, C:2*	*Natar* *A:7, C:4*	*Paraiyar* *A:4, C:3*
food (*uṇavu*)	2,160 1,180/p	6,120, 1,020/p	3000 750/p	1,260 210/p	6,000 545/p	3,600 720/p
gorcery (*palcarakku*)	240 120/p	1,440 240/p	600 150/p	1,620 270/p	1,800 164/p	150 30/p
necessary (*cōppu*)	—	126	—	—	—	—
clothing (*uṭai*)	100 50/p	2,610 435/p	1500 375/p	700 117/p	4500 409/p	400 80/p
cleaning (*calavai*)	84 42/p	350 85/p	240 60/p	180 30/p	600 55/p	192 38/p
hair-cutting (*muṭi tiruttam*)	—	—	—	120	—	—
travelling (*pōkkuvarattu*)	480 240/p	2,700 675/p	1,440 720/p	900 225/p	2,400 342/p	900 450/p
electricity (*miṉcelavu*)	66	168	720	840	300	0
medical (*maruttuvam*)	60 30/p	550 92/p	600 150/p	120 20/p	1,200 109/p	200 40/p
education (*kalvi*)	0	50 25/p	240 120/p	1000 500/p	360 90/p	360 120/p
presentation (*moy*)	25 (0.5%)	3,000 (16.9%)	1,500 (12.5%)	500 (6.5%)	1,000 (3.8%)	750 (11.1%)
offerings (*kōvilcelavu*)	450 (10.4%)	400 (2.3%)	720 (6.0%)	300 (3.9%)	300 (1.1%)	99 (1.5%)
luxuries (*āṭamparam*)	60 30/p	240 40/p	600 150/p	180 30/p	1800 164/p	50 10/p
others	600	—	840	—	6,000	75
Total	4,325 2,163/p	17,754 2,959/p	12,000 3,000/p	7,720 1,286/p	26,260 2,387/p	6,776 1,355/p
	180/p/m	247/p/m	250/p/m	107/p/m	199/p/m	113/p/m

Note: A: No. of adult members, C: No. of child members, /p: per person, /p/m: per person per month

per person per year was available, one could eat rice with each meal and have two side dishes and sometimes yoghurt. In this respect, the claim of the Paraiyar household seems to be a little doubtful, because the food expenditure of the household claimed by them does not match their actual meals, where lunch is sometimes omitted,[15] though it should, of course, be taken into account that the Paraiyars need more cash due to their not being self-sufficient as far as food is concerned.

2. The Pillais' expenses for clothing is far less than that of the other castes, even below that of the Paraiyars. This is explained by the fact that this Pillai household consists of a widowed mother (in her 70s) and her unmarried son (in his 30s), who is an ardent Murugan devotee. As the ritually highest woman, she has strictly observed a socially restricted widowhood, while her son also leads a simple life modeled around being a world renouncer. He never wears trousers, but wears traditional sarongs, called *vēṭṭi* (*dhoti*), and never uses soap or shampoo for religious reasons.

Plate 70 Recording *moy* (gift money).

3. The above-mentioned religious enthusiasm is directly reflected in the expense of the temple offerings. The offering charges occupy a higher percentage of the total expenditure in the cases of both the Pillais (10.4%) and the Acaris (6.0%), who enjoy a higher ritual status in the village. The Pantarams should be added to this group even though the expense of their temple offerings is officially a little low (3.9%), if it is taken into account that they separately spend large amounts on priestly work.
4. It seems that the expense of *moy* (presentations) corresponds greatly with the significance of kinship relationships and with the liveliness of the activities of the local caste association. This is verified by the fact that the Kallars, the Paraiyars and the Acaris spend a lot on gifts.[16] In contrast, it is noted that the amount spent by the Pillais on prestations is judged as very low. This is partly because they do not have many kinship interactions due to their dispersed distribution, and is partly due to them having economically withdrawn from patronage today. The present head, however, maintains the high status of his family line in the religious and intellectual domain, by observing a sober life as mentioned above.

The Economy of the Paraiyars

The Economic Position of the Paraiyars

Generally speaking, most of the landless and uneducated Paraiyars, who account for nearly 65 per cent of the Parayiars, make a living by working as day-labourers, called *kūliyāḷ*, in the fields of the higher caste landlords. Since they work as day-labourers, not as *aṭimaikārar or paṇṇaikārar* deeply involved within the *jajmānī* relationship, they have become freer from the traditional framework. On the other hand, it is also true that their economic position is rather more unstable than before, because the

Plate 71 Free lunch is distributed.

landlords can hire anybody, not necessarily the village Parayiars, so that whether one is engaged in labour or not becomes uncertain (cf. [Moffatt, 1979: 82]).[17] Needless to say, the large supply of labourers and the limited demand for agricultural work inevitably keep the labourers payment low.[18] How much can be earned by engaging in agricultural labour? In the case of both husband and wife going to the fields under ordinary demand, this can be calculated as follows: <husband: Rs 8/full-day 15–20 days/month = Rs 120–160/month> <wife: Rs 3.5/half-day 15–20 days/month = Rs 52.5–70/month> The total earning is estimated as Rs 172.5–230/month. Since it is said that for even a minimum standard of living Rs 250/month is required for a household consisting of five members,[19] the result shows that their earning power, even in better seasons when demand is higher, does not reach this minimum level.

Today, there are Paraiyars who hold land. Table 9.7 shows a list of 37 Paraiyar landholders (21.3% of 174 Paraiyar households)[20] in descending order of the total value of their land, which is calculated by using the prices shown in Table 9.1. According to this list, only the first two persons mentioned come close to the average land holdings of the Kallars, the value of which is Rs 33,640. The Kallars' average is *16.5 times* greater than the average value of the land holdings of the Paraiyars, Rs 2,036.[21] This obviously indicates that not only is there still a big economic differential between the Kallars, as the dominant caste, and the dominated Paraiyars but also that the economic gap within the Paraiyar community is expanding. The top two Paraiyars, KP and CV, with property values exceed Rs 30,000 are two very influential leaders of the Paraiyar community, as is shown in the discussion of problems of the Milk Society (see Chapter 12). Table 9.8 also shows the distribution of landholdings

Table 9.7
Landholders of the Paraiyars

House No.	*Lineage*	*PK*	*PKO (acre)*	*PT*	*PTO (acre)*	*NA*	*NAO (acre)*	*Property value Rs*
267	Kartananti	2.00	2.00					34,000
250	Tankalan				2.00			30,000
270	Cinnananti	1.50					0.50	25,000
332	Tankalan	1.25				0.03		21,500
246	Cahalan	0.30				0.20	0.52	19,400
292	?				1.18			17,700
304	Cahalan	0.70					0.50	17,000
261	Cinnananti	1.20				0.16		16,800
205	Tankalan		1.80					12,600
219	Tankalan	1.25						12,500
201	Mataiyan	0.75				0.08	0.08	11,500
279	Cinnananti	0.90						9,000
331	Tankalan	0.90						9,000
226	Tankalan	0.30	0.50				0.12	8,900
227	Mataiyan		0.40			0.20		8,800
373	Cahalan	0.80						8,000
206	Tankalan		1.00					7,000
241	Kartananti		1.00					7,000
299	Tankalan		1.00					7,000
300	Tankalan		1.00					7,000
371	Mataiyan						0.33	6,600
249	Cahalan		0.50				0.15	6,500
232	Mataiyan	0.40				0.08		6,400
203	Tankalan	0.60						6,000
221	Tankalan	0.20	0.50					5,500
322	Mataiyan	0.50						5,000
355	Kartananti		0.70					4,900
336	Tankalan	0.45						4,500
354	Tankalan	0.20	0.30					4,100
288	Mataiyan		0.50					3,500
284	Kartananti		0.30					2,100
290	?		0.30					2,100
214	Tankalan	0.15						1,500
215	Tankalan	0.15						1,500
326	Tankalan	0.15						1,500
222	Tankalan	0.12						1,200
331	Tankalan	0.12						1,200
Total		15.34	11.80	0.00	3.18	0.94	2.12	354,300

Note: PK: *pu̱ncey kāṭu*, PKO: *otti* land of *pu̱ncey kāṭu*, PT: *pu̱ncey tōṭṭam* PTO: *otti* land of *pu̱ncey tōṭṭam* NA: *na̱ncey,* NAO: *otti* land of *na̱ncey* among the five Paraiyar lineages. This Table indicates that the people of the *Nāṟpaṅkāḷi* (the main four-lineages of the Paraiyars) hold slightly less land than do the people of the Tankalan lineage. It is, moreover, noted that the landholding ratio of the Tankalan people, 43.2 per cent, is much higher than that of the *Nāṟpaṅkāḷi*, 17.4 per cent. If it is taken account that the Tankalan lineage is socially peripheral in the Paraiyar community, the two following points are suggested. Firstly, the socially peripheral group may be more anxious to acquire their own property in order to stabilize their economic position. Because they are rather excluded from the traditional interdependence found between the dominant castes and the *Nāṟpaṅkāḷi*, they need to independently established their economic basis by their own efforts. Secondly, the Tankalan people are economically more egalitarian than those of the *Nāṟpaṅkāḷi,* among whom there is a split between the few landholders and the landless majority.

Table 9.8

Landholding Among the Five Main Lineages of the Paraiyars

Lineage	*Number of households (A)*	*Number of landowners (B)*	*B/A (%)*	*B/C (%)*	*Land value (Rs)**		*D/E (%)*
					gr. (D)	*av.*	
Kartanantai	29 (16.7%)	4	13.8	10.5	48,000	1,655	13.4
Cirnnanati	15 (8.6%)	3	20.0	7.9	50,800	3,387	14.2
Mataiyan	41 (23.6%)	6	14.6	15.8	41,800	1,020	11.7
Cahalan	19 (10.9%)	4	21.1	10.5	50,900	2,679	14.2
Tankalan	44 (25.3%)	19	43.2	50.0	147,000	3,341	41.0
others	26 (14.9%)	2	7.7	5.3	19,800	762	5.5
Total	174	38 (C)	21.8	100.0	358,300 (E)	2,059	100.0

Note: *Land value is calculated by the same method as that in Table 9.2.

How do the Paraiyars Acquire Land?

KP's and CV's families, who are listed as the top two Paraiyar landowners, provide examples of how the Paraiyars can succeed in acquiring land. Moreover, there is an interesting contrast between these two examples. The example of CV (a member of the Kartananti lineage) can be seen to represent the central character of the *Nāṟpaṅkāḷi,* whereas KP's father (a member of the Tankalan lineage) reflects its peripheral and rather independent character. Nonetheless, since the details of CV's activities will be described in Chapter 12, I will here discuss what KP's father did, as summarized in the Note 22.[22]

The example of KP's father typically illuminates one of the possible ways through which are Paraiyar can achieve economic betterment. One starts from well-digging work, becomes a buffalo-breeder and finally acquires land. It is noteworthy that the brokerage of buffaloes is a very effective way for increasing one's property, though talent, such as that of KP's father, is also necessary for materializing this. At first, KP's father made the effort to acquire property, like equipment for well-digging and buffaloes. Then, he succeeded in taking the step towards the wider economic field beyond the village sphere as a contractor of well-digging and as a broker controlling a buffalo market. The latter development produced enough profit for acquiring the land. What is interesting is the transformation of property, from buffaloes, more generally livestock, to agricultural land. It is obvious that contrasting properties are found in land and buffaloes. Land is non-transportable, difficult to purchase, and village-oriented; whereas buffaloes are transportable, easier to purchase, and town-oriented. These characteristics of buffaloes are useful for enabling the Paraiyars to establish an economic domain rather free from the hierarchical relations of the village. In this sense, a Tankalan person, like KP's father, who is socially less involved in the village framework, tends to adopt such town-oriented work, compared with a person of the *Nāṟpaṅkāḷi*. However, it is noted that KP's father finally re-invested his gains from the outside economy into the inside economy, by the acquisition of village land. This not only provided him with more stable living conditions, but also, at least in the economic context, helped him alleviate his socially subordinate position, due to his being a Paraiyar.

Animal Husbandry and the Paraiyars

The above-mentioned example suggests that the relationship between the Paraiyars and livestock is economically important. Livestock relations are discussed in the wider perspective of the village as a whole. Table 9.9 shows the caste-wise distribution of the possession of livestock.

1. *Implication of Possessing Bulls:* Possessing a pair of bulls as draft animals is important for an agriculturalist. In this sense, it is natural that the Kallars, as the landlords, possess the most bulls.[23] Nonetheless, today six Paraiyar households each own a pair of bulls and one Paraiyar household possesses two pairs of bulls. Although only three out of these seven households hold their own land, owning a pair of bulls is in itself useful for all of them. For ploughing work using their own bulls, they can expect high reward (for example Rs 35/day, which is four or five times greater than the usual pay of an agricultural labourer). Apart from their economic use, bulls have a religious and aesthetic connotation as well [Dumont, 1986: 120].[24]

2. *Cows and Buffaloes for Milking:* Fewer cows are held than bulls, but it is noted that the number of cows seems to be gradually increasing, when the present situation is compared with Dumont's census made at the end of the 1940s [Dumont, 1986: 119]. Dumont points out that "the near total absence of milk product" [Dumont, 1986: 119] characterizes this region. In Kinnimangalam today, the recent encouragement of milk production by the government has caused an increase in the number of cows and buffaloes for milk products. This government scheme is interconnected with their policy of raising the living standards of the Harijans, so that this scheme especially increases the Paraiyars' holdings of cows and buffaloes. As is described in Chapter 12, the increase of buffaloes among the Paraiyars is doubtless partly the result of the former Milk Society (1967–1972) and of the present Milk Society (1981–). The government's policy encourages the Harijans to purchase water buffaloes rather than cows for milking for two reasons, namely, that a buffalo is a little cheaper than a cow, and buffalo milk is thicker than cow's milk so that buffalo-milking is economically more productive than cow-milking.[25]

Table 9.9
Livestock Possession

Caste	*Cow*		*Bull*		*Water-buffalo*		*Goat*		*Sheep*	
	gr.	*av.*	*gr.*	*av.*	*gr.*	*av.*	*gr.*	*av.*	*gr.*	*av.*
Pillai	0	0	0	0	0	0	0	0	0	0
Kallar	23	0.11	60	0.30	58	0.29	61	0.30	249	1.23
Pantaram	2	2	0	0	0	0	0	0	0	0
Acari	1	0.10	3	0.30	1	0.10	0	0	0	0
Natar	0	0	0	0	9	0.90	0	0	0	0
Vannar	0	0	0	0	0	0	0	0	0	0
Kuravar	0	0	0	0	0	0	0	0	0	0
Paraiyar	21	0.12	16	0.09	80	0.46	59	0.34	13	0.08
Total	47	0.12	79	0.19	148	0.36 1	120	0.29 1	262	0.64

Note: gr. and av. refer to 'gross' and 'average' respectively.

Plate 72 Milking buffaloes.

3. *Goats and Sheep:* Goats are useful, because they provide manure for agriculture, and milk and meat. In addition, a male goat, especially a young one, is the most popular sacrificial animal. Though Dumont notes that "goats are preferred by the landowners; sheep are preferred by poorer people" [Dumont, 1986: 120], this is not the case in Kinnimangalam today where the Kallars have more sheep and the Paraiyars keep more goats.

It has been made clear that the Paraiyars hold a considerable number of livestock today, and that this situation has resulted from the government's scheme of encouraging milk-production. Though there is no doubt that this scheme has directly contributed to the recent increase in livestock, it should not be ignored that animal husbandry is a relatively easy activity for even the poorer Paraiyars to adopt for their economic development, as was shown in KP's father's strategy. If Table 9.10, which shows the sale prices of the main livestock, is compared with Table 9.1, it is seen that acquiring agricultural land requires more than ten times the capital needed for acquiring livestock.

Table 9.10

Selling Prices of Livestock

Rs

Kind	*Price*
cow	1,000–10,000
bull	700–6,000
water-buffaloe	1,500–5,000
goat	250–1,300
sheep	250–1,300

The Structure of the Main Occupations of the Villagers

Today, the occupations of the villagers are diversifying with the increase in opportunities for obtaining income from the outside economy. The main occupations of each caste are shown in Table 9.11.[26] Table 9.11 is classified into two main categories, namely, category A (village-based occupations) and category B (town-based occupations), each of which has two sub-categories (A1 and A2, or B1 and B2). Those categories are defined as follows: <A1>: village-based occupations which are primarily closed within the village sphere, <A2>: village-based occupations which expand towards the outside economy, <B1>: town-based occupations which tend to be independent but are less guaranteed, <B2>: town-based occupations which can be regarded as being stable employment because of being affiliated to government bodies or big cmpanies (or associations).

Let us sum up the points made in this Table.

1. More than 60 per cent of the Paraiyars are engaged in agricultural day-labour, whereas half of the Kallars are basically independent agriculturalists.[27] This contrast indicates that the socio-economic hierarchy between the dominant Kallars and the dominated Paraiyars is still basically maintained. This, needless to say, corresponds with the fact that the land holdings of the Kallars are on average 16 times greater than those of the Paraiyars.

2. The Kallars not only dominate economically within the village but also branch out into the neighbouring town, Chekkanurani (cf. [Dumont, 1986: 19]). This is clarified by the number of Kallars classified in category B1 (Table 9.11) and is confirmed by Table 4.2, showing the shopowners' castes in Chekkanurani. Compared with this, the Paraiyars are marked by an almost total absence of occupations in category B1. This contrast suggests that the majority of Paraiyars cannot afford to invest in acquiring town-based occupations. In this sense, this point again confirms the differential of economic capital between the Kallars and the Paraiyars.

3. Roughly speaking, the distribution of occupations among the Paraiyars is characterized by a "polarization" between category A1 and category B2. It is remarkable that the extent to which the Paraiyars branch out in category B2 comes

Table 9.11
Main Occupations of Each Caste

Occupation	*Par.*	*Kal.*	*Pil.*	*Aca.*	*Nat.*	*Van.*	*Pan.*	*Kur.*
<A1: village-based occupations which are primarily closed within the village sphere)								
Farm labourer	87	32				6		
Agriculturalist	9	117	2	6	1		1	
Milk society	2	1			1			
Palm-leaf roof maker	2							
Bull-breeding	1							
Labourer-supervision	1	1						
V. A. O.'s servant	2							
Bullcart owner		2						
Milk collector		1						
Basket maker								1
Washing						6		
Sweeper								1
Priest							1	
Panchayat driver		1						
Postmaster		1						
Radio technician			1					
Crop spraying		2						
Total (<A1>)	104	158	3	6	2	12	2	2
<A2: village-based occupations which expand towards the outside economy>								
Goat sales		1						
Milk sales		3						
Paddy straw sales		2						
Moneylender		1						
Bull sales	1	5						
Kanja sales		1						
Carpenter	1	1		6				
Canal digging	1							
Cotton sales		1						
Tailor	1							
Mason	1	2						
Contractor		2	1					
Lorry-loader	16	24						
Stone cutter	1	1						
Waste paper collection					3			
Total (<A2>)	22	44	1	6	3	0	0	0

<B 1: town-based occupations which tend to be independent but are less guaranteed>								
Snack sales		3						
Vegetable sales		1						
Repairing					1			
Motor fitting		1						
Rikisha	1							
Frame maker		1						
Document writer		1						
Tea stall		1			1			
Grocery shop worker					3			
Shopkeeper		3	1					
Weaver		4						
Tailor shop		3			1			
Total (<B1>)	1	18	1	0	6	0	0	0
<B2: town-based occupations which are regarded as being stable employment>								
Forestry dept. guard	1							
Lorry conducter		1						
Electricity Board	1	1						
Company worker	2	3						
Bus driver		1						
Govt. jeep driver	1							
Railway worker	1	3						
Policeman		1						
School watcher					1			
University worker	1	1						
School teacher		1						
Accountant	1							
Lawyer	1							
Station master			(1)				1	
Central Govt. clerk			(1)				1	
Total (<B2>)	9	12	(2)	0	1	0	2	0
Total	136	232	5 + (2)	12	12	12	4	2
Unclear/non-worker	55	19	0	4	1	1	0	0

Notes: 1. Par., Kal., Pil., Aca., Nat., Van., Pan. and Kur. refer to Paraiyar, Kallar, Pillai, Acari, Natar, Vannar, Pantaram and Kuravar respectively.
2. ( ) indicates a person who stays outside the village.

close to that of the Kallars. It is very impressive that prestigious independent occupations, like lawyer and accountant are occupied by the Paraiyars, while some are employees of government bodies, such as the Forestry Department, the Electricity Board, the state government, and the University.[28] There is no doubt that this situation has been to some extent realized under the preferential policies (affirmative actions) of the government for the Harijans, especially in terms of education and employment. If the absence of occupations in category B1 and the polarization between categories A1 and B2 are jointly taken into account, this does not simply suggest that the village Paraiyars would be by and large still powerless without the help of the government, but also indicates that this government support has enlarged the gap within the Paraiyar community between the majority who are still confined to poverty, and the minority, who are enjoying success and economic privileges.

4. The so-called service castes, such as the Pantarams, the Acaris, the Vannars, and the Kuravars still primarily engage in their traditional professions, which are classified into category A1. There is a big economic differential between the former two landholding castes and the latter two landless castes. In this connection, it is notable that the Sanskritized groups, which hold economic power, like the Pillais and the Pantarams, hold the higher status and more stable jobs of category B2. As has already been argued, their property has been consumed in their pursuit of higher education by which such stable occupations are attained. In contrast, the village Natars show a strong connection with category B1. They are active as small merchants in Chekkanurani, as is shown in Table 4.2.[29]

Conclusion: Government Aid as a New Form of Patronage

The present economic position of the Paraiyars can be understood as follows: there is still generally a decisive economic gap between the dominant Kallars and the dominated Paraiyars, and only a limited number of Paraiyars exceptionally succeed in enjoying a slightly better economic position, due to both their own efforts and the special policies of the government. Since it is difficult for most villagers to make a living only by engaging in traditional occupations based on agriculture (category A) or only within the *jajmānī* relationship, they are forced to seek income from town-based work (category B). For this, it is often necessary to have some capital to invest in branching out beyond the village. This means that property holders can more easily adapt to these economic circumstances by themselves, whereas the poor people, mainly the Paraiyars, have greater difficulty doing so. In this context, the government aid to the villagers, especially to the Harijans, can be regarded as a new type of patronage, by which the traditional patronage of the dominant castes in the *jajmānī* relationship has to some extent been replaced. Though there is a fundamental difference between government aid and traditional patronage in terms of how to acquire the right of enjoying this patronage, both commonly contribute to assuring a minimum standard of living for the repressed people, such as the Harijans. It is true that the government's preferential treatment of the Harijans in various aspects, such as education, employment, housing and loans,[30] to a certain extent succeeds in raising the socio-economic position of the Harijans (e.g. their residential conditions). Nonetheless, there is a serious problem on the village level in that the government's preferential aid for them is not equally distributed among the poor Paraiyars, but rather works to extend the economic differential within the Paraiyar community. These government schemes tend to become a most attractive target which the propertied classes try to exploit, because the rather complex and opaque procedure for application which is required often results in an influential and propertied person, who is relatively more educated, being asked to act as a mediator between the government's office and the uneducated, poor applicants. Conspiracy aimed at exploitation is easily undertaken by the administrators, local politicians and local capitalists acting in the mediating process. In this sense, such an influential mediator, who can extract profit from the government, is a new type of patron, who is compared to the traditional patron by the poor. This vertical relationship forms a faction-like group consisting of a rather complex combination of power relations, new and old (cf. [Béteille, 1965: 200]). The problem of the Milk Society described in Chapter 12 provides a good example which reveals this social dynamism.

The Spread of Education among the Paraiyars

Higher Education and the Preferential Policy[31] for the Harijans

The Paraiyars' acquisition of the occupations of category B2, as mentioned above, has been encouraged by the government's preferential policy. More directly speaking, the reservation system prepared by the government has contributed to this. Not only does higher education provide a step to acquire "economic capital", but it is also part of the independent domain of "cultural capital". This is why education can be dealt with independently here, being separated from the sphere of the economy.

The education system which has been adopted in India since the 1970s is shown in Figure 9.1. The location of Kinnimangalam is rather convenient for those who want to remain in high education, because people can easily travel by bus to the College situated in Karumatur or in Madurai, and to the Madurai Kamaraj University, which is located on the way to Madurai.[32] It is very impressive that, according to Table 9.12, which shows the caste-wise distribution of people educated above Grade 10, the Paraiyars can today be compared to the Kallars. Historically speaking, the Kallars are forerunners, compared with the Paraiyars, because the Kallars were the special target of education under "the 'Kallar Reclamation' policy" [Dumont, 1986: 27] of the British government. The present situation indicates that the educational level of the Kallars[33] has rapidly been caught up with by the recent awareness by the

Figure 9.1

Educational System Since the 1970s (referring to courses such as science, engineering and letters)

Age	*Education Level*		
22		Ph.D.	
	M.Sc./M.Eg.	M.Phil	University (postgraduate)
21 20	B.Sc./B.Eg.	M.A.	
19 17		B.A.	College (undergraduate)
16 15	Plus Two Plus One		Higher Secondary School
14 10	Grade 10 Grade 6		High School
9 5	Grade 5 Grade 1		Elementary School
4 3	Upper K.G. Lower K.G.		Kindergarten

Paraiyars of the necessity of education.[34] The improvement in the educational level of the Paraiyars has been doubtlessly encouraged by the reservation system of the government, which is regarded as "compensatory discrimination" (see [Galanter, 1984: Introduction and Part One]).[35]

Table 9.12
Caste and Higher Education (1987)

Caste	*G10*		*Plus One*		*Plus Two*		*B.A.*		*M.A.*		*Total*	
	M	*F*	*M*	*F*	*M*	*F*	*M*	*F*	*M*	*F*	*M*	*F*
Pillai	—	—	1	—	—	—	1	—	—	—	2	0
Kallar	3	1	2	—	—	2	6		1	—	12	3
Pantaram	—	—	—	—	—	—	2	1	—	—	2	1
Acari	—	—	—	—	—	—	—	—	—	—	0	0
Natar	—	—	1	—	—	—	2	—	—	—	3	0
Vannar	—	—	—	—	—	—	—	—	—	—	0	0
Kuravar	—	—	—	—	—	—	—	—	—	—	0	0
Paraiyar	3	1	2		1	2	1		1	—	8	3
Total	6	2	6	0	1	4	12	1	2	0	27	7
	8		6		5		13		2		34	

Note: M: male, F: female

The Educated Youth and the Paraiyar Community

Though there is no doubt that, generally speaking, the importance of education has been, even though very gradually, recognized by the village Paraiyars, this awareness still tends to be limited to only part of the Paraiyar community. The transition process, as a result, has produced a polarization of the education levels within the village Paraiyar community (see [Oshikawa, 1981: 39–40]). What kind of conditions make the Paraiyar youth stay in higher education? The influential Paraiyars tend to encourage their sons to stay in higher education. Such people tend to be relatively better off socio-economically, which helps their children to continue studying longer. Table 9.13 to some extent verifies this correlation between a father's economic power (occupation) and his child's educational level. In this connection, I can mention the following example which shows the recent awareness by the Paraiyar youth of the importance of education. A youth of the Mataiyan lineage, CB, who is a student at the Tamil Polytechnic at Madurai told me about his experiences:

> My family is a bit complex because my mother got married twice. My mother had a son and a daughter in her first marriage and, after her former husband died, she married my father and had four children, namely, my brother, me, and my two sisters. My mother died when I was 6 years old and in Grade 2 and, after that, I was a lazy boy. But one day a Kallar acquaintance of my family advised me that I should study harder, otherwise I would not develop in future. This advice made me change and, after the incident, I began to study hard. I stayed in the government hostel from Grade 6 (10 years old) to Plus two (16 years old) during which I experienced various acts of caste discrimination. I have been provided with a scholarship from Plus one till today. Though the Polytechnic has

fixed, reserved seats (18%) for the Harijans, I did not use these special seats but entered by passing the examination of O.C. (Open Competition)[36]. In future, I would like to work to lift the social position of the Harijans, though I am now still powerless. For that, I need a good educational background. I have already begun to give advice on how education is important for us to the parents and the children of my community, reminding them that I was awakened by the Kallar acquaintance's advice.

Table 9.13

Father's Economic Power (Occupation and Landholding) and his Children's School Career Among the Paraiyars

(acre)

	Boy	*Girl*
Grade 10	* ? *Agriculturalist (PK1.25) + Farm labourer *Agriculturalist (PT2.00) + Company worker	*Agriculturalist (PK1.80) + Farm labourer
Plus One	*Electricity Board worker *Poultry farming (PK0.80, NA0.12)	
Plus Two	*Farm labourer (PK0.40)	**talaiyāri* (goverment servant) (PK0.30) *Railway worker (?)
B. A. M. A.	**talaiyāri* (government servant) (PK0.30) *Milk Society (PK4.00)	

This example shows that the preferential policy doubtlessly helped him enter the hostel and get the scholarship, even though he did not use the reserved seat for a college. It also clarifies the difficulties of social discrimination which the Harijan

Plate 73 A Paraiyar *kāriyakkāraṉs* who knows the world outside village through experience in the Indian army.

student has to confront and which may discourage him from continuing his studies[37]. Apart from the Kallar's advice and his personal excellence, it should not be overlooked that CB's father, who is a socially active Paraiyar, influenced him in various ways and that his elder brothers, who left school at early ages and began to work, support him financially. Such a family environment has made it possible for him to continue to study. Therefore, this example, as is already shown in Table 9.13, confirms that the difference between the socio-economically well off and less well off groups of Harijans within the father's generation is reproduced and enlarged in the sons' generation. The process qualitatively explains why the spread of education among the Paraiyar community has not progressed equally, but rather works for enlarging the split between the educational levels, at least in the transition phase.

Another interesting fact is made clear by the lineage composition of the 11 Paraiyars having a school career above Grade 10, which is shown in Table 9.14. In so far as total numbers are concerned, such educated persons are only from contrasting groups, namely, the most central group of the Kartananti and its affines, the Mataiyan, and the peripheral group of the Tankalan and its affines, the Manakuli.

Table 9.14

Lineage and School Career Among the Paraiyars

Lineage	*G10*	*Plus One*	*Plus Two*	*B. A.*	*M. A.*
Kartananti	0	0	(1)	1	1
Cinnananti	0	0	0	0	0
Mataiyan	0	1	1	0	0
Urkalan	0	0	0	0	0
Tankalan	2 + (1)	0	(1)	0	0
Manakuli	1	1	0	0	0

Note: Parentheses refer to women.

Nonetheless, the social gulf between the *Nārpaṅkāḷi*, deeply involved in the village caste structure, and the Tankalan, socially placed in a peripheral position of the structure, explains the clear difference in terms of the spread of higher education found among them. If the ratio of persons holding a school career over Grade 10 is calculated, the *Nārpaṅkāḷi*'s ratio is found to be 4.8 per cent whereas that of the Tankalan and the Manakuli is 12 per cent. Therefore, it is noted that a sharp split is found between the very few highly educated families and the still less educated majority among the *Nārpaṅkāḷi*; whereas there is no such split within the families of the peripheral lineages. This suggests that the socially peripheral people are more conscious of the value of education as a useful method for acquiring a more independent economic basis.

The increase in numbers of educated youth has exerted a considerable influence on the politics of the Paraiyar community. In particular, what should not be overlooked is that the monopoly of CV, the most influential man of the Kartananti, in his community began to be checked by the educated youth, such as CB of the Mataiyan an insider of the *Nārpaṅkāḷi*, and KP of the Tankalan. The appearance of young competitors like CB within the *Nārpaṅkāḷi* has had more radical effects than that of KP of the Tankalan. This is because, though KP's challenge to CV tends to be looked upon as a part of the conventional opposition between the Tankalan and the *Nārpaṅkāḷi*, the protest raised by a youth who is an insider of the *Nārpaṅkāḷi*, or from the same lineage, cannot be rephrased by such a conventional framework and has, therefore, strong and direct effects on checking CV's regime (see Chapter 12).

Education as "Cultural Capital"

So far I have dealt with education as an effective method for producing "economic capital" but, needless to say, the power of education is not exhausted by this. The more fundamental nature of education lies in the values connected with "status",[38] which cannot be fully reduced to "class". A higher academic career has, to some extent, the power of overcoming a low ritual status derived from caste membership. Although it is usually unthinkable for a Harijan man to formally marry a Kallar woman, there is an example of such an inter-caste marriage in a neighbouring village. The Paraiyar husband of this rare couple is the holder of a master's degree, and is now a high-school teacher. It is said that the Kallar relatives of his wife grudgingly accepted him because of his good educational background and his socially valued job. I do not claim that education always wins over caste discrimination but education doubtlessly widens one's choices, as Leach points out in a different context [Leach, 1988: 5]. This example reveals the positive aspect of the "cultural capital" of education, which contributes to reforming caste hierarchy. However, it should be kept in mind that, in so far as education is an independent type of "capital", it newly sets up its own hierarchy, which is not attributional in nature but tends to be "reproduced" through nurture ("habitus" in Bourdieu's concepts),[39] as argued in the previous section (see [Bourdieu, 1979b]).

Notes

1. It is well known that Béteille attempts to understand the social stratification of a Tanjore village as a combination of triadic social formations, namely caste, class, and power [Béteille, 1965]. Gough adopts basically the same concepts as Béteille's, that is, politics, caste, and class, though she also pays attention to ecology [Gough, 1989]. Bourdieu, in his analysis of French society, elucidates the contrasting concepts of "capital économique" and "capital culturel", and furthermore, adds the concept of "capital social" [Bourdieu, 1979b]. These three types of capital correspond respectively with the economy, education, and politics. These frameworks support my selection of using these three elements to analyse social power.
2. The four categories of agricultural lands are (1) *puṉcey kāṭu* (land lacking both tank-irrigation and well-irrigation), (2) *puṉcey tōṭṭam* (land having only well-irrigation), (3) *naṉcey kāṭu* (land having only tank-irrigation), (4) *naṉcey tōṭṭam* (land having both tank-irrigation and well-irrigation). Though *naṉcey* usually has a higher value than *puṉcey*, when the tank-irrigation does not work well due to irregular rainfall, the value of *tōṭṭam* rises relatively.
3. Land possession is registered by the combination of "Patta No.", which is identified with a landowner, and "Survey No.", which corresponds to the division of the land itself. This is

useful for recording the frequent movement in land ownership. The available register, called *Ciṭṭā*, records the changes in land-ownership through sale after 1963, but it is not kept up to date.

4. *Otti* was usually transacted verbally, but there is a recent tendency of drawing up a promissory note (*uṟuti moḻi*) because of an increase in associated problems. A typical difficulty arises if the *otti* giver sells the *otti* land to a party other than the *otti* taker.
5. In this sense, *otti* is "usufructuary mortgage" [Dumont, 1986: 131] so that the movement in the cultivation right of an *otti* land is usually regarded as being payment of interest. In this connection, the tax for the *otti* land is still formally the responsibility of the *otti* giver, as the owner, but in practice, it is paid by the *otti* taker, as the actual cultivator.
6. Through direct data collection, I noted that the villagers are very familiar with others' landholdings and their moves by *otti*. This means that villagers have played the role of witnessing each other's land moves. This type of mutual watch seems to still exist in the present village, in addition to the promissory note.
7. The total area of cultivated lands that I could collect directly is about 80 per cent of the area that can be calculated from the figures of the tax-fixed-cultivated-lands (*vari tīrmāṉikkappaṭṭu aṉūpōkattiliruppatu*), appearing in the Detail Notes of Kinnimangalam Revenue Village, which is based on the 1962 survey. However, the difference between my data and the revenue office data should not present a serious problem here, because my main purpose is to compare the land distribution among the different castes.
8. The two joint households, No. 129/130 and No. 123/124, are compensated for a little shortage of *puṉcey tōṭṭam* by having a little more *naṉcey*, whereas in No. 9, the shortage of *naṉcey* is balanced by *puṉcey tōṭṭam.*
9. The lands which the Pantaram priest manages are not his own private property but are temple lands, so that he cannot be regarded as another big landlord. The landholding of No. 15 is obviously greater than the maximum permissable holding (15 standard acres for a family of 5 members) fixed by the Tamil Nadu Land Reforms (Fixation of Ceiling on Land) Amendment Act (1970) [Gough, 1989: 24]. However, holding such big lands may be possible partly due to the calculation of "standard acre" [Moffatt, 1979: 68, fn.4] and partly because of tactics of registration [Gough, 1989: 41].
10. Béteille points out that, though the power of the *mirasdārs* was considerable at the beginning of the present century and the village socio-economic relations were formed on the patronage of such *mirasdārs*, in the 1960s not only was there a smaller proportion of landowners resident in the village, but also the size of individual holdings was greatly reduced. He does not clearly explain the changing processes of land dispersion, but he describes the difficulties that the present *mirasdārs* face. They cannot adequately play the role of the patrons of the village because of their reduced land holdings, their increased cost of living, the increased expense of education, the investment in acquiring urban employment, tenancy regulations for strengthening the position of tenants, and land ceilings for curbing the powers of landowners [Béteille, 1965: 201–202]. See also [Moffatt, 1979: 67–73].
11. The shift from bonded labourer to casual day labourer was encouraged under the Emergency imposed by Mrs Gandhi (1975–1977). Gough argues the influence of this policy [Gough, 1989: 149–151].
12. I should explain the methods used to obtain the data in Tables 9.5 and 9.6. The data in Table 9.5 were collected from the head of the household No. 7 by interview. He answered using round

numbers. In order to reduce his fabrication, I asked him in the following order: (1) kinds of crop, (2) each planted area, (3) cost of planting, (4) income from each crop. For, if I obtained correct answers to questions (1) and (2) at least, by comparing No. 7's case with several other cases I collected in the same way, I could check whether his answers on questions (3) and (4) were reasonable or not. I actually did so and I judged that his answers were plausible. The data in Table 9.6 were obtained by asking each head of household to write down annual cash expenses during the last one year. In this sense, there is a possibility that the data include some bias (faking), so that I deal with the data taking into account such a possibility.

13. The main agricultural period is the rainy season which starts in September and ends in January or February of the next year. Supplementary agriculture is conducted in the dry season. Therefore, the agricultural year spans two years, such as 1986–1987.
14. Several items in Table 9.6, such as travelling expenses, electricity, medical charges and education fees, which together account for about 20 per cent of the total expenditure, were not commonly incurred at the end of the 1940s. Nowadays (in 1986) it is said that in Madras Rs 1,000 per person per month is necessary for an upper-middle standard of living, and Rs 500 per person per month is required at least for a minimum standard of living. Recall that the data was given in 1986.
15. One day I visited his house in the early afternoon. He got up and told me, "I have taken a nap because I don't want to waste my energy". Not uncommonly, he had not had lunch on that day.
16. The Kallars and the Paraiyars who are the numerical majority in the village are involved in frequent gift exchanges within their lineages and among lineages. In the case of the Acaris, their activities in the caste association push up their expense of *moy*, apart from the prestations associated with their kinship relations.
17. Though Dumont points out that "field workers are apparently taken in turn" [Dumont, 1986: 43], I am not sure whether there ever was such a system in Kinnimangalam, and it is not the case today.
18. The situation has been reversed during the 1990s, because most of the village Paraiyars began to go to work in factories. As a result, the shortage of agricultural labourers is forcing the farmers to pay higher wages.
19. It is reported in the 1981 Census of India (Tamil Nadu) that the total children born per 100 married women is 311 on average in Tamil Nadu, and 315 on average in the Madurai district.
20. 42.59 per cent of the Harijans are landed householders in the village Moffatt studies [Moffatt, 1979: 74].
21. According to Moffatt, assuming that two to three acres of medium-to-poor quality land is required for the maintenance of a Harijan family, 16 out of the 108 Harijan families meet this standard in his village [Moffatt, 1979: 81]. If this standard is applied to Kinnimangalam, only two Paraiyar households, each of which holds the same amount of land as the average Kallar household, could be said to enjoy economic self-sufficiency.
22. KP's father increased his property as follows: (1) engaging in digging wells as a labourer; (2) being an independent contractor of well-digging; (3) rearing buffaloes for selling and milking, (4) being a *kuttakai* (a fixed rent tenure) tenant of two acres of *puṉcey tōṭṭam* held by a Kallar family, (5) setting up a brokerage dealing with buffaloes at the village level, (6) establishing the buffaloe markets in neighbouring towns, (7) taking *otti* land (2 acres of *puṉcey tōṭṭam*) in the mid 1950s, (8) buying 1.4 acres of *puṉcey kāṭu* in 1969, (9) buying 5 acres of *puṉcey kāṭu* in 1973. However, KP's father fell ill in 1976 and, after spending

more than Rs 25,000 on medical expenses, ultimately died. As a result, only the usufruct of two acres of *puṉcey tōṭṭam* as *otti* land remained in the hands of his son, KP.

23. However, the present ownership of the Kallars (60 bulls) seems to be very small, compared with Dumont's report on drought animals in Tengalpatti (215) [Dumont, 1986: 119].
24. During the 1990s, tractors have taken the place of bulls in agricultural work.
25. One litre of buffalo-milk is diluted with 2 litres of water for drinking, whereas 1 litre of cow-milk is diluted with only half a litre of water. The price of buffalo-milk (Rs 3/liter) is thus higher than that of cow-milk (Rs 2.5/liter). The situation of milking was again changed during the 1990s. Many private people have been promoting milking, especially cow-milking, these days.
26. The total number is greater than the number of households for the following reasons. There are two cases where the heads of the households are engaged in more than one occupation and in addition, other family members may be significant contributors to the household economy.
27. However, it is noted that many Kallar youth work as unguaranteed day labourers like agricultural labourers (32), lorry-loaders (24) and stone cutters (1). This occurs partly due to the time lag between the son's earlier independence and the delayed inheritance of lands from his father and partly because the inherited land or property may be insufficient to support the son's family.
28. The preference for employing Harijans as public servants in the central or state governments is one of the important policies for bettering the Harijans. It is, however, pointed out that the employment ratio of senior officers recruited from SC is still low [Oshikawa, 1981: 40]. This tendency seems to be valid for the case of the Paraiyars of Kinnimangalam, most of whom are only lower servants in the public sector.
29. The connection between the Natars and the town has persisted since the 19th century, when their social rise movement began under British rule [Hardgrave, 1969].
30. For example, Oshikawa [1981] and Galanter [1984] deal with the government's preferential policy for the Harijans. The policy consists mainly of a system of reservation and preference in educational, political, and administrative institutions, and of privilege in economic development. Nonetheless, the government's investment for economic development, which is more necessary for the rural Harijans, is still minor, and education has been unchangingly the central target of the policy and occupies more than half of the budget [Oshikawa, 1981: 34–40]. The main economic policies for the SC are (a) land redistribution, (b) the promotion of various industries, and (c) encouragement of the establishment of various cooperatives [ibid.: 41]. It can be seen that the establishment of Kinnimangalam Milk Cooperative comes under this policy (c).
31. The expression "preference policy" is adopted here because, though I basically agree with Galanter's argument on terminology, in which he recommends using the term "compensatory discrimination" [Galanter, 1984: 2–3], I give priority to ease of understanding here. The core scheme of the preferential policy is the system of reservation, which is laid out for the benefit of the "backward classes", namely, Scheduled Castes (SC) + Scheduled Tribes (ST) + Other Backward Classes (OBC) = "Backward Classes" [Galanter, 1984: 3]. However, as Oshikawa points out [Oshikawa, 1989: 9], the definition of backwardness is still very problematic, especially in terms of OBC, though the criteria of backwardness were given in "Report of the Backward Classes Commission" on Tamil Nadu (1970, 1985). An extensive discussion on the measures of backwardness is found in Chapter 8 of Galanter [1984]. Education is the central domain of the preferential policy to which the government has given its highest

priority. The state government is mainly responsible for educational schemes [Oshikawa, 1981: 35]. Needless to say, special treatment of outcastes did not only occur after independence, but the policy of the Indian government largely followed British policy. Policies such as land distribution to outcastes, and providing them with education, were found under British rule, even though their results were very limited [Galanter, 1984: Chapter 2].

32. In the village, there is an elementary school which developed from the school for the Kallar children founded under the British policy of "Kallar Reclamation" [Dumont, 1986: 27]. It is now open to all castes, including the Harijans. A high school and higher secondary school are available in Chekkanurani. In this area, there is another type of elementary school, called the "Panchayat Union Elementary School".
33. The Kallars are classified into the category of "Other Backward Classes (OBC)", or the category of "Socially and Educationally Backward Classes (SEBC)". This verifies their slow progress of rehabilitation.
34. Generally speaking, the educational level of women is much lower than that of men. For example, according to Maps 87 and 88 of the Census Atlas (Census of India 1981, Series 20-Tamil Nadu, Part xii), in 1981 the percentage of enrolment of males (15–24) at matriculation/secondary, higher secondary and higher levels was almost twice as great as that of females, that is, 11.11 per cent vs 5.98 per cent in the Madurai District.
35. "Compensatory discrimination" is realized in the following domains: education, employment, politics, economic development, and health, as shown in Table 6 of Oshikawa [1981: 34]. The number of reserved seats for assemblies, educational institutions, or public employment is basically determined in proportion to the ratio of the population. In Tamil Nadu, for example, a university reserves 18 per cent of its seats exclusively for the Harijans, because the Harijans occupy about 18 per cent of the total population of Tamil Nadu (for example, 18.35% in 1981). Nonetheless, it is still not easy to realize the intentions of the reservation system for various reasons. It sometimes occurs that the reserved seats cannot be filled, since the results of the entrance examination are too poor, and even after entering the university, many students drop out due to the inadequacy of their scholarships, their failure to adapt to the new environment, discrimination and so forth [Kirpal, 1978], [Oshikawa, 1981: 39].
36. 32 per cent of the total seats are secured for Open Competition, in which the examinees of all castes equally compete simply by marks. The rest are reserved for "the backward classes". Open Competition is conducted prior to the selection of the reserved seats.
37. The factors which discourage the Harijan students cannot simply be reduced to caste discrimination, but the big gap between their "habitus" acquired in their local and degraded life, and the new circumstances of school and dormitory, cause them to suffer from the difficulties of acculturation. Bourdieu and Passeron clarify this point in terms of students who are from rural areas [Bourdieu and Passeron, 1970].
38. As is well known, Srinivas takes "Western education" into account when he reconsiders his definition of "dominance" [Srinivas, 1987: 114].
39. For example, Bourdieu and Passeron deal with the complex configuration of elements for selection in the process of enrolment at higher education in their early work *Les héritiers* [Bourdieu and Passeron, 1964]. The argument is developed in *La reproduction* [Bourdieu and Passeron, 1970].

Chapter 10

Funeral Rites

A Caste-Based Strategy

This chapter concerns funeral rites, which can be thought of as ritual responses to death pollution (*tīṭṭu*) (cf. [Babb, 1975: 911]). First of all, the funeral rites of the Kallars, the major dominant caste, are described in order to provide an understanding of the whole structure of the funeral. Then, the ritual processes of the Sanskritized Pillais and of the Paraiyars are reported, in comparison with those of the Kallars.[1] These descriptions will illuminate the features of the Paraiyars' discourse on the funeral. It will be made clear that, on the one hand, there is no fundamental difference between the funerals of the Paraiyars and those of the Kallars, because both share the common basis of the less Sanskritized "popular" cultural tendency but on the other hand, the Paraiyars adopt some elements of the Pillais' funeral, fragmentally, which distinguishes them from the Kallars.

Funeral Rites of the Kallars

The Procedures of the Funeral

From Death to Burial

The following description is mainly based on my direct observation of the funeral rite conducted by the president of A. Kokkulam panchayat, who is one of the richest men in this area, but is generalized by the addition of the description of a funeral in Mavelipatti, and the general statements of informants. An ordinary, complete funeral for a "normal" death of a married person will be described here.[2]

A funeral rite is called *iḻavu kāriyam* ("funeral-function") which consists of a Tamil word *iḻavu* and a word of Sanskrit origin *kāriyam* (Skt. *kārya)*. Death is described as the state that *uyir* ("life") leaves *uṭampu* ("body"). The Kallars, especially the Kallar women, express their feelings of sorrow intensely soon after death (cf. [Dumont, 1986: 272]).[3] The corpse is washed by close relatives and clean clothes are put on it. It is then kept in a seated position facing towards the south, in the hall.[4] A Paraiyar (*tōṭṭi*) informs the villagers and the relatives of the deceased, by beating a drum called *tappu*. Digging the grave and making the ship-type of bier, called *kappal tēr*, [5] are also assigned to the *tōṭṭi*. The Kallars usually use a decorative *tēr* rather than a simple *pāṭai*, which it is thought indicates the poverty of the family. It is notable that, if a *tēr* is used, the face of the deceased will be shown to the public because of the seated posture. A temporary hut (*pantal*) is constructed in front of the house by hired labourers, and a one meter high *pantal kampu* (a miniature hut), the legs of which are made of branches of a milk-tree called *kaḷḷikkampu* (Euphorbia), is installed by the chief mourner. The necessary white cloths for making such *pantal*s are provided by a washerman. A musical band of the Harijans is indispensable for the funeral process until the burial (see [Dumont, 1986: 272] and [Good, 1978: 464]). In the case where the deceased was over fifty years old, a group of dancers called *rājarāṇi āṭṭam* is often in attendance.[6] People are believed to experience the most intense pollution until the completion of the burial. Thus eating and cooking activities are prohibited for the mourners during this time [Khare, 1976: 170–171].

The ceremony usually starts in the early afternoon, when relatives of both the husband and wife, at least the deceased's sons and their close affines like *tāymāmaṉ*, must gather in the mortuary house, because burial (or cremation) should be completed before sunset (see [Babb, 1975: 93]). It is said that, in the case of the death of a woman, *piṟantavīṭu taṇṇi* (literally, "birth-house water", namely, water taken from the parents' house) is brought by her brothers (the chief mourner's affines) for use in the ritual bathing (*kuḷippāṭṭutal*); whereas on the death of a man, the water for bathing is drawn from his village well by the classificatory "daughters" of the deceased, whose number should be odd. Nonetheless, in the case of the president's mother, the latter water was also sprinkled on the body. When a husband dies, his wife cuts her *tāli* (a gold ornament symbolizing her married state) herself, immediately after the bathing. In the same bathing place, the chief mourner causes the corpse to hold *navatāṉiyam* (nine kinds of grains) in its hand, and the chief mourner's wife then takes it from the corpse's hands and mixes it with three balls of cowdung. The balls of cowdung are pasted by her on the wall to which the corpse has its back, as is described later. A new cloth is put on the corpse after the ritual bathing which is compared to *apiṣēkam* (Skt. *aphiṣeka*) (see [Das, 1976: 253]). Following this, a ceremony called *paṭṭam eṭukkiṟatu* ("cloth lifting-up") is conducted by the chief mourner[7] and other "sons" (and "grandsons") of the deceased, who are younger than the deceased (cf. [Dumont, 1986: 274]). These, wearing garlands and holding *kumpā* (a small bowl) in their right hands, proceed under a canopy of long white cloth (8 fathoms)[8] to the junction of the village boundary, called *kuṭam uṭaikkumiṭam* (literally, "pot-breaking place"). At the head of the procession is a barber as the "funeral priest" [Dumont, 1986: 278], who officiates for this rite. At the junction, the canopy of white cloth is spread on the ground and *kumpās* are put on it. Then, those in the procession prostrate themselves to the north and recite "*corkkalōkam cēr* (reach the heaven)!" three times when the barber indicates that they should, while the barber sprinkles water over them (see [Good, 1978: 467]).

When the corpse leaves its former home, before being carried on the *tēr*, it is taken and laid under the *pantal kampu*, where it is said to experience its last sleep in this world.[9] The corpse is set in the sitting position in the *tēr*. A washerman spreads a white cloth in front of the *tēr* and, when the *tēr* passes over the cloth, one *marakkāl* of paddy is dropped on it. The paddy will be taken by the washerman as the last gift from the deceased. The order of the funeral procession is as follows; (1) *tōṭṭi* having a big hatchet (*veṭṭu arrivāḷ*) and a firepot (*akkiṉi caṭṭi*), (2) tom-tom beaters and dancers, (3) a barber having a small bowl (*kumpā*) containing *vāykkarici* (raw rice mixed with turmeric) and a small hatchet (*paṉṉarivāl*), and a washerman holding a white towel (*māttutuṇṭu*), (4) male relations, (5) the *tēr* carried by relations and friends (8 persons), (6) female relations. However, female relations are not allowed to go beyond the village border, *kuṭam uṭaikkum iṭam* (cf. [Good, 1978: 474]). They must bid farewell to the deceased there, after conducting a small ceremony called *kāikuṭam, uṭaittal*, in which a woman (the deceased's wife or eldest daughter) plays an important role and is given *muṇṭaccēlai* ("a widow"s sari") by her brother or by her *tāymāmaṉ*. This rite corresponds with that which the chief mourner performs in the burial ground. When the *tēr* leaves the village, women may express their sorrow by crying and beating their breasts (this is called *mār aṭittal*). Up to the village border the corpse on the *tēr* faces towards the village centre, but from there on its back is turned on the village and it proceeds to the burial ground (cf. [Good, 1978: 468]). After leaving the village, the procession speeds up a little. People start tearing the floral decorations of the *tēr* off. It is believed that this prevents the beloved one's ghost from returning to the village. Meanwhile, the women go back home and conduct the rite called *cītēvi vāṅkutal* (to receive the Goddess Laksmi),[10] in which the chief mourner's wife pastes the cowdung balls on the wall and lights *kuttuviḷakku*. This ritual act indicates the wealth and luck of the deceased. It seems to me that the rite typically symbolizes the dynamism of "death and the regeneration of life" by connecting together death, a woman's reproductive power, and agricultural production.

When the procession reaches the burial ground, the *tēr* is revolved clockwise[11] once and put down near the grave, and the corpse is removed from the *tēr* and laid down by the side of the pit. The direction of the head must be south. Immediately, the *tēr* is hacked down by the *tōṭṭi* with a big hatchet. The barber takes the shroud of the corpse off and cuts off any adornment, such as a garland, a waist chain or *tāli*. Further, the barber shaves the chief mourner's head (see [Good, 1978: 497]). For this service, the barber has the right to a portion of the shroud taken off the corpse (see [Dumont, 1986: 274–275] and [Good, 1978: 469] for South India and [Raheja, 1988: 148] for North India). Giving *vāykkarici* to the corpse is carried out by the male relations in turn. The rice and a 25 paisa coin put on the forehead of the deceased are finally given to the *tōṭṭi*. Further, a 25 paisa coin called *tāyvāippaṇam* ("maternal-line money") is ritually given to the senior person (*tēvār*) of the deceased's *paṅkāḷi* by the *tāymāman* of the chief mourner. The corpse is then taken down into the pit. The head is placed south and the face is turned a little to the east. After the body is covered with a white cloth, the chief mourner casts soil into the pit with the back of his right hand. Then the other relations follow him. Lastly, the *tōṭṭi* forms the mound and completes the burial (*putaittal*). *kāikuṭam uṭaittal* ("trickling-pot breaking") is conducted by the chief mourner and he finally makes a fire at the head side of the grave.[12] This is accompanied by a drum beaten by the *tōṭṭi*, which is called *kaṭaici koṭṭu* ("last drum"). People put a donation on the cloth, called *māttutuṇṭu*, which the washerman spreads on the ground, and then return home. The money collected, which is called *potupaṇam* ("common-money"), is distributed to the barber, the washerman and *tōṭṭi* for their services. Those who are seen to be heavily polluted have to take a bath on their way back, and then are again purified with water before entering their houses. Reaching home, the chief mourner goes to and worships in the place where the body was installed. He then consults a *tāymāmaṉ* on the date of *karumāti*, which is usually chosen from the seventh, nineth or eleventh day after the death. Another ritual called *koḷḷi taṇṇi* ("fire-water"), in which a potful of water and the deceased's favourite items are offered, is conducted by the chief mourner and his close male relations at the "pot breaking places" on the night of the same day, in order, it is believed, to appease the soul on the deceased.

Plate 74 *Rājarāṇi āṭṭam* which consists of Paraiyar men only.

Plate 75 *Vāykkarici* (raw rice mixed with turmeric) and *tīpeṭṭi* (a fire pot).

Plate 76 A rite at *kuṭam uṭaikkum iṭam*.

Plate 77 *Pantal kampu* kept in the backyard.

Plate 78 A palanquin type of gorgeous *kappal tēr*.

Plate 79 The broken *tēr* at the cemetery.

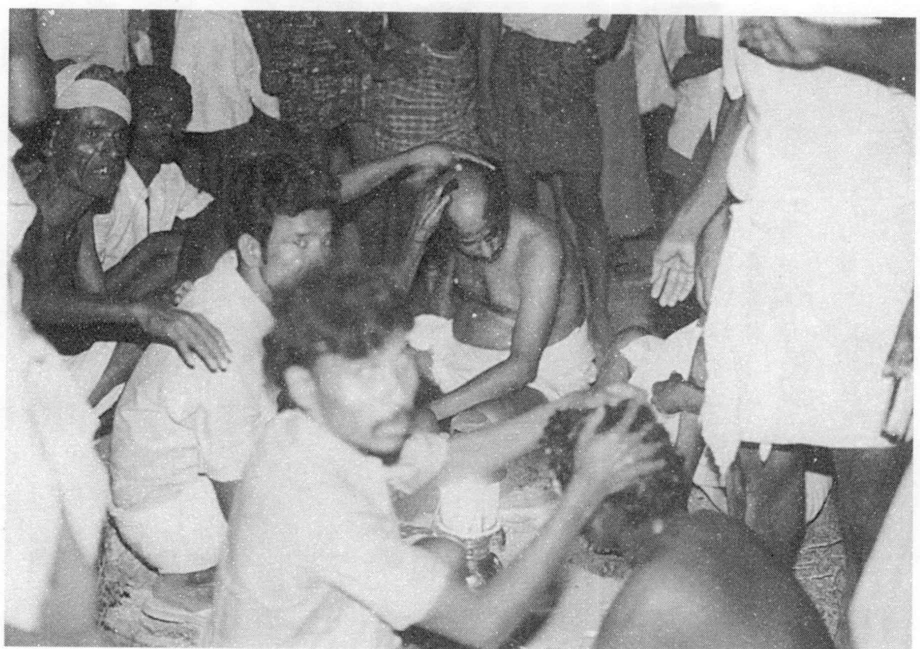

Plate 80 Tonsure at the cemetery.

Plate 81 *Karumāti* rite: Eating together.

Plate 82 *Karumāti* rite: Throwing *pantal kampu*.

Plate 83 *Karumāti* rite: *Urumā kaṭṭutal*.

The next day, the rite called *pāl ūṟṟutal* ("milk pouring") is held at the burial place. The chief mourner and his close relations pour milk and sow *navatāṉiyam* (nine kinds of grains) on the burial mound. It is said that the aim is the recovery of the fertility of the land (see [Good, 1978: 476–7]). In the evening, all the *paṅkāḷi* sit down to a vegetarian meal of one dish, made of millet and beans,[13] through which the unity of the *paṅkāḷi* is reinforced. It is expressed as *oṟṟumaiyāka taḷukai cāppiṭutal* ("single offering dining").

Karumāti

According to the Tamil lexicon, *karumāti* is a synonym of *karumantaram* which means the last funeral ceremony (the Tamil lexicon) (cf. [Good, 1978: 477]). It is said in the village that *karumāti* is the sons' last duty to their parents. In point of fact, the Kallar people consider *karumāti* very important, as they tend to think the ceremony in the main enhances the departure of the soul of the dead. This notion corresponds with their recognition of death pollution. It is believed that *tīṭṭu* is substantially reduced by the burial and, further, that it is almost completely removed by *karumāti*, though death pollution remains till the thirtieth day after the death. In the case I observed, *karumāti* started in the afternoon of the seventh day after the death.[14] It is, in general, understood that the relations above must all attend *karumāti*, whether they were on bad terms with the deceased's family or not. At the outset, there is a joint ritual dining at *tāukai* which is the first preparation of a non-vegetarian meal in the house of the deceased after the death. The male *paṅkāḷi* members eat together sharing one plate, which is placed where the corpse lay in state (see also Khare [1976: 172]). Another portion, which is served under the *pantal kampu*, is eaten by the children. It is said that consuming such food guarantees that the departed one's soul will reach heaven, and at the same time ensures that the children will live long lives. On completing this shared meal, the rite of removing *pantal kampu*, called *pantal kampu piṭuṅkutal*, is conducted by the *tāymāmaṉ* with the help of the barber.[15] The departure of the deceased is confirmed by this rite.

The central rite of the latter part of *karumāti* is *urumā kaṭṭutal* ("the tying of the turban"). After getting permission to begin *urumā kaṭṭutal* from the people, the *tāymāmaṉ* first of all ties *keṇṭai tuṇṭu* (a white towel with silver lines)[16] on the head of the chief mourner and puts *vēṭṭi* (a white sarong for a man) on him. Following this, other *māmā-macciṉaṉ* relations perform *urumā kaṭṭutal* for the chief mourner and the *uṭan paṅkāḷi* of the deceased who stand in a row. Then, the deceased's family serves an evening meal to the people of *māmā-macciṉaṉ*. The next day, the *māmā-macciṉaṉ* relations, namely, the chief mourner's Zs, his FZ, and his affinal relations, jointly buy a goat, prepare a non-vegetarian meal and serve it to the deceased's *paṅkāḷi* (see [Dumont, 1986: 276]), after which the chief mourner and his agnates take an oil bath. This ceremonial partaking of a meal is called *ākki pōṭutal* (cooking and serving). After dining, the chief mourner presents a new sari and new vessels to his sisters. This is said to be *ceymuṟai* (a traditional duty).

Thus, it is very obvious that *karumāti* presents an important opportunity both for reconfirming the unity of the *paṅkāḷi* and for re-affirming affinal relationships. Therefore, people believe that they should attend *karumāti* above all else.

Muppatām nāḷ (the thirtieth day ceremony)

Until the thirtieth day after the death, the lamp (*kuttuviḷakku*) that stands where the deceased lay in state, is lit up every morning and evening. On the eve of *muppatām nāḷ*, the rite again called *cempum taṇṇiyum vaiccu aḻukkiṟatu* is held by the close women relatives.[17] In the early morning of the thirtieth day, the mortuary house is cleaned out and old dishes are replaced with new ones. Vegetarian food is prepared and served to the relations. In the evening, the chief mourner visits the favoured temple, such as a Murugan temple, and offers a light called *mōṭcaviḷakku* (a votive light for emancipation). It is believed that death pollution (*tīṭṭu*) vanishes completely with this rite, and all concerned return to ordinary life. As is described later, only in the case of the death of a priest (*pūcāri*) or of a god-dancer (*cāmiāṭi*), in which cremation is adopted, are the more elaborate rituals for selecting a successor of the deceased, which the Brahman attend, conducted at a bank of the Vaigai river (see Dumont [1986: 277]).

The Kallars do not conduct *tivaṣam* (anniversary of death).

Reflections on the Soul and the other World

The reflections of the Kallars on the soul and the other world are as follows. Death is believed to produce two existences, namely, the *āvi* (the soul) and the *piṇam* (the dead body).[18] It is said that, although the *piṇam* is effaced by burial, the *āvi* remains with us and wanders through the world, at most until the thirtieth day after the death.[19] They feel more strongly the existence of the *āvi* before *karumāti*. On the thirtieth day, the a *āvi* is said to reach the other world. However, it is believed that an *āvi* of accidental or of abnormal death often becomes a *pēy* (ghost) and continues to roam in the world because of its strong attachment to the world. It is important that it is never thought that an *āvi* is transformed into a *pitiṛ* (the ancestor's spirit), and that the term *pitiṛ* itself is almost unknown to the community. This obviously coincides with the fact that *tivaṣam* is unobserved by them. In addition, it also indicates that their view of the other world is not very developed, indeed not well structured at all (see also [Dumont, 1986: 278]) and [Babb, 1975: 91]). Although the distinction between *corkkam* (heaven) and *narakam* (hell) is touched on by many Kallars, their answers to questions of where the other world is, that is, where the *āvi* goes to, are very vague (see [Good, 1978: 495]). The popular reply is that it goes to the upper level or to the sky.[20] As is suggested by a Kallar's statement that "We do not know where our ancestors live. Death is the end of human existence", their understanding of the other world is less elaborated and shows a this-worldly tendency. Thus, it seems to me that "ethicization" (in Obeyesekere's sense) of the Kallar's view of the other world is half way complete [Obeyesekere, 1968: 12–18].

It seems that their ideas of reincarnation are also not very clear (see also [Good, 1978: 494–5]). Therefore, although they to some extent understand the notion of *karmaviṉai* (the accumulated result of deeds done in former life) in its original sense, the notion interestingly tends to be modified by the interpretation that the actions of the previous generation influence the lives of the present generation. Corresponding with this, the concept *karumam* (Skt. *karman*) tends to be interpreted as negative and inauspicious incidents, like poverty, sin, and death, rather than as actions or deeds causing better or worse reincarnation (cf. [Maloney, 1975: 175]). Thus, this again verifies that their image of the world after life is a combination of "preliterate religion which lacks a theory of reincarnation" and "preliterate religion which includes a notion of reincarnation" in Obeyesekere's sense [Obeyesekere, 1968: 12–18]. At the same time, their understanding shows a secular tendency, in other words, they are not very concerned with abstract religious legitimacy, which they cannot directly confirm. The evidence for such a tendency is also found in their interpretation of *tarumam* (Skt. *dharma*). The Kallars understand *tarumam* as giving food, goods, or money to the poor as charity, rather than as piety (the more mental act) (cf. [Maloney, 1975: 175]). Obviously, this interpretation is a reflection of their dominant position in the village.

There is little doubt that the above-mentioned materialistic and less structured (less abstract) view of the soul and the other world corresponds with their "popular" cultural tendency crystallizing into "pollution" ideology.

Cases of Cremation

Cremation is more a matter for special cases among the Kallars, who are usually buried in the ground.

The first special case is the death of a lineage priest (*pūcāri*) and of a god-dancer (*cuvāmiāṭi* or *cāmiāṭi*). It is said that they should be cremated because they are equated with gods (*cuvāmi* or *cāmi*). In this case, cremation is done in the usual cemetery used by the Pillai. In this sense, only *pūcāri* and *cuvāmiāṭi* are thought to be ritually equitable with the ritually higher caste and are differentiated from other ordinary Kallars. In addition, they have an elaborate 30th day ceremony officiated by the Brahman priest (Aiyar) on the bank of the Vaigai river.[21] This shows that the Kallars accept the idea that cremation is a ritually higher funeral method than burial. Nonetheless, there is still room to think in a different way: that the important thing is to keep the distinction between those godly persons and ordinary persons, by which their socio-religious order is safely maintained.

The second special case is unnatural or accidental death, such as suicide, murder, or a traffic accident, where it is believed that the soul of the deceased bears a grudge and is resentful, making people afraid that it may become a *pēy* and roam the world indefinitely. It is believed to be necessary that its strong attachment must be cut off by cremation, the burning of the body to ashes (see also [Dumont, 1986: 277].[22] What should be carefully considered is the implication of cremation in this context. One way of understanding it is that cremation has a more decisive power of cutting off the deceased's attachment to this world than burial does. This understanding is not directly given by the Kallars, but is suggested by the facts and the explanation that the Pillais, who usually conduct cremation, would not cremate in the case of a child's death because they think that cremation makes the child's returning to this world more difficult.

Although the separation power of cremation, a functionalist answer, by and large seems to explain the Kallar's adoption of cremation in unusual deaths, there could be another answer: that to change the funeral method itself makes clear the distinction between the usual and the unusual. The latter point is stimulated by Das's discussion, in which cremation is deemed as a sacrificial act. According to Das, in cases of sudden death, unnatural death, and an ascetic's death, the body is not allowed to be cremated because it has already been sacrificed [Das, 1976: 255]. I take up here the phenomena she raises rather than her textual explanation. At any rate, Das's example is the reverse of the Kallars' case. It should, however, be noted that both examples share the common concern that an "unusual death" must be distinguished from a usual death by the different disposition of the body, though the adoption of cremation is contrastive. This indicates a sort of structuralist viewpoint that the significance lied in the actual distinction itself.

After considering both special cases, it seems to me that a structuralist view of handling socio-religious boundary phenomena is more relevant to the Kallars' real situation. In sum, it could be concluded that their main concern, even if unwitting, expressed through the adoption of a different funeral method, is how to cope with unusual and formidable other-worldly forces, both good (*cuvāmi*) and bad (*pēy*). In this sense, Das's functionalist explanation mentioned above has its limitations.

The Social Position of a Widow

The Kallars call a widow *vitavai, kaimpoṉṭāṭṭi or muṇṭacci*; whereas a wife whose husband is in good health is called *cumaṅkali*, which means a woman having purity. Though it is certainly said to be undesirable that a widow attend an auspicious ceremony, there is no special restriction against the remarriage of a widow. In fact, almost all widows who lose their husbands in the early stages of their lives do remarry. Related to this, it should be noted that the Kallars evaluate the custom of *satī* (or a sacrificial death of a widow) negatively. These views regarding a widow again indicate that their cultural tendency is very different from the Brahmanical one.

Funeral Rites of the Pillais

As already explained, the Pillais enjoy the highest ritual status, and are the most Sanskritized people in the village. The clearest difference between the Kallars and the Pillais lies in the fact that the funeral method of the Pillais is always cremation and that therefore their funeral procedure as a whole comes closer to the Brahmanic ceremony. In this section, I will describe the funeral rites of the Pillais by emphasizing the points which differ from those of the Kallars.

From Death to Cremation Rites

Though I deal with the case of two natural deaths of married people, I mention here two modified versions of such funerals. Firstly, in the case of an unusual death, in contrast to Das's case, the village Pillais conduct cremation, as they do in the case of a usual death. It should, however, be noted that there is certainly a distinction between a usual death and an unusual death, which is made by minimizing the ceremony. Secondly, there is one exception in which burial is found, that is, the case of the death of an unmarried youth or a child.[23] This is explained as follows: burial should be adopted so as to avoid the long wait that cremation entails before rebirth, because the soul of the deceased child must soon return to the world to complete its life (cf. [Sekine, 1984: 20]). This notion is associated with their custom that *karumāti* is not observed on the death of an unmarried person.

It is said among the Pillais that they should not weep too soon when confronted by death, because they believe that if they do so, this will prevent the soul from reaching heaven. Consequently, they are allowed to weep only after the formal procedures for the enshrinement of the deceased are completed. The corpse is kept on sand and *teṟpai* (Skt. *darbha*) in the lying position with its head towards the south, or sometimes in the sitting position with its face towards the north. The Pillais attach importance to the sound of a conch-shell being blown several times an hour, by a barber, from the death to the cremation. After conducting the water fetching rites (*nīrmālai eṭuttal*),[24] the chief mourner encircles the deceased person three times and sprinkles water on the corpse. The bereaved widow sits at the corpse's feet so as to receive these drops of water (cf. [Raheja, 1988: 148]). This act symbolizes a ritual bathing. The dressed corpse is laid in state under the *pantal kampu* which is a 4 legged miniature hut, or sometimes under a canopy called *paccai pantal*. When the chief mourner, carrying one marakkāl of paddy, encircles the body three times, he is followed by his wife, who takes a cowdung ball and puts *navatāṉiyam* (nine kinds of grain) on the ball for each turn. Then she pastes these three cowdung balls on the wall near the place where the deceased was kept (*cītēvi vāṅkutal*). Before transferring the corpse to the *tēr* the rite called *neypantam piṭittal* ("butter-oil-torch grasping") is held by the grand children as a sign of their respect for the deceased. The women must see the deceased off in the house, and *muṇṭaccēlai* ("a widow's sari") is given to the deceased's wife, lying at the corpse's feet, just before it is carried away.[25] No funeral priest is invited to this ritual stage.

The corpse is put into the *tēr* (a bier) in the seated position. The funeral procession is accompanied by the blowing of a conch by the barber, which does not occur in the case of the Kallars. At the cremation ground, the *tōṭṭi* have previously placed cowdung cakes in readiness for the cremation. The corpse is laid on the cowdung cakes with its head directed towards the south. Then the corpse is covered with cowdung cakes and paddy straws, and is further concealed by clay, except for three small holes around the head, stomach, and feet. All this work is done by the *tōṭṭi*. During this labour, the chief mourner's head is shaved by the barber. The chief mourner then encircles the clay-covered body three times, carrying a water pot. Each times he reaches the head of the corpse, the barber makes holes in this water pot. The water pouring from the holes is sprinkled onto the clay mound. Soon after breaking the pot, the chief mourner starts a fire in the hole near the head of the corpse. He then, accompanied by the others, starts on his way home. Only the *tōṭṭi* remains there, to watch the cremation (cf. [Good, 1978: 476] and [Sekine, 1984: 22].

The next day, *pāl uṟṟutal* (a rite of pouring milk) is conducted which it is believed cools down the cremation ground. Before going to the cemetery, some offerings such as cooked rice made of *paccaiarici* (raw rice), one boiled green banana,[26] seven *vaṭais* (a fried snack), most probably as *piṇṭams* (Skt. *piṇḍas*),[27] and other items are temporarily placed under the *pantal kampu*, and the female relations wail there. It is said that wailing at the *pantal kampu* is deemed as an act of *tīṭṭu*. Afterwards, these offerings and the oil used for making the *vaṭai* are taken to the cemetery. At the cemetery, cow's milk and other items are poured onto the site where the body was cremated. It is believed that these substances purify the site. The bones and ashes are then collected from the eleven parts of the body by the chief mourner and other sons. Then, the site is cultivated and *navatāṉiyam* is sown there. It is said that this action signifies the recovery of the land's fertility. The bones and ashes which have been collected are thrown into a river either on the same day or on the fifteenth day after the death. After this, the chief mourner and others return home and worship at the place where the corpse was kept. Then they eat vegetarian food which is cooked using the hearth of the deceased's house.

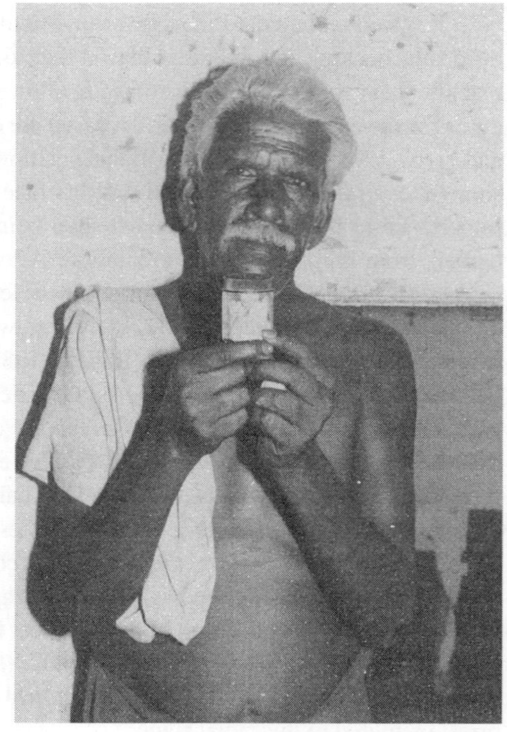

Plate 84 Father keeps remembrance of his son.

Until the thirtieth day after the death, a lamp is lit every evening at 6 o'clock. Until *karumāti*, namely, the sixteenth day, the women of the deceased's family wail ritually every morning at around 4 o'clock. On the third, eighth and fifteenth days, a consolation rite called *kiḻamai vaittal* ("connection creating") is repeatedly conducted, mainly by the close women relations, and the whole cost of the *kiḻamais* is borne by the deceased's "daughter" relations. The first *kiḻamai*, held on the third day, is associated with the rite of removing the *pantal kampu* (*pantal kampu piṭuṅkutal*), and is conducted by the barber. In the case of the death of a husband, the *tāli* is taken off from the neck of the deceased's wife on the night of the fifteenth day, i.e., the night prior to *karumāti*. This rite, called *tāli aṟuttal*, starts from midnight and finishes before dawn.[28] At the end of the rite, she receives a new sari from her brothers. Then she has a bath just before dawn, and sees the day of *karumāti* in.

Karumāti and After

Karumāti of the Pillais is ideally held on the sixteenth day after the death. It is completely different from that of the Kallars in so far as the Pillais invite a Brahman priest to officiate. A member of the family draws a square boundary with four gates in a particular place near the bank of the eastern tank. Within this sacred place a Brahman sits facing north and the chief mourner sits on his right. Paddy husks, three kinds of firewood (mango, banyan and bo) and a *kumpam* (a decorated pot symbolizing Siva) are prepared in front of the Brahman. The Brahman builds a fire using the paddy husks and firewood and recites mantras while pouring ghee (liquid butter) into the fire. Then, four *piṇṭams* (balls of rice flour mixed with green-gram, ghee, honey, sesame oil and so on) are made by the Brahman. It is said that one separate *piṇṭam* is for the crows and the other three are for the deceased, his father and his grandfather respectively.[29] The combination of these *piṇṭams* symbolizes the unification of the deceased's soul with his ancestors. This ritual act can be seen as *capiṇṭīkaraṇam* (Skt. *sapiṇḍikaraṇa*, "making a *sapiṇḍa*") which indicates a complete conservation from *preta* to *pitṛ* [Nicholas, 1981: 375] (see also [Parry, 1985: 614–616, 621–624]). Finally, the Brahman chants a *mantiram* (Skt. *Mantra*) to the *kumpam*, identified with Siva, to ensure that the soul reaches heaven and acquires peace at Siva's feet. Then, the sons of the deceased go to the tank and bath 108 times. They change their wet clothes for new *vēṭṭis* and *tuṇṭus* given by their *tāymāmaṉ* which are handed from the Brahman and return home immediately. On entering their house, their feet are washed and purified by the women of the family. Finally, the chief mourner lights a lamp at the place where the corpse was laid and worships there. The ritual finishes with a feast served by the bereaved family.[30] Though *karumāti* reduces *tīṭṭu* substantially, it is nevertheless said to remain until the thirtieth day. The thirtieth day does not involve any elaborate rite. The family just goes to a temple to light a lamp (*mōṭcaviḷakku*).

Only in the first year after a death are there mourning ceremonies for the deceased held eight days before *Āti amāvācai,*[31] on the day of *Tīpāvaḷi* (the festival of offering a fire at the end of November), and on the day of *Tāipoṅkal* (the harvest festival in mid-January when ancestral spirits are believed to visit the world). In addition, an annual anniversary commemorating the death, called *niṉaivunāḷ* ("remembrance day") or *tivaṣam* (Skt. *divasa*), is held by the Pillais, at least on the first anniversary, until which the widow must observe a restricted lifestyle, having but one meal and a light snack per day.

It has been made clear that the expression of kinship unity, which is emphasized during Kallar funerals, is not as prominent during Pillai funerals. Instead, concern for the ancestral world is increasingly demonstrated during the rituals based on Hindu orthodoxy.

Outlook on the Soul and the Next World

As is indicated by their practice of *niṉaivunāḷ*, the Pillais have a relatively clearer consciousness about ancestral spirits than do the Kallars. It is, however, also true that the Pillais' recognition of the next world still has a certain vagueness when compared with the knowledge of Hindu texts which is embodied in the funerals of the Aiyars, as can be seen from the comparison in Table 10.1 (*vide infra*). This is, for example, made obvious by their use of the word *āvi* rather than *pitiṛ* for the soul of the dead, even after the *capiṇṭīkaraṇam* rite (cf. [Gough, 1959: 256]), despite the fact that they know the word *pitiṛ* because they have heard it in the chanting of the Brahmans. Nonetheless, there is no doubt that their ritual position is much more Sanskritized than that of the Kallars. For instance, according to the Pillais, *karma* means action in the neutral sense, and they also define *dharma* not only as the giving of alms but also as performing a moral duty. Such answers obviously come closer to a textual knowledge than do those of the Kallars. A similar tendency is found in their outlook on rebirth.

Lastly, let us mention their outlook on widows, called *kaimpeṉ*. The Pillais tend to more strongly regard a widow as inauspicious and, moreover, as radiating a feeling of *tīṭṭu,*[32] than do the Kallars. The custom of *satī* is rather positively accepted by the Pillais, with the condition that she has no child. Among the Pillais, a widow's remarriage is not desirable and she must give up her enjoyments as woman and follow various restrictions.[33] Generally speaking, the Pillais tend to underestimate the status and the ability of women, compared with that of men, whereas the Kallars, in contrast, accept ultimately the equality between men and women. This demonstrates yet again that the Pillais are more Sanskritized than are the Kallars. In this connection, it can be interestingly noted that consolation rites for the bereaved wife as a widow are emphasized much more in the Pillais' funeral rites than in the case of the Kallars. Thus, it seems that the Sanskritized Pillais regard women as lesser beings, to be protected; whereas the less Sanskritized Kallars accept the ability of women as approximating that of men (see [Allen, 1982: 18]).

Funeral Rites of the Paraiyars

The funeral I describe here is that carried out by an economically better off Paraiyar family in a relative sense.[34] A funeral ceremony carried out by a poorer family would be a simplified form of what I describe below. It is useful to examine the case of an elaborate and expressive funeral ceremony, which more clearly discloses what the Paraiyars seek, in order to compare the funeral rites of the Paraiyars with those of the Kallars and the Pillais.

Since the Paraiyars basically share similar procedures with the Kallars, I will mainly emphasize their differences. The ritual parts which I ignore may be taken as being the same as those of the Kallars.

From Death to Burial

The news of death is spread not only by the cooperation of relations and friends but also by a hired messenger, who is paid Rs 100. The relatives of the mortuary family arrange the workers necessary for the funeral, such as Harijan musicians and dancers called *rājarāṇi-āṭṭam* (who are paid Rs 400), *tēr*-makers (who are paid Rs 200), flower-decorators (who are paid Rs 150), *pantal*-makers (who are paid Rs 100), the Potaravannar (who are paid Rs 20) and several labourers (who are paid Rs 50). Nowadays, these workers are often hired from Madurai city. *Pantal kampu* is made by the *māmā-maccinaṉ* side. The *pantal kampu* that I observed was a triangular form with three legs, whereas the Kallars always make a square shape of *pantal kampu* with two or four legs. Only the Potaravannars are the service caste for the Paraiyars and they play the roles of both barber and washerman, which are indispensable for the funeral.

A Paraiyar Funeral

The Paraiyars follow the same procedures as the Kallars do from death to the enshrinement of the deceased. The Paraiyars, however, believe that ideally one should not cry too soon after death. If this is taken at its face value, it comes closer to the behaviour of the Pillais than to that of the Kallars. However, the overall atmosphere of Paraiyars' funerals is rather clamorous and is similar to that of the Kallars, so that it is very doubtful that they actually practise this claim. The sons' generation of the deceased conducts the rite of *nīrmālai iruttal*, under the guidance of the Potaravannar. One of the notable points, which differs from the Kallar case, is that they each wear a *pūṇūl* ("sacred string") after bathing at the well, which is located outside their residential cluster. Another point is that they conduct the rite of *paṭṭam eṭukkiṟatu* ("cloth lifting-up"), as part of the *nīrmālai iruttal*, on their way back home, at a place just outside the village boundary (see [Good, 1978: 472–3]).

In the case of the death of a husband, a wife removes her *tāli* when the corpse is carried into the *tēr*, whereas in the case of the wife's death, her *tāli* is taken off before burial.[35] In the procession to the cemetery, a fire-pot is carried by the chief mourner himself, not by the *tōṭṭi*. A major difference is that the roles carried out by the service castes in the funeral rites of the Kallars are to a considerable extent played by *māmā-maccinaṉ* relations in the case of the Paraiyars' funerals. That is, not only is the grave dug by members of *māmā-maccinaṉ*, but also the completion of the interment is the responsibility of the *māmā-maccinaṉ* along with the Potaravannar. The Paraiyars usually adopt burial, but, as with the Kallars, a *pūcāri* and a *cāmiāṭi* are cremated. Accidental death also results in cremation. The rite *koḷḷi taṇṇi* ("fire-water") is held during the night of the burial day.

Plate 85 *Rājarāṇi āṭṭam* in front of the funeral house.

On the third day after the death, the mortuary family cook horse-gram, maize and rice, and the deceased's *paṅkāḷi* eat the meal, which must be "a bitter meal" [Khare, 1976: 171] and which is said to symbolize the body of the deceased [Parry, 1985: 617]. After eating this "bitter" meal, the removal of *pantal kampu* by the *tāymāmaṉ* and the rite of *pāl ūṟṟutal* ("milk-pouring") are conducted.[36] It is claimed by some Paraiyars that they call the Valluvar priest to the burial ground for officiating at the *pāl ūṟṟutal*. However, in practice this is not the case for most village Paraiyars.

Plate 86 The chief mourner walks under a white cloth in the rite of *paṭṭam eṭukkiṟatu.*

Plate 87 *Kappal tēr*.

Plate 88 The face of the deceased is turned towards the outside at the boundary of the village.

Plate 89 A Paraiyar man prays his wife's grave.

Plate 90 Selection of a new *cāmiāṭi* (a successor of deceased *cāmiāṭi*) at the Vaigai River bank.

Karumāti

It is especially mentioned that *karumāti*[37] is held on the sixteenth day, as in the case of the Pillais, although its content is basically similar to that of the Kallars. The procedure of *karumāti*, which consists of the *paṅkāḷi*'s dining from one plate[38] and the tying of *urumā*, is exactly the same as that in the case of the Kallars. Evening meals (vegetarian dishes) on the *karumāti* day are served to the *māmā-maccin̲an̲* by the deceased's family. The following day, conversely, a feast (non-vegetarian dishes) provided by the *māmā-maccin̲an̲*, which is called *kāycci ūrrutal* ("making food and pouring"), is given to the deceased's *paṅkāḷi*.

Some Paraiyars say that *tīṭṭu* dissipates on the sixteenth day of *karumāti*, but others maintain that *tīṭṭu* remains until the thirtieth day.[39] Among the latter people, there are a few who claim that a Valluvar priest is invited along to purify their house on the thirtieth day, although most others dismiss this idea. It is, however, true that the ceremony on the thirtieth day by the river side, which is officiated at by the Valluvar priest, assumes importance on the death of a *pūcāri* or a *cāmiāṭi*.

The Paraiyars do not observe the anniversary of death called *tivaṣam.* Nonetheless, I had an interesting experience as follows. When I met the Paraiyar whose mother's funeral I had observed one year before, he told me that he would have a *tivaṣam* for his mother on the coming 10th of August, and invited me along to the ceremony. Despite my questioning his invitation, I went to his house at the appointed time, and found there was indeed no ceremony! It would seem that this was not just a simple lie but an attempt to show off, and the experience further suggests that the Paraiyars enjoying relatively higher economic conditions tend to put on the airs of the higher status castes. In this respect, it can be noted that he would have prefered to follow the ways of the Pillais than those of the Kallars.

Outlook on the Soul and the Next World

The Paraiyars' outlook on the deceased's soul is basically not different from that of the Kallars. It is often said among them that a person who is well-behaved in his life time becomes a good *āvi*, whereas a badly-behaved one becomes a bad *āvi*, namely, a *pēy* (an evil spirit or a ghost).[40] This is possibly linked with their dichotomous view of the upper-world (*mēlōkam*) and the lower-world (*kīlōkam*). They describe the *mēlōkam* as *corkkam* (a heaven or a paradise) to which a deceased's soul goes, and then they paradoxically describe the world on earth as a *kīlōkam* comparable to *narakam* (a hell). In this connection, they also *talk* about reincarnation where good conduct in a previous life results in happiness during the present life, or where if someone killed a person he would be reborn as an animal in the next life, but their *real* intention seems to be found in their thinking of *karumam* as a synonym for difficulties or sufferings on earth. As this view is shared with the Kallars, their understanding of *tarumam* (*dharma*) is almost the same as that of the Kallars. This contradicts Maloney's claim [Maloney, 1975: 175]. Thus, if Obeyesekere's argument [Obeyesekere, 1968: 12–18] is applied, the Paraiyars' eschatological beliefs are fundamentally similar to the Kallars', in which "ethicization" is not advanced.

On Widows

The Paraiyars say that a widow is never connected with *tīṭṭu* (pollution) but is nevertheless an unhappy creature. There are no restrictions among them concerning her remarriage, though it is claimed that remarriage of a widow is very difficult. It is, nonetheless, said that a widow needs the control of some male, i.e., her deceased husband's relatives or a *tāymāmaṉ*. These rather contradictory notions reflect the ambiguity of a situation where there is a difference between actual practices and expressed ideals in terms of women. Paraiyar wives, generally speaking, have to be active and indeed go out to work, mainly as agricultural labourers, but their husbands usually claim that a wife should obey her husband and preferably stay at home taking care of the house and family. These statements tell that they are not separated from the Caste Hindus' general outlook on women and widows, but at the same time they maintain a bigger gap between the ideal and the reality.

Comparison among Castes: The Ideological Discourse of the Paraiyars

In order to compare and extract the features common to or piculiar to the various castes, Table 10.1 has been devised. It shows aspects of the funeral processes, the outlook on the next world and so on. The reason that Brahman funerals are added to this Table is that they provide a starting point for measuring the degree on Sanskritization of the other three castes. Although this Table can be read from various standpoints, I will focus here especially on the Paraiyars, as the present aim is the elucidation of their actual ideological discourse.

Features common to the Mortuary Rites of the Kallars and the Paraiyars

Table 10.1 shows that the Kallars' and Paraiyars' mortuary rites share the following features.

1. The deceased is enshrined in a seated position.

2. The regulation that one should not weep until the completion of the enshrinement of the deceased is often disregarded in actual practice.
3. The female relations send off the funeral procession at the village border.
4. The procession is preceded only by funeral drummers and there is no blowing of the conch.
5. Burial is the usual method in the case of the natural death of ordinary people. Cremation is adopted in two cases, the case of unnatural death and that of the death of a *pūcāri* and a *cāmiāṭi*.
6. One of the central rites of *karumāti* is *urumā kaṭṭutal*. This rite is not officiated at by a priest but requires the active participation of the *māmā-maccin̲an̲* side.
7. The unity of *paṅkāḷi* (a patrilineal descent group) is consistently emphasized in *karumāti*.
8. The feast of non-vegetarian food provided by the *māmā-maccin̲an̲* side is seen as the reconfirmation of the alliance between the deceased's *paṅkāḷi* and their *māmā-maccin̲an̲*.
9. *Mōṭcaviḷakku* is offered in the temple on the thirtieth day after the death.
10. There is a significant difference between ordinary people's funerals and those of *pūcāri* and *cāmiāṭi*.
11. A widow is not accorded special treatment. In practice, women, in general, are not very degraded by men.
12. A corpse is called by the pure Tamil word, *piṇam*.
13. It is, generally speaking, said that the soul of the deceased goes to the upper-world (*mēlōkam*). This indicates that their view of the next world is not very clear and is poorly developed.

Table 10.1

Components of Funeral Ceremonies: Comparison Among Castes

Caste Name / *Components*	*Ayyar Vegetarian*	*Pillai Vegetarian*	*Kallar Non-vegetarian*	*Harijan (Paraiyar) Non-vegetarian*
Expression of funerals	*amarākkirikai* (<Skt. *amara-kriyā*)	*īmakkiriyai*	*iḷavukāriyam*	*īmaccaṭaṅakukal*
Weeping soon after death	prohibition	prohibition	no prohibition	prohibition (in theory)
Posture of the dead	lying	lying/sitting	sitting	sitting
Priest (1st day)	ayyar	no	no	no
Cītevī vāṅkutal	no	3 cowdungs before procesision	3 cowdungs during procession	3 cowdoungs during procession
Farewell of women	house	house	pot breaking place	pot breaking place
Sounds in procession	no music	drum conch (barber)	drum no conch	drum no conch
Bier (Posture of the dead)	*ēnippāti* (lying)	*tēr* (sitting)	*tēr* (sitting)	*tēr* (sitting)
Rājarāni āṭṭam	no	yes	yes	yes

Cont'd ...

Cont'd ...

Dirty cloth taken by	Vannar	Vannar	Vannar	Potaravannar
Funeral messenger	?	*tōṭṭi*	*tōṭṭi*	relatives
Digging a pit	****	****	*tōṭṭi*	*māmā-maccinan*
Bier making	Ampattar	*tōṭṭi*	*tōṭṭi*	Cakkiliyar
Pantal kambu making	****	*tōṭṭi/maṭaiyan*	chief mourner	*tāymāmān māmā-maccinan*
Nīrmālai iruttal guided by	****	Vannar	Vannar	Potaravannar
Firepot holder	chief mourner with a sacred thread	*tōṭṭi*	*tōṭṭi*	chief mourner with a sacred thread
Watcher in cemetery	*tōṭṭi*/Ampattar	*tōṭṭi*/Ampattar	*tōṭṭi*/Ampattar	*māmā-maccinan* Potaravannar
Cemetery	Aiyar proper or Caste Hindus	Caste Hindus	Caste Hindus	Harijan proper
Expression for cemetery	*mayānam* (<Skt. *śmaśāna*)/ *rudráhūmi* (Skt.)	*mayānam/ cuṭukāṭu*	*iṭukāṭu/mayāna-karai/cuṭukāṭu*	?
Natural death	cremation	cremation	burial	burial
Unnatural death	cremation (minimized)	cremation (minimized)	cremation	cremation
Burial case	under 6 months	unmarried	general	general
Cremation	general	general	*pūcāri/cāmiāṭi* / unnatural	*pūcāri/cāmiāṭi* / unnatural
Shaving of chief mourner	moustache only/ hair (before Upanayana)	hair	hair	hair
A part of white cloth covered on the dead	Aiyar cuts a part and ties it on the water pot.	Ampattar cuts and takes.	Ampattar cuts and ties it on the head of chief mourner.	Potaravannar cuts and ties it on the head of chief mourner.
Priest (2nd or 3rd day)	Aiyar	no (self)	no (self)	Valluvar (?)
Bone & ash throwing/ rite in cemetery	bone: river/ ash: pintaputapati	river (2nd/ 15th)/ cultivation & sowing	***** cultivation & sowing	**** cultivation & sowing
Appeasement rites: mantra or weeping	mantra during 3rd~9th	*kiḻamai* by daughters on 3rd, 8th, 11th	*vaiccu aḻutal* on 6th, 29th	*vaiccu aḻutal* on 15th
lighting	~11th	~30th	~30th	?
Karumāti (No. of *pinṭam*)	10th AM (4 *pinṭams*)	16th AM (4 *pinṭams*)	7th or 9th or 11th PM	16th PM
Pantal kambu (shape)	no, but *kirikaippantal*	yes (rectangle)	yes (rectangle)	yes (triangle)
Pantal kambu removing (date)	*****	Ampattar (3rd)	Ampattar/ *tāymāman* (7th)	*tāymāman* (3rd)
Priest in *karumāti* (place)	Aiyar (*karumantaram*)	*Kurukkaḷ* or Aiyar (*karumantaram*)	no (house)	no (house)
Pañcāṅkam for fixing date	use	use	do not use	do not use

Cont'd ...

Cont'd ...

Urumākaṭṭutal	no	yes (sons only)	yes (*uṭaṉ-paṅkāḷi*)	yes (*uṭaṉ-paṅkāḷi*)
Tāli removing: death of husband death of wife	10th before cremation	15th before cremation	1st (bathing) before burial	1st day (before *tēr*) before burial
Ceymuṟai (kāycci ullutal)	no	no	8th by *māmā-macciṉaṉ*	17th by *māmā-macciṉaṉ*
Period of *tiṭṭu* (intence period)	10 days	30 days (16 days)	30 days (7 or 9 or 11 days)	30 days (16 days)
30th day ceremony (ordinary people)	*****	rite for widow *mōṭcaviḷakku*	purification *mōṭcaviḷakku*	purification *mōṭcaviḷakku* Valluvar (in theory)
30th day ceremony (*pūcāri/cāmiāṭi*)	*****	rite for widow *mōṭcaviḷakku*	Aiyar (river bank)	Valluvar (river bank)/ sacred thread used
Tivaṣam (anniversary)	yes	yes: *niṉaivunāl*	no	no (yes in theory)
Recognition of *pitiṛ*	yes: *pitiṛ*	yes: *āvi*	no	no
Corpse called	*pirētam* (<Skt.)	*piṇam/cavam* (<Skt.)	*piṇam*	*piṇam*
Soul of the dead called	ātman (<SivalokamSkt.)	*āvi*	*āvi*	*āvi* = *pēy*
Where soul goes	*Sivalōkam* (<Skt.)	*Sivalōkam* (<Skt.)	upper world	upper world
Images of the other world	Sivalokam	heaven (*corkkam*) & hell (*narakam*)	heaven & hell/ heaven only/ do not believe	heaven only/ do not believe
Social segregation of widow	strong separation	strong separation	weak separation	weak separation
Remarriage of widow	I no	no/yes	yes	yes
Expression of widow	*amaṅgali* (Skt.)	*kaimpeṉ*	*vitavai/muṇṭacci* (<Skt.)/ *kaimpoṇṭāṭṭi*	*kaimpeṉ*
The custom of *satī*	agreeable	ok, if without children	not good	not good (now) good (old)
Meaning of *karma*	conduct good or bad	conduct good or bad	difficulty/sin/ poverty/conducts	poverty/difficulty/ conducts
Meaning of *dharma*	moral duty	charity/moral duty	charity	charity
Patrilinial-group	*tāyātikaḷ* (<Skt.)	*kōttiram*	*paṅkāḷi*	*paṅkāḷi*

Note: *****means the absence of a component.

Furthermore, these common points can be integrated into four features as follows: (a) Both clearly lay much importance on kinship relationships, by stressing the unity of *paṅkāḷi* (parallel relatives) and the alliance with the *māmā-macciṉaṉ* (cross relatives). (b) Their cosmological view and the ritual processes consistently show a non-theological and tangible tendency. (c) The social bias against women is not strong. (d) Their ritual actions and ideas containing the above-mentioned points seem to be deeply rooted rather in the non-Brahmanical cultural basis, namely, "popular" cultural tendency in my sense. Thus, by means of the analysis of the funeral processes, we can conclude that: both the dominant Kallars, who are, however, regarded as a ritually low caste from the Brahmanical cultural viewpoint, and the dominated Paraiyars, who are placed on the bottom rung of village society, basically share a common-less-Sanskritized cultural tendency, in which the unity of kinship, including reciprocation between parallel and cross relatives, and tangible and non-abstract thinking, are pre-eminent.

Features differing between the Mortuary Rites of the Kallars and the Paraiyars

Next, I mention the features that differ between Kallar and Paraiyar funeral rites.

1. The Paraiyars tend to profess to prohibit weeping until the completion of the deceased's enshrinement, even though they do not always practice this. This prohibition appears to be actually observed by the Pillais.
2. The Paraiyars verbally insist that virginity is important for marriage, that a wife must obey her husband, that divorce should be avoided and that the remarriage of a widow is difficult, but these opinions, which seem to reflect the Pillais' ideology, are not necessarily practised.
3. Most of the duties taken charge of by the Harijans at the Kallars' funerals, are conducted by the *māmā-maccinaṉ*'s side at the Paraiyars' funerals, although only the Potaravannars work as a service caste for the Paraiyars. Apart from this, the Paraiyars will hire additional workers for cash from a town or other villages, if they can afford to do so.
4. The cemetery of the Paraiyars is separated from that of the Caste Hindus.
5. The Paraiyars enjoy the services of a separate priest, the Valluvar, and of a separate barber and concurrently washerman, the Potaravannars. The Caste Hindus do not use the Valluvar priest or the Potaravannars, though the Valluvar does visit their houses as an astrologer.
6. The date of *karumāti* is the sixteenth day for both the Paraiyars and the Pillais, though its contents are not the same in both cases.
7. The Paraiyars' *pantal kampu* has a triangular shape and is supported by three legs. It is different from the square form of the Kallars'. The *pantal kampu* is removed on the third day in the case of both the Paraiyars and the Pillais.
8. Though the Paraiyars do not have *tivaṣam* (an anniversary of death), some people verbally claim that they observe it.

We can extract three summarized features found in the practices of the Paraiyars, from the above points.

(a) A discrepancy between professed statements and actual practices or intentions is often found in the processes of their funerals. Though they tend to profess the adoption of Brahmanical cultural elements fragmentally, they do no more than "replicate" the practice of the Brahmanized Pillais superficially, and the truth is that their practices show considerable similarity to those of the Kallars. In this sense, this discrepancy seems to be a result of their manner of self-assertion.

(b) The Paraiyars have to depend much more strongly on kinship relations than do the Kallars, because they, as the dominated caste, cannot place themselves at the centre of inter-caste relations. If they intended to more closely approximate to the funerals of the dominant castes and could afford to do so, they would need to hire workers for various services from outside the village.

(c) It is obvious that the Paraiyars are discriminated against in the absolute sense and are confined to a life space separately allotted to them. This is apparent from the facts that they cannot enjoy the services of the Brahmans or the Vannars who are specialists to the Caste Hindus, and that they have to bury their dead in a separate cemetery.

Discussion and Conclusion

In order to understand correctly what is meant by the several features extracted from the Paraiyars' ritual behaviour, it is useful and necessary to introduce background information on their evaluation of caste ranking. This is shown in Table 10.2, which also includes the opinions of the Caste Hindus.

According to this Table, we find a striking and interesting difference between the evaluation of the Paraiyars and the Caste Hindus. Not only the Kallars themselves, but also other Caste Hindus regard the Pillais as a higher caste than the Kallars; whereas the Paraiyars' evaluation is that the Kallars are higher than the Pillais. Another notable point is that the Paraiyars do not rank themselves at the bottom of the social hierarchy. Rather, they tend to see the Vannars and the Kuravans, who strongly depend upon the dominant castes, and who have no practical interaction with the Paraiyars in everyday life, as lower than themselves.

I prepared cards on which caste names were written and asked villagers to line these cards up in descending order from the "socially" highest caste, without suggesting any standard to measure social ranking.[41] I also aimed to discover what kind of standards or criteria adopted by them could be extracted from their answers. As a result, I found three kinds of criteria from Table 10.2. One criterion is religious or next-worldly power, which is the so-called power associated with ritual status. This criterion is specially stressed by the Pillais, who attach importance to vegetarianism and Brahmanical knowledge. The second is politico-economic and this-worldly power, from the viewpoint of which the degree of independence is highly evaluated.[42] The third, which should not be overlooked, is the quantity and quality of interaction, because it had an important influence on their evaluations. The aspect of quantity implies the frequency or density of contacts in everyday life. This means that villagers tend to underestimate the castes with whom they have less connection. The aspect of quality is apparent in rivalry relations, which are basically found among the castes who are adjacent to each other in their social rank. Such a competing caste claims its own superiority over that of its rival castes.

After understanding these three criteria, let us reconsider the results of the caste evaluation of the Paraiyars so as to understand the features of the Paraiyars' ritual behaviour. The Paraiyars' placing of the Kallars on a higher rank than Pillais indicates that they place more importance on secular power (the second criterion) and the density of direct interaction (the third criterion), than they do upon ritual power (the first criterion). In fact, most of the village Paraiyars have had unavoidable contact with the Kallars as agricultural labourers working under the latters' control. This economic dependence upon the Kallars has forced the Paraiyars to endure ill-treatment by the Kallars. The Paraiyars fear of the Kallars is reflected in their

Table 10.2
Evaluation of Caste Ranking

Evaluator \ *Evaluated castes*	*Aiyar*	*Pillai*	*Acari*	*Kallar*	*Pantaram*	*Natar*	*Vannar*	*Kuravar*	*Paraiyar*
[Caste Hindus]									
Pillai	1	2	3	4	5	6	7	7	8
Acari	1	2	3	4	5	6	7	7	8
Kallar 1	2	1	5	3	*	4	6	*	7
Kallar 2	1	2	2	2	3	3	3	4	4
Kallar 3	1	2	6	4	3	5	9	8	7
Natar	1	2	5	4	6	3	7	9	8
Vannar	1	2	6	4	3	5	6	7	8
[Harijan]									
Paraiyar 1	*	2	*	1	6	4	3	6	5
Paraiyar 2	1	3	4	2	6	5	6	7	6
Paraiyar 3	1	3	5	2	4	6	8	9	7
Paraiyar 4	1	3	5	2	6	4	9	8	7

opinion of them. In sum, their rather harsh everyday experiences under the Kallars have led the Paraiyars to form this ranking of the castes, which differs from the Caste Hindus' view.

The problem to be answered is why the Paraiyars replicate, even if superficially and fragmentally, some elements of the Pillais' funerals, despite the fundamental ritual structure of the Paraiyars' funerals being the same as that of the Kallars. As is demonstrated by the fact that their replications are often limited to merely verbal assertions, it is suggested that their purpose is to avoid or reject their full subordination to their domination by the Kallars, by means of adding different ideological elements to their rituals. The Sanskritized village Pillais become the most suitable model for the Paraiyars to borrow such elements from. It is obvious that the Brahmans' culture could provide the most powerful model for refuting Kallar ideology, but, in practice, the Brahmans are too remote for the Paraiyars to emulate their customs, though they do know that Brahmanic customs enjoy the highest ritual value.[43] In this sense, the village Pillais, who are the most Sanskritized caste in this village, and with whom the Paraiyars have everyday contact, become the useful reference by which the monopoly of the Kallars' domination is checked, even slightly. Since the Paraiyars basically share the same cultural practices with the Kallars, it is logically inferred that the Paraiyars replicate the Pillais' Sanskritic elements not because they seriously believe in them, but rather due to their strategic action in the given social conditions (see also [Gough, 1959: 255]). That is to say, the Paraiyars adopt these Sanskritic elements as the means by which they pit their identity against the overwhelming dominance of the Kallars. Thus the Paraiyars wittingly or unwittingly aim to differentiate themselves from the Kallars ("dissimilation") by not simply replicating the practices of the Kallars ("assimilation"), but by adopting elements of the practices of the Pillais ("over-assimilation"[4]). Moffatt fails to investigate this point [Moffatt, 1979]. The Kallars' rather crude authority, which is mainly dependent on their politico-economic power and numerical predominance, results in the Paraiyars more strongly experiencing the effects of the Kallars' dominance than of the Pillais' more indirect, sophisticated dominance. The Pillais, as the ritually highest caste in the village, influence the Paraiyars by offering them an ideology from which the Paraiyars can borrow elements to use in their struggle to differentiate their ideology from that of the dominant Kallars. This enables the Paraiyars to distance themselves in some respects from the dominant Kallars and to experience some self-fulfillment in this ideological space.

Thus, a comparative analysis of funeral ceremonies results in the following conclusions concerning the practices of the Paraiyars. Although the Paraiyars primarily share the same cultural basis, called the "popular" cultural tendency, with the Kallars, the Paraiyars attempt to replicate Brahmanic cultural elements through the mediation of the Pillais, even if fragmentally and superficially, so as to shift their ceremonies away from an imperfect replication of the Kallars' funerals. This is seen as one of their practical and strategic challenges for seeking their own identity, which is not simply reduced to the hierarchically subordinate "subject", even under the Kallars' overwhelming domination. In this sense, the funeral ceremony provides one of the arenas of the Paraiyars' discourse, even a humble one, which is penetrated by their strategic attitude of seeking self-aggrandizement.

Notes

1. Firstly, the funerals of the Acaris and of the Pantarams are rather similar to those of the Pillais. Secondly, the Natars' funeral again is similar to the Pillais', but is more simple. The Vannars' funeral can be seen as a simplified form of the Kallars'. These are the reasons that I take up only the cases of the Pillais and of the Kallars for comparison with the cases of the Paraiyars.
2. Unmarried person's funerals are limited (incomplete) because, according to Dumont, this funeral type does not satisfy the following two points, "the fact that the mourners are supposed to be younger than the dead person" and "the importance of marriage and alliance" [Dumont, 1986: 277].
3. In contrast, it is said that weeping within about 1.5 hours after the death is prohibited at a Brahman funeral.
4. It is said that the corpse should be kept away from a *pūjā* room and a kitchen. After bathing, the corpse has *tirunīṟṟu* ("holy ash") for a Saivite or *tirumaṇ* ("holy soil") for a Vishnavite put on its forehead and on the back of its hands. A 25 paisa coin, called *neṟṟikkācu*, is put on its forehead. Sugar cane is stood against the wall on both sides of the corpse, which is in the seated position. Rose water is sprinkled, incense is burnt, and coconuts, betel leaves etc. are offered. A pile consisting of four *marakkāl* (*1 marakkāl* = about 6.5 liters) of paddy, on the top of which a *akalviḷakku* (a wide-mouthed clay lamp) is put, is placed near the dead person, and a *kuttuviḷakku* (a standing brass lamp) is also lit.
5. There are two kinds of biers for carrying the deceased, namely, *pāṭai* and *tēr*. The former is a simple flat bier on which the deceased person is laid in a stretched position, and the latter is a

more decorative one in which the deceased is kept in a seated position. The popular forms of *tēr* are a ship type, called *kappal tēr*, and a peacock form, called *mayil tēr*. It is said that the *tēr* must be made of green (*paccai*) bamboo newly cut down. The reason is unclear, but I guess that the use of fresh bamboo has the same connotation as the use of earthen containers and leaf plates on the occasion of death [Khare, 1976: 183].

6. *Rājarāṇi āṭṭam* consists of only male members who are recruited from the Harijans. As is indicated by the name, *rājarāṇi*, one of them disguises himself as a woman (*rāṇi*). The party, which makes a racket, creates a rather festive mood, and an early death, where the deceased is aged less than fifty years, is regarded as too sad an occasion to tolerate such a mood. See also [Dumont, 1986: 272], [Moffatt, 1979: 199] and [Srinivas, 1978 (1952): 97].
7. The eldest son becomes the chief mourner for his mother, whereas the youngest son does so for his father, as Dumont also notes [Dumont, 1986: 274]. However, the principle is not universal among the Tamils because Good reports that "the eldest S is chief mourner for both parents" [Good, 1978: 464, fn.3], and the rule is reversed among the Jaffna Tamils (the Vellalars) [Sekine, 1984: 21].
8. Ayyavu, a Kallar informant, explains as follows. These male members are polluting, and they have to be covered by a canopy of white cloth so as not to pollute the sun.
9. It is said that the lying posture, in which the direction of the corpse's head is south and its face is tilted a little towards the east, imitates a baby at the breast. The male members of the deceased's *paṅkāḷi* surround the *pantal kampu* and cry three times *"appāṭō appō, āttāṭiyō āttō!"*. The barber stops this crying by touching the shoulders of the *paṅkāḷi*. Then, margosa leaves are put on the white cloth of the *pantal kampu* and turmeric water is sprinkled on it.
10. According to the Kallars' explanation, if the grain sprouted on the day of *karumāti* (i.e., a week later), it was a good omen and the family would prosper under the protection of the Goddess Laksmi, and this would verify that the beloved one had been a person of good conduct. However, if the grain failed to sprout, this would indicate that the deceased had been a person of bad conduct. The cowdung, regardless, is kept in a pot and mixed with the grain being sown the following year.
11. It is noted that the *tēr* itself is always turned around clockwise, whereas the person who conducts *kāikuṭam uṭaittal* goes around anti-clockwise. It seems that the view that the corpse is deemed as Siva explains the auspicious turn of the *tēr* [Das, 1976: 253].
12. As Dumont notes, "the burial ceremonies show little originality. Many traits show that they are a substitute for cremation" [Dumont, 1986: 274]. The action of making a fire is one such typical trait. See also Good [1978: 475].
13. This meal seems to correspond with *kāṇam kañji*, which is a porridge made of rice and beans, in Dumont's description, and the first dish to be prepared in the deceased person's house. It seems to me that this dining almost corresponds with "a bitter meal", consisting of cooked rice and curd, which Khare mentions [Khare, 1976: 171].
14. The night before *karumāti*, the ritual called *cempum taṇṇiyum vaiccu aḻukkiṟatu* is conducted by women only. Female relations sit around a cempu (a small tray) containing water, which is put in the place where the body lay in state, and they weep in order to console the deceased's soul.
15. The barber pulls the *pantal kampu* out and pours milk into the holes. The *tāymāmaṉ* accompanied by the male relations, carries the *pantal kampu* and throws it away at the "pot breaking place".

16. It is said that if a towel without silver lines is used, it would be a terrible insult to the chief mourner's *paṅkāḷi*.
17. A woman member of the family puts the deceased's washed cloth (which is the last garment worn by the dead person) in the lying-in-state area and makes a water pot offering. Then the women gather there and wail. According to Dumont, "the pot of rice decorated with sacred ashes" is put there [Dumont, 1986: 277].
18. The textual understanding of the corpse to be cremated is much more complex. See, for example, [Das, 1976: 253-6]. It seems to me that the contrast between the Kallars' ideas and the textual understanding is already expressed by the conceptual difference between the *āvi*, as an unchanging soul, and the *prētam*, which will be converted to a *pitiṛ*.
19. The "pot breaking place", as the ritual boundary, is the focal place where the *āvi* is said to wander during the mortuary period.
20. It is noted that no one says an *āvi* goes to the south, but most villagers reply that it goes to the upper world which is not well structured in their minds. There are different opinions on the location of hell, different Kallars seeing it as in the sky, on earth, or in the under world; whereas heaven is unanimously placed in the sky. There are also a few persons who deny the existence of both heaven and hell.
21. In the case of the death of *cāmiāṭi* after the ceremony of throwing bones and ashes into a river, they endeavour to choose a new *cāmiāṭi* there and then, though the attempt is not always successful. The candidates of the *paṅkāḷi* stand in a row and are perceived to be gradually possessed by gods. The selection will be made if it is confirmed by the others that the right god or goddess has come down to a particular person.
22. Since they feel that there is in "unusual death" a tremendous power which the ordinary treatment of burial cannot cope with, an utterly different method, cremation, which is foreign to them, has to be introduced in order to manage such power.
23. There is no difference in terms of the burial of a child between the Kallars and the Pillais. If a child dies before the thirtieth day after its birth, it is buried in the nearest open space to the house, where the placenta is also buried. In terms of the Kallars, Dumont reports the classification of three stages, namely, "before the seventh day", "up to the age of four or five" and "beyond the age of five", according to which a child is buried in different places [Dumont, 1986: 277]. The village Kallars I studied do not make such a distinction. See also [Nicholas, 1981: 369–370].
24. Firstly, the deceased's daughters and granddaughters (who must be an odd number) take a bath, put flowers in their hair and draw water. Then the chief mourner and other sons and grandsons, accompanied by a barber and a washerman, draw water from the well.
25. This action is called *pukunta iṭattuk kōṭi* ("the husband's side's sari which has just come"). Since a widow is prohibited from wearing a new sari, she uses the sari after it has been wetted once.
26. It is said that the cooking should be done outside the house. The male members make the cooked rice and the boiled banana, both of which must be made of *paccai* ("fresh", "green" or "raw") materials. The boiled green banana is ultimately given to the barber. It can possibly be seen as the transfer of inauspiciousness or pollution to the barber, as Raheja emphasizes [Raheja, 1988: 161], or as the digestion of the deceased's sins [Parry, 1985: 614, 616–617]. See also [Good, 1978: 476].
27. The *vaṭais*, which are made by a widow, are usually made of black-gram powder, but on this occasion are made of raw rice powder and sugar. The *vaṭais* are made into seven balls (*uruṇṭai*). It seems to me that the *vaṭais* can be thought of as *piṇṭams* which are connected

with the seven generational ancestors forming *sapiṇḍa* [Nicholas, 1981: 375, 377], although the Pillais themselves do not give this explanation. It is significant that a fried snack is found in the offerings to the dead in this village, because this contradicts Khare's statement that "no frying in any form is done during this period" [Khare, 1976: 172].

28. Around midnight, all the gathered women wail. A little after this, one widow draws a *nīrkkōlam* (an ornamental figure drawn on the floor with water) on which cooked rice and *cāmpār* (a kind of savoury dish) served on a banana leaf is placed. Soon after the deceased's wife touches the food, it is taken away. Then the women continue to wail up to around 4 a.m. Widows must form a separate group. Before dawn, the bereaved wife sits facing a suitable direction depending on the day of the week, and one widow cuts the *tāli* and puts it into the milk in the pot, which was prepared by another widow. Only widows should attend the scene of cutting the *tāli*.
29. According to the Brahmanic and textual interpretation, one out of four *piṇṭams* is the deceased's *preta-piṇḍa* and the other three are regarded as the *pitṛ-piṇḍas* of his F, his FF, and his FFF, as Nicholas or Parry, for example, explain [Nicholas, 1981: 376] [Parry, 1985: 622]. The local interpretations are often modified in various ways. For instance, the Jaffna Vellalars give a different view that the single *piṇṭam* represents Siva and the three are the deceased, his F and his FF. Further, they believe that the crow is an incarnation of an ancestral spirit [Sekine, 1984: 25–6]. See also [Gough, 1975: 256].
30. There is no doubt that the *karumāti* of the Pillais, which I have described here, contains a combined but much simplified form of the repeated *antyēṣṭi* ("the last sacrifice") and *śrāddha* in a textual sense (see [Nicholas, 1981: 374]) and [Kane, 1973: Vol. IV, 179–551].
31. On *Āṭi amāvācai*, the new moon day of the month *Āṭi*, it is said that male ancestors come down to this world.
32. The Pillais tend to strongly believe that the appearance of a widow makes them unhappy, especially when they start a long journey or when they conduct an auspicious ceremony.
33. She cannot wear a coloured sari or ornaments and cannot put *kuṅkumam* (rouge), but only holy ash, on her forehead.
34. The deceased's eldest son (in his 30s) is a low status worker, pune, at Madurai Kamaraj University. Though his salary is low, his economic condition is rather stable compared with that of other Paraiyars, who are mostly engaged as agricultural labourers. Therefore, he could afford to pay for his mother's funeral, which was more elaborate than the average Paraiyar one. He said that it cost about Rs 2,500 in total, which is equal to nearly 5 times his monthly salary.
35. According to Good, in the funeral of a Paraiyar or Pallar, a wife of Tinda Vannar goes to the burial place and assists her husband and son there. He further notes that in the Pallar funeral he attended the deceased woman's elder sister came to the cemetery and took the jewelry off the body [Good, 1978: 374]. This is not the case in Kinnimangalam, where all women are strictly prohibited from going beyond the village boundary during the funeral rites.
36. Good also reports that the Paraiyars and the Pallars conduct *tī āṭṭutal* on the third day [Good, 1978: 477], which is compared to the second day ceremony of the Acaris. It seems to me that the Paraiyars are faithful to orthodoxy in terms of the order of the day, because there are many reports in which the collection of bones and ashes is held on the third day (see [Babb, 1975: 94] and [Chitty, 1872: 119]).
37. Good notes, "the Scheduled Castes do not carry out the *karumāti* rite" [Good, 1978: 485], but he also points out, "there is an attenuated rite on the 16th day, which the Pallar call

urimaikkaṭṭu" [ibid.: 486]. In Kinnimangalam, the term *karumāti* is shared by all villagers, although its content is not the same when carried out by the different castes.

38. It is claimed that they prepare vegetarian food for this. This is different from the case of the Kallars.
39. Among the Paraiyars, the children can take meals provided by the deceased's house (*tukkavīṭu*) after the sixteenth day, but a *kāriyakāraṉ*, a *pūcāri*, a *cāmiāṭi*, the people following *pakti*, and other persons engaged in village services like *tōṭṭi* and *maṭaiyaṉ* should not until the thirtieth day. Ordinary people thus stand somewhere between the children and the people engaged in the latter work.
40. Other people comment that if *āvi* surprised a person, the *āvi* would be called a *pēy*.
41. I only provided them with the vague expression of "social" hierarchical ranking. How the expression "social" is understood is totally dependent on those answering.
42. This criterion explains why the Kallars place the Pillais in a higher position than the Brahmans. They regard the Brahman priest as a labourer who depends on a landlord like the Pillais.
43. As to the Brahmans (Aiyars), the Paraiyars appear to show an ambivalent attitude towards them. On the one hand, the Paraiyars state that the Aiyars are a people of a different world and they make fun of them saying that the Brahmans should be walking on clouds in the sky. On the other hand, some Paraiyars have a myth which claims that the Paraiyars and the Aiyars were originally brothers. In my view, this myth is nowadays not regarded seriously by them.
44. I define "over-assimilation" as one's practice of self-assertion against one's competitor, in which one adopts the upper culture more actively than one's competitor in order to make a difference between the former and the latter.

Chapter 11

The Festivals of Lineage Deities

A Lineage-Based Strategy

In this chapter I describe the lineage deities, called *kulateyvam,* and their festivals, as important practices in village life. This aims to elucidate the social implications of the festive activities of the Paraiyars. The "performative"[1] meanings of the Paraiyars' festive activities are discussed, being compared with those of the Caste Hindus, with the same manner as the case of the funeral rites.

The Paraiyars' understanding of lineage deities, which is to a considerable extent shared by the Kallars, is based on the "popular" cultural tendency in my sense. Their understanding is characterized by the significance of (1) goddess worship and blood sacrifice, (2) the strong influence of locality on lineage segmentation, (3) the important role of cross relatives, and (4) the communicative character of deities, embodied by *cāmiāṭi* (a god-possessed dancer).

The rituals of the lineage deities and their interpretation can be understood in two ways, namely, the sacred (religious) and the secular (social).[2] Firstly, related to the sacred aspect, the lineage festival provides the members of a lineage with the shared experience of a mythological trip towards their roots, in which they can communicate with their lineage deities and reinforce (reconfirm) their identity as members of the lineage. This is an essential part of the religious festivity. The performance of lineage festivals also has a social (secular) connotation. The festivals mirror the social hierarchy found both in inter-caste relations, which is made most clear by a comparison between the Kallars and the Paraiyars, and in intra-caste ones, such as the differential between the *Nārpaṅkāḷi* (Four-lineages) and the Tankalan lineage. Therefore, it will be claimed that such festive activities tend to reinforce or reproduce the conventional social structure.

Though it is true that the ceremony works as such an encapsulating force, it does not mean people's static acceptance of structure. It should not be disregarded that the festival reflects the dynamic contests in the meshes woven by inter-caste and intra-caste relations. In other words, it provides an opportunity for socially displaying each lineage's identity competitively. It is notable that intense competition and strife are found within the lineage and this often results in the split of the festival unit. This splitting tendency has been strengthened by modernization, because the necessity of lineage cooperation is diminishing today. Most of the villagers are involved in various wider social networks, beyond traditional village relationships, under the progress of modernization. Nonetheless, it cannot be overlooked that there are earnest wishes for carrying out the lineage festival among the villagers in general, but especially among the Kallars and the Paraiyars. In this sense, as is suggested by the increase of strife within a lineage, the lineage festival tends to be used as a means of self-assertion or identity building by the more individualized members who live in the wider social space.

As mentioned above, lineage festivals are more prevailing among the Kallars and the Paraiyars in the village, though all castes have lineage deities, as has been shown in Table 4.11. This is because several lineages of both these castes have enough numbers of households within the village to conduct the festivals. In contrast, the Pillais and other Caste Hindus, who are numerically minor groups in the village, cannot maintain an extended festival. This is due to the fact that the unity of a lineage *(vakaiyaṟā)* of course based on agnatic relations, but at the same time the actual unit of aggregation is rather segmented in the local group (see [Dumont, 1986: 186]). That is, since a lineage festival is conducted mainly by lineage members living in the same village, it would be difficult for a widely dispersed lineage to maintain the elaborate festival. Thus, the Kallars and the Paraiyars occupy the main part of the following description.

Lineage Cults of the Dominant Castes

The Pillais

The Pillai households of K hamlet belong to Kiravan *kūṭṭam* of Kanicamar *kōttiram* (Skt. *gōtra*).[3] They worship 21 lineage deities,[4] of whom the goddess Aṅkāḷaīsvari is the main deity. The village Pillais regard Angalaisvari as *cuttamuka teyvam* (a deity rejecting blood sacrifice) because she is Siva's wife (see [Dumont, 1986: 433–4]). As the members of Kiravan *kūṭṭam*, they also attach special importance to the goddess Pūvayammāḷ who is, nonetheless, not included in their lineage deities. It can be confirmed that goddess worship is dominant in the lineage cult. Though the legends of the lineage deities usually not only tell of the origins of these deities but also touch on the migration history of the *kūṭṭam*, the legend held by the village Pillais is much concerned with Pūvayammāḷ and pays little attention to the lineage deities.[5] The legend includes the following information on their migration route. The ancestor, as the *karṇam*, originally lived in Purvikam, near Vattalam, North Arcot, but his family migrated down towards the south and reached Punkankulam, 10 kilometers north-west of Tirumangalam, where they settled down and built the temple of Angalaisvari. After they had moved several times around Tirumangalam, they finally came to this village, but their lineage temple, whose main deity is Angalaisvari, was built near to Cattankuti, 6 kilometers west of Tirumangalam. Since then, their lineage festival had been held there until the present family head's great-grandfather's generation, even though the festival was observed only by close relations. It is said that the grandfather consciously stopped conducting the lineage festival because he thought of the blood sacrifice and non-vegetarian offerings found in the ceremony as sinful acts. Up to that time, a pregnant goat (*ciṉai veḷḷāṭu*) or a pregnant pig (*ciṉai paṉṟi*) was sacrificed to the god Kāvalkārakaruppu (*tuṭiyāṉa teyvam* or deity accepting blood sacrifice), one of the 21 lineage deities, and then a rice ball called *cōṟṟu uruṇṭai*, which was mixed with the meat of the victim, was thrown into the air by the *pūcāri*. It is said that the ball never returns to earth because the gods in the sky take it (cf. [Hoek, 1979: 123]). This was conducted behind the temple. These acts were judged by the grandfather as blaspheming against the gods. As two generations have passed since the lineage festival was stopped, the procedures of the festival are unclear today.[6] All that is done today is that each Pillai family individually conducts a special *pūjā* to the lineage deities in a worshipping room on the day of *Makācivarattiri* ("Siva's night") (see [Mayer, 1960: 188]).

The grandfather's decision to abandon the lineage festival can be described as a radical "Sanskritization" from an outsider's viewpoint. However, if the matter was simply stated like this, it would mean a substantial shift from a culture of "Little Tradition" (a festival associated with blood sacrifice) to that of "Great Tradition" (a festival associated with *pūjā*). The level of change of field materials and the level of ideological interpretation are not separated in this sort of explanation. This is the fatal defect found in such a non-interpretative approach that I have consistently criticized in this book. The above example of change should be understood as a change of interpretative level due to an ideological shift, i.e., the permeation of Brahmanical ideology that book place in the Pillai family. This ideological shift causes the change of meaning of animal sacrifice from the positive (an inevitable conduct for getting god's grace) to the negative (an impure action to be avoided). This interpretative standpoint makes clear that what is called "Little Tradition" is, in fact, not a substantial entity but is a relative concept negatively invented by the introduction of the centripetal ideology (Brahmanical ideology here), that is named "Great Tradition" by functionalists. Animal sacrifice itself as a material does not utter any meaning. Another ideological horizon where animal sacrifice is deemed as a useful and indispensable device for a lineage festival was lost by the Pillais but is still kept among the Kallars and the Paraiyars, as described below. In that horizon, there is no such hierarchically dichotomous view of "Great Tradition" and "Little Tradition".

The Kallars

Though the Pillais gave up their lineage festival, the Kallars are in contrast very keen on conducting theirs. I will describe here mainly the lineage festival of the Kecavan lineage, which I directly observed and, in addition, the case of the Kamanan lineage, which was explained to me by the lineage *pūcāri* will be comparatively touched upon. As already noted in Chapter 4, both the Kecavan and the Kamanan occupy the head of the village system of "Two Tevars and Four Pankalis".[7] That is the reason why these two lineages show higher concerns about lineage festivals, as compared with other Kallar lineages.

Lineage Deities

The Kecavan people are said to have originally lived in Marutur, 35 km east of Madurai city, where their honorific title was *Ampalam*. Their ancestor is believed to have migrated to the west and settled down in Cellampatti, near Karumatur (see [Dumont, 1986: 175]). This shift from the eastern side of Madurai to its western side made them change their title to *Tēvār*. Their ancestors had worshipped the God Visnu, called Malaicāmi as their main lineage god in Marutur, but after settling down in Cellampatti the god Kōṭṭamantaikaruppacāmi ("fort-residing black-god), whose temple is located in Karumatur, was newly adopted as their main lineage deity, because he was thought of as an incarnation of Visnu. The Kecavan lineage which holds Visnu as its main deity is rather exceptional in this area where Siva-worship is dominant. Kottamantaikaruppacami is, in this sense, *cuttamuka teyvam*, rejecting blood sacrifice. Although Dumont touches upon the priesthood assigned to Kesan [Dumont, 1986; 368], according to a knowledgeable Kecavan elder TG, the Kecavan people hold a myth, which explains the special relationship between Kottamantaikaruppacami and them.[8] Besides Kottamantaikaruppacami, two other gods, Māyāṇṭicāmi and Muttaiyācāmi, and the goddess *Cīlaikāri* are regarded as especially important deities for the Kecavan lineage. Therefore, the attendance of these four deities' *cāmiāṭis* (possessed dancers) is indispensable to the lineage festival.

Mayanticami is a deified person and it is believed his sacrificial death saved the Kecavan lineage from its crisis.[9] He is a member of the Kattaiyan lineage and a *cakaraṉ* of the Kecavan people. The story which explains why the Kecavan people worship Mayanticami as one of their lineage deities partly illustrates their migration from Cellampatti through Cettikulam to this village. According to TG, the migration was caused by discord between them and the Paricapuli lineage (cf. [Dumont, 1986; 175]) about the proprietary rights of the Kottamantaikaruppacami temple. However, as Dumont describes in detail, it seems that the withdrawal of the Kecavan lineage from the Karumatur area may have been more fundamentally due to the rivalry between the three main lineages of Karumatur, namely, the Kecavan, the Madavanai and the Kurumban [Dumont, 1986: 175–76].[10]

Another important god, Muttaiyacami (*tuṭiyāṉa teyvam*), was originally the lineage god of an Acari caste family but has been given the position of one of the Kecavan lineage's deities since the following incident, which is said to have occurred near the Kottamantaikaruppacami temple. One day, a young couple of the Acari caste passed by the temple on their journey, and decided to stay there because it was already evening and the wife was going to have a baby. That night she had her baby, but she passed away, and the husband also died three days later. The baby was fortunately picked up by the Kecavan. Later the Kecavan people felt a special affection for the baby, having learnt that the Acari couple had migrated from the eastern side of Madurai as they had done. Not only did they rear the baby with care, but they also adopted Muttaiyacami as their lineage god in token of the brotherhood between them, or their pseudo-*Paṅkāḷi* relationship.[11] In Karumatur, the guardian deity Kottalakaruppu, whose shrine is in front of Kottamantaikaruppacami, is identified with Muttaiyacami.

It is said that the goddess Cilaikari was once reared as a human child but after reaching puberty she committed suicide, by which it was verified she was a goddess. The term Cilaikari itself, which is said to mean "a woman who has a *cīlai* (a piece of cloth which remains unburnt after suicide by fire)", indicates that her miraculous suicide is the evidence of her divinity (see [Dumont, 1986: 364]). TG claims that Cilaikari is a reincarnation of Kaṇṇaki, a heroine of Cirapatikāram and is a *caktiyuḷḷa teyvam* (a deity possessing strong sacred power, *śakti*) (see [ibid.: 364, 372]). This claim obviously contradicts the former story in which Cilaikari is a virgin goddess, *kaṇṇi* in Tamil. An important point is that the Cilaikari is strongly connected with the locality of Kinnimangalam, or the inside space of the hamlet (*ūr*) This contrasts with the chief deity Kottamantaikaruppacami, residing outside the village. There is a complementarity between them, and she occupies the position of the vice chief lineage deity. *Cāmiāṭis o*f both the Kottamantaikaruppacami and the Cilaikari are selected from the insiders (the members of the Kecavan lineage), though other secondary *cāmiāṭis* come from outside the village and also from other lineages or castes. Furthermore, the Cilaikari's *cāmiāṭi* is from the first *vāricu*, whereas the *cāmiāṭi* of the chief deity is from the second *vāricu*. The significance of the goddess should not be underestimated, even if a god is the head of the lineage deities.

Before proceeding to a discussion of their lineage festivals, I sum up the features of the Kallars' lineage deities. For this, I also take into account the case of the Kamanan lineage, adding to that of the Kecavan lineage discussed above. (1) It is believed that just as the Kecavan did due to their strife with other lineage, the Kamanan ancestors also left their original village because of the conflict between sublineages (*vāricus*) (2) As is exemplified by the Kamanan lineage, the transfer of the *putimaṇ* of the original temple is the most usual method of setting up a new temple, though the Kacavan are said not to have done so. (3) Both the Kamanan and the Kecavan lineages hold an intramural temple for storing a *cāmipeṭṭi* (a sacred chest identified with a deity) inside *ūr* (their quarter), besides the temple-outside-the-*ūr* (see the case of the Kamanan lineage shown in Figure 11.1). It is an important feature of the Kallar lineage cult that each lineage holds two temples, an inner and an outer, and their festival is conducted by moving between them. (4) Both lineages have 21 lineage deities, though all their names are not made clear. Nonetheless, the essential point lies in the complementary relationship between *cuttamuka teyvam* and *tuṭiyāna teyvam*. In other words, the presence of *tuṭiyāna teyvam* is indispensable for the cult of lineage deities.[12] (5) In both lineages, importance is attached to the goddess, who is a deified virgin, as the main deity who rejects blood sacrifice - either as the chief deity or as the sub chief deity.

Lineage Festivals

A lineage festival (*kulateyvam tiruviḻā*) is doubtlessly a highly visible discourse, as a lineage-based practice in which complex socio-cultural elements are strongly reflected. As in the case in village temple festivals, a lineage festival also bridges over both religious experience and social institutions. In this sense, the lineage festival again shows the mystificatory power of legitimating existing authority under the umbrella of the gods' unchallengeable power. Apart from this rather conservative and harmonious aspect, the lineage festival also holds a challenging or competitive aspect. It can be pointed out that the competitive aspect is found more frequently and more explicitly in the lineage festival than in the village temple festival for several reasons.

Firstly, a village is an inclusive unit in the village sphere, whereas there are plural lineages within the same caste in the village, and competition between lineages takes place. Secondly, a lineage basically maintains egalitarian values, whereas a village is structured by hierarchical values. Perceived imbalance within a lineage easily causes discord between the *vāricus* (sub-lineages) or between families, but conflict between castes is usually repressed by the vertical power relations of the village. Thirdly, generally speaking, the leadership within a lineage is more fluid than that of a village. More specifically speaking, the ritual roles at the village level are rather fixed and specialized, but in the lineage there is more room to replace the bearers of ritual roles.

Figure 11.1

Open-air Shrine of the Kamanan Lineage (The locations is outside of ūr)

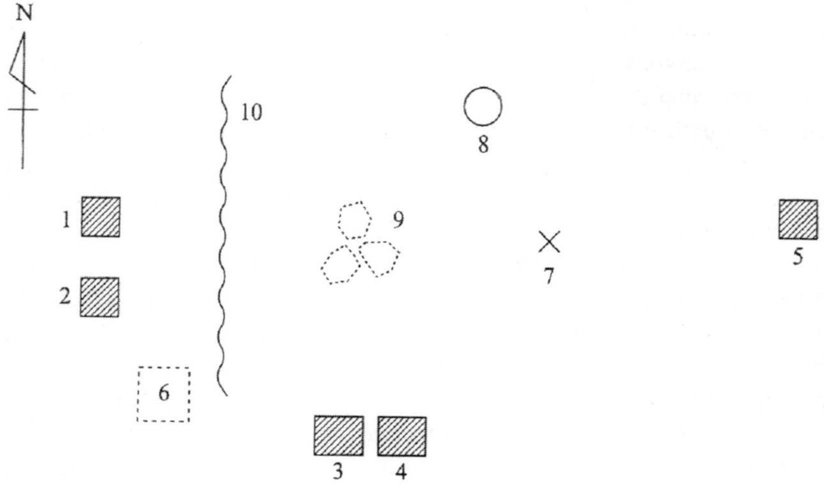

1. Ankālāisvari
2. Virapattiraṉ
3. Ciṉṉacāmi
4. Rākkāciyammaṉ
5. Kalyāṇi Karuppu
6. Position of 'sacred box' during the festival
7. Side of animal sacrifice
8. Lamp stand made of stone
9. Hearth for cooking poṅkal
10. Cloth for blindfolding blood sacrifice

This difference is based on the more rapid growth of sub-lineages, compared with changes in village composition. These arguments become the analytical point of view for the following description of the lineage festival.

The Kallars' lineage festivals are conducted during *Makācivarattiri* (an annual festival for Siva held in the night of the newmoon day of *Maci* month (February–March)). The festival is not held every year. The average frequency among the Kallars' lineages is twice or three times in ten years. This is slightly higher than that of the Paraiyars, which is once or twice in ten years. The reasons which make it difficult to hold the festival are financial difficulty, mourning due to the death of a lineage member, and discord between *vāricus*. The Kecavan lineage festival which I observed was conducted in February 1989, and was previously held in 1987. The Kecavan and the Kamanan tend to hold lineage festivals more frequently than other Kallar lineages do.[13] Since they enjoy high honour as pioneers among the Kallars, conducting the lineage festival is symbolically important for maintaining their status. This suggests that practising the festival itself is a social demonstration of the power of the lineage concerned.

Before starting the description of the lineage festival, let us look at the distribution of ritual roles, which is often a source of dispute between sub-lineages. The Kecavan lineage consists of 23 families, which are divided into two *vāricus*. Six hereditary posts (tasks), including ritual roles, are equally shared by the two *vāricus* as follows: the *pūcāri* (a lineage priest), the Cilaikari *cāmiāṭi*, and taṇṭal (a hereditary watchman of the village) are chosen from the first *vāricus*; whereas the second *vāricus* holds the privilege of selecting the Kottamantaikaruppacami *cāmiāṭi, tēvārapaṭṭam* (a representative of the lineage) and *mēlāḷar* (a temple manager). For

Plate 91 Inside shrine of the Cattai lineage.

Plate 92 Outside shrine of the Cattai lineage in the field.

Plate 93 Inside shrine of the Kecaven lineage.

Plate 94 Outside shrine of the Kecavan lineage at Karumatur.

Plate 95 Decorated *cāmipeṭṭi* kept in front of the inside shrine for starting the procession towards Karumatur (Aged lineage *pūcāri* stands near the *cāmipeṭṭi*).

Plate 96 *pūcāri's* grandson carries *cāmipeṭṭi* in the procession.

Plate 97 A lineage pūcāri moves from the main lineage deity of the Kecavan lineage, Kottamantaikaruppacami to the guardian deity, Kottalakaruppacami.

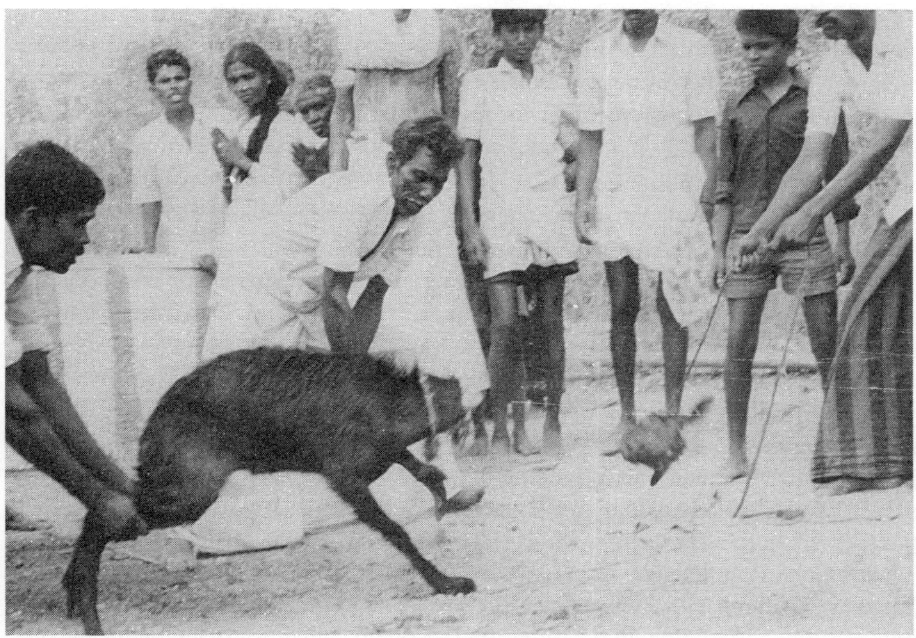

Plate 98 Cutting the head of the goat in front of Kottalakaruppacami.

comparison, the case of the Kamanan lineage is useful, because they have a quarrel between *vāricus*. Their division of ritual roles or privileges is this: (1) the first *vāricu; pūcāri*, Rakkaciyamman *cāmiāṭi*, the right of carryng the cāmipeṭṭi (a sacres chest) and *tāmpāḷam* (an offering plate) in the linage festival, (2) the second *vāricu*: *Tēvār* (the representative of the lineage), Ankalaisvari *cāmiāṭi,* Cinnacami *cāmiāṭi,* the right of making a *poṅgal* in the lineage festival, (3) the third *vāricu*: Virapattiran *cāmiāṭi*, the right of letting loose the first bull in the bull-racing called *jallikkaṭṭu* (literally, "trying the medals"). It is not an easy task to divide such ritual roles equally among multiple *vāricus*. The list in the Kamanan's case does not necessarily look equal. It seems that the third *vāricus* has the least power of the three. However, there is in fact an unsettled problem between the first and the second *vāricu*s. When the elder of the first *vāricu*, who was assigned to carry *tāmpāḷam*, died, the second *vāricu* began to claim that the bearer of *tāmpāḷam*, should be selected from the second *vāricus*. Because of this problem, they have failed to hold their lineage festival for six years (the information was collected in 1989).[14]

1. *Preparation:* In front of the intramural temple, the members of the lineage holds a gathering, called *patiṉaintu nāl kumpal* ("fifteenth day meeting"), on the day of the full moon, fifteen days before *Civarāttiri*. There, they reconfirm their decision to hold the festival, and decide on the amount to be collected from each household. In the case of the 1989 festival, it is reported that the total expenses were about Rs 3,600, and that each household paid Rs 30.[15] The rest of the cost was met by *uṇṭiyal* (donations to the temple) during the festival. From this day till the end of the festival, the *pūcāri* and *cāmiāṭis* have to abstain from eating meat, having sexual intercourse and taking meals in other people's houses. In this respect, I would like to confirm the following point. Because the persons who directly contact with deities have to be

cuttam (pure). However, as discussed in Chapter 5, *cuttam* in this context is not a hierarchical sense such as purity of higher castes but is an egalitarian sense of purity, that is, a human side's preparation for meeting deities which everybody is equally required. Therefore, although Dumont points out "the contradiction of the priest of a meat-eating god abstaining from meat" [Dumont, 1986: 380], it seems to me that this can be judged as an inappropriate question from the viewpoint of "pollution" and "pollution-sacredness", which has been clarified in Part Two.

2. *The First Day:* From the morning the god's ornaments and weapons etc.,[16] which are kept in the sacred storeroom, are cleaned. The cleaned ornaments are taken to Karumatur to decorate the main deity, and the sacred chest and other items are kept on a flat stone called *ampalakkal* ("assembly stone") in front of the sacred storeroom. In the afternoon the sacred chest is washed and decorated. Two kinds of garlands, *marikkoluntumālai* (a tendril garland) and *mallikaippūmālai* (a jasmine-flower garland), are placed on the chest. The Kecavan *pūcāri* along with, if necessary, someone to help him, arrives from Kottaiyur, at around 6 p.m.,[17] and then the festival starts. The start is indicated by the loud sound of the Harijan band.[18] *Tēvārpaṭṭam* (the lineage representative) gives the *pūcāri* a new *vēṭṭi* (cloth). Wearing this the *pūcāri* begins a *pūjā* to the sacred chest as the god. After the *pūjā, four cāmiāṭis* form a line, in the order of (1) Kottamantaikaruppacami, (2) Cilaikari, (3) Mayanticami and (4) Muttaityacami, to receive holy ash from the *pūcāri* and a garland from the *Tēvārpaṭṭam*, and they are also given particular items to carry.[19] Then they start to dance and soon each is believed to become possessed by their own deity. The first *kuricollutal* ("sign-telling"), in which problems or sufferings which people ask to be solved are answered by these possessed *cāmiāṭis*, is held in the following order; Kottamantaikaruppacami, Mayanticami, and Muttaiyacami (see [Moffatt, 1979: 230–1]).

Just before the procession starts, *kāṇikkai* (a voluntary money offering) is collected from the Kecavan people and presented to the Conaikamatci lineage as a *pūrvīkaccontam* (a hereditary affinal relation). The sacred chest is carried on the head of the *pūcāri* (actually his grandson in the observed case), and the procession leaves for Karumatur. It stops for a short time in front of the Ekanatarcuvami temple and at the *ūr* boundary near the tomb of their ancestor Palanicamitevar.[20] At the *ūr* boundary Cilaicari's *cāmiāṭi* leaves the procession because it is believed that the goddess, as a *vīṭṭukkāval teyvam* ("house-protection deity"), should not go beyond the village boundary. The procession proceeds through Cettikulam to Kottaiyur, and finally reaches the Kottamantaikaruppacami temple at midnight. On the way the sacred chest is put down on the *mantai* (a raised mound for a village gathering) of each village and people worship there. The journey from Kinnimangalam to Karumatur can be seen as the retroactive trip of their migration of their history.

The sacred chest is kept on the right side of the statue of Kottamantaikaruppacami. Not only the Kecavan people and their relatives but also other people come to worship at the temple through the night, because the temple is located on the way to the Kaluvanatarcami (Siva) temple, where a huge crowd gathers in the celebration of *Makācivarattiri.* This indicates the dual character of the god Kottamantaikaruppacami, namely as a lineage god and as a *nād* god [Dumont, 1986: 367, *Inf.* I].

3. *The Second Day:* Before dawn (around 4 a.m.) the *pūcāri* with a mask made of a banana leaves, conducts a *pūjā* by offering *taḻukais*[21] to the main deity Kottamantaikaruppacami, next to the guardian deity Kottalakaruppu (Muttaiyacami), enshrined in front of the temple of the main deity. After the *pūjā*, *mutaṉmai* (the idea of precedence) is practised, that is, *tīrttam* (sacred water), *piracātam* (a part of the offerings like *poṅkal*, banana and coconut) and holy ash are distributed in the following order: (1) *pūcāri* (2) *cāmiāṭi*s, (3) the Kurumpattevar lineage, (4) the Matayanai lineage, (5) the Kecavan lineage, (6) the Kakkuviran lineage, (7) the Cinnautaiyan lineage, and 8) the Parucapuli lineage. This order clearly reflects the traditional social system of the Karumatur area, namely, of the original Kallar *nād, as* Dumont clarifies. According to Dumont, the former three lineages are supported by the latter three lineages [Dumont, 1986: 175]. After the *pūjā*, the *pūcāri* begins to accept offerings from general visitors to the temple. In particular, the Kecavan lineage people, any *cāmiāṭis* and people who makes vows are given garlands.

Around 8 a.m. a second simplified *pūjā* in which only bananas, coconuts, coco-juice, betel and arecanut are offered is held. After this, *kuṟicollutal* is practised by three *cāmiāṭis* (Kottamantaikaruppacami, Mayanticami, and Muttaiyacami) standing in a line in front of the main temple.[22] Most people consult the *cāmiāṭi* of the deity, Kottamantaikaruppacami.

4. *The Third Day:* The third *pūjā* is carried out at around 4 a.m. The highlight of the third day is the blood sacrifice. For this, the *Tēvārpaṭṭam's* wife brings a *poṅkal* vessel and a bundle of firewood from Kinnimangalam to Karumatur. She is followed by Kecavan people carrying a goat, and women who also want to make *poṅkals*. As soon as they reach the temple, they begin to prepare the *poṅkals*.[23] At about 11 a.m., the *pūcāri* starts a *pūjā* to the main deity, and he then shifts to the Kottalakaruppu temple and does a *pūjā* to the guardian deity. There the blood sacrifice is conducted. The *pūcāri* pours the water used to wash the rice for the *poṅkal* onto the goat's head and body, and puts holy ash on its forehead. If the goat shakes its body (*kulukkutal*), this action is regarded as a sign that the god (*Brahmā*) has come into its head and accepted the conducting of the sacrifice. A Conaikamatci person, the Kecavan's affine (*pūrvīkaccontam*), cuts the goat's head off and further cuts off its right leg. The head holding the leg in its month, which is called *Viṟumā kapāla* ("*Brahmā* skull"), is put in front of Kottalakaruppu, and *kapālapūcai* ("skull-*pūjā*") is conducted by the *pūcāri*. The *piracātam* (an offering withdrawn) is distributed as *mutaṉmai* in the same order as the case of the first *pūjā*. This final ceremony at Karumatur is then over, and people prepare to return to Kinnimangalam.[24] They go back along the same routes by which they came. Reaching Kinnimangalam, the procession stops at the Pattattaraciyanman temple, where the Kecavan *pūcāri* gets holy ash from the Kauntar *pūcāri* of the goddess. When the sacred chest passes the Paraiyars' colony, the Paraiyars gather and worship the Kecavan gods by blowing *kulavai* (auspicious sounds) and by offering garlands and *kāṇikkai* (a money offering). The *Tēvār* gives holy ash to these Paraiyar worshippers. After a brief stop at the Ekanatarcami temple to receive a garland from the Ekanatarcami *pūcāri*, the Caste Hindus (the *ūr* people) also gather and worship the Kecavan gods near the Muttalamman temple. The Catayi people give garlands and money when the procession passes by the Catayi temple. Finally, the sacred chest and other items are put on the *ampalaikkal*. Then the last

pūjā, called *maṟupūcai* ("re-*pūjā*"), is held at this auspicious time by offering three bunches of bananas and three coconuts etc. The order of *mutaṉmai* in this case is this: (1) *pūcāri*, (2) four *cāmiāṭis*, (3) two *Tēvārs* (the Kamanan and the Kecavan), (4) V.A.O. (traditionally, *karṇam* and *nāṭṭāṇmai*), (5) the Conaikamatci lineage, (6) the Catayi lineage, (7) the Panniayan lineage, (8) the Cuntaravalliyamman lineage, (9) the Kattapinnai lineage, (10) the Acaris, (11) *tōṭṭi* and *maṭaiyaṉ* (12) the Four-lineages of the Paraiyars (*Nāṟpaṅkāḷi*), and (13) others. This order of *mutaṉmai* shows clearly the careful consideration given firstly, to the village power structure, (1)–(4) and (10)–(12); secondly, top the affinal lineages, (5)–(8); and, thirdly, to agnatic relations (*muṟaikkupaṅkāḷi*), (9).

After everything is put back into the storeroom, the *pūcāri* and the *cāmiāṭis* are served non-vegetarian meals in the *Tēvār's* house. This makes the end of their temporary pure state (*cuttam*). The *aṭimaikārar* (house servants) and the Paraiyar musicians are also served meals in the yard of the other Kecavan house. After the meal, only the Kecavan people gather in front of the storeroom and share the remaining bananas. At this time, one or two bananas are given to women who left the Kecavan through marriage.

Lineage Cults of the Paraiyars

The Kinnimangalam Paraiyar community mainly consists of the *Nāṟpaṅkāḷi* (Four Pankalis), who occupy the central position in the community, and the Tankalan lineage, deemed as the socially marginal.[25] It is notable that the *Nāṟpaṅkāḷi* themselves are structured by the complementarity between the first settlers, the Kartananati-Cinnananti lineages, and their affines, the Mataiyan lineages and the Urkalan lineage. Attention will be paid to this community structure, which reflects their history of migration, in the following comparative discussion.

The Kartananti-Cinnananti Lineages

Although today the Kartananti and the Cinnananti are regarded as independent lineages, they still worship common lineage deities and jointly celebrate the lineage festival. In this sense, they can be regarded as *vakaiyaṟās* ("lineages"), but in so far as they worship the same god they retain the character of *vāricu* (sub-lineages).[26]

Lineage Deities

It is believed that the common ancestor of both lineages originally lived in Uruvatti, near Sivaganga, 30 km east of Madurai city, but they were forced to leave Uruvatti in the socially chaotic period called *paṭaiveṭṭukālam*. When they left Uruvatti, they took a *putimaṇ* (a handful of earth) from the lineage temple where the goddesses *Periyanātcci* and *Ariyanātcci*, who are deified sisters, were enshrined as the main deities.[27] The present lineage temple, located in *Paṟaiya vīṭu* (cluster II), was set up after placing the *putimaṇ* on the site. As shown in Figure 11.2, the main deities are said to be in the small temple building where there is no image other than the sacred chest, made of palm-leaf (*ōlai-peṭṭi*),[28] and other subordinate deities are symbolized by the stones installed in front of the temple. They also claim that there are 21 lineage deities, though they can identify only 12 deities, as shown in Table 11.1. This table shows the character of each deity (*cuttamuka teyvam* or *tuṭiyāṉa teyvam*), and the lineage to which each deity's *cāmiāṭi* belongs (Kartananti or Cinnananti). According to it, six *cāmiāṭis* are chosen from the Kartananti, whereas five *cāmiāṭi* belong to the Cinnanati.[29] Since the *pūcāri* is from the Cinnananti, the 12 ritual roles are after all divided equally among the two lineages. It is clear that they consciously pay attention to the balance between the two lineages.

Table 11.1

12 Deities out of 21 Lineage Deities of the Kartananti-Cinnananti Lineages

Deity's name	*Sex (F/M)*	*C/T*	*Lineage of camiati*	*Sex of camiati*
Periyanatcci	F	C	Cinnananti	F
Ariyanatcci	F	C	Cinnananti	F
Periyakaruppacuvami	M	T	Kartananti	M
Virapattiracuvami	M	C	Kartananti	M
Mayanticuvami	M	C	Cinnananti	M
Muttukkaruppacuvami	M	T	Kartananti	M
Conaicuvami	M	T	Kartananti	M
Cinnakkaruppacuvami	M	T	Cinnananti	M
Rakkacciyamman	F	T		
Pattacuvami	M	T	Cinnananti	M
Latatannacicuvami	M	C	Kartananti	M
Cankilicuvami	M	T	Kartananti	M

Note: C: cuttamuka teyvam T: tutiyana teyvam

Figure 11.2

Temple of the Kartananti-Cinnananti Lineages

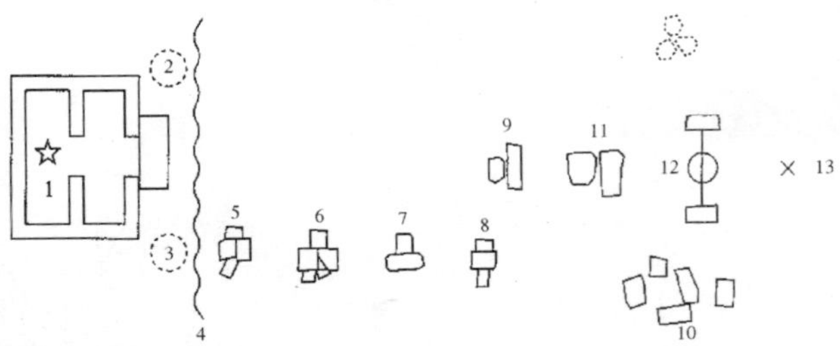

1. *karakam* only during a festival
2. Ariyanatcci during a festival
3. Periyanatcci during a festival
4. blindfold during an animal sacrifice
5. Virapattiracuvami (or Periyakaruppacuvami)
6. Periyakaruppacuvami (or Muttukkaruppacuvami)
7. Muttukkaruppacuvami (or Conaicuvami)
8. Cankilikaruppacuvami (or Cankilikaruppacuvami)
9. Cinnakarupppacuvami (or Cinnakarupppacuvami)
10. Conaicuvami (or none)
11. place for offering a light
12. bell
13. place for an animal sacrifice
14. hearth for cooking a *poṅkal*

Plate 99 Lineage temple of the Kartananti-Cinnananti lineages in Cluster II in 1987

Plate 100 Lineage temple of the Kartananti-Cinnananti lineages in 1996.

The lineage festival is held in *Paṅkuṉi* (March–April), one month after *Māci* (February–March) when the Caste Hindus' lineage festivals should be conducted. Their last festival was held eight years ago. Since then they have failed to hold a lineage festival. According to them, this is mainly because of the dispute between the Kartananti and the Cinnananti concerning the right of one house plot, rather than for economic reasons. However, it seems to me that the financial aspect is also significant. I estimate the total amount needed to cover the festival's expenses is about Rs 2,500. Members of the Kartananti and Cinnananti lineages at first claimed that their last festival cost nearly Rs 10,000, and that at least Rs 5,000 is now necessary for conducting this festival.[30] Even if it only cost about Rs 2,500 and the donations during the festival covered one third of the total costs, each household would have to pay about Rs 40, since the expenses are shared by about 44 households. The amount is not very large, but not small for the ordinary Paraiyar household which has to manage on a cash income of about Rs 200–300 per month. It is said that the dispute between the two lineages is so serious that they are about to split into completely separate lineages, each conducting its own festival.

Lineage Festival

I had no opportunity to observe any lineage festival of the Paraiyars because no festival was held during the period of my fieldwork, from 1985 to 1989. Therefore, I reconstruct the process of the festival from the data of several Paraiyar informants of both Kartananti-Cinnananti lineages. Two weeks before the festival, the lineage members gather in front of their lineage temple and formally fix the date of the festival and its budget. After fixing the date, they move to the Urkkaval temple, one of the village temples in order to obtain the god's permission.[31] Interestingly, it is said that the role of obtaining permission must be carried out by their affinal relations, i.e., by members of the Mataiyan and of the Urkalan lineages. After this, *pūcāris* and *cāmiāṭis* start to follow a disciplined life, in which they take a bath everyday and eat neither non-vegetarian food nor meals provided by others, so as to acquire the pure (*cuttam*) body and mind believed to be necessary for the festival.

1. *The First Day:* The festival starts in the evening (around 5 p.m.). The sacred chest (*cāmipeṭṭi*) of Periyanatcci-Ariyanatcci is brought to the eastern tank, where it is washed and decorated. The lineage priest (*pūcāri* and the possessed dancers (*cāmiāṭis*) take a bath and wear new clothes. Then they form a procession, accompanied by drumming,[32] to Sikkanpatti in order to receive the *karakam* (a decorated pot full of water), which is a potter has been asked to make, and which represents their main goddesses. The priest carries it on his head, through the back way, and it is installed in the temple, flour lamps (*māviḷakku*) are dedicated to the main goddesses by women. The priest, who puts on a mask of banana leaves, conducts a *pūjā* by praying 21 times for the 21 lineage deities. After this, *kuṟicollutal* ("sign-telling") is performed.

2. *The Second Day:* On the morning of the second day, the priest's wife cooks a *poṅkal*. At around ten a.m., the priest conducts a *pūjā* by offering the *poṅkal* in advance of the animal sacrifice. New cloths, garlands, donations called *pātakāṇikkai* etc. are presented to the Kavuntar priest of the Urkkaval temple. The

prestations again show the special connection between their main deities and the god Urkkaval. Though the procedure of the animal sacrifice is the same as that in the Kallars case, the decisive difference lies in the fact that the role of cutting off the head of the goat is not undertaken by an affinal relation, but by two *Tēvārs* (a Kecavan person and a Kamanan person), who are invited as honoured guests. However, the strong connection with affines is emphasized in different ways. For examples, the music during the sacrifice is played by the Mataiyan people and a possessed dancer of the Cinnacami lineage is again carried by a Mataiyan person in this scene. The main deities, as *cuttamuka teyvam*, are hidden by a curtain during the blood sacrifice. The order of *mutaṉmai* (the idea of precedence) after the sacrifice is as follows: (1) the Kartananti-Cinnananti lineage, (2) the Tankalan lineage, (3) the Matayan lineage and (4) the Urkalan lineage. It is noteworthy that a higher priority is given to the Tankalan rather than to their affines, and this seems to reflect their diplomatic judgement on the balance of power within the Paraiyar community.[33] At around 8 p.m. only the possessed dancers gather in front of the temple, and a special *pūjā* is then conducted to the guardian deities by sacrificing a hen and offering a bottle of arrack (300 ml). After the *pūjā*, they have a feast, consuming their offerings. With this ceremonial feast, the festival is substantially over.

3. *The Third Day:* In the morning the final ceremony is conducted. The priest brings the *karakam* to the tank and throws it into the water. The priest and the possessed dancers soon bath three times and then return home.

Lastly, it should be emphasized that the centrality of the Kartananti-Cinnananti lineage within the Paraiyar community is reflected in the contents of their lineage festival. Their lineage festival appears as a festival of the whole Paraiyar community, as if the Muttalamman festival is the main village festival of Kinnimangalam.[34] In contrast, they point out the peripherality of the Tankalan lineage. For example, according to them, two *Tēvārs* have the *urimai* (right and duty) of killing the goat in the lineage festivals of *Nāṟpaṅkāḷi*, but this is not the case in those of the Tankalan lineage, although this claim is denied by Tankalan people.

The Mataiyan Lineage

It is said that the Mataiyan lineage was invited to this village by the Kartananti-Cinnananti people.[35] The Mataiyan lineage was treated as an affine and was given three rights by the latter people. These rights are (1) the position of *maṭaiyaṉ* (caretaker of the sluice of the village tank), (2) the management of the Mataikaruppucami temple, and (3) a half of *māṉiyam* (lands given to village servants). The Mataiyan people also worship 21 deities, among whom Meyyanamurtti is the main god, but it is notable that they attach importance not only to the 21 deities, but also to the goddess Marattiyamman in their lineage festival. The main scene of the festival consists of processions of two sacred chests, i.e., the procession of the Meyyanamurtti's chest from Sameyanarur near the Vaigai river where the priest stays[36] and that of the Marattiyamman's from Katalanpur, east of Madurai city. It is believed that the goddess Marattiyamman is a deified Kallar woman who fell in love with one of the ancestors of the Mataiyan lineage and committed suicide. This case is regarded as the worst possible combination for a relationship, and is never allowed by the Kallars (see Chapter 7). It is believed that though her Mataiyan lover was killed by her brothers, other ancestors of the Mataiyan lineage escaped from being massacred thanks to her advance notice. Since then, they have worshipped her as a goddess. It is noteworthy that their connection with the Kallars is emphasized by the Marattiyamman worship found in the lineage festival.[37] Nonetheless, they have failed to conduct a festival for the past seven years.

The Urkalan Lineage

It is believed that the ancestors of the Urkalan lineage were forced to leave Ariyapatti during the time of *paṭaiveṭṭukālam*. According to legend, a Kamanan person met a Urkalan boy who had lost his parents, and invited him to this village. He was introduced to the Muslim Jamindar and was engaged in servant work at the Jamindar's house. As already described in Chapter 4, this Urkalan boy played a key role in the Kamanan undertaking of killing the Muslim Jaminder. The Kamanan people told the boy that they would grant his wish. The boy requested them (1) to give him a position as a village servant, (2) to give him the right to obtain a bride from the Kartananti-Cinnananti lineages, and (3) to give him the right of getting the thigh of the right foreleg of slaughtered cattle. The Kamanan people asked the Kartananti-Cinnananti people to fulfill these requests, and they did so. When the boy had a wife and a baby, the Kartananti-Cinnananti people felt sympathy for the family because they had no god to worship, and gave the god Urkalan (Urkavalcami) to him. Then, the family started to worship the 21 deities, including the main god Urkalan. However, it should be noted that they worship not only 21 lineage deities but also the goddess Cilaikari,[38] who is equated with Marattiyamman for the Mataiyan people.

The strong connection between the Kamanan lineage and the Urkalan lineage, which has been explained by this legend, still holds today. The Urkalan people enjoy special privileges[39] in the Kamanan lineage festival, while, in turn, the Kamanan people are regarded as the most important guests in the lineage festival of the Urkalan. The Urkalan lineage festival has not been conducted for ten years for financial reasons.

The Tankalan Lineage

Cutakkuti, a village near Melur, is the Tankalan's home village. According to legend, their ancestors moved to Kutiraikuti, where they were engaged in breeding the buffaloes of the Kallars and of the Konars. The "great-grandfather" (nearly equal to ancestor) of the present generation had two sons, Periyamuttukumaran and Cinnamuttukumaran, who are the originators of the present two *vāricus*. It is said that the great-grandfather was, by chance, involved in an affair, in which he murdered a king in order to help a Kallar thief, Veriyatevar. Thus he and his family decided to leave Kuritaikuti for Patti, which was Veriyatevar's village, at Veriyatevar's invitation.[40] On the way to Patti, however, the great-grandfather's family decided to settle down in Kinnimangalam, due to the villagers' good treatment of them. After several years, he happened to again see Veriyatevar in the bull-baiting festival (*Erutukaṭṭu*) held at Kokkulam. Veriyatevar again invited the great-grandfather to live in his village, Patti, but the great-grandfather explained that he lived comfortably in Kinnimangalam and did not want to move. Veriyatevar understood the situation. In order to guarantee the more stable position of the great-grandfather's family, he contacted Two Tevars and Four Pankalis in Kinnimangalam and asked them not to threaten the family in any circumstances, and to give *mutanmai* to them during their festival. The position of *taṅkaḷāṉ* was also set up and given as a sort of *naṉrikkaṭaṉ* (thanksgiving presentation) to the great-grandfather by Veriyatevar. The role of *taṅkaḷāṉ* is to be a witness to various occasions in the Paraiyar community such as engagements, and divorces.

Though their main lineage god is Muttaiyacuvani, their special preference for the God Murugan can be noted.[41] For example, this is indicated by the fact that most of the male members of the Tankalan lineage have Murugan's names, like Palani, Arumugan, and Vel. Therefore, the *pūjā* to Murugan, which is conducted during the annual festival of Tirupparankunram in *Paṅkuṉi*, is regularly practised by them.

Before describing the festival itself, it is necessary to mention the discord between two *vāricu*, i.e., Perityamuttukumaran *vāricus* (the first) and Cinnamuttukumaran *vāricu* (the second), which has continued since 1961, when the last lineage festival carried out with the cooperation of both *vāricus* was held. The strife is said to have originated over dissatisfaction with the distribution of rights and positions between the two *vāricus*,[42] making it impossible to have a united festival. In 1965, they started to hold their lineage festivals separately. Their separate festivals have not been held since 1982, mainly, according to them, for economic reasons. After the split, both *vāricu*s selected their own *pūcāri* (priest) and *cāmiāṭis* (possessed dancers), and each used different temples for their festivals. The first *vāricus* uses a storeroom for keeping the sacred chest as their temple; whereas the second *vāricu* occupies the Muttaiya temple in Pottampati, about 20 km west of Kinnimangalam. The lineage festival I describe here is, however, that held before the split occurred, because the complete form of lineage festival tells more clearly what the Tankalan people expect from these festive activities.

The sacred chest leaves the storeroom for Pottampatti at around 7 a.m. On the way, the procession must call at Sikkampatti because there they show their respect to Peyatevar who donated the land at Pottampatti for the building of the Muttaiya temple. In the early afternoon, the *pūjā* to Muttaiyacuvami and other lineage deities is conducted, and then *mutaṉmai* is given. In the night, possessed dancers do *kuṟicollutal*. A goat sacrifice, as the climax of the festival, is performed in the early afternoon of the second day. Cutting off the victim's head is followed by *kappālapūcai* and *mutaṉmai*. After the sacrifice, the sacred chest is brought back to Kinnimangalam.

The above brief sketch of the festival is made up by pointing out several differences between the Tankalan lineage and the *Nāṟpaṅkāḷi* (Four Pankalis). Firstly, the festival month of the Tankalan lineage is *Vaikāci* (May-June), which differs from the festival month of the *Nāṟpaṅkāḷi, Paṅkuṉi* (March-April). Secondly, the Tankalan people claim that the period prior to the festival when the priest and possessed dancers must observe a disciplined life is a month, which is twice as long as the purification period commonly practiced not only bythe *Nārpaṅkāḷi* but also by the Kallars. Thirdly, the Tankalan festival is characterized by a round trip between Kinnimangalam (the inside temple: the storeroom) and Pottampatti (the outside temple). In this sense, their festival is similar to that of the Kallars rather that of the *Nārpaṅkāḷi*, in which only one temple is used. Fourthly, a god or goddess specially worshipped, apart from 21 lineage deities, is often found. In the case of the Tankalan, the God Murugan is their favourite, whereas the *Nāṟpaṅkāḷi* people tend to prefer a goddess as a deified woman. There is a contrast between the former and the latter, that is, male *kaṭavuḷ* vs female *teyvam*.

As has been noted, though the *Nāṟpaṅkāḷi* people deny the attendance of the Two Tevars at the Tanaklan festival, the Tankalan people insist that those who should be invited to their lineage festival are as follows: the Two Tevars; a descendant of Veriyatevar; four representatives of the *Nāṟpaṅkāḷi*; and a person of the Manakuli lineage, as an important affine. According to them, the Two Tevars play the role of cutting off the head of the victim in the blood sacrifice.

Conclusion: The Paraiyars Strategies Concerning Lineage Cults

The following points have been made clear through the comparison between the cases of the dominant castes (the Pillais and the Kallars) and those of the dominated caste (the Paraiyars), and, furthermore, through the comparison among the lineages of the Paraiyar community.

Lineage Cults and "Pollution" Ideology

Both the Kallars and the Paraiyars share a common basis, called "the popular cultural tendency" in my sense, on which their lineage cults are practised. This means that both the Kallars and the Paraiyars, as the actors performing the lineage cults, are commonly "interpellated" by "pollution" ideology, which is the primary ideology of "the popular cultural tendency". It is now made clear that the structure of the festival process and its ideology are basically shared by the Kallars and the Paraiyars. Though the characteristics of the "popular" cultural tendency have already been highlighted in the discussion on the cults of the village deities (Chapter 6), they can be confirmed again here. That is, the lineage cult basically attaches importance to the following key traits: (i) a blood sacrifice, (ii) an affinal relationship (cross-relatives), (iii) *teyvam* and a goddess. Firstly, a blood sacrifice is indispensable for the lineage festivals both of the Kallars and of the Paraiyars, even though the main deity is said not to accept blood sacrifice. This means that the main deity and the other guardian deities are deemed as forming one whole system, as was clarified in my discussion on the structure of the village deities as well.[43] In sum, the relationship between the main deity and the guardian deities should not be interpreted as the dualism of "purity-impurity", but as the dynamism from "generation (creation)" to "conservation (maintenance)". That is, the ambiguous sacred power which is "generated" by the blood sacrifice, which is officially dedicated to the guardian deities (as *tuṭiyāna teyvam*), is controlled and "maintained" by the main deities (as *cuttamuka teyvam*).[44] Secondly, the importance of affinal relationship with cross relatives is evident in both the cases of the Kallars and the Paraiyars. The significant role of cutting off the head of the sacrificial victim is played by an affine in the case of the Kallars. Although, in the case of the Paraiyars, the role is played by the Two Tevars, this does not reduce the significance of the affinal relationship, because attention is always paid to the attendance of the affines, and is particularly emphasized in the scene of *mutaṉmai*. At any rate, it is important here that cutting off the victim's head is not done by any lineage insider but is conducted by outsiders related to the lineage.[45] Thirdly, generally speaking, their lineage deities are classified into the category of *teyvam* rather than the category of *kaṭavuḷ*. This means that the relationship between lineage deities as *teyvams* and lineage members is rather friendly and communicative.[46] In other words, their faith in lineage deities usually anticipates not only building their identities but also practical grace from the deities, as is indicated by their migration stories. In this respect, though the main deity is not always a goddess, a goddess, who is usually a deified woman after her sacrificial death, like Cilaikari, Ankalaisvari, or Marattiyamman, is certainly worshipped as one of the important deities in the lineage festival, because such a goddess is a materialized form of "pollution" ideology, which is familiar to the people.

Both the Kallars and the Paraiyars show their enthusiasm for the lineage festival which is based on "pollution" ideology, as mentioned above. This is because the lineage festival, which is held with the unity of the parallel relatives and with the cooperation of the cross relatives, provides an opportunity for reconfirming their identify in the "ritual" setting.[47] They can be seen to be reactivated through the transcendental religious experience ("*l'ordre intime*") based on "pollution" ideology, in which death is united with life, and the mythological world is fused with the present practical world. People are imagined as equal in this transcendental sphere. Especially in lineage cults, this egalitarianism infront of gods is further supported by horizontal segmentation, like lineages and sub-lineages. Thus an identity formed in this situation could be called the "ritually" egalitarian identity. This statement is exemplified in practice especially by the conduct of the animal sacrifice, and by the procession of the sacred chest symbolizing the retrospective trip. The blood sacrifice is the ritual act directly symbolizing the unification of death and life, while the procession through which historical incidents are traced provides the lineage members an opportunity of participating in their mythological world, where they not only confirm their roots, but also have their faith in their lineage deities aroused. This suggests that kinship and cosmology are strongly linked (cf. [Barnard and Good, 1984: 154–6]).

The strong connection between the horizontal unity of kinship and "pollution" ideology (logic of sacrifice) is found in the practice of the lineage festival. It is, therefore, claimed that the life-world of the villagers living under the caste institution has not only a logic of separation exemplified by caste hierarchy but also a logic of unity exemplified by the horizontal kinship relationship. It is also useful here to recall the broad range of original meaning of the word *jāti* which includes kinship groups like a lineage or a cluster of lineages [Quigley, 1993: 4–8].

Reproduction of the Hierarchical Social Order

The above-mentioned reconfirmation of identity in the "ritual" setting, or in a religious context, is necessarily associated with the social order of hierarchy and interdependence, as most explicitly shown by the custom of *mutaṉmai*. The hierarchical gap between the Kallars and the Paraiyars is not only directly indicated by *mutaṉmai*, but is also more clearly revealed by a systematic comparison of both their festivals, as is shown below:

1. The Kallars ask their affines to cut off the head of the goat in their sacrifice, whereas the Paraiyars give this important role to the Two Tevars. The Two Tevars are invited as guests to the Paraiyars' festival, but, in contrast, the Paraiyars attend the Kallars' festival as servants, like musicians.
2. The blood sacrifice is conducted on the third day among the Kallars, whereas it is held on the second day in the case of the Paraiyars, because the latter's festival lasts only two days.
3. The Paraiyars cannot conduct their lineage festival in *Māci* when the Kallars conduct their lineage festivals. One month later, in *Paṅkuni*, the *Nārpaṅkāḷi* celebrate their festivals, and the Tankalan hold it in *Vaikāci*, three months after *Māci*.
4. Generally speaking, the Kallar lineages hold their lineage festivals more frequently than the Paraiyar lineages do.
5. With the exception of the Tankalan before the split occurred, the *Nārpaṅkāḷi* have only one temple. This contrasts with the Kallars'case, in which two temples are used.
6. The lineage festival of the Kallars is open to the village community as a whole, because they are the dominant caste, whereas the Paraiyars' festival is basically closed within their community.

The above six points show that, firstly, both the Kallars and the Paraiyars share the same structure of festivity and its ideology and secondly on the shared base the Paraiyars, especially the *Nāṟpaṅkāḷi*, practice an incomplete form of the Kallars' type of lineage festival. Therefore, against the Paraiyars' will, their practices of lineage festival result in exposing the existing hierarchical order in which they are placed at the bottom. At worst, those practices, rather unwittingly, contribute to their acceptance of the conventional social order. This is the very ideological effect of non-discursive "ritual practice" (see Note 47) or "rule-governed customary behaviour". What is pointed out in the previous section is the ritual effect concerning kinship order, whereas what is argued here is the ritual effect concerning caste hierarchical order. Nonetheless, it should be noted that the caste hierarchical order here is the Kallar dominated one, so that the hierarchy legitimized by ritual is that defined mainly by politico-economic power within which "pure-impure" ideology is instrumentally utilized.

At any rate, why do the dominated Paraiyars keenly conduct such a ritual activity which tends to support or reproduce the hierarchical system suppressing them? Moffatt's answer of "true believer" is not valid. In this connection, Bloch's argument on women's position in the circumcision ceremony of Merina society is suggestive [Bloch, 1986: 173–4]. That is, the participation/contribution of women to the circumcision ceremony, even though they are humiliated as the lower positioned people in the ceremony, leads to enjoying the "victory" of the ceremony and sharing its fruits. If the women are replaced by the Paraiyars, Bloch's way of interpretation would be useful for answering the above question. As well as the case of the women, there is no other way for Paraiyars except to follow the conventional order in order to complete the festival and enjoy its fruits. Their first priority lies in getting their lineage deities' grace and in order to do that they instrumentally strategically accept or adopt the elements of village hierarchical order, such as the invitation of Two

Tevars. In other words, Tevars are invited not because that they are respectable and ritually higher but because their attendance authorizes the festival and makes it grander.[48] Despite such a rationalization of the dominated Paraiyars, however, there is no change in that their strategic practices still have a double-edged connotation. By utilizing, even if they consciously did so, the socially higher person or element they would appear to ingratiate themselves with the dominant people or ideology. In sum, (1) the Paraiyars' keen concerns for the religious fruits and (2) their instrumental usage of the hegemony holders make the Paraiyars remain within the social space encapsulated by the ruling hierarchical order.

Differentiation as a Strategy for Self-Assertion

Though I have dealt with the Paraiyars inclusively, it is very important to focus on the subtle differences between the lineage festivals of the *Nāṟpaṅkāḷi*, as the central lineage, and that of the Tankalan, as the peripheral lineage, when we consider the dynamic formation of the "subject" of the Paraiyars. Compared with the *Nāṟpaṅkāḷi*, the Tankalan people are more conscious of their identity formation and their attitude seems to predict the *Nāṟpaṅkāḷi* future. The Harijans today are not confined to the village, but live in the broader social space beyond the village social order. In this sense, the Tankalan people are top-runners in so far as K hamlet is concerned. Paying attention to the difference, therefore, leads to a discussion of "rule-examining self-reflexive behaviour" among the Harijans.

It is obvious that these differences come from the Tankalans' ambivalent social position, in which they enjoy their independence but at the same time have alienated feelings due to their social setting, being less involved in the village structure.Though the principal structure of the festival is shared by the Paraiyars, the difference derives from the given social positions which are reflected in the details of the festival.[49] (1) The Tankalan lineage has a lineage festival in *Vaikāci;* whereas the *Nāṟpaṅkāḷi* have it in *Paṅkuṉi.* The Kallar persons (Two Tevars) participate in the festival of the *Nāṟpaṅkāḷi* and play the important role of cutting off the head of the goat, but it is said that there is no Kallar participant in the Tankalan festival, though the Tankalan deny this. (2) The Tankalans' festival (before the split) was held between two temples, inside and outside, as is that of the Kallars; the *Nāṟpaṅkāḷi* have only one temple, which is built inside the colony. (3) Only the Tankalan lineage claims a one month purification period before the festival, which is twice the period the Kallars and the *Nāṟpaṅkāḷi* people observe. (4) It should be mentioned that the Tankalan people are devout worshippers of the God Murugan, apart from their lineage cult. The point lies in their enthusiasm for this *kaṭavuḷ* as compared with the *Nāṟpaṅkāḷi,* who are satisfied with the cult of a goddess as a *teyvam.* (5) The Tankalans' festival makes clear their special connection with the outside Kallars living in other villages, who helped establish their social position in Kinnimangalam. In this sense, they contrast with the *Nāṟpaṅkāḷi,* who are deeply involved in the power of inside or village Kallars. This comparison evidently shows the reflections of the Tankalan's social peripheral position and, as its reaction, their self-assertion by means of "over-assimilation" and "differentiation by citation from outside the village sphere".[50] Since there is no difference in terms of everyday lifestyle or ideological settings between the Tankalan and the *Nāṟpaṅkāḷi*, these differences are mainly caused by their feelings as "marginal men". These differences, wittingly manipulated, clearly aim at resisting the *Nāṟpaṅkāḷi* and at the same time, probably, the village Kallars. Although, for instance, as is indicated by their claim concerning Kallar guests, the Tankalan sometimes show a desire to be involved in the village conventional system, it seems that such an expression of desire is rather reinforced by their rivalry feelings to the *Nāṟpaṅkāḷi*. This sort of reaction among the Tankalan results in their "differentiation of over-assimilation", such as a strong connection with an outside influential Kallar, Murugan worship, a long purification period etc. In this sense, differentiation and assimilation are not separable but are deemed as different facets of their stıategic self-assertion.

The strategic self-assertion of the Tankalan associated with the citation of components from the broader social sphere beyond the village, in other words, the Tankalans' decentripetal tendency against the centripetal power working in the village sphere doubtless takes in advance the trend that the *Nāṟpaṅkāḷi* will definitely follow in the near future. It is noted, however, that this level of decentripetal movement against the village system is most probably again encapsulated by another urban-centred dominant ideology which can cover the much broader social sphere. This prevailing dominant ideology is grasped as a combination of market-oriented consumerism and new-fashioned and popularized Brahmanical culture, both of which have been developed since British colonization and are more and more deeply permeated in the society these days. I call this complex ideology "contemporary popular Brahmanical culture". The main conveyor of this ideology today are, needless to say, people caught by the middle class syndrome. It is extremely difficult for anybody to escape from this new hierarchical ideology, so to speak, the modified "pure-impure" ideology whose appearance is not a religious ideology but a taste for high culture. In the light of the above framework, therefore, the strategy of the Tankalan found in the practice of their lineage festival is regarded as a challenge to the conventional village system by using some elements of "contemporary popular Brahmanical culture". There is an irony here that the attempt to disregard the immediate village caste hierarchy rather supports the modified "pure-impure" ideology circulating in wider societies. It is of course possible still to claim from the Tankalans' subjective viewpoint that "pollution" ideology is materialized through the practice of the lineage festival anyhow, even though the twisted "pure-impure" ideology is instrumentally adopted. Anyhow, the Tankalans' deviation from the *Nāṟpaṅkāḷi* in the practice of the lineage festival provides an important example of the reflection of "non-ritual" knowledge, like socio-economic conditions, upon "ritual" knowledge. In this sense, it is at least true that the Tankalans' challenge breaks through the village level of closed circle of "ritual communication" in which the *Nāṟpaṅkāḷi* are rather confined,[51] even though another new trap is waiting for their attempt, as mentioned above.

As a corollary of the above arguments, it is suggested that ideological difference (what they actually believe) should not be confused with strategical difference (how they behave), which is strongly determined by socio-economic conditions. This claim is exemplified by the contrasts between the *Nāṟpaṅkāḷi* and the Tankalan lineage, such as the socially central vs. the socially peripheral (degraded), and the economically dependent vs. the economically independent. The adoption of different cultural components *per se* does not imply an actual ideological difference. This point is a fundamental criticism of Moffatt, but it also reveals the defect often found in disjunction theories that the distinction between the level of ideology and the level of strategy is blurred.

It is now obvious that the analysis of ritual practices at a collective level is limited as a methodology for disclosing social reality in its full sense. In the next chapter, therefore, my focus of discussion will shift to "non-ritual" everyday practices (or politico-economic aspect of practices) and to individual-centred practices.

Notes

1. The concept "performative", which is usually contrasted with "constative", is borrowed from Austin's work on the speech act [Austin, 1970: 233–252]. Tambiah's work entitled "A Performative Approach to Ritual" [Tambiah, 1985: Ch. 4] is also useful.
2. The usage of the sacred and the secular here is basically derived from Bataille's dualistic concepts "l'ordre intime" and "l'ordre réel" (see Chapter 2). This distinction also seems to correspond with that of Tambiah, namely, the sacred as an aspect of symbolic or iconic meaning and the secular as that of indexical meaning [Tambiah, 1985].
3. Though *kūṭṭam* is a sub-category of *kōttiram*, *kūṭṭam* rather corresponds to the *vakaiyaṟā* of the Kallars in size. Their account of *kōttiram* suggests the Sanskritized tendency of the Pillais.
4. The present generation of Pillai families can identify only five deities out of twenty-one, namely, Ankalaisvari, Virapattirar, Latacanyaci, Kannimarkai and Kavalkarakaruppu. The identification of the deities' names is not very important for them, but the number 21 itself holds a significant connotation. Dumont explains that the number 21 itself is important for them because it has the value of totality. Not only 21 but also 18, 24, or 108 holds the same connotation [Dumont, 1986:166].
5. The legend of Pūvayammāḷ is as follows: Their ancestor, as the *karṇam* (a village accountant), lived in the village Purikam, near Vettalam, North Arcot. One day, his daughter was combing her hair on the upstairs veranda. The Nayaka king passed by and saw her. The king fell in love with her at first sight. Her father, the *karṇam*, soon noticed the king's feelings and decided to leave the village because he was afraid that the king would take his daughter to the palace (the Pillai family is ritually higher than the Nayaka king). Though the *karṇam* family left the village at night, the soldiers of the king chased them by horse. The family reached a river bank, but they were worried when they noticed that there was no way to cross the river. They soon noticed a small shrine of the goddess Puvayammal and a big Baniyan tree on the other side of the river. The *karṇam* prayed to Puvayammal, "Please topple the Baniyan tree so as to make a bridge". Suddenly, what he asked was realized, and they crossed the river safely. Again he asked the goddess, "Please raise the tree". The tree stood as it was before. Thus, the family could escape from the king's chase. The *karṇam* swore to the goddess that the eldest child of his descendents would always be named after the goddess. Since then, the family and its descendents have worshipped Puvayammal and have observed their promise by naming their eldest sons Puvannanatam

or Puvattapillai, and their eldest daughters Puvayammal. This is a ceremonial name for them; the registered name is often different.

6. It is believed that unless the ritual is "properly" conducted, it will be harmful to them. It is, therefore, difficult to revive the lineage festival, since the detail of its procedures are obscure. The father of the present head of the family once told his sons, "If the Goddess appeared in a dream and told you how to do the ceremony, we could have the festival again", but this has not yet occurred.
7. It is said that the Kamanan ancestors who migrated from Ariyapatti were asked to settle down in Kinnimangalam by the Kecavan people. The Kamanan people agreed to the invitation on condition that the Kecavan gave them house plots and fields for cultivation. Moreover, the Kamanan lineage was also given the privilege of receiving the *mutaṉmai* (the order of honour) next to *karṇam* and *nāṭṭāṇmai* in the village. Therefore, the order of *mutaṉmai* found today, namely the system of "Two Tevars and Four Pankalis" was fixed at that time. The order is this: (1) *karṇam*, (2) *nāṭṭāṇmai*, (3) the Kamanan lineage, (4) the Kecavan lineage, (5) the Acaris, (6) *tōṭṭii* and *maṭaiyaṉ*, and (7) *Nāṟpaṅkāḷi* (the Harijans).
8. The myth I heard is this: The place (*mantai*) where Kottamantaikaruppacami resides was originally the fort of a notorious lord called Tanappamutali (who probably took over Nayakkar's rule [Dumont, 1986: 366–67]. The people suffered a lot under the evil rule of the lord, and the God Siva, of the Kaluvanatarcami temple, became angry and commanded the god Kruppacami, as the incarnation of Visnu, to "go" and destroy the lord. Karuppacami went to the fort and killed the lord. Karuppacami did not return, but remained there, because Siva told him only to "go" and did not command him to "go and come back". The local people asked Karuppacami to return to the Kaluvanatarcami temple but he did not do so. When the Kecavan people entreated him by touching his feet, he replied, "I will stay here and protect your lineage people." Since then, Karuppacami began to be called Kottamantaikaruppacami, and become the main lineage deity of the Kecavan.
9. The following myth is held. After the Kecavan people settled down in Cettikulam, they went one day to Karumatur and worshipped the gods there. The Paricapuli people found them and got angry. The Kecavan people soon returned to Cettikulam in order to avoid an attack by the Paricapuli people but, finally, they were cornered by the Paricapuri in Cettikulam. Fortunately, a man named Mayanticami rushed to the scene to help them. Thanks to his help, the Kecavan narrowly escaped to Kinnimangalam, but Mayanticami lost his life in the fight. In compensation for his sacrificial death, the Kecavan people gave the Kattaiyan lineage their land in Cettikulam and the Ellappacami temple, in which the beloved man was deified as the god Mayanticami. The Kecavan people also began to worship Mayanticami as one of their lineage deities.
10. Such discord seems not to be settled completely even today. I realized this clearly when TG suggested to me that I should stop asking about the history of Kottamantaikaruppacami during my stay in Karumatur to observe the festival.
11. The pseudo-*Paṅkāḷi* relationship between the Kecavan lineage and the Acari family's descendants has continued to the present time. They may provide meals for each other.
12. The Kamanan lineage especially holds active *tuṭiyāṉa teyvams*. The Cinnacami (a god) is famous for the fact that the deity's *cāmiāṭi* drinks the blood of a sacrificed goat. Another god Kalyanikaruppu is said to be too violent to be controlled by the Kanamam *pūcāri*, so that they have had to give up conducting a *pūjā* for the god.
13. In 1989, I heard that both the Kecavan and the Catayi lineages would conduct lineage festivals, but only the Kecavan did so.

14. The death of a member of the lineage is also raised as a reason for the lineage festival being suspended in 1989.
15. The dependence upon *uṇṭiyal* is very high. The Kecavans' exceptional dependence on *uṇṭiyal* is possible since their lineage temple has a public aspect as one of the *nād* (*nāṭu*) temples of Karumatur.
16. The god's weapons, belongings and ornaments etc. are these: *muttukkuṭai* (a big umbrella), *iṭuppumaṇi* (a waist bell), *cilampu* (bangles), *parivaṭṭam* (a headband), *kilukiluppai* (a kind of musical instrument), *arivāḷ* (a hatchet), *pirampu* (a knife), *karuṅkālikkampu* (a kind of weapon), and several facial ornaments such as *puruvam* (eyebrows), *kaṇṇatakkam* (eyes), *mīcai* (a moustache), *rāmaṉ* (a forehead mark of the Visnavite) and *neṟṟikkirīṭam* (a forehead decoration). Musical instruments and weapons, particularly, have sesame oil applied to them.
17. In the case I observed, since the *pūcāri* was very old, his grandson carried the sacred chest to *Karumatur.*
18. The band consisted of six Harijan musicians (4 drummers and 2 clarinetists) on the occasion I observed. Two of them are Paraiyars of Kinnimangalam, namely, a member of the Kartananti lineage and one of the Mataiyan lineage. The other four are from neighbouring villages.
19. Kottamantaikaruppacami's *cāmiāṭi* and Muttaiyacami's *cāmiāṭi* are given *arivāḷ* (a hatchet) and *karuṅkālikkampu* (a weapon); Cilaikari's *cāmiāṭi* is given *kilukiluppai* (a musical instrument) and *pāḷaikiri* (coco-palm flower); and Mayanticami's *cāmiāṭi* is given *pirampu* (a knife). Besides important guests, the *aṭimaikārar* of the Kecavan lineage and the Harijan musicians are given garlands and sacred ashes as well. In this stage, I myself was also given both, as a special guest.
20. It is said that Palanicamitevar, who lived three generation ago, was an outstandingly influential man. The memorial stone is put on his burial place, for which the *ūr* boundary was especially chosen. This burial style called *camātiaṭi* is adopted only for a man of high repute. There the garland taken from the chest is put on the tomb. It seems strange that the Kallars, who do not clearly recognize *pitiṛ* (an ancestral soul), do worship their ancestor's tomb. In this sense, it is important that he was buried at the village boundary, because this means that people understand the ancestor in the this-worldly spatial framework, rather than this being so-called ancestor worship.
21. Around three a.m. the *pūcāri's* wife begins to boil a sort of gram (*tuvaraipayaṟu*) and to cook a *Poṅkal*. The *taḷukai* includes *poṅkal*, boiled gram, and *mārupaṉai* (raw rice powder mixed with jaggery). Besides the *taḷukai, iḷanīr* (tender coconut juice), *karumpu* (sugarcane), *veṟrilai pākku* (betel and arecanut) and bananas are also offered. Two *taḷukais*, five bunches of banana and five coconuts are offered to the main god; whereas one *taḷukais*, two bunches of bananas and two coconuts are offered to the guardian deity. After the *pūjā*, the former two *taḷukais are taken by the pūcāri* and the Kottamantaikaruppacami's *cāmipeṭṭi* respectively, and the latter *taḷukais* is given to the Muttaiyacami's *cāmiāṭi*.
22. The *pūcāri* put holy ash on each *cāmiāṭi* and they are soon possessed by their respective deities. They lapse into an unconscious state of trance called *aruḷ*,which can be distinguished from conscious possession (*maruḷ*). A distressed person offers *veṟrilai pākku* (betel and arecanut) to the *cāmiāṭi* and prostrates himself or herself. Then it is believed that the *cāmiāṭi* correctly diagnoses his or her problem, and makes suggestions about how to solve it. Lastly, a promise of help is made by the *cāmiāṭi*. Moffatt provides an example of the dialogue between the *cāmiāṭi* and the client [Moffatt, 1979: 238–39].

23. The materials of *poṅkal* as follows; *paccarici* (raw rice), *pacumpāl* (cow's milk), *pacuney* (cow's butter), *pacipparuppu* (broken greengram), *muntiriparuppu* (cashews), *ēlam* (cardamom), *cukku* (ginger), *kismipaḻam* (raisins), *tāvara eṇṇey* (vegetable oil) and *vallam* (sugar).
24. The beheaded goat is taken back to Kinnimangalam, though only the head of the victim is given to the *pūcāri*. The *pūcāri* takes four garlands from the main god and puts one on himself and the other three on the *cāmiāṭi*.
25. The Tankalans' marginal character is clearly indicated by the fact that they are not included in the *mutaṉmai* order which is repeatedly expressed in the village temple festivals and in lineage festivals.
26. The usual ramification of a lineage, namely, the change from *vāricu* to *vakaiyaṟā* is caused by an increase in the members of a *vāricu*, and the change is marked by an independent lineage festival. It seems that their case being an exception is partly due to their small increase in population.
27. According to the legend, which lineage members apparently confirmed in Uruvatti in 1983, Periyanatcci and Ariyanatcci were the sisters of the ancestor of the Kartananti-Cinnananti lineages. One day a quarrel between their neighbours took place. Periyanatcci and Ariyanatcci arbitrated between them, but the dispute was unsettled, and finally they went to the panchayat court. Periyanatcci and Ariyanatcci took the witness stand, but, since one party would not accept their witness, the sisters came to the end of their patience and warned the opposing party. They said, "If we told a lie, our lineage will disappear but if we were right, your lineage should end." They also commanded another party who accepted the witness, "Your lineage people should go out of the village, but they should live within three miles of it because you must attend the festival to worship us." The lineage of the opposing party soon vanished, and the people of the 8 lineages living within 3 miles of Uruvatti started to worship the deified sisters. It is noted that the goddesses were originally enshrined not only as their lineage deities, but also as local deities.
28. In the chest, the following things are placed: *mani* (bell), *tīpārātaṉaittaṭṭu* (lamp-stand), *caṅku* (conch), *cēkaṇṭi* (a kind of gong), *vipūtikkopparai* (pot of holy ash), *parivaṭṭam* (dresses of the possessed dancers), and *tūpakkālam* (increase-vessel). The *ōlai-peṭṭi* is often renewed because it is easily damaged. It contrasts with the strong wooden chest of the Kallars.
29. Though this seems to be a type of traditional device for creating balance between two lineages, they believe that the main deities, Periyanatti and Ariyanatti, definitely possess a Cinnananti person, whereas the head of the guardian deities, Periyakaruppacami, always possesses a Kartananti person. It is interesting that the main deities are said to have come to the Cinnananti through the younger brother's line, because this reflects the prevailing notion that the younger is superior to the elder.
30. It seems to me that the amount Rs 2,500 sounds reasonable when it is compared with the cost of the Kecavan case, Rs 3,600. The big disparity between what they claim verbally and what they actually do is deemed as further evidence of their overconsciousness about their inferior position.
31. In those days the festivals of the Urkkavalcami temple and of the Kartananti-Cinnananti lineage were held on the same day. One year, the start of their lineage festival was delayed, so that it was believed that their lineage deities appeared in the Urkkavalcami temple. Since then, it is said that they have to get permission from Urkkavalcami for conducting their festival.

32. It is notable that the possessed dancer of the god Cinnacami rides on the shoulders of a Mataiyan person in the procession. This provides an example of the contribution of their affinal lineage to their festival.
33. As the Tankalan people claim, there is consensus among five lineages of the Paraiyar community that the Tankalan also can receive *mutaṉmai*, but the order of *mutaṉmai* is not always agreed upon by them. The Mataiyan and the Urkalan people do not accept this order in which the Tankalan come before them.
34. Interestingly, two points are common to their lineage festival and the Muttalamman festival. Both festivals are held in *Paṅkuṉi* (March-April); and in both cases the symbol of the main goddess(es), i.e., a statue or a *karakam*, is prepared by a potter living in Sikkanpatti.
35. It is said that the Mataiyan ancestors are originally from the Sivaganga area. Though they progressed after settling down in Vatavaranji, just west of Madurai city, one *vāricus* was picked on by other *vāricu* in their lineage festival. This *vāricu*, therefore, decided to leave the village, and they happened to meet Kartananti-Cinnananti people on their migration. The present Mataiyan lineage of Kinnimangalam consists of two *vāricu*, i.e., a first *vāricus* called Meiyan, and a second *vāricu* called Vettaiyan.
36. Because it is said that the main god, Meyyanamurtti, who dislikes dry areas, requested the Mataiyan people to keep the sacred chest near the river.
37. Besides the lineage festival, the goddess Marattiyamman has an independent festival in *Āṭi* (July-August).
38. The annual *pūjā* to the goddess Cilaikari is regularly conducted in *Āṭi* (July-August), even though the lineage festival is not held.
39. The Urkalan people are given *parivaṭṭam* (a decorated headband) as a token of the right/duty of *aṭimaikārar*, garlands and *piracātam* (an offering withdrawn) as *mutaṉmai*.
40. The legend is as follows. Veriyatevar committed theft in the palace of the local king. The king himself chased the thief on horseback. The thief came across the great-grandfather (GGF) resting under a tree and asked him for help. GGF judged it was *dharma* to help him, since GGF did not know that the man was a thief, and GGF hid him in a drove of cattle. Soon after this, the king came and asked GGF whether he had seen the thief. GGF thought if he replied honestly, the thief would be killed, and if he told a lie and the thief was found later, he himself would be killed. So, GGF suddenly snatched a spear from the hands of the king and struck the king and the horse with the spear. GGF urged the thief to return to his village, but the thief asked GGF to come to his village, Patti, since GGF and his family could not live in Kutiraikuti any longer. The thief told GGF, "Ask someone where Vertyatevar's house is, when you reach my village". Sometime later, GGF and his family left for Patti.
41. The migration story includes an episode which shows the special connection between Murugan and the Tankalan people. On the way to Patti, the great-grandfather (GGF) and his family stayed in the Murugan temple of Tirupparankuntram. When GGF saw people urinating near the temple, he said that the place was nasty. Hearing his words, the God Murugan became angry and made him blind as a punishment. He regretted his words, and prayed to the God with all his might, and his sight was restored. On the following day, they proceeded to Tanakkankulam. There he suddenly noticed that he had forgotten his wallet under a wheel of the festival cart. When he was at a loss, having lost his money, the God Murugan appeared and told him, "Don't worry. Your money will be found". After doing a *pūjā* to the God, he returned to Tirupparankunram and found his wallet as the God had predicted.

42. Periyamuttukumaran (PMK) *vāricu* has the right of receiving *mutanmai* on various occasions as the representative of the Tankalan lineage, whereas the position of *tankaḷān* belongs to the Cinnamuttukumaran (CMK) *vāricu*. This is the traditionally approved distribution. Nonetheless, the PMK *vāricu* began to claim that the role of *tankaḷān* should be carried out by the PMK. Of course, the CMK rejected this claim. According to the CMK's explanation, the PMK make such a demand because the PMK regard the role of *tankaḷān* as being more remunerative than the right of receiving *mutanami*.
43. No members of the lineage can identify the names of 21 deities. This fact seems to be a strong evidence for my claim that 21 deities should not be seen as separate deities but grasped as one whole body.
44. From this point if view, I cannot accept Moffatt's statement that "As a group, the lineage gods are almost uniformly low in nature, ..." [Moffatt, 1979: 229]. I do not believe that the villagers of Kinnimangalam rank their lineage deities in the hierarchical ladder of the pantheon as is shown in Figure 8-1, provided by Moffatt [ibid.: 232]. This point has already been argued in Part One.
45. The affines, who are ambiguous between insiders and outsiders, seem to be very suitable for conducting a liminal action of animal sacrifice, i.e., an introduction of death as an ultimate "outside".
46. For example, the people can give or take a lineage deity to or from other lineages and they can easily build a new temple using *putiman* taken from the former temple site. This reveals that the deities not only require people's faith, but also are controlled by people's will.
47. I have learnt much from Bloch [Bloch, 1986] in terms of the usage of the concept "ritual". That is, a "ritual" act is non-discursive and, therefore, there is little room for accepting everyday thought. Furthermore, the important "ideological" effect of a "ritual" is derived from its symbolic devaluation of this life by introducing the still transcendent [Bloch, 1986: 195] [Bloch, 1989: 407].
48. This point is clarified by Paraiyar people legitimating social position by stressing their strong connection (interdependence) with a particular Kallar lineage or person.
49. Though Bloch focuses on the stability of the ritual [Bloch, 1989: 405], it is also possible and important to throw light on the subtle differences found in the details of the ritual.
50. Being different from the case of funeral ceremonies, the Pillais' practice of lineage festival, which was stopped, cannot provide a model to be replicated by the Paraiyars. I guess that this is one of the reasons why the Tankalan jump to the generally circulated knowledge of Hinduism.
51. Concepts of "ritual" and "non-ritual" are used following Bloch's definitions. Bloch distinguishes non-discursive "ritual communication" from discursive "non-ritual communication" found in the knowledge of the everyday world [Bloch, 1986: 182–189]. The usage in the present context is this. It is usually true that, though in their everyday thinking the Paraiyar people consciously reject hierarchical discrimination, their lineage festivals, as "ritual communication", do not reflect this practical knowledge of defiance. As Bloch also notes, ritual communication cannot be completely separated from non-ritual knowledge, like politico-economic change, though we can recognize the relatively unchangeability of rituals [Bloch, 1989: 398, 406].

Chapter 12

The Politics Around the Cooperative Society

An Individual-Based Strategy

Departing from ritual analyses, this chapter is devoted to an investigation of the politico-economic behaviour of the village Paraiyars, particularly by dealing with the ongoing problems which have emerged around the activities of the village cooperative society of milk producers (hereafter, the milk society). In the course of investigation, individual behaviour will be paid attention to.

There are three main reasons why I deal with the problems of the milk society. Firstly, the activities of the milk society involve many village Paraiyars, so that a study of its activities provides a good opportunity to comprehensively understand the Paraiyars' behaviour. The milk society was established originally at the suggestion of the village Paraiyars and is now almost monopolized by them. The problems concerning the milk society since its inception have thus involved most of the village Paraiyars. This problem-oriented investigation makes it possible to vividly observe the Paraiyars' fundamental attitudes which sustain their everyday practices. Secondly, the difficulties of the milk society not only concern the Paraiyars, but also directly involve part of the Kallar community, and indirectly affect other members of the Caste Hindus. As a result, faction-like groups cutting across caste boundaries have been formed. This study will provide a good chance to examine the relationship between the Paraiyars and the Caste Hindus. The third reason is that, since the milk society is one of the state government's schemes, an investigation of its activities or problems will, to some extent, disclose the connection between village politics, especially the politics of the Paraiyar community, and party politics at the state level.

The Harijans under "Gift Politics"

The Milk Society as One of the Preferential Schemes

The argument here in fact follows that which I summarized under the title of "the government aids as a new patronage" in Chapter 9. As shown below, and as many writers point out, the politics of the Tamil Nadu state government after independence have been aimed at being easily understood by the ordinary people. This political line has been adopted especially by the DMK (Dravida Munnetra Kazhagam) and AIADMK (All India Anna Dravida Munnetra Kazhagam) and governments [Barnett, 1976: 295].[1] As a result, the governments have tended to work out inconsistent and *ad hoc* politics [Gough, 1989: 161], such as direct cash-distribution to the suffering people.[2] The state government provides various subsidy loans for buying land, houses or domestic animals, or for supporting agriculture, which are issued through the Panchayat Union or through the village co-operative societies such as the village co-operative agricultural credit society and the village co-operative society for milk producers. These subsidy loans can doubtless be regarded as important aspects of such politics and, therefore, have not often been fully returned by the debtors. Having the loans, therefore, means partly enjoying a cash gift from the state government.[3] I call this sort of politics "gift politics". This characteristic of present Tamil Nadu politics, which increases people's dependence on the government, seems to invite corruption or bribery (*lanṟcam or kaiyūṭṭu*).

In these political circumstances, the Kinnimangalam Co-operative Society of Milk Producers (*Kiṇṇimankalam kūṭṭuṟavu pāl uṟpattiyāṉarkaḷ caṅkam*) was formed in 1982, as a link in the chain of the preferential policy of the state government. The chief purpose of the scheme is to raise the economic conditions of the Harijans through the benefits of buffalo milk production. The Harijans are treated better than the Caste Hindus in the scheme. The state government makes loans to the members of the cooperative society in order to enable them to buy water buffaloes (Rs 2,500 per member). The loans are given through the society from the Kanara Bank.[4] Harijan members pay back only half of their loans to the bank, through the society, by the production of milk; whereas members of the Caste Hindus must return two thirds of their loans. Therefore, it is more beneficial for the Paraiyars to participate in the milk society. The scheme is also attractive for the Paraiyars because it does not require any special qualifications or conditions, so that propertyless Paraiyars can apply to it. This point is made clearer by comparing the scheme to the village co-operative agricultural credit society (hereafter the agricultural society) which provides loans only to land-holders.[5]

The milk society scheme for helping the poor Harijans may at first glance look good and appear to have no problems, but this is not in practice the case. The problems do not lie in the contents of the scheme but in the procedure through which such government schemes are actually set up in the village. Setting up the milk society in the village was not an easy matter for the ordinary Harijans, requiring various abilities such as filling in application forms, negotiating with administrative officers, obtaining permission from the higher castes, and reaching a consensus among the Paraiyars themselves. Thus a talented member of the village Paraiyars, such as CV, had to act as a leader in order to facilitate the co-operation of both concerned villagers and the administrators. CV, who is the main founder of the present village milk society, is not only knowledgeable, but also has political connections, as an old member of the Congress party. In the situation of a particular person leading the powerless, it is obviously easy for that person to monopolize the management of the society. CV's monopoly of the milk society causes ongoing problems for the society. These problems deepen the divide within the Paraiyar community and have some repercussions on the Caste Hindus. This is because an undertaking as big as the milk society is invaluable for the villagers, especially for the Paraiyars, who in the village situation find it difficult to have opportunities for making a profit, and most of whom are suffering from poverty. Therefore, it is in a sense natural that such government subsidy schemes as the preferential policy, generally speaking, tend to be regarded as good opportunities for gain by shrewd villagers.

Villagers are thus interested in politics and they are very concerned about political parties. This suggests that it is useful for a better understanding of people's behaviour to clarify the political consciousness of the villagers, and of the Paraiyars, and to more clearly appreciate the characteristics of Tamil Nadu politics, before proceeding to the details of the problems of the milk society.

Political Parties and the Village Paraiyars

As Béteille points out [Béteille, 1965: 221], there is no doubt today that politics (power in Béteille's sense) forms a relatively independent domain apart from caste and class. This is, for example, suggested by the fact that no political party can ignore, and must take into account, the Harijans as the "dominated majority".[6] This means that it is crucial for a political party to respond to the urgent needs of the Harijans in order to have a chance of winning an election. It is a historical fact that all the parties which have ruled Tamil Nadu, such as Congress, DMK and AIADMK, have stressed the necessity of a rise in the socio-economic conditions of the Harijans, especially before the election. As I noted at the outset, the tendency towards concrete and more readily understandable politics has increased through the DMK and AIADMK governments. It was mainly the AIADMK government which introduced *ad hoc* politics like the direct supply of cash to the social sector suffering from poverty. The socially repressed people rather welcome such policies, because they believe that only political power can overcome the haughty and inefficient bureaucracy with which they are disgusted and cannot cope.[7] It is said that M.G. Ramachandran, an outstanding charismatic leader of AIADMK [Barnett, 1976: 296–7], especially responded to these demands of the people.[8] This, to some extent, explains the villagers' relatively great concern with politics, which is concretely expressed as their preferences for particular political parties. The interdependent link between the poor seeking quick welfare, and the political party seeking supporters, which generally characterizes recent Tamil Nadu politics, is called "gift politics" by me.[9] This also explains that a person with political connections has more influential power than villagers lacking such connections, as Béteille also points out [Béteille, 1965: 200].

Generally speaking, who the supporters of a particular party are is a well-known fact among the villagers. This implies that politics is actually part of their life. The selection of a party to support is one of the important means of people's self-expression today. Table 12.1 shows the caste-wise distribution of support for a party. Though the survey was conducted only in terms of the heads of households, most of whom are men, it is possible to claim that its findings, as shown in the Table, represent the villagers' general tendency, because a wife tends to vote for the same party as her husband (or she follows her father or brother when she has no husband), as Gough points out [Gough, 1981: 141].

It is impressive that more than half of the Kallars clearly support particular parties whereas about two-thirds of the Paraiyars do not specify their preferred parties. The difference is also made clear by the ratio of numbers of party members to numbers of supporters (72% in the Kallars' case vs 36% in the Paraiyars' case). This difference seems to indicate the relative backwardness of the Paraiyars in terms of social consciousness and their accumulated despair, both of which are results of their long history of social repression. Even though this difference is found, it is also true that certain leading Paraiyars very consciously concern themselves with politics.

Table 12.1, furthermore, indicates several features of village politics in the wider framework of Tamil Nadu politics. The following discussion aims at elucidating the significance of politics for the Paraiyar community today. For the discussion, more detailed information, namely, the lineage-wise distribution of supporters in terms of the Kallars and the Paraiyars, is shown in Table 12.2 and 12.3.

Generally speaking, it is natural that AIADMK, the present party-in-government (at my survey time 1986), enjoys the largest number of supporters. The AIADMK, moreover, has the characteristic that its supporters are from various castes and lineages, as is shown in Table 12.1, 12.2 and 12.3 (see [Gough, 1989: 343]). The distribution of DMK[10] supporters shows almost the same tendency as that of AIADMK, but support for the DMK is less than that for the AIADMK. There is a tendency that villagers move to support the party-in-government due to their practical motivation. That is, DMK support was eroded by AIADMK because both draw on the same type of supporters.[11] It is an important feature that Congress is less supported by the village Kallars, with the notable exception of the Catayi lineage (see Table 12.2). Another remarkable feature is that the FB (Forward Bloc)[12] still gains strong support from the Kallars, especially the Panniyan lineage (see Table 12.2).[13]

Table 12.1

Caste-wise Distribution of Support for a Party (1986)

Party / *Caste*	*AIADMK*	*Congress*	*DMK*	*FB (see Note 12)*	*Janata (See Note 15)*	*CPI (M) (See Note 14)*	*Others*	*Total*
Pillai	0	0	1	0	1 (p)+ 0	0	1	3
Kallar	27 (p) + 19	8 + 5	10 + 3	26 (p, s)+ 2	5 + 0	1 + 0	96 (47.5%)	202
Pantaram	0	1 + 0	0	0	0	0	0	1
Acari	1 + 2	1 + 0	1 + 0	0	1 + 0	0	4	10
Natar	1 + 1	2 + 2	1(s) + 1	0	1	0	1	10
Vannar	4	0	1 + 0	0	0	0	2	7
Kuravar	0	0	0	0	0	0	1	1
Paraiyar	1 + 16	14 + 10	5 + 10	0	2 + 1	1	114 (65.5%)	174
Total	34 + 38	26 + 17	18 + 15	26 + 2	9 + 2	1 + 1	219	408
	72	43	33	28	11	2		

Note: No.: number of party members
No.: number of supporters (not members)
(p): party president at a village level
(s): party secretary at a village level

Table 12.2

Lineage-wise Distribution of Support for a Party Among the Kallars (1986)

Party / *Lineage*	*AIADMK*	*Congress*	*DMK*	*FB*	*Janata*	*CPI (M)*	*DK*	*Total*
Kecavan (23)	4 + 1	1 + 0	3 + 1	1 + 0	1 + 0	0	0	12
Kamanan (2 1)	2 + 2	1 + 0	3 + 1	3 + 0	1 + 0	0	0	13
Cattayi (28)	3 + 1	4 + 3	1 + 0	3 + 0	3 + 0	0	0	18
Panniyan (65)	8 + 4	0	1 + 0	*13 + 0	0	0	0	26
Katta. (18)	5 + 4	1	0	0	0	0	0	10
Cuntra 1 (17)	3 + 3	0	1	1 + 1	0	0	0	9
Cuntra 11 (4)	0	1 + 0	0	0	0	0	0	1
Conai. (9)	0	1	1 + 0	1 + 1	0	0	0	4
Kanni (3)	0	0	1 + 0	2 + 0	0	0	0	3
Others (14)	2 + 4	1 + 0	0	2 + 0	0	1 + 0	1	11
Total (202)	27 + 19	8 + 5	10 + 3	26 + 2	5 + 0	1 + 0	1	107
	46	13	13	28	5	1	1	

Note: No.: party members, No.: party supporters (not members)
Mark*: indicates a party president at village level.

Table 12.3

Lineage-wise Distribution of Support for a Party Among the Paraiyars (1986)

Party / *Lineage*	*AIADMK*	*Congress*	*DMK*	*FB*	*Janata*	*CPI (M)*	*DK*	*Total*
Kartananti (29)	4	5 + 0	1	0	0	0	0	10
Cinnananti (15)	1	3 + 0	3	0	1	0	0	9
Mataiyan (41)	5	2 + 0	1	0	0	0	0	8
Urkalan (19)	3	1 + 0	1 + 0	0	1 + 0	0	0	6
Tankalan (44)	1 + 0	5	3 + 1	0	1 + 0	1	0	12
Manakuli (6)	0	3	1	0	0	0	0	4
Cappatai. (3)	2	1 + 0	0	0	0	0	0	3
Others (17)	1	2 + 1	1 + 3	0	0	0	1	8
Total (174)	1 + 16	14 + 10	5 + 10	0	2 + 1	1	0	60
	17	24	15	0	3	1	0	

Note: No.: party members, No.: party supporters (not members)

The distribution of supporters in the Paraiyar community shows almost the opposite tendency to that of the Kallars. First of all, Congress is ranked in the top position, even if narrowly. The contrast between the Kallars and the Paraiyars can be made clearer if attention is paid to the numbers of party members, that is, if the ratio of Congress members to members of AIADMK and DMK is compared among both castes (8:37 in the case of the Kallars and 14:6 in the case of the Paraiyars). Thus, there is a splitting tendency in that, in so far as party members are concerned, while the Kallars support AIADMK, DMK and FB, the Paraiyars tend to support Congress.

The unpopularity of CPI (M)[14] among the villagers is also obvious. This situation is very different from that of Tanjore, where the Communist party is popular among the Harijans [Gough, 1981; 1989]. This clearly indicates that ideological consistency or class consciousness is not given importance by the villagers in general. Although Janata is a minor party in Tamil Nadu, several party members are found in Kinnimangalam due to the personal influence of BS, a Pillai leader who is the village president of the party.[15]

The significant feature to note is that Congress is the most popular party among the village Paraiyars even today (cf. [Béteille, 1965: 218], [Gough, 1989: 343]). In so far as Kinnimangalam is concerned, as mentioned above, the DMK and AIADMK have failed to establish a firm basis among the Paraiyars. It should be pointed out that, although the Dravida movement has doubtlessly involved the Paraiyar people as well, this means that the movement did not make the Paraiyars change to become opponents of Congress.[16] According to Barnett, the frustrated non-Brahman youth, rather than the Harijans, led the vanguard of the anti-Congress campaign, especially at its initial stages [Barnett, 1976: 153–155] [Béteille, 1965: 218]. Secondly, since the ecological setting of this area is very different from that of Tanjore, and the area lacks a class of dominant Brahman landlords ruling over Paraiyar agricultural labourers, the anti-Congress campaign did not have as great an impact on the Paraiyars of this area (cf. [Gough, 1981] and [Gough, 1989]). Thirdly, it is said that the Harijans were better treated and more protected in Congress's ruling period [Béteille, 1965: 218] than under the DMK government. Since there is no significant difference in policy towards Harijan affairs between Congress, DMK and AIADMK [Gough, 1989: 475], the difference between them depends upon executive ability. This was because in the Congress ministry, led by Kamaraj, there were two Adi-Dravida ministers, P. Kakkan for Harijan affairs and Jothi Venkatachalem for health. Kakkan was especially powerful.[17] On the other hand, the DMK government had only one Adi-Dravida representative, Satyiavani Muthu, who was thought of as a person lacking executive ability [Barnett, 1976: 263–4]. According to Barnett, since DMK took power, the gap between the non-Brahman Caste Hindus and the Harijans has been rather widened [Barnett, 1976: 300]. This generally proves that the political line is quicker and more effective than the administrative line and specifically explains why Congress members of the village Paraiyar community were influential in Kinnimangalam. The central figure of the Milk society, CV, is a typical example. His personal connections with the Congress party were his "social capital", which he mainly used to enable his social rise.[18] In this sense, CV himself verifies that politics forms an independent domain in which a social rise can be realized, apart from caste or class [Béteille, 1965: 202-3].

In addition to this general situation, several local factors specific to the Paraiyars of Kinnimangalam should be taken into account in order to explain the dominance of Congress among the Paraiyar community. One is the fact that Congress greatly contributed to the awakening of the village Harijans through its policies of modernization. For example, one of the middle-aged village Paraiyars, CB's father, SP (Mataiyan lineage) told me his own striking experience as follows:

> It was Congress's ruling time (around 1960). One day, in Chekkanurani, I was taking lunch in a restaurant. I was sitting on the floor, as usual. At that time a higher caste man came into the restaurant and stepped on the banana-leaf on which my meal was put. So I said, "please pay attention. I am eating here". Suddenly, he took my meal and threw it away, and said to me, "Why do you eat on the floor? You sit on a chair and eat! I will pay for it". He furthermore continued, "We are now under Congress government. We don't mind your sitting on a chair even if you are a Harijan". However, I still hesitated to do so because of my fear. Then, since the Kallar owner of the restaurant kindly urged me, "All right, you can eat sitting at the table", I did so. This was my first experience of eating at a table in a restaurant.

SP confessed that he had naively regarded himself as "ugly and unclean" (*aciṅkam* and *acuttam*)[19] thinking that a god would be angry if he entered a temple, until he experienced this incident. This example well conveys the contribution of Congress to the reformation of the Harijans' social conditions.

Another example showing Congress's support of the Harijans, which is well known and rather unforgettable among the village Paraiyars, is the series of incidents caused by the violent clash between the Kallars and the Harijans in the village of Ramanathapuram, called Mutukulattur, in 1957.[20] Since the village was the birthplace of Mutturamalingatevar (a Maravar), a charismatic leader of the FB of Tamil Nadu, the clash was politicized and soon developed into an all-out confrontation between the Congress government and the FB. Though Mutturamalingatevar was arrested, the Kallars, instigated by FB, began to attack the Harijan colonies in the Ramanathapuram and Madurai regions,[21] in reaction to the Congress government's (actually Kakkan's) drastic action of executing seven Kallars of Mutukulattur for their violence against the Harijans. Kinnimangalam was also influenced by the troubles. My Pillai informant, adopting an "objective" stance, relates what happened in the village.

> The Kallars supporting FB, particularly the Panniyan lineage,[22] attacked the Paraiyars and the Natars.[23] In the case of Kinnimangalam, the situation was rather complicated because anti-Panniyan Kallars rather supported the Paraiyars' side. The attacks continued for about two years, during which the powerless Paraiyars suffered enormous damage. The Paraiyars could not directly resist the Kallars, so some Paraiyars adopted a rather indirect means of resistance. For example, they themselves set their houses alight and then complained to the police that the Kallars were responsible.[24] Fortunately, after this harsh experience, there were no other terrible disturbances in the village. However, the Paraiyars still hold feelings of hatred and fear towards the Kallars, especially towards the Panniyan lineage.

This incident again provides an example in which Congress took the Harijans' side. The incident, which includes three levels of conflict, namely the Kallars vs the Paraiyars, FB vs Congress, and the Panniyan group vs the anti-Panniyan group, suggests that politics tends to cross boundaries of castes.

The most visible and concrete benefits which the Congress government provided for the village Paraiyars were the free supply of house plots and houses to them under the housing scheme in 1961. This housing scheme formed the basis of

Cluster III, and greatly improved the Paraiyars' housing conditions. Of course, the DMK and AIADMK governments have also successively made great efforts to supply better houses to the Harijans. Table 12.4 shows that only the initial housing scheme carried out by the Congress government is, even today, clearly connected with the Congress support of the people who enjoyed its benefits (see Table 12.4–(1)). This is not always the case with the second housing scheme (the free supply of houses and plots) carried out by the DMK government in 1974–5 (see Table 12.4–(2)), and in the preferential scheme of housing loans for the Harijans, carried out in 1981 and 1982 under the AIADMK government (see Table 12.4–(3)). There is no doubt that those who received the benefits have been the core group of Congress supporters, as Party members. Moreover, the Kartananti lineage and its brother lineage, the Cinnananti lineage, benefited much from the scheme (9 houses out of 17). Why has this taken place? The main reason lies in the activity of CV, whose lineage is the Kartananti. A Paraiyar informant explain the situation at that time, as follows:

> At that time, there was no person among the village Paraiyars who could negotiate with the administrative officers, except CV, who was educated, even though only at a primary level. All official matters were left to him. When the Congress government introduced the housing scheme for the Harijans, CV became the general agent of the Paraiyar community for negotiating with the authorities concerned. It is significant that, since CV was active as a party member of Congress, his monopoly not only is due to his being literate, but also depended on his personal connections with Harijan politicians of the Congress party, who work under the influence of Kakkan. At any rate, CV fully used the scheme for his own money-making, by himself dealing with all tenders for house construction. Other Paraiyar people believed in him, and they were at his beck and call.

There is no doubt the CV did in fact contribute to the introduction of the housing scheme in the village through his political connections. As Table 12.4 tells, it seems that CV gave first priority to his own relatives among the Kartananti in the distribution of the benefits of the scheme. By this means, he probably elicited or increased their support for the Congress party.

By citing these examples, I have demonstrated why Congress has maintained its popularity and has enjoyed the most stable support among the Paraiyar community in this village. The last example most clearly suggests that politics (power in Béteille's sense) as "social capital" provides the landless and propertyless Paraiyars a chance of establishing their socio-economic position in a wider social network. CV is a typical Harijan who has accumulated his social power by mediating between the state level of politics and the everyday activities of his community. However, the community has changed in the past 30 years (as of 1986). This is verified by the ongoing problems of the milk society which appears to be CV's other big undertaking to develop himself. The current social situation is not the same as that of the early 1960s, in which CV's authority was simply accepted. His attempt to monopolize the milk society has not been easily accomplished and his social power has been challenged by other active Paraiyars. In this sense, the problems of the milk society, which are discussed below, are regarded as an epitome of the social dynamism of the Paraiyar community (at the end of 1980s). It will also be shown that government schemes, which basically have good aims, on the contrary often create social problems.

Table 12.4

The Paraiyars who Enjoyed Government Housing Schemes and their Present Support for a Party (1986)

(1) Congress' housing scheme (1961)

Party / *Lineage*	*AIADMK*	*Congress*	*not specified*	*Total*
Kartananti	0	3 + 0	3	6
Cinnananti	0	1 + 1	1	3
Mataiyan	0	0	2	2
Manakuli	0	2	1	3
Others	1	1 + 0	1	3
Total	1	5 + 3	8	17

Note: No.: party members, No.: party supporters (not members)

(2) DMK's housing scheme (1974-5)

Party / *Lineage*	*AIADMK*	*Congress*	*DMK*	*Janata*	*not specified*	*Total*
Kartananti					2	2
Cinnananti				1	2	3
Mataiyan					3	3
Urkalan	1 + 0	1 + 0				2
Tankalan	1		1 + 0		4	6
Others					1	1
Total	1 + 1	1 + 0	1 + 0	1	12	17

Note: No.: party members, No.: party supporters (not members)

(3) AIADMK's housing scheme (1981-2)

Party / *Lineage*	*AIADMK*	*Congress*	*DMK*	*Janata*	*not specified*	*Total*
Kartananti		1 + 0			2	3
Cinnananti			1			1
Mataiyan	1		1		8	10
Cahalan				1 + 0	2	3
Tankalan		3	1 + 0		4	8
Manakuli					1	1
Others			1 + 2		2	5
Total	1	1 + 3	2 + 4	1 + 0	19	31

Note: No.: party members, No.: party supporters (not members)

The Problem of the Milk Society and the Paraiyars' Strategies

The Milk Society and Its Difficulties

Poverty is undoubtedly the enemy of the village Paraiyars. This leads us to the simple but important fact that the village Paraiyars are always struggling to earn their livelihood. Therefore, they naturally show interest in any opportunities to make money. The pressure of poverty forms the basic social environment in which the difficulties of the milk society take place.

I clearly note in advance that my concern here is not to address the problem of the milk society from the ethical standpoint but to observe and clarify the political attitudes of the Paraiyar people. Though so far I have rather fragmentally dealt with the behaviour of several individuals, such as KP, KP's father, CB, SP (CB's father) and CV, the on-going difficulties of the milk society, which involve most of the influential persons of the Paraiyar community, are useful for disclosing the dynamic interactions between these Paraiyar leaders and their strategic attitudes.

CV (the Kartananti lineage) is consistently the focal person of the problems. As has already been explained, social conditions in 1980s are not the same as those of the 1960s. Several educated young leaders, like KP (the Tankalan lineage) and CB (the Mataiyan lineage), have begun to voice their opinions in the Paraiyar community and therefore CV's monopoly has begun to be checked. It is said that KP is the first person who openly opposed CV. The problems of the milk society have two stages so far, that is, the first stage in which KP opposed CV, and the second stage in which RJ (a Kallar) and TK (of the Cinnananti lineage) have jointly opposed CV.

It was necessary to gain the all-out support of the Paraiyars and the Kallars' cooperation in order to found the milk society. At first, CV had to persuade the young leader KP who was basically opposed to him. CV narrowly gained KP's support by giving him the position of the first director of the milk society and, then gained the Kallars' cooperation through RJ, who was given the position of vice-president of the society. The milk society started with a governing body which consisted of the following persons: (1) the president VM, CV's eldest son (a Paraiyar, the Kartananti lineage); (2) the vice-president RJ (a Kallar, the Keçavan lineage); and three directors, (3) KP (a Paraiyar, the Tankalan lineage), (4) SP (a Paraiyar, the Mataiyan lineage) and (5) ST (a Kallar, the Cuntravalliyamman (II) lineage). It is obvious that CV manipulates his son, the president VM. Each member of the society purchased buffaloes, and the society's activities progressed well for a while. After some time, however, trouble began. This was the start of the stage in which KP actively opposed VM and CV. The incident is as follows:

> One day VM asked the milk society to pay an amount, which was claimed to be expenses incurred by the activities of the milk society. This demand was refused by the other directors. After this incident, KP began to check the account book every day in order to prevent VM from embezzling the profits of the society. CV and VM plotted to drive out KP from the society through some trickery. However, their trickery failed, but they began to rather openly do wrong by various crooked schemes. Despite the warnings of other directors, VM repeatedly did such crooked things. So the other directors appealed to the administration office supervising the milk society, but after all they did not do anything but rather noticed that there was something wrong behind the scenes. These incidents finally made KP leave the milk society because he was fed up with those situations.

After KP left the society, the vice-president and other directors still maintained a working relationship. However, it is alleged that CV, VM and their families more and more insolently attempted to exploit the milk society. In time, another Kallar director, ST, also left the society. Then, the trouble in the milk society entered the second stage.

It is claimed that CV's group saw the other directors as obstacles in their attempt to monopolize the milk society. They thus planned to reorganize the governing body of the society by holding an election. The election, which it is claimed was manipulated high-handedly by VM and CV, caused the spread of the trouble outside the society. The vice-president, RJ, who had co-operated with VM and CV before this incident, became a strong opponent of them after the election. He criticises CV as follows:

> CV's aim in conducting the election was to expel all the Caste Hindus and the Paraiyar members who were opposed to him, from the milk society. Though the election was not necessary, CV persuade the superintendent of the milk society to grant permission for the election by saying that it was impossible to fill two vacant director's posts through negotiation among the members. In order to achieve their purpose, VM and CV remade the voters' list, so that it consisted only of members supporting them, by imposing new criteria[25] of qualification for a voter. As a result, VM reported that only 38 members out of the 210 members[26] of the society satisfied the qualifications for a voter. RJ and one of the directors, SP, were omitted from the voters' list. Since it was obvious that the criteria were arbitrarily applied so as to retain only the supporters of CV on the list, not only the Caste Hindus but also the Paraiyar members expelled from the society got angry with VM's and CV's absurd ways. The Paraiyars held a community gathering which all the heads of household had to attend, which is called *makā-cavai*. It is said that about 75 per cent of all the household heads of the Paraiyar community actually attended this gathering. The gathering decided that the president VM should resign. However this decision was not upheld, being simply turned down by VM and CV. The election was held and the intentions of VM and CV were achieved, that is to say, the privatization of the milk society by them was realized. Those opposed to the privatization, including both Paraiyars and Caste Hindus, claimed the invalidity of the corrupt election. The opposing group, led mainly by a Kallar, RJ, and a Paraiyar, TK, are preparing to file a suit against CV in the District Cooperative Assistant Registrar Office's Court, which specializes in suits relating to the activities of the cooperative societies.

The focus of the second stage is the problematic reorganization of the milk society, which it is claimed was carried out high-handedly by CV's family, and the preparation of the suit by their opponents. RJ explained to me that he aims to have the election declared invalid by the court, and the election re-held. According to him, the series of deviant acts carried out by CV and VM is not the point at issue in this suit. This suggests that villagers are currently less concerned with the ethical aspects and more concerned with more practical aspects, reflecting their self-interest. This corresponds with the shift of the leadership of the opponents of CV from KP in the first stage, to RJ in the second stage. This difference is confirmed by KP's opinion that while he for the time being supports the people preparing the suit, this does not mean that he trusts RJ, whom he regards as having had good relations with CV. RJ himself does not deny what he did, so that he knows that he cannot raise the issue of CV's deviant acts in the court.

Why has TK, who is not a member of the milk society, been deeply involved in this trouble? According to TK, RJ came and explained to him the problems of the milk society just after the election. TK sided with RJ, and decided to attend the preparation of the suit. TK has his own motivation. He was angry to learn that memberes of his lineage (the Cinnananti) who had been members of the milk society were omitted from the voters' list. Moreover, according to RJ, TK has been opposed to CV because TK regards CV as responsible for many of the problems within the Paraiyar community.[27] Since TK himself has not been directly involved in the society's activities, his attitude towards the suit is a little different from RJ's. TK tends to place stress on stopping the selfish acts of CV's family, rather than on seeking for the election to be re-held. This shows that one's attitude is much determined by one's social position or the condition in which one is placed.

I myself recognize that the above-mentioned description lacks the views from CV/VM's side regarding these incidents. I did not talk with CV or VM about this problem, partly because it is too serious for them to speak about to an outsider like me, and partly because I am not concerned with judging who is wrong or right in these incidents; rather, my basic concern is to observe how they respond and behave. Of course I made an effort to grasp what actually took place by interviewing the people who are in a rather neutral position.

Four Levels of Confrontation Distinguished

There is no doubt that various levels of social relationship are complexly entangled in this problem. At least four levels of confrontation can be distinguished, although my ultimate concern is to clarify the patterns of the Paraiyars' behaviour.

The Level of Inter-caste Relations

Table 12.5, which shows the caste-wise distribution of the supporters and opponents of VM (and thus also CV), indicates that their supporters are found only among the Paraiyars, whereas Caste Hindus either stand on the opposing side or have no interest. However, this does not imply a simple confrontation between the Paraiyars and the Caste Hindus, because a considerable number of Paraiyars oppose the president. There are two ways in which the general opposition between the Paraiyars and the Kallars influences the present specific problem. One is found on CV's side, which tends to use conversely people's stereotyped view that the Kallars often bully the Paraiyars in order to weaken the Kallar opponents' criticism of CV. This is a kind of technique to make a particular personal problem appear to be a more general inter-caste problem. Another is on the Kallars' side. It cannot be denied that the Kallars' discrimination against the Paraiyars works to strengthen their repulsion of CV, as was indicated by RJ's attitude mentioned above. Thus, even though the present problem does not directly have an inter-caste character, the basic hostility between the Paraiyars and the Kallars seems to influence the present escalation of the problem indirectly. This makes us understand that the joint struggle of a Kallar, RJ, and a Paraiyar, TK, against CV does not necessarily indicate the cooperation of RJ and TK, but rather can be seen as a convenient means of achieving their respective aims. In other words, though RJ and TK have their own strategies, their contingent cooperation is due to their sharing the common purpose of wanting to defeat CV.

Table 12.5

Caste-wise Distribution of the Supporters and Opponents of VM

Caste	*Supporter*	*Neutral position*	*Opponent*	*Unclear*	*Total*
Pillai	0	0	1	2	3
Kallar	0	0	31	171	202
Pantaram	0	1	0	0	1
Acari	0	0	3	7	10
Natar	0	0	3	7	10
Vannar	0	0	0	7	7
Kuravar	0	0	0	1	1
Paraiyar	32	1	31	110	174
Total	32	2	69	305	408

Table 12.6

Lineage-wise Distribution of the Supporters and Opponents of VM Among the Paraiyars

Lineage	*Supporters*	*Opponents*	*Unclear*	*Total*
Kartannanti	12	0	17	29
Cinnananti	0	6	9	15
Mataiyan	7	7	27	41
Urkalan	5	2	12	19
Tankalan	5	10	29	44
Cappataiyan	0	1	2	3
Manakuli	0	1	5	6
Necavan	0	0	1	1
Others	3	4	9	16
Total	32	31	111	174

It is notable that TK, who tends to adhere to a traditional lifestyle, cooperates with the Kallars. TK could be called a "traditional" type of influential man (*Kāriyakāraṉ*), because his life-basis is still much embedded in the traditional village framework. TK, as a servant (*Paṇṇaikāraṉ*), has a strong connection with the Catayi lineage of the Kallars and also engages in agricultural labour. In addition, he is very religious and has played an important role as a "god-possessor" (*cāmiāṭi*) at functions. I am not implying that TK is simply subordinate to the dominant caste,[28] but that his cooperation with the Kallars is part of his conscious strategy, taking into account his actual social situation which is deeply involved in the conventional village system. Because TK lacks "economic capital", he can only manipulate the "social capital" of his confined personal network, namely, his traditional connection with his Kallar patrons and with his lineage (the Cinnananti) members.

The Level of Inter-lineage Relations

The confrontation between CV and TK is certainly regarded as an inter-lineage conflict between the Kartananti and the Cinnananti. However, since both lineages are close enough to share the same lineage deities, the confrontation is almost an internal competition within the same lineage. Another strong opponent of CV is KP, a member of the Tankalan lineage, who has blamed CV from the time the milk society was set up. Table 12.6, which shows the lineage-wise distribution of the supporters and opponents of VM, makes it clear that the opponents mainly consist of the Cinnananti lineage and the Tankalan lineage, while the Mataiyan lineage is split, and the Urkalan lineage backs the president.

This result well reflects the internal structure of the Paraiyar community. The affinal lineages of the Kartananti, such as the Mataiyan and the Urkalan, tend to support, even if not fully, VM as their affine.[29] In contrast, the lineages which are prohibited from having marriage relations (*paṅkāḷi muṟai*) with the Kartananti for different reasons, such as the Cinnananti and the Tankalan, openly oppose VM. The contrast can be to some extent explained by the alleged distribution of the profits that CV's family acquired from the government schemes such as the milk society. There are various opportunities for the exchange of property between affinal relations, so that the property of one party flows into its affinal party in the course of time. This is, however, not the case between *paṅkāḷi muṟai* At this juncture, it is understandable that TK, as an *uṭaṉpaṅkāḷi*[30] of the Kartananti lineage, strongly complains about CV's selfish monopolizing of the profits, rather than of CV's injustice in an ethical sense. The Tankalan people, who are placed in a peripheral social position, originally had no possibility of sharing the benefits of CV's undertaking. Therefore, they behave more independently towards the Kartananti people than other lineages do. This is typically represented by KP's straightforward attitude to CV. Here again, it is possible to point out that an individual's behaviour wittingly or unwittingly reflects his social position, like his kinship relations within the Paraiyar community.

The Level of Intra-lineage Relations

As shown in Table 12.6, though nearly half of the Kartananti people express their support for VM, it should not be overlooked that more than half of the lineage members reserve their judgement. In this sense, CV's family is far from enjoying the all-out support of their lineage members. This suggests that being a member of the Kartananti lineage does not automatically make one a supporter of VM, but whether one supports him or not is dependent on one's individual judgement. In this sense, the evident monopoly of CV's family would cause more serious friction even within the Kartananti lineage, if CV's family failed to distribute their profits property among the Kartananti lineage members. Another lesson from Table 12.6 is that there are several supporters of VM in the Tankalan lineage. This seems to be a reflection of the strife between two sublineages PMK and CMK.

The Level of Family

I have often heard in the village that it is not unusual for there to be tension between a father and his first son. It is rumoured that there is conflict between CV and his first son VM, which is still rather suppressed. VM, who is around thirty years old, is said to want to seek independence from his father's domination. Even though VM is nominally the president of the milk society, villagers think VM is under the control of CV. Therefore, VM is not regarded as a *kāriyakāraṉ* among the Paraiyar community, even though he is the president. It is said that VM began to feel frustration about this situation and saw the recent election as a chance of taking an initiative by himself. Nonetheless, the situation after the election is not much different from that prior to the election. There is no doubt that this supressed tension between the father, CV, and his first son, VM, is a potential source of further conflict between them.

The description of these four levels of confrontation clearly show that the Paraiyars behave strategically according to their individual judgement. Moreover, the variety of their behaviour can be to a considerable extent explained by their respective social circumstances, like caste, lineage and family. This does not mean that their attitudes are unambiguously determined by the given social conditions, but rather means that they consciously manipulate the "capital" available to them in their given social positions for seeking "self-aggrandizement".

Conclusion: The Paraiyar Community as an Immediate Arena

Patterns of Leadership and State Politics

The main Paraiyar actors in the troubles of the milk society are CV, VM, KP and TK. The reason that I mention CV, KP and TK especially is that they seem to represent three possible patterns of leadership within the Paraiyar community. I attempt here to clarify these patterns, by briefly illustrating the characteristics of the behaviour of these three people. Not only will this confirm their strategic attitudes for seeking self-aggrandizement, but it will also suggest the strong impact of state politics upon the village social sphere.

KP's father achieved his social rise economically. His economic success enabled his son, KP, to obtain higher education (KP is a graduate of ITI), and helped establish his current leadership in the Paraiyar community. KP's economic basis is a combination of a landed farmer and a shop-worker in the nearest town, so that he is less involved in the village economic structure, as was his father. Such independence from the village structure is the general tendency of the peripheral Tankalan lineage, and KP typically represents this tendency and the "independent" type of leadership. There is no doubt that his straightforward attitude, as shown by his accusation against VM and his father CV, is possible due to his independent and peripheral socio-economic position. KP can afford to keep his distance from the troubles of the milk society, though he led the accusations against CV in the first stage of its troubles. In this sense, KP embodies an "independent" type of leadership.

CV has also succeeded in economic accumulation, but the means he adopted were very different from those of KP's father. CV has profited from his ability to make connections between the village Paraiyar community and the politico-administrative sphere. His abilities are mainly due to his personal connections in the political field, which were cultivated through his activities as a member of the Congress party. It is said that for his money-making, CV has consistently used the preferential schemes of the government, such as the housing scheme for the Harijans and the scheme of the milk society. CV's undertakings have been successful because the poor Harijans have participated due to their strong desire for profit-making. As his monopoly of the milk society shows, it is possible to say that CV has probably exploited the poor village Paraiyars. It should be noted that this strategy is made possible not only by his personal ability, but also by his membership of the Kartananti lineage, which is the most central lineage of the Paraiyar community. This centrality makes him have deep links with other Paraiyars, especially with the people of the Four Pankalis (*Nāṟpaṅkāḷi*) who are the basic "social capital" of his undertaking. Thus, CV's strategy can be called a "mediating" type of leadership.

There is a third type of leadership, namely, the "traditional" type, which is represented by TK, as already to some extent explained. TK has a much more traditional life-style than KP or CV. He still attaches importance to conventional social institutions, such as socio-economic dependence on the dominant castes and the unity of the lineage, because he himself profits from this dependence. Though TK's social position is not very different to that of CV, TK has probably chosen his conservative strategy due to his personality, his religious beliefs, his lower education etc. This tendency is clearly verified by his manner of accepting cooperation with a Kallar, RJ, in order to defeat his *paṅkāḷi* ("brother"), CV, whose apparent selfishness violates the unity of the lineage.

It is important to note the common features in the strategic behaviours of these leading Paraiyars. The different types of leadership, apart from personal talents and characters, can be regarded as reflecting the differences in the social positions of the individuals, and of the qualitative and quantitative differences in their capital-holding. The feature common to all these types of leadership is the attitude of aiming to aggrandize one's social power by effectively manipulating one's accessible capital under given social conditions.

The "mediating" type of leadership is by necessity the most influential in the village Paraiyar community, at least in the village situation of 1980s and 1990s. This is because the government's preferential schemes in fact become opportunities for money-making. The mediator who introduces the scheme into the village can be compared to a new type of patron (*jajmān*), who distributes profits to the people, but at the same time exploits them.

In terms of the minimum welfare for the Harijans, the role that the big landlords of the dominant caste played in the *jajmānī* relationships was replaced by the central and the state governments in the process of nation-building after Independence. In the social environment of inadequate and uneven economic development, however, preferential policies or affirmative actions of the state are crucial for sustaining the minimum life standard of the people of the bottom like the poor Harijans. The necessity of such urgent economic support strongly corresponds with "gift politics", which particularly characterizes the policies of the state government. This politico-economic situation produces the "mediating" type of leaders as mini-patrons who rather quickly connect, by using political means, the lowest villagers with top-down state measures. Needless to say, this tendency is ironically promoted by the inefficiency of administration routes. It is, therefore, to be noted that the combination of this political quick bypass and dull administration bring up the "mediating" type of mini-patrons and at the same time prepare the space where social evils come in, as shown by the problem of the milk society.

Individualistic Rivalry and the Penetration of "Class" Ideology

The troubles of the milk society have revealed the individualistic and strategic behaviour of the village Paraiyars. Though they are not sufficiently free from conventional social relationships such as the *jajmānī*-like and inter- and intra-lineage ties, it is also true that their behaviour cannot be explained adequately only by such conventional social idioms. This was made clear by the description of the four levels of confrontation. The strategic manoeuvrings around the milk society are not simply determined by traditional, collective groupings, like caste, lineage and sub-lineage, though they do to some extent reflect these conventional social categories. In these manoeuvrings, an individual's self-interest tends to take precedence over the collective interest. On the one hand, this individualistic behaviour to some extent appears to reproduce the conventional relationships (cf. [Béteille, 1991a, 1992]). On the other hand, it also works to change, and moreover, dismember conventional "caste culture" [Barnett, 1975: 151].[31]

A strategic behaviour requires at least some capital for constructing it. It has already been made clear in Chapter 9 that there is a decisive difference between the Paraiyars and the Kallars in terms of the possession of agricultural land. Moreover, this difference in "economic capital", based on land, between them tends to have been preserved even after the wave of modernization and urbanization, because generally only capital possessors can invest in taking advantage of a new situation. There are two ways for maintaining higher social status in the new situation, that is, (1) to invest in establishing modernized agriculture and (2) to invest in higher education so as to facilitate engagement in urban employment. A weak group, like the village Paraiyars, are obviously blocked from both ways without the aid of the government. Though it is true that the preferential schemes of the government have worked to help the Paraiyars, these schemes do not help them sufficiently. At the present stage, the aid of the government has rather enhanced hierarchical distinctions within the Paraiyar community. Most of the village Paraiyars remain at the bottom of the hierarchy, unchangingly suffering from poverty. In this respect, the scheme of milk society also cannot escape from this problem. Rather than contributing to assisting the poor Harijans to raise their living standards as a whole, the milk society has increased the differentials within the Harijan community. The analysis of the troubles of the milk society has disclosed the split between the leading Paraiyars who are relatively richer, and the passive, poor Paraiyars.

In sum, the Harijans' social situation where the milk society scheme has been implemented shows at least two features, i.e., their individualistic and strategic attitude manipulating several social segments for self-aggrandizement and their absolutely limited capital holding preventing from self-help. These features explain why they so eagerly struggle for profits from the government subsidiary schemes. In this connection, I recall that the ethical aspect of the accusation of deviated acts in the case of the milk society has been reduced in the course of time. The point at issue has been shifted to the more practical purpose of stopping CV's monopoly and seeking to share the profits. This shift is impressive, and, in a sense, natural for those who are suffering from poverty. This suggests that most of the Paraiyars tend to engage in short-sighted struggles to seek a chance to make a profit, because they are blocked from planning their lives steadily due to lacking capital. The leadership found among the Paraiyars must be understood in terms of this background situation and atmosphere. Therefore, it is natural that the "mediating" type of leader, who can obtain sanction for government schemes in reply to the demands of the poor Harijans, most attracts the Paraiyars in general. However, in reality the profit is small but the Paraiyars' demand is high, so that, as the milk society problem shows, the internal rivalry and conflicts within the Paraiyar community become extremely intense. As a result, most of the energy of the Paraiyars is consumed competing with their immediate rivals, as Burghart also suggests in a different context [Burghart, 1983: 641]. It is notable, furthermore, that a very few "mediating" leaders may economically rise by skillfully deploying their political and economic capital, whereas the majority of the Paraiyars as followers are betrayed, exploited and after all left in the unchanging poor situation. Thus, after draining energy this ultimately results in the "class" hierarchy and its ideology penetrating into the Paraiyar community (see also [Gough, 1989]).

Since economic improvement is the goal of their competition, there is no doubt that the identity interpellated by individualistic "class" ideology is formed through these struggles. The identity can be seen as secular and self-assertive, and at the same time, hierarchical. That is to say, although "class" ideology appears or is said to be democratic and egalitarian because "class" is not determined by birth and therefore enables open competition as "equality of opportunity", it should not be overlooked that "class" ideology is in fact penetrated by hierarchical values. It would be obvious if "class" ideology was checked from the viewpoint of "equality of result". Poverty and the stigma of pollution are two major sufferings for most Harijans. As I observed, they tend to think their economic improvement would solve or mitigate those sufferings. This is to some extent true. However, I have to mention the following ironical fact. The acute struggles among the powerless Harijans that seek economic betterment and social equality, that is, that aim at eradication of both poverty and the social stigma (caste ideology based on "pure-impure") finally do not improve the situation but, on the contrary, tend to serve the acceptance of "class" hierarchy, at the bottom of the ladder of which most Harijans are again placed.[32] This connotation is not small, because the acceptance of the "class" ideology today almost automatically leads to the dominant ideology conquering the broader societies, that is, "contemporary popular Brahmanical culture" in my terms that provides the modified hierarchical norm of high culture vs. low culture in the prevailing atmosphere of the so-called middle class syndrome. This shows how difficult it is for the people to get rid of caste hierarchical norms.

Notes

1. After independence, Congress first ruled Tamil Nadu for nearly 20 years after 1946. Dravida nationalism reduced Congress's power, and finally DMK came in power in 1967. In 1972, DMK was split into two parties, DMK of Karunanidhi and AIADMK of M.G. Ramachandran (MGR). AIADMK became more popular and ultimately gained power in 1977. The AIADMK government ended with MGR's death in 1987 and was again replaced by the DMK.
2. The political attitude of the AIADMK (ADMK) is typically found in their "ten point plan" to uplift the poor, which was stated in the campaign of the State Assembly elections of May 1980 [Gough, 1989: 162].

3. The repayment of loans is supervised by the Panchayat Union or the co-operative societies, but the debtors very often delay their return.
4. The Kanara Bank is one of the nationalized banks. The Kanara Bank was chosen as the society's bank because it has a branch in Chekkanurani, the nearest town.
5. The Agricultural society which the Kinnimangalam people join was established in 1958. The present number of members is 890 from seven villages, which includes 172 Harijan members. Though even a landless person can obtain membership, a borrower must have land. In 1986 there are 240 members who have taken loans out of the 890 members (106 borrowers from Kinnimangalam), of whom only eight (four from Kinnimangalam) are Harijans. The society uses MDCCB (Madurai District Central Co-operative Bank) for its activities.
6. The Brahmans are sometimes called the "dominant minority" [Nair, 1969: xiii]. In contrast, it seems that the Harijans (SC and ST) who occupy 19.5 per cent (SC: 18.4%, ST: 1.1%) of the total population of Tamil Nadu (about 48.41 million in 1981) can be called the "dominated majority" [Government of India, 1988].
7. This attitude corresponds with the case studies done by Barnett. Five case subjects of various castes, including two Adi-Dravidas, agreed with the idea that a few strong leaders would do more for the country than all the laws and talk [Barnett, 1976: 167–185].
8. For examples, Mathur notes, "AIADMK's attitude generally and MGR's particularly towards the bureaucracy was calculatedly hostile" [Mathur, 1988: 126] and, furthermore, "MGR introduced certain administrative innovations and welfare schemes for the poor and the down-trodden and pushed them through despite all odds" [ibid.]
9. As Béteille states, mobility of power is relatively higher than that of class or of caste [Béteille, 1965: 221]. Due to its quick and radical nature, politics is expected to provide quick and effective solutions by the socially repressed people.
10. DMK was established by C.N. Annadurai in 1949. DMK is a political party which was derived from the long stream of anti-Brahman movements, such as the Justice Party (1916), the Self-Respect Movement (1927) and Dravida Kazhagam (1944), which was led by E. V. Ramaswamy (Periyar) [Perumal and Padmanabhan, 1986: 431]. DMK successfully obtained the support of the non-Brahman masses, particularly that of the Backward Classes, in the wave of Dravida Nationalism.
11. Since this Kallar area, a part of the southern part of the state, was among the weakest areas of DMK influence, AIADMK could obtain considerable support by using the good image of MGR [Barnett, 1976: 298]. Barnett also analyses the shift in power from Karunanidhi to MGR. That is, the people chose a charismatic leader, or "some sort of benevolent dictator" [Barnett, 1976: 173] like Annadurai and MGR, rather than a strong organizer like Karunanidhi [Barnett, 1976: 302] [Mathur, 1988: 123]. More objectively, DMK had faced political difficulty due to its factionalism and narrow nationalism [ibid.: 310], when the Emergency (1975–7) was imposed by Mrs Indira Gandhi [Gough, 1989: 149–154].
12. The FB is said to have been originally a separate stream of Congress whose active base is Bengal, but it has a radical tendency of resorting to violence beyond its parliamentary activities. In Tamil Nadu, since the FB was founded in 1939 and has been almost monopolized by *Mukkulattōr* (Kallar, Maravar and Akampatiyar), it has basically tended to be hostile to the Harijans and not to hide its feelings of caste discrimination.
13. It is not strange that Congress, which tends to be dependent on the Brahman community and minority groups, is not very popular among the Kallars, as one of the Backward Classes. However, it is a notable feature of this area that the FB has checked not only Congress's development, but also later the advance of the DMK [Barnett, 1976: 91, 298].

14. CPI (M) was formed by the leftists within CPI in 1964 because the rightists of the CPI cooperated with Congress. Although the history of the communist party prior to independence is one of internal splits and of suppression by the governing power, after independence they have by and large participated in the parliamentary system. The communists of Tamil Nadu draw their support chiefly from the urban labourers and from the agricultural labourers of Tanjore [Padmanabhan, 1987: 234]. During my fieldwork, members of CPI (M) sometimes came to the village and agitated, but not many villagers gathered to listen, and they did not intently respond to their ideological assertions.
15. Janata is a new party which was formed by an alliance between the left wing of Congress (the Congress (O)), the Socialist Party and so on, in the 1977 elections for the central government. In this election, Janata defeated Congress (I), and was in power until 1980. Janata is estranged from the Tamil masses not only due to it being a nation-wide party, based mainly in northern India, but also because of its upright image. Therefore, Janata tends to be supported mainly by the socially higher intellectuals.
16. The political streams of the Dravida movement are not simple. For example, there was a 1954 incident in which the DK led by E.V. Ramasami supported the "Kamaraj Congress" against DMK [Barnett, 1976: 91]. This is because "DMK ideology had been assimilated into the political culture" beyond party boundaries, as is clearly shown in case study B of Barnett's survey [Barnett, 1976: 171–176].
17. Barnett cites K.V.S. Mani's statement that "The villagers were afraid on Kakkan. They thought if they did anything, Kakkan would come and so they were afraid" [Barnett, 1976: 263].
18. It is said that CV has good connections with a Sittan who is a MLA (Member of Legislative Assembly) of Tamil Nadu and a member of the Congress party.
19. The reason I translate the term as "unclean" is that SP emphasizes mainly his physical dirtiness and his unsophisticated manners in those days. This interpretation given by him already reflects his modernized attitude.
20. It is said that in the village an untouchable Pallar man called Immanuvel was killed by the Kallars and this triggered the clashes between the Pallars and the Kallars, in which many people died.
21. The extreme southeastern *Mukkulattōr* area is the only area in which the Kamaraj Congress did not have stable support, because the area was dominated by FB, even though the Harijans did support Congress [Barnett, 1976: 91, 94, 152]. The trouble spread readily in this area.
22. As Table 12.2 shows, the strong connection between the Panniyan lineage and FB is still maintained today. Nearly half of the supporters of FB are from the Panniyan lineage and, moreover, all are party members, including the local president.
23. The reason the Natars were also attacked by supporters of FB is that the chief minister of the Congress government, K. Kamaraj was from the Natar community. In Kinnimangalam, it is said that a Panniyan broke a mud pot filled with faeces and urine in front of a Natar house.
24. It should be recalled that there is the special police for the abolition of Untouchability and the police worked to some extent effectively under the power of Kakkan. If not for the presence of a person like Kakkan, this tactic of the Paraiyars would not have been successful.
25. According to RJ, the new criteria they imposed required 1) a voter to have given the milk society more than 300 ml of milk during the past four months and 2) to have never failed to pay proceeds to the society in the past. But SP told me another criterion: that the right to vote was reserved for only those members who registered after 1985.

26. Before the election, the society had 177 members from the Kinnimangalam panchayat village, which consisted of 109 members from the Kinnimangalam hamlet and 68 from other hamlets. Of these 109 members, 80 were Paraiyars, 22 were Kallars, 4 were Natars and 3 were Acaris.
27. For example, CV allegedly converted common land given to the Paraiyar people by the government to private land, and gave it as an *otti* land to a particular Paraiyar (CV's affinal lineage). This caused a confrontation between the Kartananti lineage and the Cinnananti lineage, which is still unresolved.
28. It is evident that TK has a conscious and critical mind about the caste hierarchy. For example, he refused to answer when I asked him to tell me the conventional caste order or the myths of the origin of the Paraiyars.
29. The reason why the Mataiyan has more opponents than the Urkalan can be explained by the scale of the lineage. It is natural that the bigger Mataiyan lineage (41 households) can hold more independent positions than can the Urkalan lineage (19 households).
30. TK thinks that the relationship between CV and himself is very close and that it is thus a matter of course to share the profits among both the Kartananti and the Cinnananti.
31. In other words, the change is described as the process of giving a new interpretation to more or less modified conventional social categories. For example, Kolenda recaptures the concept of subcaste by referring to "kin-community" in the contemporary Indian context [Kolenda, 1978].
32. Although the irony pointed out is a reality, the Paraiyars' statement that the economy will save them should be accepted in its deep sense. In its deep dimension, their insight about the symbolic power of money (economy) should be paid attention to. They may know intuitively that money has the power to compensate them for their degraded status, which is fixed by birth. It seems to me that the symbolic power of money, in this context, is related to something defined as "the superiority of the giver" (the deep connection between power and generosity) in anthropological arguments on exchange. Economic power will never erase caste boundaries completely, but its symbolic power can reduce the gap in social status in practice (A good example is the case of the Nadars [Hardgrave, 1969].) In this context, it is possible to regard CV's activity as an unwitting practice in which the Paraiyars' radical (maybe selfish) challenge against "caste" ideology is carried out through the introduction of the "class" ideology.

Part Four

Conclusion and Discussion

Chapter 13

Conclusion

The main description and arguments of this book consist of two parts, Part Two and Part Three. The arguments of Part Three are developed on the basis of the discussion in Part Two. In order to overcome the limitations of the conventional research attitude found in studies on caste society, the consistent methodological standpoint penetrating both Parts is characterized as the interpretative approach associated with the decentripetal, i.e., the "other-worldly", "bottom-up" and "dynamic (generative)" viewpoint.

In Part Two, the concept of pollution or impurity was reexamined in the Tamil village context, in the light of the review discussion of Chapter 2. It was an indispensable task to properly examine the concept of pollution in order to break the strong spell of the Dumontian understanding of the Hindu society. My basic claim is that, though the villagers (both Caste Hindus and the Paraiyars) to some extent accept "pure-impure" ideology, the value in which they truely believe is "pollution" ideology in my sense, which should be distinguished from the Dumontian "pure-impure" ideology.

In Part Three, the village Paraiyars' practices are analysed with the theoretical perspective discussed in Chapter 3. It is revealed that the Paraiyars' practices can be regarded as strategies for seeking their self-aggrandizement, based on an interpretative understanding, which encourages progress from the static and unproductive dispute between the disjunction and consensus theorists.

"Pollution" Ideology and the Strategizing Harijans

"Pollution" and "Impurity": An ideological distinction

The construction of an inner order leads to the expulsion and creation of an outer existence. Ironically, pollution (*tiṭṭu*) is a sense of crisis (a boundary or liminal situation) that is produced when one feels the exterior being as an other-worldly power infringing and destroying the inner order. The nature of pollution is a subjective feeling of the "menace of death (the destruction of the inner order)".

In this connection, pollution tends to be avoided or suppressed because it appears destructive. A knowledge of (1) the deep connection between the life crises, accompanied by rites of passage, and the generation of pollution, and of (2) the villagers' ardent worship of village deities and of lineage deities, in which blood sacrifice is indispensable, clearly indicates that pollution is positively accepted and used in order to acquire newly increased life-energy. Thus there are two ways of interpreting pollution, according to the different attitudes towards pollution. One is the rejective manner of shutting out and degrading pollution due to its fearful connotation. The other is the affirmative manner, in which the destruction of the existing order is positively accepted and used as an opportunity for reconstructing a new order.

The rejective manner towards pollution invites the unambiguously negative implication of pollution, which is dominant in the shallow conscious level of the villagers' minds. This expulsive attitude results from the mindset that creates the viewpoint at the centre of the inner order. It serves as a centripetal logic that defines ritual hierarchy, in which pollution *(tiṭṭu)* is reduced to "impurity" as the lower pole, the opposite to "purity" as the higher pole. This manner of interpretation of pollution represents the Dumontian sense of pollution. This dimension of interpretation is no different from "*normalization*" in Foucault's terms, that is, the justifying of "pure normal self" (centre) by producing "impure abnormal others" (periphery). Contrastively, the affirmative attitude towards pollution reveals the creative aspect of pollution, which embodies the dynamic process of "death and the regeneration of life" (the logic of sacrifice). This dimension of interpretation of pollution is suitable to be called "pollution" as an independent concept that does not require any opposite pole, because the ambiguity of pollution is accepted as it is with the on-boundary decentripetal viewpoint.

At the outset it is necessary to recognize the interpretative, or ideological, differences between "impurity" and "pollution". I use the term "ideological" because the differentiation of "impurity" from "pollution" refers to a fundamental difference in terms of the locus of viewpoint, which leads to quite different interpretations in practice. That difference does not indicate a simple epistemic distinction between two different value categories coexistent on the same ground. There occurs a profound difference depending on whether one examines the boundary situation, i.e., "pollution", from the outside or from within the "pollution". The notion of "impurity" is the result of seeing "pollution" from outside the boundary area, that is, seeing from the centre of order. It is actually a static, substantialist concept looking down from the viewpoint of the privileged, although it looks like a structuralist concept with binary opposition. In contrast, the notion of "pollution" is an interpretative product of the viewpoint residing within the boundary situation of pollution, in other words, a product of a truly structuralist viewpoint [Oda, 1994], which focuses upon the moment when interior and exterior domains are generated. In this work, I make a distinction between "impurity" and "pollution" as symbols of centripetal and decentripetal (not anti-centripetal) ideologies. These ideologies are not on the same cognitive ground, but belong to different spheres, which in my terms are "pure-impure" and "pollution" ideologies.

We may take a closer look at the features of these two different ideologies through the example of the ambiguity surrounding the menstrual "pollution" of Hindu women (for details, see [Sekine, 1999]). The essence of the "pure-impure" ideology is a *nomos*-oriented attitude characterized by the perception of what are regarded as peripheral elements, i.e., an off-boundary centripetal viewpoint. It first defines the existence of women as a marginal, peripheral event regarded as "impure" from the viewpoint of the centre of a governing androcentric and Brahmanocentric order. Then, having posited such a hierarchical relationship, it apotheosises women's subordinative self-sacrifice (blank denial of "impure" self), sublimating the "impure" woman and in a single stroke fabricating a "pure" and "sacred" woman and then taking her into the centre. This is a highly arbitrary ethical mechanism for the reproduction of women's position. Under this ideology, then, women are subjected to the dangers of leaping between the contradictory poles of "impurity" and "purity".This mystification, by force and assumed unification, of the "impurity" and "purity" categories that are logically incapable of coexisting, is realised via the heavy burden of coerced "sacredness" which is borne by women. In contrast, the essence of the "pollution" ideology is that it takes its viewpoint in what is socially defined as the boundary, and hence expresses a dynamic of intent to exist on the boundary directly linking *chaos* with *cosmos*, eluding the grasp of *nomos*. As argued in Chapter 8, for example, this ideology maintains an attitude of positive acceptance toward the existence of the "pollution" brought about by the natural phenomenon of female menstruation (*chaos*) as "pollution" with independent potentiality, and it celebrates the flowering of productivity and fertility (*cosmos*) as sacred. "Pollution" ideology is free of the oppression of a centripetal order, and that is enough to give consistency to the female identity without any forced refraction.

Thus these two ideologies conflict with each other in their interpretation of identical phenomena occurring in the bodies of Hindu women (from menstruation to the manifestation of reproductive power). Those who face this reality will clearly see that to speak of "the ambiguity of Hindu women" is quite inadequate and causes unnecessary confusion. The confusion is rooted in a high-handed reading of the actual conflicts between the two ideologies by "pure-impure" ideology, which dominates the arena of conflict, and so reduces them to the ambiguity of "purity" and "impurity". Scholars who are inept at detecting the power of the dominant ideology ("pure-impure" ideology) have described the reduction as an objective fact, thereby overlooking the proper ground of "pollution" ideology. Those scholars must seriously reflect on their responsibility for the propagation of a misleading discourse of "ambiguous Hindu women" which tends to hide the reality.[1]

It is now appropriate to examine what kind of interpretative perspective is formed on the ground of "pollution" ideology. For that purpose, it is necessary to adopt a somewhat broader scope with regard to the ideological distinction between "impurity" and "pollution". Suppose that on the ground of "pollution" ideology, the direct generation of cosmos from "pollution" can be termed "pollution-sacredness". Then "pure-impure" ideology, from its viewpoint at the centre of the dominant order, would translate the same flower of the fertility of women as the ultimate in "purity", as "purity-sacredness", persistently delivering the flower back into the centralized *nomos* framework.

Awareness of this distinction between "pollution-sacredness" and "purity-sacredness" which grows out of the distinction between "pollution" and "impurity" is typically found in the discussion of the relationship between village goddesses and village gods (See Chapter 6). Both types of deities are necessary in villagers' lives not because of the importance of a hierarchical, complementary relationship between goddesses on the impure side and gods on the pure side in the sacred pantheon, but because the goddesses who embody "pollution-sacredness" create *cakti* (Skt. *śakti*), and the gods who embody "purity-sacredness" maintain it. In this way the villagers, whose basic values rest on "pollution" ideology, provide their own views on the values of Brahmanical culture ("pure-impure" ideology). This dynamic relationship can be described as complementary cycles between the intimate order (*l'ordre intime*) and the real order (*l'ordre réel*) in Bataille's terms. Needless to say, this is not something that can be reduced to binary opposition between "pure" and "impure" phases.

Those fundamental considerations illuminate the dimensions of "pollution" ideology as a viable discourse which has been pushed into the shadows by the dominant discourse of the "pure-impure" ideology, and overlooked as a result of being mixed with some nonsensical confusion. "Pollution" ideology retains a viewpoint positioned within the gap at the margin of order between the internal and the external. It is vital to recognize that it has a value's vector that is utterly different from that of "pure-impure" ideology, with its viewpoint located at the centre of the internal world of order. Dumontian "pure-impure" ideology represents centripetal thinking that defends the existing secular and hierarchical orders, reflecting the conservative attitude of viewing boundaries from the centre and discriminating and solidifying them as the lower point in the binary opposition. In contrast, "pollution" ideology inverts that attitude and advocates what may be defined as an other-worldly egalitarianism. In other words, as it resides in the boundary phenomena of death and the generation of life, "pollution" ideology maintains a decentripetal, generative attitude that enables it to convert the energy produced from the internal-external gap to creative power. Thus there occurs conscious and unconscious friction between interpretations made from the off-boundary viewpoint of the former and the on-boundary viewpoint of the latter, concerning what are defined as marginal or peripheral phenomena by the secular order. These contrasting characters illuminate the fundamental difference in viewpoint between "pollution" ideology in my sense and Dumontian "pure-impure" ideology,[2] and at the same time indicate the mutual relationship between the two ideologies, in particular between the "discrimination" of the latter and the "boundary transgression" of the former. To reach a systematic understanding of the conceptual framework of "pollution", we must grasp the dynamics (the cyclical relationship) of the simultaneous existence of an ideology of "maintenance on the surface" and another of "innovation (generation) in depth".

It must be emphasized that an interpretative approach is used here to draw the distinction between "impurity" and "pollution". This is because the true nature of *tīṭṭu* cannot be sufficiently grasped by means of the substantialist approach that assumes the possibility of an objective, unambiguous definition of a phenomenon (and hence conceals its unconscious connection with the viewpoint of the privileged). It can only be determined through an interpretative approach guided by subjective postures towards "pollution". It is necessary to be aware of both interpretations: one based on centripetal thinking at an easily perceived level, and the other possessing a decentripetal moment at a level that is more difficult to perceive. Towards that end we must adopt a decentripetal, transboundary approach that is other-worldly, bottom-up and dynamic (generative), in order to access the inside of boundary phenomena. To seek out such an approach, reform at the methodological level is indispensable.

The Ideological Configuration of Village Society

"Pure-impure" ideology is certainly dominant in the form of centripetal thinking, i.e., as the scale of values defining the village caste hierarchy, especially the distinction between Caste Hindus and Paraiyars. Nonetheless, there are some differences among the dominant castes in terms of how the "pure-impure" ideology is manipulated, depending upon their socio-cultural conditions. The Pillais, the dominant minority in village K who are ritually the highest caste in the village, are relatively more keen on following the "pure-impure" ideology in all aspects of their activities. They tend to suppress the "pollution" ideology, whether consciously or unconsciously. By doing so, they differentiate themselves from people of other castes. Meanwhile the Kallars, who are ritually low but socio-economically dominant, believe half-heartedly in this ideology but emphasize it chiefly for maintaining the vertical distinction between Caste Hindus and Harijans (see also [Deliège, 1992: 166]).

Although there is no doubt that "pure-impure" ideology (expressing the political nature of culture) functions as a dominant ideology in the village social sphere, the villagers' principal source of values in daily life is the "pollution" ideology described above, which attaches importance to productive power or vitality. It is "pollution" ideology, with its transboundary (decentripetal) nature, that is basically shared by both Caste Hindus and Paraiyars, irrespective of caste ranks, as the viable culture of the village.

Why is "pure-impure" ideology a powerful dominating tool in the village setting? To answer this question it is necessary to consider the wider framework of the post-colonial situation in which India finds itself today [Sekine, 1994b]. That situation is supported by the permeation of what I shall call "contemporary popular Brahmanical culture", i.e., a newly invented and objectified Brahmanic culture that arose in tandem with the Westernization and modernization of India that began under British colonial rule. From another angle, the situation is that of the arrival at the village level of the modernization phenomena that have engulfed all India, in a preliminary fashion during the colonial period and at an accelerating pace after Independence. Modernization has impacted village life in several notable ways. On the one hand, the strong pressures of the urban-based market (cash) economy on village life have obviously made the villagers give more importance to classes (economic hierarchy). On the other hand, there is the revival of Brahmanical culture among the masses as the contemporary sense of social morality, in the guise of urban sophistication, in connection with the rise in importance of academic qualifications.[3] This tendency is spread through modern schools and mass media. Thus the Brahmanical culture re-invented during the colonial period developed to display its effects of differentiation broadly and deeply as a dominant culture along with the progress of urbanization after independence. That is the social situation in which all of the villagers, including the Paraiyars, are placed today; of course it is inconceivable that the Paraiyars could alone be free from those effects of differentiation.

The Paraiyars today are strongly opposed to the overt use of "pure-impure" ideology (by which they are seen as impure Harijans) by the higher castes in the village. Yet they tend matter-of-factly to accept and internalize the "pure-impure" ideology in the form of the high culture with an urban-style atmosphere of sophisticated manners and taste, due to its non-ideological appearance. Particularly vulnerable to that ideology are the social climbers among the Harijan elite who have picked up the individualistic, middle-class mindset. The extraordinary permeability of "contemporary popular Brahmanical culture" survived even a Dravidian movement (Tamil Nationalism) which campaigned with anti-Brahman slogans, and lately seems to have found new strength with the rise of communalism [Sekine, 1995].

However, we should not simply regard the above discussion as proof of the validity of Dumont's static, substantialist encompassing theory, as Moffat does. Rather, we should clarify the dynamics of why and how the Paraiyars, whose lives are arranged principally around "pollution" ideology, are attracted by "pure-impure" ideology in the form of high culture.

The Lived Value System of the Paraiyars: Productivity-Centred Basic Values

My task is to answer such questions as what the present value system (the cultural situation) of the village Paraiyars is and how they actually practise in their socially repressed situation.

The Paraiyars share with Caste Hindus the above-mentioned ideological configuration, in which "pollution" ideology is primarily important for them. They are not, therefore, segregated from "pure-impure" ideology and they also manipulate it more or less. However, the difference between Caste Hindus and the Paraiyars lies particularly in their attitudes towards the ritual hierarchical ideology. There is no doubt that the social hierarchical barrier between the Caste Hindus and the Paraiyars remains strong in the village sphere. However, today the Paraiyars refute and deny the ritual hierarchy (the social hierarchy based on "pure-impure" ideology), at least on a conscious level, and they thus tend to explain the remaining social hierarchy as an economic differential between the dominant castes and them. The same observation is also reported by other writers like Freeman [1979] and Vincentnathan [1987]. This attitude of the Paraiyars is not unfound and reflects the social reality that today the Paraiyars are not always confined to the traditional village system associated with the ritual hierarchy, but that they can (or must) live in the wider social framework beyond the village system, where "class" ideology is more prevalent. The government's preferential schemes, which work as a form of new patronage, especially for the Harijans, tend to encourage this attitude of the Paraiyars.[4]

This attitude of the Paraiyars, in which the ritual hierarchy is replaced by the economic hierarchy [Deliège, 1992: 166], however, is not only motivated by their feeling against the imposed "pure-impure" ideology, but also is naturally derived from "pollution" ideology which attaches importance to "productivity". This point can be made clear by their subjective understanding of caste boundaries. That is, it looks objectively contradictory that on the one hand, the Paraiyars deny caste hierarchy based on "pure-impure" ideology, but on the other hand, they tend to preserve their caste boundaries, as Caste Hindus do. However, from their subjective viewpoint this is not contradictory for them. The answer is this: generally speaking, although this caste barrier is objectively seen as the result of the penetration of "pure-impure" ideology, it is important that the subjective understanding of each caste member of it cannot be fully explained by the logic of "pure-impure". This is valid, not only for the higher castes, but also for the Paraiyars who are also keen on preserving their own caste barriers. It is embedded in their minds that the mixing of different "kinds" of people should be avoided. The point is that the reason for their wanting to preserve caste boundaries does not lie in "pure-impure" ideology, but lies in the Paraiyars' subjective understanding that the violation of a caste boundary invites danger leading to social disorder and threatening their identity. In other words, their fear of inter-caste mixing is connected with the possibility (anxiety) of decreasing the "productive power" of their own caste by losing their own property ("flower"), as is clarified in their attitude towards inter-caste marriage (see Chapter 7). Recalled here is that they evaluate women not due to their purity but due to their power or productivity. Thus, in this context, their subjective understanding derives not from the hierarchical caste order based on "pure-impure" ideology but from the horizontal cooperation based on the value of "productivity", which is the primary value of "pollution" ideology.

The same interpretation is also found in the following example. Though the Paraiyars follow "pure-impure" ideology in the religious context, it is because they think that the "pure" state of worshippers is instrumentally necessary for obtaining gods' grace or power, such as security and productivity. For them, there is no contradiction between this notion and the conduct of blood sacrifice, embodying "pollution" ideology.[5] In other words, their religious behaviour, which objectively appears to be an acceptance of "pure-impure" ideology, can be seen to be subjectively based on the ideology of "pollution" or "pollution-sacredness". This interpretation is more clearly extracted as their strategic attitudes in the following sections.

The Paraiyars' Subjective Interpretations and Strategies: The Disparity between Behaviour and Beliefs, and Its Fluctuation of Meaning

As has been suggested, we must be conscious of the disparity between what the Paraiyars do and what the Paraiyars believe. For instance, the custom of *mutaṉmai* (priority) conducted in the village or lineage festivals in which the Paraiyars are the last receivers appears problematic for them because it works as an ideological device to legitimate the conventinal social hierarchical order in the name of god. In practice, the Paraiyars do not take the *mutaṉmai* order seriously, but accept it as part of the necessary ritual peocedure in order to achieve their primary purpose of enjoying god's grace. This suggests that they sometimes, despite not believing in it, accept or utilize "pure-impure" ideology as a means for seeking their "self-aggrandizement".

This suggestion of their strategic viewpoint is further confirmed by other examples. The Paraiyars have primarily replicated aspects of the culture of the Kallars, as the dominant caste, in order to establish more satisfying cultural styles (for example, those of rites of passage and of lineage festivals), if they can afford to do so. In addition, as is shown by the comparative analysis of funeral ceremonies of the Pillais, the Kallars and the Paraiyars, elements of the Pillais' ceremonies, which are much Sanskritized, are also fragmentarily replicated by the Paraiyars. This "over-replication (over-assimilation)" can be thought of as a manoeuvre of asserting their respectability or autonomous identity [Deliège, 1992: 167], in contrast to that of the Kallars, by using cultural elements given ritually higher values.

Thus their receptive behaviour of replication does not appear to result from a true belief in what they are replicating. It should instead be regarded as an aspect of their strategies for pursuing self-aggrandizement. Still, it is true that an action in itself contributes to the generation of values. Externally their action contributes to the reproduction of a value, while internally, their action allows the value to penetrate the self. The effect of this replicatory action corresponds to the encompassing aspect of the performative effect of a rite. As a result, the strategic intent of the replicatory behaviour brings about reform (independence), while its performative effect yields conservativeness (subordinacy), and therefore the meaning of the behaviour fluctuates between those poles. In this respect, active Harijans who intend to use the dominant culture experience a strong fluctuation (irony).

The point here is that it is necessary to move to a higher level of interpretative discussion by inserting a parameter of strategy between action and belief, thereby stepping away from Moffat-style substantialism, which short-circuits action and belief.

Individualistic Strategies in the Arena of Paraiyar Society

Strategies are not constructed free from outside influences and are not determined only from the Paraiyars' point of view, but are made and remade in the course of social interaction with higher castes and with their fellows. Therefore it is necessary to take into account both internal and external conditions. Though it is doubtless true that the Harijans' position has been strongly restricted by social power relationships, there is still room, albeit limited, for the free choice by which their strategies are constructed. In other words, there is a certain space of freedom even under strong social compulsion among the Harijans, as Freeman makes clear through his ethnography using the life history method [Freeman, 1979].

The kind of strategies which are adopted by the Paraiyars are influenced by two types of social relationships, inter-caste relationships and intra-caste ones, both of which Vincentnathan takes into account in her argument dealing with social strategies for self-esteem management [Vincentnathan, 1987: Chapters IV,V,VI] (see Chapter 3). Both types of social relationships are important, but my observations suggest that the Paraiyar community itself is rather the main arena where rivalry is intensely present and much energy is consumed.

Though the village Paraiyars still observe their traditional duties (*toḻil*) as menial village servants, their main contact with the dominant castes is found in the fields, where they work as agricultural labourers. Generally speaking, the Paraiyars cope with the rather crude dominance of the Kallars by limiting their contact with the Kallars to necessary businesses, which can be described as "avoidance and withdrawal" in Vincentnathan's terms. The Paraiyars know well that their oppressed situation is unlikely to change, even if they resort to "defiance" or "escape" by conversion to another religion. They also have no hope in terms of "positive transactions" in her terms.[6] Therefore, as discussed in Chapter 12, they tend to seek a way out by using politics and the economy connected with the wider social dynamics, which are conceptualized as "political movements and protests" and "non-caste-based status" by Vincentnathan. In sum, their concerns are found mainly in the sphere beyond the village caste system, rather than in the sphere of inter-caste relationships within the village.

This tendency of extending beyond the village sphere is also reflected in intra-caste relationships. Through an investigation of the milk society's problems, three types of Paraiyar leaders can be recognized. It is also made clear that their leadership tend to be defined by each different socio-economic condition. They at times co-operate with, and at times oppose, one another in their quest for self-aggrandizement. Firstly, the "independent" type of leader KP represents the peripheral Tankalan lineage's type of attitude. He tends to show the combined attitude of "disassociation" (in Vincentnathan's terms) and "straightforwardness" due to his economic independency from, and his social peripherality in, the village system (see Chapters 9 and 12). He is influential and admired by many of the youth of his community, but he ultimately avoids becoming too deeply involved in community matters, as is shown in Chapter 12. It is judged that he adopts "optimal" (giving but not receiving like Brahman) strategies, like "disassociation" and "exemplary behaviour" in Vincentnathan's (or basically Marriott's) terms. In contrast, the "traditional" type of leader TK, who represents the conservative aspect of *Nāṟpaṅkāḷi* (the four-central lineages), still makes a profit from the conventional village institutions, like the *jajmānī* relationship, and, therefore, tends to act relatively more in concert with the dominant castes. He is an ardent follower of the village level of deities. He, being less economically active, but more religiously active, seems to adopt the "minimal" (having the minimum transaction like Vaisha), but in a sense "optimal", strategy. Among these three types, the "mediating" type of leader, who bridges between the politico-administrative sphere and the village sphere, is most influential, and at the same time a trouble-maker in the Paraiyar community today. Because the politics of the state government have begun to work as a new type of patronage, instead of the traditional *jajmānī* relationships, the mediator plays the role of a new patron for the village Paraiyars. The Paraiyars' strategic attitude is rather exaggeratedly exemplified by a "mediating" type of leader, CV, who seeks self-aggrandizement, even by exploiting his own community. This "mediating" type of leader represents the innovative aspect of the *Nārpaṅkāḷi*, and his strategy, fully dependent on political power, is typically the "maximal" (having the maximum transaction like Kshatriya) but, at the same time, "pessimal" (receiving but not giving like Shudra), due to his deviant behaviour.

Although the three types of leaders engage in different strategies, their common purpose is self-aggrandizement. These scheming and calculating individuals sometimes come into conflict with each other. As the problem of the milk society shows, the competition or conflict within the Paraiyar community forms a significant portion of his everyday concerns. This intra-caste conflict appears to be more energy-consuming in their everyday life than are inter-caste relationships. It is also suggested that the social unit of competition tends to be dismembered to a family or to an individual, and this minimal unit attempts to strategically manipulate various social boundaries, like sub-lineage, lineage, caste and village, for its self-aggrandizement.

Conclusion: The Illusion and Paradox of Urbanized Society for the Paraiyars

The spread of urbanization turns even the villagers individualistic. As explained above, there is a shift towards the family or the individual as the unit for competition and strategizing. Furthermore, the advancement of urbanization has given the villagers increased chances for participating in broad-based economic and cultural activities. As a result, even the Paraiyars are not necessarily bound to their lives in their home village. One aspect of this situation is that Paraiyars are led to the illusion that they have increased freedom to implement strategies for self-aggrandizement. It is therefore necessary to point out that since they are still Harijans, the situation sets them in a new trap.

In reality the individual struggles and strategies found in the arena of the Paraiyar community are of necessity rather short-sighted and profit-seeking, because the Paraiyars are in an oppressed position and in the propertyless class. I have identified three leadership types to illustrate three styles of self-aggrandizement strategy. Leadership of the *mediating* type appears best suited to coping with the actual conditions at present. However, the attitude of the *independent* type of leadership exhibited by the peripheral Tankalan lineage appears to be helpful for forecasting the future trends of the village Paraiyars. The Tankalan are becoming independent from the conventional order in the village through reliance on the outside economy, and they are going over to the "contemporary popular Brahmanical culture" (as symbolized by their devotion to Murugan, a son of Siva). Their behaviour, therefore, most sensitively reflects the current conditions of urbanized society.

The trend among the Tankalan does not occur in isolation, but rather as a counteraction against the *Nāṟpankāḷi* central group of the Paraiyar community. That is, their behaviour is driven by a sense of rivalry, a will to self-aggrandizement through differentiation. In fact, whether consciously or unconsciously, they are so eager for differentiation that they incorporate values contradictory to the "pollution" ideology emphasizing productive power in which they basically believe. In the process of differentiation they tend to adopt what is highly valued by the society, which leads them to an ambivalent position as the result of replication of the so-called high culture. To restate: although this type of situation originates from a power-oriented attitude rooted in the horizon of *kinship* associated with the "pollution" ideology that is the basis of their thinking, in the course of their actual strategic behaviour as individual or family units, they nonetheless welcome the "contemporary popular Brahmanical culture" that is generally considered to be of high quality. As a result, they unwittingly approach the hierarchical "pure-impure" ideology developed on the horizon of *caste*. Hence most propertyless Harijans not only sink again to the bottom of the economic hierarchy of urbanized society, but also are likely to be positioned at the bottom of the ritual hierarchy based on the "pure-impure" ideology dressed up in the new moral style of sophisticated manners and taste. The illusion of liberation and its ironical result for the Paraiyars corresponds to Béteille's argument on current urban trends, in which the sense of loyalty that drives the pursuit of self-aggrandizement for one's own family ends up acting as a conservative force which paradoxically works to retain the caste structure [Béteille, 1991a, 1992].

The paradox certainly exists that the reforms attempted in the hope of individualized self-aggrandizement reverse their course to support conservative power. However, it should be noted that this does not necessarily mean simple sustainment of caste culture. It should be recognized that a "transformation of caste culture" [Barnett, 1975: 151] is indeed occurring at the same time, albeit with fluctuations. Hence the above-mentioned ironical trap which Harijans experience today can be seen as a process that they should undergo to improve their social standing in the long run. I mention this because their short-sighted individualistic struggles can be seen as practice (*pratique*) in Bourdieu's sense, which is based on *habitus*. That is, on the one hand their practices may contribute to the reproduction of the social hierarchy, but, on the other hand, their dynamic sense of practice (*le sens pratique*) [Bourdieu, 1980] may mount a renewed challenge against the situation which absurdly confines them. In this sense, we must carefully explore the potential field in which two separately pursued goals, the acquisition of a sense of salvation within the lives of individual Harijans and their improvement as a whole through institutional reforms, may ultimately merge.

Theoretical Contributions to Studies of "Untouchables"

The findings presented above point to the following conclusions with regard to the debate on the nature of the culture that is maintained and followed by Harijans. First, inquiry in a substantialist manner which is confined to the choice between whether or not Harijans hold the same culture as the higher dominant castes is not only unessential, but also mistaken in that it departs from reality through inadvertent simplification. This realization is the fundamental premise of my criticisms of both cultural disjunction and cultural consensus theories, although I certainly accept their advantages.

My criticism derives from two key findings in terms of the comparison between the dominant castes and the Harijans, namely, (1) the cultural consensus based on "pollution" ideology and (2) the disjunction in the interpretative or strategic dimension. Furthermore, in order to illuminate the actual conditions, it is absolutely necessary to adopt a methodology that takes full account of the above conclusion, which first separates the lived values and beliefs (ideology) from the actual practices that emerge under social constraints, and then develops a fresh linkage between them in the dimension of interpretation.

Firstly, it seems to me that both disjunction and consensus theorists share the common tendency of placing the Brahmanical culture in the centre of their arguments, though there is a difference whether it is overestimated or underestimated. In this sense, their investigation of local cultural values (ideologies) seems to be inadequate. The naive and superficial dispute about whether the Harijans' culture is same as the culture of the upper castes obviously fails to take into account the depth of the local culture, which is elucidated by the distinction between "pollution" and "impurity". "Pollution" ideology, as the deeper dimension of culture, is basically shared among all the castes, high and low, in the village. In this sense, it can be claimed that there is a cultural consensus between the dominant castes and the Paraiyars, but my claim is not the same as Moffatt's. Cultural consensus in my sense does not lie in "pure-impure" ideology but lies in "pollution" ideology, as the key value of the shared basic Tamil culture. This point should be firmly kept in mind. Thus, I agree with Moffatt's claim of cultural unity, but cannot accept his assertion that this cultural concensus is realized by the Harijans' replication of the higher castes' culture. My disagreement with Moffatt does not imply my denial of the Harijans' replicatory acts, but such acts should not be simply seen as the Harijans' true acceptance of "pure-impure" ideology. We have to be wary of a Moffatt-like "non-interpretative" viewpoint. This naturally leads us to the second point of the "interpretative" approach.

The interpretative viewpoint not only highlights the difference between the Harijans' actions and their real beliefs, but also reveals that it is misleading to think that there is a one-to-one correspondence between a particular ideology and a particular social section. Needless to say, there is "pollution" ideology as a primary cultural value shared among all castes and "pure-impure" ideology regulating the village social hierarchy. However, village life today has not only these conventional ones but also other ideologies brought by urbanization such as class ideology associated with consumerism and "contemporary popular Brahmanical culture". All ideologies are manipulated by the people of all social sections, including the Harijans. Moreover, such manipulations or interpretations are motivated by their desire for seeking self-aggrandizement. In other words, their strategic behaviours are diversifying in appearance, but they are integrated under the ultimate goal of self-aggrandizement. For example, the custom of meat-eating is sometimes hidden from outsiders, and is sometimes positively claimed by the Harijans. Such responses look contradictory but consistently reflect the desire for self-esteem. In sum, their rather diversified behaviour, such as replication, denial, disregard, etc. (passing, positive transactions, defiance, escape, avoidance in Vincentnathan's terms), should be regarded as part of their strategies for self-aggrandizement.

From this point of view, the Harijans' "subculture" which the disjunction theorists describe must be carefully reconsidered. For instance, if the Paraiyars' subcultural compornents listed by Deliège [Deliège, 1988: 115] were checked, it would be soon made clear that most of them are shared by the Kallars, the dominant caste in Kinnimangalam, with the exception of eating dead animals, beef-eating and restrictions of dress and study (which is now abolished). Therefore, it is difficult to claim that the Harijans exclusively hold a separate subculture, though there is a difference between the Brahmanical culture and the non-Brahmanical one. It should be again pointed out that the level of ideologies should not be mixed up with the level of social sections. I think that the difference between the Caste Hindus and the Harijans rather lies in the strategic behaviour which strongly reflects their social positions. Compared with the Caste Hindus, the Harijans' manipulation of the available ideologies is very much limited and complicated by their socially constrained situation, such as abject poverty, menial duties, degraded status, physical labour, and various restrictions on their way of life (see, for example, [Vincentnathan, 1987: 176–178], [Moffatt, 1979: 51]). Therefore, it seems to be problematic to naively describe the Harijans as if they lived in a sort of self-contained world, without taking into consideration their socio-historical background. I am afraid that disjunction theorists fail to sufficiently investigate the Harijans'standpoint and their theories unwittingly adopt (or repeat) the Caste Hindus' view which wants to distinguish the Harijans' culture from their culture. However, I should also note that I highly evaluate the attempt of the disjunction theorists to make it clear that the Harijans are not incompetent subordinates, but are rather conscious interpreters. In addition, the notion that different strategies derive from different social conditions can explain the variety of strategies among the Harijans, ranging from the strategy of the educated, active, urban Harijans to that of the illiterate, passive, rural Harijans.

Thus, it can be concluded that the Harijans' culture does not form a separate world, but is doubtless a part of the village culture, which is penetrated by "pollution" ideology, though there is the disjunction at the behavioural level reflecting the Harijans' socio-economic and historical background.

Reconstruction of Theory on Caste Society and Conceptualization of a "Common-Ground" Anthropology

The application of Dumontian theory to caste society [Dumont, 1980 (1966)] has stimulated a great deal of controversy and criticism, as described in Chapter 2. Various value systems have been proposed as additions or alternatives to Dumontian hierarchical "pure-impure" ideology, including those that are described as: reciprocal ([Das and Uberoi, 1971]), egalitarian ([Parry, 1974], [Holmstrom, 1976]), mutual ([Raheja, 1988]), kingly ([Dirks, 1987], [Hoek, 1979]), central ([Raheja, 1988]), transcendental ([Heesterman, 1981, 1985]), and matrilineal ([McGilvray, 1982]. While these critical studies have all made valuable contributions, as a whole this body of work cannot be said to have succeeded in mounting a complete criticism of Dumont, or in *systematically* illustrating the actual aspects of Hindu society. My fundamental objection is that simply juxtaposing an alternative complementary value from a top-down viewpoint does not constitute a thoroughgoing criticism of Dumontian theory. There are two key points. First, the relationship between Dumontian "pure-impure" ideology and an alternative ideology must be properly explained; second – and this must be emphasized – a bottom-up viewpoint is necessary.

On the first point, [Burghart, 1978] is noteworthy as a comprehensive investigation of the mutual relationships among the Brahmanical, kingly and transcendental hierarchic models. The merit of Burghart's work lies in an interpretative approach that brings to light the gaps among the three viewpoints of Brahman, king and renouncer (see also [Malamoud, 1981]). A recent work worthy of special mention is Quigley's critique of Dumont, including a criticism of Orientalism [Quigley, 1993]. After historically and logically identifying problems of Dumontian theory, Quigley present a consistent picture of Indian society on the basis of a ritual practice model founded on Hocart's theory of divine kingship (for details see [Sekine, 1994b]). Yet while much may be learned from these two works, their arguments are still based on the standpoint of the dominant centre of society (top-down viewpoint), with no conscientious effort to incorporate an other-worldly and bottom-up (or on-boundary decentripetal) standpoint. This is the second key point that was mentioned above. I emphasize this limitation because it is essential to shift from the *off-boundary viewpoint* (viewing the periphery from the centre) to the *on-boundary viewpoint* (viewing from within what the *off-boundary viewpoint* sees as the periphery), in order to criticize Dumontian theory. As mentioned previously, the decisive shortcoming of Dumontian theory is that it stops at the off-boundary viewpoint and so the analyst's so-called objective theory, which conceals a privileged viewpoint, unwittingly overlaps the value perspective of the dominant group in the society.

From the position of emphasizing the other-worldly and bottom-up viewpoint (hence a generative viewpoint), I would note the need to devote more attention to research findings concerning such phenomena as blood sacrifice and *pakti* cults which are categorized under popular religion or popular culture,[7] as well as the acute need to properly re-examine them. In this regard I would again call special attention to the dimension of the "sharedness of ordinary values" [Caplan, 1980: 235] in those studies. This holds potential as a base for relativizing viewpoints that are based on dominant values. To obtain the full picture of the pollution concepts in villagers' minds, which are considered to embody "ordinary values" and are not exhausted by a Dumontian understanding, investigation from a decentripetal, bottom-up, interpretative viewpoint is required. An in-depth approach to pollution concepts is possible only from that viewpoint. The deeper connotations of "pollution" that may be thus explored are not always consciously recognized by the villagers, as indicated by Caplan [1980: 234], but will be revealed through analysis of their practices.[8]

The present work, as I have already made clear, is an attempt to overcome shortcomings in the conventional theory of caste society. By educing the dimensions of "pollution" in a manner embodying the decentripetal interpretative viewpoint (an other-worldly, bottom-up and dynamic [generative] viewpoint), this book relativises Dumont's view of "impurity" which is patterned on centripetal thought (a this-worldly, top-down and substantialist viewpoint), and also explains why the relationship between the dimensions of those two approaches should be understood as interpretative struggles between differing ideologies. As the methodology of this work, I have used a revision of social theory derived by going back to liminality theory which has been investigated as a theory of "pollution". The innovation that I propose is to separate "pollution" from "impurity". This evokes Karatani's conceptual categorization of individuality (see Note 1), and denotes a shift from the Leach-style theory of liminality as *particularity* to the Bataille-style theory of liminality as *singularity*. This basic innovation makes it possible to relativise the Dumontian theory of caste society which like Leach conceals a privileged, universal viewpoint, as well as the perception of the Harijans that is set forth by Moffatt (who is an adherent of the Dumontian theory), by pointing out how their non-interpretative attitudes obscure the dynamics of actual ideological conflicts. It is necessary to properly reposition Dumontian theory as one underpinning of an overall scheme comprising the existence of differing ideologies engendered by differing viewpoints and the dynamic relationships among them. I view those dynamics as differences in the depth of interpretation which I denote as "maintenance on the surface" and "innovation in depth". With regard to difference in the location of the point of view, I refer to friction between the *off-boundary viewpoint* which looks down on the margin as the periphery from the centre of order (centripetal motion), and the *on-boundary viewpoint* of those who live at the periphery (decentripetal motion). Both of those motions are distributed in the internal worlds of people of every caste, where they produce a cyclical movement. The cyclical movement may begin with a *symbolic* state in which a certain order is constructed, pass through an immature, creative *semiotic* state, and proceed to another *symbolic* state [Kristiva, 1974]. This understanding makes it clear that Dumontian theory is a static perception of only the centripetal motion, which is merely one facet of a cyclical dynamic. The two dimensions are articulated as friction between dominant discourse and de-dominant discourse at points that are defined as marginal within social power relationships. This is the comprehensive theoretical framework within which I have repositioned Dumont's "pure-impure" theory.

The above summarises my critique of Dumontian theory and my approach for subsuming it. The essence of my theory, to repeat once again, consists in the importance for the villagers of the affirmative and creative dimension of "pollution" in a sense that cannot be reduced to "impurity". It should be noted here that "pollution" is actually more strongly connected with a kinship horizon orientated towards equality and productivity (in contrast, "impurity" has an affinity to the caste horizon that places importance on ritual hierarchy). Furthermore, to focus afresh on the kinship horizon in Indian society is to re-examine *jāti*, a word that has been translated as "caste" and acquired a fixed image as such but which originally had a wider meaning. In particular, it is to rediscover the sense of *jāti* that also refers to kinship community [Quigley, 1993: 4–8]. To do so in the context of Indian society is to find internal continuities between caste society and tribal society[9] as pointed out by Kolenda [1978]; and in a broader context to be led towards the discovery of external commonalities between caste society and other societies including those of various Southeast Asian peoples. In other words it opens up the possibility of comparative sociology in a different sense than Dumont's.

While Dumont's comparative sociology notes *differences* (contrasts) between self (the West) and others (the non-West),[10] the comparative sociology I am proposing here looks at *similarities*. Hocart also took the latter standpoint, as indicated by a valuable commentary in Inden's critique of Indology [Inden, 1990]. Denying the view that West and East are extremes, Hocart takes a standpoint that emphasises similarities among Western, Oriental and "uncivilized" cultures, and argues that caste is not some sort of curiosity indigenous to India. He also clearly perceives that introducing *varṇa* theory is arbitrary and deceptive, and warns that the actual realities of India ought to be examined [ibid.: 74–75]. As Dumont and Hocart are both basically cultural relativists, the occurrence of that sort of difference between them verifies a conceptual difficulty of cultural relativism [Shimizu, 1992: 445]. A thoroughgoing relativism will negate the universalism that is actually a hidden premise of relativism, and therefore the basis of comparison will be lost. I think the contradiction is rooted in an idealistic, essentialistic conceptualization of the notion of the autonomy of individual cultures. The facile comparisons of evolutionism which are based on a uniformistic view of human society, as well as the converse denial of comparisons that close off individual cultures in the isolation of perfect endemism, are both products of intellectualism that are blind to reality. Here the confrontational scheme of relativism versus universalism reaches an impasse. The open notions that there are commonalities (similarities) and at the same time differences among cultures, and that culture inherently consists of processes of creation and transformation, conform more closely to actual conditions. A person is fundamentally an open being who continually interprets ambiguous experiences. Such is the ground of possibility for comprehending "other culture". Accordingly the question is, as Quigley puts it, "how do we gain access to that world without resort to an extreme relativism (or ethnosociology) which defies comparison?" [Quigley, 1993: 15].[11] In his attempt to answer it, he ends up reevaluating Hocart's method which gives weight to the discovery not of differences but of similarities. As a result, Quigley was led to make a comparison and contrast of Indian kingship and Balinese *negara* [Geertz, 1980] and point out the similarities between them (see also [Dirks, 1987: Chapter 13]).

But just what is this *similarity*-oriented comparative sociology? It is easy to anticipate the critics: is not this a reactionary solution that falls back on the evolutionist premise of the uniformity of human culture? If any false step is made, how would this be any different from the consensual identification that Said cites as a characteristic of modern Orientalism? [Said, 1978]. However, we must remember the context in which I am making this claim, which is on the way back after visiting the impasse of relativism (in what Quigley calls "intellectual limbo" [Quigley, 1993:14]) which was a difference-oriented comparative sociology (see Note 11). My approach to a sociology of *similarity* in this context is neither a return to the illusion of consensual identification based on romantic intuition nor a Radcliffe-Brown-style comparison of a row of target societies from a modern transcendental viewpoint.

Then what distinguishes this new *similarity*-oriented comparative sociology from other comparative sociologies? It is that in the comparison it adopts *the attitude that identifies self and other as being within the inner part of boundary phenomena that have decentripetal, fragmentational moment*, instead of the attitude of discovering through objective comparison the similarities in centripetal phenomena, phenomena oriented towards the centre of the existing order (the attitude of the laboratory scientist analysing the subject of an experiment). A prerequisite to the former attitude is a Nietzschean turn in the attitude towards our life, a turn from *recognition* to *valuation* as the principle of experiencing the world [Takeda, 1993: 2–3]. Valuation means interpretation of the world as the chaos of existence, on the basis of *eros* (capacity for life). Hence there arises the necessity to enter into that location known as the boundary, which will reveal to us the world as the chaos of existence. To draw comparisons by means of a decentripetal attitude, it is essential to avoid taking a stand on the side of the logic of the dominant societal order, i.e., engaging in interpretation that suppresses chaos, or in socially triumphant valuation that overpowers the other. It is therefore essential that interest be directed where *eros* (capacity for life) manifests, rather than where the moral order penetrates. Since the method I advocate aims at comparison that incorporates *extériorité* in Deleuze's sense, I call it "common-ground" anthropology rather than similarity-oriented comparative sociology. The former term better conveys the intended nuances of a break with the viewpoint which, in the name of objective comparison, soars to the centre of order, and of an approach towards and shared perception of the underlying chaos, from which culture is generated.

What is a lived culture? I found an answer to this question through my field experience in the South Indian village and my preparation of this book. The answer is this: *The core of a lived culture lies in the affirmative management of boundary phenomena and, through that process, the derivation of life energy.* A culture that lacks this core cannot be called a lived culture, and in a radical sense should not exist. From this point of view, the core of the Tamil culture is not to be found in the rigid "pure-impure" ideology that has been thought of as defining the caste order. "Pure-impure" ideology speaks only of the ruling principle of a this-worldly societal order (negative management), and has no interest in the affirmative management of boundary phenomena where people can live. In Foucault's terms, "pure-impure" ideology works as a *normalization* grid to produce a distinction between a normal self and an abnormal other inside the same society, and serves as a value scale for repressive control through differentiation that creates social hierarchy. Thus the boundary, which is inevitably produced by the existence of order, is contained by the centre of order as a necessary evil. In direct opposition to that, the affirmative management of boundary phenomena entails entering and exposing oneself to the boundary area where the other world is encountered. Here is how my "pollution" theory comes into the discussion. Regarding boundary phenomena such as death or birth which bring people into the state of "pollution", the villagers to some extent accept "pure-impure" ideology as the logic of the *caste* horizon, which translates the phenomenon negatively. However, judging from what they actually do, the villagers fully embrace the phenomena and thus convert them into their own capacity for life (fertility). This can be defined as affirmative management of boundary phenomena on the *kinship* horizon where pollution is shared. It is precisely by means of practices based on such "pollution" ideology that village culture is vitalized and becomes a lived culture.

Re-examined from the viewpoint of affirmative boundary management, the deep relationship between divine kingship and sacrifice, which Hocart observes from a cross-cultural perspective, can occur on a common ground beyond individual cultures precisely because it is management of a boundary phenomenon that incorporates other-worldly power. This has nothing to do with what Hocart himself thinks, but is rather my way of understanding the depth at which his work deals with the subject matter. Quigley seems to assess Hocart in the same way, although he uses the term "similarity". In presenting my methodological notion, I adopt the term "common ground" instead of "similarity", on the basis of the above-stated comprehension of the core of a lived culture. My intention is to establish the level of comparison by considering that a boundary phenomenon, in that it signifies decentripetal motion or reveals a limit of the systemic order, occurs at a point where a basic common language like a prote-mother tongue is capable of penetrating the dominant languages of individual cultures. I base my claim on the universal fact that a boundary phenomenon occurs always where the inner logic of an individual culture faces a limit (a gap); in other words, where a culture encounters that which is beyond itself (i.e., the outside) and is paradoxically created by the existence of the culture. This universal fact does not lead to the uniformity (universality) of human mentality (i.e., reason) that is postulated by developmental stage theory (evolutionism) as a premise for the *normalization* grid that places Western rational man at the summit of development. But it leads to the human universality found in the decentripetal moment of *eros* that provides an opportunity of de-*normalization*, which makes nonsense of the very existence of differences within the *normalization* grid. In Bataille's terms, it would be a universality that appears not in a worldly oriented moment of "prohibition", but in a supra-mundane oriented moment of "violation".[12]

Hence it is of vital importance for today's anthropology to focus upon boundary phenomena, such as untouchability or pollution, as the subject of discussion, because they have the potentiality of becoming truly far-reaching "common grounds". The perspective of "common-ground" anthropology that I present here is my way of wandering in "intellectual limbo" as one who is alive and studying. Perhaps this requires a Creole spirit which steps out of the integrity of the inner logic of the self and tries to live in the abyss between inner and outer worlds, that is, at the boundary.

Students specializing in South Asia, including Indian scholars, are still bound by the Orientalist knowledge framework that originated in the West, a point that has been fully treated as a problem of the post-colonial situation [Breckenridge and van der Veer, 1993]. In that intellectual climate, this book is an attempt by a non-Westerner to criticize and transcend Dumontian theory, an emblem of the spell of Orientalism in the post-colonial era (see e.g. [ibid.: 13]), in order to search for a new sense of "universal" common language for the understanding of "other culture". I intend to continue my research along this line in the hope that it may ultimately be fully worthy of being called "common-ground" anthropology.

Notes

1. Kojin Karatani (a Japanese critic) emphasizes the distinction between an individuality as "particularity" (I) and an individuality as "singularity" (this I). He provides the following explanation in the premise of distinction between generality and universality; "While particularity is an individuality disposed on the yardstick of generality, singularity (which is deeply connected with universality) is an individuality that has no place on the yardstick of generality"[Karatani, 1994 (1989): 11], and "the singularity is not able to be explained by the cognitive terms such as subject and object" [ibid.: 19]. Borrowing the Karatani's concepts mentioned above, the ideological struggles in the present argument would be described as follows. That is to say, the struggles are regarded as the complications taking place at the gap between the dimension of "particularity" of "pure-impure" ideology and the dimension of "singularity" of "pollution" ideology. It becomes evident that the image of women, that is, the view of women as being "impure" but also "pure" when certain conditions are fulfilled, is a discourse or narrative produced by relatively particularizing women with the dominant values of Hindu society (viz. Male-centred or Brahman- centred values) i.e., "pure-impure" ideology working as a yardstick of generality (cf. Foucault's *normalization* [Foucault, 1975]). By developing a suppressive narrative typical of a centripetal ideology which would regard menstrual blood and sexual intercourse, representing the starting point of reproductivity, as "impure" while interpreting the resulting fruit of fertility as exalted "purity" (or "purity-sacredness"), the existence of "pollution" as representing the dimension of "singularity", in which women are actually living, ends up being concealed.

Unwitting tracing of the discourse trapped by the dominant ("pure-impure") ideology reproduces the image of ambiguity of Hindu women which is circulated in general. What I want to make clear is that the nomostic dominant ideology tends to conceal the fact that there is a decisive and crucial difference in terms of the locus of viewpoint between the dimension of particularity (the centripetal) and the dimension of singularity (the decentripetal). In this respect, it is important to percieve the reality that Hindu women are the arena where two ideologies clash and not to reduce the reality to the ambiguous image of women that the "pure-impure" ideology high-handedly produces.

2. My criticism of Dumont theory and my alternative proposal of the necessary distinction between "pollution" and "impurity" corresponds with the necessity of the paradigm shift in Social Anthropology from the popular structuralism that does not sufficiently escape functionalism to the Levi-Straussian structualism which inclines to post-structuralism (cf. [Oda, 1994] [Bourdieu, 1987: Chapter 1]).
3. Nowadays Brahmanic ideology in the form of "sophisticated manner" or "cultured behaviour" permeates among the people and succeeds in unchangingly grasping the social hegemony. For example, you can imagine that a Harijan elite who climbed up a social ladder by the help of reservation often suffers from the gap between his embodied sense of manner nurtured in the Harijan habitus and socially expected sophisticated manner. These negative experiences form his inferiority complex which leads to deep acceptance of Brahmanical ideology against or regardless of his will. This example suggests the mechanism through which the Brahmanical ideology permeates into the bottom of society and perpetuates its hegemonic power.
4. The Paraiyars' claim seems to be partly sustained by the materialized reality such as the improvement of their housing conditions under the state government schemes [Sekine, 1993a]. As shown by this example, politics is practically important for most of the Paraiyars who lack self-help capability. This to some extent explains why they naively worshipped hero politicians like MGR.
5. In this connection, I am reminded of Dumont's naive question of why people stop eating meat to see the meat-eating deity [Dumont, 1986: 380 fn.8]. It seems to me that this question appears due to Dumont's strong adherence to the dichotomous notion of "pure-impure". The confusion lies in his misleading term, a meat-eating god, because the essential nature of animal sacrifice is not eating meat but the sacrificial act itself. (Though I do not fully agree with Fuller's argument in his work [Fuller, 1988], he doubtlessly points out this problem of Dumont.)
6. Vincentnathan raises and discusses the following examples as "positive transactions": the Aiyappan puja and pilgrimage, Praha shakti cult, friendship, intercaste marriages and so forth. In sum, "positive transactions" imply the degraded Harijans' positive attempts in that they overcome caste discrimination and enjoy an atmosphere of no caste feelings by mixing with higher caste people [Vincentnathan, 1987: 210–229].
7. For example, [Caplan, 1980, 1981], [Holmstrom, 1971, 1976], [Parry, 1974, 1980, 1982], [Fuller, 1976], [Obeyesekerc, 1978, 1981], [Shulman, 1980], [Beck, 1981], [Das, 1983] and so forth.
8. It is crucial to carefully recognize the gap between what the villagers consciously know and speak out and the analytical findings by an observer. For instance, Good points out the necessity of the methodological recognition of this gap when he criticizes ethnosociology of the Chicago school [Good, 1978: Ch. 12].

9. Quigley also points out that Indian society is not fully captured by caste, but among tribes and hunter-gatherers there are social spaces ruled by the principle of kinship which could be an antithesis against the hierarchical principle of "pure-impure" [Quigley, 1993: 17–8].
10. There is no doubt that Dumont tried to deepen his thinking by comparing the West dominated by egalitarian individualism with India dominated by hierarchical holism. That is, his anthropology is a comparative sociology focusing on the difference between self and other. Béteille says that the approaches of Dumont and Marriott can be described as contrast, not as comparison [Béteille, 1991b: 10]
11. Relativism could be found even in the absolutism of the Orientalist cultural view in so far as one has to imagine Other as a counterpart of Self. The more thorough relativism is propagated by the deconsructionists like Inden et al. who criticize the optimistic and haughty manner of Orientalism in terms of Other, that is, the view that both Self and Other can be located within the same homogeneous space. It seems, however, that this thorough relativism ultimately leads you to the despair of impossibility of understanding Other or the impossibility of difference-oriented comparative sociology. Therefore, although Quigley recognizes the importance of deconstructionist works, he tries to keep away from such an extreme positon [Quigley, 1993: 14]. He is also conscious that this conundrum cannot be solved by ethnosociology or an emic approach.
12. Needless to say, a series of Foucault's works show his strong concerns about the liminal phenomena such as insanity, crime and sex. This is because he clearly understands the mechanism of *normalization*, that is to say, the reality that those liminal phenomena are the sensitive locus which the ruling culture is very keen on controlling and suppressing and at the same time from which the dominant culture generates the justificatory power for perpetuating its rule. Therefore, his precise archaeological study of these liminal phenomena reversely discloses the fabrication and limitation of the dominant culture. This is his manner of "outside thinking" in his sense, which claims that the very locus of "subjugated knowledge" has the possibility of reversely becoming the foothold of "popular knowledge" escaping to the outside of power working in the form of knowledge.

Chapter 14

Discussion Extended for a "Common-Ground" Anthropology

Differentiating Discrimination against "Untouchables" from Caste Discrimination

The final chapter is laid down in the light of current argument on "crisis of representation", and it constructs a general theoretical frame with a verification and confirmation from the present ethnographic study to elucidate the structural mechanism of social discrimination, which appears as the differentiation the discrimination against "Untouchables" from caste discrimination in Indian social context. This frame, liberating from a perspective of destructive circuit of social discrimination naturalized in the Orientalist discursive space, helps to build up a "common-ground" horizon of anthropology characterized by liminality and indeterminancy, providing a stage where creative interactions between ours and others are made possible. Emphasized is again the significance of the change of attitude that is the shift of our standpoint from the "pure-impure" ideology to the one of "pollution", without which a "common-ground" anthropology could never be materialized.

Still Think based on "facts" after the Critique of Anthropology

The problem of the "crisis of representation" critically hit the foundation of anthropology that has professionally represented other cultures. Anthropology must be reconstructed by overcoming that problem. I argue that it is an important issue to evaluate and distinguish between "bad representation" and "good representation" ("accurate representation" in my word). People will be sensitive and delicate about how they themselves are represented, and dislike to be seen in a stereotyped way. People can really nose out "bad representations" of themselves. Nevertheless, people tend to assertively speak about others, or easily press "bad representations" on others without hesitation. Moreover, we can see before our eyes today that we ferment real conflicts depending on those very "bad representations" (especially, it is a grave phenomenon that such an ideologically rough argument as "the clash of civilizations" by S. Huntington is made in the name of a scholar).

This situation will make us understand that considering the anthropologically critical problem on representation also means reconsidering the fundamentals of frictional phenomena such as opposition and discrimination. The present question "can't we speak about others as if about ourselves?" is set to analyse the mechanism of opposition and discrimination (here, again, Orientalism will be the main topic), and to search the way to dissolve it. Our purpose is, by acquiring "good representations" or "accurate representations", to seek a horizon that enables us to divert from the way of excluding others to the way of understanding others. Therefore, this chapter will be added as a further discussion or an application of my ethnographic conclusions (shown in the previous chapter "Conclusions") in this book in order to ascertain that the urgent theme of contemporary anthropology is a change from "cross-cultural study" to "understanding towards others".

Nowadays, smokers are not comfortable in the society anymore. The persecution against them sometimes seems like "non-smoking fascism". Although the bad effects of smoking have been known to society in such a degree, there still are those who don't stop smoking, or those who can't. Young women smokers are said to be even increasing in the number. People still smoke in-between addiction and fashion.

I started this section from this everyday topic because we need to recognize that the choice of the starting point of an argument can influence the course of it. There is a difference between when we start from the viewpoint of "we should stop smoking for our health" or "the world as it should be" (ideology) and when we start from the viewpoint of "we are smoking" or "the world as it is" (reality). I have pointed out this difference certainly because I would like to start from the viewpoint of "the world as it is". It is like an attitude of smoking addicts who say, "May be we should stop smoking", but are still smoking. Such attitude has a vector to reality and individuality, not to ideology and generality, and I think that is a virtue and a manner of anthropological thought.

It gets more and more difficult for contemporary Japanese to separate modern Japan and the modern West. We are obviously the addicts of the modern West. We might be irritated by this situation, and try to separate and rescue something Japanese. However, no matter how we deny the reality from the viewpoint of "the world as it should be", it is only to generate new oppression (Distorted neo-nationalism is such an example. We have misgivings about the recent surge of this sentiment in Japan). Our scheme is to clearly recognize the reality that we are like addicts who try to escape from such situation, starting to think from the viewpoint of "the world as it is". That is the manner of anthropology. When we start like this, we could be aware of the variety of facets of reality of addicts and their change in the time scale. Similarly, I would like to grasp the positioning of Japanese anthropologists in the eyes of reality and its variety, not only judging from the viewpoint of ideology and generality.

Today, we might be allowed to say that it was unavoidable that the Orientalistic structure had penetrated in anthropological practices in the world system under the hegemony of the modern West. However, it is also the fact that the Western anthropologists themselves had developed self-criticism from within that structure.[1] Especially Lévi-Strauss's structuralism, which is symbolized with the title of *La pensée sauvage* (1962), is obviously one of such great accomplishments. It seems like a marriage of relativism and universalism, or a masterpiece of interweaving of romanticism and scientism.[2] Of course, it was even then obvious that the anthropologist, who was not the experimental scientist, couldnot stand outside of the experimental devices. That is, not everyone innocently believed the possibility of the functionalist anthropology, which casually ignored the existence of researchers as if they had been invisible in the fields.[3] Nevertheless, anthropologists had avoided describing in ethnographies the existence of anthropologists in the fields, since they were bound by the relativistic thought combined with objectivism. The sense of duty to set up anthropology as a social science had prevented to be aware of the existence of the describing subject. In this sense also, we can look back on the Lévi-Strauss's structuralism, as a masterwork that had passed through, in a magically clever way, this complicated problem by getting the hints and foundations from linguistics that was more or less natural scientific and in that sense a rare success of social sciences.

Then after the 70's, the era of so called the postmodern passed over anthropology before people knew it.[4] Anthropology had stopped opening up a new vista of the contemporary thoughts, and in reverse, the contemporary thoughts (new criticism, philosophy, psychoanalysis and so on) started leading anthropology. *Orientalism* by Edward Said (1978) and its critique of anthropology, as an outer pressure from the contemporary thoughts, had direct impact to overtly pull out anthropologists' inner awareness and self-reflection. After 1980's, the academic style of the postmodern anthropology and the postcolonial anthropology, which centered on the thought-methodological concepts such as discourse, text, and representation, started to set the new tone in anthropology. Then, *Writing Culture: the Poetics and Politics of Ethnography* [Clifford and Marcus, 1986] was written as a complete book of self-criticism. It advocates to break with the premises of traditional ethnography such as naïve ontology, empiricism (directness of experience) and objectivism, and to reconsider the poetic and politic foundations such as language, rhetoric, power, history for justifying the writer's authority. These criticisms of anthropology sent from both inside and outside basically strike at the heart of the problem. Anthropologists must reflect on themselves and anthropology must be reformed.

Anthropologists must be aware that their own representing privilege has been supported by the historically generated power relationship (in fact, the first world has always produced anthropologists). Anthropologists often like "entropic metanarrative" but it does not match with the actual conditions of the lived cultures. It is premised on the existence of the self-completed, pure, and authentic culture, but such one-sided understanding (or the discourse of a mouthpiece) is only possible within the suppressive condition in which the speaker deprives the represented object of the utterance position. No one has the right to represent others as the separated objects. "Ethnographic present" is also an example of the way of such one-sided discourse. It is a fictional tense to make up the wholeness of pure culture, and is also a device to separate the object out of the historical context and the background of the world system. These points are already-accepted and well-known criticisms against the discourse of the "Orientalistic" knowledge (of course it includes the critique of "identity politics") that separates those who know from those who are known. (It is another problem whether the every research practice has been improved as taking these criticisms in practically).

Based on these well-recognized points, the authors of *Writing Culture* go one more step forward. This collection of essays, based on the text theory and focusing on "writing" (or ecriture), asserts that ethnography is cultural fiction (it doesn't mean it is falsehood but is something made up). As same as text, under the condition of system and history, ethnography can only clarify "partial truths" and cannot reach "the whole truth". Moreover, the very truth is constructed with the strong 'falsehood' of elimination and rhetoric. This reminds us of Derrida's notion of différance and supplément. Accordingly, they argue that "ethnography is always writing" in this sense. James Clifford, forecasting the rebuttal, adds; these self-critical reviews on ethnography are not for disorganization of ethnography but for encouragement to write ethnography, and their intension of focusing on the poetics and politics of culture does not require that "one give up facts and accurate accounting".[5]

I am willing to take such self-criticism of anthropology by Clifford (because not every author of *Writing Culture* has the same opinion, I restrict the object for argument to his), and also to take it into my own anthropological practice as far as I can. However, I still feel fundamental discomfort in his way of self-criticism, both in his basic stance of anthropology or ethnography, and in the way of grasping the notion of culture. As already been pointed out, the basic objection to *Writing Culture* is caused by its tendency of reducing the whole work of anthropology to mere ethnography-writing by focusing on "writing" from the viewpoint of the text theory. Thus, as a result of his taking ethnography-writing as creation of text, there are relating two points I can't accept when I read the introduction written by Clifford [Clifford, 1986: 1–26].

First, it is on "partial truths". This is his assertion of taking ethnography not as work but as text. Probably, he tries to say that the ethnography as ecriture is a supplément of the unborn real society (or the primary world to be assumed), by insisting that ethnography can reveal the "partial truths". But here, I would like to question whether the term 'partial' is sufficient or not. I understand they intend to deprive the authority of the work that pretend to be "the whole truth" (it is a conduct to universalize the voice of Occident, blocking the voice of the Orient) by emphasizing that anthropologists only can describe "partial truths". In that case, however, both the discourse to be accused and the discourse to accuse the former are equally relativized and eventually we can't defend ourselves as accusers. In reality, we need to distinguish the "bad", violent, and Orientalistic "partial truth" to-be-overcome from the "better" "partial truth" to be counter-constructed. In order to do this, it is important to consciously make the bad "partial truth" confronted with what is presented as "the contingent whole truth", that is, the better "partial truth" composed in the each historical setting. It is not enough only to tell that both the Orientalistic ethnography and the counter ethnography are writing "partial truths".

They are too naïve and ignorant to the mercilessness of power, if they believe that writers of the dominant ethnographies (or ideology producers) will feel sorry just because they are criticized as their representations are only "texts as a partial truth" (Besides, the majority of society is always insensitive to the criticism like this, and also accustomed to put it down in the name of the public benefit). Here, the neutral and restrained way of criticism saying such as "partial truths" and "the whole truth" lose its effectiveness. We, the living humans, are always living in the concrete positions in the real time and space. Taking such positions, we must live in reality by distinguishing the "better" texts from the "bad" texts. It is not impossible. I set the criterion in whether a representation is open and creative ("open representation" or "good representation") or closed and violent ("closed representation" or "bad representation") for the represented. As shown later in this chapter, naturally I seek the way to create the former style of representations.

The second point I can't accept is that "always writing ethnography" [ibid.: 26] in the endlessly relative world of text seems too compulsory. We always have to face with the compulsory question; what desire and confusions was it smoothing over? [ibid.: 14] Moreover, Clifford argues that "truth" is constructed with "falsehood" such as elimination and rhetoric, and praises ethnographers who try to decrease the "falsehood", such as James Walker who tries to erase the authorship [ibid.: 15–17]. Judging from this, it is another attempt of selfless anthropology, although it is different from the one based on the scientific objectivism. I have no objection to deny the vision-centralism, but is it really the ideal style that erases the author's voice by the various voices studded in ethnography?

This idealism and compulsoriness mentioned above are related each other. On this point, I cannot follow their way anymore. As mentioned later, my central concept of the reformation of anthropology is for anthropologists who live limited lives as members of this society, and who develop their own *problématique* and search for the "truth" valid to their own *problématique*. As far as this sense concerned, the valid "truth" can be presented as "the contingent whole truth". Self will not be erased but utilized in this style of anthropology. In my opinion also, ethnography will still continue to be written. However, it occurs because Self incessantly renews the *problématique*, not because endlessly driven by the hunger for "the whole truth". When the author signs his/her name on the text (I am writing in a contradictory way on purpose), the text will be open to conversations grounded on the "singularity" in Karatani's sense. Self, in this context, is an antenna sensing and sending the *problématique*. It is the existence of antenna that opens up the communications.[6]

These are the reasons why I, with Clifford and the others, criticize the Orientalistic "identity politics", and later, part with them. I know we can't thoughtlessly do anthropological research anymore, but what I hope is to properly and productively accept the critiques of anthropology, not having excessive obsession about them. This is my motive to write this chapter.

Therefore, even if I am criticized as too simple, and even after I heard many criticisms of anthropology, I believe that fieldwork, the central method of thinking based on the individual "facts" (that are a pile of phenomena separated from the primary seamless reality and grasped by fieldworkers with their own *problématique*) collected from the fields, is still important (Clifford also admits that). To keep the field-oriented attitude, or to learn from "certain real world" on its concrete phases, will have been a basic method not only of anthropology but also of other social sciences. The quality of the "facts" grasped out of fields wholly depends on the *problématique* (it is conditioned by dominant paradigms though) of the individual researcher. The way of writing ethnography alone should not be discussed, being separated from the whole process of writing culture. It is the *problématique* of the writer that shall be firstly centered in the discussion. There, researcher's individuality meets the real field and then, something comes out of "the world as it is". It is not sufficient to name the something revealed "partial truth". What the "facts" tell based on certain *problématique* is sufficiently proper to be called "the contingent whole truth". As mentioned above, this is where I break away from *Writing Culture*. In short, even if ethnography seems nearer to fiction than science, not everything becomes just relative. It is an important point that ethnographers write ethnographies moved by the otherness of the "facts" grasped by Self's *problématique* (in phenomenological terms, it is a problem of intentionality, or the problem of noesis/noema. Self, which is shaped by others, is not a simple world of subjectivity). It is an unreliable assertion that general objective-positivism is valid anywhere and anytime, but I argue that the valid positivism backed with the individual *problématique* is reliable.

In this sense, the easy generalization such as "anthropology is…" or "Japanese anthropology is …" should be avoided. Too much use of such general nominatives will only contribute to set argument into the ideologically closed logic of "the world as it should be". It is important to go forward keeping the good balance of general nominatives and individual nominatives on a basis of "the world as it is". It is practice of researchers who are put in the ever-changing "real world" (or researchers as living humans who are conditioned in the social situation of the times) that create contingent ethnographies. Each of them keeps questioning his/her *problématique*, and the process consequently takes the form of ethnography. In this sense, there cannot be a fixed format to write ethnography.

The discussion on the Orientalistic problem of ethnography writing goes nowhere when it is discussed only within the narrow sense of representation or description. At best, it only can reach the halfway resolution such as the experimental ethnography (to give positions to the objects for speech and diminish the authorship within the ethnographical description). It can't provide essential solution and will just make writing difficult (or impossible) by increasing the compulsion to write. On coming to this dead-end, raising this problem itself is turned out to be fruitless. We should think this is a result of the wrong way of questioning. As we have seen above, we should realize where the true problem is before exploring a limited problem of questioning the methodology of writing of ethnography. That is, the attitude or *problématique* to the object comes first as the important point, and then, appears the problem of ethnography writing as the next step. What we should discuss is this whole process of representation in a broad sense, and we should fight against the Orientalistic mechanism in every phase of this process.

On the Problem of Orientalistic Representation as Structural Discrimination: A Direction of Anthropological Practice

The problem of Orientalistic representation is only a part of more general problem of representation. To represent others could be a violent and oppressive deed even when those who represent and the represented are on an equal footing. On such a basic level, the problem of representation has higher generality, which is not left only for the privileged writers such like anthropologists. But here I insist that it is very important to clearly separate "the problem of Orientalistic representation" and "the problem of representation under the equal relationship". It is theoretically important to be aware of the difference.

The difference will be recognized as what exists between "the triangular relationship" composing the hierarchical social relationships and "the dual-confronting relationship" found in the face-to-face relationships. Representation, in the first place, has a violent and suppressive nature. However, especially in the triangular relationship, the way to represent is structurally decided and the representations already have socially persuasive power as stereotypes. Even the represented themselves have already been trapped in such stereotypes, they will not be able to recognize exactly against whom they should fight. This will be explained concretely in the later argument on the discrimination against Untouchables. At the outset, the monopolistic (self-righteous) characteristic of representations generated in the triangular relationship under the Orientalistic condition will be pointed out here.

Orientalism is not the simple way of dichotomous recognition of the vertical social relationship between the superior Occident and the inferior Orient. It is more importantly noted that Orientalism is an ideology of "the politics of identity", which contains the structure to reconstruct the same inclination. That is the structure to constantly reproduce the triangular relationship among (1) the Occident as those who discriminate, (2) "the good Orient (the Orient assimilated)" as the accomplice, and (3) "the bad Orient (the alienated Orient)" as the discriminated.

How is it possible? Because of the intervention of the accomplice, the Occident as those who discriminate can produce the discourse of self-justification at will, and stabilize the monopoly system of knowledge as "those who know". "The Tempest", by Shakespeare, is a well-known allegory which is often quoted to explain the nature of the Orientalism as a colonial discourse. Caliban, the monster, who learned language from Prospero, the white magician, being contrary to Prospero's expectations, rises against him. Ohashi Yoichi call our attention to the fact that Orientalism, as the monopoly system of knowledge, has a tough logic which can utilize even the series of apparent failures in taming the primitive, uncivilized, and ungrateful Orient for testifying the superiority of the Occident. (The Occident already "knows" the betrayal of the Orient!). Ohashi also illustrates the mechanism that a woman (wife) in a primitive society, who was rescued from a savage man (husband) and civilized by a white master as her merciful father, works to civilize her own son in that society. Even if the son, who is seen as the grand son of the white master, rises against the white master, the grand son can be said as a fruit of the Occidental civilization. In this way, the Orientalism succeeds in taking even such the ungrateful Orient into its discourse. This closed and enduring circuit of discourse is grounded on the triangular relationship, which can be formed thanks to the existence of "the good Orient" (such as the woman who are rescued by the white master, or the native elite who are civilized as an honorary White) as the accomplice.

Compared to this, the dual-confronting relationship naturally leads to the direct negotiation between the two, even though the two are the powerful and the powerless. This means that those who discriminate could be talked back by the discriminated since the latter could identify the former who utter such discriminative representations. The logic is this. Lacking the accomplice, those who discriminate cannot stably press the one-sided representations to the others. In other words, those who discriminate cannot ensure the superiority in the relationship without making ceaseless efforts to create it. Thus, the dual-confronting relationship, which is opened to the negotiable transaction between the parties concerned, must hold the potential locus in which self-innovation or self-transformation could take place.

As mentioned above, we have surveyed the representational difference between the dual-confronting relationship and the triangular relationship. The difference obviously shows the theoretic potential of the dual-confronting relationship to break up the representational closed-ness and the one-sided discrimination seen in the triangular relationship. Therefore, we should carefully examine the relationship between these two mechanisms. To say in advance, the link between them is inevitable. Because the communally closed system produced from the triangular relationship inevitably ends at its fringe. On the fringe, the closed system has to directly sense its outside, and inevitably start the dual-confronting relationship between the known inside and the unknown outside. There, the suppressive power of the triangular relationship doesn't work anymore. Therefore, there is logical possibility to suppose that it is strategically important to be aware of the limits of such system in order to get a key to the disorganization of it.

Nevertheless, our actual feeling tells something reverse. We don't get violent impression from the triangular mechanism of representation that produces the serious social discrimination in reality. This happens because the socially dominant perspective has already obtained the authority of the truth as if it embodied the neutral sense of values. On the other hand, the violent impression of the dual-confronting relationship is easily sensed because its representations are subjective, naked and direct. As a matter of fact, however, it is rather healthier all the more for the easiness of sensing. This means that even the same discriminative representations produce different impressions between the dual-confronting relationship and the triangular one. Paradoxically, they could be more natural and less violent, when they are used in the structure of the triangular relationship. The discriminated become, therefore, the constant victims whose cry for help is not easily heard. Anthropology, which tends to treat of the social cultural level united with the triangular relationship of the society concerned, also failed to relativize the violent force of dominant representations which has already become natural within the object society. Thus, even the stereotyped representations of discrimination are easily overlooked just because they are produced in the triangular relationship of those who discriminate, the accomplice and the discriminated, not in the dual-confronting relationship of those who discriminate and the discriminated.

Following the Alfred Schutz's way of classification of others in social world, this is the situation where the discourse on the level of generalized "contemporaries" has primacy and where the face-to-face relationship of "consociates" based on the communal space sharing goes backward. Schutz says, there, a mechanism works to produce the stereotyped representations of both of others and selves [Schutz, 1982: 15–18]. In this situation, it is difficult to specify the offender and the victim because the sender or producer of discriminative representations is the part of the community as the reproductive structure. It is neither easy to declare for or against, nor to blame someone. Lacking the imagination for the relationship of "consociates", even the rare response tends to be made in the name of the collective and obscure social unit.

Kurihara Akira illustrates this situation with a remarkable case. He focused on "the Minamata Tokyo Exhibition" held in an empty lot in Shinagawa, in autumn 1996, and noticed the significance of specifying every Minamata victim on the portrait as the individual with the name and character such as "the best master of catching octopuses in Minamata" [Kurihara, 2000: 6]. There, the individuality and the face of every victim of Minamata disease, who had been only represented as "patients" collectively even by the supporters, were revealed and recovered. At that place, people "experienced to realize that the mere representation of 'patients' is incapable of describing every patient's rich existence" [ibid.: 7]. However, the sensitive view like this will be often ruined unknowingly.[7] This fact itself suggests the difficulty of relativizing the structural discrimination based on the triangular relationship.

Discrimination in the society with the triangular relationship model easily escapes and delays people's reflection, because there is a distance or a discontinuity between the actual feeling on the individual level and the ideology on the social level. This difficulty also affects the work of anthropologists. We should do the anthropological practice with great care to find out the mechanism of the Orientalistic representation.

Under the structural discrimination, it is very difficult for individuals to find out the way of voicing their resistance by themselves. Most of the individuals will remain silent with unsatisfied feeling in their minds. Orientalism, or the ideology (discriminative structure) working on the social (world system) level, will be mentionable by the individuals only after when the whole society is ready for self-examination. That is true not only for the ordinary people but also for anthropologists. It was not until the trend of the criticism of Orientalism symbolized by Edward Said rose worldly that many anthropologists began to participate in this renewed discussion on the newly opened field. I know that I myself am the one of them. At least, I want to relativize myself as that I am reflecting within the newly appearing potential of finding out the discourse to analyse and resist the structural discrimination of Orientalism (since this is also important to avoid the easy mix-up between the reflection of the modern West and that of the modern Japan). In any case, anthropology seems to finally start the work to find out the words to resist the structural discrimination, after the long delay. Each Anthropologist should make efforts to clearly describe the way of resistance, being concerned with his/her own field.

The ultimate end of such studies is, by the practice of resistance against the structural representation within the academic arena of anthropology (or the critique and reformation of improper theories on representation), to enforce the trend of getting-over Orientalism as a whole society. The true goal of the attempt to overcome the crisis of anthropology is not the salvation of anthropology, but to start a paradigm shift in the whole society by socially establishing the new thinking attitude developed by the attempt of overcoming the crisis. In the various arenas constituting the whole society, the attempts at innovating have started. Various activities resonate with each other, by using the power of analogies and metaphors, and seek the possibility to set interactions forward. When these activities reach a critical point, a surge of innovation will rise up. For that purpose, we need to look for the logic of resistance and also the space where analogies can be productively discovered.

I will briefly sum up the following argument in advance. The overcoming practice argued here becomes possible by switching the stance from the cross-cultural study (the representation of "the described culture") to the understanding towards otherness (the representation of "the lived culture"). This is an attempt to find out the dual-confronting relationship at the fringe of the dominant structure of the triangular relationship (the ideology of "the world as it should be"). This is a search for the existence of "the lived culture" that is set up in "the world as it is" with the help of the openness (liberated-ness) and the creativity of the new representations. I myself call such project to renew the improper representations into the "accurate representations" (the "good representations" in my word) the " 'common-ground' anthropology". Here I demonstrate this attempt by taking up the case of discrimination against Untouchables in Indian society.

From the Cross-Cultural Study to the Understanding Towards Otherness

To the Depth of Culture, or to the Fringe of Culture

By discussing the discrimination against Untouchables as the concrete example, the link between "what to be represented", or the decision of the target of representation, and "how represent it", or the content of the representation, will be revealed. The *problématique* of the researcher penetrates both the target and the content. The researcher, therefore, should examine the target and the content of the representation altogether.

Let's think one by one. Generally speaking, the anthropologist takes another culture as the target of representation. However, it is not easy to decide what another culture really is. I am a social anthropologist or, if possible, simply an anthropologist in my own conceit, but it doesnot make me free of the notion of culture. (I never mean to banish the notion of culture). Culture is a mysterious notion that seems to exist in reality but easily slip away when we try to grasp. Culture is generally thought as a principle constructing formula that is commonly and uniquely kept in a specific society (if it could be specified). But when it comes to be taken out as a pattern, no one is sure to tell if it really is unique to the society concerned. Even if we leave the difficult problem of the correspondence between culture and society to one side, deciding the range of specific culture itself becomes out of hand. The butterfly-collecting-like difficulties still remain unresolved even by using the Wittgenstein's concept of "family resemblance". It is because culture has its own depth that refuses to be placed side by side on one level. The superficial differences sensed at first are invalid, when we get to know the depths.

For example, Yamaguchi Masao has once tried to show the depth by grading the cultural structure of the Japanese post-war anthropologists in three levels [Yamaguchi, 1966: 31]. Firstly, there is the level of "the logic of the civil society where he belongs". Secondly, behind the first level, there is the level of "the small world as a system of interaction between he and his surrounding world". Thirdly, as the whole background, there is the level of "the world where people can have the time of the best fulfillment as a human", in other words, "the world where symbols or myths, arts and religions can be most eloquent". (It should be noted that Abe

Toshiharu has emphasized the significance of the third level of culture by advocating the concept of "hinterland" in his own sense [Abe, 2005]). Yamaguchi also adds that "every culture always has the passage to the (third level) world of its own" (the words in brackets are added by the author). If we can say that the functionalist view of culture corresponds with the second level, Lévi-strauss's concept of culture will be surely related to the third level.[8] In Iwata Keiji's words, it represents the change over from the viewpoint of "pattern" to the viewpoint including both of "pattern" and "ground". There is a big difference in the understanding of culture between the way to see culture as the plane pattern and the way to see it as a world of combination of "pattern" and "ground", taking the cultural depth into account. Iwata shows the latter way as the view of grasping the true life, not the illusion.[9]

People are likely to argue that the West has the culture of sin and Japan has the culture of shame, and that the West has culture of individualism and Japan has the culture of groupism. These contrastive understandings come from the representations on the level of the generalized "pattern" based on the substantial view of culture. We should get ahead of this shallow view and make the comparison taking the depth of culture into account. This attempt will inevitably make us search for the viewpoint where the "pattern" lands on the "ground". This viewpoint is, in other words, to see the world from its boundary and not to forget the moment of restriction in the sense of structuralism. It is to think from the place of "singularity" in Karatani Kojin's terminology. For example, the groupistic culture is established by restricting the individualism in the public space. The individualistic culture originates from the restriction of groupism. Like this, to get outside of the "pattern" and to get into the point of touching the "ground", we need to clearly see the world, being aware of the dynamics in the beginning point of emerging culture. At that deep point, the society still remains unidentified (not yet established) and open to both the individualism and the groupism.

Then, why we have to move to such standpoint? Because the argument to show the difference between cultures on the level of "pattern" as a substantial difference is only to support the dominant cultural order, which is established at the price of restrictions, as "truth". We need to go to the point to touch the "ground" in order to disorganize this dominant discourse and get outside of it. The dominant discourse shows nothing but the "poetics and politics" of cultural representation. It is obvious that the cultural representation of Japanese groupism contrasted with the western individualistic culture is penetrated by the Orientalistic "poetics and politics" to the core. Therefore, if we really need to deconstruct the dominant discourse, the framework of "cross-cultural study" that ultimately misleads us to the cultural substantialism is better to be thrown away. It is because our strategy is to find out the open dual-confronting relationship at the fringe of the dominant system in order to relativize the domination of triangular relationship. The reason why I advocate the change over from the cross-cultural study to the understanding towards otherness is because I want to formulate the shift to the viewpoint having its basis in the cultural depth. It is a change concerned with both the target of representation (from other cultures to otherness) and its content (from triangular relationship to dual-confronting one). It is an attempt of the cultural genealogy, so to speak.

From "The Described Culture" to "The Lived Culture"

As the argument of the "invented tradition" has already clarified, people have been creating culture by putting together anything at hand on the spot in every time and space. This is reality of "the lived culture". Because it is obvious that the elements of culture are crossbred in their origins, people try to emphasize the consistency of the composed culture, all the more for the hybridity (and also in order to conceal the hybridity). This is how the culture to be lived and described. Therefore, it is important to distinguish "the lived culture" from "the described culture" when we discuss culture.

When a culture is described from the essentialistic viewpoint, there are often seen the conservative tendencies in the way of emphasizing its purity and uniqueness. On the other hand, the lived culture is a concept to grasp the present culture that is always dynamically innovated, and that has the hybridity and receptiveness of outer things. We can say that "the described culture" has a vector of centralization (discourse of the dominant) or a vector of counter-centralization (the resisting discourse of the dominated), and that "the lived culture" has the vector of de-centralization. If we say that the former two have stayed within the "identity politics" of the triangular relationship (it is established at the price of the third discriminated), we can also say that the latter will get out of such "identity politics", with the help of the inclination to hybridity and pluralism, by practicing the dual-confronting relationship. Because the closed "identity politics", such as Orientalism, has created the structural discriminations, our aim, as anthropologists, is to represent "the lived culture" without letting it be taken back to "the described culture". It is a restitution of the dual-confronting relationship, so to speak, standing on the place called "fringe" of the system of the triangular relationship, or on such possible "boundary" emerging there in-between inside and outside.

By posing this theme, I intend to make a change towards the creativity of representation, controlling the violence of representation. It is to treat others delicately like treating ourselves, and to stop utilizing them as materials or victims for establishing our identity. This is the motive of posing the question of "can't we speak about others as if about ourselves?" To focus on the dual-confronting relationship or interactions with outsideness or otherness at the fringe of the social order means to undermine the centripetal power of the dominant culture, in resisting the identifying power of the culture. It will also lead us to break away with the monolithic cultural substantialism.

On this intention, I propose adopting the words "understanding towards otherness", which can directly mention the open dual-confronting relationship, and disposing the words "*cross-cultural study*". The latter, in which an other culture is seen as the different from the *"transcendent"* viewpoint, is too coarse in grasping the object correctly. It is a way to the pitfall of cultural relativism. Our destination is the emerging point of culture filled with generating dynamism. This is where we can encounter the unknown otherness. Therefore, adopting the word "otherness" also means to deal with the opening event of the transition from nature to culture, with the attitude of *"transcendental* recognition" depending on the subjective perspective towards the unknown object (the otherness).

The attitude of the *"transcendental* recognition", which is aware of the possibility of the other viewpoint different from what temporary we take, can bring the innovation of self understanding through the process of the development of the understanding towards otherness. The discovery of otherness will correspond with the discovery of self-ness. To emphasize the nuance of this self-innovation, I will adopt the word "understanding", distinguishing it from "study" that has the nuance of the *"transcendent"* recognition about otherness made from the fixed point of self. This distinction is made to emphasize, in using the "understanding", the attitude of acceptance of otherness with the effort of self-innovation to "understand in the bodily thought and experience" (the words of Tsurumi Yoshiyuki introduced in [Sakiyama, 1999: 220]).

To Disorganize the Theory Particularizing India: The Discrimination against Untouchables cannot be Reduced to the Caste Discrimination

"The Described India" and "The Lived India"

I have made anthropological research in India as the main field since 1985. Naturally, I cannot be indifferent to the politics of representation about India. We, the contemporary Japanese, have the image of India that was basically formed in the mainstream thought of *Datsu-a nyu-ou* (following the West and getting out of Asia) in the Meiji period, and then it had been strengthened and distorted during the post-war era of the high economic growth. Although there still is a basic image of Buddhist country [Yamazaki/Takahashi, 1993], the logic of Orientalism and civil society introduced from the West surpasses it in influence. That is, Japanese journalism repeatedly conveys the gloomy keywords such as caste, religion, poverty and discrimination by veiling them with the mysterious and eternal atmosphere (for example [Oshikawa, 1994]). (There is a sign of change under the influence of the rapid economic growth led by the IT industry after 2000 though.)

The very fact that the Ministry of Tourism of India itself uses the catch phrase of "Eternal India" shows today's complicated situation. This is an obvious example that shows the politics of representation has already been "naturalized" and "transparent" in today's post-colonial India. The representations of India, which are naturalized to make India the object of "the mission of civilization" in the colonial era and the object of the selvation and aid in the present post-colonial day, has been penetrating. (I am curious how the new sense of "Incredible India" in rapid economic growth will change the representations of India). At least, up until now, India was yearned only when it acted the subordinate role, in the image, to supplement the faults of the rationalism of the modern civilization. I must point out that anthropologists have deeply contributed to establish such situation of representation. Shortly, the representations of the public view of Indian society, which were produced by the British colonial government in the dialectic of the modern rationalism and Orientalism, were reused by the post-war anthropology mainly in the UK and France. Then, in due course, they were reinforced and settled.[10]

My experience in India [Sekine, 1995a] made me notice the gap between "the described India" and "the lived India". The social structure and the human relationship in India do not always work centering on the caste system. When we notice the importance of the kinship [Raheja, 1988] and the connection between the kinship and the sub-caste [Kolenda, 1978], we can clearly understand the image of "Caste India" is a rough and inaccurate representation. For example, Dumont describes the image of "Religious India" arguing that the pure-impure principle penetrates the society, where the religion overwhelms the secular world under the authority of Brahmans. However, my actual feeling tells that it is a one-sided view failed to describe the reality of the Indian villages, the majority of which are non-Brahman villages [Quigley, 1993]. Of course, the secularization is going on in some phases of modernizing India, but it is not necessarily true that the secularization extinguishes the religion [Sekine, 1995b, 1998c, 1999a, 2000a] [Sekine, 1999]. The dichotomous view of religious and secular doesn't correspond with the reality at all, and the connection between them should be questioned at first. The image of "Discriminative India" is also be utilized to make people believe that India is particularly discriminative society. It is based on the inaccurate recognition that the discrimination both in the status (caste) and in the class (poverty) is influential in the suppressive society, and this recognition is produced from the thoughtless but dominant view of those who represent. This is how the representations of "the described India" essentialize the biased image of Indian society both consciously and unconsciously.

Anthropologists should not ignore the influence of these distorted representations that even cuts into the arena of anthropology. We should firmly set the target of our practice at searching for the representations to describe "the lived India". Here, in the limited space, I will focus on, out of the many representational problems of "Discriminative India", the argument about representations of the caste discrimination and the discrimination against "Untouchables" (in order to correct the inaccurate representations). In the course of the argument, the viewpoint noted as "the depth of culture" will show the deep relationship with it.

The Caste Discrimination and the Discrimination against "Untouchables"

What I want to clarify here is the necessity of distinguishing the caste discrimination from the discrimination against "Untouchables". This necessity is not fully recognized even among the expert researchers of Indian society, and this fact might show the blinded spot of the area studies that are indifferent to the human study. The reason why I insist the necessity of this distinction is just because it can deconstruct the representations establishing the image of particularized Indian society. To represent the other society specifying as "a mysterious society" is almost a renunciation of thinking. No one can say that India is particularly discriminative society in comparison with Japan. India has its own principle of equality just like any other societies ([Parry, 1974] for example). I want to open up the place where we can have such sober views. In order to do this, we must get out of the framework of "the cross-cultural study". It is indispensable for this quest to see the individual faces in the various social positions, especially the views of those who are sent to the fringe of the society by the suppressive centripetal thought. We don't need the views of the society in general or the culture in general any more. This is the reason why I use the word "understanding towards otherness", as I have mentioned, to focus on the de-centripetal thought.

It is true that the caste discrimination and the discrimination against "Untouchables" are related each other in some aspects, but it will make the reality of discrimination invisible to subsume the discrimination against "Untouchables" into the caste discrimination (as the worst part of it), and then we will lose the way to get out of the discourse of the particularized India. In order to clarify the reality of the discrimination, the both need to be clearly distinguished and, then, properly analysed the relationship between them. In short, the caste discrimination is the relative discrimination against others as the lower caste within the system, and the discrimination against "Untouchables" is the absolute one against others who stand at the fringe of the system. When we clearly recognize the triangular relationship in this discrimination, we will understand the difference between the caste discrimination and the discrimination against Untouchables, even if these phenomena are mentioned by the same term, discrimination. This argument relies on the discovery, in the notion of pollution, of the distinction between the relative "impurity" and the absolute "pollution" concluded from my own ethnographic research in an Indian village.[11]

"Impurity" and "Pollution"

Pollution is a notion that has been used when people senses something outside in the subjective perspective. Mary Douglas defines pollution (impurity, dirt or defilement) as the border situation in-between things by saying "matter out of place", but this definition is not sufficient. The border must be the one between inside and outside, in other word, the boundary.[12] This means that the essential point of the notion "pollution" is "menace of death". The inside fears to be decayed by the unknown outside. However, it is also a moment for self-innovation. The utterances and acts of the villagers attest this. When the villagers face something polluted, they show two contrastive attitudes; one is exclusion, and the other is acceptance. This is why I choose the analytic terms "impurity" and "pollution" to exhibit their comprehension of pollution that includes these both attitudes. On one hand, "impurity" is a relative concept (centripetal concept) placed in the inferior pole of the dichotomous relationship contrasted with "purity". On the other hand, "pollution" is an independent concept (de-centripetal concept), which connotes the logic of innovation by accepting the symbolic death and regenerating out of it. They are completely different in the way dealing with the outside that generates "the menace of death". "Impurity" tries to forcibly tame "the menace of death", and "pollution" tries to creatively convert "the menace of death", the way of the latter seems somewhat passive though.

The folk terminologies for pollution mainly used in Tamil society are *tīṭṭu* and *acuttam*. *Tīṭṭu* is an original Tamil word and has no antonym. *Acuttam* has its origin in the word *aśuddha*, the Sanskrit word, and constitutes an antonymous pair with *cuttam* (*śuddha* in Sanskrit) that means purity. *Tīṭṭu* and *acuttam* are sometimes compatible and sometimes distinctive. Caste Hindus assume that the birth, menarche/menstruation, death and Untouchables are *tīṭṭu*. Spits, fallen hairs, cut nails and spilt sperm are also *tīṭṭu* in their recognition. These things and phenomena can be also expressed as *acuttam,* and these two words are compatible and used at the same time. However, there is an object that can only be mentioned as *acuttam*, never *tīṭṭu*. The dominant caste in the village takes Untouchables as *tīṭṭu*, but never mentions the lower castes as *tīṭṭu*. In their words, the lower castes are only *acuttam* relatively. This distinction is shown not only in words. Between the higher castes and the lower castes, we can't observe the decisive discrimination in the every day life. They share the living space and live side-by-side except the restrictions of inter-marriages and to dine together. Both live in the same world of the Caste Hindus. If seen from the longer perspective of several generations, there are some cases, like Nadar caste, the lower caste almost near to Untouchables, could go up to the middle caste and more or less overcame even the restrictions of inter-marriage and to dine together by utilizing the economic power, academic career, and social position [Hardgrave, 1969]. Compared to this, the dividing line between the Caste Hindus and *tīṭṭu* "Untouchables" is striking. "Untouchables" cannot share the living place, well and graveyard with other villagers (Caste Hindus) and cannot get into the precinct of the village temple. It is uneasy for "Untouchables" to go into the house of the Caste Hindus freely. The decrease of direct and violent deeds of discrimination by the higher castes doesn't mean the discriminative mind to thin down. Rather, the discrimination has been structurally established and naturalized.[13]

The Lower Castes and "Untouchables"

Then, what is the difference between the lower castes and "Untouchables"? That is whether they play the role of "the boundary marker" of the village order or not. The essence of the concept of *tīṭṭu* is to be on-boundary (the outside-ness or the other world-ness in insiders' view) always adjoining the outside. It holds the de-centripetal vector to keep the position remaining unidentified and undecided on the boundary, and I name the vector the "pollution" ideology. That lies in the core of the word *tīṭṭu*. Only "the boundary marker" can shoulder the task to be *tīṭṭu*. The lower castes that have become the inside other can be *acuttam* but can't be *tīṭṭu*. They are already assimilated to play the role of inferior pole of the dichotomous "pure-impure" ideology that establishes the order of the village society. They are discriminated as the lower castes in a relative way, but never discriminated as "Untouchables".

There is one thing to be noted. That is, the dominant caste people sometimes mention "Untouchables" not only as *tīṭṭu*, but also as "very *acuttam*", overlapping the usage of words. This is a deed to send Untouchables to the double-bind situation by using the dominant "pure-impure" ideology. "Untouchables" are placed on the boundary as *tīṭṭu* on one hand, and re-placed at the bottom of the inside order as the worst *acuttam*, being deprived of their last weapon of the outside-ness, on the other hand. By using both the absolute discrimination and the relative discrimination, it creates the fictional double-bind situation.

As a result, "Untouchables" are, on surface, represented as the discriminated like the lower castes, although they are, in reality, discriminated in the absolute way as the boundary marker. Many anthropologists and researchers of the area or the society of India also, unfortunately, have repeatedly made a mistake to follow the fictional discourse of the dominant caste, without reflecting on their own perspectives. As long as we fail to discuss the Indian pollution theory from the outside of the Brahman's perspective and also fail to distinguish "impurity" and "pollution", we cannot get the standpoint which enables us to grasp the reality of the discrimination by distinguishing the caste discrimination and the discrimination against Untouchables. When we stay in the rough perspective swallowing the discourse that Indian society is a Brahman-centric Hindus society, we cannot notice such difference, and therefore, we cannot liberate India from the curse of the discourse of Particularized India, lacking the perspective open to the comparison as noted in the next section. The consideration concerned with the otherness is truly needed, by getting out of the rough perspective "described" by the centripetal thought of the cross-cultural study, and by standing on the "lived" reality of those who are placed on the fringe of the centripetal order.

The Structural Discrimination as the Triangular Relationship

The structural discrimination described in the former section has rather high generality. It cannot be restricted to the discourse of particularized India, because we can extract the common formula of the structural discrimination from it, that is, "the discrimination in the triangular relationship". First, I will certify its generality, putting the case of India aside.

Auschwitz, as well known, is a symbol of the cruel and massive violence that the Jewish were suffered from. The violence burned on both body and mind, including Shoah, itself is a wordless grief. In order not to repeat such tragedy, we should not be blinded by the grave result of Shoah, but find out the mechanism of the Nazism (ideology) that brought the tragedy, in the context of the historical situation of Germany. *Dialectic of Enlightenment* (*Dialektik der Aufklarung)* by Max Horkheimer and Theodor Adorno [Horkheimer and Adorno, 1972] is a painstaking work trying to reveal such mechanism by struggling with the negative legacy. According to them, the mechanism is like this. First, the Jewish people were represented as those who contaminate the German blood and as those who bring in the social disorder. Motivated by the ideology of the elimination of the Jewish people, the cruel social mechanism started to justify Shoah. Horkheimer and Adorno analyse this social mechanism like this. The German industrial capitalists, who had grown powerful by actually victimizing the German people, offered the Jewish people as the outlet for the swelling discontent and angst of the German people, lest they themselves became the target. At that time, they utilized the unpopular image of the Jewish who work as financiers in cities and made them up as the socially harmful people. The German people were completely trapped in this trick, and mistook the Jewish, "the villain nearby", as enemies, failing to recognize the true enemy of their lives (the exploiting industrial capitalists). Horkheimer and Adorno called this phenomenon "a false projection" [Horkheimer and Adorno, 1972: 187].

This analysis of the cruel mechanism perfectly illustrates the social discrimination formed from what is mentioned as the triangular relationship in the sociology of discrimination [Sato, 1990]. The three are, in this case, "those who discriminate" (the German industrial capitalists), "the accomplice" (the German people), and "the discriminated" (the Jewish people). The accomplices, who are, in reality, discriminated by those who discriminate as the social rulers, barely escape from being placed on the social fringe by participating in the hegemonic ideology and discrimination against the people of the lower classes or ranks, and try to get the nearer position of the rulers. As a result, they come to play the role of the toady who helps to reproduce the discriminative ideology. The accomplices parrot the discourse of those who discriminate, "the Jews are dirty". When the two out of the three collude, the majorities can safely and steadily exclude the last one out of the community. More precisely, they can place it on the boundary between inside and outside. The former two can steadily identify themselves by repeating the same ideology in the codependent situation (or the community illusion), but the excluded one is permanently left deprived of the self-identification in the miserable situation. (It is sad that structurally the same tragedies take place everyday in school as "bullying".[14])

Anyway, this is the basic model of the social discrimination with the minimum three to form a society. In this model, conflicts tend to take place between the accomplices and the discriminated because the direct practitioners of the discriminative deeds are often the accomplices. Those who truly discriminate can keep their power without getting their hands dirty, as long as the other two, who are discriminated in different ways, fail to find out the true enemy and fight the fruitless fight with each other.

At the same time, the community illusion is created, which absorbs the angst of the people. In this case, the German identity (the Deutsch nationalism) was created as the imagined community by eliminating the Jewish people as the common enemy. The German people, who were isolated each other, felt angst and misfortune between the ideal of freedom and equality, and the reality of restriction and inequality. In order to dissolve such negative energy of angst, they were willingly trapped into participating in the imagined community guided by the dominant ideology of Nazism as the racism. The pureblood German ideology involved the people into the utopian longing to cleanse themselves of the annoying disturbance.

The space of "the discrimination in the triangular relationship", typically illustrated by this case study, one-sidedly drives the discriminated third party into the hopeless situation of "the closed representation" (for example, "the mad" is a representation to utilize such person as the skin of a body of the sane people, to keep them safely inside "the sane" community by isolating and keeping the mad on the boundary), and gain stability and permanence that are typically seen in the social discriminations.[15] This space corresponds with the social space suppressed by the "second violence" in Derrida's classification. There works the dominant ideology, which takes the figure of the social norm (moral) or common sense, as "concealing violence" that socially conceals the violence of discrimination [Derrida, 1976: 112].

Let me go back to the context of the Indian society. As we have seen, the three in this case are; the dominant caste as "those who discriminate", the lower castes as "the accomplices", and "Untouchables" as "the discriminated". In the Indian village society, the dominant caste and the lower castes consist of the same category as Caste Hindus, and expel "Untouchables" alone out to the fringe (accurately, on the boundary of inside and outside). We cannot overlook the important role of the lower castes. The lower castes play the double role; they are relatively discriminated within the same category on one hand, and they discriminate Untouchables, agreeing the dominant ideology on the other hand. This stabilizes the discrimination by the dominant caste. In other words, the lower castes, in order to stay within the Caste Hindus, are involved in the "pure-impure" ideology as "legitimation" that legitimates the authority of the dominant caste, whereas being forced to play the impure part, they practices the very "pure-impure" logic to discriminate Untouchables. The mimetic discriminative practices of the accomplice provides "the validating experience" of the dominant ideology of those who discriminate ("legitimations") and also produces the "plausibility structure" (approval by others) (cf. [Berger and Luckmann, 1971]). This layered relationship of collusion embodies the mechanism of reproduction and establishes the whole structure of discrimination that enables the majority to exclude the discriminated third party constantly and one-sidedly. This is the skeleton of the structural discrimination of the stratified society.

In comparison with this, the discrimination in the dual-confronting relationship is partial. Even if the one is discriminative and the other is discriminated, the relationship is always shaky unless the one who discriminate directly presses such relationship in every occasion. This means the one who discriminate is likely to have a fear against the discriminated in the case of partial discrimination. As we will see below in the cases of social discriminations in many parts of the world, the fear for the discriminated seen at the beginning seems, as the common historical development, to be diminished as the modern period is drawing near. That is to say, the shift from the partial discrimination to the entire discrimination has taken place during the course of the time. What is more, the entireness takes on the stronger closed-ness as it getting near to the modern period.[16]

In any case, if the distinction and the relationship of the caste discrimination and the discrimination against "Untouchables" are explained by the general logic, as shown above, the theory particularizing India will lose its foundation and get disorganized.

The Perspective from the Indian History

To make the disorganization of the theory particularizing India more persuasive, I will review the Indian history briefly. For this purpose, I will revise and quote a part of my book review on *Fukashoku-senmin to Kasuto Seido no Rekisi* (that means; *the History of Untouchables and the Caste System)* [Kotani, 1996] written by Kotani Hiroyuki, the expert of the modern and medieval history of India.

> We can verify at least two epochs on the history of the castes and Untouchables. The first one is the formation of the village community (with the settlement of "Untouchables" in the village) that had the system of the division of labor by castes (*Watan* system), and it seemingly developed from the 7th century to the 12th century. In the previous Gupta period, it was not common for the people to be conscious of the *varṇa* classification *(Brahman, Kṣatriya, Vaiśya* and *Śūdra*), and it was only a ruling idea among *Brāhman.* After this change, however, the system described as *varṇa-jati* system came into existence. In that system, the division of labor in the local society, the endogamous unit called *jati* and the ideal social classification called *varṇa* were combined. (There seems to leave room for the more argument how far the framework of *varṇa* was prevailed in reality though). Kotani states the *varṇa-jati* system had developed as the five *varṇa* system, that is, the four *varṇa* plus "Untouchables". The description on this process is interesting also for me as an anthropologist, because it allows us to understand that the

> ascent movement in *varṇa* was motivated by the self-assertion with the rivalry sense against *Brāhman*, not by the mimetic longing for the *Brāhman* culture. It is remarkable that Kotani brings many examples of the *jati*, who belonged to *Śūdra*, claimed for *Kṣatriya varṇa* against *Brāhman*. It is obvious that their purpose of this ascent is to break through the conceptual discrimination between *Śūdra*, the *ekaja,* who are deemed as the once-born and *Kṣatriya,* the *dvija,* who are as the twice-born. I myself understand that these facts shows there was structural potential for such struggle in the society, and that its concrete outcome was what Kotani calls the five *varṇa* system. If my interpretation is correct, "Untouchables" took over the social role as the boundary marker of the *Śūdra*, the *ekaja*, in course of the formation of "Untouchables" class as the fifth *varṇa*. The role as the boundary marker is, as mentioned repeatedly, to show the limits of the social order with the boundary-ness, placed inside and opened outside at the same time. *Śūdra*, the *ekaja*, was once placed on the boundary in the four *varṇa* system, but they were completely integrated as the Caste Hindus in the five *varṇa* system, then "Untouchables" were to be placed on the boundary instead. Stimulated by Kotani's description, I logically deduce that this change made it possible for *Śūdra* to go up in *varṇa* system. [Sekine, 1998a: 101]

In this long quotation, I suppose the readers can understand the historical process of the formation of the triangular relationship among (1) the upper three *varṇa*, (2) *Śūdra* as *ekaja*, and (3) "Untouchables". It is obvious that the role of the boundary marker of the social order was taken over from *Śūdra* to "Untouchables". The fact that we can hypothesize the existence of logical generality in the particular history of the social discrimination in India shows that this historical phenomenon in India has the social logics of higher universality, and it reduces the necessity of the theory particularizing India.

To make our viewpoint clearer, I must additionally point out the inaccuracy in this analysis of mentioning Untouchables as the fifth *varṇa,* because it blurs the distinction between the caste discrimination and the discrimination against "Untouchables". We are trying to disorganize the problem representation that "tends to subsume the discrimination against 'Untouchables' into the caste discrimination". However, in reality, this representation had become more naturalized in the second epoch, the reintroduction of the four *varṇa* system in the Indian society. To make it sure, I again make quotation from the book review.

> The second epoch was caused by the power structure of the colonialism. In the process of introducing the modern state system, the British colonial government reintroduced the four *varṇa* system as the ruling concept of the ancient India (1830's, "Hindu law" approved), imposing it on the real situation of the five *varṇa* system. Under this situation of "further castization" [Kotani, 1996: 126] by the colonial rule, the concepts of *dvija* and *ekaja* reintroduced, that had not been significant in the medieval. Kotani points out that this stimulated the ascent tendency in the *varṇa* system and made it escalate without brakes. (This is the outset of the phenomenon that M.N. Srinivas described as "Sanskritization" later). At the same time, the double structure came into existence, which, on one hand, tended to integrate "Untouchables" into *Śūdra* on the law level by introducing the four *varṇa* system, and on the other hand, tended to maintain the discrimination against "Untouchables" on the level of the real conventional world. This

is a new stage of "concealing violence". Adding to this, the modern consciousness for the civil rights started prevailing. We may read between the lines that the ascent movement both in caste and in *varṇa* took on the more complicated matters in such mingling situations. [Sekine, 1998a: 102]

Since the situation of Indian society after the colonial rule is complicated to such a degree, we must adopt more precise and analytic framework, anatomize and disorganize the deception of representation.

The Perspective from the World History

Now, we need to broaden our horizons and survey the contemporary cases in the world history scale in order to relativize the theory particularizing India.

"When we notice that it is about the 10th century that the five *varṇa* system, with 'Untouchables' as the lowest, had established, and that it is also the same period that the discriminated classes were formed in many parts in the world simultaneously, we should know the limitation of the deduction on 'Untouchables' system as a particular case produced from the caste system" [Sekine, 1995a: 5–6]. "It is important to distinguish the particularity of the local phenomena and the universality of the developing paradigm of the world history, but we still be aware of the link between these two" [Sekine, 1998a: 101].

In other occasion, Kotani indicates that the village communities were formed in the course of the development of the social relationship which is mentioned as the Indian Medieval, since the 7th century AD and that, as the result of it, the system of Untouchables were formed about the 10th century. However, Kotani also points out that the ambiguous discrimination against Untouchables during the medieval turned into the one-sided discrimination as the modern times was drawing near [Kotani, 2003: 7–303]. This change, in my words, could be described as the change from "pollution" to "impurity" in the view to Untouchables, and also corresponds with the change from the partial discrimination to the entire discrimination.

In Japan too, it is after the 10th century that the notion of pollution started developing in the ruling class and that the *Hinin* group (so-called *Kiyome-no–Hinin*, those who are deemed to hold special abilities of purifying things) was formed. However, the *Hinin* group had started to lose their originally attributed magical power and authority since around the 14th century, then become the object of simple rejection, and finally, the discrimination against them took root [Amino, 1989: B-349]. In the Korean peninsula, the *Yi* dynasty started in the 13th century had established the feudal system by the first half of the 15th century, and it produced the steadily discriminated class called *Baekjeong* [Inoue, 1992]. The discrimination against the Kago among the Basque in the north of the Iberian Peninsula also appeared in the record of the latter half of the 13th century [Ishihara, 1989: B-328]. The Roma, appeared at the beginning of the 15th century in Europe, immediately became the target of suppression, and they are thought to have been obviously discriminated in the 16th century [Ogawa, 1992].

This is not the sufficient demonstration, but it is possible, in high probability, to deduct that the social discriminations, in general, start systematically in the medieval societies and become stabilized by the modern period. Besides, this deduction is also supported by the study made by Miki Wataru on the ecological world history mainly dealing with the Islamic social history. In his accomplishment, he points out the shift from the horizontal development to the vertical development of the civilizations that happened following to the Mongolian conquest during the 11th century to the 13th century. On this critical point, I will note a longer quotation in order to avoid our misunderstanding it.

> This big change on the Old Continent, which started in the 11th century and resulted in the Mongolian conquest, ...has consequently closed the world. Almost all the parts of the Old Continent have been covered with some civilizations. ...The uncultivated frontier, which used to be the generating area of the new civilization energy, has disappeared and the boundary groups generated in-between the different civilizations have started to play the role of the creator of a new civilization. It surely was a start of the new stage of the world history. ...Before that stage started, a new civilization used to form itself by creating the system to integrate the new part of the uncultivated into the preceding civilization. However, after that stage started, there was no more room for such horizontal development. Then, started the new process that the existing universal civilizations precipitated and deposited, so to speak, and changed into something mentioned as the indigenous civilizations. ...However, the world religions that had been normalized and documented with their own universal logics have survived this big change, rather activated by means of their popularization, and even spread over. Kamakura Buddhism in the Japanese archipelago, New Confucianism of *Zhuzi* and *Wang Yangming* in China, *Bhakti* cult in India, Sufism in Islamic area and the mysticism movement in Christian area are the examples. Each of them succeeded in connecting itself to the broad popular movement by reinterpreting the existing text and survived. In this case, the public itself could be said as the new boundary groups. In contrast with the horizontal development of civilization in previous times, this is the vertical development of civilization so to speak. That is the process of thickening of human relationship within the social space [Miki, 1998: 37–39].

I will point out one more parallel phenomenon. Talal Asad shows this in the argument about the change of the manner of reaching the truth in the Medieval Christian world. In his words, "the practices of defining the truth" has changed. We can grasp it as the shift from the "ordeal", which is done by appealing to the supernatural (the outside), to the "torture as a technique belonging to inquisitorial procedure" (the way of deciding the truth depending only on human ability). It was the sign of the trend towards the rational development of European law, and according to Asad, this decisive change happened also in the 12th century [Asad, 1993: 83–87].

What I try to say is that the spot of the fringe of civilization has moved from the outside of the system to the inside of it. I suppose the historical facts of the shift from the medieval discrimination to the modern discrimination in many areas mentioned before were the outcomes of the local development of this big change. When a civilization lose its outside, it starts to produce the inner others and to classify people (or differentiate people into the superior ruling elite and the inferior mass). Because there is no more room for the civilization to expand outside, the civilization cannot help hardening the walls of boundary in order to maintain the system of civilization from within. The fringe of the system is not the "boundary confronting the outside" anymore, but has changed into "periphery inside the system". This could be the outset of the societies with the discriminative structure of the triangular relationship that guarantees its spontaneous reproduction. If the system has its outside, the fringe of the civilization can create something new by taking the outside in. This is what I call the situation to live with "pollution" or to live in the dual-confronting relationship (the partiality). But if the system loses its outside, it cannot mix with the outside and is suffocated in the enclosed world with high walls of "impurity". The walls are naturally loaded with the pressure of the entire discrimination.

According to the Miki's historical view of "primitive-civilization-savagery", so called the modern world is the end of "civilization" stage and the beginning of "savagery" stage under the hegemony of the modern West. The Miki's theory suggests that the social discrimination of the modern India reorganized after the British colonial rule is also a development of the modern structure of the entire discrimination classified in "savagery".

Although still leaving many insufficient points in the argumentation, it may not far off in reasoning that it is valid, logically and as the historical facts, to disorganize the theory particularizing India produced from the suppressive Orientalistic representations. This is the conclusion I reached by wrestling with "the world as it is" as far as I can. When we get out of the particularizing theory and keep such open viewpoint, there comes out the possibility to stand on the "common-ground".

Searching for "The Accurate Representation": Remaining Indeterminate to be Sensitive

Our essential aim is to stand on the place where we can develop the creativity of the representations, escaping from the violent-ness of the Orientalistic representations. To search for "the accurate representations" or "good representations", is to proceed in such direction. In other words, it means to speak from "the world as it is" viewpoint, without being trapped by "the world as it should be", to keep the space where the represented others "can live". Such way of speaking will also make our lives "livable", because the understanding towards otherness really means the self-innovation. This is what I mean by asking "can't we speak about others as if about ourselves?" In the same sense, it is also possible to ask "can't we speak about ourselves as if about others?" To liberate one "Indian' out of the violence of representation is, at the same time, to set a "Japanese" like myself free.

When we are attacked by violence of representation, we are very sensitive and easily get hurt. However in the reverse situation, we are surprisingly insensitive. Not even aware of hurting the others. If we are in the dual-confronting relationship, there is always the chance for feedback. But if the same thing happens in the triangular relationship or in the community, it is difficult for us to recognize it and to have feedback. The delay of recognition makes them more difficult because such violent situation gets naturalized and becomes transparent. Then the coarse discourse starts to prevail. Therefore, in order to get rid of this communality, we take the strategy of getting off the stance of the cross-cultural study. Instead of this, we set the perspective of the understanding towards otherness depending on the dual-confronting relationship that is based on the singularity born at the fringe of the community. To stand on the fringe or the "boundary" only allows us to gain the sensitive viewpoint capable of recognizing the subtle "existence of the indeterminacy".[17] When we ourselves live, we always stay in such sensitivity. The sensitivity can tell us that our lives are always open to the outside. So, I would like to face the objects with such sensitive viewpoint, being against the "identity politics" in "the described culture" manipulated by the ruling power.

Some people may be hurt in defeat against the discourse of the ruling ideology and driven to the "periphery". However, the fringe of the ruling order is the place where the sincere concern for the "existence of indeterminacy" springs up in people's mind; "it is not like that", "it is not what you say". The place, featured in the openness of indeterminacy, has the potential to link itself to various arenas crossing the boundaries. Imaginary power of analogy produces and creates the possible world. I name this manner as the reinterpretation of "periphery" into "boundary".

I am going to emphasize this again. Even if the ruling power tries to conceal the trace of something driven out to the periphery of the order by identifying it as "impurity", it rather becomes "pollution", the existence with the potential for resistance against the order, breathing outside because of its given location of periphery of the discursive space of the dominant ideology. We have to search for the profound level of resistance beyond the superficiality of the simple resistance that directly say no to the ruling ideology. In such the profound level, people can undermine the ruling discourse that demands for identification (or determination) of yes or no, and widen the common space to remaining indeterminate. Its profundity lies in noticing that both those who discriminate and the discriminated have shadows of the outside in each individual life, or in noticing the otherness inside. Our impossibility of identification, or to be suspended in indeterminacy, and to share such recognition, will open up the "common-ground" place.

Through studying the triangular relationship among (1) those who discriminate (the ruling caste), (2) the accomplice (the lower castes) and (3) the discriminated (Untouchables) in the target society (Indian society here), we can analogically and metaphorically infer the similar relationship of (1) the modern west, (2) the modern Japan, and (3) the Third World in the contemporary world, and similarly in academism, (1) the western anthropologist, (2) the Japanese anthropologist, and (3) people of the third world, and so on. It may also be important to consider the way to get out of the position of the accomplice as the Japanese anthropologist in this construction, but all the more for that, it is eventually more important for the each self to encounter the otherness with the attitude of the singularity in the place where we put down the communal title of Japanese. The field of anthropology is covered with the Orientalistic representations, but never gets covered up completely. On the fringe of the covering of representations, we will see "the world as it is" lived by each person with the sensitive view as if seeing ourselves. I think this is the attitude to create the "accurate representations" or "open and good representations". Here lies a window of hope to get out the structural discriminations and conflicts that we are suffered from.

Notes

1. There also were unique, critical and productive practices in Japanese post-war anthropology, For example, Yamaguchi Masao highly evaluates the folklore of Yanagita Kunio as an attempt to avoid the confusion of the Modern in Japan and the Modern in the West, and to construct the spontaneous anthropology [Yamaguchi, 1966]. According to Yamaguchi, "Japanese ultimate sense of values is decided based on the absolutization of the two-pole time, 'something very old' and 'something very new' " [ibid.: 21]. Because of this, he acutely points out, Japan accepted anthropology as "something very new" from abroad and never linked it to the spontaneous critical mind. However, originally in the West, Anthropology was a movement of self-criticism in the tense relationship between the positivistic rationalism and something irrational and unusual that reject such quest. From this viewpoint, he highly evaluates the attempt of Yangagita Kunio as to transplant such tense *problématique* seen in the West, by converting the question of "what is human?" to the question of "what is Japanese?" However, he also adds that Yanagita should have returned to the question of "what is human", because the Yangagita's concept of "*Jōmin* (common people)" had potential power to tackle that question. Miyamoto Tsuneichi, the folklorist and one of the successors of Yangagita, is also important in Japanese anthropology. He has left a lot of records of the fieldwork made much of the living people's view or the ethnography of living. His legacy is an inexhaustible well to the following researchers. Umesao Tadao, Kawakita Jiro, Iwata Keiji, and Wazaki Yoichi are also solid anthropologists who were trained in the atmosphere of the Kyoto university school in the pre and post war era. Each of them can be evaluated that they sought the anthropology by persisting in their own singularity, and not just rehashing the Western anthropology.
2. There is a detailed description in [Stocking, 1992] on the history of the fatal duality of anthropology between romanticism and scientism in the shaky balance.
3. James Clifford notes that the explanation-oriented manner of ethnography writing restrained by the objectivism has been cracked since 1960 [Clifford and Marcus, 1986: 13–14]. There, in the publication of the diaries of Malinowski in the Mailu Island and the Trobriand Islands, he notices the sign of new trend in it. The first publication of *a Diary in the Strict Sense of the Trem* in 1967 (in 1987, it was published in Japan titled as *Marinohusuki Nikki* (means; the diary of Malinowski)) has revealed the vivid reality of the generating process of the scientific functionalist anthropology and the human conflict in body and soul of the anthropologist in the field.
4. After the main works of Jack Derrida on ecriture such as *L'ecriture et la différence* was published in 1967, the influence spread through the 70'.
5. *Writing Culture* contains many articles with different views and sometimes they are not harmonious with each other. Here I take the introduction by Clifford as its manifest.
6. The credibility (prestige) of the identified antenna is, in the actual sense, polyphonically judged from his or her series of works (for example, I trust and buy the magazine with the signature of Karatani Kojin).
7. The speculation of Kurihara Akira on "*Shukkon-gi* (ceremony of receiving the souls)" in "Minamata Tokyo Exhibition" successfully describe the gap between the supporters as the conscientious citizens and the Minamata patients.
8. Nakazawa Shinichi properly points out the tense relationship between this symbolic level of the world noted by Yamaguchi and the structuralism of Lévi-Strauss. "Symbolic anthropology is a new genre of knowledge objectifying the human symbolic activities. However,

when it forget that the teleological reason (Husserl), which restricts the rhizome-like polymorphism and tends to construct the world of meaning, always lies in the basic ground of the human symbolic activities, it only can produce the catharsis illusion of easy getting-over of the modernity. The greatness and glory of the Lévi-strauss's "static" structuralism lies in the point that it clearly recognized the much consequence of what this restriction will bring." [Nakazawa, 1984: 70].

9. The distinction and interchange of "pattern" and "ground" is the main motif penetrating the Iwata's anthropology. For example, there are lines like these in *Sozo Jinruigaku Nyumon* (means; introduction to the anthropology of creation). "Anthropologists usually think like this. They think our culture or society technically adopts itself to the environment at first, then makes the social self-adjustment, and lastly orients itself with the ideology and religion. That is, they think our culture or society has a kind of pyramid structure. But according to our argument, our society or culture is floating on a sea. The bottom of the pyramid is actually a sea. In other words, it is rooted in the blank or in the space where *Kami* (a kind of spirit) has not came into being yet and is constructed upon it. By thinking like this, the structural recognition of the world will be completely renewed [Iwata, 1982: 79]. "There are many words and concepts about this world and the other world, and their boundary is blurred. …Such images seem to be more suitable to the reality of the folkloric life. I think this way of thinking could be valid. …However, no matter how it is maybe true to the image of the worlds in everyday life associated with illusions or cultural traditions, it is not interesting unless we take these worlds are logically separated. If we don't separate these two worlds, this world can't get the reality. This world can't maintain the sublimity. By disconnecting these two worlds, our viewpoint can be interchanged. … Without distinction, there is no interchange. …The change of the viewpoint itself is the reality of our momentary lives. By changing it, we can grasp the whole world. So, if there is no interchange, we cannot live vividly. We cannot connect the every moment of life incessantly." [ibid.: 79–80]. After these lines, he severely criticizes the Boulding's concept of "Spaceship Earth" as it is closed to the level of "pattern".
10. The study on this phase is flourishing both in history and in anthropology. In Japan, Fujii Tsuyoshi energetically produces many works. (for example, [Fujii, 1988, 1993, 1994a]). From the anthropological viewpoint, see [Sekine, 1994a].
11. See especially [Sekine, 1995a: the third and the fourth chapter].
12. The case study of the secret ceremony of the pangolin in Lele culture illustrated by Mary Douglas has the potential for the interesting argument, but the book [Douglas, 1972], as a whole, doesn't succeed in extracting and theorizing the crucial essence of the case. It only tends to note the aspect of reproduction of the cultural order by something driven out to the "periphery", but it fails to understand the view of "boundary" in the place occupied by the pangolin.
13. Kurihara illustrates the subtleness of this problem like this. "In *Kishu Kinokuni Nenokuni Monogatari* (means; *Kishu*: a story of the land of woods and roots), Nakagami Kenji says, recently people didn't openly utter the discriminating words. At least, such people are getting fewer. That is, discrimination has come to be structural. …For example, when a Korean resident in Japan rents an apartment, the landlord never says "I don't rent it to Korean". Of course the landlord says "O.K.", but will add, "the guarantee should be Japanese." This gives an impression that the landlord is not discriminative, and the Korean also doesn't think he/she is insulted. At least it is difficult to talk back". [Kurihara, 2000: 11].

14. Morita Yoji and Shimizu Kenji [Morita/Shimizu, 1994] analyse bullying as "the four layered structure" among the bully, the bullied, audience and onlooker. In comparison with the triangular relationship, audience and onlooker play the same role of the accomplice. Both formulas match basically. And it is also certain that their analysis is more detailed and important theory reflecting the reality of bullying.
15. The theory of the process of identity construction is based on the argument of Peter L. Berger and Thomas Luckmann [Berger and Luckmann, 1971]. According to them, the process of identity construction consists of the two stages; one is legitimations (the stage that the self finds out the coherent meaning to experience) and the other is the plausibility structure (the communicative stage to get the validating experience). In this theory, the representation of discrimination not only suspends the discriminated in the incomplete process of identity construction but also denies their legitimations. It is the cruelest example of the "closed representation" that deprives them of the chance to get the approval of their own legitimations by the others. Human's life as Dasein is a process of incessant disorganization and reconstruction of identity, which Serizawa Shunsuke calls "sophistication of Eros". Obviously, we cannot easily solve this human problem by saying "modern people live multi-identities" or "this is the era of Créolism".
16. On this point, we can confirm that the Oda Makoto's work [Oda, 1994: the third chapter] is also important in the context of the discrimination theory. He analyses the difference between chiefdom and kingship by using the concept of partiality and entirety. According to his theory, there are many holes as the partial outsides within "the society against the state" like chiefdom, and there is neither exclusion from the entire society, nor exclusion from the higher to the lower. On the other hand, the kingship society never allows the existence of the dotting place for outside, tries to form the small universe and synthesizes the outside into the king-central order. There emerges the exclusion both to the higher end and to the lower end around the focal point of the king. As I have depicted the needed point from Oda's argument, now I dilate it in the context of the present argument. It is true that the outside is placed under the entire rule in the kingship society, but it still keeps the last openness because the center is apparently connected to the outside. However, the emerging modern state will conceal and suppress the very connection between the center and the outside. This difference may be told as the shift from the dynamic entirety to the static entirety.
17. Some conflicts took place between the patients and the supporting civil activists about the ceremony of receiving the souls of the victims from Minamata to the hall of "Minamata Tokyo Exhibition". Kurihara interprets the feelings of the Minamata patients about this "*Shukkon-gi*" (ceremony of receiving the souls) as that they tried to see the "existence of indeterminacy" in "soul". This means that the soul is also deemed as the others who are the outside of self. It is expected for the patients that the place of the "*Shukkon-gi*" could have been the space to share such existence of indeterminacy [Kurihara, 2000: 6].

Appendix

The Myths of the Origin of the Paraiyars

It is noteworthy that there is a common pattern among the various versions of the Paraiyar myths which are reported by Moffatt [Moffatt, 1979: 120–127] and which I myself have collected. It is not difficult to find from their myths the message that the greediness and stupidity of the Paraiyars resulted in their social fall, as Moffatt points out [ibid.: 124]. It is very clear that what they wish to most emphasize is that the Paraiyars originally enjoyed high status, similar to that of the Aiyars, though they are at the bottom of the hierarchy today. This is in a sense verified by the fact that the core part of the myth, the story of the brother relationship between the Paraiyars and the Aiyars, has been well preserved, even though other parts have been changed often, partly due to lapses of memory.

1. A Man of Tankalan Lineage in his 40s

[Myth] Once upon a time, an elder brother, Aiyan, and a younger brother, Paraiyan, worked together under a landlord. They engaged in cattle rearing there. One day, they were as usual in the pastureland for feeding cattle. The landlord came to them and, pointing at the cattle, he asked the two the following: "If I give you these cattle, which would you want, the standing cattle or the reclining ones?" The brothers looked at the cattle and found that most cattle were reclining except for a few. The younger brother replied that he preferred the reclining cattle, while the elder brother said he preferred the standing ones. According to their requests, the landlord gave his cattle to them respectively. Since then, it has been said that Paraiyan means "a reclining person" and Aiyan signifies "a standing person".

[Comment] As the myth tells, Aiyan (the Brahmans) and Paraiyan (the Paraiyars) were originally brothers. Thus, whenever we the Paraiyars have a ceremony we used to invite the Aiyars and give *piracātam* (Skt. *Prasāda*) them, but as time passed, the Aiyars began to reject our invitation and the acceptance of our *piracātam*

2. A Man of Mataiyan Lineage in his 50s

[Myth] Once upon a time, there were two brothers who reared cattle in co-operation. At length, the time for division of their property came. For this, they went to a pastureland and the younger brother asked his elder brother, "Which cattle do you want to take, the standing or the reclining?". The elder brother replied that he would take the ones lying down because he saw that all the cattle except one were lying.

However, he had no sooner answered than the standing cattle suddenly fell down, and the lying cattle stood up all together. As a result, the elder brother took the single dead cow, and all the other ones belonged to the younger brother. Since then, the younger brother began to call himself Aiyan and his elder brother Paraiayyan, which is an original form of Paraiyan.

[Comment] It should not be overlooked that our (the Paraiyars') ancestor was originally a brother of the Aiyar (the Brahmans), although only the Aiyar are socially given importance. The story of the origin of caste names seems to be clear evidence for this. I heard such a myth from my grandfather.

References

Abe Toshiharu

2005 "'Kohaichi' kara: Afurika no Yojutsu (Out of 'Hinterland': the Witchcraft in Africa)." *Shukyo to Shakai*, 11, pp. 241–245. (in Japanese)

Abercrombie, N., S. Hill and B.S. Turner

1980 *The Dominant Ideology Thesis*. London: George Allen & Unwin.

Ahmad, I.

1973 Introduction. In I. Ahmad (ed.) *Caste and Social Stratification among the Muslims*. Delhi: Manohar Book Service.

Allen, M.

1982 Introduction: The Hindu View of Women. In M. Allen and S.N. Mukherjee (eds) *Women in India and Nepal.* Canberra: Australian National University

Althusser, L.

1971 Ideology and Ideological State Apparatuses: Notes towards an Investigation. *Lenin and Philosophy and other Essays*. London: New Left Books.

Amino Yoshihiko

1989 'Kiyome to Senshi: Nihon no Hisabetsumin (Purification and Contempt: The Discriminated in Japan).' *Shukan Asahi Hyakka Nihon no Rekishi*, Vol. 52, B–349, Asahi Shinbun-Sha, p. 237 (in Japanese).

Ardener, E.

1967 Review of M. Douglas: Purity and Danger. *Man* (N.S.) 2, 139.

Austin, J.L.

1970 *Philosophical Papers*. Oxford: Oxford University Press.

Asad, Talal

1993 *Genealogies of Religion: Discipline and Reasons of Power in Christianity and Islam*, Baltimore: The Johns Hopkins University Press.

Babb, Lawrence A.

1975 *The Divine Hierarchy: Popular Hinduism in Central India*. New York: Columbia University Press.

Bailey, F.G.

1959 For a Sociology of India? *Contributions to Indian Sociology* III, 88–101.

Barnard, Alan and A. Good

1984 *Research Practices in the Study of Kinship*. London: Academic Press.

Barnett, Marguerite R.

1976 *The Politics of Cultural Nationalisim in South India.* Princeton: Princeton University Press.

Barnett, Stephen A.

1975 Approaches to Changes in Caste Ideology in South India. In Burton Stein (ed.) *Essays on South India.* Honolulu: The University Press of Hawaii.

Barnett, Stephen A., D. Fruzzetti and A. Ostor

1976 Hierarchy Purified: Notes on Dumont and his Critics. *Journal of Asian Studies* 35(4), 627–650.

Bataille, Georges

1976 (1948) Théorie de la Religion. *Œuvres Complètes de G. Bataille VII.* Paris: Gallimard.

1957 *L'erotisme.* Paris: Editions de Minuit.

Beck, Brenda E.F.

1969 Colour and Heat in South Indian Ritual. *Man (N.S.),* 4(4): 553–572.

1972 *Peasant Society in Konku.* Vancouver: University of British Columbia Press.

1974 The Kin Nucleus in Tamil Folklore. In T.R. Trautmann (ed.), *Kinship and History in South Asia (Michigan Papers on South and Southeast Asia,* 7). Ann Arbor: Center for South and Southeast Asian Studies, The University of Michigan.

1976 The Symbolic Merger of Body, Space, and Cosmos in Hindu Tamil Nadu. *Contributions to Indian Sociology* (N.S.) 10(2), 213–243.

1981 The Goddess and the Demon: A Local South Indian Festival and its Wider Context. *Purusartha* 5, 83–136.

Berger, Peter and Thomas Luckmann

1971 *The Social Construction of Reality: A Treatise in the Sociology of Knowledge*, London: Penguin University Books (Originally published in 1966, and then published by Allen Lane 1967).

Beidelman, T.O.

1959 *A Comparative Analysis of the Jajmani System* (Monograph of the Association for Asian Studies VII). New York: J. J. Augustin.

Berreman, Gerald D.

1962 Caste and Economy in the Himalayas. *Economic Development and Cultural Change,* 10, 396–394.

1966 Caste in Cross-cultural Perspective. In G. De Vos and H. Wagatuma (eds) *Japan's Invisible Race.* Berkeley: University of California Press.

1971 The Brahmanical View of Caste. *Contributions to Indian Sociology* (N.S.) 5, 16–23.

1973 *Caste in the Modern World.* Morristown: General Learning Press.

Béteille, André

1965 *Caste, Class, and Power: Changing Patterns of Stratification in a Tanjore Village.* Berkeley: University of California Press.

1991a The Reproduction of Inequality: Occupation, Caste and Family. *Contributions to Indian Sociology* (N.S.) 25(1), 3–28.

1991b *Society and Politics in India: Essays in a Comparative Perspective.* London: The Athlone Press.

1992 Caste and Family in Representations of Indian Society, *Anthropology Today*, 8(1), 13–18.

Biardeau, Madeleine

1976 Le sacrifice dans l'hindouisme. In M. Biardeau and C. Malamoud (eds*) Le sacrifice dans l'Inde ancienne*. Paris: Presses Universitaires de France.

Bloch, Maurice

1986 *From Blessing to Violence: History and Ideology in the Circumcision Ritual of the Merina of Madagascar.* Cambridge: Cambridge University Press.

1989 Construction of Ideology and History. In S. Tanabe (ed.) *Jinruigaku-teki Ninshiki no Bōken (An Adventure of Anthropological Recognition).* Tokyo: Dobunkan (in Japanese).

Bouglé, C.

1971(1908) *Essays on the Caste System.* Cambridge: Cambridge University Press (*Essais sur le regime des castes*, Paris: Alcan, 1927 (1908)).

Bourdieu, Pierre

1977 (1972) *Outline of a Theory of Practice*. Cambridge: Cambridge University Press. (*Esquisse d'.une thérie dela pratique: précedé de trois études d'ethnologie Kabyle.* Geneve: Droz. 1972).

1979a (1977) Symbolic Power. *Critique of Anthropology* IV–13 and 14, 77–85 ("Sur le pouvoir symbolique. *Annales* 3, 405–411, 1977).

1979b *La Distinction: Critique sociale de jugement*. Paris: Éditions de Minuit.

1980 *Le sens pratique*. Paris: Éditions de Minuit.

1987 *Choses dites*. Paris: Éditions de Minuit.

1990 *Cho-ryoiki no Ningen-kagaku* (Pierre Bourdieu: A Human Science beyond Domains). Translated by H. Kato, Tokyo: Fujiwara-shoten.(in Japanese)

Bourdieu, P. and A. Accardo et al.

1993 *La Misère du Monde.* Paris: Editions du Seuil.

Bourdieu, Pierre and J. C. Passeron

1964 *Les héitiers, les étudiants et la culture.* Paris: Éditions de Minuit.

1970 *La reproduction, Eléments pour une théorie du système d'enseignement.* Paris: Éditions de Minuit.

Bradford, N.J.

1983 Transgenderism and the Cult of Yellamma: Heat, Sex and Sickness in South Indian Ritual. *Journal of Anthropological Research* 39, 307–322.

Breckenridge, C.A. and Peter van der Veer (eds)

1993 *Orientalism and the Postcolonial Predicament.* Philadelphia: University of Pennsylvania Press.

Breman, Jan

1974 *Patronage and Exploitation*. Berkeley: University of California Press.

Brubaker, R.L.

1979a The Ambivalent Mistress: A Study of South India Village Goddess and their Religious Meaning. Ph.D. dissertation, The University of Chicago.

1979b Barbers, Washermen, and other Priests: Servants of the South Indian Village and its Goddess. *History of Religion* 19(2), 128–152.

Buckley, Thomas and Alma Gottlieb

1988 *Blood Magic: The Anthropology of Menstruation*. Berkeley: University of California Press.

Bulmer, R.

1967 Why is the Cassowary not a Bird?: A Problem of Zoological Taxonomy among the Karam of the New Guinea Highlands. *Man* (N.S.) 2, 5–25.

Burghart, Richard

1978 Hierarchical Models of the Hindu Social System. *Man* (N.S.) 13, 519–536.

1983 Renunciation in the Religious Traditions of South Asia. *Man* (N.S.) 18, 635–653.

1985 Introduction: Theoretical Approaches of Anthropology of South Asia. In R. Burghart and A. Cantlie (eds) *Indian Religion*. London: Curzon Press.

Caplan, Lionel

1980 Caste and Castelessness among South Indian Christians. *Contributions to Indian Sociology* (N.S.) 14(2), 213–238.

1981 Morality and Poliethnic Identity in Urban South India. In Adrian C. Mayer (ed.) *Culture and Morality: Essays in honour of Christoph von Furer-Haimendorf*. Delhi: Oxford University Press.

1985 The Popular Culture of Evil in Urban South India. In D. J. Parkin (ed.) *The Anthropology of Evil*. Oxford: Blackwell.

Carroll, L.

1978 Colonial Perception of Indian Society and the Emergence of Caste(s). *Journal of Asian Studies* 37(2), 233–250.

Clifford, James and Marcus, George (eds),

1986 *Writing Culture: The Poetics and Politics of Ethnography*, Berkeley: University of California Press.

Chitty, Simon C.

1872 *The Castes, Customs, Manners and Literature of the Tamils*. Colombo: The Ceylon Printers.

Cohen, Abner

1974 *Two-Dimensional Man: An Essay on the Anthropology of Power and Symbolism in Complex Society*. London: Routledge & Kegan Paul.

Cohn, Bernard S.

1954 The Camars of Senapur: A Study of the Changing Status of a Depressed Caste. Ph.D. dissertation, Cornell University.

1955 The Changing Status of a Depressed Caste. In McKim Marriott (ed.) *Village India*. Chicago: The University of Chicago Press.

1958 Changing Traditions of a Low Caste. In Milton Singer (ed.) *Traditional India: Structure and Change*. Philadelphia: The American Folklore Society.

1983 Representing Authority in Victorian India. In E. Hobsbawn and T. Ranger (eds) *The Invention of Tradition*. Cambridge: Cambridge University Press.

Commander, Simon
1983 The Jajmani System in North India: An Examination of its Logic and Status across Two Centuries. *Modern Asian Studies* 17(2), 283–311.

Daniel, E.V.
1984 *Fluid Signs: Being a Person the Tamil Way*. Berkeley: University Press.

Das, Veena
1976 The Uses of Liminality: Society and Cosmos in Hinduism. *Contributions to Indian Sociology* (N.S.) 10(2), 245–263.
1977 *Structure and Cognition: Aspects of Hindu Caste and Ritual.* Delhi: Oxford University Press.
1983 Language of Sacrifice. *Man* (N.S.) 18(3), 445–462.

Das, V. and J S. Uberoi
1971 The Elementary Structure of Caste. *Contributions to Indian Sociology* (N.S.) 4, 33–43.

David, Kenneth A.
1973 Until Marriage Do Us Part: A Cultural Account of Jaffna Tamil Categories of Kinsmen. *Man* (N.S.) 8, 521–535.
1977 Hierarchy and Equivalence in Jaffna, North Sri Lanka: Normative Codes as Mediator. In K. David (ed.) *The New Wind: Changing Identities in South Asia.* The Hague Mouton Publishers.

Davis, Marvin
1976 A Philosophy of Hindu Rank from Rural West Bengal. *Journal of Asian Studies* 36, 5–24.

de Heusch, Luc
1971 (1964) Structure et praxis sociales chez les Lele du Kasai'. *Pourquoi l'épouser? et autres essais.* Paris: Gallimard.

Deliège, Robert
1987 Patrilateral Cross-Cousin Marriage among the Paraiyars of South India. *Journal of Anthropological Society of Oxford* 18, 223–236.
1988 *Les Paraiyars du Tamil Nadu* (Studia Instituti Anthropos Vol. 42). Nettetal: Steyler Verlag-Wort und Werk.
1992 Replication and Consensus: Untouchability, Caste and Ideology in India. *Man* (N.S.) 27, 155–173.
1993 The Myths of Origin of the Indian Untouchables. *Man* (N.S.) 28, 533–549.
1994 Comment: Replication and Consensus among Indian Untouchables (Harijan) Castes. *Man* 29(2), 460–461.

Derrida, Jacques
1976 *Of Grammatology*, (translated by Gayatri Chakravorty Spivak), Baltimore: Johns Hopkins University Press(1967, De la grammatologie, Les Editions de Minuit). (A corrected edition of the translation was published in 1998.)

Dickey, Sara Ann
1988 Going to the Pictures in Madurai: Social, Psychological and Political Aspects of Cinema in Urban Working Class South India. Ph.D. dissertation, University of California.

1993 *Cinema and the Urban Poor in South India.* Cambridge: Cambridge University Press.

Dimock, Edward C., Jr.

1962 The Goddess of Snakes in Medieval Bengali Literature. *History of Religions* 1(2), 307–321.

Dirks, Nicholas B.

1987 *The Hollow Crown: Ethnohistory of an Indian Kingdom.* Cambridge: Cambridge University Press.

Douglas, Mary

1966 *Purity and Danger: an Analysis of Concepts of Pollution and Taboo,* London: Routledge and K. Paul.

1968 Pollution. In D. L. Sills (ed.) *International Encyclopedia of the Social Sciences.* New York: The Macmillan Company & The Free Press.

1975 (1972) Self-evidence. in M. Douglas, *Implicit Meanings*: Essays in Anthropology. London: Routledge.

1985 (1972) *Owai to Kinki,* (T. Tsukamoto trans.). Tokyo: Sichousha. (in Japanese)

Dumont, Louis

1957a *Une sous-caste de l'Inde du sud: Organisation sociale et religion des Pramalai Kallar.* Paris: Mouton.

1957b *Hierarchy and Marriage Alliance in South Indian Kinship* (R.A.I. Occasional Paper no.12). London: Royal Anthropological Institute.

1961 Marriage in India, the Present State of the Question I: Marriage Alliance in South-east India and Ceylon. *Contributions to Indian Sociology* 5, 75–95.

1970 A Structural Definition of a Folk Deity of Tamil Nad: Aiyanar, the Lord. in L. Dumont, *Religion, Politics and History in India.* The Hague: Mouton.

1980 (1966) *Homo Hierarchicus: The Caste System and its Implications* (complete revised English edition). Chicago: The University of Chicago Press (*Homo Hierarchicus*, Paris: Gallimard, 1966).

1983 *Affinity as a Value: Marriage Alliance in South India, with Comparative Essays on Australia.* Chicago: The University of Chicago Press.

1986 (1957) *A South Indian Subcaste: Social Organization and Religion of the Pramalai Kallar* (M. Moffatt and L. & A. Morton trans.). Delhi: Oxford University Press (*Une sous-caste de l.Inde du sud: Organisation sociale et religion des Pramalai Kallar.* Paris: Mouton, 1957).

Dumont, L. and D.F. Pocock

1958 On the Different Aspects of Levels in Hinduism. *Contributions to Indian Sociology* 2, 31–44.

1959 Pure and Impure. *Contributions to Indian Sociology* 3, 9–39.

1960 For Sociology of India: A Rejoinder to Dr. Bailey. *Contributions to Indian Sociology* 4, 82–9.

Eagleton, Terry

1983 *Literary Theory: An Introduction.* Oxford: Basil Blackwell.

Eliade, M.

1965 *Rites and Symbols of Initiation.* New York: Harper Torchbooks.

1977 Virgin and Mother. In I. Lewis (ed.), *Symbols and Sentiments.* London: Academic Press.

Fardon, Richard

1985 Introduction: A Sense of Relevance. In R. Fardon (ed.) *Power and Knowledge: Anthropological and Sociological Approaches.* Edinburgh: Scottish Academic Press.

Ferro-Luzzi, G.E.

1974 Women's Pollution Periods in Tamilnad (India). *Anthropos* 69, 113–161.

Foucault, Michel

1975 *Surveiller et punir: Naissance de la prison.* Paris: Gallimard.

Fowler, Roger (ed.)

1987 (1973) *A Dictionary of Modern Critical Terms* (revised and enlarged edition). London: Routledge & Kegan Paul.

Freeman, James M.

1979 *Untouchables: An Indian Life History.* Stanford: Stanford University Press.

1986 The Consciousness of Freedom among India's Untouchables. In Dilip K Basu and Richard Sisson (eds) *Social and Economic Development in India: A Reassessment.* New Delhi: Sage Publications.

Fuchs, Stephen

1965 (1908) *Rebellious Prophets*: A Study of Messianic Movements in Indian Religions. London: Asia Publishing House.

Fuji, Tsuyoshi

1988 "Indo Kokusei-shi niokeru Shudan: Sono Gainen Kitei to Houkatsu Han'i (the Group in the History of Indian Country System: on its Definition and Range)," in Sato Hiroshi (ed.), *Minami Ajia Gendai-shi to Kokumin Togo*, Tokyo: Ajia Keizai Kenkyu-Sho, pp. 23–103 (in Japanese).

1993 "Shokuminchi-Ki Indo niokeru Shakai Ninshiki to Chiho-Shi Hensan (the Social Recognition and Compilation of the Local Histories under the Colonial rule)," *Rekishigaku Kenkyu*, 641, pp.10–16 (in Japanese).

1994 "Rekishi no nakano Kasuto: Koten-teki Indo Shakaikan no Jittaika wo megutte (the Caste in the History: on substantialization of the View of Classic Indian Society)," *Gendai Shiso*, Vol. 22, no.7, pp. 99–111 (in Japanese).

Fuller, C.J.

1976 Kerala Christians and the Caste System. *Man* 11, 53–70.

1977 British India or Traditional India? An Anthropological Problem. *Ethnos* 3(4), 95–121.

1979 Gods, Priests and Purity: On the Relation between Hinduism and the Caste System. *Man* 14, 459–476.

1984 *Servants of the Goddess*: *The Priest of a South Indian Temple.* Cambridge: Cambridge University Press.

1988 The Hindu Pantheon and the Legitimation of Hierarchy. *Man* (N.S.) 23, 19–39.

1989 Misconceiving the Grain Heap: A Critique of the Concept of the Indian Jajmani System. In J. Parry and M. Block (eds) *Money and the Morality of Exchange.* Cambridge: Cambridge University Press.

1992 *The Camphor Flame: Popular Hinduism and Society in India*. Princeton: Princeton University Press.

Gail, A.

1977 *Parasurama Brahmane und Krieger*. Wiesbaden: Otto Harrassowitz.

Galanter, Marc

1984 *Competing Equalities: Law and the Backward Classes in India*. Berkeley: University of California Press.

Geertz, C.

1973 *The Interpretation of Cultures*. New York: Basic Books.

1980 *Negara: The Theater State in Nineteenth Century Bali*. Princeton: Princeton University Press.

Giddens, A.

1977 *Studies in Social and Political Theory*. New York: Basic Books.

Glucklich, A.

1984 Karma and Pollution in Hindu Dharma: Distinguishing Law from Nature. *Contributions to Indian Sociology* (N.S.) 18(1), 25–43.

Good, Anthony

1978 Kinship and Ritual in a South Indian Micro-Region. Ph.D. dissertation, University of Durham.

1980 Elder Sister's Daughter Marriage in South Asia. *Journal of Asian Research* 36(4), 474–500.

1982 The Actor and the Act: Categories of Prestation in South India. *Man* (N.S.) 17, 23–41.

1985 The Annual Goddess Festival in a South Indian Village. *South Asian Social Scientist* 1(2), 119–167.

1987 The Culture of Kinship. *Edinburgh Anthropology* 1, 71–86.

1991 *The Female Bridegroom: A Comparative Study of Life-Crisis Rituals in South India and Sri Lanka*. Oxford: Oxford University Press (Clarendon Press).

Gough, Kathleen

1956 Brahmin Kinship in a Tamil Village. *American Anthropologist* 58, 826–853.

1959 Criteria of Caste Ranking in South India. *Man in India* 39(2), 115–126.

1960 Caste in a Tanjore Village. In E. R. Leach (ed.) *Aspects of Caste in South India, Ceylon, and North-West Pakistan*. New York: Cambridge University Press.

1973 Harijans in Thanjavur. In K. Gough and H. Sharma (eds) *Imperialism and Revolution in South Asia*. New York: Monthly Review Press.

1975 (1958) Cults of the Dead among the Nayars. In M. Singer (ed.) *Traditional India: Structure and Change*. Jaipur: Rawat Publications.

1981 *Rural Society in Southeast India*. Cambridge: Cambridge University Press.

1989 *Rural Change in Southeast India: 1950s to 1980s*. Delhi: Oxford University Press.

Government of India (Director of Census Operations, Tamil Nadu).

1988 Census of India 1981, Series 20-Tamil Nadu, Part II-B, Primary Census Abstract, and Part XII, Census Atlas. Madras: Government Press.

Government of Madras.

1933 Madras District Gazetteers: Statistical Appendix for Madura District. Madras: Government Press.

1960 Gazetteer of the Madura District. Madras: Government Press.

Government of Madras (Director of Animal Husbandry).

1965 Statistical Information of the Department of Animal Husbandry. Madras: Government Press.

Government of Tamil Nadu (Commissioner of Statistics).

1986 Season and Crop Report of Tamil Nadu for the Year 1983–1984. Madras: Government Press.

Halverson, J.

1976 Animal Categories and Terms of Abuse. *Man* (N.S.) 11, 505–516.

Hardgrave, Robert L., Jr.

1969 *The Natars of Tamiland: The Political Culture of a Community in Change*. Berkeley: University of California Press.

1973 Politics and the Film in Tamil Nadu: The Stars and the DMK. *Asian Survey* 13(3), 288–305.

Harman, W.P.

1989 *The Sacred Marriage of a Hindu Goddess.* Bloomington: Indiana University Press.

Harper, E.B.

1964 Ritual Pollution as an Integrator of Caste and Religion. *Journal of Asian Studies* 23, 151–197.

Heesterman, J.C.

1981 Householder and Wanderer. *Contributions to Indian Sociology* (N.S.) 15–1 and 2, 251–271.

1985 *The Inner Conflict of Tradition: Essays in Indian Ritual, Kingship, and Society.* Chicago: The University of Chicago Press.

Hershman, P.

1974 Hair, Sex and Dirt. *Man* (N.S.) 9, 274–298.

Hiltebeitel, Alf.

1981 Draupati's Hair. *Purusartha* 5, 179–213.

1988 *The Cult of Draupati* 1. Chicago: The University of Chicago Press.

1991 *The Cult of Draupati* 2. Chicago: The University of Chicago Press.

Hocart, Arthur M.

1950 *Caste*. London: Methuen and Company.

1970 (1936) *Kings and Councillors: An Essay in the Comparative Anatomy of Human Society* (R. Needham, ed.). Chicago: The University of Chicago Press.

Hoek, A.W. van den

1979 The Goddess of the Northern Gate: Cellattamman as the 'Divine Warrior' of Madurai. In the Proceedings of Colloques Internationaux du C.N.R.S. No.582 (Asie du Sud. Traditions et Changements), 119–129.

Holmstrom, Mark

1971 Religious Change in an Industrial City of South India. *Journal of the Royal Asiatic Society* 1, 28–40.

1976 *South Indian Factory Workers: their Life and their World.* Cambridge: Cambridge University Press.

Horkheimer, Max and Theodor W. Adorno

1972 *Dialectics of Enlightenment*, (translated by John Cumming), New York: Herder and Herder (1947, *Philosophische Fragmente (Dialektik der Aufklarung)*, Amsterdam: Querido Verlag).

Houska, William

1981 Religious Belief and Practice in an Urban Scheduled Caste Community. Ph.D. dissertation, Syracuse University.

Hubert, H. and M. Mauss

1964 (1899) *Sacrifice: Its Nature and Function.* Chicago: The University of Chicago Press.

Imada, T.

1989 Rihurekushon-Siso: Kindai no Chōshutu (Reflection-thought: Beyond Modernity). *Gendai Shakaigaku* (Contemporary Sociology) No. 25 (in Japanese).

Inoue Tomitaka

1992 "Chosen: Senmin 'Pakuchō' no Keifu (Korea: the Genealogy of 'Baekjeong' the Humble people)," in Isomura Eiichi (ed.), *Zoho Gendai Sekai no Sabetsu Mondai*, Tokyo: Akashi Shoten, pp. 11–46 (in Japanese).

Ishihara, Terutoshi

1989 'Basuku no Tami to Kago Sabetsu (the Basque and the Kago discrimination)' *Shukan Asahi Hyakka Nihon no Rekishi*, Vol. 52, B-328, Asahi Shinbun-Sha, p. 237 (in Japanese).

Iwata, Keiji

1982 *Sozo Jinruigaku Nyumon* (Introduction to the Anthropology of Creation), Tokyo: Shogaku-kan (in Japanese).

Inden, R.

1986 Orientalist Constructions of India. *Modern Asian Studies* 20(3), 401–446.

1990 *Imagining India.* Oxford: Basil Blackwell.

Inden, Ronald B. and Ralph Nicholas

1972 A Cultural Analysis of Bengali Kinship. In P.J. Bertocci (ed.) *Prelude to Crisis: Bengal and Bengal Studies in 1970* (Michigan State University Studies Series). Michigan: East Lansing.

Iwata, Keiji

1995 *Iwata Keiji Chosakushu (The Writings of Iwata Keiji)* I-VIII. Tokyo: Kodansha (in Japanese).

Kamimura, K.

1981 *Indo Shinwa (Indian Myths).* Tokyo: Tokyo-shoseki (in Japanese).

Kane, Pandurang Vaman

1973 *History of Dharmasastra,* Vol. IV (Second Edition). Poona: Bhandarker Oriental Research Institute.

Karashima, N.

1980 (1969) Minami-Indo Shakai no Rekisi-teki Hatten (The Historical Development of South Indian Societies). In T. Matsui and T. Yamazaki (eds) *Indo-shi ni okeru Tochi-seido to Kenryoku-kōzō (Land Institution and Power Structure in Indian History).* Tokyo: University of Tokyo Press (in Japanese).

Karatani, Kojin

1992 Tankyu I (*Quest I*), (Kodan-sha Gakujutsu Bunko 1015), Tokyo: Kodan-sha. (in Japanese)

1994 (1989) *Tankyu II (Quest II).* Tokyo: Kodansha. (in Japanese)

Karve, Irawati

1968 *Hindu Society: An Interpretation* (2nd edition). Poona: Deskmukh Prakashan.

Kaushik, M.

1976 The Symbolic Representation of Death. *Contributions to Indian Sociology* (N.S.) 10(2), 265–292.

Kemper, Steven

1979 Sinhalese Astrology, South Asian Caste Systems and the Notion of Individuality. *Journal of Asian Studies* 38, 447–497.

Keyes, C.F. and E.V. Daniel

1983 *Karma: An Anthropological Inquiry.* Berkeley: University of California Press.

Khare, R.S.

1962–63 Ritual Purity and Pollution in Relation to Domestic Sanitation. *Eastern Anthropologist,* 15 and 16, 125–139.

1976 *The Hindu Hearth and Home.* Delhi: Vikas Publishing House.

1984 *The Untouchable as Himself: Ideology, Identity, and Pragmatism among the Lucknow Chamars*. Cambridge: Cambridge University Press.

Kinsley D.

1988 *Hindu Goddess: Visions of the Divine Feminine in the Hindu Religious Tradition*. Berkeley: University of California Press.

Kirpal, Viney

1978 Higher Education for the Scheduled Castes and Scheduled Tribes. *Economic and Political Weekly*, 18 January–4 February.

Kolenda, Pauline Mahar

1960 Changing Religious Practices of an Untouchable Caste. *Economic Development and Culture Change* 7(3), 279–287.

1963 Toward a Model of the Hindu Jajmani System. *Human Organization* 22, 11–31.

1964 Religious Anxiety and Hindu Fate. *Journal of Asian Studies* 23, 71–82.

1976 Seven Kinds of Hierarchy in Homo Hierarchicus. *The Journal of Asian Studies* 35(4), 581–596.

1978 *Caste in Contemporary India: Beyond Organic Solidarity*. Illinois: Waveland Press.

1982 Caste and Female Pollution. In M. Allen and S.N. Mukherjee (eds), *Women in India and Nepal.* Canberra: Australian National University.

1984 Woman as Tribute, Woman as Flower: Images of 'Woman' in Weddings in North and South India. *American Ethnologist* 11(1), 98–117.

Kotani, Hiroyaki

1989 *Indo no Chūsei-shakai: Mura, Kasuto, Ryoshu* (*The Medieval Society in India: Village, Caste and Lord*). Tokyo: Iwanami-shoten (in Japanese).

1996 *Fukashoku-Senmin to Kasuto Seido no Rekishi* (The History of Untouchables and Caste System), Tokyo: Akashi Shoten (in Japanese).

2003 "Indo no Fukashoku-Senmin: Kindaika to Kasuto-sei (Untouchables in India: Modernization and Caste System)," *Shukan Asahi Hyakka Nihon no Rekishi*, Vol. 70, modern times I–10, Asahi Shinbun-Sha, p. 303 (in Japanese).

Koto, Y.

1975 Weber to Imi no Shakaigaku (Weber and Semantic Sociology). *Gendai-Siso (Contemporary Thought)* 3(2) (in Japanese).

Kristiva, J.

1974 *La Révolution du langage Poétique*. Paris: Éditions du Seuil.

Krygier, J.

1982 Caste and Female Pollution. In M. Allen and S.N. Mukherjee (eds) *Women in India and Nepal.* Canberra: Australian National University.

Kumar, Dharma

1965 *Land and Caste in South India* (Cambridge Studies in Economic History). Cambridge: Cambridge University Press.

Kurihara, Akira

2000 "Hyosho no Seiji: Hikettei no Sonzai wo Sukuidasu (Politics of Representation: to Rescue the Existence of Indeterminacy)." *Shiso*, 907, pp. 5–17 (in Japanese).

Leach, E.R.

1960 Introduction: What Should We Mean by Caste? In E.R. Leach (ed.) *Aspects of Caste in South India, Ceylon and North-West Pakistan.* Cambridge: Cambridge University Press.

1961 *Rethinking Anthropology* (London School of Economics, Monographs on Social Anthropology). London: The Athlone Press (University of London).

1971 Esprit' in Homo Hierarchicus. *Contributions to Indian Sociology* (N.S.) 5, 13–16.

1972 (1964) Anthropological Aspects of Language: Animal Categories and Verbal Abuse. In P. Maranda (ed.) *Mythology.* Hammondsworth: Penguin Books.

1976 *Culture and Communication.* Cambridge: Cambridge University Press.

1988 South Africa and India. *Anthropology Today* 4(4), Royal Anthropological Institute.

Lévi-Strauss, Claude,

1962 La pensée sauvage, Paris: Plon.

Ludden, David

1985 *Peasant History in South India.* Princeton: Princeton University Press.

Madan, T.N. et al.

1971 On the Nature of Caste in India: A Review Symposium on Louis Dumont's Homo Hierarchicus. *Contributions to Indian Sociology* (N.S.) 5, 1–81.

Malamould, C.

1981 On the Rhetric and Semantics of Purasartha. *Contributions to Indian Sociology* 15, 35–54.

Maloney, C.

1975 Religious Beliefs and Social Hierarchy in Tamil Nadu. *American Ethnologist* 2(1), 169–191.

Mandelbaum, David G.

1970 *Society in India*. Berkeley: University of California Press.

Marglin, F.A.

1977 Power, Purity and Pollution: Aspects of the Caste System Reconsidered. *Contributions to Indian Sociology* 11(2), 245–270.

1985 Types of Oppositions in Hindu Culture. In J.B. Carman and F.A. Marglin (eds) *Purity and Auspiciousness in Indian Society*. Leiden: E. J. Brill.

Marriott, McKim

1976 (1973) Hindu Transactions: Diversity without Dualism. In B. Kapferer (ed.) *Transaction and Meaning: Directions in the Anthropology of Exchange and Symbolic Behaviour.* Philadelphia: Institute for the Study of Human Issues.

Marriott, McKim (ed.)

1955 *Village India.* Chicago: The University of Chicago Press.

Marriott, McKim et al.

1989 Special Issue: Toward an Ethnosociology of India. *Contributions to Indian Sociology* 23(1), 1–202.

Marriott, McKim and Ronald B. Inden

1977 Toward an Ethnosociology of South Asian Caste Systems. In K. David (ed.) *The New Wind: Changing Identities in South Asia.* The Hague: Mouton.

Marx, Karl and F. Engels

1970 *The German Ideology*: Part One (C.J. Arthur ed.) London: Lawrence and Wishart.

Mathur, A.B.

1988 Dravidian Heritage: MGR and Tamil Nadu. *The Indian Journal of Political Science* 49(1), 121–128.

Mayer, Adrian C.

1958 The Dominant Caste in a Region of Central India. *South-western Journal of Anthropology* 14(4), 407–427.

1960 *Caste and Kinship in Central India: A Village and its Region*. Berkeley: University of California Press.

1980 Review of Michael Moffatt's An Untouchable Community in South India. *Bulletin of the School of Oriental and African Studies* (University of London) XLIII, 397–398.

McGilvray, Dennis B.

1974 Tamils and Moors: Caste and Matriclan Structure in Eastern Sri Lanka. Ph.D. dissertation, The University of Chicago.

1982 Mukkuvar Vannimai: Tamil Caste and Matriclan Ideology in Batticaloa, Sri Lanka. In D.B. McGilvray (ed.) *Caste Ideology and Interaction.* Cambridge: Cambridge University Press.

1983 Paraiyar Drummers of Sri Lanka: Consensus and Constraint in an Untouchable Caste. *American Ethnologist* 10, 87–115.

Meigs, Anna S.

1978 A Papuan Perspective on Pollution. *Man* (N.S.) 13, 304–318.

Mencher, J.P.

1974 The Caste System Upside Down, or the Not-so-mysterious East. *Current Anthropology* 15(4), 469–478.

1978 *Agriculture and Social Structure in Tamil Nadu*. New Delhi: Allied Publishers.

Miki Wataru

1998 *Sekai-shi no Dai-ni Raundo wa Kano ka: Isuramu Sekai no Shiten kara* (Is the Second Round of the World History Possible?: from the Viewpoint of Islamic World), Tokyo: Heibon-Sha. (in Japanese)

Miller, Barbara D.

1980 Female Neglect and the Costs of Marriage in Rural India. *Contributions to Indian Sociology* (N.S.) 14(1), 95–129.

Miller, Robert J.

1966 Button, Button…Great Tradition, Little Tradition, Whose Tradition? *Anthropological Quarterly* 39, 26–42.

1967 They Will Not Die Hindus: The Buddhist Conversion of Mahar Ex-Untouchables. *Asian Survey* 7, 637–645.

Milner, Murray, Jr.

1988 Status Relations in South Asian Marriage Alliances: Toward a General Theory. *Contributions to Indian Sociology* (N.S.) 22(2), 145–169.

Mines M.

1984 *The Warrior Merchants: Textiles, Trade and Territory in South India*. Cambridge: Cambridge University Press.

Moffatt, Michael

1975 Untouchables and the Caste System: A Tamil Case Study. *Contributions to Indian Sociology* (N.S.) 9(1), 111–122.

1979 *An Untouchable Community in South India: Structure and Consensus*. Princeton: Princeton University Press.

Moore, M.A.

1989 The Kerala House as a Hindu Cosmos. *Contributions to Indian Sociology* (N.S.), 23(1): 169-202.

Morita, Yoji and Shimizu Kenji

1994 *Shintei-Ban Ijime: Kyoshitsu no Yamai* (a new revision Bullying: Illness in a Class Room), Tokyo: Kaneko-Shobo (in Japanese).

Mosse, David

1994a Catholic Saints and the Hindu Village Pantheon in Rural Tamil Nadu, India. *Man* 29(2), 301–332.

1994b Comment: Replication and Consensus among Indian Untouchables (Harijan) Castes. *Man* 29(2), 457–460.

Mukherjee, Nilmani

1962 *The Ryotwari System in Madras*. Calcutta: Firma K.L. Mukhopadhyay.

Nair, Kusum

1969 *The Lonely Furrow*. Ann Arbor: University of Michigan Press.

Naka, H. (ed.)

1990 *Gendai Shakaigaku no Shoriron* (Theories of Contemporary Sociology). Tokyo: Sekaishisōsha (in Japanese).

Nakazawa, Shin'ichi

1984 "Jizoku-suru 'Toki' Bibun-suru 'Toki' ('Time' of maintaining and 'time' of differentiating)," *Gendai no Jinruigaku 4 Shocho Jinruigaku*, (a separate volume of *Gendai no Esupuri* edited by AOKI Tamotsu), Tokyo: Shibun-Do, pp. 65–70 (in Japanese).

Natarajan, C.N.

1978 The Piramalai Kallars of Tamil Nadu: A Study of their Marriage, Kinship and Clan System. Ph.D. dissertation, Madurai Kamaraj University.

Needham, R. (ed.)

1971 *Rethinking Kinship and Marriage* (ASA Monographs 11). London: Tavistock Publications.

Nicholas, R.W.

1981 Sraddha, Impurity, and Relations between the Living and the Dead. *Contributions to Indian Sociology* (N.S.) 15–1 and 2, 367–379.

O'Flaherty, Wendy Doniger

1973 *Asceticism and Eroticism in the Mythology of Siva.* London: Oxford University Press.

1976 *The Origins of Evil in Hindu Mythology.* Berkeley: University of California Press.

1988 *Texual Sources for the Study of Hinduism.* Manchester: Manchester University Press.

Obeyesekere, G.

1968 Theodicy, Sin and Salvation in a Sociology of Buddhism. In E. Leach (ed.). *Dialectic in Practical Religion.* Cambridge: Cambridge University Press.

1977 Social Change and the Deities: Rise of the Kataragama Cult in Modern Sri Lanka. *Man* (N.S.) 12, 377–396.

1978 The Fire-Walkers of Kataragama: The Rise of Bhakti Religiosity in Buddhist Sri Lanka. *Journal of Asian Studies* 37(3), 457–476.

1981 *Medusa's Hair: An Essay on Personal Symbols and Religious Experience.* Chicago: Chicago University Press.

Oda, Makoto

1994 *Kōzō-Jinruigaku no Fīrudo* (*The Field of Structuralist Anthropology*). Tokyo: Sekaishisōsha (in Japanese).

Ogawa, Satoru

1992 "Roma ni taisuru Sabetsu no Jittai to Kaiho Undo no Ayumi (the Actual Situation of the Discrimination against Roma and the process of the Liberation Movement)," in Isomura Eiichi (ed.), *Zoho Gendai Sekai no Sabetsu Mondai*, Tokyo: Akashi Shoten, pp. 281–315 (in Japanese).

Ohashi, Yoichi

1996 "Fuhensei demonaku, Sai demonaku: Said Orientalism Saiko (Not universally, not differently: Rethinking Said's Orientalism)." *Daikokai*, Vol.11, pp. 30–35 (in Japanese).

Ojha, C.

1981 Feminine Asceticism in Hinduism: Its Tradition and Present Condition. *Man in India,* 61(3): 254–285.

Omori, Shozo

1992 *Jikan to Jiga (Time and Ego)*. Tokyo: Seidosha (in Japanese).

Oppert, Gustav

1978 (1893) *On the Original Inhabitants of Bharatavarsa or India*. New York: Arno Press.

Orenstein, H.

1968 Toward a Grammar of Defilement in Hindu Sacred law. In M. Singer and B.S. Cohn (eds), *Structure and Change in Indian Society*. Chicago: Aldine Publishing Company.

Ortner, S.B.

1978 The Virgin and the State. *Feminist Studies,* 4(3): 19–35.

Oshikawa, Fumiko

1981 Dokuritu-go Indo no Sitei-kāsuto (Scheduled Castes of Independent India). *Ajia Keizai* (*Asian Economy*) 22(1), 26–45 (in Japanese).

1989 Indo Shakai-zō niokeru Kāsuto (Caste in the Image of Indian Society*). Ajia Keizai (Asian Economy)* 30(3), 5–29 (in Japanese).

1994 "Terebi Dokyumentari nitotte 'Shinjitsu' towa: NHK "Ajia Haiwei" eno Gimon (What is 'Truth' in TV Documentary program?: a question to NHK's "Asian Highway")", *Sekai*, Vol. 2, 212–216 (in Japanese).

Padmanabhan, V.K.

1987 Communist Parties in Tamilnadu. *The Indian Journal of Political Science* 48–2, 225–250.

Pandian, J.

1987 *Caste, Nationalism and Ethnicity: An Interpretation of Tamil Cultural History and Social Order*. London: Sangam Books.

Parry, J.P.

1970 The Koli Dilemma. *Contributions to Indian Sociology* (N.S.) 4, 84–104.

1974 Egalitarian Values in Hierarchical Society. *South Asian Review* 7(2), 95–121.

1979 *Caste and Kinship in Kangra.* London: Routledge & Kegan Paul.

1980 Ghosts, Greed and Sin: The Occupational Identity of the Banaras Funeral Priests. *Man* 15(1), 88–111.

1982 Sacrificial Death and the Necrophagous Ascetic. In M. Bloch and J. Parry (eds) *Death and the Regeneration of Life*. Cambridge: Cambridge University Press.

1985 Death and Digestion: The Symbolism of Food and Eating in North Indian Mortuary Rites. *Man* (N.S.) 20, 612–630.

Parsons, Talcott

1951 *The Social System*. Glencoe, Ill.: The Free Press.

Peacock, J.L.

1986 *The Anthropological Lens: Harsh Light, Soft Focus*. Cambridge: Cambridge University Press.

Perumal, C.A. and V.K. Padmanabhan

1986 Congress and Non-Congressism in Tamilnadu. *The Indian Journal of Political Science* 47(3), 421–434.

Pfaffenberger, Bryan

1980 Social Communication in Dravidian Ritual. *Journal of Anthropological Research* 36(2), 196–219.

Pinney, C.

1988 Representations of India: Normalisation and the 'Other'. *Pacific Viewpoint* 29(2), 144–162.

Platenkamp, J.D.M.

1979 Out of Mind, Out of Sight: Suppression and Taboo in the 'Leach-Theory'. *Bijdragen tot de taal-, land- en Volkenkunde* 135, 172–180.

Poirié, Francois

1987 *Emmanuel Lévinas, Qui etes-vous?* Paris: Manufacture.

Prigogine, Ilya and Isabelle Stengers.

1984 *Order Out of Chaos: Man's New Dialogue with Nature*. Toronto: Bantam Books.

Prinde, P.H.

1977 The Jajmani System: A Nepalese Example. *Journal of Anthropological Research* 33.

Quigley, D.

1993 *The Interpretation of Caste*. Oxford: Oxford University Press.

Radcliffe-Brown, A.R.

1922 *The Andaman Islanders*. Cambridge: Cambridge University Press.

Raheja, G.G.

1988 *The Poison in the Gift: Ritual Prestation, and the Dominant Caste in a North Indian Village*. Chicago: Chicago University Press.

Rajayyan, K.

1974 *History of Madurai (1736–1801)*. Madurai: Madurai University.

Reiniche, Marie-Louise

1975 Les <<demons>> et leur culte dans la structure du panthéon d'un village du Tirunelveli. *Puruṣārtha,* 2: 173–201.

1979 *Le dieux et hommes: Étude des cultes d'un village du Tirunelveli, Inde du sud*. Paris: Mouton.

1981 La maison au Tirunelveli (Inde du sud). *Bulletin de l.Éole Française d'exrême-orient*, LXX. Paris: École Française D'extrê*me-Orient.*

Retzlaff, Ralph H.

1962 *Village Government in India.* New York: Asia Publishing House.

Reynolds, H.B.

1980 The Auspicious Married Women. In S. Wadley (ed.), *The Powers of Tamil Women.* Syracuse: Syracuse University.

Richards, J.F. and R.W. Nicholas et al.

1976 Symposium: The Contributions of Louis Dumont. *The Journal of Asian Studies* 35(4), 579–650.

Rosaldo, Renato

1989 *Culture and Truth: The Remaking of Social Analysis*. Boston: Beacon Press.

Sachchidananda

1977 *The Harijan Elite: A Study of their Status, Networks, Mobility and Role in Social Transformation*. Faridabad; Thomson Press.

Sahi, J.

1980 *The Child and the Serpent.* London: Routledge & Kegan Paul.

Said, E.W.

1978 *Orientalism*. New York: Georges Borchardt Inc.

Sakiyama, Masaki

1999 Itami wo wakaru (to Understand Pain). *Gendai Shiso*, 27–2, 214–221. (in Japanese)

Sartre, Jean P.

1943 *L'êre et lenéant: Essai d'ontologie phénoménologique*. Paris: Gallimard.

Sato, Yutaka

1990 "Sansha Kankei toshiteno Sabetsu (the Discrimination as the Triangular Relationship)", *Kaiho Shakaigaku Kenkyu*, 4, 77–87 (in Japanese).

Sawada, Akio

1994 PC Undō to 'Amerika no Bunretu' (PC Movement and the 'Disruption of America'*). Shosai-no-mado* Nos. 432–436 (in Japanese).

Schneider, David M.

1968 *American Kinship: A Cultural Account* (second edition 1980). Chicago: The University of Chicago Press.

Searle-Chatterjee, Mary

1979 The Polluted Identity of Work: A Study of Benares Sweepers. In S. Wallman (ed.) *Social Anthropology of Work*. London: Academic Press.

1981 *Reversible Sex Roles: The Special Case of Benares Sweepers*. Oxford: Pergamon Press.

Sekine, Yasumasa

1983 Jafuna-Tamiru no Shoji no Girei: Kegare no Kukanron ni mukete(Birth and Death Rites among the Jaffna Tamils: Towards a Spatial Theory of Pollution). *Kikan Jinruigaku* 14(4): 67–166 (in Japanese).

1984 Birth and Death Ceremonies among the Jaffna Tamil: A Study of Pollution from the Viewpoint of Spatial Structure. In K. Iawta and Y. Ikari (eds) *Religions and Cultures of Sri Lanka and South India*. Osaka: National Museum of Ethnology.

1985 'Hujyō' to 'Kegare' no Aida: Jahuna Tamiru no Kegare no Kūkan (Between 'Impurity' and 'Pollution': The Space of Pollution among the

Jaffna Tamils). In E. Ishikawa, K. Iwata, and K. Sasaki (eds) *Sei to Shi no Jinruigaku* (*Anthroplogy of Life and Death*). Tokyo: Kodansha (in Japanese).

1986 Tamiru Shakai no Kegare Kannen no Shoso: Hieraruki to Shutaisei no Sokoku no Basho (Some Aspects of the Conceptions of Pollution in Tamil Society: A Place of Conflict between Hierarchy and Subjectivity). *Minzokugaku Kenkyu* 51(3): 219–247 (in Japanese).

1989 Theory of Pollution: Theoretical perspective and practice in a South Indian Tamil village (Monumenta Serindica), Tokyo: Institute for the Study of Languages and Cultures of Asia and Africa.

1993a Jyūkyo no *Kosumoroji to Ideorogi ni* kansuru Dotai-teki Kenkyu (The Dynamic Approach towards Cosmology and Ideology of Houses: South India and Japan). *Jyūtaku Sōgō Kenkyū Zaidan Kenkyū Nenpō* (Annals of the Foundation for Integrated Studies on Houses 19, Tokyo: Jyūtaku Sōgō Kenkyū Zaidan (in Japanese).

1993b 'Ten de Kakou' Hūkei to 'Sen de Kakou' Hūkei: Minami Indo Tamiru-jin no Kukan Ninshiki kara (Landscape 'surrounded by Points' and Landscape 'surrounded by Lines': the Spatial Recognition among the South Indian Tamils). In S. Sugimoto and T. Nakamura (eds) *Hendō suru Genndai Sekai no Naritati: Tiiki, Minzoku, Bunka (Construction of the Changing Contemporary World: Region, Ethnic Group and Culture).* Kyoto: Kōyō-shobō (in Japanese).

1993c Pollution Theory and Harijan Strategies among South Indian Tamils, Ph.D. Dissertation, University of London.

1993d Chi no Kugi to Kegare no Ronri: Mura no Kami kara mita Tamiru-jin no Shinko (Blood Sacrifices and a Logic of 'Pollution': The Belief World of the Tamils as seen in their 'Village Gods'). In Y. Nagano and Y. Ikari (eds), *Indo: Fukugo Bunka no Kozo (India: The Multiplex Structure).* Kyoto: Hozokan (in Japanese).

1993e The Belief World of the Tamils as seen in their 'Village Gods': Blood Sacrifices and 'pollution'. In Y. Nagano and Y. Ikari [eds], *From Vedic Altar to Village Shrine: Towards an Interface between Indology and Anthropology (Senri Ethnological Studies,* No. 36). Osaka: National Museum of Ethnology.

1994a Kiyome to Girei: Tamiru no Seijyoshiki (Purification and Rituals: A Coming of Age Ceremony among the Tamils*). Indo Nyūmon II: Doravida no Sekai (Introduction to India II: The Dravidian World)* Tokyo: University of Tokyo Press (in Japanese).

1994b 'Orientalism' to Indo-Shakai-jinnruigaku eno Siron ('Orientalism' and Social Anthropology of India). *Shakai-Jinruigaku Nenpō* (Annals of Social Anthropology) 20, 27–61 (in Japanese).

1995a *Kegare no Jinruigaku: Minami-Indo Harijan no Seikatsu Sekai (The Anthropology of Pollution:The Life-World of South Indian Harijans).* Tokyo: University of Tokyo Press (in Japanese).

1995b "Indo Shakai de 'jitsuduki' no Jinruigaku wo Kangaeru: 'Shomin bunka' Kenkyu no Igi (Thinking the 'Common-ground'Anthropology in Indian

Society: the Significance of 'Folk Culture'Study')", *Sobun*, 368, 9–11 (in Japanese).

1995c Boryoku, Seiji, Shūkyō: Madorasu-shi no Sairei Vinayaga Chaturuti no Genzai kara no Kōsatu (Violence, Politics, and Religion: from a Observation of Vinayaga Chaturthi in Madras City). In Yoshio Sugimoto (ed.) *Shūkyō Minzoku, Dentō: Ideorogī-teki Kosatu* (Religion, Ethnic Group, and Tradition: An Ideological Consideration). Nagoya: Anthropological Institute of Nanzan University (in Japanese).

1998a "Book Review: *Fukashoku-Senmin to Kasuto Seido no Rekishi (The History of Untouchables and Caste System)* by Kotani Hiroyuki" *Rekishi Hyoron*, 579, 100–103 (in Japanese).

1998b "Minami Ajia no Kaihatsu to Kokumin Togo no Genjitsu: Indo ni okeru Keizai Jiyuka to Hindu Nashonarizumu no Taitou (the Development of South India and the Reality of Nation Building: Economic Liberation and the Rise of Hindu Nationalism in India)", in Kawada Junzo (eds), *Iwanami Koza: Kaihatsu to Bunka 4: Kaihatsu to Minzoku Mondai (Development and Ethnic Problem)*, Tokyo: Iwanami Shoten (in Japanese).

1999a Rethinking the Ambiguous Character of Hindu Women. In M. Tanaka and M. Tachikawa (eds) *Living with Śakti: Gender, Sexuality and Religion in South Asia* (Senri Ethnological Studies 50). Osaka: National Museum of Ethnology.

1999b "Communalism and Modern Thinking". In Fumiko Oshikawa (ed.), *South Asia under the Economic Reforms* (JCAS Symposium Series 6), Osaka: The Japan Center for Area Studies, National Museum of Ethnology, 263–274.

2000 Indo ni okeru 'Shukyo Tairitsu' Gensho to Datsu-Kindai no Mosaku: 'Komyunarizumu' no Kanata e ('Religious Conflicts' Phenomena and the search for the de-Modernization in India: Beyond 'Communalism').' In Sogo Kenkyu Kaihatsu Kiko and Nakamaki Hirochika (eds), *Gendai Sekai to Shukyo*, Tokyo: Kokusai Shoin, pp. 89–111, 215–278 (in Japanese).

Shibatani, A. and K. Ikeda, (eds)

1992 *Sabetu toiu Kotoba (A Language of Discrimination)*. Tokyo: Akashishoten (in Japanese).

Shigematsu, Shinji

1976 Igirisu-Sihai-mae no Minami Indo ni okeru Sonrakuyōtai to Nominken'eki (Village Patterns and Peasant Rights in the Pre-British Ruling South India). In N. Karashima (ed.) *Indo-shi ni okeru Sonraku-Kyōdotai no Kenkyū (The Studies on Village Communities in Indian History)*. Tokyo: University of Tokyo Press (in Japanese).

Stutchbury, E.L.

1982 Blood, Fire and Mediation: Human Sacrifice and Widow Burning in Nineteenth Century India. In M. Allen and S.N. Mukherjee (eds), *Women in India and Nepal*. Canberra: Australian National University.

Shimizu, Akitoshi

1992 Eien no Mikai-bunka to Shuen-Minzoku: Kindai-Seiou-Jinruigakushi Tenbyo (The Eternal Primitive Culture and Marginalized People: Re-interpretation of Modern Western Anthropology). *Kokuritu-*

Minzokugaku-Hakubutukan Kekyu-Hokoku (The Bulletin of National Museum of Ethnology) 17(3), 417–488 (in Japanese).

Shindo, Yuzo

1990 Rikai Shakaigaku no Keihu (A Genealogy of Comprehensive Sociology). In H. Naka (ed.) *Gendai Shakai no Shoriron (Theories of Contemporary Sociology)*. Sekaishisosha (in Japanese).

Shulman, David D.

1976 The Murderous Bride: Tamil Versions of the Myth of Devi and the Buffalo-Demon. *History of Religion* 16, 120–146.

1980 *Tamil Temple Myths: Sacrifice and Divine Marriage in the South Indian Saiva Tradition*. Princeton: Princeton University Press.

Singer, Milton

1966 The Radha-Krishna Bhajanas of Madras City. In M. Singer (ed.) *Krishna: Myths, Rites and Attitudes*. Honolulu: East-West Center Press.

Sivathamby, Karthigesu

1981 *The Tamil Film as a Medium of Political Communication*. Madras: New Century Book House.

Sperber, Dan

1985 *On Anthropological Knowledge*. Cambridge: Cambridge University Press.

Srinivas, M.N.

1952 *Religion and Society among the Coorgs of South India*, London: Oxford University Press.

1955 The Social System of a Mysore Village. In McKim Marriott (ed.) *Village India*. Chicago: The University of Chicago Press.

1978 (1952) *Religion and Society among the Coorgs of South India* (reprinted 1978). Bombay: Media Promoters & Publishers.

1987 (1959) The Dominant Caste in Rampura. In *The Dominant Caste and Other Essays*. Delhi: Oxford University Press.

Stevenson, H.N.C.

1954 Status Evaluation in the Hindu Caste System. *The Journal of Royal Anthropological Institute of Great Britain and Ireland* 84, 45–66.

Stevenson, S.

1971 (1920) *The Rites of the Twice-Born*. New Delhi: Oriental Books Reprint Corporation.

Stirrat, R.L.

1984 Sacred Models. *Man* (N.S.) 19, 199–215.

Stocking, George W., Jr.

1992 *The Ethnographer's Magic and Other Essays in the History of Anthropology*, Madison: University of Wisconsin Press.

Schutz, Alfred

1982 *The Problem of Social Reality* (edited and introduced by Maurice Natanson; with a preface by H.L. van Breda), (Collected Papers 11), Hague: M. Nijhoff.

Tachikawa, Musashi

1990 *Joshin-tati no Indo* (*Goddesses' India*). Tokyo: Serika-Shob (in Japanese).

Takeda, Seiji

1993 *Erosu no Sekai-zō (A World View of Eros)*. Tokyo: Sanseido (in Japanese).

Tambiah, S.J.

1972 Review of Homo Hierarchicus. *American Anthropologist* 74(4), 832–835.

1973 From Varna to Caste through Mixed Unions. In J. Goody (ed.) *The Character of Kinship*. Cambridge: Cambridge University Press.

1985 *Culture, Thought, and Social Action: An Anthropological Perspective*. Cambridge,Massachusetts: Harvard University Press.

Tapper, B.E.

1979 Widows and Goddesses: Female Roles in Deity Symbolism in a South Indian Village. *Contributions to Indian Sociology* (N.S.) 13(1), 1–31.

Therborn, G.

1980 *The Ideology of Power and the Power of Ideology*. London: Verso.

Thompson, Kenneth

1986 *Beliefs and Ideology*. Chichester: Ellis Horwood.

Thurston, E. and K. Rangachari

1987 *Castes and Tribes of Southern India*. Vols. 1–7, New Delhi: Asian Education Services.

Tokunaga, Muneo

1981 *Tamil* (Asian and African Grammatical Mannual No.13). Tokyo: Institute for the Study of Languages and Cultures of Asia and Africa, Tokyo Gaikokugo Daigaku.

1985 Shukyoteki Shinsei: Hinzūkyo towa Nanika (Religious Mentality: What is Hinduism?). In N. Karashima (ed.) *Minzoku no Sekaisi 7: Indo Sekai no Rekisi-Zō (Ethnic World Histories 7: The Historical Image of Indian World)*, Tokyo: Yamakawa-shuppansha (in Japanese).

Trautmann, Thomas R.

1981 *Dravidian Kinship*. Cambridge: Cambridge University Press.

Turner, Victor

1969 *The Ritual Process: Structure and Anti-Structure*. Chicago: Aldine Publishing Company.

Turton, Andrew

1984 Limits of Ideological Domination and the Formation of Social Consciousness. In A. Turton and S. Tanabe (eds) *History and Peasant Consciousness in South East Asia* (Senri Ethnological Studies 13). Osaka: National Museum of Ethnology.

Uberoi, J.P.S.

1967 On Being Unshorn. *Sikhism and Indian Society*. (Transactions of the Indian Institute of Advanced Study, Simla.

University of Madras.

1982 *Tamil Lexicon*. 6 Vols and Supplement (reprint). Madras: University of Madras.

van der Veer, Peter

1988 *Gods on Earth: The Management of Religious Experience and Identity in a North Indian Pilgrimage Centre*. London: The Athlone Press.

van Gennep, A.

1960 (1909) *Rites of Passage* (M.B. Vizedom and G.L. Caffee trans.). London: Routledge & Kegan Paul.

Vincentnathan, Lynn

1987 Harijan Subculture and Self-Esteem Management in a South Indian Community. Ph.D. dissertation, University of Chicago.

Wadley, S.S.

1975 *Shakti: Power in the Conceptual Structure of Karimpur Religion.* Chicago: Dept. of Anthropology, University of Chicago.

1980 The Paradoxical Powers of Tamil Women. In S. Wadley (ed.), *The Powers of Tamil Women.* Syracuse: Syracuse University.

Watase, Nobuyuki

1990 *Manu Hōten: Hindukyō Sekai no Genkei (The Laws of Manu: The Prototype of the Hindu World).* Tokyo: Chuo Koronsha.

Whitehead, D.D.H.

1921 (1907) *The Village Gods of South India.* Calcutta: Oxford University Press.

Wiser, William H.

1958 (1936) *The Hindu Jajmani System.* Lucknow: Lucknow Publication House. (Originally published in 1936.)

Wittgenstein

1980 *The Blue and Brown Books: Preliminary Studies for the Philosophical Investigations*, Oxford: Blackwell.

von Wright, G.H.

1971 *Explanation and Understanding.* Ithaca, N. Y.: Cornell University Press.

Yalman, Nur

1963 On the Purity of Women in the Castes of Malabar and Ceylon. *Journal of the Royal Anthropological Institute* 93, 25–58.

Yamaguchi, Masao

1966 Jinruigakuteki Ninshiki no Shozentei: Sengo Nihon Jinruigaku no Shiso Jokyo (The premises of Anthropological Recognition: the Thought Condition of the Japanese Post-War Anthropology). *Shiso*, 508, pp. 21–33 (in Japanese).

Yamazaki, Toshio and Takahashi, Mitsuru (eds)

1993 *Nihon to Indo Koryu no Rekishi* (the History of exchanges between Japan and India), Tokyo: Sansei-do (in Japanese).

Yamashita, Hiroshi

1989 Deivamu to Kadaburu: Kodai Tamiru Sekai no 'Kami' (Teyvam and Katavul: 'Deities' in an Ancient Tamil). *Indogaku Shukyogakkai-Ronshū* 15 (in Japanese).

Yoshimoto, Takaaki

1982 (1966) *Kaitei-Sinban: Kyōdo-Gensō-ron* (A Renewed Version*: Communal Imagination).* Tokyo: Kadokawa-shoten (in Japanese).

Yoshioka, Masanori

1989 Engumi to Shinzoku (Alliance and Kinship). In T. Gōda (ed.) *Gendai Shakai Jinruigaku (Contemporary Social Anthropology*), Tokyo: Kobundo (in Japanese).

Glossary

The important Tamil words referred to in the main text, except caste names and proper names for places, temples, kingdoms and persons, have been included below. The words are listed in English alphabetical order with the added condition that short vowels take precedence over long vowels.

acinṁkam: ugly, unsightly.

acuttam: impure, unclean.

amman̲: goddess.

aṇṇan̲-tampi: literally, elder brother-younger brother; ego's parallel relatives between whom inter-marriage is prohibited.

an̲n̲iyam: non-relatives.

*apiṣēkam (*Skt. *abhiṣeka*): libation on an idol.

aṭimai/aṭimaikārar: slave or tied labourer.

cakalan̲: the relations between sisters' husbands; an ego-centred group of male parallel relatives.

cakti/catti (Skt. *śakti*): divine power or energy.

*camāti (*Skt. *samādhi*): a tomb; the ultimate state attained through deep meditation.

can̲n̲iiyāci: religious renouncer or mendicant.

caṭaṅku: religious ceremony; a rite associated with puberty.

cuttamuka teyvam: a Sanskritized deity rejecting blood sacrifice.

cuṭukāṭu: graveyard or cremation ground.

cuvāmi/cāmi: god; a common term of address of a superior by an inferior.

cāmiāṭi: a god-dancer; a person possessed by a god or a goddess.

cāmipeṭṭi: a sacred chest which symbolizes a deity.

cēri: the older term for a residential quarter inhabited uniquely by Untouchable castes.

in̲ām (from Arabic): tax-free grants of land by rulers to subjects.

jajmānī (from Hindi): a village system of customary payments in kind at harvest time, from landowning patrons to clients who perform services for them.

jamīn̲tār: zamindar, a person with dominant rights over land, usually a large tract including several villages.

kamalai: a device for raising water from a well.

karai: the traditional right and duty of marriage preference.

karakam: a flower-decked water-filled brass pot representing a goddess.

karṇam: a village land-accountant.

karumāti: final obsequies; a funeral ceremony for sending the spirit of the dead to heaven or the ancestral world; a purificatory rite which ends a funeral rite.

kaṭavuḷ: God; a great Hindu god who is unseeable by villagers.

*kirāmam (*Skt. *grāma)*: a village, the term tending to be used in an administrative sense.

kulateyvam: a lineage deity.

kummi: girl's dance accompanied by clapping.

kuravai/kulavai: an ululating cry made by women to mark auspicious transition points in ritual.

kurukkaḷ: Brahman temple priests; a subcaste of Brahman priests in Saivite temples.

kuṭimakaṉ: lower status people who engage in services.

kāriyakkāraṉ: an influential person who is regarded as an opinion leader in the traditional village community.

kāval: protection.

kōṭāṅki: exorcist; soothsayer who carries the hour-glass hand drum.

*kōttiram (*Skt. *gōtra*): patrilineal exogamous grouping which is comparable to clan.

kōvil: a Hindu temple.

kūliyāḷ: a daily wage labourer.

mantai: a raised platform for men's gatherings; a traditional gathering or court of the village panchayat.

*mantiram (*Skt. *mantra*): a sacred utterance.

mantiravāti: sorcerer; a person who uses *mantras* for black magic.

marakkāl: dry measure, usually of paddy, about 6.5 liters.

maṭaiyaṉ: one of the village menial offices carried out by Untouchables; a caretaker of the sluice of the village tank.

moy: presents or donations given on special occasions like a life-crisis rite.

mukkai: three handfuls of grain as part of prestation at harvest time.

mukti/mutti (Skt. *mukti*): stage in salvation.

muḷaippāri: a little grown sprout of nine kinds of grains planted in a small bowl.

muṉi: the most powerful evil being or deified being, who resides under an old tree.

muṟaikkupaṅkāḷi: a group of patrilineal lineages who can not marry each other because they believe they are brothers.

mutaṉmai: primary importance; the order of honour which is indicated by the order of distribution of consecrated leftovers.

māmā-macciṉaṉ: ego's cross relatives with whom marriage occurs.

māṉiyam: land the usufruct of which is associated with an office.

naṉcey: irrigated 'wet' land drawn from a tank or a river.

narakam: hell.

nāṭṭāṇmai (kirama muṉcīf): a village headman; a village official who could try suits brought by the ryots of the village.

nāṭu: a state; a country.

otti: an institution whereby people transfer the usufruct of their property, such as land and houses, as a mortgage for the loan of money.

pakti (Skt. *bhakti*): devotion to god, piety.

*pali (*Skt. *bali):* offering given to gods, manes etc., in sacrifice.

pañchāyattu: a panchayat; a council; a body of villagers which settles disputes according to custom and god conscience.

paṇkāḷi: a group of brothers and other male parallel relatives; shareholders of property.

paṇṇaikārar/paṇṇaiyāḷ: farm labourer; contracted farm labourer in Kinnimangalam.

pantal: a temporary shed with a roof made of plaited coconut leaves or cloth for a function, purpose, etc.

*piracātam (*Skt. *prasāda):* consecrated leftovers; sacred offering to deity distributed to devotees.

poṅkal: ceremonially-boiled rice, cooked at a temple.

puṉcey: unirrigated 'dry' land.

puṉitam: sacredness.

*purōkitar (*Skt. *purohita*): a Brahman priest who officiates at marriage and other rituals.

pēy: an evil being, usually the spirit of a human who died unhappily.

pūcai/pūjai (Skt. *pūjā*): worship; adoration of the gods with proper ceremonies.

pūcāri: a non-Brahman priest for local deities or lineage deities at the village level.

ratta uṟavu: blood relations.

talaiyāri: village watchman and policeman appointed by the government to assist the village headman.

taḷukai: meals offered to the gods.

teyvam: deity, a local deity who is seeable by villagers.

toḻil: traditional service or occupation to which a given caste's identity and rank is referred and which is usually rewarded in kind.

tuṭiyāṉa teyvam: a fearful (and active) deity who requires blood sacrifice.

tāymāmaṉ: mother's brother.

tēr: a temple car; a funeral bier.

tīṇṭāmai: untouchability.

tīṭṭu: pollution, impurity.

tōṭṭam: a garden; land with well-irrigation.

tōṭṭi: one of menial offices carried out by Untouchables; a funeral messenger, a grave-digger, a sanitary worker; or a sweeper, etc.

urimai: a right associated with a duty.

uṭaṉpaṅkāḷi: a group of people the relationships of whom can be actually traced patrilineally.

ūr: a village the territory of which is defined contextually from an ego-centred viewpoint

vakaiyaṟā: patrilineal lineage.

vāstu: site or the tutelary deity of the house site.

vēlai: work or individual occupation which is often rewarded in cash.

Index